Calvin
and Social Welfare

Calvin
and Social Welfare

Deacons
and the
Bourse française

Jeannine E. Olson

Selinsgrove: Susquehanna University Press
London and Toronto: Associated University Presses

Associated University Presses
440 Forsgate Drive
Cranbury, NJ 08512

Associated University Presses
25 Sicilian Avenue
London WC1A 2QH, England

Associated University Presses
P.O. Box 488, Port Credit
Mississauga, Ontario
Canada L5G 4M2

The paper used in this publication meets the requirements
of the American National Standard for Permanence of Paper
for Printed Library Materials Z39.48-1984.

Library of Congress Cataloging-in-Publication Data

Olson, Jeannine E.
　Calvin and social welfare.

　Bibliography: p.
　Includes index.
　1. Bourse française (Geneva, Switzerland)
2. Reformed Church—Charities—History—16th century.
3. Church work with the poor—Switzerland—Geneva—
History—16th century.　4. Church work with refugees—
Switzerland—Geneva—History—16th century.　5. Deacons—
Reformed Church—History—16th century.　6. Calvin,
Jean, 1509–1564.　7. Geneva (Switzerland)—Church
history.　I. Title.
BX9423.B45045　1989　　362.8　　　86-43234
ISBN 0–941664–85–6 (alk. paper)

PRINTED IN THE UNITED STATES OF AMERICA

To Karen, Daniel, and Rebecca

Contents

List of Tables   9
List of Illustrations   10
Preface   11

1   The *Bourse française* and Its Setting: An Introduction   17
2   Ideology and Origins of the *Bourse française:* John Calvin   29
3   Welfare, Refugees, Publishing   37
4   International Activities   50
5   Pastors and Deacons   70
6   Volunteers and Paid Personnel   92
7   Donors   107
8   Recipients   127
9   Jean Budé and the *Bourse française*   148
10 Summary and Conclusions   161

Appendixes
  A. Payments to Paris, Copyist of John Calvin's Sermons, from
      the "Great Book of the Assisted," 1561–1564   184
  B. Selected Expenditures from the Extraordinary Accounts of
      the *Bourse française:* August 1559–November 1562   189
  C. Payments to Paris, Copyist of Calvin's Sermons, from the
      "Great Book of the Assisted," 1568–1575   201
  D. Guidelines of the *Bourse française*, January 1581   206
  E. Notarial Documents Pertaining to Jean de Borne in His
      Appeal to the Deacons of the *Bourse française* for His
      Inheritance from Damoiselle Gabrielle de Borne   208
  F. Text of a Genevan Decision for Five Boys in a Case of
      Sodomy, 7–16 March 1554   211

G. A Résumé of the Confessions and Sentencing of Charles Lourdois and His Wife, Jeanne Varrot, and an Opinion in the Case by Germain Colladon, 8–27 August 1568   215

H. Real Estate Transactions from the Family Papers of Jean Budé de Vérace   219

I. The Will of Marguerite de Morel, Wife of François Budé   220

Notes   223
Select Bibliography   278
Index   291

Tables

1. Selected Expenditures from the Extraordinary Accounts of the *Bourse française:* August 1559–November 1562   58

2. Deacons of the *Bourse française:* 1550–1577   87

3. *Bourse* Accounts   97

4. Donors to the *Bourse française:* 1550–1559   120

5. Criminal Procedures against *Bourse française* Aid Recipients of the 1550s   146

6. Real Estate Transactions from the Family Papers of Jean Budé de Vérace   155

Illustrations

Geneva	19
John Calvin	31
John Calvin's Signatures	35
A Map of the Walled City of Geneva in 1564	41
A Page from an Account Book of the *Bourse française*	85
First Expenditures of the *Bourse française*	96
Coins of Geneva	102
Church of the Auditoire	130
Interior of the Cathedral of Saint Pierre	137
Cathedral of Saint Pierre	159

Preface

John Calvin stands head and shoulders above the rest of the leaders of the French and Swiss Reformation. He made his major impact on Europe and the rest of the world from Geneva. Powerful as was his influence there, he was always somewhat of a sojourner in a foreign land. In a sense he was but one of the many refugees living in Geneva with their eyes on their homeland, hoping that someday all of France would be evangelized and that the Reformed religion would be allowed to prosper freely. Awaiting that day, he and his friends provided for the continuing stream of Protestant refugees from Roman Catholic areas by offering them food and shelter in Geneva. It is characteristic of Calvin's Reformation that this hospitality was institutionalized into a welfare fund known as the *Bourse française* or "the French fund for poor foreigners," intended for those who came to Geneva to live according to the "reform of the Word."

Calvin's personal impact on the Geneva Reformation was tremendous, but the lasting effectiveness of his reform owed much to those institutional structures through which he worked and that he also to an extent created. Just as Luther influenced millions of people through his writings and established a permanent institutional base for the Reformation through the reform of the University of Wittenberg and the founding of Protestant universities and many secondary schools, so Calvin's influence was implemented through the academy that he founded that became the University of Geneva. Educational institutions were clearly important. Like Luther, Calvin promoted secondary school education and insisted on compulsory primary education for boys and girls. The reformers also understood the importance of charitable institutions for the welfare not only of the totally indigent and disadvantaged but also of the many victims of the historical events of their times. Thus within the organizational structure for charity in Geneva, the *Bourse française* was a fundamental institution that cared for not only many humble refugees and the poor of Geneva but also for French refugees of

11

importance and consequence. Luther understood that things were changing, that there was a shift from ecclesiastical support of the poor, and that the change was necessary because gifts to the poor were often considered salvific works. He also saw that city councils with a tax structure could provide more secure support. Just as Luther, for example, urged the people at Leisnig to establish a common chest to support the poor and integrate them into society by encouraging them to work, so Calvin, in line with the general trend in urban society, urged the institutional organization of charity. As a French reformer he was, of course, particularly concerned with the welfare of the French refugees in Geneva whose numbers swelled day by day. Calvin's response to this difficult problem was to accept an initial gift that grew into a fund that became the financial base for the *Bourse française*. The *Bourse française* with its deacons became a fundamental institution in Calvin's Geneva alongside the disciplinary body of the consistory with its elders and the ministerial association of the Venerable Company of Pastors.

Social welfare in Geneva resembled welfare organization in many other early modern Europe cities of the times in its conversion of urban welfare systems from decentralized institutions run by religious orders to centralized systems controlled by city councils. In cities that became Protestant like Geneva this conversion often coincided with the local Reformation; it was necessary to replace the welfare functions of the Roman Catholic religious orders. Thus, when Geneva became Protestant, the city's welfare institutions were taken under the control of the city council and centered in the city hospital. The creation of the *Bourse française* represented somewhat of a departure from this tendency toward centralization, because the *Bourse* was supervised by deacons and pastors and financed independently of the city council.

The social welfare system of Geneva responded to the theological emphasis of the reformers. The reformers had undermined the medieval recognition of giving alms to the poor as a worthy act counting toward the remission of the temporal punishment for sin that otherwise would need to be purged in Purgatory. Protestants emphasized charity as a response of love to God and one's neighbor. Within this context, the Reformed church found it necessary to care for the needy in an organized manner. The haphazard aspects of traditional almsgiving in Geneva were minimized by encouraging people to channel their benevolence regularly through a fund administered through deacons who would ensure that the welfare would be distributed systematically, comprehensively, and compassionately. The *Bourse française* was an important part of that system of welfare because it was dedicated to foreigners in a city popular to refugees.

In a sense, this work is a biography of an institution. Its purpose is to bring to light new information on Reformation Geneva by looking at one particular institution, the *Bourse française*, a fund for poor Protestant refugees from Roman Catholic France founded by John Calvin and his friends and run by deacons of the Reformed Church of Geneva. Most of my research was with unedited manuscripts, primarily the account books of the *Bourse française*, carefully preserved in the Archives of the State of Geneva, Switzerland. These mid-sixteenth-century documents have largely remained unexamined, perhaps because of their difficult handwriting or their repetitious nature. In addition to my research at the Archives of Geneva, I did auxiliary work in the manuscript room of the library of the University of Geneva and in the rich collection on sixteenth-century Geneva there. The materials at the Museum for Reformation History were also especially useful.

The project was largely paleographical in its overwhelming challenge to acquire the skill and practice necessary to read the sixteenth-century hands accurately. Knowledge of the handwriting was the key that eventually unlocked the past, opening for examination not only the account books but also the ancillary records and notarial documents that pertain to the *Bourse française*. This study intends to present as thoroughly, systematically, and accurately as possible the information that the documents divulged, and to interpret those documents so that their extraordinary story will not be lost to posterity.

A word about terminology is necessary to avoid confusion. This text follows traditional usage of the term "Reformed," which when capitalized is used in much the same manner as one would use the label "Lutheran" for the churches emanating from Germany and Scandinavia as part of the reform movement begun by Martin Luther. "Reformed" refers to those churches emanating from the Swiss Reformation or looking to Switzerland as a model, that is, by and large, churches that spread into France, the Low Countries, and across the English Channel to the British Isles whence they eventually expanded to the New World through our Puritan and Presbyterian ancestors.

In addition, dates cited from the sixteenth-century manuscripts are as they appear in the documents, without adjustment for the Gregorian calendar reform of 1582. The names of sixteenth-century persons are given in French rather than anglicized with the exception of John Calvin. Original spelling and accents are retained in tables and in transcriptions from the original manuscripts, especially in names. Names are alphabetized under the various possibilities, which often creates several entries, especially for names that include *de* or *la* that are listed under *d* and *l* as well as under the name itself.

This study of the *Bourse française* was made possible by the preservation of the account books of the deacons of the *Bourse française* in the Archives of the State of Geneva. The archive, now directed by Catherine Santschi, provides a rich source of information about the *Bourse* and its religious and social function in Geneva. The resources of the archive were graciously made available to me with the help of Bertrand Chouet. The archivists who were especially helpful were Barbara Lochner-Roth, Micheline Tripet, and Jean-Etienne Genequand. Among the scholars at the archive and at the Museum of History of the Reformation I wish especially to thank Professor Pierre Fraenkel and Professor Gabrielle Berthoud, Robert Roth, Lillian Mottu, Bernard Lescaze, Sabine Citron, Marie-Claude Junod, and Claire Chimelli for having introduced me to the intricacies of archival scholarship of early modern Geneva.

I owe a debt of gratitude to Dr. Alain Dufour and Dr. Robert M. Kingdon for having suggested to me the particular set of documents I investigated and for their encouragement and expert advice. I also received a helping hand from Professors Nancy Roelker, E. William Monter, Natalie Zemon Davis, and Dr. Jean-François Gilmont. I am grateful especially to Professor Lewis W. Spitz of Stanford University who served as my mentor in Reformation history and consultant in writing this volume. Professors Louis Binz, Alfred Soman, and George Brown assisted me very substantially in mastering paleography of a difficult sort. In this regard Madame Gabriella Cahier, editor of the *Registres de la Compagnie des Pasteurs de Genève,* has been of tremendous assistance in transcribing passages and deciphering difficult readings. A word of appreciation is in order for Henri Bordier, one of those who went before, whose nineteenth-century transcription of parts of the early account books was the key to deciphering the handwriting of Jean Budé, the first deacon-accountant. The modern aspects of the manuscript were handled capably by Dr. Colleen Redmond, Mary Lucas, and Rebecca Prichard, who helped me proofread the typescript.

The research abroad was funded through the Danforth Foundation, the American Council of Learned Societies, the National Endowment for the Humanities, the Lutheran Brotherhood, and San Francisco Theological Seminary; fittingly, I was also *boursière de la France* while studying this French *bourse* and had the help of scholars in France, Professors Daniel Olivier of the L'Institut supérieur d'études oecumeniques de Paris and Claude Nordmann of the University of Lille. I have made ample use of the collections in the Stanford libraries and the University of Geneva library. Professors Benjamin Reist, Jorge Lara-Braud, and Surjit Singh; Dean Walter Davis, and President J. Randolph Taylor of San Francisco Theological Seminary kindly made time available for the completion of this volume as did Dean Claude Welch and President Michael Blecker of the Graduate Theological Union. Rhode Island College, Professor Norman Smith, and the department of history supported my work.

While in Geneva I enjoyed the hospitality of both the Protestant and Catholic university centers and that of the Home St. Pierre. The *Collège de la Florence* of the Genevan public schools educated my daughter in French, and we enjoyed the fellowship and support of the churches of the old city: the Scottish church, the Lutheran church on the Bourg de Four, and the Congregation of St. Pierre-Fusterie, especially the chorale and the Forum of St. Pierre.

Calvin
and Social Welfare

1
The *Bourse française* and Its Setting:
An Introduction

The founders of the *Bourse française* were neither reactionaries nor social revolutionaries in the modern sense. They were unaware that they were setting precedents for social welfare and philanthropy that would endure; they were looking to the past and the present rather than to the future. The foundation of the *Bourse française* was both the consummation of high ideals and a pragmatic response to need. It was based on centuries of precedent and yet it met the practical needs of the poor foreign refugees to Geneva. The founders of the *Bourse,* who seemed so progressive, tended to idealize antiquity, for they were scholar-reformers educated as humanists. John Calvin was not the least among them. As humanists they looked to ancient Greece and Rome for their models for the present. As reformers they were most attracted to the institution of the early church. They found precedent therein for much of what they did. They looked especially to Scripture for inspiration, explanation, and sometimes, indeed, rationalization of what they did. They knew the Bible well and therefore believed that "You always have the poor with you" (Mark 14:7). They did not believe that poverty could be entirely eliminated, but this did not immobilize them.

This chapter surveys the precedents for the *Bourse française* and considers the sixteenth-century world in which the *Bourse* was founded. It explains what the *Bourse française* was and where information about it was found. It touches on the broader implications of the study of the *Bourse* and sets the parameters of this study.

The early precedents for the *Bourse française* lay largely but not entirely in Scripture, where one finds the history of the early church's relationship to the poor. The church had always been an advocate of the disadvantaged. Early Christians took care of their own and some others as well. They fed the poor, nursed the sick, housed the homeless, and rescued newborn infants abandoned to die. One of the earliest stories of the church was that of the apostles of Jesus Christ selecting seven men from the Christian community to manage the daily distributions to the widows, recorded in the Acts of the Apostles 6:1–7. Among those selected was Stephen, the first Christian martyr according to Acts 6:8–15 and 7:1–60. Stephen and others were assumed by many, including John Calvin and his friends, to be the first deacons, even though they were not called deacons in the Bible. By the time Paul wrote his first letter to Timothy, the office of deacon had become so institutionalized as to merit a description of what deacons should be like. In 1 Timothy 3:8–13, Paul described deacons as people of good character who were temperate and faithful, both men and women. These Scriptural citations were used by the reformers of the sixteenth century to describe the diaconate, for they considered the Bible the primary document of church institutions for all time. These reformers sometimes spoke of the church as if it existed before Christ. They thus looked to earlier precedents such as the Levitical Code, for instance, with its provision for the poor of the gleanings of the fields and the leftover grapes (Leviticus 19:9–10). There were also the tithe and the traditions of the synagogues in which many of the first Christians were nurtured.[1]

In addition to ancient Israel and Jewish culture, the classical world of Greece and Rome influenced the church through the Roman example of bread and circuses and the ancient system of patronage. Patrons, even after death, offered aid to clients who in turn gave support. Christians were influenced by some of these traditions although they did not replicate them exactly. In the fourth century, when Christianity became the religion of the Roman empire, the system of patronage lived on. Emperors asked the bishops of the church to act as judges in the courts; the bishops were then able to act as patrons of the poor in the courts and to protect the disadvantaged.

With the fall of the Roman Empire in the fifth century, the situation changed drastically. Government and institutions collapsed in many areas. Only the church and its monasteries kept social welfare and education alive in Europe by providing hospitality and schooling. In addition, the Synod of Tours in 567 made each parish responsible for the poor dependent upon it, charging its priest and budget with the welfare of the indigent.[2] Certain monks and nuns dedicated themselves to the care of the poor and to teaching.

Eventually, entire medieval religious groups were committed to service, such as the Knights of St. John Hospitaler. Lay people of generosity and foresight gave land and money in return for prayers and Masses for the souls in Purgatory. Institutions called hospitals were founded to help the needy. Many of them were much smaller than the hospitals of today; they were less

Geneva from the north, P. Chouet, 1655. "A" is the Cathedral of Saint Pierre. From Émile Doumergue, *Jean Calvin, Les hommes et les choses de son temps*, vol. 3, *La ville, la maison, et la rue de Calvin* (Lausanne: Georges Bridel, Éditeurs, 1905), p. 35.

intended to care for the ill than to provide food and shelter for the disadvantaged. They housed orphans, the elderly, and those who were incapacitated in any way, mentally or physically. They sheltered sick people too, but sick people, in general, stayed home and died in their own beds. Other needy people received food and clothing at the hospitals in weekly handouts. Lay people also took on charitable projects such as feeding the poor, endowing hospitals, and providing Christian burial for themselves and the indigent. Lay people also worked through societies called confraternities, organized around patron saints.

The church, then, through its clergy and its laity, strove to provide for the poor. It had developed a system that included everyone in Christendom, in theory at least. It was not centralized, however, and left enormous gaps. These gaps were less apparent in times of prosperity and in some locales. Since the poor could not rely on the church alone they relied on themselves. They begged for alms at the entrances to churches or wherever people gathered. Sometimes they inflicted wounds on themselves or crippled their own children to appear more pathetic. Begging became a way of life for some families that was passed on from one generation to the next. It became the unorganized all-pervasive form of welfare in the new urban centers.[3] Cities, as they developed, attempted to eliminate begging or at least to control it; some tried to license begging, in effect, by requiring authorized beggars to wear badges or some other sort of identification. They attempted to drive the other beggars out of town.

When cities and secular governments revived after the barbarian and Viking invasions, institutions other than the church could enter into education and welfare. The new governments were eventually able to coordinate the welfare establishments in their midst. Sometimes they created a special board of trustees responsible for welfare, or appointed overseers responsible to the city council. They also consolidated overlapping institutions. This coordination proceeded much faster in some areas than in others, into the sixteenth century. There was resistance to many of these changes, of course, particularly when changes appeared to involve confiscation of church property or impinged upon individual prerogatives. Growing need forced greater change. Expanding population and limited resources led to higher prices, and the sixteenth century witnessed a period of personal distress and social unrest.

The social history of the centuries immediately preceding the sixteenth is mixed. The great disaster of the mid-fourteenth century was the bubonic plague. Whole villages were wiped out and the general population was decimated. The plague continued in diminishing waves into the seventeenth century. It killed some of the major donors and activists in the *Bourse française* such as Laurent de Normandie, the great financier of books, and Jean Crespin, the publisher and martyrologist.

As population increased in the sixteenth century so did pressure on the land. In some areas the enclosure system turned agricultural land over to sheep grazing. This was less labor-intensive than agriculture and contributed to the problem of vagrancy. In England enclosure was perceived as a critical problem and denounced by a rising tide of socially conscious people, such as the humanist Sir Thomas More, author of *Utopia,* but enclosure continued with the rise in population. The unemployed went from area to area seeking work or a place to beg or something to steal. Years of bad harvest complicated the picture, as did inflation. The authorities attempted to send everyone home, where the local parish was to take care of its own poor. Legislation that sent people home did not solve the problem, even though its penalties went from bad to worse. In England, harsh words were replaced by branding and banishment for those vagrants who refused to "go home." Nevertheless, a great crowd of floating poor moved at will across the countryside.

By the beginning of the sixteenth century socially conscious people were trying to do something about the situation. They preached, wrote, and agitated about it. Before the Protestant Reformation, John Geiler von Kaisersberg alerted the population of Strasbourg.[4] Juan Luis Vives, the Spanish humanist, proposed on 6 January 1526 a comprehensive system of social welfare for the city of Bruges in the Low Countries, which has been thought to be a model for many reforms that followed elsewhere.[5] While Bruges did not implement it, other cities did act, although not because of Vives necessarily. South German cities such as Nuremberg are often given credit for inspiring subsequent reforms, but there is some discussion as to whether the credit should go to the Lutheran influence there since the city was still Catholic when many of the reforms occurred.[6]

The overall tendency in welfare reform was to centralize, rationalize, and "laicize" the systems (that is, to get more lay people involved). A typical reform was to establish a central welfare system or a hospital. Some of these new institutions coordinated or replaced the existing multifaceted systems, but others were established alongside older institutions. The new systems and administrators were usually responsible to some governmental body, often the city council in the case of a city reform. Many of the reforms did occur in cities, where the influx of the transient poor exacerbated the congested living conditions of late medieval and sixteenth-century urban settings. Many social welfare reforms included hiring a paid administrator to manage the institutions, keep the books, do the purchasing, hire the servants, and oversee the entire operation. The administrator would sometimes be supervised by a board of trustees or a committee of the government that would make major decisions, provide for income, see to the auditing of the books, and hire and fire the administrator. In Geneva, as in other cities, the person in charge of the hospital was called the hospitaler. The hospitaler and his wife had a great deal of responsibility as a team, so much so that a man without a wife was considered inadequate to do the job well. As cities established new sytems of welfare they would write them up as ordinances. These ordinances were printed and sold. The general interest in welfare reform was great enough to make the printing and sale of hospital ordinances viable.

The sixteenth century brought to a head these reforming tendencies in social welfare. Some have said that sixteenth-century reforms were the beginning of a new era. Others feel they were a product of cumulative changes in social welfare in the late medieval era. Still others have attributed changes in social welfare to the Renaissance and particularly to interested humanists or to better business practices during the Renaissance. Some also attribute the changes in social welfare to the Protestant Reformation, but this denominational theory of social welfare reforms is less in vogue, particularly with recent research on social reform in Catholic areas.[7]

Whatever one might say about the similarities of Catholic and Protestant social welfare in the sixteenth century, institutional differences did exist in the manner in which social welfare was conducted. The Protestant states and cities took over land and buildings that had belonged to the Roman Catholic church and dedicated them to social welfare and to education. Responsibility for the disadvantaged shifted from religious orders and confraternities to city councils and boards of trustees. Catholic areas had religious orders and confraternities to do some of the work and provide some of the resources; Protestant areas did not. As the Catholic religious orders disappeared, their services as teachers and helpers of the poor went with them. In Protestant areas lay workers filled some of the roles that Catholic clergy had occupied. Sometimes these workers were given the title of deacon, an office that was conceived differently from the diaconate in the medieval Catholic tradition. The ways in which money was handled also changed with the demise of the old institutions. The reformers of the sixteenth century appealed to the city councils and to the people to support hospitals and schools generously. This was often accomplished through the founding of a common chest that was often an actual locked chest in which donations to the poor were deposited or conserved. Smaller "poor boxes" were available to collect donations in the churches.

Both Catholics and Protestants tried to eliminate begging. Neither was successful, but the Catholic areas faced an additional obstacle in mendicancy. Mendicant orders such as the Dominicans and the Franciscans had been founded just a few centuries before to serve in the new urban areas. Believing that begging was a pious act of abnegation, they established mendicancy as part of their religious way of life. Some Roman Catholic legislation against begging made exceptions for religious mendicants, but there was further opposition to laws against begging in Catholic areas on the grounds that such laws were "Lutheran." This accusation ignored a long Catholic history of such legislation—for instance, in 806 Charlemagne had forbidden giving alms to lazy beggars circulating through his countryside.[8]

The differences between Catholic and Protestant social welfare were noted at the time. There even appears to have been some competition between them. For instance, a Catholic bishop speaking on the occasion of the establishment of the general hospital at Nîmes in the seventeenth century remarked that the example of the Protestants was putting the Roman Catholics to shame. There were no beggars among them, they took a collection every Sunday, and they taxed themselves to provide for those who fell in need and could not work. "Imitate your adversaries," he said.[9] On the other hand, French Protestants might have praised St. Vincent de Paul and the Ladies and Sisters of Charity, but Protestant opposition to vows of celibacy limited their appreciation of Catholic charitable individuals and institutions.

The decisive factor in the relative success of new Protestant welfare systems may have had less to do with theology than with endowment. The fate of Catholic lands and possessions was central to the new welfare systems in Protestant regions, since without money or goods no welfare system could succeed. An adequate endowment was preferable to daily contributions. The property of the church was in danger of being diverted in the shift to Protestantism and local secularization. The reformers were aware of this. John Knox bemoaned that much of what had been intended for the poor fell into other hands when Scotland became Protestant. On the other hand, Martin Luther allowed that some of the property should return to the families of the original donors rather than go to the common chest for the poor. This was only if the donor families were needy, however.[10] In many cases city councils rather than avaricious individuals gained control of the endowment, and, at least in the case of the town of Leisnig, Martin Luther favored the parish regaining control of the endowment of the city council. He wrote a letter to the Elector Frederick on behalf of the parish.[11] When endowments passed over to city councils they were not necessarily lost, but councils did not always reserve the endowment of the church for welfare and schools. Another complication was that in some areas, notably Lutheran, salaries for the pastors and schoolteachers came out of the common chest for the poor. This was not true in Strasbourg where Calvin developed precedents for Geneva.[12]

Discussion of the relative success of welfare systems is hampered by lack of quantifiable information. How much money was spent? How many people were helped? What were the sources of financial support? To answer such questions one must study the old account books and records of the period. Important research has already been done in primary sources, but much more remains to be done.[13] This study of the *Bourse française* in Geneva is a part of that basic research.

Before dealing with the content of the manuscripts, it would be well to consider just what the *Bourse française* was and what it did. The *Bourse des pauvres estrangers français*, as it was called in the mid-sixteenth century, was a fund for the poor founded sometime after the city accepted the Protestant Reformation (1536), while John Calvin was there (1536–38 and 1541–64). The *Bourse*, intended for foreigners, was an innovation among contemporary welfare institutions of Europe, which were dedicated primarily to meeting local needs. In welcoming Protestants to Geneva, it was instrumental in making it possible for the city to accommodate an enormous influx of refugees who otherwise would have overwhelmed the local welfare facilities. It stands out among European institutions of the period in that it circumvented local sentiments against supporting foreign poor people and helped make Geneva a city of refuge in early modern Europe.

The momentum behind the *Bourse* came from the French residents in Geneva. Those first refugees helped the others who followed. Although the *Bourse française* was created by foreigners to help foreigners, it survived because of a shared conviction of Genevans and French that people who came for religious reasons should be helped. Geneva would not easily have tolerated an agency aiding large-scale immigration were it not for a conviction that persecuted people should not be turned away; although there was pride in the city's popularity and in the opportunity it offered to live according to the "Reform of the Word," as the phrase went, this pride existed alongside animosity toward the growing number of foreigners that threatened to overwhelm the local population by taking away jobs and political power.

The religious purposes of the *Bourse française* guaranteed its survival in the city. The *Bourse* was destined for those who came to Geneva for "religious" reasons and was not intended to help everyone who passed through town, though in fact, it sometimes appears to have done just that. Its goal, specifically, was to help refugees from areas less safe or congenial to come to Geneva to live according to the "Reform of the Gospel."

A second factor in the survival of the *Bourse* during its early years was its dependence on foreign money. This took some of the load off the indigenous Genevans who had their own hospital to support. The *Bourse* depended on resources from the local French immigrant population and from sympathetic donors living abroad. Survival was ensured by the contacts in France of the Venerable Company of Pastors and the local French donors. (The pastors of mid-sixteenth-century Geneva were largely French in origin.) These contacts served as a conduit of money from supporters outside Geneva. Initially the Genevans appeared to give relatively little financial support, although they permitted the *Bourse* to exist and occasionally applauded its activity.

Foreign funding expanded rapidly as Reformed churches spread in France and across Europe and the *Bourse française* became part of the international network of Reformed churches. Many local churches founded in reformed areas tried to imitate the Genevan model. They established funds for the poor under the charge of deacons, parallel to the *Bourse française*, and they organized consistories of elders and pastors. The leaders of these institutions maintained ties with one another and with Geneva. Sometimes they relied on each other and on Geneva for help. This mutual dependence helped make it possible for Reformed churches to survive as minority institutions under persecution. No small element in the strength of these churches was their ability to transfer funds and maintain a place of refuge in Switzerland. The *Bourse française* was thus a part of the discipline and order of the Reformed Church, a church that was held together, in part, by personal acquaintances and a common organization.

With time, as the French settled down in Geneva, the fund became indigenous and lost the international character of its financial support while retaining its goal of aiding poor foreign religious refugees. The *Bourse française* grew pragmatically according to need, first helping the trickle of early immigrants, and then later being almost overwhelmed by the influx of refugees during years of crisis in France such as the St. Bartholomew's Day Massacre in 1572 or the revocation of the Edict of Nantes in 1685. But as the French became Genevan, the fund became Genevan too. The problem of the refugees was one for the whole city to face. Eventually, when persecution in France ceased, urgent aid to religious refugees was replaced by simple help to immigrants. By the nineteenth century the *Bourse*'s stipulation that aid should go to Protestants seemed discriminatory and was a significant factor in its dissolution. A well-known Genevan politician named James Fazy, whose name still today elicits strong opinion, accused such welfare institutions of being parochial.

This study examines the *Bourse française* primarily during the mid-sixteenth century when the fund functioned in an international setting. Some of the information, however, was taken from later periods when better records were kept of internal functioning. Later evidence was used only when it was corroborated by hints and references in the sixteenth-century documents.

Overall, the institutional character of the *Bourse* was what one would expect. It was flexible and even makeshift in the beginning and later stabilized as the organization took firm shape. Daily practical decisions of individuals became policies enforced by a group of people informed by precedent.

The fund in the mid-sixteenth century escaped some of the legalisms that developed in the course of the seventeenth century. In the beginning the spontaneous generosity of even one person, particularly a deacon, was decisive. Those also were the days when one family, and especially a younger son of that family, did much of the work and provided a great deal of the impetus behind the *Bourse française*.

The surviving records of the *Bourse française* date from September 1550 and are surprisingly complete. They consist of daily account books that the deacons kept of donations and expenditures. By 1560 there are additional records of expenditures initially included in the daily accounts, but these are merely an elaboration of the basic system of record keeping set out in 1550. The first substantial, essentially new record that was not a product of the deacons' accounting system was a huge volume begun in the later sixteenth century listing bequests to charitable institutions in the city. This document includes the *Bourse française*, as listed in individual bequests, alongside the *Bourse italienne*, the city hospital, and the Genevan academy.[14]

More complete records belonging to the *Bourse* alone survive after the turn of the century. For example, the minutes of the business meetings of the deacons survive from the seventeenth century.[15] Although one would wish to have such records from the inception of the fund as well as a simple list of the names of the deacons who ran the fund, such as exists for a comparable Genevan fund for Italian refugees of this period, the daily account books of the sixteenth-century *Bourse française* are a rich source indeed; they contain substantial information about both the fund's management and daily life in Geneva.[16]

The search for information about the *Bourse française* only began with the account books. Other documents in the Genevan archives from the mid-sixteenth century were also valuable to this study: the records of the city council and of the consistory; the *procès criminels;* lists of baptisms, marriages, and deaths; and notarial records of various types such as wills, marriage contracts, real estate negotiations, and the like. All of these provided information about the individuals named in the account books. For at least two key individuals, Jean Budé and Laurent de Normandie, family papers are on deposit in the archive. While one could occasionally find direct references to the *Bourse française* indexed under its own title, in contemporary records the legal activities of the *Bourse* were usually listed under the names of the responsible individuals, the deacons.

These rich documents have obviously served scholars before. Especially for the study of the seventeenth and eighteenth centuries, the *Bourse* records have provided valuable information on the philanthropic patterns of Genevans, but there is much more to be garnered. The last major foray into the mid-sixteenth-century account books occurred in the nineteenth century when the paleographer Henri Bordier began extracting names from them, apparently for the second edition of *France Protestante*, an encyclopedia of early Protestants, but he did not get all the names, having stopped after the first sixteen years of the account books.[17] Much more remains to be done, both in the retrieval and identification of names and in the accumulation of other information. The geographic origins of the poor remain to be sorted out systematically, for instance, and the daily nature of the accounting offers economic historians a valuable source for calculating prices and the rate of inflation. The accounts of the *Bourse française* also need to be compared to those of the city of Geneva to determine how much the French deacons spent in comparison to the city government. These are but a few of the account books' possible future uses.

Other possibilities include studying the *Bourse française,* with its frequent direct involvement of John Calvin, for a new perspective on Calvin's social and economic thought. This is an area in Calvin research that, as with so many other areas, has been studied in the context of his theological writings and not of his actions in real life. The *Bourse française* contains concrete examples of Calvin's thought put into action, revealing that he not only preached charity but generously supported the poor as well. Similar specific information is available on the philanthropical habits of Calvin's contemporaries, such as Robert Estienne and Jean Crespin to name but two.

Another aspect of Calvin's thought exemplified in the *Bourse française* is his idea of the diaconate, an office of the church that for Calvin constituted one of four parallel offices alongside ministers, elders, and doctors (teachers). A traditional popular source for his ideas on these offices is the Ecclesiastical Ordinances that Calvin and others wrote for the city after he came back in 1541, but the section on deacons in these ordinances was formulated around the image of the city hospital, and that description does not fit the deacons of the *Bourse française,* whose responsibilities were a modification of the pattern laid out in the ordinances.[18] Yet this modification apparently occurred with Calvin's blessing. One of the elections of these deacons, in fact, occurred at Calvin's house. He was apparently less concerned with an exact replication of his original ideas than some of his followers would allow.

The *Bourse française* by and large honored the germinal ideas of John Calvin on charity and on the role of the deacons. It would be wrong to view this institution solely as the product of his mind, however, for at the same time that the *Bourse* institutionalized his ideas and those of other people involved in it, the institution also met its daily demands in a manner that was generally acceptable in the standard welfare practice of the world in which it existed.

This interplay between practical considerations and ideology makes a study of this institution captivating, and it interjects a note of caution into any temptation to grandiose speculation on the theoretical implications of the activity of the *Bourse* and the people involved in it. For instance, it is tempting to attribute the hard work of the people involved in the *Bourse* to the so-called "Protestant ethic," but in seeking the ideology that inspired the *Bourse* and those behind it, one would do well to be careful about pulling them too far out of the context of their sixteenth-century world. The people involved in the *Bourse française* were not created, after all, by the Reformation; they were already present in sixteenth-century European society. What Geneva did was to bring them together in one place and to provide them with an opportunity to use their organizational skills in the "service of the Lord." This involvement in the church and in society was a logical outgrowth of the concept of the priesthood of all believers. It sprang not only from the working out of an idea, however, but also from the needs of a minority church to survive in an alien society. The Reformed Church had to organize to survive, unlike the more state-protected Lutherans in the Holy Roman Empire and in Scandinavia. More than any other Protestant denomination of the time except perhaps communal Anabaptist agrarian sects, it put everyone to work. In the case of the *Bourse française*, practical considerations and ideology generally supported each other so that there does not appear to have been any particular conflict of ideals.

Another aspect of this study of the *Bourse française* is the delineation of its role in the history of the larger Reformed Church. As local Reformed churches were organized and a network of communication developed, the *Bourse* became a model for deacons' funds, much as so many other aspects of Reformed polity and worship in Geneva became a prototype for other communities. Much local research remains to discover just what form these other deacons' funds took and how contacts were maintained; this can only be touched upon here. Such considerations are some of the broader implications of the study of the *Bourse française*.

2
Ideology and Origins of the *Bourse française:* John Calvin

The *Bourse française* had roots both in ideology and in real life. The ideas of Calvin combined with practical needs to produce a unique institution that blended pragmatism, social theory, and theology. The creation of the *Bourse* was typical of the Reformation in that the thought of a single great individual strongly influenced the social organization of daily life. It was Calvin's vision about the duties of Christians toward the less fortunate and the role of deacons in the church that provided the conceptual framework within which the *Bourse française* grew.

Specifically, Calvin's conception of four offices within the church formed the theoretical basis for the organizational structure of the *Bourse*.[1] These offices were those of the pastors or ministers, elders, deacons, and doctors (teachers).[2] Calvin derived this four-part division from precedents in the Bible and the early church and from his own experience, particularly in Basel and Strasbourg. An understanding of this fourfold system of church organization is fundamental to placing the *Bourse française* within the structure of Reformed polity. Within this scheme, ministers were responsible for preaching, elders for discipline, deacons for money, and doctors for teaching. The basic idea was division of labor, but there was some overlap, even in theory. Both ministers and elders sat on the consistory (a disciplinary body), for example, and all four offices had some part in the nurturing of the flock. Yet the four offices were not indistinguishable. Calvin was specific about their mutually exclusive roles. The ministers of Geneva preferred, for instance, that deacons take charge of financial responsibilities.[3] This general dictum was also applied to other Reformed churches, but the ideal of a four-part division of ministers, elders, deacons, and doctors was not always realized outside of Geneva. Doctors were often absent and in some areas deacons as

29

well, so that financial responsibilities then fell on the elders.[4] Ministers were often called pastors. Calvin and his followers used both terms interchangeably based on the New Testament example where pastor meant shepherd and minister meant servant.

It was primarily with the office of deacon that the *Bourse française* was concerned, because deacons carried on the daily activities of the fund. According to Calvin the office of deacon originated in the early church when the apostles, overburdened with work within the growing community of believers, gave the responsibility of caring for the widows to Stephen and six others.[5] References to deacons elsewhere in the New Testament indicate that this office continued within the church.[6] Deacons originally dealt with the social welfare needs of the community, and this was their role with the *Bourse française* as well.

Calvin insisted that this early pattern was to be emulated in the sixteenth century. Over the centuries the diaconate had been merged into the church's hierarchical structure and had become a steppingstone to the priesthood. The relationship of deacon to priest became sequential. However, Calvin leaned toward an ideal relationship between deacons and ministers as separate equals. Thus, as with many other aspects of the Reformed tradition, the reform of the diaconate and the fourfold division of the offices of the church were considered a return to the pristine practices of earlier times. It is well to be aware, however, that the theory was purer than the practice and that in Geneva the ministers tended toward a supervisory role. Also, occasionally a deacon became a minister, the diaconate thus again serving as a stepping-stone to the ministry, but this was the exception rather than the rule and did not entirely undermine Calvin's theory.[7]

The situation in Geneva illustrates that Calvin's ideas about deacons as well as his opinions about other aspects of church organization did not remain theoretical abstractions. His ideas were applied concretely to the city and appear to have been formulated to some extent to fit its situation. The office of deacon, for instance, fit most comfortably within the framework of an institution already organized to handle the sick and the poor, the city hospital of Geneva.[8] The Ecclesiastical Ordinances of 1541 described the office of deacon in a manner conforming to the organization of the hospital. In that document Calvin spoke of two kinds of deacons, procurators and hospitalers, which were two offices that already existed in Geneva—procurators ran the hospital and hospitalers dealt with the clientele. He gave these positions the new title of deacon.[9]

This new title did not seem to catch on quickly. The procurators and hospitalers continued to be referred to by their original titles and to consider themselves responsible to the city council and not to the ministers or to a formal church structure. Toward the end of the century, the title of deacon came into greater use with reference to hospital personnel, but this did not

John Calvin. From M. Audin, *Histoire de la vie, des ouvrages, et des doctrines de Calvin*, vol. 1 (Paris: Maison, Libraire-Éditeur, 1841), frontispiece.

appear to indicate any change in orientation. The problem was that the city hospital was already functioning when the Ecclesiastical Ordinances were written. This apparent attempt by the early reformers to make the secular sacred was not really successful. The hospital remained an institution that relied on the city council, even though some of its functions were religious, such as saying grace before the weekly handouts and purchasing Bibles and Psalters for the poor.[10]

Meanwhile, however, a new institution came into being that fit much more closely the ideal of an organization headed by officers of the church. This was the *Bourse française*. The *Bourse* was not mentioned in the Ecclesiastical Ordinances and probably did not exist at the time. The ordinances were written before the large influx of refugees overwhelmed local resources and the need for a separate institution dedicated to them became apparent. Initially, the primary institution engaged in social welfare in the city was the city hospital. Sometime in the 1540s the need for alternate provisions for the refugees became apparent, and by 30 September 1550 the fund had been established and three men had been chosen as its leaders.[11] These men were not formally referred to as deacons in the account books until July 1554 at an election held at Calvin's house.[12] The title apparently caught on; by the late 1550s and the 1560s they were cited with increasing frequency in notarial records as administrators and deacons of the fund for the poor foreigners. Contemporary records referred more and more to the "deacons" of the *Bourse française*.

The existence of these two sets of deacons, one for the hospital and the other for the *Bourse française*, has confused modern understanding of the situation. The reference to the deacons of the city hospital in the Ecclesiastical Ordinances, so readily available to modern scholars, has tended to diminish awareness of the deacons of the *Bourse*, whose record remains largely in unpublished manuscripts. But the people living in the sixteenth century were not confused. In colloquial usage "deacon" apparently referred to an administrator of the *Bourse française* rather than to one of the hospital. If the speaker were Italian or English, it might mean a deacon of the Italian *Bourse* or of the English church, who was charged with the care of these communities. In any case, the term "deacon" was habitually used to refer to those men chosen to administer funds for religious refugees, and references to deacons in Genevan documents of the mid-sixteenth century should be considered with this in mind.

Calvin had more to say about deacons than is expressed in the Ecclesiastical Ordinances. In his sermons and correspondence he explained that the duties of deacons, as well as of widows over sixty years old, was to visit the poor and the sick.[13] In this, as in so many other matters, Calvin used the Bible as a basis. Both theory and practice played a part in Calvin's thought at this critical juncture in history when new institutions were being formed.

The Bible and the early church offered precedents, and the particular situation provided practical guidelines. Thus, stipulations about deacons visiting the sick were included in the 1581 ordinances for the *Bourse française*.[14]

It is easier to trace the doctrine behind the office of deacon and the theories about Christian duty to the poor than it is to document the concrete details of what actually happened in social welfare at the time. In particular, the origins of the *Bourse française* are ambiguous because there are no specific records that go back to its beginning. It is evident that money had been collected and distributed well before the first existing record of the *Bourse*. There are indications that before that date some of the refugees from France were handled by their compatriots rather than by the city hospital, which was intended primarily for the indigenous poor. There could have been an early practice of aiding refugees within the immigrant community itself, a policy that would have been both practical and politically advantageous because of growing resistance to refugees in Geneva, but aid to refugees on a large scale would have required an organized means of collecting and distributing money. This could very well have been centered around the ministers. It might have eventually been expedient to designate others for the task, following the biblical example of the deacons. This is what surfaced in the records of the *Bourse française*.

There is more concrete evidence of the origins of the *Bourse* than this speculation, however. Specifically, the beginning of the *Bourse* has been traced back to the will of an early refugee, David (de) Busanton (of the Hainault, who died in Geneva in 1545), who willed a sizable sum to the poor of Strasbourg and to the poor of Geneva (at least one authority says to "foreign refugees").[15] Emile Doumergue, Calvin's biographer, stated categorically that it was with this money that Calvin founded the first funds of the *Bourse française*, but Busanton's actual will, which would substantiate this claim, has not been located.[16] Historians thus have questioned the association of Busanton with the *Bourse*.[17] This association is traced back to the Genevan chronicler Michel Roset, who claimed that shortly after the legacy was made the contributions and distributions for the poor were organized into a fund under the charge of deacons and receivers.[18] Roset may have been telescoping events since he was a boy when the legacy was made, or he may have been quoting his father, who was an active civic leader.[19]

The issue of the legacy of David Busanton involves more than him, however, for if his will was instrumental in organizing relief for poor refugees in Geneva, then Calvin may have been involved as well. The details of the founding of the *Bourse* elude us. There is no positive proof that Calvin created it, nor that Busanton's legacy constituted the original funds, but the possibility of a connection does exist. Calvin intimated to Pierre Viret that he knew Busanton well and even witnessed his death.[20] He commented on

Busanton's death: "A little afterwards he gave up his soul into the hands of Christ with a constancy of faith rare and admirable."[21] Moreover, half of the legacy was willed to the poor of Strasbourg, the city where Calvin had been minister to the French congregation. Was this mere coincidence, or was it Calvin's influence?

As for the date of the Bourse's origins, it is possible to be more precise than simply the decade of the 1540s. Clearly the *Bourse française* did not exist when Calvin returned from Strasbourg or he would have mentioned it in the Ecclesiastical Ordinances of 1541 when he described the role of the deacons with reference to the city hospital. At that time no mention was made of any deacon other than the procurators and hospitalers. In the early 1540s the city seems to have been coping with the refugee problem directly (by providing work, for instance), but by 1545 there were indications that the refugees may have been putting pressure on the city's resources. On 9 March 1945 the city council acted on Calvin's request to put the hospital's accounting in order, to list the revenue in writing, and to keep track of those who were given assistance.[22] Then on 15 June the council attempted to chase the poor foreigners out of town. They were to be assembled, given alms of bread, and commanded never to come back to Geneva again.[23] It was just ten days later that Calvin announced to the city council David Busanton's legacy, a considerable sum for the time. There are no records showing how this money was distributed except for a slur by Jerome Bolsec suggesting that Calvin misused it, nor is there any concrete indication of whether or not the legacy immediately caused the establishment of what later was called the *Bourse française*. In any case, sometime before the end of September 1550 the fund was apparently functioning.[24]

It is evident that when record keeping began, the *Bourse* activities were already in progress, because the first pages of the account books give evidence of previous activity. The first expenditure was to the copyist of Calvin's sermons, who had begun his work a year earlier with the sermon of 25 August 1549.[25] The entry in the account book refers to a payment for sermons of the month of September 1550 for which the *Bourse* was in arrears. (The copyist continued to be salaried by the *Bourse* until December 1560.[26]) In addition, the first list of donors included twenty-nine separate contributions (plus four that were crossed out) including the proceeds of what seems to have been a collection box, all of which hint at some anterior activity.[27] Moreover, in Calvin's correspondence there is evidence of prior contributions, including a gift of ten ecus from an unnamed woman. Calvin wrote to her that he had placed this contribution in someone else's hands to distribute. This occurred twenty months before the formal records of the *Bourse* began.[28] In the first month of its recorded activity there were 118 disbursements, and some of these persons were to receive money from the *Bourse* for years.[29] It is difficult to imagine that they were all called together

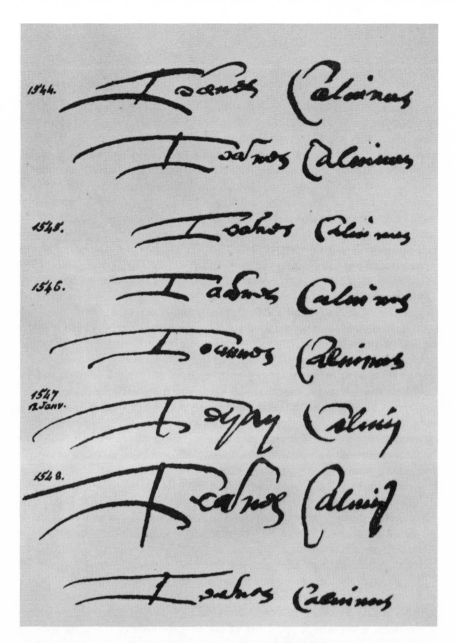

These signatures of John Calvin, 1544–48, are in Latin, "Ioannus Calvinus," except for that of 12 January 1547, which is in French, "Iehan Calvin." The "I" and the "J" are often interchanged in this period, and there is an "h" in the sixteenth century version of Jean. Letters are shaped differently, such as "a," "e," "h," and "o"; and abbreviations are frequently used, such as the curved stroke substituted for the first "n" in Ioannes that is attached to the "a" in all of the Latin signatures except for the first, in which it is over the middle of the name, and the fifth, in which there is no abbreviation. Calvin often makes a capital "C" with the use of two strokes of the pen. From M. Audin, *Histoire de la vie, des ouvrages, et des doctrines de Calvin,* vol. 2 (Paris: Maison, Libraire-Éditeur, 1841).

by chance for the first time that month. Although there is no definite proof of this hypothesis, the accounts themselves give the distinct impression that *Bourse* activities were already in progress when the accounts began. The first surviving account book apparently marks a step in the organization of the fund when accounts were to be formally kept and administrators officially chosen. To further substantiate this thesis, it should be noted that the first three deacons to administer the *Bourse* were probably on the job before they were formally committed to that office. All three men were entered into the lists of the inhabitants of Geneva in May and June of 1549.[30]

There are thus four concrete dates to work with: the death in 1545 of David Busanton, the entry of the three future deacons in May and June 1549 as inhabitants of Geneva, the start of the copying of Calvin's sermons by Denis Raguenier on 25 August 1549, and the opening of the accounts on 30 September 1550. Sometime within this span of five years the *Bourse française* was organized. Sometime within the year prior to the opening of the account books the three deacons may have begun their work.

One possible conclusion is that aid to the refugees had been going on for some years, both through legacies such as those of David Busanton and by acs of personal charity. Eventually, what began informally could have been organized into a common fund, financed by a cadre of donors from which were chosen several administrators. These men would have been called deacons to conform to Calvin's idea of an office in the church dedicated to helping the poor. The institution's framework seems to have grown both from the needs of the time and the theology of Calvin.

Calvin's involvement was more concrete than merely the provision of guidelines if he was instrumental in influencing the will of David Busanton. His regular presence as both a donor and a recommender of individual poor people in the account books also suggests an ongoing concern on his part.[31] Although to assert that Calvin created the *Bourse française* would be to overstate what the facts allow, he can fairly be allocated a major role in its activities without detracting from the important role of numerous other individuals whose names are less well known today. Part of Calvin's genius was his ability to assign responsibility and mobilize the energies of others. Ultimately, it is perhaps most fair to say that the *Bourse française* was the work of a group of peole and not the creation of just one man. In this, as in other areas of Genevan life at the time, too much can be attributed to Calvin, who would have acknowledged the involvement of others. The Reformed Church and its institutions were in many ways the product of a group effort, and the *Bourse française* was no exception.

3
Welfare, Refugees, Publishing

In considering the *Bourse française* as a welfare institution and refugee agency, it is important to place it solidly within its context in the sixteenth century. In some ways it was very much like other welfare institutions of the period, largely because the needs of the poor were similar. Everywhere the needy included the poverty-stricken and the disabled, the overnight travelers and the long-term pensioners. Some had fallen into momentary inconvenience or were temporarily unemployed, while others belonged to the world of the chronically poor. Some were wealthy people and those of noble birth who had fallen on hard times. (These "shamefaced poor" felt that begging was intolerable for anyone of their status, although some joined religious orders that deemed it a meritorious and humbling act.) Some poor came from families that had learned the art of begging and passed down its tricks from father to son and mother to daughter. Some were the victims of circumstance or environment: drought, famine, or the population growth of the later sixteenth century. Poor widows and orphans tended to dominate the rolls. These were the facts of life from which no welfare institution, including the *Bourse française*, could entirely escape.

But the *Bourse française* also differed from other contemporary institutions because it dealt largely with refugees, which created peculiarities of its own, notably high turnover on the welfare rolls. The special predicament of the refugees had forced onto the welfare rolls many who would not have been there in a more stable environment. Many of them apparently became self-supporting within a short while after resettling in Geneva, or they moved on or went back home. This made it possible for the *Bourse* to expect that it would not have to support them for a long time. This hope was not always realized, but it encouraged optimistic policies toward rehabilitation that would have been unrealistic if the sole clientele had been the intransigent poor.

37

The role of the *Bourse française* as a refugee agency made it unique. In the sixteenth century welfare administrators, not unlike those today, attempted to exclude outsiders from local welfare rolls. Thus the fact that the *Bourse* had been founded to aid foreigners made it somewhat of an anomaly. In reality, it functioned in two capacities, as welfare fund and as refugee agency.

Keeping in mind, then, these dual functions of the *Bourse française*, one can consider the activities of the *Bourse* at closer range and in greater detail. The temptation in evaluating any Genevan institution of this period is to consider it more original than it actually was, because Geneva has become a casebook for social theorists studying the impact of Calvinism on the modern world. Not all observers, when concentrating on Geneva, have kept an eye on the rest of Europe; modern historians have often failed to see beyond contemporary American conceptions of church and state. In a community of the sixteenth century, an institution of the church such as the *Bourse française* may not have been much different from similar civic welfare institutions. With these considerations in mind, it is, nevertheless, illuminating to consider the welfare and refugee activities of the fund.

As a welfare institution, the *Bourse* intended to help the poor in every conceivable way. It was guided, apparently, by a judicious combination of pragmatism and precedent. The administrators of the fund acted according to what they understood as normal in sixteenth-century welfare practice, but they were also practical men. They responded with ingenuity to the needs of the immediate situation in Geneva to produce an institution that was at once similar and dissimilar to its counterparts across Europe. It illustrates how practical sixteenth-century Europeans came to grips with the need for organized welfare.

The role of the *Bourse* as a fund for refugees implied that its aid was temporary, but for many individuals this was not the case. In reality, the deacons cared for virtually every type of poor person, including those who spent the rest of their lives on welfare. On one end of the budget were the passersby who received a small sum adequate for an overnight stay, and on the other end of the welfare spectrum were the aged, the disabled, and the terminally ill who had no hope of becoming self-supporting. Between these two extremes there was substantial variety. Although in many ways a description of the range of people whom the *Bourse* helped reads like any welfare roll of the period, the refugee component made it unique.

The shortest term aid that the *Bourse* offered was the traditional viaticum to travelers. This practice stemmed from the pre-Reformation custom of helping pilgrims along the way to their destinations. Geneva had long been a stopover point for those on pilgrimage. The Protestant city's continuance of the long-established viaticum testified to the extent to which patterns of propriety in giving had become ingrained, but it also reflected the expedience of aiding travelers. It was better to give voyagers a small sum for their promise to leave on the morrow than to risk having them steal or break the city's ordinance against begging, and it was better to give poor travelers a little money to move on than to have them linger in town long enough to become ill or fall into long-term indigence. The account books do not reveal the religious affiliation of the passersby, only that the viaticum was a welfare handout practiced from the beginning of the *Bourse*. As good sixteenth-century men, the deacons continued it as a normal part of welfare.[1]

The influx of overnight guests blended almost imperceptibly into that of the religious refugees, because many of the refugees also appeared to be transient, moving on or staying in town for awhile and then returning home. Possibilities for exodus for those who came truly seeking refuge were limited, however. Either rooms or jobs had to be found for them in the city or arrangements had to be made for them to move on to a safe place elsewhere. Not all of them were poor, of course, for some had escaped with their possessions intact.

In addition to the true religious refugees, many people who decided to move to Geneva had felt no religious pressure to leave their homeland. This latter group could more aptly be called "religious immigrants" or just "immigrants," because their motivations were sometimes mixed, unclear, or nonreligious. Many came with entire families, including young children and even servants. On arrival in the city some of these individuals and families needed help.

For whatever reasons they came, many of the newcomers arrived with virtually nothing: limited clothing, no blankets or bedclothes, no beds or household utensils. Artisans brought skills but no tools with which to work. Professional men came ready to use their talents, but they could not always be absorbed into the Genevan economy. Some of these people moved on, but others had no place to go. There were also those who had no usable skill, such as priests who had become Protestant. The solution of the deacons was to retrain them.

The goal of the deacons was apparently to get able-bodied refugees back on their feet as soon as possible, by providing temporary housing, short-term support, and job retraining when necessary. The deacons paid for tools to set up artisans in trade and provided some of them with raw materials. Cards were purchased for carders of wool, for example, and woodworking tools for a woodworker.[2] Such relatively modest expenditures could make people financially independent with little outlay, and since loans were preferred to handouts, the deacons had an opportunity to recover some of their outlay.[3] Occasionally the *Bourse* advanced larger sums, paying the rent for a shop for someone in business, for instance.[4] Disbursements to an individual were often occasioned by the special recommendation of a donor or a pastor. In a number of cases John Calvin himself was personally concerned.[5]

The Genevan economy absorbed many refugees, no doubt including those whom the *Bourse* helped back into productive employment, but it is difficult to determine with any precision how often this happened, because when names disappeared from the welfare rolls, the account books did not specify why. In the seventeenth century there were records of the poor thanking the deacons and bidding adieu in the minutes of the deacons' meetings, but the account books of the sixteenth century recorded departures irregularly, usually only when a financial expenditure was involved, such as when the deacons paid people to help them go home.[6] At times the deacons appear to have encouraged people to leave in order to relieve the welfare roles. For instance, the deacons gave eight florins to a widow who took her children and left for the country, saying she had a way to support her family there without relying on the church for support.[7]

Refugees who stayed in Geneva certainly might have set themselves up in business or sought employment with a master craftsman once they were furnished with tools, retrained, or given a loan, and the *Bourse's* help sometimes did not stop at that. Printer-publisher Jean Crespin and other donors to the *Bourse* may have employed and trained refugees.[8] With the help of the *Bourse* in finding a job, the chance of successful employment for refugees must have been enhanced.

Of course, not everyone who came wanted to work, and the city tried to protect itself and the *Bourse* by requiring that newcomers register their profession or craft and the names of those who would witness for them. This ordinance of 7 December 1568 also stipulated that no more people would be received who were without profession or craft. One wonders if this ordinance was as difficult to enforce as those that the city made against begging.

> For as much as several of those who retreated here now are poor and do not want to do anything, charging the *Bourse* to relieve them, it is ordered that from now on one receive no more of these who have no profession and that those who witness for them promise that they will not be a charge, and that in order that they can be summoned, when they come, that they present themselves at the *Bourse*, that one put in their letters their crafts and the name of those who witnessed for them.[9]

Despite frustration with some refugees who did not want to work, adult males with marketable skills were relatively easy for the *Bourse* to handle, even though the families that many of them brought presented a heavier initial charge. The sad fact of the welfare rolls, however, was that families that came intact did not always stay that way, and some families arrived already broken. Not that divorce was common in Reformation Geneva. It was practically nonexistent, although Geneva allowed divorce in cases of proven adultery or prolonged desertion. Death rates were high in the mid-sixteenth century, however, so many families were broken by death. When the heads of households died with no viable pension plans to fill the gap, the

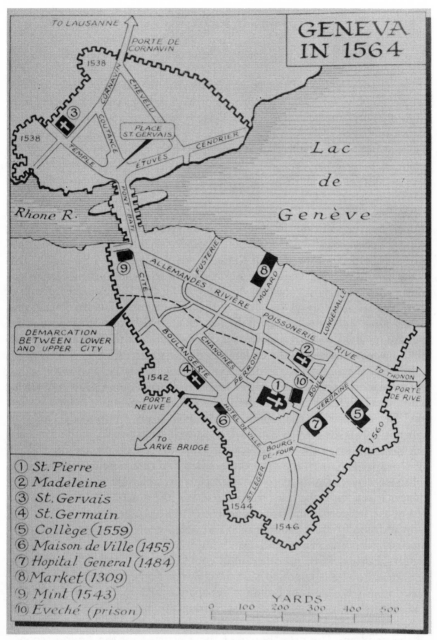

GENEVA
IN 1564

TO LAUSANNE
PORTE DE
CORNAVIN
1538
CORNAVIN
CHEVELU
COUTANCE
③
1538
TEMPLE
PLACE
ST. GERVAIS
ÉTUVES
CENDRIER
PONT BATI
Rhone R.

L a c
d e
G e n è v e

⑨
CITÉ
ALLEMANDES
FUSTERIE
RIVIÈRE
⑧
MOLARD
POISSONERIE
LONGEMALLE
RIVE
TO THONON
DEMARCATION
BETWEEN LOWER
AND UPPER CITY
BOULANGERIE
CHANOINES
PERRON
②
⑩
⑤
1560
PORTE
DE RIVE
1542
④
①
VERDAINE
PORTE
NEUVE
⑥
HOTEL DE VILLE
BOUL
⑦
⑤
TO
ARVE BRIDGE
ST LEGER
BOURG
DE FOUR
1544
1546

① St. Pierre
② Madeleine
③ St. Gervais
④ St. Germain
⑤ Collège (1559)
⑥ Maison de Ville (1455)
⑦ Hopital General (1484)
⑧ Market (1309)
⑨ Mint (1543)
⑩ Éveché (prison)

YARDS
0   100   200   300   400   500

A map of the walled city of Geneva in 1564 showing the streets and the location
of the churches, collège, city hall, hospital, market, mint, and prison. The map is
by Russell H. Lenz with the permission of John Wiley & Sons, Inc., and of
E. William Monter from his book, *Calvin's Geneva* (Huntington, N.Y.: Robert E.
Krieger Publishing Company, copyright © 1967), p. 116.

Bourse was left to support a person's dependents. There were also cases of abandonment.

The deacons did what they could to alleviate the plight of these solitary people, mostly women. They provided them with piecework sewing and additional orphaned children to care for to relieve their poverty. They rented rooms for them.[10] Nevertheless, many a widow lived off a pittance of a handout per week, a sum that at times may have been less than enough to maintain an adequate caloric intake unless a recipient received outside support or food or was able to buy her staple of bread at prices below the legal minimum.[11]

The most promising positive solution for widows was remarriage, although marriage did not necessarily move one off the welfare roles. Moreover, poor women did not attract the prospects that the widows of wealthy men did. Some widows brought whole business enterprises with them, such as the famous masters' widows of European printers who sometimes married journeymen already involved in their former husbands' businesses. Despite their bad financial prospects, some of the poor widows did remarry, and in some cases the deacons alleviated the burden on their prospective spouses by continuing child support payments to the "children of the first bed," as the phrase went, referring to the children of the first marriage.[12]

Death of the mother in a refugee family, leaving the father a widower, does not appear to have had as serious financial repercussions. But even then, when small children were involved, the deacons sometimes helped a man out. The *Bourse* paid the monthly stipends of many wet nurses. This was true not only if the mother had died, but also if she were sick, and on at least one occasion when the mother was declared to have absolutely no milk at all.[13] Apparently even the minimal fees for child care were enough to put a subsistence level family onto the welfare rolls, although in some such instances it was only the bill for the nurse that the deacons paid, leaving the rest of the support of the family apparently up to the parents.

In addition to these children who had only one living parent, there were orphans who apparently had lost both father and mother. In sixteenth-century Europe when no other adult could step in, a welfare organization was sometimes called upon to raise the children. Some of these orphans were raised in city hospitals or buildings set apart as orphanages, but the *Bourse* had no such institutions of its own during this period. This led to what appear to have been foster home arrangements, perhaps in the best interests of the children. The great books of those assisted by the *Bourse* records names of orphans along with the names of those to whom money for child care was paid. Many of the recipients, foster parents so to speak, were widows, but other foster parents were married couples. Sometimes it is difficult to determine the marital status of a foster parent.[14] Typically a child changed foster homes before reaching maturity.[15]

One can trace a number of stories of parents, poor or terminally ill, who fell on welfare, died, and left their children to the *Bourse* to support. Subsistence payments, gifts of clothing, and medical bills were regularly recorded after the children's names. At adolescence the *Bourse* would often cover their apprenticeship fees.[16] These were typical arrangements, not only for the *Bourse française*, but for the city hospital, which handled the orphans of Geneva. The two differed in that the city hospital had a separate building in which to care for some of its orphans, at least after they were past the age when they needed a wet nurse.

The *Bourse*'s goal for these orphans was to provide them with a means of making a living and to get them out into the workaday world. There are no indications in the account books that any of them were adopted, although that does not preclude the possibility. Children were legally adopted in Lyons, France, during this period, from the city hospital.[17]

The responsibility of the *Bourse* for children included support for children in families that were still partially intact, particularly when the surviving parent was a widow who was herself a welfare recipient. In these instances, the *Bourse* apparently gave the same type of aid as for children with no surviving parents except that sometimes the deacons may have been able to get by with partial support. Some people appear to have asked for help with their children only for occasional major expenditures, such as apprenticeship fees.[18] Any poor family, even one with both parents alive, could apparently make this type of request.

When the *Bourse* was responsible for child support, the deacons apparently felt that they had some say in the children's future. In 1580, for instance, when a women refused the apprenticeship arrangements that the deacons had made for her son they judged her "unworthy to receive assistance from the money of the poor." She then "recognized her faults" and acquiesced, but she apparently had a better idea of her son's mind than the deacons, who later recorded that the boy did not stay with the apprenticeship they had arranged for him.[19]

The deacons helped many young people who were not necessarily orphans on their way to making their own livelihood. The early account books contain references to a number of young men who received money from the deacons while waiting to find a master, and sometimes the donors to the fund helped provide employment. The printer and martyrologist Jean Crespin took as apprentices young men on the welfare rolls.[20] The deacons also paid school fees for both boys and girls and occasionally for adults, even married women.[21] They helped students who were in need, poor, or ill.[22] They even paid ten florins to a schoolboy to depart for England.[23]

The *Bourse* appears to have had more young people to support than just those whom death would leave in need. One wonders if some of them had ever had family in town. The entries in the accounts give the impression of many young men and boys coming to Geneva by themselves, even before the academy was founded, perhaps leaving family to follow the reform or to seek their fortunes, but falling quickly into need.

Women arrived on their own, too, but not, at least so far as the welfare rolls reveal, young women seeking their fortune. Rather they were widows, often with dependent children, or married women whose husbands were not with them. Some of these women were from families that were later reunited in Geneva. The deacons made frequent disbursements to people returning to France to bring back a member of the family or personal possessions that they had left behind. These were frequently men seeking wives, children, or possessions.[24] The plight of the solitary woman was often a product of the religious strife in France; some of their husbands were dead, imprisoned, or serving on the galleys because of the reform. Geneva and the *Bourse française* provided a haven of refuge for these women. The wives and families of martyrs were helped, too.[25] And at least one man's wife was a prisoner; he was a bookseller from Paris.[26]

Occasionally the prisoners themselves were able to make their way to Geneva, such as a poor man of Paris leaving the galleys and Nicolas Campin, a cutler, who had been one of four prisoners released by decree from prison in Paris.[27] Some came fleeing for their lives; there were ministers among them.[28] Some came alone and some in groups, as when four or five couples arrived in the summer of 1560, "chased for the Gospel."[29] The stories of these fugitives must have fueled awareness of persecution and fired the efforts of the *Bourse* to continue to meet the needs of the incoming refugees. One wife of a minister, for instance, whose husband was listed as absent for several months in 1559 and then finally as "hung for his witness to the gospel" in December 1560, appeared a month later as a widow on the welfare rolls, and the deacons were paying for her room.[30]

Such stories must have contributed to the anger at persecution in France. The welfare rolls, however, were not usually as exciting as the record of these recipients would imply. Ex-prisoners and the families of martyrs were a decided minority. More often the rolls were a regular repetition of the same people coming back again and again to the weekly distribution; a paleographer of the nineteenth century making a transcription of the accounts threw up his hands in despair over the tedium of the same names.[31]

This boring repetition of names, however, was evidence of the work of the deacons with those who needed persistent support. The *Bourse's* perseverance year after year with the same needy people indicated its commitment to the indigent. These were the sort of recipients who also appeared on the rolls of welfare funds that served a less transient population: the aged and the invalids, those mentally and physically incompetent to make it on their own. The deacons provided them with a weekly subsistence dole, a bed, clothing, and medical care, or whatever combination of these was deemed necessary.

In its handling of long-term support, the *Bourse* resembled many other contemporary welfare funds of a more stable nature. It had its own peculiarities, however. It apparently gave no regular handout of bread, for instance, as did the city hospital during this period. Not until the inundation of refugees in the late seventeenth century with the revocation of the Edict of Nantes in France did the *Bourse française* made arrangements for the hospital to cook bread regularly in its ovens.[32] In the sixteenth century the *Bourse* sometimes gave out quantities of grain that the recipient could pass on to the baker to prepare, but no bread lines were mentioned. Instead there was a dole of money, usually weekly, but at times twice a week or biweekly. Gifts of grain were less the practice at the beginning of the account books than later on in the century, perhaps due to the increase in gifts of grain received by the *Bourse*.

Superficially there appear to have been certain inequities in the handouts. People who seem to have been in the same situation, widows for example, received different amounts of money. The amount was usually relatively consistent for any individual over a period of weeks, as if a specific sum had been decided on for that person. The variation in the amounts paid to similar people may have been caused by a different number of dependents. Children were not necessarily listed in the account books in the early years, but the deacons would have been aware of how many children a person had to support and could have adjusted the stipend accordingly. Occasionally, when an aid recipient was unable to come to the weekly distribution, a previously unmentioned child would appear instead. For the first years of accounting it is simply not possible to determine the number of dependents with any accuracy.

Other areas of aid were equally ambiguous, that of housing for the refugees, for instance. The accountant did not often state where an individual aid recipient lived (although he did on occasion, which provided information about who took refugees into their homes). The deacons paid out money to many aid recipients for their rooms or for their beds, or even for the rent of their houses, but for other people on the regular welfare rolls room rent was never mentioned.[33] Did they get free housing somewhere? Did the *Bourse* have its own accommodations at this time? (It owned some real estate that it might have used to accommodate refugees, or it could have rented houses.) Or were the poor expected to pay their rent out of their weekly subsistence allowance? It appears to have been inadequate for that.

Wherever the recipients lived, the fund provided for specific aspects of their existence that one might well have expected to be left up to them. It lent out mattresses, for instance, and bedclothes. During cold weather the deacons bought firewood or arranged for the distribution of wood that had been received as gifts to the poor.[34] They also provided people with clothing. In the early years they sometimes allowed individuals to buy their own clothes, but as the *Bourse* grew it tended to purchase cloth in quantity and employ tailors and seamstresses to sew garments, as the city hospital did.[35] Shoes were provided, apparently purchased on the open market at first, in contrast to the hospital of Geneva, which periodically employed a cobbler.[36] The account books specified if a pair of shoes was new or used. (There apparently was a market for secondhand shoes.) The *Bourse* also paid for shoe repairs.[37] The deacons also paid for a variety of services and individual purchases, such as the laundering of a shirt and a basket for a small boy.[38]

Medical care was an important part of the *Bourse*'s provisions. The deacons spent a lot of money for it and helped many people. The great books of the assisted reveal the large numbers of people who were served at some point in their lives by the apothecary of the *Bourse française* and the fees that were paid out to the doctor and the barber-surgeon.[39] The deacons were especially called upon when a child was born.[40] The records occasionally reveal the nature of medical care, because sometimes the accountant specified what type of service was offered, and later in the history of the *Bourse* drug bills were itemized.[41] These expenditures reveal that the deacons apparently accepted the medical practices of the age, paying regularly for contemporary procedures such as bloodletting and on one occasion giving thirty sous to someone to go and "change air" on the recommendation of a doctor.[42] Dubious as was the value of these expenditures, in other respects the efficacy of care met modern comprehensiveness. For instance, the deacons hired guardians for those who were ill or disabled and provided for their dependents.[43] The deacons arranged for the care of the sick, at first in private homes and inns, and later in the city hospital.[44] After its first few years the *Bourse* took to using the city hospital more and more, as indicated by the regular bills the *Bourse* paid to the hospital for its services.[45] In the eighteenth century the *Bourse* established its own facility on the Bourg-de-four, across the street from what was then the city hospital.[46]

The *Bourse* was comprehensive and versatile in medical care, as in its other activities. It exhibited a surprising degree of flexibility during its early years, both in short-term and in long-term support, and, when all its functions are considered, it appears to have been quite thorough in its efforts to provide for the needs of the refugees. In providing for their resettlement, its contribution to the success of the refuge of Protestants in the sixteenth century must have been considerable.

The flexibility of the *Bourse* was apparently enhanced by a willingness to consider any legitimate request; indeed, the list of demands on its resources was greater than any ordinary welfare fund would expect. The community behind the *Bourse* apparently allowed it a scope so broad that it could meet any need that arose; in fact, it was allowed and perhaps even encouraged to become involved in activities that were not strictly welfare in nature. This was perhaps an inevitable tendency for an institution that represented the interests of the ardent immigrant French Protestant community in Geneva.

The welfare functions of the *Bourse française* shaded off into other projects that were more commonly governed by a church budget, which for the first generation of its existence, is perhaps a more accurate description of the fund. It was regularly involved, from the very first, in expenditures only indirectly related to its commission to help the poor. The very first expenditure on the surviving accounts, in fact, was not a welfare recipient at all but to an employee: in October 1550 the *Bourse* paid two ecus to the copyist of Calvin's lectures and sermons, and, as the account books suggest, the deacons were already in arrears to this man, who had apparently started work a year before.[47]

Master Denis, as the copyist was called in the accounts, was a long-term employee of the fund by the name of Denis Raguenier. In a catalogue of Calvin's sermons Denis stated that he had begun copying them the penultimate day of September 1549, which would have been exactly a year before the first surviving account book begins. Actually the first sermon was dated earlier, 25 August 1549.

> Since the penultimate day of September 1549, I, Denis Raguenier, writer, have collected the sermons of Monsieur Calvin, and these furnished into the hands of the deacons directed to provide for the needs of the poor French who are in the church of Geneva. . . . On the Acts of the Apostles . . . beginning the first of the said sermons Sunday the twenty-fifth day of August, 1549 in the morning.[48]

For almost eleven years Denis Raguenier copied the sermons of Calvin. He was able, by a form of shorthand, to write down word for word what Calvin said, with few words escaping him. He then copied the shorthand into longhand. This apparently became Raguenier's full-time occupation, since Calvin averaged over four sermons per week in a period of ten and one-half years prior to 21 February 1560.[49]

The deacons paid Denis Raguenier several times per month for this work. The record of these payments was entered into the account books of the *Bourse française* regularly alongside the handouts to the poor and the other expenditures. He also received periodic advances on his salary and financial assistance for his relatives from the *Bourse*, and he did not go without recognition in the larger community. On 21 January 1556 the city entered his name in the *Livre des Bourgeois* without the usual fee, in recognition of a book of eight sermons by Calvin that he presented.[50]

The precise date of his death is not known, but he ceased copying Calvin's sermons before Calvin stopped preaching them. His last payment from the deacons was in December 1560. That payment carries no exact date but falls sometime between the fourth and the twelfth of the month. He may have died during a lacuna in the death records of Geneva between 11 July 1560 and 8 May 1561. He was mentioned as deceased in a 19 January 1562 letter of the printer Conrad Badius in an edition of Calvin's sermons.[51]

Whatever the exact date of Raguenier's death, the *Bourse française* hired someone else to copy Calvin's sermons. Raguenier's replacement was named Paris, perhaps Paris Prostat, writer, entered into the book of inhabitants 4 September 1572. He first appears in the account books on 7 February 1561 when the deacons paid thirty sous to "Paris who writes the sermons." Thus began a regular outlay of money to him approximately twice a month. He began at a rate of two florins six sous for each pay period and reached a rate of nine florins three sous on 15 May 1562. He continued to receive that amount twice a month until Calvin's death on 26 May 1564. Paris then was paid at a lesser scale and less frequently until the end of 1564. His last payment in 1564 was on 26 December. The regularity of the payments during Calvin's lifetime would seem to indicate that Paris received a salary of a fixed sum, although there is some indication in the extraordinary account books of piecework payments for a stated number of sermons. The wife of Paris received several disbursements also.[52]

Thus for a period of at least fourteen important years the *Bourse française* paid for the copying of Calvin's sermons and lectures. The deacons appear to have supervised closely, sometimes buying the paper, paying for the binding, and seeing to the rewriting of sermons that were poorly transcribed. This was an activity appropriate to the French immigrant community in Geneva but was not within what one considers the ordinary activites of a welfare fund. Hence the *Bourse française* should be understood as more than a welfare institution.[53]

The motives behind some of these nonwelfare projects were clearly mixed. The deacons did not intend to squander welfare money; in fact, they hoped to realize a profit for the poor from what otherwise was a laudable project in itself, the preservation of Calvin's sermons. The project was similar to the publication of Théodore de Bèze's Psalms, the proceeds of which were also intended for the poor.[54] In exchange for the eventual proceeds, the *Bourse* made arrangements and paid at least some of the expenses. What a disappointment, then, when, as was to happen with the Psalter, some of the sermons were published in France without paying royalties to the *Bourse française*. Cries arose of stealing from the poor, but these very first efforts at copyright were difficult to enforce outside of Geneva. Unfortunately, the extent to which the poor benefited from either project is not substantiated, as the surviving receipts of the *Bourse* for the first generation of its activities contain no entries that specifically mention profits from either one, but most of the account books in which one could reasonably expect to find some record of profits from the Psalters and the sermons have not survived. Profits might have at one time been recorded and subsequently lost.

The outcome of this project of copying Calvin's sermons was not as happy as it might have been. Some were published within the century. Others were deposited at the college, which eventually became the University of Geneva. Of these a large number were sold and lost early in the nineteenth century, partly to make room on the library shelves. Attempts to recover them were largely unsuccessful, but the project of publishing the remaining sermons continues into the twentieth century. It began again in 1936, was interrupted by World War II, and goes on to the present.[55]

There may have been other employees of the fund in addition to the copyist of Calvin's sermons. Other people periodically received money from the *Bourse*, possibly for some type of service rendered, but, except for the doctor and the barber-surgeon, they are more difficult to identify and substantiate as employees.

Despite its other activities, the *Bourse française* was a fund primarily involved in direct welfare expenditures. It was by no means a "secular" institution, however. Even in its welfare functions, the religious convictions of the administrators and donors clearly influenced the sentiments of those distributing the money. The deacons aided the wives and families of prisoners, martyrs, and pastors. (The presence of a number of ministers on the welfare rolls is of particular interest and will be considered later.) These people, of course, might have come within the general purview of the *Bourse* anyway, but it is worth noting that the deacons made a point of mentioning extenuating circumstances that involved persecution, and these circumstances may have influenced their decisions. The religious motivations of the deacons are also prominent in the publishing activities of the *Bourse* involving Théodore de Bèze's Psalms and Calvin's sermons. There was a profit motive in these projects too, but the profits were destined for the poor.

The publishing activities of the *Bourse* blended into its functions as an international agency. It is with this role that the next chapter is concerned.

4

International Activities

The *Bourse française* was primarily a welfare fund, but several years prior to the outbreak of the Wars of Religion in France (April 1562) it became a missionary enterprise as well. It sent colporteurs and books into France in an attempt to win the nation for the religious reform at a time when tempers were heated and feelings of inequity were rising among the Protestants. This was the era when Geneva was also involved in strenuous efforts to supply the Reformed churches in France with ministers, an enterprise that has already been ably documented.[1] The action of the *Bourse* in sending religious literature into France confirms and expands what is already known about that zealous generation's activities in France. The *Bourse* functioned, in effect, as a bank, collecting funds from Protestants, channeling them through Geneva, and using them to send Bibles and Psalters into France at a time when this was illegal and dangerous.

Of all the activities in which the *Bourse française* engaged, its work as an international agency is the most astounding. Yet this missionary enterprise has long been hidden from modern view. The record of these acts was discreetly preserved among the other daily expenditures in the *Bourse* account books. The disbursements that pointed to missionary activity were stated with varying directness. Purchases of religious literature were clearly stated, for instance, as were some of the disbursements to a wealthy supporter of colporteurs and some of the financial support for missionary pastors and their families. Other disbursements were decidedly more vague, such as payments to individuals being sent by the Company of Pastors of Geneva into France for undesignated purposes. The deacons appear to have dispensed sums of money considerably larger than the usual welfare handouts to numbers of nameless or vaguely identified individuals, often at the behest of the company of Pastors. These individuals seem to have included couriers, emissaries, and missionary pastors. Only occasionally does the accountant reveal explicitly the details of these suspect expenditures. That there is any account of such clandestine events at all owes much to the deacons' practice of keeping scrupulous account of expenditures. The entries that suggest international activities in France are cloaked in vague phrases that could give away little of what was being done to the casual reader.

The disbursements that indicate missionary activity by the *Bourse* between 1559 and 1562 consist of three distinct categories: (1) entries referring to a wealthy supporter of colporteurs named Laurent de Normandie; (2) entries mentioning purchases of Bibles, Psalters, and catechisms; and (3) entries listing miscellaneous, ill-defined disbursements. Together they constitute what proof survives from the accounts of the *Bourse* that it became, for a few years, a missionary arm of the French refugee community in Geneva.

Most of these disbursements were inconspicuously recorded in an account book of the *Bourse française* that was classified among documents pertaining to the city hospital, somewhat apart from the other manuscripts of the *Bourse*.[2] There are no surviving account books in sequence immediately before or after it. This volume of the account books is crucial for its references to the missionary work of the *Bourse française*. It covered the extraordinary expenses of the *Bourse française* from 1 August 1559 to the end of July 1570. The extraordinary expenses of the fund are important because they listed the clandestine activities. The ordinary expenses are less significant because they were the regular welfare expenditures. It was the custom in Genevan bookkeeping of this time to divide expenditures into these two categories, and the deacons of the *Bourse française* conformed by keeping two parallel sets of books. The account book of ordinary expenses for the 1560s is apparently lost.[3] It was during the first three years of the account book of extraordinary expenses that entries indicate missionary activities. These were in the form of exceptional disbursements scattered among the traditional welfare expenditures. The nature of these entries rendered the evidence somewhat circumstantial, so they bear closer scrutiny.

The first of the three types of disbursements that indicate international activity were those to Laurent de Normandie, a wealthy supporter of colporteurs. Laurent de Normandie was a financier and distributor of books.[4] It is well known that Laurent de Normandie sent booksellers to his native France. His contracts with them are contained in the minutes of the notaries, and the scope of this business is documented in the extensive litigation over the settlement of his estate. The core of these documents has been published, revealing the extent and nature of the arrangements he made with the men carrying books from Geneva to sell in France.[5] The distribution itself was clandestine because it was both illegal and dangerous: the purchase and sale of books printed in Geneva were formally prohibited in France in April 1548. This was reinforced in 1551 in the Edict of Châteaubriand.[6]

The deacons' disbursements to Laurent de Normandie were outstanding for their regularity. Between August 1559 and May 1561 the *Bourse française* channeled money to him twice a week, on Sundays and Wednesdays. It was as if a planned event, supported by the fund, occurred regularly at his house on the court of the Cathedral of St. Pierre. Nothing quite like it had been entered in the books before.

The account book did not elaborate on what was going on at Laurent de Normandie's house. The brief entries of disbursements provided only hints, but there are several possibilities. On the face of it, the event at his house would appear to have been a handout to the poor. Some of the entries even specified that the money was intended for poor people at his house, but there are several reasons why this does not seem to be the whole truth. A handout at Laurent de Normandie's house would have been a duplication of effort, for the *Bourse* already had a regular dole to the poor that it had conducted for years, and, by the late 1550s, the accountant who recorded these disbursements was paying considerable attention to the names of aid recipients, sharpening up the records, whereas the "poor" at Laurent de Normandie's house were rarely named and those who were named were not typical indigent welfare recipients.[7]

The destination of the money, as well as the names of recipients, was vague. Many of the allocations to Laurent de Normandie were entered simply as "rendered to Monsieur de Normandie" with no indication of how they had been used.[8] This ambiguity was particularly noticeable on those occasions when he was also given money alloted to the poor. It was as if he were conducting two activities simultaneously, only one of which involved the poor. This was in keeping with his personal background, for he had been an active supporter of the *Bourse* for years. At the same time he may have been engaged in other activities with the *Bourse* through his profession as a financier of books and colporteurs.

It would have been inprudent for the *Bourse française* to have admitted its involvement in such affairs with detailed entries in the account books; it seems likely, therefore, that the undesignated activities that the *Bourse* funded through Laurent de Normandie had to do with the illegal export of religious books into France. The entries in the accounts lend credibility to this hypothesis. The accounts contain citations such as the following: "At Monsieur de Normandie's, distributed to diverse people, four florins," and "more to him again for another party, twenty-nine florins, two sous."[9] The ambiguity of the first entry and the quantity of money in the second imply that the recipients were not on welfare. Who were Laurent de Normandie's "people"? Could they have been the colporteurs whom he used in France? If they were colporteurs, the money from the *Bourse française* might have been to help support them in France, at least while funds were being channeled through Laurent de Normandie. There were numerous references of this nature.

Actually, supporting such individual men and families they left behind in Geneva was nothing new. The earliest indications of such activity were entered in the account books in the early 1550s, so that this support in the late 1550s represented only an acceleration of an already established practice, apparently enlisting the help of the person most highly organized in such affairs, Laurent de Normandie.

Before accepting this conclusion of what might have been happening at Laurent de Normandie's house, one other hypothesis should be explored: Could the anonymous people that the *Bourse* was helping have been the ministers being sent to serve congregations in France? Could these men even have been carrying along loads of books to supply the congregations to which they were being sent?

There is definite evidence that the *Bourse* was helping pastors and their families whom they sometimes left behind in Geneva. The extent to which this occurred and the degree to which this aid extended into France is difficult to determine. On at least one occasion the *Bourse* rented a room for a minister.[10] The deacons rented a whole house for some of the ministers' wives, and they gave direct handouts to several of the women: "to two wives of absent ministers, five florins"; "Also for the rent of a house for the wives of some ministers sent into France that belongs to the Prevost of Cluny, fifty-two florins, one sou."[11] These disbursements were intended for local uses and these expenditures were entered in the account books in a straightforward manner. Funds intended for international use were a different matter. It would have been highly incriminating for the bookkeeper to have recorded openly the disbursement of funds to be forwarded to France to help the subversive missionary effort there. They may have found other ways to keep track of the money, such as through the many indefinite entries in the accounts, for instance. There was, nevertheless, at least one specific reference to direct aid to a minister sent to France. In October 1559 the deacon, Jean Budé, recorded: "Likewise I gave back to Monsieur de Normandie nineteen ecus pistoles that he had advanced for a minister who had been sent to Gascony for which there is the signature of Antesignanus as a guarantee."[12] Thus, Laurent de Normandie was definitely implicated on at least this occasion of having given aid to someone being sent as a pastor to France. This raises the question of how many other undesignated disbursements channeled through him were being used to this end.

There are other considerations with regard to the ministers' support: the funds for ministers sent to France sometimes came from the congregations who called them. It is entirely possible that they were not always able to pay the full travel expenses and that the deacons made up the difference. It is also possible that the *Bourse* functioned as a channel through which funds from sponsoring congregations passed.

All these factors lead one to suspect that Laurent de Normandie was dealing with more than colporteurs at his house. Even if there were mainly colporteurs involved, that would have represented a considerable missionary effort, for Geneva had recently discovered the power of the printed word. These extraordinary activities of the *Bourse* coincided with what is considered a peak in the city's publishing activity and may have contributed to the dissemination of these books.

The details of how the *Bourse* supported the flow of books into France are not spelled out in the account books. There are no lists of titles, for instance, but numerous references to purchases of Bibles, Psalters, and catechisms indicate what books might have been involved. In itself the purchase of such books was not incriminating, because for years the deacons had bought religious and other kinds of books for individual poor people as the need arose.[13] Clearly books were considered a basic necessity of life along with food, clothing, and shelter. The deacons appear even to have accommodated infirmities, as when they bought a Psalter with large print for one poor man.[14] However, earlier purchases for individuals had identified the person to whom a book was going. For these mass purchases no recipients' names were indicated.

There seems every reason to suspect that some of the books were transported into France. Even a deluge of refugees that could have moved the *Bourse* to buy up a stock of books for them does not provide a full explanation; such a motivation should have been repeated at intervals to respond to the flow of immigrants. Also, the fact that the increased buying coincided with the activities at Laurent de Normandie's house is suspicous, although the purchases continued somewhat beyond the last reference to him in the account books in May 1561.[15]

At one point the account books reveal that some of the Psalters, at least, were shipped away. In January 1562 the deacons paid for the binding of Psalters that were sent to Théodore de Bèze by means of a person named Simon, who was afterward reimbursed for his trip to Paris: "For the Psalms sent to Monsieur de Bèze, that is to say, for the binding of forty-four, forty-eight florins, nine sous." "To Simon who carried the said books, advanced, first, ten florins," and "to Simon again for the completion of his trip, at the return from Paris, where he stayed thirty-two or thirty-four [*sic* thirty-three] days, nineteen florins, six sous."[16]

This is the only point at which the account books specify the shipment of books to France, and it is of special note that it involved Psalters. The *Bourse française* had a vested interest in Psalters because it had been given the rights to proceeds from the translation in verse of the Psalms of Theodore de Bèze. It was directly involved in arranging for their binding.[17] At one point this was done through a bookseller named Denis who had also bound New Testaments and catechisms for the fund.[18] The expenditures for Psalters disappeared from the accounts after the spring of 1562. During that year the various printshops of the city proceeded with the printing of the Psalters.

They were supposed to retain a percentage of sales for the *Bourse*, but the percentage was difficult to collect from the printers. De Bèze himself had to intervene on behalf of the poor.[19]

While it could be argued that the *Bourse* involvement with Psalters was a special case because of the deacons' direct interest in the profits from their production and sale, there was no clear financial benefit to account for the *Bourse* purchases of Bibles and catechisms. The purchase and transportation of all three may well have been a part of a missionary endeavor in France, and the overall motivation may have been more evangelical than monetary. Whatever financial benefit accrued, in any case, was not for the pockets of the deacons but for the poor.

In addition to the purchase of religious books and the expenditures through Laurent de Normandie, a third category of references in the account books points to exceptional activities by the *Bourse*. This was a group of miscellaneous, ambiguous disbursements that consisted of money paid to messengers and unnamed individuals for ill-defined purposes. Most of the recipients cannot be identified with certainty. Some were apparently insignificant figures who do not appear elsewhere in the records, and others may have been refugees passing through Geneva for a brief stay at most. What is remarkable is the variety of ambiguous people that the *Bourse* apparently used, over the years, for its purposes, or (it might be more accurate to say) that the Company used, since the Venerable Company of Pastors of Geneva was the guiding hand in many of these disbursements. Individual pastors were mentioned in support of such disbursements as well, specifically the pastors Pierre Viret and John Calvin, the latter usually referred to as "Monsieur Calvin" in the account books.

The ambiguous disbursements were apparently destined for a variety of purposes. Some may have been local, but many appeared to have been international. Overall, it appears that the deacons paid for a considerable amount of travel. There were people coming or going from Basel, Lyons, Lausanne, Paris, Grenoble, Dieppe, and even England. Some of them were sent expressly, perhaps carrying either money or messages. Others appear to have been on voyages that the *Bourse* supported but may not have initiated. Some of the people involved were well-known figures, but others are a mystery, either because they were not named, or because only their first name was mentioned. Who, for instance, was Pyramus, "who escaped from the hand of the executioners and tyrants" at Paris?[20] There was a Pyramus in the Candolle family of immigrants to Geneva from France who was an editor and printer, a likely profession for involvement in the *Bourse* during this period, but his known activity in the city dated from later in the century.[21]

The miscellaneous expenditures that hint at international activity are recorded in the extraordinary accounts of the *Bourse* between the years 1559 and 1562. They are scattered among the other disbursements for traditional welfare expenditures such as health care and cloth purchases, and they represent only a minority of the entries for the period. The ambiguous descriptions of these expenditures stand out in marked contrast to the deacons' efforts by 1559 to be precise and to identify by name those who received regular handouts. A selection of these suspicious entries from table 1 reads as follows:[22]

To a poor Burgundian boy to convey him to Basel by the order of the Company,	15 s		
To a young man in order to go to Lyons by the order of the Company,	20 s		
To Master François, having come from Lausanne, to render to Master Pierre Viret,	10 f		
To Pyramus, who has come from Paris, having escaped from the hand of the executioners and tyrants,	20 f		
To a good man of this church by the communication of the counsel of Monsieur Calvin,	30 f		
Paid back to Monsieur Remé [sic; René, a deacon] that he advanced by order of the Company,	11 f		6 d
To a poor boy whom we sent expressly to Grenoble,	2 f	3 s	
Rendered to Monsieur de Saint Germain that he gave to send to a poor prisoner of Grenoble,	5 f	2 s	6 d
To one unidentified person recommended by Monsieur Viret who was going to England,	2 f	4 s	4 d
To poor Pyramus, given again,	10 f		
Likewise and Monday the fifth [February 1560] by order of the Company,	20 s		
To the wife of Master Barthelemy, who went to Chartres[?] and then to Dieppe,	2 f		
To a poor young man in order to make his voyage into Normandy,	18 s		
To Monsieur René to reimburse to the Prevost Bergevin that he gave in our name to several companions,	7 f	6 s	
Tuesday the seventeenth [September 1560] by order of the Company,	3 f	9 s	

Such expenditures were not new to the account books. They were scattered here and there in the accounts from the early 1550s. As the decade progressed, they increased in frequency and diversity. The activities between 1559 and 1562 thus did not represent an entirely new departure, but rather an acceleration of practices already in effect. One is tantalized by possible meanings of some of these expenditures, made in a period that witnessed the Conspiracy of Amboise and intensified activity leading to the Wars of Religion in France. Sometimes the account books are startlingly clear; for instance, in November 1562, after the Wars of Religion had begun, the deacons purchased a halberd and a sword by order of the company.[23] The company referred to was probably the Venerable Company of Pastors of Geneva, an organization of the Genevan pastors.

At the very least, one is forced to acknowledge that whatever the money was used for, a strong precedent was set for using the funds of the *Bourse française* for nonwelfare expenditures. By 1559 it had become, in effect, a church budget rather than just a welfare fund. It was, in fact, a missionary arm of the Company of Pastors.

Table 1 is a translation of the expenditures from the extraordinary accounts of the *Bourse française* that seem to indicate nonwelfare activities during the period 1559–62. It includes entries from the three suspect categories: (1) those referring to Laurent de Normandie, (2) purchases in quantity of Bibles, Psalters, and catechisms, and (3) miscellaneous vague disbursements, often ordered by the Company of Pastors.

A word of caution: The list of expenditures in table 1, because it is a selection of entries scattered throughout the accounts, disproportionately emphasizes the extent to which the missionary effort of the *Bourse française* dominated its activities. Moreover, these disbursements were taken only from the part of the accounts of the *Bourse* that survived, the extraordinary accounts. There were also presumably ordinary accounts for this period that have not survived. Therein should have been listed the weekly handouts to the poor who were on the regular rolls of the fund.

Instead of the ordinary account books for the decade of the 1560s, there is an enormous manuscript volume called the "Great Book of the Assisted, 1560–1579."[24] This huge volume, together with the predominance of welfare rather than nonwelfare expenses in the years that precede it, attests to the primacy of the *Bourse's* role in helping the poor. Its missionary effort, important as it was, constituted ancillary activity that lasted a proportionately short time in the long history of the fund. Despite all its other functions, the *Bourse* was primarily a welfare institution. The press of refugees was too great for it to stray far from its charter role of helping the needy; its daily concern was for the poor, the widows and orphans, the unemployed and the sick.

Table 1
Selected Expenditures from the Extraordinary Accounts
of the *Bourse Française:*
August 1559–November 1562[25]

All the extraordinary expenditure since the first of August 1559

To two wives of absent ministers,	5 f		
For a dozen and a half of New Testaments from Monsieur Maccard,	4 f	6 s	
To three poor people at Monsieur de Normandie's,	3 f	1 s	
Rendered to Monsieur de Normandie,	12 f		
Rendered to Monsieur de Normandie again,	7 f	4 s	
Rendered to Monsieur de Normandie,	36 f		6 d

The extraordinary expenditure for the poor in the month of September 1559

To Denis for the binding of two dozen catechisms in leather,	4 f	
To himself for fifteen New Testaments, part in leather, part in parchment,	5 f	
Rendered as much to Monsieur de Normandie as to Monsieur de Saint Germain by the hands of Monsieur de la Touche,	33 f	2 s
To a poor Burgundian boy to convey him to Basel by the order of the Company,		15 s
To a young man in order to go to Lyons by the order of the Company,		20 s
Rendered to Monsieur de Normandie,	32 f	8 s

Extraordinary expenditure for the poor in the month of October 1559

Likewise I repaid Monsieur de Normandie 19 ecus pistoles that he had advanced for a minister who had been sent to Gascony for which there is the signature of Antesignanus [Pierre Davantes] as a guarantee. The said 19 ecus pistoles worth	95 f	
To Master François, having come from Lausanne, to render to Master Pierre Viret,	10 f	
Likewise for the rent of a house for the wives of some of the ministers sent into France that belongs to the Prevost of Cluny,	52 f	1 s
Rendered to Monsieur de Normandie that he had advanced for several days,	21 f	8 s
More to himself again for another party,	29 f	2 s

Table 1 *(Continued)*

Extraordinary expenditure for the poor in the month of November 1559

To the wife of Master Helye, absent minister, charged with five small children,	4 f		
For the preparation of 9 cords of wood at the house of Monsieur de Normandie at 7 sous per cord,	5 f	3 s	
To a poor man at Monsieur de Normandie's house,		9 s	
Rendered to Monsieur de Normandie,	15 f		
To Pyramus, who has come from Paris, having escaped from the hand of the executioners and tyrants,	20 f		
To a poor German recommended by Monsieur de Bèze in order to return to his country,	5 f	2 s	6 d
To a good man of this church by the communication of the counsel of Monsieur Calvin,	30 f		
To Julienne for the fashioning of the clothes that she made, other than 3 florins that she received from Monsieur de Normandie,	4 f	3 s	
To the son of Gohier for a bound Greek New Testament,		15 s	
To several poor people by the order of the Company,		31 s	
Likewise to Master Jacques Chapel, minister,	2 f	6 s	
Likewise sent to Estienne Girar by his man by whom he sent me a request for money, one Portuguese, 5 ecus sol, and 8 testons worth all of it together,	104 f	2 s	6 d
At Monsieur de Normandie's house distributed to diverse people,	4 f		
Likewise given to a poor glassmaker at Monsieur de Normandie's,		12 s	
Rendered to Monsieur Remé [sic; René] that he advanced by order of the Company,	11 f		6 d
To Baltazar for the fashioning of the clothes that he made other than two florins that he received from Monsieur de Normandie. I gave to him again,	4 f	6 s	
To a poor boy whom we sent expressly to Grenoble,	2 f	3 s	

Table 1 *(Continued)*

Rendered to Monsieur de Saint Germain that he gave to send to a poor prisoner of Grenoble,	5 f	2 s	6 d

Extraordinary expenditure for the poor in the month of December 1559

Likewise rendered to Monsieur de Normandie,	10 f	7 s	
Given, Wednesday the twelfth, at the home of Monsieur de Normandie,	3 f	4 s	6 d
To Pierre Bourgeoys, under the credit of Monsieur René, loaned,	10 f		
Sunday the seventeenth at the home of Monsieur de Normandie, to several poor people,	3 f	9 s	6 d
To a good person of this church, Chaperon,	20 f		
To one unidentified person recommended by Monsieur Viret who was going to England,	2 f	4 s	4 d
Likewise Wednesday the twentieth, at the home of Monsieur de Normandie to several poor people,	7 f		
Saturday at the end of the preaching, . . . the Company gave to several poor people,	5 f		
Sunday, the twenty-fourth, given at Monsieur de Normandie's,		18 s	
Likewise Tuesday the twenty-sixth, at Monsieur de Normandie's,	4 f	8 s	
Wednesday at Monsieur de Normandie's,	6 f	4 s	
To poor Pyramus, given again,	10 f		
To Monsieur de Normandie rendered,	13 f	2 s	
To several poor people at Monsieur de Normandie's, the last day of December,	7 f	8 s	

For the month of January 1560

To Charles Hernes, by order of the Company, in order to have some leather in order to work,	5 f		
To Denis, bookseller, for the binding of fifty Psalters [Psalms] at 2 sous each,	8 f	4 s	
Wednesday at Monsieur de Normandie's to several poor people,		23 s	
To a poor boy for having carried some fagots,			9d

Table 1 *(Continued)*

To Henry Gon for some fagots that he sent to Monsieur de Normandie's,		18 s	
Sunday at Monsieur de Normandie's, for several poor people,	6 f	3 s	
Again, the same day, to a poor person at Monsieur de Normandie's,		10 s	
Likewise to Jean de Tere for getting some small merchandise,	5 f		
To Denis for the binding of fifty Psalters [Psalms],	5 f	6 s	3 d
To Master Symon,		12 s	
Wednesday, the seventeenth, at Monsieur de Normandie's,	6 f	2 s	6 d
Sunday, the twenty-first, at Monsieur de Normandie's,	2 f	7 s	
To Denis, bookseller, again in order to finish the binding of fifty Psalters [Psalms],	2 f	9 s	9 d
Rendered to Monsieur de Normandie,	22 f	7 s	
To several poor people at Monsieur de Normandie's, Sunday, the twenty-eighth,	6 f	6 s	
Wednesday, the thirtieth [*sic;* Wednesday the thirty-first or Tuesday the thirtieth] at Monsieur de Normandie's,	9 f	3 s	

Extraordinary expenditure made in the month of February 1560

Sunday, the fourth, at Monsieur de Normandie's,	8 f	4 s	
Likewise and Monday, the fifth, by command of the Company,		20 s	
Wednesday, the seventh, at Monsieur de Normandie's,	6 f	2 s	
To Denis, bookseller, for the binding of twenty-four New Testaments,	6 f		
To Hierost who was a prisoner, by the order of the Company,	5 f		
To Denis, bookseller, for the binding of two dozen Testaments,	6 f		
Sunday, February eleventh, at Monsieur de Normandie's,	4 f	6 s	
Wednesday, the fourteenth, at Monsieur de Normandie's,	9 f		

Table 1 *(Continued)*

Sunday, the eighteenth, at Monsieur de Normandie's,	8 f		
Wednesday at Monsieur de Normandie's,	2 f	8 s	
To a poor soldier recommended,		12 s	
Sunday, the twenty-fifth, at Monsieur de Normandie's,	11 f	2 s	
Extraordinary expenditure in the month of March 1560			
Sunday at Monsieur de Normandie's, including therein a poor boy, brother of the brother-in-law of the registrar,	11 f	4 s	
To Jean de Tere for the children whom he teaches,		18 s	
Wednesday, the sixth, at Monsieur de Normandie's,	2 f	5 s	
To Trucheron for several parties,		12 s	6 d
Wednesday, the twentieth, at Monsieur de Normandie's,	3 f	3 s	
Sent to a poor man, prisoner at Grenoble, by Monsieur Perlier[?],	5 f		
Reimbursed to Monsieur de Normandie for several parties that he facilitated,	19 f	11 s	
To Piramus,	2 f		
To several poor people at Monsieur Normandie's, Sunday, the last of this month,	3 f	4 s	
To Salomon Camuz[?] by order of the Company in order to pay for his house,	6 f		
Extraordinary expenditure for the poor in the month of April 1560			
To a few poor people at Monsieur de Normandie's, Wednesday, the third,		21 s	
To a few poor people by the order of the Company,	2 f	6 s	
Sunday, the seventh, at Monsieur de Normandie's,	3 f		
From the side of Monsieur René as much for this trip as for that which he advanced last week	28 f	9 s	
To several poor people for the week,	2 f		
To several poor people at Monsieur de Normandie's, Wednesday, the seventeenth,		9 s	3 d
To several poor people at Monsieur de Normandie's, Sunday, the twenty-first,	3 f	11 s	11 d

Table 1 *(Continued)*

Sunday, the twenty-eighth, at Monsieur de Normandie's,	9 f	3 s	3 d
Likewise again to another, that is to say, Pierre Conseil,		18 s	9 d
Rendered to Monsieur de Normandie,	12 f		

Extraordinary expenditure made for the poor in the month of May 1560

To another poor person at Monsieur de Normandie's,		9 s	
Wednesday, the fifteenth, at Monsieur de Normandie's,	7 f	7 s	
Loaned to Monsieur de Besze[?] for Master Jean Randon, sick,	52 f	1 s	
To Master Jacques Chapel by order of the Company,	5 f		
Sunday, the twenty-sixth, at Monsieur de Normandie's,	10 f		
Wednesday, the twenty-eighth, at Monsieur de Normandie's to several poor people,	4 f	5 s	
To the wife of Master Barthelemy, who went to Chartres[?] and then to Dieppe,	2 f		

Extraordinary expenditure for the poor in the month of June 1560

To Master Jacques Chapel, Sunday the second,	4 f	8 s	
Sunday, the ninth, at Monsieur de Normandie's, to several people,	11 f	11 s	9 d
Reimbursed to Monsieur de Normandie for several parties,	15 f	7 s	6 d
Wednesday, the twelfth, at Monsieur de Normandie's,	2 f	3 s	
To several poor people at Monsieur de Normandie's,	2 f		
Sunday, the twenty-third, at Monsieur de Normandie's,	8 f		9 d
Wednesday, the twenty-sixth, at Monsieur de Normandie's,	13 f	5 s	3 d
This said day at Monsieur de Normandie's,	4 f	6 s	9 d

Extraordinary expenditure for the poor in the month of July 1560

Wednesday, the tenth, at Monsieur de Normandie's,	6 f	6 s	
The same day: Rendered to Monsieur de Normandie,	41 f	6 s	
To a certain person by the hands of Monsieur Autin [Antin?],		31 s	3 d

Table 1 *(Continued)*

Sunday, at Monsieur de Normandie's,	6 f	6 s	
Sunday, the twenty-first, at Monsieur de Normandie's, to several poor people,	10 f	7 s	6 d
To a poor young man in order to make his voyage into Normandy,		18 s	
At Monsieur Normandie's to several poor people by the hands of Monsieur Paré,	5 f	4 s	
Reimbursed to Monsieur de Normandie for money that he had advanced on several occasions and even for Master Jacques Besson to whom had been given three ecus sol for him,	28 f		3 d
From the preceding Sunday, the twenty-eighth, at Monsieur de Normandie's,	11 f		
Wednesday, the thirty-first, at Monsieur de Normandie's,	6 f	9 s	

Money expended extraordinarily for the poor in the month of August 1560

At Monsieur de Normandie's Sunday, the fourth,	12 f		
To Denis, bookseller, for the New Testaments, advanced,		27 s	
Wednesday at Monsieur de Normandie's,	9 f	8 s	
To Denis, bookseller, for the completion of the binding of two dozen New Testaments,	3 f	9 s	
To Jean de Tere to depart to his homeland,	12 f	11 s	
To Monsieur Maccard for twenty-four New Testaments,	6 f		
To Monsieur René in order to pay for the room of a minister,	8 f	7 s	
To Denis for the binding of thirty-eight Testaments,	6 f	4 s	
Saturday, the thirty-first, after the preaching, given,	3 f	8 s	

Extraordinary expenditure for the poor in the month of September 1560

Sunday, the first day of the said month, at Monsieur de Normandie's,	8 f	6 s	
Sunday, the eighth, at Monsieur de Normandie's,	6 f		
Wednesday, eleven, at Monsieur de Normandie's,	5 f	8 s	
Sunday, the fifteenth, at Monsieur de Normandie's,	5 f	11 s	

Table 1 *(Continued)*

To Monsieur René to reimburse to the Prevost Bergevin that he gave in our name to several companions,	7 f	6 s	
To a young man of Provence by order of the Company,		15 s	
Tuesday, the seventeenth, by order of the Company,	3 f	9 s	
Wednesday, at Monsieur de Normandie's,	11 f	9 s	9 d
Sunday, the twenty-second, in the morning, given at Monsieur de Normandie's,	3 f		
To Pierre Helon of Rennes in Brittany,	5 f		
Reimbursed to Monsieur de Normandie for several parties,	68 f	2 s	
More given two times at Monsieur de Normandie's, [one time] delivered by the hands of the Sieur Boucher, ten florins, the other by Monsieur du [*sic;* de] Paré, 12 florins, 6 sous, in my absence, for this,	22 f	6 s	
Likewise for three dozen and a half New Testaments from the deceased Monsieur Maccard at three sous the piece,	10 f	6 s	6 d
Sunday, the twenty-ninth, at Monsieur de Normandie's, given by the hands of Monsieur Paré,	10 f	3 s	6 d

Extraordinary expenditure for the poor in the month of October 1560

At Monsieur de Normandie's, Wednesday, the second,	7 f	7 s	9 d
To Monsieur de Paré for eight Bibles in French,	9 f	4 s	
Likewise to the good man of Brittany, Pierre Helon,	5 f		
For binding five Bibles in small volume to Monsieur de Paré,	4 f	2 s	
For the binding of three small Bibles,		30 s	
Wednesday, the sixteenth, at Monsieur de Normandie's to several poor people,	11 f	10 s	
Paid back to Monsieur de Normandie,	5 f	11 s	
To a poor man in order to depart for Nîmes,		14 s	
To Monsieur Cordernis[?] by order of the Company,	16 f		
To three others at Monsieur de Normandie's, Wednesday, the thirtieth,	2 f		

Table 1 *(Continued)*

To Master Jean du Taulne[?] by the hands of the collectors of Anjou,	5 f		

Extraordinary expenditure for the poor in the month of November 1560

Again to the bookseller who is teaching the trade to Balthasar for this second month as it was accorded to him,	5 f	3 s	
To two poor boys in order to return to France,		15 s	
Given to a poor Provençal recommended by Monsieur Du Four,		8 s	
For the binding of two dozen Psalters [Psalms],	4 f		
To Anthoine Ogier for a Bible,		9 s	2 d
To a good man of Anjou, Taulne[?] by the hands of those of the collect,	5 f		
Sunday, the twenty-third,		19 s	
To the bookseller for the binding of eighteen Psalters [Psalms],	3 f		

Extraordinary expenditure for the poor in the month of December 1560

To two poor people, Wednesday, the third,		12 s	
To several people, Tuesday, the seventeenth,	2 f	6 s	
Reimbursed to Sieur Jean Personne 15 florins, 6 sous, that he had advanced by our order to several poor sick people,	15 f	6 s	
Rendered to Monsieur de Normandie,	5 f	1 s	
Given to three poor people,		22 s	6 d
Wednesday, given to three poor people,		12 s	
Again for the fashioning of a few shirts,		5 s	
To a young man of Grenoble in order to depart to his country,	4 f		

Extraordinary expenditure for the poor in the month of January 1561

For the binding of two New Testaments and twenty-two Psalters [Psalms],	4 f	2 s	
To Madamoiselle du Plessix by the order of the Company,	5 f	6 s	3 d
To a poor minister, fugitive from the valley of Augroigne [a valley of Piedmont, 'Angrogna' in Italy],	5 f		

Extraordinary expenditure made for the poor in the month of February 1561

Wednesday at Monsieur de Normandie's,	4 f		
Wednesday, the twenty-sixth, at Monsieur de Normandie's,	9 f		

Table 1 *(Continued)*

Extraordinary expenditure for the poor in the month of March 1561

To Loys Mile for binding several books that
he had pawned [placed as surety],   12 s

To a poor boy in order to return to Paris,   6 s

Reimbursed to Monsieur de Paré that he
advanced by order of the Company,   10 f   8 s

Extraordinary expenditure for the poor in the month of April 1561

To Pierre Cousturier in order to return to
Paris by order of the Company,   10 f   6 s

To a poor wife of the minister sent to
Coutance,   2 f

To the minister of Angroigne,   15 f

Extraordinary expenditure made for the poor in the month of May 1561

To a poor person found near the city hall for
the rent of a room,   8 f[26]

To the wife of Jacques Vilet [?] in order to
help them rent a room,   15 s

To Jean Singlant in order to go to Lyons,   2 f   1 s

Rendered to Monsieur de Normandie,   3 f

Extraordinary expenditure for the month of June 1561

To Monsieur de la Court for having
transcribed the Psalms of Monsieur de
Bèze in order to send them to Court,   12 f   6 s

To himself for having transcribed the
privilege of the said Psalms,   8 s

For a dozen Bibles bought from
Madamoiselle du Plessis,   12 f

Reimbursed to Monsieur de Paré that he
furnished diverse parties,   7 f   2 s

To Master Pierre for having put the Psalms
to music,   10 f

To Jean Parran by order of the Company,   2 f

Extraordinary expenditure made for the poor in the month of July 1561

Reimbursed to Monsieur de Bèze that he
had given again to Master Pierre, the
singer, for the Psalms in music other than
the ten florins above,   20 f   5 s

Extraordinary expenditure for the poor in the month of August 1561

Sunday, the third, to several poor people in
the Place Saint Pierre,   34 s   6 d

Given to Cornille for one time by order of
the Company,   50 f

Table 1 *(Continued)*

To the said Cornille, even again the said day, it was advised to give him again 25 florins,	25 f		
To Master Jean Le Roux, poor schoolboy, by the order of the Company,		15 s	
Sunday, in the Place Saint Pierre, to several poor people,	3 f	2 s	
To Monsieur de Paré, rendered for the binding of several New Testaments and palettes,	4 f	5 s	
To the one who transcribed the first copy of the Psalms of Monsieur de Bèze before Monsieur de La Court wrote them down in order to send them to the Court,	12 f	6 s	

Money expended extraordinarily for the poor in the month of September 1561

Reimbursed to the Lord Jehan Personne that he had advanced to Master Bevigne several times,	16 f	
To Monsieur the clerk,		15 s

Extraordinary expenditure for the poor in the month of October 1561

To Paris,	5 f		
To the bookseller for two Bibles and five volumes,		20 s	
To Jacques Bruyere according to that which had, for a long time, been ordered,	5 f	3 s	9 d

Extraordinary expenditure for the poor in the month of November 1561

All the extraordinary expenditure for the poor in the month of December 1561

Extraordinary expenditure for the poor in the month of January 1562

To Noel, poor baker, that which had been ordered for him by the Company,	50 f	
Likewise and again to Noel, the baker, by the notice awarded in order to pay a person named Bastier,	25 f	
Paid back to Jean Personne for some money that he had advanced for several people of his quarter,	12 f	2 s
To Master Aynierant[?] for the Psalms [Psalters] sent to Monsieur de Bèze, that is to say, for the binding of forty-four,	48 f	9 s
Likewise for the ribbon other than that which the said Aynierant furnished,	3 f	
To Simon who carried the said books, advanced first,	10 f	

Table 1 *(Continued)*

				one
To him again on leaving,	13 f	6 s	7 d	florin*
				one
For the waxed cloth for the packing,		9 s	3 d	florin
To Simon again for the completion of his voyage, at the return from Paris where he stayed thirty-two or thirty-four [sic; thirty-three] days,	19 f	6 s		

Extraordinary expenditure for the poor in the month of February 1562

Expenditure made extraordinarily for the poor in the month of March 1562

To Thomas Dourteau [sic; Courteau] for a dozen Psalms [Psalters] to send to Monsieur de Bèze,	5 f	
To a poor boy for the binding of some Psalters [Psalms] again,	1 s	

Extraordinary expenditure for the poor in the month of April 1562.

Extraordinary expenditure for the poor in the month of May [1562]

Extraordinary expenditure for the poor in the month of June 1562

Extraordinary expenditure for the poor in the month of July 1562

To Robinet for the binding of 56 Psalms [Psalters] by agreement made by Monsieur René, 2 s, 6 d,	11 f	8 s

Extraordinary expenditure for the poor in the month of August 1562

To Master Artus the said day given for his pains for having worked on the accounts of the Psalms [Psalters] for the poor, six pistoles,	30 f	7 s	6 d

Extraordinary expenditure for the poor in the month of September 1562

To the officers who went to see the booksellers three diverse times for the making of the Psalms [Psalters],	22 s	6 d

Extraordinary expenditure for the poor in the month of October 1562

To a minister of Mascons,	5 f	3 s	9 d
To some others as it was ordered by the Company, Wednesday, the thirteenth,	4 f	4 s	

Extraordinary expenditure for the month of November 1562

Paid back to Jean Combez for a halberd and a sword that he bought from a poor man by the order of the Company,	26 s

*In the original manuscript, these one florin entries are located to the right of the columns ordinarily used by the bookkeeper.

5

Pastors and Deacons

The *Bourse française* was run by volunteers under whom there was a cadre of part-time help. In the early years the overall administration was in the hands of the Company of Pastors of Geneva and the deacons. Working with them was a group of collectors and auditors who were apparently volunteers. The only person employed on a certain full-time basis when the account books began in 1550 was the copyist of Calvin's sermons. The *Bourse* also paid regularly a doctor, a surgeon, and apothecary. It hired wet nurses, guardians for the sick, foster homes, inns, and private dwellings on a fee for services basis, although much of the hosting of refugees was done voluntarily. It paid tailors by the piece and also seamstresses, many of whom were poor women on the welfare rolls. The poor were also used for various odd jobs such as carrying wood or conveying messages. The overall philosophy seemed to have been to pay when it was necessary, but to use volunteers whenever possible.

PASTORS

Within this organizational structure there was a hierarchy of authority that, if examined category by category, reveals a pragmatic institution responding to need rather than conforming to a preconceived constitution. At the top of this hierarchy were the city pastors. Although they represented only one of four offices in the church, alongside elders, doctors (teachers), and deacons, they frequently appear to have told the deacons what to do. Numerous entries in the account books specify "by the order of the Company," or "recommended by Monsieur Calvin,"[1] "Master Jean Fabri," or another of the city pastors.[2] Other entries imply that, at the very beginning, the deacons hesitated to make a long-range commitment to a poor person without the approval of the Company of Pastors: "To a poor woman of near Pommier, wife of Jean Le Roy, waiting for the Company, three sous."[3] There is also evidence in the notarial acts that the deacons consulted the pastors before making policy decisions. For instance, the deacons consulted with the pastors and followed their advice before giving to one Jean de Borne a legacy from a will whose conditions he did not entirely meet because he had left Geneva. This was a financial loss to the deacons of two-thirds of one hundred ecus because the money was to escheat to the *Bourse* if the heirs did not fulfill their obligations.[4]

As the *Bourse* evolved, the Company of Pastors assigned one of their members to counsel the deacons. A list of ten ordinances adopted 5 January 1581 and copied into the account book of 1582 included an ordinance stating that the ministers were to choose "one of the ministers of this church" to sit for a six-month term in the assembly of deacons.[5] If a difficulty arose, he was to report it to the assembly of ministers, who would advise the deacons on what to do. He was to take the lead in the "censure" that the deacons held among themselves before the quarterly Communion services, "in order to mutually encourage and admonish each other fraternally in their duty."[6] A minister's presence with the deacons was also valued because he was thought to enhance their credibility. According to the ordinance, a minister was assigned to the deacons "so that the poor respect so much better and as they ought the said deacons in their administration."[7] This was a telling statement of the prestige of ministers in sixteenth-century Geneva, for the deacons were among the wealthiest and most influential men of the day.

The ordinances of 1581 revealed further evidence of supervision by the pastors. Every six months, after the books were audited and signed by the auditors, they were to be passed on to the Company of Pastors, who would sign them. This formal system of auditing contrasts with the more informal arrangement during the *Bourse's* early years, if there was any arrangement at all. By 1582 the positions had become institutionalized, and, clearly, the Company of Pastors was the body of final responsibility.[8]

One would think that the deacons might have chafed under this yoke of authority, but there is no indication of major dissension between deacons and pastors, at least that appeared in the account books, nor should one necessarily expect dissension in this age when hierarchy and authority were acceptable facts of life. The Company of Pastors may well have served as an umbrella over the *Bourse*, lending a measure of security and certitude to those engaged in activities that were innovative and sometimes even dangerous.

The Company of Pastors, moreover, allowed the deacons a great deal of autonomy and initiative. Most of the daily decisions were made by them, and, in any case, their activities were so vast that close supervision would have required considerable effort. One reason for having deacons, after all, was to enlist people other than the pastors in the work of the church. Therefore, although the pastors were, in a general sense, in charge, the deacons were the visible administrators whom everyone associated with the *Bourse*.

DEACONS

There was no fixed number of deacons. The first page of the surviving accounts lists three such men, but in July 1554 four were elected.[9] By 1569 there were five, and by 1576 there appear to have been six, but in the election of 1582 the number was back to five. By the early seventeenth century there were six again. At the end of the seventeenth century there were eight.[10] This seems to reflect the general pragmatic pattern of growth, but such growth must have profoundly affected the nature of their interrelationships.

Whatever the number of deacons, they served three functions; they received money, disbursed it, and visited the poor. They thus had both financial and pastoral responsibilities. Deacons' duties involved them in almost daily contact with the poor, both those who came to them and the sick whom they visited in their homes. They also did the purchasing, paid salaries, and tended to legal and administrative work. In addition, although a group of men called collectors seemed to be formally charged with the collection of money, the deacons became involved in the informal soliciting of funds.[11] All in all, managing the *Bourse française* was very much like running a business with an added component of pastoral work, and since many of the responsibilities were open-ended, such as visiting the sick and soliciting funds, there was a real sense in which a deacon's work was never done.

One might well ask whom the community got to do this unpaid and often thankless job. That they were able to recruit the capable people that they did was a credit to the zeal and dedication of those who supported the *Bourse*. The large expenditure of time that this office entailed is revealed by examining the deacons' individual responsibilities.

Of the deacons' three tasks (receiving money, disbursing it, and visiting the poor) the easiest should have been taking in money, but even this was tedious, because everything had to be recorded and some of the gifts came with legal encumbrances. The deacons received donations of various kinds, but basically there were two broad categories: donations from living people and inheritances from the dead.[12] Gifts were received either as money or as gifts in kind, such as grain. The gifts frequently involved processing or delivery before they could be used. The deacons arranged for the cutting and transporting of firewood, for instance, and the processing of cloth.[13] More often, donations were actual specie, in currencies that reflected the origins and trade relations of the donor. Even coin was not without its headaches, because some of the foreign monies had to be exchanged for usable currency. The account books include entries recording small fees that the *Bourse* paid for such transactions.[14]

The deacons entered donations into the regular account books, usually on one or two pages of receipts at the beginning of each month before they listed the expenditures. They also apparently solicited donations, to judge from the names of relatives, friends, and house guests of deacons that appear in the receipts. They used their business and diplomatic voyages to collect for the poor, and even when they were not traveling they served as channels for money from their native region. René Gassin, a deacon originally from Provence, brought in money from the Provençals, for example.[15]

Such donations from living people seem to have dominated the early years, although it is difficult to determine this exactly because the first accountant, Jean Budé, appears to have kept track of some of the inherited money in a separate journal, now lost. Despite the absence of the exact records, it is clear that there were willed legacies from the very beginning; the *Bourse* may even have been started with one. As time wore on and the first generation of supporters began to die, inherited money became an important component of *Bourse* income. This brought the deacons the additional work of settling disputed estates and managing gifts in Geneva and also in France.[16]

As property accumulated, the deacons became involved in real estate management, renting and selling houses. Sometimes the execution of a will or the disposition of some of the property would be left in their hands, perhaps in part as insurance by the donor that the poor would actually get what was willed to them.[17] Collecting sums willed to the poor from the other heirs was a problem. Calvin spoke of this problem at an early point, calling any attempt to turn aside money to the poor a real theft and sacrilege.[18]

Policing the execution of wills was time consuming, in part because of the concomitant procedures with the notaries that such action entailed. At times the deacons seemed to be acting as trustees responsible for passing money from one person to another. This especially occurred in inheritances that included the *Bourse*. At times the deacons appear to have transferred money from benefactors to heirs.[19] In at least one instance the lieutenant of justice, the judge who presided over Genevan civil matters and over the tribunal of the police, deposited a large sum with the deacons awaiting the heirs.[20] Some of the notarial procedures involved in these activities were of international dimensions as, for instance, the procuration made to two inhabitants of France for the goods left to the poor by one Pastor François Felix.[21]

Properties willed to the *Bourse* were not all large inheritances. The deacons became involved in the disposition of some very minor estates because of an apparent custom of passing on to the *Bourse* the belongings of those who had received aid from it. This left the deacons with the task of arranging for the inventory and sale of the personal possessions of the poor. These inventories, which detailed lists of the total earthly goods of some very poor people, provide a rich insight into what sixteenth-century life was like for the poor, since every article of clothing, book, and eating utensil was listed. Many of these poor people owned no books other than a Psalter, a catechism, or a Bible. That they owned even that is remarkable in light of their poverty.[22] Such detailed inventories were tedious work, which implies both that not a penny escaped the *Bourse* and that insufficient concern was shown for the value of the volunteer deacons' time, since this was only one of their many tasks.

Taking money in and managing the capital of the fund was only one side of the financial management, for the deacons also spent the money. They gave away substantial amounts to the poor, and they also paid the employees. They bought what the *Bourse* needed, and, in the early years, they disbursed funds at the request of the Company of Pastors for particular projects. Some of these expenditures were mechanical, but most of the purchases or handouts, except those requested by the Company of Pastors, required a decision at some point by the deacons, and this lengthened the procedure. It seems to have been true in the sixteenth century, as it is today, that giving away other people's money could be more complicated than spending one's own.

For the *Bourse* to work effectively there had to be some coordinated effort among the deacons in dealing with the poor, but there also had to be enough flexibility to allow deacons to make individual decisions in case of emergencies. To facilitate matters the deacons held regular meetings. The ordinances of 1581 stipulated that they should be held once a week at the same time as the handout to the poor.[23] It is not clear that this was the pattern from the beginning, and the deacons may not even have met together formally since there were only three of them. The account books also reveal that there was a considerable amount of individual initiative. In the early years, deacons and apparently even others made handouts and then solicited the fund for reimbursement. Those who were not deacons were usually people who were active contributors to *Bourse* or who had some special attachment to the fund, such as the innkeepers on whom the deacons relied. Occasionally, however, it appears that a virtual unknown made claims on the fund, such as a barber-surgeon or an apothecary, who perhaps rendered a service and then requested the deacon for payment of his fees. The deacons soon brought order to this haphazard system by employing a doctor, a surgeon, and an apothecary.

The deacons also promoted an orderly system of disbursement by arranging for the poor to receive their allotments at the regular handouts. Although the ordinance of 1581 stipulated that these regular handouts should coincide with the weekly meeting of the deacons, the earlier account books reveal that the deacons experimented with various schedules ranging from twice a week to twice a month. There was no mention in the early account books of where the handouts were held, but the *Bourse* eventually acquired a building.[24]

Despite efforts to consolidate disbursement, the clientele of the *Bourse* made it difficult to be as systematic as other welfare institutions that dealt with a stable population. The refugees did not come and go on schedule. This irregularity, combined with other emergencies common to welfare, meant that some transaction was entered into the books almost every day. In times of illness, childbirth, or death of a nursing mother, people were driven to the edge of their resources and the deacons' door.[25] Many a traveler passing through town must also have stopped at their door since, in the beginning, the *Bourse* apparently operated to a large extent out of the homes of the deacons. The ordinances of 1581 provided for the travelers who arrived between weekly meetings and for emergencies by leaving those situations up to the judgment of the deacons: "As for extraordinary affairs, that they most diligently and conveniently advise what to do according to the requirements of the case," and "that they thus among themselves advise the subvention of those passing through according to what they judge most proper and expedient."[26] To facilitate this system the deacons frequently would advance money from their own resources, at least in the early years, and they were reimbursed later from the fund.[27]

Allowing the deacons to make decisions on their own was a practical necessity, but it placed the burden of responsibility on them. It was not always a pleasant task to deal directly with the poor. Some were ungrateful, and some disagreed with the deacons over the extent of their need. Others tried to put something over on the deacons, as was apparently the case with a Parisian named Guillaume Maurice who was called before the consistory for having played with money that he had received from the deacons. He was reported to be an idler who did not want to work.[28]

The deacons had strong adjectives for those whom they felt had deceived them, but underlying the venomous language was a current of disappointment in those whom they tried to help. Sometimes people borrowed items from the *Bourse*, such as bedding, for instance, and then left town with it, and many just forgot to thank the deacons.[29] Sometimes the deacons recorded their irritation in the permanent records, and their attitude appears to have angered some people and left others bitter. For instance, one woman was brought before the consistory after the death of a deacon for having said at his burial: "The devil had this fine prey." The deceased deacon was Pierre Maldonnade, who contributed regularly to the *Bourse*. Clearly, the deacon's role could be a thankless one.[30]

Then, too, the deacons made mistakes, since they could not possibly know the personal circumstances and needs of the flood of refugees. Transient people were difficult to monitor, but the church seems to have devised early a system for knowing its own that distributed the responsibility of deciding whether or not a person needed aid. At first an informal custom of recommendation appears to have begun by word of mouth. This soon evolved into a full-fledged international scheme, complete with letters of recommendation.[31] From the very first account book in 1550 people came to the deacons at the recommendation of some person associated with the *Bourse*. The recommender was usually a donor, often a pastor, but sometimes merely someone of recognized responsibility whose name appeared nowhere else in the accounts. The first recommenders were people in Geneva, but as Reformed churches sprang up elsewhere, the *Bourse* received recommendations from the deacons or pastors of churches in any number of places, usually in France. The Reformed churches became a veritable network, with congregations in places such as Lyons and Nîmes helping refugees along the way. It became a custom to make sure that a legitimate traveler had the means to get from one Protestant church to the next.[32]

These travelers were not all coming to Geneva, of course. Indeed, the *Bourse* itself paid the travel expenses of many people who were leaving town. Some were returning temporarily to France to try to recover their belongings and members of their family, but others were departing permanently. There seems some evidence that people were encouraged and given the wherewithal to move on, but in the sixteenth century there were more people coming to Geneva than leaving it.[33]

As a prime city of refuge, Geneva was the permanent destination of many of these voyagers. Under these circumstances, good communication was important so that the residents could guard against becoming inundated with crowds of opportunists who professed allegiance to the Reformation but who, in reality, were merely seeking their fortune. The city, cramped between walls that it was still building in the sixteenth century, had limited facilities even for the bona fide refugees who came seeking to live according to the reform of the "Word," as they put it. Just as Geneva did not intend to open the floodgates of immigration, the *Bourse* wanted to devote its limited resources to this group of religious refugees rather than to the general masses of the poor. Despite these restrictions, in the early years the deacons' activity seemed to lean more toward generosity than to stinginess. Often confronted by human need that required no recommendation, the deacons helped those who in years to come would be shuttled off to other funds or rejected entirely as ineligible. They helped people of all nationalities and, apparently, religions, assisting even a Jew passing through.[34] At times they seemed ready to believe almost any story.

One way to avoid being hoaxed was to get to know the poor as well as possible, and the accounts leave the impression that the deacons were familiar with the aid recipients, especially those who were on the regular rolls. It was part of the deacons' job to know everyone's economic situation, but they also had a charge to visit the poor and sick and offer spiritual and financial aid. The ordinances of 1581 stipulated that it was the duty of the deacons to visit the poor even when they were sick, apparently despite dangers of contagion of which sixteenth-century Genevans were well aware. On such occasions, it was up to the deacons to ask the doctor, barber-surgeon, and apothecary employed by the *Bourse* to care for the sick person.[35] There is no doubt that such visits had already been taking place for years before the ordinances of 1581 formalized the requirement; one can follow for years in the account books the visits that the deacons made: Monsieur René [Gassin] for "his district," and Monsieur Dalamont for "our district."[36] Since a sum of money was listed after each of these weekly expeditions, the deacons were probably also handing out financial aid at the door because they were given money for their visit. It is impossible to tell from the accounts just how much neighborly visiting and spiritual solace the deacons brought with them as they made their rounds. Perhaps they were too busy or afraid of contagion to have made more than a quick stop. There are no references to the actual nature of the visits. Does the fact that the regulations of 1581 left out any mention of Bible reading and prayer imply that that did not occur? Perhaps the pastoral duties of the deacons were neglected with the pressure of all their other responsibilities for the *Bourse*, but perhaps these duties were so commonly performed that they were not remarked upon.

The account books suggest that the visits were made to the sick poor, perhaps only those who were bedridden and could not come to the weekly handout. There is no mention of the poor per se being visited regularly in these expeditions by the deacons, although one cannot preclude the possibility of impromptu visits to check on a person's needs. That they actually visited the homes of the sick was alone a great accomplishment that set this fund apart from many other sixteenth-century welfare institutions. The number of deacons who died after only a few years in service suggests that the danger of contagion was to be taken seriously, although it is difficult to ascertain whether or not the life expectancy was any shorter for deacons than for anyone else in sixteenth-century plague-infested Geneva. The long-living deacon was an exception, however, and Jean Budé was a marvel. His first two colleagues had died within four years of their tenure as deacons, yet he continued to outlive their successors.[37] Before he died in 1587, he had seen almost everyone of his generation pass away. But his responsibility was primarily for the accounts, not the visitation of the sick, so he may not have been as frequently exposed to contagious disease as the other deacons.[38]

The account books were an important responsibility. Because they were thoroughly detailed, keeping them must have occupied a good share of the private time of at least one of the deacons. The deacons handed this duty around somewhat, even before the ordinances of 1581 institutionalized a rotation. They specified that one deacon was to be charged with the books for six months, which was the interval between audits. He could be kept on for a subsequent term if necessary.[39] This was a departure from the earliest practice, when, for more than a decade, the accounts almost always seemed to be in the hands of one person, Jean Budé, except when he was out of town.

Finally, the deacons were responsible for making large-scale purchases for the poor. The account books listed regular purchases but do not reveal who made them. This was a considerable task, for the *Bourse* bought much of its own cloth and arranged for it to be sewn into clothing.[40] It also occasionally bought firewood and food. Conceivably the responsibility for purchasing could have been in the hands of some deacon other than the accountant, just as in the early 1560s the visitation of the sick was apparently given over primarily to two of the four deacons.

But even though some of the work load could be lightened by dividing the responsibilities among the deacons, there still was a great deal for each to do. The *Bourse* needed people who could both meet the qualifications and persevere. Good will alone was clearly not enough, although of course they needed that too.

A deacon had to be, at the very least, conscientious, hardworking, and competent. The "typical" deacon varied somewhat over the centuries of the existence of the *Bourse française*, but the fact that they were responsible for large sums of money commanded that they had to be honest, trustworthy, and respected by the community. It was important that they be well enough established in the world to be trusted with other people's money. During the early years, they tended to be well-to-do. They were regular contributors to the *Bourse* and often advanced sums from their own pockets to the poor. Of course, they also had to be able to read, write, and keep track of money, and they had to be familiar with the legal customs of the day in order to transact the *Bourse*'s business. These were practical considerations useful to any person of affairs. In the sixteenth century deacons were often businessmen like René Gassin and Antoine Popillon and nobles like Jean Budé, Seigneur de Vérace, and François Buynard, Seigneur de la Touche. These men shared a fundamental ability to get along in the world of affairs. With the exception of Jean Budé, who initially had to polish up his accounting skills, the deacons seemed to have had to learn very little that was new to them, at least as far as the business aspects of running the *Bourse*. They were busy men bringing into the administration of the *Bourse française* skills that they had already learned in the everyday management of their own businesses and fortunes. The minutes of the notaries are the proof of this, because the notaries, in keeping track of legal transactions, recorded the personal business affairs of the deacons as well as the deacons' activities on behalf of the *Bourse*. The deacons' names appear repeatedly in pursuit of their own concerns: buying and selling property, concluding business arrangements, drawing up marriage contracts, and dictating wills. These records are an impressive testimonial to their financial expertise, and so much legal activity in their names is no accident; during the first few years of immigration it was difficult for French immigrants to enter the Genevan bourgeoisie, but soon the French deacons became bourgeois of Geneva, active in local life.

But business acumen was not all that was desirable in a deacon. This was an office of the church, mentioned in the Bible, and the injunctions about deacons in the early church were applied to their sixteenth-century counterparts. The 1581 list of regulations for the *Bourse* cited 1 Timothy 3:8 and Romans 12:8 as guides to the choice of deacons: "Deacons likewise must be serious, not double-tongued, not addicted to much wine, not greedy for gain"; "he who exhorts, in his exhortation; he who contributes, in liberality; he who gives aid, with zeal; he who does acts of mercy, with cheerfulness."[41] Beyond verse eight of 1 Timothy 3 were listed other criteria for deacons that extended to their families, but the ordinance of 1581 did not mention these. Verses nine through thirteen suggest that deacons should be Christian with a clear conscience and should have been tested before being given the job. A deacon should have one wife, and she should be serious and temperate, not a slanderer. They should manage their children and households well. The injunction ends on a positive note, "for those who serve well as deacons gain a good standing for themselves and also great confidence in the faith which is in Christ Jesus" (1 Timothy 3:13). The Biblical injunction, in short, called for experienced people with stable family lives who were recognized by the community as responsible Christians.

This was essentially the type of individual that the *Bourse* chose as deacons in sixteenth-century Geneva. They were established figures who met both the character and business criteria for deacons, such as Charles de Jonvilliers, a former secretary to John Calvin, and Antoine Calvin, John Calvin's brother, a merchant and bourgeois of the city.

The Biblical injunctions about family appear to have been less critical than the general requirements about character. Charles de Jonvilliers never married, and Antoine Calvin was divorced from his first wife, a convicted adulteress. He also partially disinherited two disobedient sons.[42] The sixteenth-century mentality would not necessarily have laid any part of the blame for these eventualities on Antoine, but it is, nevertheless, interesting to note that the ordinances recorded in the account book of 1582 neglected to cite the verses in 1 Timothy 3 that include the references to marriage and well-managed children as a prerequisite for the diaconate, although verses nine through thirteen would seem to be as pertinent as verse eight to the choice of deacons: "They [deacons] must hold the mystery of the faith with a clear conscience. And let them also be tested first; then if they prove themselves blameless let them serve as deacons. . . . Let deacons be the husband of one wife, and let them manage their children and their households well" (1 Timothy 3:9–10, 12).

Marital and family instability, however, was the exception and not the rule among the deacons, judging from their attitudes toward their wives and children in their wills, where a disinherited child or a wife's inheritance stripped down to the legal minimum could have revealed family quarrels. Perhaps certain individuals were eliminated from consideration as deacons for domestic reasons. Could Robert Estienne, for instance, Geneva's most renowned printer-editor, ever have been elected deacon? Active as he was as a contributor and supporter of the *Bourse,* he seemed to have been at odds with his children and his wife, except for his son Henri, at the time that he wrote his will.[43] It was probably a moot question, as he already had enough to do, although many of the deacons were busy men. Sheer busyness did not seem to disqualify one, but judgment by the community that whatever else one was doing was too worthwhile to allow a diversion of time may have eliminated likely candidates, and this would have been the case with Estienne's publishing business.

Although one cannot determine to what extent a man's family situation figured into the election of a deacon, the *Bourse* would have been unwise to ignore it, for a deacon and his family were privy to confidential information about the private lives of many people. Pejorative as it may sound, the statement in 1 Timothy 3:11 that the women should be serious and temperate, not slanderers, was a practical injunction for deacons' wives, who probably had ample material for gossip, but then so did the deacons.[44] The Genevans apparently applied this verse to deacons' wives rather than to women deacons or deaconesses of which they had none. Moreover, if a deacon had a "good" wife, the *Bourse* got two workers when they had only elected one.

Some of the deacons' wives may have taken active roles in the *Bourse;* Maldonnade and his wife, for instance, hosted contributors.[45] One can imagine the deacons' wives handling the work with the poor who came to the door while their husbands were out of the house. The work of women filling in for their husbands was not often recorded in the account books, except when the deacons died and their wives continued as donors or participants. For instance, the account books mention that the deacons "also received [ten ecus] from the will of Monsieur de Maldonnade [the deacon] by the hands of his wife."[46]

The daily account books recorded by name many women who, though not necessarily wives of deacons, were active as donors, hostesses, landladies, nurses, and recommenders of the poor to the deacons.[47] So, although the diaconate of the *Bourse française* and of the city hospital was a man's role in Reformation Geneva, many women were also involved in the *Bourse,* and their time and money were apparently welcomed. The records of the *Bourse française* thus shed some light on the lives of these sixteenth-century women.

Although there were no women in the formal diaconate of Geneva, women were not necessarily excluded from diaconal functions. John Calvin, in fact, emphasized women's role in the care of the poor and the sick, using Biblical precedent. Care of the poor and sick was for him the lesser of two grades of diaconal service, distinct from the deacons' administration of the affairs of the poor reserved to men. He wrote in his *Institutes of the Christian Religion* that "women could fill no other public office than to devote themselves to the care of the poor. . . . There will be two kinds of deacons: one to serve the church in administering the affairs of the poor; the other, in caring for the poor themselves."[48] This did not necessarily mean that the women were called deacons, however, for the ancient office of widow designated women who cared for the poor. Although Calvin allowed that this office was of lower rank than that of magistrate or of pastor, he felt that it was important and clearly Biblical. Its absence in Geneva as a distinct office was something of which he felt the city should be ashamed.[49]

Whatever Calvin might have said, there were widows in Geneva who were serving the poor. For example, widows cared for orphans supported by the *Bourse*. Foster care was not exclusively in the hands of widows, but they seemed fundamental to the continuing placement of orphans in foster homes by the deacons of the *Bourse française*. These widows were not merely gracious women over sixty devoting themselves to the bedside care of the sick and poor. Although they may have been gracious, they were usually hard pressed themselves. Many had no family or other means of support in line with the ancient office of widow. Hence a practical drawback to widows serving as foster parents seemed to be that when such a single person died a whole household of children needed a new home. Nonetheless, while there was no formal ordained office of widow in Geneva, quite a few such women seemed to be hard at work.[50]

As Reformed churches spread women were not necessarily excluded from the diaconate and surely not from diaconal service, although their presence in office was exceptional. In at least one region, in the town of Wesel along the Rhine, there were deaconesses. Their role was approved by the first general synod of that region in 1568. Their services were specific: they were (1) to serve as nurses in caring for women who were sick or in childbed (a service that was indiscreet for the male deacons to perform), (2) to buy and sew cloth, and (3) to care for the poor in case of need. The deaconesses were elected. Some of them were married, which disturbed some of their contemporaries who equated them with the Biblical office of widow. Some of the sixteenth-century widows of Wesel were under sixty years of age as well, which also conflicted with the Biblical description of the office.[51] The practice of electing women deaconesses apparently died out by the early seventeenth century. Some thought that the wives of deacons could do the work of the deaconesses. Apparently some Protestants of this era considered the diaconate to some extent as a husband-wife team.[52]

The title of deaconess became important again in the nineteenth century, especially in German-speaking areas of Europe but also in the New World. The title was given at that time to women who, often when they were young and single, served as social workers or nurses. They were somewhat analogous to Roman Catholic sisters, but Protestant deaconesses did not necessarily continue celibate. Some of them married, able to change roles with much greater ease than their Roman Catholic counterparts of the nineteenth and early twentieth centuries.

The apparent absence of women in roles such as the diaconate was typical of sixteenth-century Geneva and of most of society at the time. The *Bourse française* was one of many institutions with no female officers. In other respects the *Bourse* was more inclusive than other contemporary institutions, particularly in that it was initially run almost exclusively by foreigners. While it was not, apparently, a requirement that one be foreign to work for the *Bourse,* it seemed inevitable in the early years of immigration.

Residency requirements for public office were normal in early modern European cities, a way of preserving power in the hands of the old guard. Although in the first half of the sixteenth century Geneva's city fathers employed foreigners, sometimes in important positions such as engineering the city walls or serving as pastors in the city's churches, they did not wish to relinquish control. When the number of foreign refugees to the city became threatening in midcentury, the Genevans restricted admission to the governing councils of the city. After the defeat of Ami Perrin and the anti-Calvinist faction in 1555, these laws were loosened, and important persons of foreign origin were admitted to the Council of Two Hundred. The small council, the body that ran the city on a daily basis, remained exclusive for a long time.[53] Such restrictions were normal for the age, and less tightly drawn in Geneva than in many other cities, but they did restrict the potential leadership roles of Protestants newly arrived in Geneva. Some of these people had been leaders in their home communities, such as the Candolles, whose home region sent a letter to the Genevan government inquiring as to why the family had left home where they were so well thought of and well received.[54] The organizational skills of such people could not be fully realized when they were barred from leading civic offices, but this restriction may indirectly have been a boon to organizations such as the *Bourse française* that were run by foreigners.

In the early years when the *Bourse* depended on the community of French-speaking immigrants to staff its administration, it tapped a reservoir of talented leaders who, while not being used to their full capacity in

Genevan government, were by no means dormant in Genevan society. They were active in business and even bought up land around the city, all the while keeping their eyes on their homeland.[55] Many never thought of themselves as permanent residents and were prepared to go home when the situation improved in France. The *Bourse française* was an ideal organization for them, and its early success depended much on the talent they brought to Geneva in the 1550s. Its international links depended on their foreign contacts, and its missionary activities were inspired by their zeal.

The administration of the *Bourse*, like the city itself, brought together French-speaking immigrants from many regions, and even countries. Of the first three deacons, one was from the Low Countries, Pierre Maldonnade from the Hainaut in Belgium, and the other two were from Paris and Gascony, Jean Budé and Guy de Serignac (Monsieur de [du] Thillat, du Tillac, or du [de] Thillac).[56] There is no way to know if deacons were chosen for geographical diversity, but the *Bourse* would seem to have had a vested interest in wide distribution of its key figures because of the close contact they maintained with their home regions. Through such contacts, funds were channeled to the *Bourse* from these people's native regions.

The qualifications for deacon were probably many—financial, moral, personal, and region of origin. With these criteria in mind, the office of deacon was filled through elections. We cannot be sure how they proceeded in the early years, but by 1582 a system of annual elections had been set up. According to the ordinances of 1581, the ministers of the church and the contributors to the *Bourse* were called together by the collectors at the beginning of the year to elect or reconfirm the deacons in their posts by a plurality of votes.[57] The earlier accounts, however, give no record of such regularity of elections, nor can we be sure that they were carried out by an assembly of both donors and ministers.

The earliest evidence for the selection of deacons, found on folio one of the first account book, dated 30 September 1550, did not call the administrators deacons nor refer to the fund as the *Bourse française*. The scribe, Jean Budé, simply stated that "in order to keep the account of the money that has been received for the poor . . . the Company committed to that office the Lord Maldonnade, Monsieur de Thillat, and myself, which was the penultimate day of September, the year 550 [sic], the Company assembled at the home of the brothers de Burcy [de Bury?] and d'Aimery [d'Aimen?]."[58]

The text did not say that the men were elected, only that they were committed to the office. The company mentioned by Budé could very well have been the Company of Pastors rather than any joint meeting of ministers and donors, because that is what that term usually referred to in Genevan parlance. The location of the meeting at the home of brothers who were donors, not ministers, suggests, however, the presence of others. One must at least consider the possibility that subsequent references to "the Company"

by Budé refer to a company of donors who might have met regularly to
direct the *Bourse*. As for the location of the meeting, the notarial records
reveal that in 1559 one "Seigneur de Bursy, Noble Jacques de Sainct Martin"
had a house on the rue des chanoines. If this was his home nine years earlier,
the meeting may have taken place there.[59]

Selection of deacons was noted from the first page of the account books,
but not every year and at no fixed time of the year. It appears that it was
occasioned as much by the death or retirement of a deacon as by any attempt
to conform to a regular pattern. After the selection of the first three deacons,
no election was recorded until July 1554. The accounts only reveal that the
three men mentioned in September 1550 continued in their post. On 12
October 1552 Monsieur de Thillat died.[60] His replacement seems to have
been Monsieur de Saint Germain, Guillaume Prevost. The death of Lord
Maldonnade may have prompted the next election. A new account book for
July 1554 states on the first page that on the fifth at John Calvin's house there
was an election of "Monsieur de Sainct Jeremie [*sic*, Germain], Monsieur
René, Monsieur de la Touche," and Jean Budé.[61] Then from 1554 to 1582
there is no mention of elections in the surviving account books, but changes
in the deacons were sometimes clear from other evidence, particularly
notarial documents.

Since in the early days there seems to have been no regular system of
recording, it is possible, even probable, that elections were simply not
remarked upon, especially in the late 1550s and the 1560s when deacons
were replaced with no elections mentioned. But it seems presumptuous to
suppose that elections were held on a regular annual basis, at least until
shortly before January 1582, because what evidence there is shows an
irregular pattern.

In the 1570s the registers of the Company of Pastors began to take note of
the elections of the deacons. They mention an election on 3 September 1572,
just eight days after two deacons had died on 25 and 26 August. One of these
two newly elected deacons was Antoine, brother of John Calvin, but his
tenure as deacon was soon interrupted by death, so that less than five months
after the previous election, another one was held on 6 February 1573.[62] Two
men were chosen in his stead. The next election was the first that simply
confirmed those deacons already in office, on 26 May 1575, but annual
regularity did not yet seem to be established, because the next election was
held eight months later on 30 December. When Jean Budé and Charles de
Jonvilliers stepped down from the accounting in favor of Monsieur de
Campefleur. Within a year there was another election of 28 December 1576
confirming Budé, Jonvilliers, and three other deacons and replacing a sixth.
Thus, available information seems to indicate that it could not have been
many, if any, years before 1582 that an annual pattern of election at the

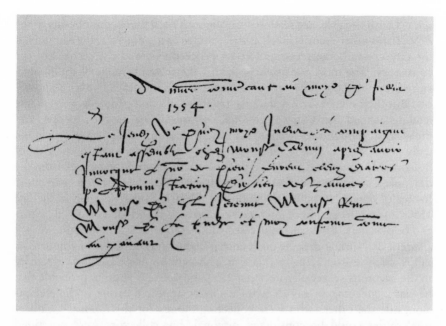

This first page of the fourth account book of the *Bourse française* announces
the results of an election of deacons that took place on 5 July 1554 at John Calvin's
house. The scribe is Jean Budé, son of Guillaume Budé. Note the abbreviations,
letter formation, absence of modern punctuation and accents, and additional
consonants typical of sixteenth-century French and bastard cursive handwriting.
Some letters, such as "s" and "e," can be formed in different ways depending on
where the letter falls in the word. From Archives d'État de Genève, Archives
hospitalières, Kg 15, *Bourse française* (July 1554–July 1555), p. 1.

beginning of the year replaced the practice of calling an election only when
there was a need for new deacons.[63]

Thus the pattern of annual elections developed over several decades. Once
the Company of Pastors began to record the names of deacons their names
are easily retrievable, but in the 1550s and 1560s there were many changes in
deacons for which there was no election noted. A variety of possible circumstances might be responsible: missing account books, unrecorded administrative changes during the early years, and perhaps, though this cannot be
proved, the selection of new deacons without an election.

The net result is that there is no sure way to find out who all the deacons
were. There is no convenient list to refer to as for the Italian *Bourse* of the
same period, but there are clues. The names of the deacons, though not

always with the title, are scattered throughout both the account books of the *Bourse* and other records, such as the minutes of the notaries, the registers of the city council, the reports of court proceedings, and the records of the consistory. The most consistent source is the account books of the *Bourse*, since they cover the daily expenditures for which the deacons were responsible. But their names are listed alongside those of other people who were just lending a hand, including occasional substitutes for absent deacons, and those who, though they were never official deacons, were very active in the daily work of the *Bourse*. Since the early account books used the title of deacon only at election time, it is difficult to distinguish the helpers from the deacons. This is particularly true in the early 1550s when the *Bourse* used the homes of donors to house the poor and the sick. It is true again in the late 1550s during the period of missionary activity in France that involved editors and booksellers. One is hard pressed to know, for example, whether or not Laurent de Normandie, the great entrepreneur and supporter of colporteurs in France, was ever actually a deacon, although his name appears repeatedly in the accounts, especially between 1559 and 1562. It appears probable that he was a collector, in any case, for his name appeared earlier in the receipts alongside the others who were collecting money for the *Bourse*.[64] Collectors' duties could be considered diaconal, but collectors were not titled deacons. Beyond that, Laurent de Normandie performed functions that were similar to those of the deacons. For instance, on 21 January 1569, he paid a widow eleven ecus sol for having assisted and served two children who were ill for two months with the plague.[65] He was also mentioned in the "Registre du Conseil" of the city government as an agitator in the name of the *Bourse des pauvres français*. On 16 June 1561 he had a woman imprisoned for being unwilling to keep a small girl with her. The girl had been confided to her by her husband who was preaching at "la Côte de Saint André," and the woman, Rogette, wanted to join her husband and leave the girl. The council pointed out to the woman her temerity and audacity and let Normandie find another lodging for the girl.[66]

Only if a name is mentioned along with the title can one be sure that someone was a deacon. This seems to have been the type of information that was so commonly known that no one bothered to write it down, with the exception of the notaries, who, in their formal legalistic language, began in the late 1550s to refer by name to the "deacons and administrators of the fund for the poor foreigners."[67] From this time on the legal activities of the *Bourse*, as recorded in the minutes of the notaries, revealed the names of the deacons, making it possible to check the names that appear in the accounts against the minutes of the notaries and come up with a list of the deacons. This list, supplemented by vital statistics, especially death records, gives a fairly accurate picture of who the deacons were and when they served, but it is not perfect, because there are lacunae in the records.

Table 2 lists the names of all the deacons from 1550 to 1577, with the possible exception of the late 1550s and early 1560s when the *Bourse* activity expanded to include the missionary enterprise that involved so many other active contributors. Dashes indicate a probable missing deacon; a question mark indicates uncertainty about the particular dates. Evidence substantiating someone's role as a deacon was gathered from several contemporary sources, including notary minutes, criminal records, consistory records, the registers of the city council and of the Company of Pastors. Such information did not always reveal the exact day, month, or even the year that a deacon began and ended his tenure in office, but this list records what information we have available now on the men who filled this important role. Biographical articles and even monographs have been written on some of these men without reference to their activities as deacons nor with any understanding of what that task involved in their lives.

For instance, a century ago Jules Bonnet's biographical chapter on Charles de Jonvilliers, Calvin's secretary and friend, commented that toward the end of his life Jonvilliers lapsed into colorless semiretirement: "these works accomplished he returned to the shadows."[68] This was not the case at all. On 20 March 1569 Charles de Jonvilliers was cited by the notary Jean Ragueau as a deacon, and he still held that post in 1582 when the ordinances that governed the *Bourse française* were recorded.[69] He died on 20 May 1590 at the age of about seventy-four. As a deacon he had not lapsed into obscurity. His name appears in the notarial records and in the registers of the *Bourse française*, but he may not have had the time to do much else of note while he was a deacon. The duties of a deacon were so demanding that they seemed to limit literary activity in particular, although Jonvillier did manage to edit the commentaries of John Calvin on Jeremiah.[70] The absence of the deacons from the ranks of the great writers and theologians has effectively hidden them from modern notice, for history remembers those who leave their names in print. The following list should correct that lacuna, give credit where credit is due, and also better reconstruct a period that held in honor its businessmen, nobles, and church leaders.

Table 2

Deacons of the *Bourse française*: 1550–1577[71]

1550
Pierre Maldonnade[72]
Jean Budé, Sieur de Vérace[73]
Guy de Serignac, Monsieur de Thillat,[74]

1551
Maldonnade
Budé
Thillat

Table 2 *(Continued)*

1552
Maldonnade
Budé
Thillat (Died 12 October)

1553
Maldonnade
Budé
Guillaume Prevost, Monsieur de Saint
  Germain[75]

1554
Maldonnade (Died)
(5 July election at John Calvin's house):
Budé
Saint Germain
René Gassin[76]
François Buynard, Monsieur de La
  Touche[77]

1555
Budé
Saint Germain
Gassin
La Touche

1556
Budé
Gassin
La Touche

1557
Budé
Gassin
La Touche
Antoine Popillon, Monsieur de Paré[78]

1558
Budé
Gassin
La Touche
Paré

1559
Budé
Gassin
La Touche (January–September)
Paré

1560
Budé
Gassin
Paré

Table 2 *(Continued)*

1561
Budé
Gassin
Paré
Jean Dalamont (3 November)[79]

1562
Budé
Gassin
Paré
Dalamont

1563
Budé
Gassin (reported sick, 30 August)
Paré
Dalamont

1564
Budé
Paré
Dalamont

1565
Budé
Dalamont
Prévost Yves Bergevin[80]

1566
Budé
Dalamont
Bergevin
Renaud Anjorrant, Sieur de Souilly[81]

1567
Budé
Dalamont
Bergevin
Anjorrant

1568
Budé
Dalamont
Bergevin
Anjorrant

1569
Budé
Dalamont
Bergevin
Anjorrant
Charles de Jonvilliers[82]

1570
Budé

Table 2 *(Continued)*

Dalamont
Bergevin (Still alive, 18 June)
Anjorrant
Jonvilliers

1571
Budé
Dalamont
Bergevin (?)
Anjorrant
Jonvilliers

1572
Budé
Anjorrant (Died 25 August)
Dalamont (Died 26 August)
Jonvilliers
(3 September election):
Budé
Jonvilliers
Antoine Calvin[83]
Louys André[84]

1573
Budé
Jonvilliers
Antoine Calvin (Died 2 February)
André
(6 February election):
Philippes du Pas, dict de Feuquières[85]
   and
Artus Chauvin[86] (For Antoine Calvin)

1574
Budé
Jonvilliers
André
Du Pas
Chauvin

1575
Budé
Jonvilliers
André
Du Pas
Chauvin
(30 December election):
Budé (?)
Jonvilliers (?)
André
Du Pas
Chauvin
Monsieur de Campefleur[87]

Table 2 *(Continued)*

1576
Budé (?)
Jonvilliers (?)
André
Du Pas
Chauvin
Campefleur

(28 December election):
Budé
Jonvilliers
André
Du Pas
Campefleur
Bernardin de Candolle[88] for Chauvin

1577
Budé
Jonvilliers
André
Du Pas
Campefleur
Candolle

6
Volunteers and Paid Personnel

The deacons appear to be the busiest of the volunteers who ran the *Bourse française*. So all-encompassing was their role that it strayed into the other offices of the *Bourse*, particularly that of the collectors, who were in charge of soliciting and collecting money. In a sense, the collectors could be considered deacons too, for they shared in the responsibility for the *Bourse* and they filled some of the functions that Calvin reserved for the diaconate in the Ecclesiastical Ordinances of 1541.

The Genevan ordinances of 1541 organized church offices in Geneva, theoretically finding precedent in the ancient church for dividing the diaconate in two. The ordinances of 1541 found a contemporary example of the two types of deacons in the procurators and hospitalers of the Genevan city hospital, the procurators "deputed to receive, dispense, and hold goods for the poor," and the hospitalers "to tend and care for the sick and administer allowances to the poor."[1] The procurators functioned as a board of trustees and the hospitalers dealt directly with the poor; both were considered deacons.[2]

COLLECTORS

This division of the office of deacon does not apply to the *Bourse française*, for the *Bourse* combined both administrative work (like that of the procurators of the hospital) and personal contact (like that of the hospitaler) in the single office of deacon. A separate group of men was assigned to collect money, a task that assumed significant proportions in an institution that relied on freewill support rather than government funding. These men were called collectors. As recipients of goods for the poor, the collectors' duties for the *Bourse française* appear to be less burdensome than those of the deacons. Besides collecting money, the collectors also were charged, in the regulations laid out in the account book of 1582, with calling together the assembly of the ministers and contributors for the annual elections, a task easily enough performed by a group of men in touch with the contributors in the quarters of the city assigned to them.[3]

As the organization of the *Bourse* evolved, collectors were subordinate to deacons, but that was less clearly defined in the early years, although there seems to have always been more collectors than deacons. In the election that accompanied the ordinances listed in the account book of 1582, fourteen collectors were elected. Among them were two of the five deacons, Bernardin de Candolles and Claude Mollet. The offices thus were not mutually exclusive in 1582, and they had overlapped for some time. In 1575 there were complaints recorded in the minutes of the Company of Pastors because of the excessive work this gave to the individuals who held both posts and because of the financial suspicions aroused.[4]

It seems entirely possible that at the beginning of the *Bourse* the office of collector may have been part of an informal system that looked to all who were associated with the *Bourse* to do whatever they could to solicit funds. The office of collector seems to have emerged early, however. A formal division of labor seems to have occurred by the early 1550s, when entries such as the following began to appear in the account books: "From Monsieur de La Touche for those of his quarter," and "From Monsieur de Normandye for himself and those of his charge." Unexpected in these lists of receipts is evidence that the collectors were apparently bringing money from France, clear from entries such as these: "From the bailiff Potier for those of Orleans, ten florins, nine sous, three deniers"; "From those of Lyons by the hands of the Lord Estienne Trembly, eight ecus sol and nineteen sous tournois, worth forty florins, three sous, nine deniers"; "On the part of those of Provence by the hands of Monsieur René, 28 florins, 11 sous, 6 deniers."[5]

Actually, the role of collecting seemed to have functioned on two levels: at home and abroad. Some people were apparently responsible for collection from a part of the city of Geneva itself, and others apparently channeled funds into the *Bourse* from abroad. In the early years when the foreign connections were strong, the international network seemed to dominate, but as time went on the *Bourse* became more of a local affair. The foreign funding seemed to work by way of the refugees' contacts with their homelands or areas with which they conducted business. Thus, for example, the merchant Estienne Trembley brought in contributions in the 1550s from Lyons, his home city and an area with which he had business ties.

Other merchants and nobles were also pressed into service on their trips into France; the collection activity benefited from a wide representation of people from many areas. Although it is difficult to determine from the account books whether these men were mere couriers aiding the *Bourse* or official collectors, the result was the same.

The organizational flexibility of the early *Bourse* allowed it to recruit every potential worker. In fact, anyone on an errand to Geneva could bring in contributions from France, and the *Bourse* thus benefited from travelers to town. Often people who came to Geneva for other errands, such as a message to the pastors or a request for advice on what to do in a home congregation, would also carry money for the *Bourse*. We cannot determine the number of these voyages with dual purposes, but in the early years the *Bourse française* was truly an organization with international links of impressive magnitude and breadth.

AUDITORS

Although the offices of deacon and of collector could be held by the same person, it does not seem that a deacon could be an auditor. Of the deacons named during the *Bourse*'s first thirty-two years none was apparently also an auditor, nor would one expect to find a deacon auditing his own books.[6]

The ordinances in the account book of 1582 provided for three auditors, elected by the same assembly that elected the deacons. Every six months the auditors were to audit and sign the accounts and pass them on to the Company of Pastors to sign. Then they were to be placed in a cupboard containing the papers of the poor, so that they would always be available to show how the fund was administered. One of the collectors elected that year, Jean Boucher, was also an auditor. These two roles apparently were not seen as conflicting.[7] When Jean Budé began keeping the books in 1550 the auditing procedure, if one existed at all, was clearly not as elaborate as it became by 1582. Throughout the initial fourteen years when he was accountant, none of the books was signed by an auditor. He signed the first account book on the cover as if to identify it as his own, and the second account book on the anterior plate.[8] During the 1550s and 1560s there were no auditor's signatures in the surviving account books.[9] Finally, on 3 September 1572 the Company of Pastors ordered that the deacons who had been in office hand over their accounts to three men who were elected to audit them. This was accompanied by exhortations from Pastor Théodore de Bèze to do better because of faults committed in the past. By 28 December 1576 the three men elected were formally referred to as auditors of the accounts. The office of auditor had definitely begun.[10]

By that date the accounting procedure had also become better organized. It may not even have been possible to audit the very first account books, not because of dishonesty but because they were such a mess. The covers and flyleaves of the first account books are veritable scratchpads of computations and haphazard notes, some of which were written upside down. The deacons almost always spent more than they received in donations, and month after month Jean Budé reported in the red. During these years the *Bourse* either had outstanding debts or another source of money that was not entered into the regular accounts. Budé's habitual phrase after he had totaled the figures for the month was, "Thus the receipts owe to the disbursement for having put out more than received, 127 florins, 5 sols, six deniers." The sum changed but the phrase remained the same month after month.[11] Typically no comment was made in the account books about this unfortunate situation, but that may have been due to the brevity of the account books. The minutes of the Company of Pastors for 28 December 1576 do express alarm at the situation. In fact, at the election that day the group was asked to reassemble again the following Friday to review the accounts and see how far the expenditures exceed the receipts. The pastors feared that all would be used up if God did not provide and each one did not force himself to do his part.[12] It is likely that much more such rhetoric about the state of the *Bourse*'s affairs did not appear in print.

A task that remains is to compare the sums collected and disbursed by the *Bourse française* with the budgets of the city government. This would give an approximate idea of the magnitude of the deacons' work in comparison with other city activities. The incompleteness of the account books, especially in the early years of *Bourse* activity, would make such a comparison difficult, of course.

As for the accounts themselves, Jean Budé and the other early accountants used an unsophisticated method of single-entry bookkeeping prevalent in Geneva at the time and kept their accounts in roman numerals in small unlined paper journals bound in parchment. They used a sixteenth-century notarial hand known as bastard cursive because of the eclectic nature of its paleographical influences. Budé's handwriting was difficult, but not impossible, to read. What would have been more disturbing than his handwriting to an auditor would be his habit of not consistently separating different currencies one from another. On occasional pages in the account books money from France, Italy, and Geneva are aligned in the same column.[13] These columns are impossible to add up without mentally translating them into a common currency. Long before the early 1560s, when his handwriting disappears from the accounts, Jean Budé's record keeping had improved considerably. He soon conformed to the Genevan system of multiples of twelve based on the Genevan florin. In this system one florin equaled twelve sous and each sou equaled twelve deniers. This produced a three-column pattern of florins, sous, and deniers that was awkward by modern standards of divisibility by ten, but that was at least uniform. With this standardization, Budé did not immediately cease recording the original currency of many of the donations. He merely translated the currency in which he received a donation into the

These first expenditures of the *Bourse française* of September and October 1550 are typical of those which follow. They are recorded on paper in an unlined account book with a description of the expenditure on the left and the money expended on the right. The expenditures are totaled at the end of each month. The expenditures for each month are typically preceded by the receipts. From Archives d'État de Genève, Archives hospitalières, Kg 12, *Bourse française* (30 September 1550–September 1551), fol. 2.

Genevan system for bookkeeping purposes in the right-hand columns of the page, but he continued to record the original foreign currency in his description of expenditures on the left-hand side of the page. This redundancy left a record of actual currency exchange rates that supplements what is known about the official exchange rates of the city. See, for instance, the contribution of Mademoiselle de Boynville of July 1554: "From Mademoiselle de Boynville, one ducat, worth five florins, two sous, 6 deniers."[14]

The Genevan system was emulated further by the deacons of the *Bourse* in the early 1550s when the accounts were split into ordinary and extraordinary accounts, a practice prevalent in city accounting at this time. The account book that covers July 1553 to June 1554 specifies that it contains ordinary receipts and expenditures.[15] Apparently no extraordinary account books survive from July 1553 to August 1559, but there are some extraordinary contributions in the account book that covers August 1557 to February 1559. The extraordinary contributions from September 1557 include: 165 florins from "Monsieur de Vérace" [Jean Budé] and five florins from "some other particular person by the hands of Monsieur de Villeneuve" [François Budé, brother of Jean Budé]. The extraordinary contributions seem to include legacies, donations from unnamed individuals, and possibly large special contributions. Perhaps extraordinary contributions were those not collected by the collectors of the city.[16]

Table 3

Bourse Accounts

Archive Number	Inclusive Dates		Comments
Kg 12	30 Sept. 1550	Sept. 1551	
Kg 13	Oct. 1551	Sept. 1552	
	Oct. 1552	June 1553	No account book extant
Kg 14	July 1553	June 1554	Ordinary receipts and expenditures
Kg 15	July 1554	July 1555	
Kg 16	Aug. 1555	June 1556	Ordinary receipts and expenditures
Kg 17	July 1556	July 1557	Ordinary receipts and expenditures
Hj 1	Aug. 1557	Feb. 1559	Ordinary receipts and expenditures and some extraordinary receipts
	Mar. 1559	July 1559	No account book extant
Hj 2	Aug. 1559	July 1570	Extraordinary expenditures only
	Aug. 1570	Dec. 1579	No account book extant
Kg 18	Jan. 1579	June 1579	Ordinary and extraordinary receipts and expenditures
	July 1579	Dec. 1581	No account book extant
Kg 19	Jan. 1582	Dec. 1582	Receipts and expenditures
Kq 1	1560	1579	*Grand Livre des Assistés*
Kq 2	1580	1599	*Grand Livre des Assistés*

No account books at all survive from March to August 1559. Then only an extraordinary account book that covers August 1559 to July 1570 survives. These extraordinary accounts include expenditures such as cloth purchases, payments to medical personnel, and unanticipated handouts, but do not include the regular weekly dole or donations.[17] From August 1570 to December 1578 there is neither an ordinary nor an extraordinary account book. The two "Great Books of the Assisted" cover the years 1560–99.[18] Table 3 shows which account books exist from 30 September 1550 to December 1582, including the two "Great Books of the Assisted."

The auditors formed the third of the main categories of the *Bourse* personnel that were apparently unsalaried. They, with the collectors and deacons, were the volunteers who ran the *Bourse*. In contrast, the medical personnel were paid, as also was the copyist of Calvin's sermons and the various piecework employees whom the deacons employed. Yet even in matters where the *Bourse* paid employees the deacons were not loath to accept free services when they were offered them. This was particularly true of people who were willing to host refugees.

MEDICAL PERSONNEL

The medical personnel consisted of a doctor, a barber-surgeon, and an apothecary.[19] From the earliest pages of the accounts the deacons paid for medical services on a fee for service basis, but this system lacked controls. Bills were occasionally presented by apothecaries and barber-surgeons who were new to the account books and perhaps even strangers to the deacons themselves.[20] Initially there appears to have been nothing to prevent someone from aiding a poor person and then going to the deacons to collect the fees. Eventually the ordinances of 1581 closed this loophole by providing that the deacons were to visit the sick first and then, if necessary, "order that they be cared for by the doctor, the surgeon, and the apothecary employed to this end," but there was no indication that this procedure was tightly adhered to at the beginning of the *Bourse* in the early 1550s.[21] It did not take long, however, for the deacons to coordinate medical care. A certain measure of control was achieved within even the first few years simply by relying on one person for each service (one doctor, one barber-surgeon, and one apothecary) while continuing to pay on a fee-for-services basis. This arrangement appears to have been satisfactory, for the deacons retained the same medical people for several years. In the early 1560s they modified the fee system somewhat by hiring a doctor on a monthly or annual salary.[22] He would occasionally be granted supplements to his regular wage in times of a great deal of illness in the city or of a high influx of refugees. The early account books do not indicate for certain if the doctors were ever full-time employees of the fund. One suspects that they were not full-time employees at the beginning at least, and that the deacons' stipend to them was therefore only a part of their income. By the end of the seventeenth century the relationship of the deacons to the doctor they employed had been formalized; on 16 January 1688 a doctor was chosen by the loudest voice of the assembly at a fixed salary of ten ecus per year with an additional payment at the end of the year if there had been many sick people.[23] One can assume, however, that the relationship of the deacons to the doctor in their employ had been formalized earlier, since the deacons often recorded procedures only after they had been going on for a long time.

The system seemed to work well enough, but the cryptic entries in the sixteenth-century account books reveal little more than that a doctor, a barber-surgeon, and an apothecary were regularly paid for services that presumably they rendered. The records of the sessions of the deacons (which only survive from the seventeenth century on) indicate periodic problems with the logistics of the medical arrangements: a doctor asked to quit because there was more work than he could possibly manage, and an apothecary had to be warned that his services were to be rendered only under the prescription of the doctor and at reasonable rates.[24] There may very well have been similar problems in the sixteenth century, but the early account books did not contain this information.

The quality of medical care is more difficult to determine than that it was provided. The deacons appear to have honored the conventional wisdom about what constituted appropriate care. This meant that they paid for such practices as bloodletting, but it also meant that they concerned themselves with the overall welfare of the patients. They paid guardians for the sick and disabled who stayed at home; they placed people in the hospital or the pesthouse outside the city walls reserved for those who were bedridden with the plague. They also gave financial support to needy families of patients when the breadwinner was ill, and they paid for child care when the mother was incapacitated. They attended to details like light and heat, providing candles and wood for people incarcerated in the plague hospital, for instance, and they paid for burials, much as the confraternities did in Roman Catholic areas. They even paid a locksmith to unlock a door at Plainpalais.[25] When one considers the nature of medical care in the sixteenth century, it may well have been in these auxiliary services rather than in the actual medical care itself that the *Bourse* made its greatest contribution to the sick.

THE COPYIST OF CALVIN'S SERMONS

The *Bourse*'s only other long-term employee in the sixteenth century who received a regular salary was the copyist of Calvin's sermons, initially Denis

Raguenier and later a man named Paris. An exception to the usual method of payment for services, their record as salaried personnel may reveal why the deacons seemed to shy away from hiring full-time help and preferred to pay for individual services. If these two men were any example of what a full-time employee could mean in long-term financial obligation, there is ample evidence of their expensive dependency on the *Bourse*. The deacons not only paid the two men, but they also made frequent advances to Denis Raguenier, gave handouts to his relatives, paid Paris after Calvin's death, and provided for him periodically in the years that followed.[26] The two men clearly constituted an ongoing burden over and above their base salaries. Paying only for services rendered may thus have protected the *Bourse* from becoming a patron on whom employees relied for their total incomes. By avoiding such employee expenses as claims for sick leave and unemployment allowances, the deacons would have freed more of their resources for other poor people, but even the piecework employees occasionally solicited the deacons for financial aid. Apparently patronage relationships were difficult for the deacons to avoid.

PIECEWORK EMPLOYEES

Most of the people who worked for the *Bourse* received compensation for each individual item they manufactured or service they rendered rather than a regular salary. People who worked under this arrangement included tailors and seamstresses,[27] mattress makers and innkeepers, wet nurses and foster mothers. The copyist of Calvin's sermon may even have been paid per sermon for a time after the death of Denis Raguenier, although it seems more likely that Paris received a regular salary.[28]

When the deacons purchased goods from a craftsman, the payments were itemized in the account books. Similarly, workers were paid directly for what they had done or for the time they had taken to do it. Wet nurses, for instance, were paid for as long as a month at a time or more. In a sense, the deacons were purchasing goods and services on the open market, except that they tended to hire over and over again the same skilled workers and child care personnel, just as they tended to purchase items in large volume, such as cloth, from the same entrepreneurs.[29] There is no evidence of seeking bids to obtain the most competitive price, but one need not assume that the deacons paid an inflated price. The business acumen of the deacons should have protected them from paying too much. Also the concept of a just price still prevailed, at least to some extent, in the sixteenth century. The deacons were so careful as to ask for items in security when they advanced money; it is difficult to imagine them any less careful with the money of the fund when they made purchases.

It may have been for convenience as much as economy that the deacons tended to hire the same workers over and over again, but the result was that in a sense there was a *Bourse* tailor and a *Bourse* seamstress just as there was a *Bourse* doctor and a *Bourse* surgeon, although none necessarily relied on the deacons for his or her sole income. The *Bourse* relied on its own craftspersons for most services, with the exception of such services as shoemaking and shoe repair; no particular cobbler was mentioned in the early years. Sometimes, especially in the early years, the deacons also left the purchase of clothing up to the individual, paying for it rather than arranging to have it sewn, but when they chose to commission a service themselves, they seemed to prefer familiar craftspersons.

The deacons apparently did not always rigorously seek out the lowest price. They may have paid more for a tailor to make something, for instance, than a seamstress. If so, the deacons might have reflected the values of their age in which they lived by discriminating according to sex, or the difference in payment may have meant that the nature of the goods was different. At any rate, one cannot expect these businessmen and nobles to have been social revolutionaries or even to have been more democratic than the era in which they lived. Had they been, they would never have been selected as deacons, for no one would have trusted them with money.

On the whole, the deacons do not appear to have been spendthrift. On the contrary, they economized when they could. For instance, by hiring poor people to a job they may have saved welfare funds that might otherwise have had to be given to these people. The deacons hired the poor for many tasks, especially sewing, errand-running, and child care, and although the level of compensation sometimes seemed woefully inadequate, it was an age when labor was cheap compared to the price of the material. Since the poor usually provided services rather than goods, their very low wages may actually have been the prevailing rate.

Low wages were particularly common for child care, work that has never paid well, perhaps because it employs women almost exclusively. One wonders if the money that wet nurses received covered the cost of additional calories needed to produce the milk for the children for whom they were caring. Guardians of older children were not overly compensated either. It is entirely possible that the deacons did not believe they were paying the women for work per se; they may have felt they were making it possible for women to render service. The money paid to a child's guardian would thus have been only to cover the estimated extra cost of keeping an additional child in the house rather than to compensate the woman for the hours of work involved. This would have conformed to the Reformed principle, enunciated by Calvin, that widows played a special role in helping the poor. Whatever the motivation of the deacons, child care may have been the only opportunity for work that many women had, especially if they were caring

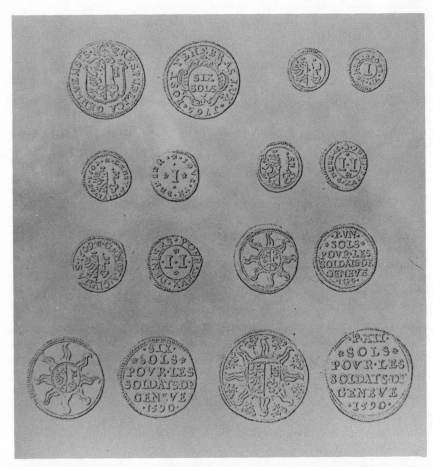

These are coins of Geneva with both sides of each coin displayed, from left to right: a coin worth six sous from 1765, an undated copper denier, a copper denier of 1609, an undated copper two denier coin, a copper two denier coin of 1609, a copper sou of 1590, a copper six sou coin of 1590, and a copper florin of 1590. Note the Reformation motto of Geneva on the back of the first coin, "Post Tenebras Lux," (After the darkness light), and the Genevan coat of arms on all the coins, half an eagle and a key, sometimes set within a radiant sun. Geneva also minted coins of greater value in silver and gold. From Eugène Demole, *Histoire monétaire de Genève de 1535 à 1792*, Mémoires et documents publiés par la Société d'histoire et d'archéologie de Genève (Geneva: J. Jullien, Libraire-Éditeur, 1887) 1:428 and plate 5.

for young children of their own; they were thus not in a good position to bargain over their wages.

The level of women's wages tends to make the deacons appear chauvinistic and stingy. This may not have been the case at all. Their economic policies may have sprung less from miserliness than from a stringent budget. In fact, there were complaints in the centuries that followed that the deacons were too generous with money rather than too strict. Judgment on these issues awaits a more thorough study of the economics and prevailing prices of the age.

HOSTS, HOSTESSES, AND ACCOMMODATIONS

A large part of the deacons' work was providing housing for refugees. They seemed to rely primarily on two types of accommodations: private homes and inns. Private homes were available in the early years because the *Bourse* enjoyed the generosity of large numbers of private individuals, many of whom were originally religious immigrants themselves, who opened their doors to refugees, apparently often without financial recompense. The deacons also used several inns in the city to accommodate refugees and apparently also occasionally relied on other accommodations organized for refugees.

During the first few years of record keeping the accountant specified with whom some of the poor were staying. These entries reveal that many a donor and deacon took in guests (clear evidence of their involvement with the poor beyond their financial commitments), but other hosts and hostesses were less well-to-do than the deacons and donors. Almost all of the hosts and hostesses appear to be French, immigrants to Geneva themselves, who were in turn receiving their countrymen and women. A number of women took in guests, responding enthusiastically to what was apparently an acceptable means of philanthropy for them.

The *Bourse* had charge accounts, in effect, with two of the city's inns, the Green Dog and the Crescent, the latter apparently located on the *Place du Molard,* a square in central Geneva.[30] The host of the Crescent was Henry Gon also known as Jaquet. Monsieur Giles Bobusse regularly received monthly payments for refugees that he housed, including the direct ancestor of Jean Jacques Rousseau, one Didier Rousseau.[31] Many of the payments to Master Bobusse and to the two inns were made after the fact for guests identified by description rather than by name. This might indicate that the innkeepers received guests on behalf of the *Bourse* without necessarily obtaining the prior approval of the deacons.

The *Bourse*'s charge accounts with the Green Dog and the Crescent do not preclude the possibility that the deacons subsidized the accommodations of refugees elsewhere, in other city inns or in private homes, since many of the entries in the account books specify only that a sum was paid for rent for an individual. Hence it is impossible to know exactly where all these people stayed, but evidently those who housed the refugees also sometimes cared for the sick among them, at least for the first few years before the deacons began using the city hospital. The *Bourse* subsidized the care of sick people at Henry Gon's place, the Crescent, presumably where he was host. The wife of Bobusse collected money for ill or injured people whom she was hosting. The deacons also employed guardians for the sick, usually one guardian per person. The account books do not reveal whether these guardians provided room and board within their own homes or went out to the bedsides of the sick.

The city's facilities were soon outdistanced by the number of refugees, sick or well. Overcrowding prompted expansion, but since Geneva was building defensive walls in the sixteenth century, it has to grow up rather than out, adding onto existing houses and filling in its gardens.[32] The deacons adjusted to limited facilities. They rented beds rather than rooms for many of the poor. Since the deacons also gave out mattresses and bedclothes, the accountant may have been referring only to the loan of the bed itself, leaving its location up to the individual. The deacons may also have accommodated the poor in some of the houses that were given to the fund, for the *Bourse* was accumulating real estate, particularly from bequests of the deceased. In addition, private individuals, such as Jean Crespin, were apparently setting up special accommodations for the refugees. In October 1550 the deacons gave money to a poor tapestry maker of Flanders staying "at the lodging of Monsieur Crespin." Eleven years later, in 1561, Crespin's wife housed a nun for what appears to have been at least half a year.[33] Altogether, the arrangements for housing were extensive and diverse.

In summary, the organization of the *Bourse française* centered around a group of deacons, donors, and volunteer helpers who periodically employed people on a piecework basis for goods and services that could not be obtained for nothing. When it was necessary to pay, the deacons did, but whenever possible they relied on the good will of their supporters, particularly for hosting the refugees in their homes. The institution was chiefly a volunteer agency, but one that had grown so large that it could not rely exclusively on unpaid help. Nevertheless, the manner in which it mobilized the energies of so many people in service to the poor is a testimonial to the zeal of that first generation of religious immigrants to Geneva and to the organizational genius of the Reformed Church.

The following are the rules of January 1581 that guided the *Bourse française:*

It is the order that has been held until now for the most part in the election of the deacons and in the administration of the pennies of the fund of the poor foreigners confirmed as much by the opinion of the ministers of this church as by the approval of the said deacons and a good part of the contributors to the said fund assembled for this fact the fifth of January, 1581.

1. That the number of the deacons will be five for the present and their charge annual and that at the beginning of each year one will elect or confirm those of the preceding year, all or in part.

2. That one will elect the most fitting that is possible according to the rule of the apostle, Romans 12:8 and 1 Timothy 3:8, that is to say by the plurality of the voice as much of the ministers of this church as the contributors to the fund who will meet together with them, being for this called by the collectors.

3. That the deacons consider committing to one among themselves the receipt and the distribution of the pennies belonging to the said fund as much the ordinary that will be gathered by the collectors each in his quarter as all the rest that there can be, and this for the time of half a year except if they continue the same receipt in the same person by their advice for another consecutive half year if there is need, and that the person who receives the said pennies register the sums received by him in order to render a good and loyal account.

4. That the deacons assemble ordinarily one time per week as much to distribute the alms that they advise are required for the poor widows and others who are in need according to the condition of each as in order to make provision for all other affairs concerning the subvention of the said poor, and as for extraordinary affairs that happen, that they inform themselves thereupon the most diligently and conveniently as is possible according to the requirements of the case, doing the duty of attentively visiting the persons of the said poor even when there are sick people, giving order that those sick ones be cared for by the doctor, surgeon, and apothecary whom they employ for this purpose.

5. That they consider also among themselves the subvention of the passersby according to what they judge to be the most fitting and proper.

6. And to the end that the poor respect much better and as they ought the said deacons in their administration that there be one of the ministers of this church chosen by these ministers who for the space of six months is present in their assembly and who when there befall some difficulty report it to the assembly of the said ministers in order to advise them; following the advice of the said ministers, the said deacons will rule after having been heard in the company of the said ministers.

7. That he who receives and handles the pennies of the said fund draw up the accounts at the end of the half year and render them to the auditors of the said accounts, then, having been signed by the said auditors, present them to the company of the ministers in order that they also be signed by two of them, then that they put them in the armoire of the papers of the poor in order that one can always show how one is governed in this administration.

8. That one elect three auditors of the accounts or that one confirm

those who have already been elected in the same fashion as has been said of the deacons. The same thus the collectors should do when it is time.

9. That from Communion service to Communion service there be censure in the said company of the deacons, the minister deputied to be with them gathering the judgments and subject the first to censure in order to encourage and fraternally to inform them in their duty.

10. That at the time of the elections of the above said there will be read the present articles at the beginning in order that all the assembly hear better how it is necessary to proceed.[34]

7

Donors

The *Bourse française* depended for its survival on the contributions of donors, and its whole elaborate system of welfare would have faltered had it not been for the generosity of large numbers of people who supported it. The identity of these contributors reveals a great deal about the nature of the institution. Lists of contributors survive for the first nine years of the *Bourse* and then, after a considerable lapse, resume again in early modern times. These later records have received some scholarly attention, but the earlier ones have not.[1] Who, then, gave to the *Bourse française* during the first decade of its recorded existence?

The donors were essentially men and women of French ancestry. There were occasional donors of other nationalities, but few Genevans were mentioned during the first decade. Some of the French donors were religious refugees living in the city, others were travelers and house guests buttonholed for contributions while passing through Geneva, and the remainder were people who sent their contributions to Geneva from France itself. Money came both from individuals in France and from Reformed congregations. As the word spread through the extensive communication network of the Reformed churches, gifts came from Lyons, Paris, Provence, Orleans, and elsewhere. The regularity of the giving and the geographic spread of the donor network reveal that Reformed churches in France had mobilized themselves behind this institution within a few short years after its inception in Geneva.

The funding of this great institution during this early period, when contributions had such an important international dimension, has never been studied before. It would be worth examining on two levels, local and international, but it is difficult to distinguish the two because the bookkeepers entered receipts from Geneva and from abroad pell-mell one after the other, without any consideration of region of origin, as if they thought of the Reformed churches as one contiguous community. The registers of the city council occasionally recorded large foreign gifts, such as eight hundred ecus for the poor foreigners and two hundred ecus for the students of theology from England on 5 August 1584,[2] but smaller foreign gifts did not receive special attention. Therefore, it is expedient to consider the *Bourse* from the perspective of the deacons, and to study the financing as a whole.

Several aspects of the *Bourse's* financing have already been touched upon in chapter 3. This chapter examines: (1) the nature of the giving, (2) the motivations behind the donations, (3) the use of deacons and other intermediaries in lieu of direct almsgiving, and (4) the influence of contributors on the *Bourse française*.

THE NATURE OF GIVING

Donations to the *Bourse* ranged from occasional gifts to long-term commitments. The account books reveal a considerable number of one-time contributors, that is, donors whose names appear only once in the receipts. These individual donations should not be minimized, for they indicate the extent to which the word about the *Bourse's* activities was being disseminated. Frequently made by people traveling through Geneva, these gifts may have reflected longer-range commitments from local congregations in France. Moreover, there were important names among these one-time donors, including such notable figures as Monsieur d'Andelot, the brother of Admiral Coligny.[3] Furthermore, the receipts of the *Bourse française* constitute only the tip of the iceberg. They list many individuals who may have contributed regularly but whose names appear in the account books only once or irregularly. This irregularity appears in part because not all lists of contributors in the sixteenth century survive, and also because the system of collection tended to subsume the names of individual donors under those of the collectors assigned to them.

At the very beginning, the bookkeeper apparently attempted to name all the contributors, but once the system of collection developed, only the names of a few individual donors were recorded and the rest were represented anonymously in the sums of money brought forward by the collectors in Geneva or carried to the deacons by messengers and merchants from France. Thus people who had lived in Geneva for years may have given regularly through the collector assigned to their quarter of town but be named in the receipts only once or twice. There were, no doubt, many others whose records of contributions were lost to posterity entirely. This might explain the relative absence of native Genevans from the formal lists of contributors in the period 1550–59, although some important Genevan contributors were recorded, such as Guillaume Chiccand, a leading procurator of the city hospital at the height of Calvin's ministry, 1556–61. He was an active elder on the consistory from 1546 on. He supported Calvin against his local enemies, the Perrinists. He was elected to the small council in 1556, and the next year he became a ruling syndic. But although this deacon of the city hospital contributed to the *Bourse française*, not many names of Genevans were among the donors.[4] That native Genevans had their own city hospital to support may explain why so few of them are listed in the receipts of the *Bourse française*.

This is not to say that the city of Geneva did not support the *Bourse française*. On the contrary, the city council applauded its activities and even attempted to take over supervision of the *Bourse* in the seventeenth and eighteenth centuries.[5] The council also contributed to the *Bourse*. The council authorized collections for the *Bourse* and for the city hospital and put alms boxes in the churches on their behalf. In 1568 the city council and the ministers put poor boxes in the churches at each door and chose men in each parish to exhort people to give. In 1569 the city council gave one hundred ecus, wheat, and rye to the deacons. After the Massacre of St. Bartholemew's Day on Sunday, 24 August 1572, the city council lodged refugees fleeing France in the city hospital and authorized the deacons of the hospital to provide them with furniture and clothes. Members of the council gave five hundred florins from their own money and instructed the preachers to prepare the people for a collection. The people were convoked in one of the churches of the city, and, as an example, the ministers and members of the city council led in the collection. Many of those who could not give immediately promised to do so later and their pledges were noted.[6] Thus in various ways the city made extraordinary efforts to help the poor refugees. The city council helped the *Bourse française* both directly and indirectly. Nevertheless, few names of native Genevans are found on the rolls of the direct contributors to the *Bourse française*.

Those whose names appear repeatedly in the lists of contributors were apparently either collectors, donors who began giving before the system of collection had fully developed, or contributors of such generosity or stature that their names were worthy of special notice. This latter category included the pastors John Calvin and Michel Cop; the printers Robert Estienne and Jean Crespin; and the financier of colporteurs, Laurent de Normandie. All of the early deacons were substantial donors, Jean Budé, Pierre Maldonnade, Monsieur de La Touche, René Gassin, and Antoine Popillon. There were several regular female donors, too, many of whom hosted refugees as well: the widow of the humanist Guillaume Budé, who was mother of the deacon Jean Budé, and Marguerite Vernon, sister of the martyr Jean Vernon.

Many of the contributors apparently pledged to give regularly to the *Bourse*, perhaps from the very beginning, because their pattern of giving was consistent before the collectors took over; they tended to give one fixed sum each month, and when they lapsed for several months, they would make up the difference later. When they gave an amount above their regular pledge, the bookkeeper noted it as an extraordinary contribution.

The deacons could thus expect each month a certain fixed sum of money from a solid core of donors. The supporters of the *Bourse* apparently realized early that the institution depended on sound financing. Indeed, some of these pledges went on year after year with fixed regularity.

The Achilles' heel in this system of pledging to the *Bourse* was inflation, a problem that was augmented by the pressure of the growing refugee population on the city's basic resources. The price of food and rent went up as demand increased faster than supply, despite the indignation of the ministers at the unreasonable burden that this placed on the poor.[7] Yet the contributors did not necessarily raise their pledges to accommodate increasing prices. For instance, a noted Italian donor, Galeazzo Caracciolo, consistently gave thirty sous to the *Bourse,* monthly, for a period of years, during an era of inflation.[8] Although his failure to increase his donation may have been because he had no more to give, such practices were reinforced in the sixteenth century by economic theories that not adequately allowed for inflation.[9] Nevertheless, one would have had to realize that virtually everything in Geneva seemed to be going up in price except for incidental items that lagged behind for a time, such as the price of burials.[10] Of course, for donors living on fixed sums of money or annuities, it must have been a hardship to maintain their original pledges.

Although some contributors did not raise their donations to compensate for inflating prices, overall giving to the *Bourse* seems to have increased in the late 1550s to accommodate a larger budget and diversified activities. This was in large part due to the expansion of the network of donors outside Geneva. It would be helpful to know more about these foreign gifts. We do know of a number of attempts to secure aid from Protestants outside Geneva especially in times of crisis. For instance, after a series of edicts in 1568 ordered all ministers to leave France, inundating the city with ministers and students, the Germans and the other Swiss came to the aid of Geneva. Théodore de Bèze and the deacons had corresponded with the ministers of Basel and of Zurich on behalf of the refugees. In turn, Henry Bullinger and his colleagues approached the Zurich city council, and on 9 January 1569 Zurich sent a donation of one thousand francs as a first envoy. The next year the councils of *Payerne* and of *Moudon* sent money for the poor fugitive ministers from the *pays de Vaud*. These appeals to Protestant neighbors were not always successful. After the Massacre of St. Bartholomew's Day the Company of Pastors sought help from the city councils of Berne and of Neuchâtel. The city council of Berne replied it was already too charged with responsibility. Nevertheless, Geneva was greatly assisted by the other Swiss cantons. The soliciting of funds was thus done in various ways, especially through correspondence and direct visits by pastors and deacons.[11]

In addition to these extraordinary contributions in times of crisis there seemed to be a strong regular network of foreign donors. Because of the poorly detailed account books in Geneva and the scarcity of surviving Protestant church records in France for this period, however, a regular pattern of foreign contributions is difficult to substantiate. There certainly were frequent gifts from some localities. Did this mean that they were trying to raise a given minimum fixed amount? Or were they just taking up a spontaneous collection whenever someone on the way to Geneva passed through? Théodore de Bèze reportedly received subsidies for the poor French when he made trips to France, for instance. Were these spontaneous gifts?[12] Surely cities such as Lyons must have expected periodic visits from Estienne Trembley and other merchants from Geneva, which would have allowed donors there to organize their giving. Records of local churches might provide some information about the arrangements for collecting money and sending it on to Geneva. Where local church records have disappeared, manuscripts of the local notaries might indicate what happened, just as in Geneva the books of the notaries contain records of some of the money willed to the *Bourse française* by people residing in France. The full ramifications of this international network of deacons and welfare funds has yet to be explored.

As for the local scene, regular giving apparently did not preclude fundraising for occasional special purposes. Alongside the records of fixed pledges, the account books reveal that special collections were made for projects beyond the ordinary work of the *Bourse*. For instance, in January 1551 a special collection was taken up for a Breton that for some reason did not fit under the ordinary rubric of the disbursements to the poor.[13] More interestingly, a year later, at the end of the January 1552 accounts, the bookkeeper entered the receipts and expenditures for sending a party to rescue a group of nuns who apparently had fled their convent in France. The nuns were imprisoned at Vienne near Lyons and were seeking refuge. The *Bourse's* usual donors gave separate sums to finance this expedition, and the accounts are so detailed that they reveal how much the deacons paid to rent horses and what was expended to clothe the nuns.[14]

These special collections were entered into the accounts within the first year and a half of the surviving record books. The special aid to the Breton and the expedition to rescue the nuns occurred early, before the fund had diversified its activities. Other special collections may have been recorded elsewhere in records that did not survive, but it is also possible that within a few years of the inception of the account books the expanding activities of the *Bourse* made special collections unnecessary.

There were other special financial arrangements as well, most notably that some of the money came encumbered with restrictions limiting how it could be spent. Such money was apparently handled separately from the regular budget, since the bookkeeper sometimes remarked that he was taking money from a particular donor's contribution. At times the deacons seemed to be acting less as free agents than as trustees, especially in the execution of wills. It was even possible for people to give or will money to be administered by deacons intended for a specific individual. For example, on 5 June 1561 a student named Master Jacques Perrin received ten pounds through the *Bourse* from the deacon Antoine Popillon to provide room and board for another student, Antoine Chanluin. The money was from the will of his godfather, Antoine Rebut.[15] In cases such as this one, it appears that the deacons were simply administering private gifts that stipulated in detail how the money was to be used. The *Bourse* might have agreed to do this because, if the recipient was poor, it saved the *Bourse*'s own money. It thus may have been in the interests of the *Bourse* to administer even very restricted gifts, especially if the volunteer time of the deacons was not taken into account, and there is little evidence that it was. The deacons might also have felt that in acting as trustees they were rendering a service to the parties involved.

It seems difficult to imagine that an organization of such breadth could have functioned as effectively as it did, encumbered by so many complicated administrative entanglements. At least the bookkeeping aspect of the finances was made more efficient with practice; after the first few account books, references to specific special gifts disappear form the running accounts. Thus, as the bookkeeping became more streamlined, the practice of attaching strings to gifts either subsided or the accountant chose to keep track of such gifts separately so that they did not appear in the general accounts. References to special gifts continued to appear in the minutes of the notaries, however, and it would be surprising if the deacons had turned down any money whose destination was compatible with their overall purposes.

In essence, the deacons had become such trusted members of the community that they represented the trustworthiness that people sought in financial transactions. This no doubt enhanced the credibility of the *Bourse* and contributed toward its growth, but it also increased the workload of the deacons, who were called upon for any number of financial transactions unrelated to their official charge of administering a welfare fund.

This happened not only on the local but on the international level. The offices of the church were becoming respected positions that linked Reformed congregations everywhere and made possible legal and financial transactions that would otherwise have been difficult to conduct at a distance. This may help to explain the relative prosperity of some of the religious refugees in Geneva who through their links with the Reformed churches in France kept account of the estates that they had left behind. Thus, for instance, one of the deacons in Geneva attempted in 1665 to recover the estate willed to him by his deceased wife, selecting another deacon as one of the procurators and stipulating that the arbitraters should be the deacons, ministers, and elders of the church at Meaux in France.[16]

Some of this extra work for the deacons was a blessing to the church, and some of the legal restrictions on donations worked to the benefit of the *Bourse*. This was particularly true in bequests to the *Bourse* from the deceased, for a popular sixteenth-century practice limited inheritance to those heirs who adhered to certain requirements, and in Geneva some of the first generation of French refugees willed their estates to their children on the condition that they remain in Geneva and practice the Reformed religion. This was an attempt to discourage the return to Roman Catholic France that was a constant threat to some of these families. If an heir did not remain in Geneva and practice the Reformed religion, the inheritance would be forfeited to someone else, sometimes a brother or a sister, but often "the fund for the poor foreigners," as the *Bourse française* was called in legal documents. The will of printer Robert Estienne was a classic example of such restrictive clauses and is well known because of its importance for the Geneva printing industry. In particular, Estienne's printing equipment was not to be removed from Geneva.[17] Sometimes the legal restrictions on an heir's activities were carried to illogical extremes. For example, a woman willed money to her bastard brother or nephew and to two women on the condition that they remain "in the church of Geneva or another of this country reformed according to the Gospel."[18] At the time the will was written, on 9 April 1560, this would have included some surrounding Swiss cantons where French was spoken and some German-speaking areas. The Reformed church had spread to other areas, but it tended not to be the government-approved church. If the heirs "retreated to the country of the papacy," they would lose their inheritance.

By the time she died, sometime before 18 April 1566, one of the prospective heirs lived in a town near Nîmes in France where he was serving as schoolmaster and deacon of a Reformed church. The Church had spread! Yet the man risked disinheritance because he lived in France, so he sent attestations back to Geneva pointing out that at the time that the woman wrote her will she could not have known that "it pleased God to enlarge his favor to establish the Church" in France. Moreover, because he was a deacon and a schoolmaster in his local church he could not leave to accomplish more precisely the condition of the will. The backup heir, if the other heirs did not fulfill the conditions of this will, was the *Bourse française*, so one would have thought that it was the responsibility of the deacons to decide what to do since the inheritance was to escheat to the *Bourse*. The deacons, however, asked the pastors. Then, following the advice of the pastors, they awarded the would-be heir an inheritance, since he was fulfilling the spirit if not the letter of the law.[19]

Not all wills contained such conditions of forfeiture. Many awarded money to the *Bourse* directly. Legacies became a major source of funding as more and more people died who were familiar with the work of the deacons. Eventually legacies constituted, together with long-term pledges and extraordinary contributions, one of the three major ways in which people donated to the *Bourse française*.

Of course, it is one thing to be willed a legacy and another to collect it. The book of legacies reveals money that was not collected—sometimes because the person who willed money to the *Bourse* did not have it at death, other times because it was difficult to collect. The minutes of the notaries of 15 June 1612 record that the deacons eventually employed one François Bernard for eighty florins per year to collect debts owed to the poor in Geneva and elsewhere. Presumably this included money borrowed from the deacons and perhaps unpaid royalties for the Psalter and Calvin's sermons.[20]

THE MOTIVATIONS BEHIND THE DONATIONS

The ways in which people gave donations to the *Bourse* is possible to decipher, at least in part, from the account books. Why they gave is more difficult to ascertain. Nevertheless, some clues to the personal motivations behind donations rest in the documents of the period, specifically, in the account books of the *Bourse*, in the notarial documents, and in the laws of the city of Geneva.

It seems there were two basic reasons for giving to the poor, because one wanted to give and because one had to give. This was true everywhere. In the sixteenth century charity was basically voluntary, but with a strong religious encouragement that suggested one should give for the sake of one's neighbors or for one's immortal soul. Thus people felt obliged to give, fearing that if they did not they would suffer for it in this world and the next. The late medieval and sixteenth-century world was alive with vivid images, both verbal and pictorial, of life after death in hell and purgatory. Protestants did not believe in purgatory but they did believe in hell, and the imagery that Dante had created in his *Inferno* and *Purgatorio* lived on for centuries in the popular mentality, whatever the theologians might have said about suffering after death being a "state" of alienation from God rather than a place.[21]

In addition to religious motives, people of means were expected by their communities to give generously. Social pressure combined with a desire to maintain one's own good name and that of one's family. For example, the city council of Geneva attempted to organize the whole city to help the poor in January 1587. A fund drive began with a systematic grassroots canvas in each quarter of the city to identify the needy. Teams of four men made home visits: a member of the city council, a pastor, the person responsible for the quarter, and one other individual. Then heads of households were convoked to the city's churches under penalty of a ten-florin fine for nonattendance. They were exhorted either to take charge of feeding several poor people, to pay a certain amount per month to support the poor, or to give a large sum in one contribution. During this fund drive the members of the city council taxed themselves between three and twenty florins each, but, on the advice of the ministers, they decided to contribute like everyone else in the quarter of town in which they lived. In that way they showed that they did not want to exempt themselves. Thus a combination of social pressures and pride urged everyone in the city who was able to contribute.[22]

Roman Catholic areas also had effective institutions for organized charity. Confraternities in particular operated as institutions of social welfare. These quasireligious, quasisocial groups allowed people to support formally their favorite charities, including even entire institutions such as hospitals. Members of a confraternity could hope that the other members would help in time of need or at least at time of death. Upon death, fellow members would be expected to attend the funeral, participate in the funeral procession, and ensure a proper burial. Before the Reformation Geneva had confraternities.[23]

The ultimate in social coercion was taxation or imprisonment for failing to do one's share voluntarily. On the whole, in sixteenth-century Europe taxation as a compulsory form of providing for the poor had not yet reached sophisticated proportions. Taxes were very limited in scope, although there were some special levies for the poor.[24] The graduated income tax was largely an institution of the future. Many people still felt the church and not the government was responsible for charity, if an institution was to be responsible at all. The Catholic church had its own taxes, such as the "tithe," and, at least in some areas, the patrimony of the church was still considered the patrimony of the poor.[25] Whether the property of the church was actually the patrimony of the poor was another question. In sum, the lack of a sophisticated system of taxation limited the effectiveness of outright compulsion as a means of obtaining funds to support the poor.

Fortunately for the poor, however, they did not depend only on the generosity of their own generation. They benefited from the endowment income of gifts given in the past. This was particularly true of Catholic regions where the church held considerable land and property. With the Protestant Reformation the endowment of the church was not necessarily lost, but was often partially dissipated in the change in ownership of church property. In some Protestant areas, therefore, the resources of the church had shrunk because of loss of property during the transition from Catholicism to Protestantism. Sometimes this was simply because city councils or other government units took over church properties and managed welfare and education directly, as in Geneva. Other times it was because some of the church property was taken back into private hands. John Knox bemoaned this in Scotland, but Martin Luther approved on a limited scale. Generally, Protestant areas were satisfied that they were following the original intentions of the benefactors if they diverted church properties to educational and charitable purposes. The prayers and masses for the souls of the dead benefactors in purgatory were abolished even though they had often been a condition of the original donation. Testators in Protestant areas continued to will property to the poor, building endowments and establishing new endowments as their interest and purposes shifted.[26]

Overall, considerable confidence was placed in the efficacy of voluntary giving. For instance, the system of social welfare that the Spanish humanist Juan Luis Vives proposed for the city of Bruges in the Low Countries was based on voluntary giving, although it proposed that poor people should work, even the disabled and the blind.[27] Work for the able-bodied was suggested and implemented elsewhere. In Geneva, for instance, the silk industry was brought to the city hospital, but only some time after John Calvin's suggestion in December 1545 that the poor of the hospital be given a craft and that an industry such as drapery be established in the city.[28] That the treatise of Vives was widely read, indicates the interest at the time in resolving the needs of the poor.

At bottom, ongoing individual charity was still very much needed to support charitable institutions in the sixteenth century, and the individual donor could be important. One need not assume that donors' reasons were perverse or self-seeking. For instance, on 2 April 1557 a Dame Anes de Remy(?) in Geneva gave fifty-five angelots to the poor in one donation because the price of grain and provisions was up and many people were in need: "considering the great abundance of the poor foreigners who are present in this city, having retreated in order to live according to the holy Reformation . . . and also the high price of grain and provisions that causes greater need for the said poor. . . ."[29] That she chose to give in the face of such necessity should not be surprising, but it is worth noting that she chose to give through the hands of a deacon to an institution such as the *Bourse française* rather then directly to the poor. This raises the question of why Christians in Geneva and elsewhere in Europe gave through an intermediary such as an institution or a deacon.

THE USE OF DEACONS AND OTHER INTERMEDIARIES IN LIEU OF DIRECT ALMSGIVING

Protestants gave to the *Bourse française*, or to similar funds, simply because it was a substitute for giving alms directly. They believed that giving alms directly would encourage beggars on the streets just when many cities were attempting to cut down on begging. This was true of both Catholic and Protestant cities, but the effort in Protestant areas was bolstered by the doctrine of justification by faith, which eliminated the emphasis on works of merit for salvation, among which direct handouts to mendicants, secular or religious, had been important. As long as Catholics recognized some merit in either asking for or giving alms directly, it would be difficult to do away with the phenomenon entirely, and the strong mendicant orders in many Catholic areas reinforced the conviction that mendicancy was meritorious. In contrast, many reformers were outspoken critics of mendicancy of any sort.

But theory aside, in the everyday world, Protestant areas were likely no more successful than Catholic in completely abolishing begging. The crucial factor may not have been theology at all but relative levels of poverty. At any rate, begging was obviously open to abuses, and there was growing opposition to it.

Begging was the only recourse that many poor people had in the sixteenth century. The frequency with which laws were passed to eliminate the problem was evidence of the prevailing inability to do away with it; the only clear long-range solution would have been to eliminate poverty. Short of that, society had to provide welfare agencies to which the poor could go in times of hardship. Where social agencies provided an alternative to begging, policing had some chance of diminishing the problem. Thus, for instance, Geneva tried a combination of social welfare, laws against begging, and guardians stationed at the churches to entrap beggars.[30] Catholic cities tried similar measures, but they clearly did not solve the whole problem. Evidence of continued mendicity crept up here and there in the records of Geneva.[31] For instance, in 1554 a boy who was begging was reportedly seduced into homosexual acts by a Messire Le Blanc.[32] Nevertheless, the Reformation brought changes that may have had some effect on mendicancy.

Dealing with the beggars themselves was one way to attack mendicity; the other approach was to discourage the well-to-do from giving direct handouts. Perhaps for the theological reasons indicated earlier, there is some evidence that in Geneva the contributors to the *Bourse française* made a concentrated effort to channel their donations through the deacons rather than give to the poor directly. Similarly, some of the poor people who were lodged or employed by contributors to the *Bourse* did not apparently go to their patrons for handouts but to the deacons. There could, of course, have been direct handouts from patrons that would not have appeared in the account books of the *Bourse*, and there is some evidence that deacons reimbursed individuals who had given out of their own pockets directly to the poor. Also, many of the first generation of contributors to the *Bourse* clearly thought of their donations as alms, that is, as money or food usually given directly to the poor. The bookkeeper Jean Budé in particular liked to refer to his contribution as "mon aulmosne," my alms.

A whole literature is devoted to the presumed transition from a medieval conception of the poor as representative of Christ Incarnate to a more detached unemotional, institutional view of poverty. The medieval view is usually associated with Catholicism and the institutional view is associated either with Protestantism or with modern secularism.[33] Whether or not a Protestant deacon was less likely to see the face of Christ in the poor than his medieval ancestors, an organized welfare fund could at least potentially deal with the poor more systematically, thoroughly, and equitably than a system that relied on individual impulse.

The danger in creating dichotomies between so-called Catholic and so-called Protestant views on social welfare is a tendency to attribute to one or the other changes that were instead products of the times, such as the rationalization of local welfare arrangements and the creation of new institutions. Examining welfare practices in light of church affiliation can lead to oversimplifications, particularly when welfare reform was carried out on a city-wide basis without particular attention to denominational allegiances. This is not to say, however, that social welfare progressed evenly throughout Europe or that in certain areas one denomination did not take the lead in providing efficient measures for helping the poor.[34]

An emphasis on the institutional aspects of welfare, however, can give the mistaken impression that early modern charity was simply a matter of channeling individual generosity through central funds. In reality considerable personal volunteer work was also encouraged. In Geneva hosting refugees could be a voluntary deed as could caring for and visiting the sick. An enormous amount of such help went on without being recorded anywhere. On the other hand, not all giving in Geneva appeared to be self-generated. Those who were able were expected to give. The collectors assigned to each quarter of the city knew people's financial wherewithal so they could approach them with realistic requests for donations. This kind of social pressure by one's peers was important to the effective functioning of the welfare system. Over the years a system of careful record keeping developed, documenting in detail Genevan philanthropy in the seventeenth and eighteenth centuries.

In Geneva one could also give spontaneously through collection boxes designated for the poor. The city hospital and the various welfare funds were beneficiaries of the collection boxes. These boxes played more than a perfunctory part in overall charity; quarrels often resulted when efforts were made to designate the proceeds for one institution rather than another for even one day of the week. The minutes of the deacons of the latter seventeenth century indicate that the *Bourse* received the money collected in these boxes on Thursdays. When the city hospital apparently attempted to take over the Thursday proceeds, the deacons of the *Bourse* in October 1688 registered an objection and sent two deacons to the Sunday assembly of the city hospital board to represent their interests. The deacons stated that they had no extra money, that the *Bourse* was heavily charged with French refugees, and that the people expected their Thursday donations to go to the *Bourse*. After an exchange between the deacons of the city hospital and those of the *Bourse française*, the proceeds were given to the *Bourse*.[35]

Charity in Geneva seemed to be a judicious combination of free will and mutual encouragement. The city's notaries, who recorded wills and other legal documents, were encouraged to remind their clients of the needs of the city's welfare institutions and to register their bequests. A registry was created, perhaps to facilitate collection of these legacies, listing the bequests to the city hospital, to the academy, and to the funds for the poor foreigners, French or Italian. The typical donation supported several of these institutions, usually a combination of the hospital, the academy, and either the Italian or the French *Bourse*. When the bequest was collected, the fact was entered into the margin. Not all of them were collected, by any means. Thus in death as well as in life the inhabitants of Geneva were encouraged to raise their sights above their own immediate needs and those of their heirs.[36]

THE INFLUENCE OF CONTRIBUTORS ON THE *BOURSE FRANÇAISE*

Contributing to welfare in Geneva, as everywhere, had its own rewards. One gained social prestige and recognition, and, if one gave on a large enough scale, power to influence the charity institutions. During the first years of the *Bourse française*, the contributors controlled the destinies of the institution very directly. They not only assembled and voted, they also recommended individual poor people to the *Bourse* on a regular basis. There is no evidence that in the early years the deacons ever turned down a specific recommendation of a contributor, although such a decision would not have been entered in the accounts because no expenditure would have been made. Nevertheless, the frequency of donors recommendations indicates the donors' intimate involvement with the activities of the fund and their apparent desire to have something to say about the dispensing of their alms. Hence the contributors turned over their money to the deacons but retained some power to help specific individuals simply by recommending them.

Others who were not listed in the record of the receipts as contributors could also recommend a poor person. The power to recommend stemmed more from one's acknowledged reliability than from solely the power of one's pocketbooks. This was particularly true of the pastors who recommended poor people to the *Bourse*. Not all of them were able to donate large amounts themselves, but their role in the *Bourse* remained important. At one point, when the city council wanted a magistrate to supervise the deacons, opponents argued that the poor felt comfortable going to the pastors, who were familiar with them and their needs. Apparently the pastors continued to suggest people whom the deacons should aid even after their names as recommenders dropped out of the account books. It appears that in very tangible ways the members of the Venerable Company of Pastors continued to make their influence felt over the *Bourse française*.

After the first few years, when the bookkeeping became more concise, less was recorded about recommenders. This may have been a function of streamlining the entries, or it may have been that contributors became more confident of the judgment of the deacons and, as the existence of the fund became more widely known, the poor came directly to the deacons for help.

Table 4 lists the names of the contributors to the *Bourse française* that appeared in the receipts of the account books in the period 1550–59. Orthography was not yet fixed at this time, so the accountant spelled the names with various phonetic spellings. Therefore, alternate spellings or variants frequently follow an individual's name, in parentheses. Information enclosed in brackets further identifies people, and question marks indicate a lack of reasonable certainty. Where a person is identified with more than one name or a name and a title, both are listed, usually with a cross reference in brackets. Short phrases that identify the donor as the relative of another donor are included, as are indications that the donation was a will. This list replicates the spelling of the manuscripts; it does not attempt to conform to commonly accepted spelling of today. Needless to say, the variant spellings tend to suggest several people when only one existed. Despite considerable help from the archivists in compiling this list, a number of names look improbable indeed. They are included, however, in an attempt to make this a thorough, genuine working list of the donors to the *Bourse française*.

Table 4

Donors to the *Bourse française:* 1550–1559[37]

Alban, Jehan de Montauldan or Montaulban
Alphonse, Monsieur
Anjorrant, Regnault or Regnauld [Monsieur de Souilly]
Aubelin (Aulmosne, Alphonse), Monsieur
Autin, Seigneur Rene
Autour, Estienne [Seigneur de Beauregard]

Baduel, Claude[38]
Barrault, Monsieur Pierre or Maistre Pierre
Bartholemy, Maistre
Baudechon, feu Seigneur
Bayf or Baif, Monsieur Rene de [Seigneur de Cre][39]

Table 4 *(Continued)*

Beaucastel, feu Monsieur
Beaulieu, Monsieur de [François Prevost]
Beauregard, Monsieur de [Estienne Autour]
Beguin (Begnin, Begnyn), Monsieur or Sire Jehan
Bellegarde, feu Monsieur de
Benoist, Seigneur Estienne
Bergevin, Monsieur de
Bernard, Maistre or Seigneur Jaques
Bernire (Bernier), Francois
Bernot, Monsieur
Besson, Honorat (Besson, Anton Charle)
Bienassis, Mademoiselle de [Marguerite Vernon, femme de Rene Bienassis]
Bonneterye or La Bonneterye, Monsieur de [François de la Botiere, Prevost de
    Cluny?]
Bonueni (Bonuemi, Bonuevi), Testament de
Bosquet, mon frere de [Jean Budé's brother?]
Bouchard, François [Vicomte d'Aubeterre]
Bouche (Boucher), Jehan
Bourgoing, Francois [Seigneur d'Aignon or d'Agnon]
Boynville (Boyenville, Boinville), Monsieur de [Guillaume Le Comte or Le
    Cointe][40]
Boynville, Mademoiselle de
Boysbossart (Boiboyssard), Monsieur or Seigneur de [Seigneur de Boisbossart,
    Pierre Gorin]
Brachet, Damoiselle Francoise [widow of feu Noble Guillaume Aubelin, Seigneur
    de la Bruyere]
Bredan (Bredain, Bredehan), Monsieur de [Jacques de Bourgogne, Seigneur de
    Falais et de Breda? See Monsieur de Fallaix]
Brichauteau, Charles de [Seigneur de Saint Martin, alias de Saint Lauren]
Bronet, Monsieur de, and son frere
Brusquin, Monsieur de
Budé, Francois [Monsieur de Villeneuve]
Budé, Jehan [Seigneur de Verace]
Budé, Louis [Monsieur de la Motte or Mothe]
Budé, Mademoiselle [Jean Budé's sister or mother], also "ma soeur," "ma mere,"
    "feu ma mere"
Burcy or Bursy, Monsieur de [Monsieur de Saint Martin, alias de Saint Lauren,
    Jacques?]

Calvin, Jehan
Camiailles (Camiealles, Carnicalles), Jehan
Camiailles, pere de [Yves?]
Candolle, Monsieur de
Canut
Carracciolo, Galiazo (Galeazzo), le Marquis [de Vico]
Carre, L'Escuyer [Esquire?]
Caves, Seigneur de
Cenesnid (Cenefnit), Mademoiselle de
Chabart (Chabert?), Maistre Anthoine
Chandieu, Monsieur de [Antoine de la Roche Chandieu]

Table 4 *(Continued)*

Charpon (Senarpont?), Monsieur de
Chervault (Clairvant?), Monsieur de
Chican (Chiccand, Checcant), Guillaume [Le seigneur Chicquan]
Claude, Le Maistre[41]
Claude, Maistre 'le coustalier'
Claude, Maistre 'le tincturier'
Cluny, Prevost de [François de la Botiere, see Bonneterye]
Colladans, Messieurs les [Germain et Nicolas Colladon?]
Colonge (Collonges), Sire de [Francois de Morel][42]
Cop, Monsieur
Cornaron, Monsieur
Cornavit, Monsieur [Seigneur Amend Cornevet?]
Cornillaudt (Cornillaudit), feu Seigneur, "de la femme du Seigneur . . . testament"
Coumarron or Armarron, Monsieur
Courteau (Aourteau), Thomas
Cre, Seigneur de [Rene de Baif or Bayf]
Creil, Monsieur de
Crespin, Jehan
Crulannes (Crulaines), Monsieur de

Daguat (d'Aguat), 'par les heriteurs de'
d'Aguile (d'Aguilles, d'Aguylle, d'Aguilhon, des Aiguilles, d'Aguillon), Monsieur [Jehan d'Esguille de Genas, or René Gassin, deacon], and "la soeur de" and "la belle soeur"
d'Aignon (d'Agnon), Monsieur or Seigneur [Francois Bourgoing][43]
d'Aimee, Seigneur
d'Allemant (d'Allemand), Seigneur
Danieres (Danere), Monsieur de or Siegneur de
d'Aubeterre, Monsieur [Francois Bouchard, Vicomte d'Aubeterre]
d'Audelot (d'Audelont), Monsieur [François de Coligny, Sire Andelot, Seigneur Châtillon?]
David (Damo), feu Monsieur
Denis
Des Arenes [Monsieur de Varennes, Guillaume Try or de Trie?]
Des Combres (de Combes), Monsieur
Des Crignelles (Crignelles, Coignelles, Criquelles), Monsieur
Des Crignelles, Mademoiselle
Des Dant or Des Daut
Des Forestz [region?]
Des Garennes, Mademoiselle
Des Vaulx [region?]
Desprit (Despoit), Monsieur
Domcevol[?], Mademoiselle de
Domques
Du Bois, Mademoiselle
Du Clare, Francois [d'Orleans]
Du Mas, Jehan [Seigneur de Lisle]
Du Mont, Monsieur
Du Pont, Monsieur [Phillippe Corquilleray, Claude Du Pont, or Françoys Du Pont?]

Table 4 *(Continued)*

Durand, Zacharie
Du Tillat (de Thillac), Mademoiselle
Du Val, Seigneur Estienne
Du Vanneau, Monsieur
Du Vivier, Monsieur

Enard (Eynard?), Maistre
Estienne, Seigneur Robert

Fallaix or Falaises, Monsieur de [Jacques de Bourgogne, Seigneur de Falais et de
    Breda][44]
Fanon (Favon), Seigneur
Farel, Guillaume
Fay, Etienne [Monsieur or Seigneur de la Tour]
Florentin, Seigneur Michel
Fontaine or Haute Fontaine, Monsieur de
Forestz, Monsieur de
Frappe, Jehan

Garnier, Seigneur Francoys
Girard (Gerard), Seigneur Estienne
Gon, Henri
Gorin, Pierre [Seigneur de Boisbossard or Boysbossart]
Grene, Philibert, "L'esleu Grene" et son frere
Grule or Goute, Seigneur Henry
Guerin, Seigneur Francoys Loys or Loys

Haute Fontaine, Monsieur de [Monsieur de Fontaine]

Jehan de Lyon
Jeremie, Monsieur de [Monsieur de Saint Germain]
Jonniane[?]
Jonvilliers, Charles de or "mon frere de"
Jonvilliers, Mademoiselle de [Marye de Jonvilliers, femme de Jean Budé]

La Barde (La Barie, La Barre), Mademoiselle de
La Bonneterye, Monsieur de [François de la Botiere?, Prevost de Cluny, see Bon-
    neterye]
La Borde, Monsieur de [Pierre Borde?]
La Boullaye, Mademoiselle de
La Boullaye, Monsieur de [Françoys Eschallat, dict de la Bolayie]
La Bruere, Dame de (La Bruyere, Mademoiselle de) [Mademoiselle Francoise
    Brachet, widow of Guillaume Aubelin, Seigneur de la Bruyere or Geneviève
    Aubelyn, his daughter]
La Garde or La Gard, Monsieur de
Lalir or Labier, Seigneur Thomas
La Monnoye (le Monneraye [Bretagne]), Maistre de [Master of the Money?]
La Motte or Mothe, Monsieur de [Louis Budé]
La Nalliac (Malliac), Monsieur de
Lanere, Seigneur
Langlis (Langlys, Lanys), Monsieur

Table 4 (*Continued*)

La Planche, Monsieur de [Louis Regnier], et son cousin
La Pommeraye, Monsieur de, Charles
La Porte, Monsieur de, Claude or Eustache de la Porte
La Prade, Monsieur de
L'Archeveque
La Ripantiere (Repautiere, Ribautrere, La Repauldiere), Monsieur de
La Roche, Mademoiselle de
La Roche, Seigneur Estienne de
La Roche, Seigneur Francois de or des Roche(s)
Lassere, Seigneur or Seigneur de [Denys Lacere?]
La Touche, beaufrere de Monsieur de
La Touche, cousin de Monsieur de
La Touche, Jehan de
La Touche, Monsieur de [Francois Buynard]
La Tour, Monsieur or Seigneur de [Estienne de Faye]
Laufmoins, feu Monsieur David [see also David]
Laurdes (Laurere), Jehan
La Valleyere (Vallayere, Valliere), Monsieur de
Le Blanc, Messire Lambert
Le Coint
Le Court, Monsieur [Andre Le Court]
Le Drerur (Derier), Nicolas
Le Fer, Monsieur Nicolas
Le Grand, Seigneur Pierre
Le Maistre, Claude
Le Marquis [de Vico, Galiazo Carracciolo]
L'Emery, Monsieur de [Jean de Lemerey, l'Hemery, l'Humery, Lumery]
Lenfant, Bailly
Le Villain, Nicolas
Lisle, Seigneur de [Jehan du Mas]
Lonnir, Jehan de
Lorestz [see Des Forestz]

Macart (Maccar, Macar, Macquard, Macard), Jehan
Maillaiges (Maillaignes), Monsieur de
Maillane (Maillain, Maillant, Maillame), Seigneur de [Ardoin de Percellet, Porceller]
Maldonnade, Madame [Pierre's wife]
Maldonnade, Nicolas, le frere de Seigneur de Maldonnade
Maldonnade, Pierre de
Mangiron, le niesce de Monsieur de [Maugiron, gouverneur catholique de Lyon?]
Marheron or Macheroy, mon cousin de [Jean Budé's cousin?]
Marillac (Marillat), Monsieur [Pierre Marillac]
Marrot, Monsieur
Meigret (Megret), Laurent [Le Magnifique Meigret]
Monon, Ysabeau [Madame la conseilliere de Scienous or Chinon, veuve Charles Quinal]
Montiguy, Monsieur de or Jehan de Montigne [Seigneur de Villiers?]
Montrohe, Mademoiselle de
Morin, Pierre
Mot, Mont, or Mon, Monsieur de [Monsieur de la Motte, Louis Budé?]
Moulins, Monsieur de

Table 4 *(Continued)*

Normandie, Laurens de
Nour'bre, Monsieur de [Could this be Normandy?]
Nuegler (Nueglno, Nurglne), Vincent

Olivier, Maistre

Pallai, Monsieur de [Falais?]
Pare, Monsieur de [Anthoine Popillon]
Peroulies (Poliet, Polier, Poulier), Monsieur le Secretaire
Personne, Seigneur Jehan
Petit Loys, espicier
Picot, Nicolas, apoticaire
Pierre, Maistre, le tourneur (tondeur?)
Plainchamps, Monsieur de
Porceller, Monsieur de [Seigneur de Maillane?]
Potier (Pothier), Nicolas, Baillif
Prade, Monsieur
Presle(s), Mademoiselle de
Prevost de Cluny [see Bonneterye or La Bonneterye, François de la Botiere]
Prevost, François [Monsieur de Beaulieu]
Prevost, Guillaume [Monsieur de Saint Germain]
Prieur (Prien), Seigneur Guillaume
Pron (Prou, Prov, Prot), Monsieur de

Quard (Guard, Girard, Quaile, Quanil, Quail)

Rabier (Rabir or Rubir), Estienne [Latin: Rabirius—libraire?]
Ramus (Ramuz) [Latin: Ramuses]
Remont (Remond, Raymond), Monsieur [Raymond Chauvet?]
Rene [Monsieur Rene Gassin]
Renier (Regnier), Louis
Ribautrere (Repautiere, La Repauldiere) [see also La Ripantiere, Monsieur de]
Richard, Maistre, de Vauville or Vanville
Rocquebrun (Roquebrune), Monsieur de 'pour l'oncle de'
Ruffy or Rufy, Monsieur [Jacques Ruffy?]

Saint Andre, Monsieur de
Saint Germain, "la mere de"
Saint Germain, Monsieur de [Guillaume Prevost, Seigneur de Saint Germain]
Saint Laurent, Madame de
Saint Laurent, Mademoiselle de
Saint Laurent, Monsieur de [Charles de Brichauteau, Seigneur de Saint Martin, alias de Saint Lauren]
Saint Michel, jeune homme nommé
Saint Ramy (Rany, Ravy, Ranvit), Monsieur de
Salai (Falai?), Monsieur de
Saules, Saulx, or Sautes
Saulx, Madame de
Savalier (Sanaliere, Savaliere), Monsieur de
Savion (Savyon, Panien), Monsieur de
Scandillat, Mademoiselle de

Table 4 *(Continued)*

Segriynard (Seguynard), Robert
Sertiers, Nicolas or Nicolas de Sartieres (Sertieres)
Souilly, Monsieur de [Regnauld or Regnault Anjorrant]
Stample, Seigneur Jehan or Stampes
Sylvestre, Jacque

Thillac, Ma soeur de
Thillac (Thillat), Mademoiselle du [see also Du Tillac]
Thillac (Thillat), Monsieur [Guy de Serignac]
Thologe, La Dame de [Tholouse, the city?]
Thomas
Tirl . . . , Monsieur
Toucheron, Seigneur [Jehan Toucheron?]
Tremblay, Maistre Jehan
Tremblay, Seigneur Estienne

Valleyere, Monsieur de
Varennes, femme de Monsieur de, or "mere de," or "soeur de"
Varennes, Monsieur de, et son cousin [Guillaume de Trie or Try is Monsieur de
    Varennes]
Varquey
Varro, Michel [Seigneur de Brassu]
Velu, Monsieur de
Verace, Mademoiselle de
Verace, Monsieur or Seigneur de [Jean Budé]
Veqnon (Vequon), Maistre Jehan
Vernon (Vernou), Monsieur
Vigne (Vigny), Monsieur de
Villan, Francoys
Villemongez, Monsieur [Adrian de Prignault, Seigneur de Briquemault or de Pri-
    quemaut]
Villeneufve, Monsieur de [François Budé]
Villiers or Villers, Monsieur [Jehan Moreli]

Ynit (Yvit, Yuiv), Anthoine

8
Recipients

Much less is known about those who received money from the *Bourse française* than about those who contributed to it. The recipients came in great numbers as refugees to Geneva. There was a great influx in the 1550s, the most active decade of Calvin's ministry. They came from France, primarily, but also from other countries including Italy and Britain. A recent study estimates that Geneva's population grew from 13,100 to 21,400 between 1550 and 1560, a more than 60 percent increase in one decade.[1] Many of the refugees went home when it was safe to do so; most of the English returned to England after the death of Mary Tudor in 1558, although some of them stayed a few years more until the completion of the Geneva Bible.[2] Many refugees of other nationalities were never able to go home. Some moved on to other parts of Switzerland or Protestant Europe, while others stayed and made Geneva their home. Those who could afford to buy property invested in houses, fields, and vineyards.

Considerable information is available on the wealthier of these religious immigrants.[3] They left contracts and wills in the notarial records. Far less is known about the poor, because they left few permanent legal documents. The poor are virtually absent from the minutes of the Genevan notaries and appear only occasionally in the registers of the consistory and in the criminal records, less frequently than one would suppose for a group of poor people who might have been tempted to steal.[4] In fact, in these records the contributors to the *Bourse* are much more evident than the poor, although usually as witnesses or employers rather than as people accused of wrongdoing. The relatively low number of French refugees in trouble with the consistory or the city council belies the popular conception in France at the time of the refugees as thieves, brigands, and drunkards.[5] Many poor refugees left to posterity no permanent trace of their existence except their names on a welfare roll, but the information found there is enlightening.[6]

The early account books contain considerable information on some of the refugees, including their sex, marital status, profession or craft, and region of origin. In very broad terms they indicate refugees' approximate age, condition of health, and financial status. They sometimes briefly recount the particular circumstances of refugees who fled religious persecution or survived prison or the galleys. In the mid-sixteenth century Protestants were apparently already condemned to row on ships alongside beggars and debtors just as John Knox served on the galleys before coming to Geneva with the English refugees. This was to become a characteristic fate of the Huguenots during the next two centuries.[7]

Despite this wide variety of detail in the earliest account books, the deacon used very approximate categories in the first decade of record keeping. For instance, the deacon indicated age by noting if individuals were children, youths, or old people; everyone else apparently fell into the broad category of adult. Information about health was simply whether they were sick or well, injured, or incapacitated in some way. The financial information he offered was merely whether or not they were poor, or looking for a job. Sometimes he indicated for whom they worked, especially if they were servants or employees of someone who was well known to the deacons, as when the former servant of Théodore de Bèze received aid from the deacons in April 1561.[8]

Sometimes the account books reveal why people came to the deacons for help, whether it was because they were poor, sick, unemployed, temporarily in difficult straits, or because they needed a loan, a tool, child care, school fees, or money for a trip. The amount of information that the bookkeeper included in the short entries to explain his expenditures was considerable. In one terse phrase he covered a wide spectrum of detail about an aid recipient.

If all of this information were available for every aid recipient the accounts would be a statistical treasure, but in the first decade of record keeping the deacons apparently made no attempt to be consistent. For some entries they gave only recipients' names, and for others they recorded much more. They appear to have been primarily interested in accurate identification of the people to whom they gave money and in justifying each expenditure, rather than in keeping systematic records about the aid recipients. Some of the descriptions were very long, but other entries included only the recipient's name, and often the bookkeeper felt it was not necessary to add other information. Thus the data was very irregular.

From this information one can form an approximate picture of the refugee population in the early years, but one cannot compile complete detailed statistical tables.[9] One exception to this haphazard recording of information about the recipients was during the month of August 1557 when the bookkeeper, Jean Budé, carefully recorded in the margin of the accounts the geographic origins of the welfare recipients for that month.[10] He was apparently struck by the regional variety of those who were coming to him for aid, but he was not concerned with presenting any other information about them in a systematic manner either here or elsewhere.

This one-month geographical profile did not include all the regions or cities from which refugees came, according to the first ten years of the records of the *Bourse*. Scattered throughout the accounts were references to other parts of France and French-speaking parts of the Low Countries,[11] as well as non-French-speaking areas such as England, Italy, Spain,[12] and Germany. There were even a few exotic refugees, such as the Jew who said he was on his way to England. This wide range of refugees' national origins and religions was evidence of a considerable generosity on the part of the *Bourse* and its deacons during these first years of its existence.[13]

Some of these non-French foreigners were eventually referred to other welfare funds created to handle the various ethnic groups that were arriving in Geneva. The Italians were received by an Italian *Bourse*, an institution supported by the Italian community in Geneva and staffed by the deacons of the Italian congregation.[14] German-speaking people later had their own *Bourse allemande*, and the English-speaking church apparently also cared for their own once they were organized to do so.[15]

The *Livre des Anglois* in Geneva lists two deacons in 1555, three in 1556, and four in 1557 and 1558, which indicates welfare activities or a *Bourse anglaise* of one sort or another. The limited presence, in both numbers and length of stay, by the English in Geneva may have made it unnecessary for a highly organized institution to develop.[16] Eventually the responsibility for the English fell to the *Bourse allemande*. By the end of the eighteenth century it was also responsible for Swedes, Poles, the Dutch, the Flemish, and German-speaking people of the Germanies and Switzerland.[17] Thus it appears that the *Bourse française* served refugees of many nationalities until the national communities in Geneva organized their own systems of welfare.

This division of the welfare load by nationality led to eventual conflicts of interest. By the seventeenth century the lines were so finely drawn between the welfare institutions in Geneva that a shifting regional boundary in Europe could realign each institution's responsibility and lead to bickering over which refugees belonged to which fund. The proceedings of the deacons of the *Bourse française* for this period recorded disagreements, particularly with the city hospital, that may have harmed and confused the poor people, who on occasion were shuttled from one institution to another. In all fairness to the welfare institutions, however, it must be said that the diversity of sources of aid in Geneva allowed some poor people to use first one institution and then another, and perhaps even to get themselves on more than one welfare roll at once.[18] Drawing strict nationality lines among the welfare funds might have in part expressed the need to prevent abuse of the welfare system.[19]

The church of the Auditoire, formerly Notre-Dame-La-Neuve, with the Cathedral of Saint Pierre in the background. John Knox preached here, and the English congregation met here in the 1550s. It was also used for lectures, as its name, auditorium, would suggest. In modern Geneva it is sometimes used for concerts, and the Scottish Church meets here on Sundays as do other Reformed groups, such as the Waldensians. There is a beautiful room over the sanctuary called the Salle de Théodore de Bèze. This illustration is based on a drawing of C. Bastard, from Émile Doumergue, *Jean Calvin, Les hommes et les choses de son temps,* vol. 3, *La ville, la maison, et la rue de Calvin* (Lausanne: Georges Bridel, Éditeurs, 1905), p. 343.

Whatever the circumstances for tighter institutional policies, the situation had clearly changed by the seventeenth century. The first generation of deacons of the *Bourse française* often ignored ethnic lines; on at least one occasion, they even aided a native Genevan.[20] A mitigation of the crisis situation by the early seventeenth century might have made more flexible policies possible, but instead, the open-handed spirit apparently gave way to one concerned with protecting limited funds. The latter-day deacons appear in a less favorable light than their first-generation counterparts, although the seventeenth-century deacons may have been working with a tighter budget than their sixteenth-century counterparts as the ravages of inflation ate away at the available funds. Perhaps they could not afford to be too openhanded.

In addition to inflation, the latter half of the seventeenth century brought a large influx of refugees to Geneva. The policies of the French government toward Reformed Christians living in France became increasingly repressive, forcing many Reformed Christians to flee France. A key event in the policy of repression was the revocation of the Edict of Nantes (1685) during the reign of the French king Louis XIV. The Edict of Nantes (1598), promulgated after the era of the Wars of Religion in France, had granted Reformed Christians (Huguenots) the right to public worship in France wherever the Reformed Church had existed in 1597 except for Paris, Reims, Toulouse, Lyons, and Dijon. It had admitted Huguenots to public office, and it had provided that Huguenot children could not be forced to receive Roman Catholic training. These rights were gradually eroded after the assassination in 1610 of Henry IV, the tolerant king of France who had once been a Protestant. By the latter half of the seventeenth century conditions had become very difficult for French Protestants. Many of them fled the country, causing what the Genevans call the "second refuge," sometimes dated from 1660 to 1720. The "second refuge" began a century after the so-called "first refuge," sometimes dated from 1549 to 1560.[21]

The "first refuge" coincided with the decade when the Genevan population increased by over 60 percent. This "refuge" is documented in the first book of the inhabitants of Geneva, which covers the period 1549–60. But to understand the dynamics of the refugee situation it might be useful to extend the dates of the first refuge. Refugees continued to come to Geneva after 1560, especially when forced out by royal edicts or by such a tragedy as the Massacre of St. Bartholomew's Day of 24 August 1572.[22]

Many of the sixteenth-century refugees returned home after the particular crisis that had driven them out subsided. In the seventeenth century it became difficult for the refugees to return to France because the oppressive policies of Louis XIV caused them to lose possessions and their right to worship. They needed to find a permanent home outside of France.

Geneva, of course, could not house all the refugees. Many refugees were therefore sent on to more distant parts of Switzerland or elsewhere. Some did not stop in Geneva at all but headed directly for Lausanne or other regions.[23] Yet Geneva's convenient location at the headwaters of the Rhone River provided a natural stopping point. It was the first safe city across the border from Roman Catholic France. Many refugees stopped in Geneva; more of them wanted to stay than Geneva could accommodate.

Geneva did not leave the departure of excess refugees to chance. Many were encouraged to move on. The deacons of the *Bourse française* gave financial aid to refugees who were headed elsewhere and saw to their transportation. The deacons' minutes of 26 September 1687 discuss the boats that took refugees across Lake Geneva to other destinations; boat trips were planned up until there was no longer a sufficient number of people to fill a boat.[24]

The willingness of the first generation of deacons to help a diverse group of refugees left its imprint on the account books. The records of the *Bourse française* reveal the coming and going of the refugee population in rather minute detail. For instance, months before the number of Marian exiles warranted the formation of an English-speaking church in Geneva, the deacons of the *Bourse française* noted the arrival of the English. An English person made a donation in August 1552, another received help in November 1553, and a third was given woodworking tools in September 1554.[25] The account books also reveal where people had been and where they were going. The deacons recorded, for example, a number of French people, from the north and west regions of France in particular, who made their way to Geneva by way of England. Overall there seems to have been a great deal of traveling about, for both those who eventually made their way to Geneva and those already implanted in the city. Some of the latter returned to their home regions to recover their possessions and to bring back the rest of their families.

THE BOOK OF INHABITANTS

The account books of the *Bourse française* are not the only surviving records of the refugees. New inhabitants are also listed in the book of inhabitants of Geneva, a registry started at about the same time as the records of the *Bourse*. The account books of the *Bourse* and the book of inhabitants overlapped to some extent, but a large portion of the aid recipients who were mentioned by name in the welfare rolls were absent from the book of inhabitants. Considerably fewer than half the names of those who were recorded in the accounts of the *Bourse* were included in the first book of inhabitants for the overlapping period of 1550–60. Of course, there is no way to determine what percentage of the nameless *Bourse* aid recipients were named in the book of inhabitants, but it seems likely that if their names escaped the deacons of the *Bourse française* they might have been so obscure or transient as to have escaped the book of inhabitants as well.[26]

The book of inhabitants and the account books of the *Bourse* complement each other: the welfare rolls broaden the spectrum of immigrants to include the poor. The rolls, as one would expect, included many women and children who were absent from the book of inhabitants, but they also named men who did not appear on the list of inhabitants. Some of these men were described as "impotent," a term that in the sixteenth century referred to an inability to support oneself and a lack of strength and health. Others were considered lazy though able-bodied; the city was loath to accept them. On 7 December 1568 the city council ruled that the city would no longer accept those who were not willing to work. Refugees were to register with the *Bourse* stating their profession and to provide a witness who would promise that they would not be a charge to the *Bourse*. Whether or not this regulation was effective over time was not indicated, and in any case the poor continued to arrive. The ordinance of the city council reads as follows:

> For as much as several of those who retreated here now are poor and want to do nothing, charging the *Bourse* for relieving them, it is decided that henceforth one will not receive more of those who have no estate, and that those who witness for them promise that they will not be a charge, and, in order that they can be summoned when this happens, that they present themselves to the *Bourse*, that one puts in their letters their professions and the name of those who will have witnessed for them.[27]

The image of "the refuge" as an influx of worthy artisans and a few professional people is somewhat mitigated by the lists of those who went on welfare soon after they arrived in Geneva and stayed on the rolls for the rest of their lives. Here were the abandoned women, the widows with dependent children, the elderly, the blind, and the "impotent" who were too debilitated to care for themselves. Those who came to Geneva to follow the Reformation included more than just the able-bodied. The book of inhabitants and the account books of the *Bourse* together reveal that a considerable sociological spectrum came to Geneva.

This spectrum was reflected even among those who were aided by the deacons. The *Bourse* dealt particularly with the poor, of course, but also well-to-do people in temporary straits received money. Didier Rousseau, a direct ancestor of Jean-Jacques Rousseau, was one notable figure apparently aided by the *Bourse* who did not belong to the chronic poor. It is possible that the money the deacons gave him on 6 April 1551 was to pay the host's bill for other people's accommodations rather than his own, but the entry in the account book suggests he was given more money for his own use than the typical welfare recipient of the period received. This perhaps indicates that the deacons did not practice total equality in their dissemination of funds. Whether they did or not, it may have been an investment in the future; almost two decades later, in his will of April 1570, Didier Rousseau remembered the *Bourse*.[28]

Didier Rousseau was not an isolated example. For instance, a relatively large sum was given to one Madamoiselle du Plessix (Plessis) by the order of the Company of Pastors and sums were given to a Dame Anne, to a Madamoiselle de la Tour, and to a Monsieur Hennequin. There were also sums entered for a bourgeois sent to the city hospital, one Mangis Merlin.[29] The deacons seem to have reflected in their practices the prevailing view of society that frowned on treating a gentleman the same as a poor one from lower strata in society. The deacons may have honored the concept of "the shamefaced poor," providing more discreetly for those of high birth. To have done otherwise would have been out of place in early modern society and would have offended the prevailing sense of propriety. Before criticizing such blatant inequality, it should be noted that the help rendered to those who turned out only to be in temporary straits was sometimes paid back in abundance. Overall, the deacons could very well have been ahead financially for having helped generously. It has been argued as well that the elite were motivated to help the shamefaced poor out of a sense of brotherhood and sisterhood, just as, elsewhere, brothers and sisters of the same confraternity received preferential aid.[30]

That the *Bourse française* gave special treatment to the shamefaced poor shatters any illusions about the *Bourse* being a completely democratic institution. But the *Bourse française* did not apparently intend to modify the existing social order, only to improve the lot of those within the social order. Nevertheless, by making it possible for refugees with a wide variety of skills to establish themselves in Geneva, its activities did affect the economic, political, and religious history of that city. And, by providing books and apprenticeship and school fees, it enabled people who might otherwise have had negligible opportunity to rise in society to do so. The deacons' efforts to train people and to help them learn to read may have had a considerably greater impact on social mobility than the deacons themselves could possibly have realized at the time. Indirectly, the *Bourse française* may have helped foster democracy just as the Reformation as a whole did through its campaign for literacy.[31] The Reformation encouraged people to learn to read so that they could read the Bible for themselves. They could then read other books too, of course, including secular works that opened new horizons to them. In this age when literacy divided society between upper and lower strata and was a powerful component of social mobility, the *Bourse française* did its part to enable people to become literate.

DOCTORS AND MINISTERS ON WELFARE

That the *Bourse* was not totally democratic in its handouts should come as no surprise, considering the values of the world in which the deacons lived, but in the long run the *Bourse française* may have indirectly promoted equality in several ways. The fund's aid for so many people who would never have needed assistance had they not been uprooted by the Reformation may have ameliorated their judgments about those who received welfare help. For instance, the fund aided a number of ministers and at least one doctor.[32] The ministers appear to have been mostly refugees from France who found themselves with no congregation to serve in Geneva. Whatever the extenuating circumstances, their presence on the welfare rolls may have suggested to others around them that bad times could fall on anyone, even those in what was considered a high calling.[33]

The arrival of more ministers than the city could handle presented Geneva with a problem. Respect for the ministry was sufficient to appreciate the difficult position in which some of these men were placed, particularly since some were fleeing persecution.[34] The city could not provide salaried positions for all the pastors who came to town, however, nor would the city fathers necessarily have found them all qualified. These ministers came from France, where, in the early years of the Reformation, the requirements for leadership were apparently less than stringent. Before schools were established to train pastors to meet fundamental educational standards, some people served as pastors or lay preachers with little formal education. Some of these men were artisans, for example. One wonders how many of the mid-sixteenth-century refugee ministers coming to Geneva were charismatic leaders, either self-selected or chosen by a local congregation without reference to the standards that were soon to prevail for the Protestant pastorate. Where the situation in France was dangerous, leadership fell at times to whomever would step to the fore. Nevertheless, these men were minister enough for the accountant to designate them as such, and they appeared on the welfare rolls with that profession after their names.[35] Meanwhile, the Company of Pastors of Geneva was making a tremendous effort to supply qualified missionary ministers to France. In a sense, this missionary project offered a possible outlet for surplus ministers, although the endeavor was not meant to serve as an employment agency. The risks were so great that employment itself provided scant motivation, although it may have moved some to at least consider serving as ministers in France.[36]

At any rate, the missionary project did not offset the influx of refugee ministers, and persecution in Roman Catholic areas, focused particularly on pastors, periodically flooded the city with refugee ministers. The Wars of Religion in the latter half of the sixteenth century in France contributed to the ebb and flow of refugees.[37] Pastors were sometimes singled out as a group and pressured to leave the country. In 1568 ministers were ordered to leave France within fifteen days. Many of them arrived in Geneva without food or proper clothing. Despite the efforts of the Genevans to meet their needs there were always malcontents who were dissatisfied. The refugee ministers and the students complained about the procedures to meet their needs and to pay their support.[38]

Again in 1572 after the Massacre of St. Bartholomew's Day ministers arrived from France among the other refugees. By 15 September about twenty ministers were in Geneva who had just fled France. Money set aside for poor students at the academy was made available to them. The Company of Pastors of Geneva wanted to put newly arrived ministers to work by adding a supplementary worship service, but the city council felt there was already enough of a diversity of pastors in town. By 16 December there were about fifty foreign ministers in the city, all poor and most with wives and children. To complicate their situation they had no craft because of their social status or "quality." The city fathers of Geneva expressed exasperation at the presence of such a large group of people whose dignity of office as ministers would not allow them to pursue other means of livelihood.[39]

Once, on 13 August 1585, many ministers of the churches of France who had fled the repressive policies of Henry III asked to meet together in Geneva to pray and discuss affairs concerning their churches. They were allowed to meet in the place of the Company of Pastors.[40]

The periodic influx of foreign pastors did not end with the sixteenth century. The seventeenth century brought an increasingly difficult situation for French Protestants, culminating in the revocation of the Edict of Nantes in 1685. Already the year before important foreign refugee pastors had preached at St. Pierre from April to June, but in July the city council forbade them to preach. This time the city council was concerned about its delicate diplomacy with France and avoiding offense to Louis XIV. It had the city's own independence to be concerned about.[41]

At times throughout their refuge ministers found themselves at the mercy of their Genevan hosts and hostesses for food and livelihood. Sometimes they accepted welfare. It should be noted, however, that Geneva did not customarily allow its own ministers to end up on the welfare rolls, although there were partially justified complaints about the adequacy of their salaries and about the quality of the grain that they were allotted. In Geneva the city council paid the ministers in grain, wine, and money.[42]

Of eleven men designated as ministers during the period 1560–79 in the book of those assisted by the *Bourse française*, ten were apparently refugees and only one was a local pastor.[43] His case was somewhat bizarre because he lived well beyond his usefulness and transgressed the pattern of respectability expected of Reformed pastors. His name was Jean Boulier, called La Roche or de la Roche. He served a pastorate at Vandoeuvres in 1560 under

This is the interior of the Cathedral of Saint Pierre. The pews are grouped in a semicircle around the preacher, emphasizing the Reformation and post-Reformation preaching of the Word. John Calvin frequently preached here until his death in 1564. From Emile Doumergue, *Jean Calvin, Les hommes et les choses de son temps*, vol. 3, *La ville, la maison, et la rue de Calvin* (Lausanne: Georges Bridel, Éditeurs, 1905), p. 281.

the aegis of the Company of Pastors of Geneva, between two pastorates at Lyons in 1558 and 1562–65.[44] He died on 26 January 1580 at the age of eighty-seven, if the death records are accurate.[45] His family life appears to have been troubled. His son was censured at the academy, and both he and his wife were called before the consistory. On 10 June 1578 Jean Boulier, the twelve-year-old son of Pastor Jean Boulier, was condemned to be whipped at the college for having thrown some notes at his father on which he had written: "I am the devil!"[46] Pastor Boulier was reproached before the consistory for not having done much of anything and was asked to occupy himself with educating his family. One of his sons of nine or ten years of age could neither read nor write. He also had withdrawn five hundred pounds from the *Bourse des pauvres*. He reportedly spoke rudely to Théodore de Bèze and conceitedly to the Company of Pastors.[47] When this latter incident occurred, a short time before his death, his advanced age and the relative youth of his wife, who was pregnant at the time, may have had something to do with their troubles. He and his family appeared on the welfare rolls of the *Bourse française* even before he died. On 29 December 1579 he was admitted to the hospital, and his wife and children continued to receive aid for years afterward,[48] just as did the wives and widows of other ministers.[49]

He surely cannot be considered a long-term pastor of the countryside around Geneva because of his short tenure in office. Moreover, the *Bourse française* in Geneva appeared to be channeling, at least in part, funds from Lyons to support the family.[50] These could be considered an early modern form of pension rather than a typical welfare handout. There were examples of pensions elsewhere in Europe even before this date.[51] Thus, this example of a Genevan pastor on welfare is the exception that proves the rule.

Whatever the circumstances, if people as respected in Geneva as ministers could find themselves on the welfare rolls, stereotypes of the poor and ther causes of poverty must have changed. Perhaps attitudes toward the poor improved.

WORTHINESS AS A CRITERION FOR WELFARE

There was an effort in Geneva to maintain the image of the *Bourse française* as a fund to help people who were considered worthy, rather than as an institution that indiscriminately aided everyone. The funds were intended for those who were in genuine need, particularly those who were ill or handicapped. The deserving poor were numerous in this age before modern medicine or surgery, when a simple hernia or a poorly aligned broken bone could render one unable to work.[52] The limited funds of the *Bourse* were not intended for the derelict poor, those who were considered unwilling to work, lazy and slothful vagrants and vagabonds, to use the popular English terminology of the era.

The assumption that welfare recipients should be worthy of aid had long been common in Europe, but the definition of worthiness varied from one milieu to another. For instance, in Venice at the end of the fifteenth century it was usual to dispense charity according to the recipient's performance of outward acts of piety. In Catholic Venice this meant, in part, participation in religious processions. In the Middle Ages, the confraternities of Venice enforced attendance in these processions through visits by confraternity officers to members' homes. By the mid-fifteenth century the confraternity officers' visit was to determine if a fellow member was ill or in need of alms. These later visits appear to be similar in purpose to the visits that the deacons of Geneva made to the poor, although the deacons of Geneva went especially to the sick poor. The confraternities of Venice, like the *Bourse française*, used physicians. In Venice physicians were admitted with no charge to the confraternities with the understanding that they would visit the sick poor. Some of the sick poor were eventually housed in confraternity hospitals and poor houses. It was assumed in all of this attention to the poor that those who received alms were worthy.[53] Although confraternities were absent from many Protestant areas, similar social welfare practices were continued by Protestant Christians.

Despite the distinction between the deserving and the derelict poor, the deacons were sometimes accused of being overly generous and hesitant to turn anyone away. One can well imagine this to be true of a volunteer staff. In the mid-seventeenth century attempts were made to curb their generosity. On 11 January 1660, the company (of pastors or of deacons and contributors) resolved at the suggestion of Monsieur Dufour, a pastor, that people who came to the fund who were not dependent on it should be aided only that one time. Passersby would be given six sous unless they could attest that they were "of the religion," in which case they could be given up to four florins with the consent of two or three of the deacons.[54]

This example indicates that the monies of the *Bourse* were intended primarily for refugees of sincere Reformed religious convictions. The very title of the *Bourse française* in the formal legal language of the notaries confirmed this. In the notarial documents the *Bourse* was "the fund for the poor French foreigners who have taken refuge in this city for the Word of God" or some variant on this phrase.[55]

The documents of the sixteenth century reveal other attempts to preserve the good name of the *Bourse française*. Apparently criticism of the *Bourse* was not allowed. For instance, one man named Esprit Nielle was thrown into jail and fed bread and water for five days because, when solicited for a donation, he said that he would give nothing to the *Bourse française* since it supported debauchers and prostitutes. This seems to have been a case of sour grapes, for he had once been refused help from the deacons. Indeed, he confessed in a hearing that he had criticized the *Bourse* seven or eight years before because, when he had lost many of his possessions, the deacons would not give him anything. He was very sorry he had criticized the *Bourse*.[56]

The deacons seem to have tried to concentrate their aid on those who were clearly worthy of it, and worthiness, in their eyes, apparently consisted of a healthy blend of religious conviction, humility, appreciativeness, and good behavior, in addition to genuine need, of course. Someone initially judged worthy could become unworthy by inappropriate behavior. For instance, Huguette Martin, the wife of Jean Boulier, insulted the ministers and elders during a session before the consistory by suggesting that the real reason they had called her before them was not to discuss marital discord but to encourage her to get an abortion, a suggestion that was a scandal to sixteenth-century ears. She was then pregnant, with a houseful of children and a husband in his eighties.[57]

She was taken off the welfare rolls until "Messieurs" of Lyons, where her husband had been pastor for a time, requested clemency, and then only with the caution that she behave more modestly in the future. She confessed to the consistory and the assembly of the deacons that she had spoken with many injurious words against all those in charge of the church. She was told no longer to use such words. She was to behave modestly or she would be chased from the distribution as unworthy of receiving it. She received twelve sous or the equivalent at each distribution from 3 July 1581, to 12 November 1593. Her sons also received assistance. In fact, Jean and Timothee were both apprenticed in February 1580, the month after their father died. Jean, who received clothes and shoes in the month of March, subsequently left the apprenticeship with a printer that the deacons had intended to last three years. This may have been the same son Jean who had received aid in December 1565 and who had been in trouble at the college. Timothee had a five-year apprenticeship with a *Passemantier,* and nothing is said about his leaving that apprenticeship. He received clothing as well, the last of which was received in November 1586. A third son, Antoine, apparently the youngest child, was also helped. Perhaps this was the child that was not aborted, who would have been born after the death of Jean Boulier.

The case of this pregnant woman may be an extreme example. Nevertheless, welfare recipients were definitely expected to maintain certain standards of acceptable behavior. Thus, relatively few of them are found in the criminal records, since recipients of *Bourse* funds were expected to be honest. Of 769 names recorded in the first decade of *Bourse* activity, only 11 were registered in the criminal records of the city, some for incidents such as criticizing native Genevans. Even allowing for the gaps in the criminal records for the period, that is a relatively insignificant number.[58] Moreover, in Geneva in the sixteenth century one could be in trouble with the city council for such activities as dancing or playing chess. On 23 March 1587 Pyramus de Candolle was accused of those offenses after celebrating at the wedding of Jean Crespin.[59] The accusations against individuals named in both the account books of the deacons and the criminal records include matters that would ordinarily not be handled in a court of law today. The sumptuary laws of the Genevans can be understood better if one considers similar laws in other cities of the period. Genevans were truly afraid that they would provoke God's anger if they did not prosecute so many superfluities.[60] Thus there were accusations of popism, bad character, unwillingness to work, charging an elevated price for wine, and selling wine while ill and in danger of the plague. These latter two accusations involving the sale of wine were against Didier Rousseau and his wife. There are also more serious cases of spouse beating, counterfeiting, mishandling of funds, usury, extramarital sex, and "soliciting a young girl to abandon herself" to the accused.

Table 5 at the end of the chapter lists the ten recipients of *Bourse* funds from its first decade who were in trouble with the law. While most were not in serious trouble, the exception was a poor woman who resorted to stealing to supplement her family's needs. She was convicted of theft.[61] Her name was Jeanne Varrot. She claimed that her subsistence allowance from the *Bourse* was inadequate because of her numerous children, and it may well have been. She stole money and goods repeatedly. The text of her hearing reports that "she abandoned herself to larceny . . . in several diverse places using all the means at her disposal . . . at the market, or at the butcher's, or even in taking wine from the pot." With the proceeds from this activity she had fed and maintained her family in a style that allegedly was beyond their needs and their place, even amassing a large quantity of furniture. She had also lent money, up to twenty ecus at one point. Meanwhile, over periods of time, the family had received aid from the *Bourse française*. The woman and her children had been clothed by the *Bourse*, and, just the year before her troubles with the law, the doctor and the apothecary had treated the family at the expense of the *Bourse*. Taking unneeded charity from the deacons was in itself considered a kind of theft and sacrilege.[62]

During all this her husband, Charles Lourdois, a cloth fuller, had stood by, content to be supported by these means. He did not stop her, nor did he report her, although he had accused others of wrongdoing in the past.[63] Thus they were both condemned to be whipped through the city, branded on their right shoulders, and banished. If they returned they were to be hanged.

There were less serious instances in which the deacons seemed exasperated rather than scandalized. One of the deacons of the *Bourse française* reported to the hospital that a woman who was the hospital's dependent had once received support from the *Bourse française* and that he knew her to be a scandalous drunkard and thief.[64]

In 1631 a separate section of the hospital was created called the "discipline."[65] It was a place of punishment for the poor. On 12 October 1683 the deacons of the *Bourse française* asked the syndic of the hospital to have Catherine Chevalier, who had been convicted of diverse larcenies, to be put in the "discipline." She was taken there that very day.[66]

Names of people who appear in the deacons' account books can be found more frequently in the consistory records than in the criminal records. The consistory was a weekly gathering of the pastors and of elders chosen from the city councils to reprimand people for lesser offenses. The names of those who received welfare appeared more often among the accused than the names of those who contributed to the *Bourse*, but the donors were not immune from accusation, such as of adultery, for instance.

Attempts to limit aid to the worthy poor may have eliminated some who may have been unable to do anything about their situation, including the mentally ill. The *Bourse* withdrew aid for a while from one woman because "the deacons did not want to support fools."[67]

The deacons, like their contemporaries, may not always have had the best of insights into the causes of people's behavior. On the other hand, in 1613 a woman was awarded a monthly grant because her daughter was afflicted with a melancholy illness. It could be that the deacons made a distinction between depression and bizarre behavior, but the deacons also hoped to be reimbursed by her brothers.[68]

The deacons, after all, were volunteers, not professionals. They expected a certain appreciation from the people whom they helped, and they apparently considered assistance from the *Bourse* a privilege and not a right. They valued people doing what they were told, acting sanely, and expressing gratitude for the aid they received. Indeed, the records of the sessions of the deacons in the seventeenth century recorded the visits of aid recipients who came to thank the deacons for their help.[69] This may also have been a practice in the sixteenth century, because then the deacons sometimes made a note of aid recipients who left town without stopping to thank them for help. Some even took or sold articles that the deacons had lent them. Benoiste, wife of Louis Arnault, left without saying good-bye, much less thank you, and carried with her the linens that the deacons had lent to her. Françoise, widow of Jean Guemin, sold the mattress and linens that the deacons had lent her.[70] Gratitude was apparently not always expressed, for there were repeated references over the years to a need for respect for the deacons. One of the reasons for assigning a pastor to the deacons was to enhance their credibility and encourage the respect of the poor.

The recipients of assistance from the *Bourse française* in the sixteenth century were expected to be worthy, upright people. They were thought of as religious refugees who retreated to Geneva to live according to the reform of the Word. This was not always the case, but it was the popular conception of the *Bourse*. The donors apparently had this in mind when they made their contributions, and the deacons tried to enforce it.

WELFARE AS SOCIAL CONTROL

Giving out alms was not merely a matter of selecting the worthy. The deacons also tried to keep those who were already on the welfare rolls in line. Huguette Martin, the disrespectful wife of Jean Boulier, for example, had to apologize and conform to the will of the pastors and elders of Geneva before being returned to the welfare rolls.[71]

The ability of the deacons to take someone off the welfare rolls was a powerful incentive to conform to their will. In fact "welfare as social control" might well be described as "welfare as deacon control" since it was the deacons who were able to remove people from the rolls. Yet an element of social pressure was involved, too, since Genevan society expected commonly accepted norms of behavior. The entire welfare structure of Geneva contained an element of social control in that it prevented riot and theft. Feeding the poor was a preferable alternative to allowing them to go hungry and risking the food riots that occurred in other parts of early modern Europe.[72]

It was in dealing with individual poor people, however, that pressure to conform was applied, in part through the threat of having one's support cut off by the deacons. This was sometimes more than a threat. Alex, widow of Pierre Herman, was judged unworthy of assistance because she did not allow her son Jean and her daughter to leave home to begin apprenticeships. The account book record states that after she recognized her faults her son was placed in an apprenticeship. However, he did not stay with it, and the money for the apprenticeship was reimbursed to the deacons. Perhaps she knew her son's mind better than the deacons did. She continued to receive aid from the deacons after this incident.[73]

Clearly the deacons were frustrated in their attempts to get the aid recipients to do what they wanted them to do. Whether or not this can be called social control is another question. At times the deacons seem to have done their best with people who were difficult or stubborn. For instance, a blind woman named Barbe Vioche refused to stay with the widow with whom they had placed her, questioning that the deacons had allowed enough money for her food. The deacons agreed to pay more. Nevertheless, Barbe Vioche left without saying good-bye or thanking the deacons for their assistance.[74]

At other times the deacons were not able to do what they could for the

poor because the city government intervened. For instance, the wife of a
locksmith who was receiving aid from the deacons was ordered to leave town
by the city council because her husband was gone. The poor woman gave
back the blanket that the deacons had lent her. The last payment to her in the
deacons' account books is in March 1586.[75]

The city's commitment to help the poor refugees did not extend as far as
one might have wished, and women without men to support them were
particularly vulnerable in times of hardship. Perhaps they were not seen as
potentially productive members of society, although women in this era did
heavy labor, and laborers were needed in sixteenth-century Geneva, particularly when the city was building the city walls. On 16 December 1572
the city council wrote to the council of Berne that there were seven hundred
on the welfare rolls and a great number who were working in the city's
trenches who would fall onto welfare as soon as the work ceased or the
weather became too bad for work.[76] It was not unknown for a city to use its
welfare institutions to encourage the poor to take work that was not desirable. In Venice, for example, the confraternities were expected to encourage
poor people to serve at sea.[77]

In Geneva the ministers did what they could to discourage the city council
from turning the poor out of the city. On 5 August 1586 they reminded the
council that "those who God has sent us here, who are refugees for the Word
of God, do not know where to go. They will go to the papacy. There are the
impotent, widows, and small children. When Messieurs put them out and if
they die, that will be on their coffins. Observe that the church of God is the
refuge of the poor. They are those of whom our Lord Jesus Christ speaks,
saying: You have seen me naked, etc."[78]

On the other hand, the ministers were willing to send away from Geneva
those who were useless, old people who did nothing, the ordinary drunks,
and debauchers of youth. The ministers were right in observing that the
most vulnerable people were the impotent, the widows, and the small
children. Many of them were without other resources than those that the
deacons could provide. Widowhood may have been the most advantageous
position for wealthy and noble women in this period, as has often been said,
but it was a miserable condition for the poor.[79]

In light of pressures on the poor from the city, it would have been in the
interests of both the deacons and the poor French refugees to avoid any
behavior that the city council might interpret as deviant. The Genevans
already had reservations about the foreigners; they did not know much
about the refugees' pasts, and were upset that they could not even determine
whether or not the refugee couples arriving in town were married. This
matter was discussed in the city council in August of 1550, when it was
decided that men who brought women with them to town must prove the
legitimacy of their marriages. Otherwise they must be presented in the

congregation and brought into the church. Perhaps this means that they were to go through a marriage ceremony again. The precedent had been set by one lord already. Of course, requiring a marriage ceremony for newly arrived couples might only have encouraged bigamy. It is not clear how well this edict was enforced. With concerns like these in Geneva, the poor foreigners would have been wise to behave as discreetly and appropriately as possible to not loose what support they had. The deacons may have felt pressure, then, to keep the foreign poor in line, intensifying their own feelings of what was respectable and decent.[80]

The poor were vulnerable, even if they were well behaved, as the case of the woman abandoned by her locksmith husband attests. Women were particularly vulnerable, and they constituted a large segment of the welfare roles. But if a woman had some property, even if it was not enough to support her completely, she was in less difficult straits. Apparently the *Bourse*, like the city hospital, would agree to support someone on condition that they transfer the ownership of some property, a piece of real estate especially, over to the deacons. For instance, on 1 March 1613, the widow of Nicolas Saget was awarded assistance of two florins per week on the condition that she transfer a large boutique over to the profit of the poor.[81] The hope was that she would pay all or part of her own support. Other women, of course, were not so lucky as to be able to exchange property for care.

The Company of Pastors and the consistory made sure that the rules of discipline would be strictly observed among the refugees. The rules governing idolatry were particularly enforced. Anyone who had attended a Catholic Mass, sermon, or burial had to acknowledge their fault and make a public confession in church. The city council thought this was too severe for those who had come from Catholic countries and would rather have only enforced the law against those who has prostrated themselves before an "idol" or image, but the ministers insisted.[82]

There seemed little inclination among the pastors to let matters of discipline slide. There were complaints about the life and morals of the city by the most scrupulous amongst its inhabitants, but outsiders such as John Knox and John Bale found it exemplary. John Knox said of Geneva that it was "the most perfect school of Christ that ever was in the earth since the days of the Apostles. In other places, I confess Christ to be truly preached; but manners and religion to be so sincerely reformed, I have not yet seen in any other place."

John Bale remarked:

Geneva seemeth to me to be the wonderful miracle of the whole world; so many from all countries come thither, as it were into a sanctuary, not to gather riches but to live in poverty. . . . Is it not wonderful that Spaniards, Italians, Scots, Englishmen, Frenchmen, Germans, disagreeing in man-

ners, speech and apparel, sheep and wolves, bulls and bears, being cou-
pled only with the yoke of Christ, should live so lovingly and friendly,
and that monks, laymen and nuns, disagreeing both in life and sect,
should dwell together, like a spiritual and Chrisitan congregation[?][83]

Not everyone was so enthusiastic, of course, but it is difficult to imagine
anything occurring in Geneva that would approach the scandal at the hospital of Lyons earlier in the sixteenth century where the Catholic sisters in
charge allowed illicit rendezvous in the evenings.[84]

The story of the recipients of aid from the *Bourse française* is one of mixed
blessing. Many were helped, but some were forced to leave town despite the
efforts of the deacons. Some were given a great boost to learning, literacy,
and social betterment, but others gave up their children to apprenticeships
that neither they nor their children had chosen. Some were happily
domiciled in the homes of friends and fellow countrymen and women.
Others had to put up with less than desirable housemates and foster parents.
The deacons apparently did the best that they could for those they served,
but they sometimes succumbed to the temptation to make decisions on
behalf of the poor that the poor could well have made for themselves.

One need not assume that the morale of the poor was low just because
they were vulnerable. For some refugees exile was living death, but for
others it was a gift of life. As their last wills and testaments reveal, many
religious refugees came because they felt called by God. Their very homelessness could be understood as union with the rejected Christ. The poverty
of the recipients fostered in the wealthier refugees a lively sympathy for their
less fortunate countrymen and women. The refugees forged a new community, intent on realizing the reform of the Word in their daily lives.[85]

The table that follows describes the aid recipients named in the *Procès
criminels* of Geneva in the 1550s. That they are so few in number testifies to
the moral stature of those who received aid from the deacons.

The preceding chapters described how the *Bourse française* was organized
and what its activities were, who ran it, who contributed to it, and who
received its help. The next chapter looks at one family that was very active in
the *Bourse française* in its early years, the Budé family. It centers especially
on Jean Budé.

Table 5

Criminal Procedures against *Bourse française* Aid Recipients of the 1550s

Augier (Ogier), Antoine, an inhabitant who had been a priest, received nine sous,
two deniers for a Bible in November 1560. He was banished in a procedure of
16–19 September 1561 for having solicited a young girl to "abandon herself" to
him.[86]

Table 5 *(Continued)*

Carion, Claude, inhabitant of Geneva, and his wife Etiennette of Orleans were accused on 18 November 1551 of having fought. Etiennette struck her husband with a knife.[87]

Dimenche. On Wednesday 13 April 1552 Dimenche received five sous from the deacons. On 27 May 1552 the wife, burdened with five children, received five sous. From 19–22 August 1552 Dimenche and Nicolas Guard were accused of having carried false money. They were imprisoned but released on 22 August 1552.[88]

De (Du) Chesne, Pierre, was a printer from Auvergne. In December 1553 his wife received five sous from the deacons. On 8 April 1557 his case and that of another man was sent from the consistory to the small council. They were accused of having asked several people if they had been confessed, an allusion to popery (Catholicism).[89]

La Loubiere received aid from the *Bourse française* in March 1552. On 1 February 1558 her case was placed before the small council of Geneva because René Gassin, the deacon of the *Bourse française,* had complained to the procurators of the city hospital, where she was lodged, that she was "a drunkard, thief, beggar, chatterer, and in all and by all scandalous."[90]

Maillard, Guillaume, draper, received in April 1552 from the *Bourse française* eight sous. From 27 July to 6 August 1565, Guillaume Maillard of Rouen, haberdasher, inhabitant of Geneva, was charged with mishandling the funds allocated to Martha and David, children of the deceased Louis Flambert, his wife's first husband.[91]

Michau (Micaux or Michault), Barthelemy, a miller of Provence, was sent by the administration of the hospital to the small council on 1 February 1558 and ordered to leave the city because he would not do anything, even though his son was hungry and was going around the city begging.[92]

Navet, Jean, a maker of velvet of Tours, was banished forever in a procedure of 17–30 May 1554 for having said that all the children of Geneva were *Gouliards* and worthless and for having wanted to burn the handle of his halbard when he had disarmed the foreigners.[93]

Rousseau, Didier, son of Antoine, of Paris, bourgeois of Geneva, was condemned to three days in prison and censured along with another man in a procedure of 13–16 October 1562 for having charged too much for wine. He and his wife, Marguerite Trousset, were condemned in a procedure of August to September 1568 to ask forgiveness and pay a fine of thirty sous for having sold wine while they were sick and in danger of the plague despite the ordinances forbidding this.[94]

Sylvestre, Jacques. The wife of Sylvestre received four sous, three deniers, in November 1554. He was accused of usury in a procedure of 15 July 1557.[95]

9

Jean Budé and the *Bourse française*

A mere description of the organizational structure, activities and origins, and donors and recipients alone cannot capture the spirit animating the *Bourse*. In the final analysis individual personalities, religious convictions, political motivations, social status, and personal idiosyncrasies—particularly of those who were in charge of the institution for the early formative years— shaped it into what it was. The study of the *Bourse* simply as an institutional structure can imply that it functioned autonomously and that its success was a foregone conclusion.

But in the early account books the influence of the people who ran the *Bourse française* manifests itself on almost every page. This is in part because all of the account books are written by hand and so appear much more personal than a printed page; it is also because one finds a network of relationships throughout the various documents of the period among the individuals who wrote them. Acquaintances, friends, and kin worked together. The history of the *Bourse* at the human level is a collection of minibiographies that have yet to be written.

The accounts of the *Bourse* bring home the interrelatedness among these personalities, for they were all joined together through their cooperation in the *Bourse française*. They were linked in many other ways as well, because of the close proximity of everyone who lived within the walls of this little city and the ties of kith and kin. Indeed, for the first thirty years of the recorded activity of the fund, one family was centrally involved in it. This was the Budé family, or the "De Budé" family as it was known in later Genevan history. The family worked particularly through one of its members, Jean Budé, who was one of the first three deacons and bookkeeper of the accounts for many years. The family as a whole was active in support of the *Bourse*'s activities, but Jean, in particular, was ever present, both in the overall administration of the fund and in its daily activities with the poor, disbursing funds, soliciting gifts, and publicizing the name and work of the fledgling institution. This chapter on the influence of personality on the *Bourse* is thus devoted particularly to Jean Budé and his family.

The Budé family was already well known before many of its members came to Geneva from Paris. Perhaps its most notable figure in France had been the famous humanist Guillaume Budé, listed in *The Book of Inhabitants* of Geneva as the father of Jean Budé and "counselor and Master of Requests, ordinary, of the house of the king of France," indicating his special relationship to Francis I, although his enduring fame was in the realm of scholarship and education. Guillaume Budé was an eminent Greek scholar and philologist who contributed to the creation of the *Collège de France*.[1] The family had a long acquaintanceship with John Calvin, which dated from Calvin's student days at the *Collège de Montaigu* in Paris when he was welcome in their home.[2] After Guillaume died, his widow, in her old age, was encouraged by Calvin to move to Geneva which she did in 1549. His famous letter to a widow is presumed to have been written to her. Some of the adult children came too at about the same time, at least Jean, Louis, and Marguerite. François established himself in Geneva in 1554. Catherine apparently came later. Matthieu had passed through Geneva earlier. There is some indication in John Calvin's correspondence with Matthieu and his brothers that he intended to return there. He died, it seems, in 1547.[3]

The family members settled in town and bought land close by—pastureland, orchards, and vineyards. This suggests that they considered the move permanent. The purchase and sale of land continued after this initial transaction, making it possible to follow the many members of the family and their descendants who stayed in Geneva, prominent and active in the community. The record of their real estate and legal transactions can be traced in the city's notarial documents, and a living testimonial today is the park named after the De Budé family.[4] John Calvin brought them to town, and they stayed on to become pillars of the community.

When the surviving account books of the *Bourse française* opened on 30 September 1550, they were in the hand of Jean Budé (1515–87). He may have begun keeping records earlier. It was noted in the registers of the Company of Pastors that he had served as deacon for twenty-six years when, on 30 December 1575, he stepped down from the accounting. The editors of the registers suggest correctly that this note would imply that the formal foundation of the *Bourse française* dates from 1549. The reason given for Jean Budé's retirement from the accounting in 1575 was his age, cited as sixty years old. He was thanked for his good witness and his willingness to serve and asked to help when it would please him. He apparently continued as deacon, however. He was referred to as deacon again in the registers of the Company of Pastors in February 1576, less than two months later. At that time the deacons presented the account books of 1575 to the Company of

Pastors. On 28 December 1576 he was confirmed as deacon for the year 1577.[5]

During his era as deacon he apparently remained as bookkeeper, with brief interruptions, at least until 1564, when his hand seems to disappear from the account books.[6] One can tell something about the man from the way he kept the books, particularly that he was verbose. His wordiness must have cost him hours of time as an accountant, but left a veritable goldmine for the historian. The first accounts included a wealth of detail that is unnecessary to modern accounting. This detail produced records of the first few years of *Bourse* activity that create a useful picture of the life of the times. The early account books are much more useful to historians than the more efficient, brief, and concise entries of a later date.

While Jean Budé's verbosity is of value to the historian, his contemporaries seem to have been peeved by his inability to remember names. Of course, a simple list of names would have been a more orderly and concise record than the wordy descriptions Budé sometimes used. Nevertheless, his lengthy entries conveyed a warmth and familiarity that surely indicate a wide circle of friends. He was as likely to record on a list of donations, "from my Mother," or "from my brother and from me," as to use names, and he used the same personal touch for other relatives and friends. As a result, the identity of some people has been lost to modern times, for the unnamed cousins and the gentleman friends passing through town were known only to him and to knowledgeable contemporaries.[7]

At one point, Jean Budé resolved to record names, and increasingly did so as time went on. By 1560 the records were so complete that it was possible to list the names of those who were assisted by the *Bourse*. This may, unfortunately, have been the excuse for disposing of the original "ordinary" account books. They are missing completely for the decade of the 1560s, and thereafter are intermittently incomplete. At a later date a copyist with a more legible hand recorded each recipient family separately with expenditures in the enormous volumes called the "Great Books of the Assisted." Each of these two volumes for the sixteenth century covers a twenty-year period, the first from 1560 to 1579 and the second from 1580 to 1599.[8] Many of the original account books that record the daily expenditures of the deacons are missing for these years, whereas they are almost completely extant for the decade of the 1550s before the great books of those assisted were established. The initial disorderly recording, which did not allow for an efficient extraction of names, may have been a factor in preserving these first account books.

At any rate, one admires the compassion of a man who, even when he did remember a name, felt compelled to write down a little more about each person whom he recorded. If the aid recipient was unemployed or passing through, ill or injured, Jean Budé was likely to comment. Fortunately, much of the information from the daily accounts was included in the great books of the assisted, but the daily record of events of the times has been lost. Accounts of the plagues and severe winters, the ebb and flow of refugees, the fat years and the lean are simply gone, whereas this panorama emerges when one reads through the running accounts as they were originally recorded.

As animator of the *Bourse française*, Jean Budé seems to have been a central figure among the first generation of the family in Geneva. He was mentioned often in the family's notarial documents, and he was relied upon as a responsible party in family legal transactions. He was also a leader within the larger French immigrant community, and he served the city as an ambassador to the Protestant churches of Switzerland in 1553, to the Protestant princes of Germany in 1558, to the Elector Palatine in 1565, and to Admiral Gaspard de Coligny in 1567. He served on the Council of Two Hundred in 1559 and then on the Council of Sixty. He was one of the people responsible for the physical construction of the academy.[9] He was instrumental in collecting and editing John Calvin's commentaries on the Prophets.

Calvin spoke warmly of Jean Budé as "one of the most intimate friends that I have, and a man on whom one can rely to the end." This was in a letter that Budé carried for him to the Duchess of Ferrara dated 8 January 1564.[10] Calvin apparently associated with Jean Budé regularly. The nineteenth-century author Jules Bonnet lists the brothers Budé as Calvin's habitual companions, along with Nicholas des Gallars, Laurent de Normandie, Colladon, and the Marquis de Vico.[11]

As far as one can ascertain from an account book, Jean Budé seems to have had sincere religious convictions. That he was giving his time as a deacon and his money as a donor testifies to that, but the account books tell more. On the last surviving page of the first account book he jotted down the following remarks, which appear to be either notes on a sermon or his thoughts on the seventh chapter of John: "The first and sure address to lead us to the knowledge of good is to have the will to obey him as it is written: If one wants to obey his will he will know and will judge all doctrine whether it is of God or not, seventh John. Secondly, [it] is to be noted that it is a true sureness of knowledge that it is a doctrine when by it we glorify God."[12] Overall, Jean Budé seems to have been congenial, reliable, and well liked, an ideal person to animate the first few years of a fund that needed to raise large amounts of money and to establish itself in the community.

Some thought that they saw a negative side to his personality, however. There exist a number of criminal procedures in which people less powerful than he were punished for having treated him badly. For instance, in October 1558 a woman was convicted of having slandered both Monsieur and Madame de Vérace (Budé's formal title) and the consistory. She was condemned to ask pardon of God, the magistry, and those whom she had outraged and to appear before the consistory. In May 1562 a man who had led a dissolute life and had been impertinent to Monsieur de Vérace was condemned to three days in prison on bread and water. In March and April 1584 a man who had badly ground the grain of the Lord of Vérace was condemned to make up the loss, to pay a fine of ten florins, and to appear before the consistory.[13]

Perhaps these seemingly excessive actions stem from Jean Budé's wife, Marie. On 17 December 1599, twelve years after his death, information was taken against Marie's chambermaid. She was detained on an accusation of having committed several small thefts, then banished from the city and the territory around it despite her denials. Jean Budé's will revealed that Marie and their son Jean were having problems. Could Marie have had a difficult or demanding personality? That is perhaps too much to assume from this scant evidence. Servants and children could be exasperating.[14]

An accusation of a more serious nature for a deacon-accountant came on 15 November 1580. At a meeting of the Company of Pastors, Théodore de Bèze and a Monsieur Rotan denounced the excesses of Jean Budé in the name of the Company of Pastors. He was accused of having abused the fortune of his nieces, Jeanne and Judith, daughters of his deceased brother François, for whom he had legal responsibility. On 22 November 1580 the procurator general asked Budé to hand over account books that he kept for the girls on the assumption they contained exaggerated amounts for pensions and trips. On 28 November Jean Budé attempted to justify himself by pointing out that his nieces had not complained. The spouse of one niece had approved the account book for her, and the Marquis of Vico had approved the account book for the other niece. Nonetheless, the city council insisted that the procurator general see the account books.[15]

Having seen the account books on 4 March 1581, the city council decided to reduce the amounts for trips and pensions. Was Jean Budé using his position to charge excessive amounts at the expense of his nieces? Or did he just live at a more expensive level than the pastors? One shudders to think of what this could have meant for the expense accounts of the *Bourse française*. There is no evidence therein, however, of his reimbursing himself for expenses he might have incurred in the line of duty.[16]

Jean Budé has also been criticized by modern historians. In his genealogy of Genevan families, J. A. Galiffe called Jean Budé a religious bigot. It is true that the language Budé used in the account books of the *Bourse* reveals a keen awareness of religious opposition in France: he referred to Catholics as tyrants and hangmen on occasion. No doubt his dealings with refugees made him keenly aware of the plight of the religious minority in France. He was not alone among the first generation of religious immigrants to Geneva to be acutely sensitive to persecution, for some of them had experienced it personally.[17]

Jean Budé may well have seen the world in black and white rather than in shades of gray, but this did not seem to affect his magnanimous spirit. It may even have made him more generous, at least to other Protestants. Moreover, the list of the people who received aid from him as a deacon crossed ethnic and religious lines. The dominant impression, from what traces of him remain in the records, is that of a man with an open and cheerful disposition and a wide circle of friends. His last will and testament is perhaps the document that is the most revealing of all, for there is a marked absence of any tone of frustration and manipulation. This is in contrast to the wills of other ardent Protestants of his generation who used provisions in their wills to attempt to control the future of members of their families.

Jean Budé's will suggests that he was on good terms with those about him: his wife, his children, and his friends. When he actually dictated his will, apparently in the presence of a group of friends that may have included a notary, he seems to have been in characteristic good spirits, despite the fact that he could not sign it because of "the infirmity and imbecility of his right hand."[18] Could the years of writing verbosely in the account books have helped debilitate his hand? He expressed sincere affection for his "beloved wife," *Damoiselle* Marie de Jonvilliers,[19] and a warm friendship for this brother-in-law, Charles de Jonvilliers, to whom he commended his children and whom he guaranteed both continued residence in the Budé home and a portion of the harvest of his fields and orchards: "in consideration and recognition of the good and singular amity that I have always carried and that I carry toward Noble Charles de Jonvilliers, my dear and beloved brother-in-law, and for the right affection that he has always carried toward my house and toward the welfare and the succor of myself and of my children that I pray he wants to continue. . . ."[20]

The will reveals that the family of Jean Budé may have had its problems. It hints of possible tension between his wife and the children, at least between her and Jean, their son. Yet there are no vindictive threats of financial repercussions such as could be found in other wills of the period for those who did not conform to a father's plans. Instead Budé appealed to his children to get along with their mother, while he also made it possible for her to have quarters of her own if she chose not to reside with their son. He willed that she should have all that was necessary for someone of her quality to furnish two rooms if she could not or would not live with her son. He charged his children also to "honor and respect her in all things as a good child ought who is well instructed in the fear of God. . . ."[21]

In his will Jean Budé gave generously to the charitable institutions of the city: to the *Bourse française*, six hundred florins; to the city hospital, one hundred florins; and the same amount to the academy.[22] He also provided well for the members of his family who fell heir to his estate. His generosity was facilitated by the possession of considerable worldy goods: gold and silver, livestock, orchards, pasturelands, real estate in the city, and a library of sufficient books to divide and will to his son and son-in-law (both of whom were also named Jean, Jean Budé and Jean Du Lac).[23] The will portrays a man of means, and the family papers reinforce this with their record of regular real estate negotiations and land purchases in the vicinity of the city.[24]

Table 6 substantiates the real estate transactions of the Budé family.[25] Jean Budé also had wealth in France, as did some of the other religious refugees in Geneva.[26] It is of interest that Jean Budé included in his estate his rights to an annuity on the city hall in Paris.[27] He might thus be categorized as an urban aristocrat and a rentier, someone who relied on interest, rents, and dues for part of his income.[28]

Except for having been wealthier than many, Jean Budé seems to typify the first generation of Protestant immigrants to Geneva among whom he lived, and his attitudes about religion reflected theirs. He shared with them a concrete sense of Providence working in everyday life and an antipathy toward the Catholic church that they had left behind. Chance had a small role to play for those who conceived of God as active in the world of human events. In his will Jean Budé included the standard thanksgiving that appeared in Genevan wills of this period, thanking God for being called from the superstitions and idolatry of Catholicism. However, Budé's own exuberant language paraphrased the standard preamble as follows:

In the first place, I give thanks to my God that, through our Lord Jesus Christ, it pleased him to pull me back from the horrible darkness and from that infernal abyss where I was plunged under the tyranny of the Roman Antichrist, when, through his pure goodness and according to what he ordained from the beginning, he introduced me into his true Church, under the reign and empire of our Lord Jesus Christ, through the death and sacrifice of whom, all my sins are pardoned, and however much that of myself I am a poor and miserable creature, who senses only in me every material of death and condemnation, nevertheless, I know that his blood is my true purgation, and his merit and obedience acquired for me the true and unique justice through which I am waiting and hold assurance that God will know me and receive me as his child with all his saints at the day of our Saviour Jesus Christ. Such is my faith and assurance according to his Holy Gospel, in which I am ready to give up my soul to God when it will please him to call me to himself, holding, furthermore, in general, to all the doctrine contained in the Old and New Testament as it is summarily understood in the confession of faith made in this church of Geneva, received and approved by all the churches of France and others, detesting all other doctrines contrary to this which have null certitude and firm foundation in Scripture. Also, I desire and will that directly after my decease my body be buried Christianly in the manner accustomed in this city of Geneva, waiting the day of the blessed Resurrection, and, as for the

Table 6

Real Estate Transactions from the Family Papers of Jean Budé de Vérace[29]

Date	Transaction
17 December 1551	Purchase by Jean de Budé of possessions on the fief of Nicolas de la Biellée.
17 November 1556	Purchase by Jean de Budé from Nicolas and Amblard de Lonnex of the land . . .
26 June 1571	Purchase by Jean de Budé from Pierre Delapierre.
27 September 1573	Sale to Jean de Budé by Jean Thuril de Gaillard . . . of three poses for 172 florins.
18 December 1573	Purchase by Jean de Budé from Claude Debarge at Thonex.
27 October 1573	Purchase by Jean de Budé . . . for two poses meadow and vineyard, the said place at the Chatelet, price: 120 florins.
1 January 1577	Sale to Jean de Budé of a vineyard by Jean Turil de Gaillard.
12 March 1582	Sale to Jean de Budé by Guillaume, of one house . . . price 1700 florins.
14 December 1583	Purchase by Jean de Budé from Bertrand, of one vineyard . . .
29 April 1584	Purchase from Pierre Polliens by Jean de Budé of one vineyard.
10 September 1584	Purchase from Bertrand, son of the deceased Pierre Polliens, by Jean de Budé, of one vineyard.
31 January 1585	Purchase from Pierre Du Cimitiere by Jean de Budé of a piece of land at the Salève.
25 February 1587	Purchase of Jean de Budé of a vineyard.
9 December 1607	Purchase from Claude Debornand by Jean de Budé of a vineyard.

goods that it has pleased God to give me in this world, I dispose of them and ordain through this present, my last solemn will, and by writing, in the following manner. . . .[30]

Jean Budé then disposed of his property, dividing it as described among the members of his family and the charitable institutions of Geneva. He remembered his beloved *Bourse française* by willing to it a sum six times greater than that which he willed to the city hospital and to the academy, although he treated them all generously. He continued at some length, affectionately providing for those he loved, then he closed the will and had it put away in one of his chests. It was sealed with his coat of arms, inside and on top, on 9 March 1587. That same day it was turned over to the notary Jean Jovenon in the presence of witnesses.

After the decease of Jean Budé on 5 July 1587, the will was put into the hands of the lieutenant of justice. On 7 July he authorized the publication of the will at the judicial bench. The decree was signed by the secretary of justice, Butini, and carried the seal of the ordinary justice. The will was then handed over to the notary Jean Jovenon who copied it into the notary minutes where it remains today, one of the great Protestant wills of the sixteenth century.[31]

The usual procedure in Geneva was for a notary to draw up a "minute" or draft of a will, sometimes even at the deathbed. This would be turned into an official protocol for deposit with the city courts. A city law of 28 January 1568 provided that if a testator wanted his will to be secret he could write the will or have it written, close it, seal it, and declare in the presence of a notary and seven witnesses that it was his last will. They would endorse it, and the will would be valid.[32]

Although Jean Budé's will is one of the best sources of insight into his mentality, other city records indicate what he was like. For instance, he is mentioned incidentally as the host and kinsman of Lambert Le Blanc, a young man who was convicted of sodomy. Le Blanc had paid a boy five sous to go outside the city gates and engage in homosexual acts. In his confession Le Blanc admitted to having solicited boys on several occasions. He was "tempted by a bad spirit," as he put it.[33]

Le Blanc's plea for clemency revealed that Jean Budé knew about his kinsman's sexual orientation when he accepted him as a guest in his home but that he did not turn him away. He surely could have refused him hospitality, for a homosexual pattern of life was no more acceptable in Geneva than elsewhere in Europe in the sixteenth century. Indeed, the manuscript in which Lambert Le Blanc was condemned cited as precedent a law of Charles V that prescribed the death sentence within the Holy Roman Empire. Europeans of the era identified sodomy as the crime of Sodom. God had destroyed the cities of Sodom and Gomorrah for their wickedness, according to Genesis, chapter nineteen. Only Lot and his two daughters were saved.[34]

Sixteenth-century mentality conjectured, from the Biblical example of the destruction of the city of Sodom, that God would punish any city that allowed sodomy. They considered it an enormous crime against nature. Genevans and other Europeans felt that God wanted them to punish such a sin to make everyone share in the horror of it. Thus they condemned Lambert Le Blanc to be burned at Champel, a place of execution that was then just outside the city but which is now near the city hospital. He was to be an example to others who might want to commit such an act.[35]

Lambert Le Blanc's kinsman Jean Budé was out of town when he was convicted. His absence leaves unknown whatever stand he might have taken in the matter. Le Blanc spoke with affection of Budé, saying that when he had come to town to live according to the Reform, Jean Budé had extended a hand of friendship and welcomed him into the Budé household. Although Budé apparently suggested to Le Blanc that he change his ways, Le Blanc's pleas for clemency reveal that they had a good relationship. Le Blanc looked to Jean Budé for help in his predicament, but he was absent, unfortunately.[36]

Thus despite the tenor of the preamble to his will and some of his remarks in the account books, at times Jean Budé appeared more flexible in his attitudes than many others of his era. He comes through the records as a sensitive and intelligent man, one whom his homosexual kinsman could regard with affection as a person in whom he could confide and in whose home he had been received humanely.

Jean Budé continued for many years with the *Bourse* after his handwriting dropped out of the accounts. He outlived most of his colleagues as deacons. By the time that he died in 1587, at about seventy-two years of age, he was practically alone among those of his generation.[37] It was an old age for the epoch. He and his wife, Marie, outlived many of their own children, even those who died as young adults.

The death records reveal that Jean Budé and his wife lost a number of children at a tender age as well as several who died as young adults. On 31 December 1551 they lost a son in their home for whom no age nor name was given.[38] In January of 1567 they lost a three-year-old daughter named Jeanne.[39] On the last day of January 1569, they lost their five-month-old daughter Sera.[40] On 11 May 1573 they lost another daughter, Madelene[?]. No age was given.[41] On 21 November 1584 their son Jacob died at approximately twenty-three years of age.[42] On 20 October 1586 their daughter Marie died at their home at the age of approximately twenty-nine years of age.[43] The death records are not complete; there may have been more.

The children who survived to mature adult years were apparently Jean and Elisabeth. Both of them appear as heirs in their father's will. Jean lived from 1558 to 1610. He was a member of the Council of Two Hundred in 1587 and of the small council in 1599, a syndic in 1603 and 1607, and a representative of the city to Henry IV, king of France, in 1600. Elisabeth married Noble Jean de Saussure, seigneur de Bussens.[44]

Because he was such a stellar figure, it is tempting to describe the *Bourse* as if it took shape through the efforts of Jean Budé alone, but in reality it was more of a group effort. One of Budé's key attributes as an administrator was his apparent ability to involve other people around him in the work of the *Bourse*. This was particularly true of his own family.

A number of the people involved in the *Bourse* at this time were members of the Budé family or had links with it. Among the regular donors were the widow of Guillaume Budé, her children, their spouses, and an unnamed relative mentioned by Jean Budé in the receipts simply as "mon cousin." These included Budé's brothers Louis, seigneur de la Motte, and François, seigneur de Villeneuve, and his sisters Catherine and Marguerite.[45] Catherine married Jean Anjorrant. After his death she lived with her brother François and his wife Marguerite. Marguerite Budé married Guillaume (de) Trie, seigneur de Varennes, a notary. She lived until 27 April 1618, when she reportedly died at the age of eighty-eight. Jean Budé also apparently had two brothers and two sisters who settled in France, Dreux, Antoine, Isabeau, and Anne. Dreux remained Catholic. Isabeau was a nun. *France Protestante* states that Antoine became an inhabitant of Geneva, 10 December 1554, but returned to France, a Protestant. This is perhaps a confusion with François who became an inhabitant of Geneva on that date.[46]

Many of this first group of supporters from the Budé family soon died off. Jean Budé's mother was listed by the genealogist J. A. Galiffe as "the widow Budé," Isabeau de Lailly, who died in Geneva on 15 April 1550,[47] but almost two years later Jean Budé recorded that at the end of January 1552 "My mother gave 12 sous."[48] Was Galiffe wrong about the date of her death? If so, it is not proved by this entry, for more than two months earlier, on 5 November 1551, Jean Budé gave twelve sous to a servant of his mother, who he then described as deceased.[49] Was the January 1552 contribution from his mother a posthumous donation from her estate? Or perhaps was it a delayed recording of an earlier collection, since it was a special collection recorded separately from the regular receipts? It is less easy to discount the receipts of May 1551, still a full year after Galiffe reported her as dead, when Jean Budé recorded a donation of six florins "for my mother and for me."[50] Was this donation in memory of her or at her request before she died? Or was she still alive and Galiffe's date wrong?

At about the same time that Jean Budé lost his mother he also lost his brother Louis Budé, who died 23 May 1551. His legacy to the *Bourse française* was of sufficient magnitude to come to the attention of John Calvin and to evoke comment from the city council.[51] Part of it was used immediately to help bail out the deacons' accounts from an overexpenditure of sixteen pounds, sixteen sous.[52] Louis Budé's larger legacy to posterity was the Psalms in French prose on which Théodore de Bèze relied so heavily for his own rhymed versions.[53] He also had infants who died at a young age. The death records list him as "scientific Louis Budé, doctor."[54]

One of Jean Budé's fellow deacons married Louis Budé's widow. The widow's name was Barbe Le Bouc du Berry and the deacon was Guy de Serignac, usually referred to in the account books as "Monsieur de Thillat" or "de Thillac" but elsewhere as "Seigneur du Tillac." She in turn was widowed a second time.[55]

The Budé family's involvement with the *Bourse* went on, apparently despite the deaths of these significant members. Jean continued as deacon and another brother, François, stayed on the rolls as a supporter of the *Bourse*. He eventually remembered it in his will by bequeathing five hundred pounds plus continuation of his monthly pledge, and he instructed his wife to double the amount of the pledge, "if," he hoped, "it would please God to bring peace to France," so that she could realize her fortune there.[56] After his death his wife, in turn, remembered the *Bourse* in her will and entrusted

The Cathedral of Saint Pierre before the restoration begun in 1889. This is the church from whose pulpit John Calvin frequently preached. From Émile Doumergue, *Jean Calvin, Les hommes et les choses de son temps*, vol. 3, *La ville, la maison, et la rue de Calvin* (Lausanne: Georges Bridel, Éditeurs, 1905), p. 265.

the care of their two daughters, Jeanne and Judith, to Catherine and Marguerite Budé, her sisters-in-law.[57]

A trail of legacies and continued support followed the deaths of members of the family and their spouses, even of those who were only indirectly tied to the family. Charles de Jonvilliers, Jean Budé's brother-in-law who lived in his home and was so fondly remembered in his will, spent a good share of his last years as a deacon. Budé's son-in-law Jean Du Lac was a deacon from 1586 to 1589 or longer. He is mentioned in 1595 as having interrupted his charge because of illness. The phenomenon of the close extended family apparently made it possible for much of the work of the fund to be accomplished within one large household.[58]

The Bourse française was truly a family endeavor for the Budé family, but other families were involved as well as friends and acquaintances of the deacons. Some of these people apparently responded individually, but the overall impression is one of community, one that encompassed many of the French refugees in Geneva. It later spread to include friends and associates in France and eventually to Reformed churches elsewhere on the Continent and across the channel in England. The personal links that the business of the Bourse française forged helped form the international Reformed community. That community was the context within which the Bourse itself was shaped. The people who made up this early Reformed community were fundamental in shaping the Bourse française, and more remains to be said about many of them.

The Bourse was thus the product of the hard work of a considerable number of individuals, unaware, perhaps, that they were engaged in one of the first great efforts of Protestant philanthropy. The precedent set by these French nobles and businessmen, refugees in Geneva, would resound throughout the world. This study is just the beginning of that story.

10
Summary and Conclusions

This study has examined a specific institution in the most critical Calvinist situation, Geneva itself. This chapter places the *Bourse* once again in its European context, summarizes what has been said about the *Bourse*, and ventures a few generalizations.

THE EUROPEAN SOCIAL WELFARE CONTEXT

Various solutions to the need for poor relief developed in different regions of Europe. To put the *Bourse française* in context, it is necessary to look briefly at the alternate systems of social welfare outside Geneva, specifically in Lutheran, Reformed, Catholic, and Anabaptist regions.

Lutheran examples of poor relief were found in Wittenberg, Leisnig, and Nuremberg. They were similar in many respects, but each had its own unique characteristics. The poor relief system closest to Luther was in Wittenberg, where he lived most of his adult life. A Wittenberg church order of 24 January 1522 is of particular interest because it set up a welfare system for post-Reformation Wittenberg. The order provided for a common chest to assist the poor, a foundation typical of areas that became Protestant. The phrase "common chest" referred to a cash fund for the poor with all the property that stood behind it. Often an actual chest was locked with several keys, which were distributed among several responsible people to ensure the security of the properties, incomes, monies, rights, and goods in the chest. Perishables such as food were kept elsewhere. The common chest was funded both by current donations and by property inherited from the pre-Reformation period. In Wittenberg this included property from the church, confraternities, and endowments. From these funds the magistracy helped the poor, supported orphans, and made interest-free loans to artisans. Begging was outlawed. The common chest was run by people whom the magistrates selected: two from the city council, two from the citizens at large, and a secretary. The secretary collected money, supervised the distribution of aid, and kept the books.[1]

At the time this system was instigated, Luther was in hiding at the Wartburg Castle because of his excommunication by Pope Leo X and his banishment by Emperor Charles V, but Luther was not without influence in Wittenberg. Andreas Karlstadt, Luther's colleague on the theological faculty of the university, was also at work there. With the advice and consent of Luther and Karlstadt the city council drew up an "Ordinance for a Common Purse" with more specific provisions. A money box with three keys was set up in the city church. The city was divided into four quarters and the ruling *Bürgermeister* or mayor appointed a citizen over each quarter. These men were to find out who the poor were and support them. They were also to buy grain and wood and report to the mayor on Sundays.[2]

Eleven years later the elector of Saxony prescribed a church order for Wittenberg that was somewhat different from that of 1522. The order of 1533 provided for a common chest for the poor, but the chest was also to pay teachers, clergy, an organist, and the secretary of the common chest. The chest was responsible for upkeep of the school and church buildings. The number of directors of the common chest was increased to four instead of two from the citizens at large. Of the total of six directors, three were to be elected at a time by the council and the pastors. Each would serve for two years.[3]

The ordinance for a common chest in Leisnig was perhaps closer to Luther's heart than that of Wittenberg. The Leisnig ordinance was drawn up on his advice, had his approval, and was published by him together with a preface that he had written. Luther had visited the parish of Leisnig in electoral Saxony on 25 September 1522, while the city was undergoing reform. The congregation subsequently took over the church properties and asked Luther's advice on their social welfare ordinance. Luther responded with approval and a preface for the ordinance.[4]

Leisnig's common chest was to be administered by a board of ten trustees: two from the nobility, two from the city council, three from among the town citizens, and three from the peasants. This board of trustees was to be elected by the Leisnig parish assembly at its annual meeting in January. There were to be weekly meetings of the board on Sunday, a fairly common practice for welfare boards in this era. The trustees were not only to take care of the poor but also to run the schools, to maintain the church buildings, and to pay the pastors and custodians. To support the common chest, every family was to contribute according to its means. This compulsory taxation was omitted in later Lutheran ordinances. The care of the poor provided from the chest was similar to that in other regions. The common chest supported the poor living in their own homes, cared for and fed orphans, apprenticed and educated children, provided dowries for marriageable girls, and lent money to worthy artisans and merchants. Luther also suggested that the citizens of Leisnig establish schools for boys and girls in monastery buildings. Unfortunately for the parish assembly of Leisnig, the city council would not turn over the properties and endowments of the pre-Reformation church to the directors of the common chest, and the city council gained control of the chest.[5]

Unlike the funds in Wittenberg and Leisnig, the welfare funds of Geneva did not pay for the ministers' salaries nor for the maintenance of church buildings. In Geneva the city council was responsible for these expenditures. Some Lutheran church orders divided the common chest into two parts; one to pay for teachers and pastors, the other to pay for the poor and for church buildings. This two-part division also applied to some of the church orders written for north Germany by Johann Bugenhagen, the parish preacher of Wittenberg.

The Nuremberg system of social welfare was perhaps the most famous of Lutheran welfare systems. Its welfare legislation was widely read, and it became a model of reform elsewhere. Its ordinances were printed in Basel, Berlin, Leipzig, and Strasbourg; it may even have influenced Catholic Ypres. The Catholic humanist Juan Luis Vives wrote a social welfare plan for the city of Bruges in 1526 that espoused certain principles of workfare rather than mere welfare and other features familiar from the Protestant welfare ordinances. Emperor Charles V asked for a draft of the Nuremberg welfare legislation before issuing his own 1531 ordinance, the adoption of which he urged on the cities of the Low Countries.

Reform in Nuremberg actually began when the city was still Catholic, in the spring of 1522, when the imperial diet was meeting in the city. Nuremberg had a system of badges for legitimate beggars, but the council found itself embarrassed by its inability to keep beggars away from the important people who had come to the city for the diet and asked two men to study the situation. A new system of poor relief was enacted in an ordinance of 24 July 1522. Then directors were chosen from the citizens to serve under two chief directors. Under these directors were four salaried officers, one for each of the four wards of the city. These four officers were to study the needs of their wards and report to the directors. Collection boxes were erected in churches and collection plates and later collection bags were passed in church. After the city formally broke with Catholicism in March 1525, the city council appropriated church endowments and property. It replaced the ten directors with five and created a common chest.[6]

The appropriation of church property was a common feature of social welfare in areas that became Protestant. No one, except the expropriated, thought it strange. When the Church of Rome was replaced by a Lutheran or

Reformed church it was thought natural that church property should remain in local hands to be used for purposes for which the endowment had originally been intended. Unfortunately, the revenues of church endowments were sometimes used for other purposes. It was a temptation when governmental bodies took over the supervision of property, as was often the case, to use the revenues for expenses other than social welfare, education, church maintenance, and clergy salaries. In particular, the expenses of war and self-defense were often more than a local city council could afford, and church property was auctioned in Lausanne to pay public debts. Part of the proceeds went to Catholic Fribourg as a peace tribute. In Zurich, after the two battles of Kappel, the city council argued that the wars had been fought for the sake of the church. The reformer Heinrich Bullinger, who succeeded Zwingli as the leading reformer, objected, but on 30 July 1533 a new office of *obmann* was created. The *obmann* was the overseer of all monastic property, elected from the small council of the city to administer the surplus income. Sometimes he used it for church needs, at other times for civic needs. That was perhaps better for the church than having the property slip back into private hands as happened elsewhere. Once church property came under city council control the new Protestant churches could not completely supervise the use of funds.[7]

In various ways the social welfare system of Zurich was a model for other Reformed churches. In 1520, before the city became Reformed, the city council centralized the welfare system and took it under its own control. In 1525 when the convents were suppressed, their possessions were given over to the needs of the poor. Begging was forbidden, since begging was associated with the Catholic theological belief in earning merit by the giving of alms. Moreover, the presence of beggars in the streets was considered demeaning for the city. In each quarter of the city an ecclesiastic and a lay person were responsible for making the necessary investigations and gathering donations. A large cauldron was set up before one of the city's churches, where early in the morning people could come for soup. Zurich served as a model for other cities such as Berne when they became reformed.[8]

The reformers of Strasbourg may have fared better than those in Zurich in controlling funds taken from the pre-Reformation church, at least those for education. The problem of obtaining funds for teachers' salaries was resolved in Strasbourg by the use of canonical prebends for the teachers, but funding social welfare in Strasbourg remained a problem. The civil authority took over responsibility for the distribution of poor relief and asked that all contributions henceforth be handed over to the city authorities. A committee of the magistrat called *almosenherren* was created. An administrator of poor relief was created and nine helpers called *almosenpfleger* were appointed, each responsible for a parish. There was to be no begging; each week an allowance would be delivered to each needy home. This well-conceived system impressed John Calvin during his sojourn in Strasbourg from 1538 to 1541. Like any welfare system, it depended on adequate funds, and these were often wanting. Strasbourg, like Geneva, provided refuge for many religious exiles, which strained the social welfare system. John Calvin, in fact, served a congregation of French-speaking refugees while he was in Strasbourg. Unlike Geneva, the reformers of Strasbourg appeared not to be involved in the administration of poor relief. John Calvin was nevertheless aware of the needs of refugees in both cities. It should be noted that the legacy of David Busanton in 1545 provided for the refugees both in Geneva and in Strasbourg. Perhaps this was administered through the congregation of French refugees that Calvin had served.[9]

One commentator on the Strasbourg scene suggested that "voluntary contributions, given in faith and love, never yielded the same quantity of revenue as that obtained when the donors believed their gifts would guarantee a better life in the world to come."[10] It is true that Protestant theology eliminated the concept of an accumulation of merit toward eternal life for deeds well done, but this theological shift was not necessarily the reason for a less successful welfare system. In some regions, welfare seemed to work better after a city became Protestant than before, as may very well have been the case in Geneva. Two crucial factors in the success of post-Reformation welfare systems seem to have been the size of the endowment from the Roman Catholic period and the organizational skills of the collectors of contributions. A third factor may have been the extent to which contributions were solicited from outside the immediate locale. This was especially true where there were needy refugees such as in Geneva and Strasbourg. The collectors for the Bourse française in Geneva cast a very broad net, since contributions came in from several different countries, especially from France.

In Strasbourg, preaching of welfare reform began before the Protestant Reformation. Geiler von Kaysersberg urged a new system of poor relief that included a suggestion that able-bodied people should work. Only those incapable of work, he argued, should receive relief. The dissolution of the monasteries and convents at the time of the Reformation facilitated the process, but long before that the city had taken over considerable responsibility for the funding and administration of public welfare.[11]

As in Strasbourg, centralization and rationalization of social welfare occurred in other cities and regions before they became Protestant—in the city of Lyons, for example. In Geneva itself in 1508 the small council attempted to combine all of the hospitals, travelers' hostels, asylums, and other beneficent institutions. But Geneva, in general, went less far in the direction of secularization and centralization of institutions before the Reformation than many European cities. The political revolution that cast out the prince-bishop of Geneva and the Protestant Reformation occurred almost simultaneously. Many other cities had eliminated ecclesiastical control of their governments long before.[12]

Welfare reform also occurred in regions that never became Protestant. In Catholic areas where centralization and rationalization of welfare institutions had barely begun, welfare was not necessarily dominated by the clergy. Catholic welfare administration was often considerably laicized because of the role of the confraternities in caring for the poor. Confraternities performed a variety of central religious, economic, and fiscal functions, supporting the collective life of communities even in rural areas.[13] One wonders how the new Protestant areas did without confraternities except that they may have had their drawbacks. Luther pointed out that their funds were sometimes spent on themselves and in his opinion, were squandered in entertainment and banqueting. Nevertheless, in some cities the confraternities played a central role in maintaining institutions of welfare, hospitals, and poor houses. This was true in Venice, for instance. Some of the confraternities of Venice divided the town into sections, then placed members in charge of supervising a section and seeing especially to other members' needs. The confraternities of Venice admitted physicians as members and used their services. They took particular care of their own members, of course, but this was true of many welfare institutions. For the confraternities in Venice as for the deacons in Geneva, worthiness was a criterion for assistance, but in Venice it took the form of punctiliousness in performing external acts of piety that were considered idolatrous in Geneva. The confraternities of Venice were also compelled by the city to offer incentives to serve Venice at sea, an early modern form of workfare.

Catholic confraternities continued their efforts in the area of social welfare in the Catholic Counter-Reformation period. Competition from Protestants in some areas perhaps intensified their efforts. A number of recent studies have examined the role of Catholic confraternities in social welfare. In seventeenth- and eighteenth-century Grenoble, France, three groups were particularly active: a women's confraternity that cared for orphans and rescued prostitutes; the Company of the Holy Sacrament, a secret organization that ran the general hospital; and the Congregation for the Propagation of the Faith that devoted itself to the elimination of Protestantism. It was typical of confraternities to specialize in particular welfare concerns.[14]

Social welfare in Catholic and Protestant areas varied in institutional form, but both intended to work within the existing social order rather than to modify it. The notion of the shamefaced poor, for instance, seems to have been honored across Europe. The shamefaced poor were people of wealth and prominence in society who fell on hard times. They received special treatment that must have been a consolation to them but was not necessarily fair to others. Welfare may have also been a force for a more egalitarian society in several ways, however. Social welfare supported literacy, especially in Protestant areas. Literacy opened doors for many people that would have been closed to them before. Likewise, providing dowries for young girls and apprenticeships for young people must have offered many a young person a start in life that he or she otherwise would not have had. Social welfare in the sixteenth century thus equalized opportunity for some young people, but it most certainly was not the intention of the reformers to revolutionize the hierarchy of society through social welfare.

In many respects poor relief in Catholic and Protestant areas shared common features: they used poor boxes in the churches, encouraged able-bodied people to work, aided the indigent and travelers, and suppressed or limited begging. Both Catholic and Protestant welfare systems left the ownership of property in private hands. The only religious groups of this period that successfully advocated communal ownership of property were some Anabaptists. The Hutterites, with their practice of community property, have endured to the present. Their communities were relatively small and self-contained. As they grew larger they became even more self-contained. They may have been a model of the good life within their own communities, but they did not have a significant impact on the society around them.

Although little socialism was practiced in Europe at this time, there was a sincere desire on the part of many reformers, both Catholic and Protestant, to alleviate poverty. In fact, Calvinism is characterized more by a struggle against poverty than by a justification of lending money at interest or of keeping one's profits to oneself. Moreover, John Calvin did not see material possessions or success as a sign of God's blessing for personal merit. None of the magisterial reformers considered poverty a virtue, and it certainly was not considered a blessing. They felt that the church had an obligation to be concerned for its members' social and economic lives. In Geneva, Calvin and the other city pastors repeatedly pressured the city council to protect the poor and to pass laws that would favor social welfare. They wanted to limit the allowable rate of interest on loans in the city to what they considered a reasonable amount, often lower than the market would bear. Calvin opposed hoarding, speculation, and profiteering on commodities that were essential, especially food.[15] The welfare system that evolved in the city during his lifetime was a living testimonial to the commitment of his generation to provide for the poor. It was based almost exclusively on free will donations beyond what the city was willing to provide. Calvin and the other magisterial reformers believed the Christian was a steward of the gifts of God. Good stewardship of God's gifts committed one to a generous and open spirit toward the less fortunate. Stewardship was expressed concretely in Geneva through regular monthly contributions to the poor by some donors.

The social and economic thought of Calvin has been analyzed at length elsewhere.[16] Social welfare systems in other parts of Europe have been examined in depth. The purpose of this study has been to examine one institution, the *Bourse française* of Geneva, as a specific solution to a specific set of problems. The solutions arrived at in Geneva were influential in subsequent Protestant development, but this is a study of a particular case.

THE *BOURSE FRANÇAISE*

To describe accurately the *Bourse française* during the first generation of its existence does not call for elaborate hypotheses but rather straightforward questions about the nature of the institution, how it began, how it worked, and who controlled it. Its manuscripts reveal some concrete answers. Most startling is that although the *Bourse* was primarily a welfare fund, it became for a time a missionary arm of the Reformed Church. In the late 1550s and early 1560s it bought Bibles, Psalters, and catechisms and apparently distributed them in France via colporteurs associated with that great financier of books, Laurent de Normandie. The *Bourse* paid for countless nameless messengers, often at the behest of the Venerable Company of Pastors, and it became involved in the production and distribution of Théodore de Bèze's translations of the Psalms, perhaps because he had designated the proceeds for the *Bourse*.

On a broader scale, the fund functioned in a dual role as a fund for the church and as a welfare fund. This should come as no surprise, considering that it was probably the largest sum of money available to the pastors and officers of the church in Geneva that did not have to be channeled through the city budget. Since the church buildings and the pastors' salaries were taken care of through the city, the financial needs of the local church were largely paid for, but there was no obvious freestanding budget from which the ministers could draw for special projects except for the deacons' funds of the various immigrant groups.

Since the contributors to the *Bourse française* apparently determined how its monies were spent under the influence of the French pastors of the mid-sixteenth century Genevan church, it is small wonder that the fund was used to serve both the needs of the poor refugees and those of the Company of Pastors. The constituents of the *Bourse* drew no particular lines between welfare and religion; no one in the sixteenth century would have thought it inappropriate to use this private fund for both purposes.

In its dual role as church budget and welfare fund, the *Bourse* reflected an interplay between ideology and practicality. It was the creation of John Calvin and his compatriots, but it was also an everyday institution that evolved pragmatically and conformed to generally acceptable welfare practices of the sixteenth-century world. This was reflected in the *Bourse*'s continuation of the long-standing tradition of handouts to travelers passing through town for a night, as well as in its custom of treating the shamefaced poor in a special manner appropriate to their rank in society. The ideas of Calvin were evident in the organization of the fund around officers known as deacons and in the general philosophy that we are to be "our brother's and sister's keeper" that permeated the fund's activities. This idea was not original with Calvin, of course, but he surely emphasized it in his social and economic thought.

Alongside these broader considerations, some very specific information emerged from the manuscripts about how the *Bourse* originated, how it was administered, and how it carried out its functions on a daily level. This information can be divided into three categories: origins, organization, and functions.

Origins

The tradition about the origins of the *Bourse française* claims that it began with a large legacy in 1545 by a person named David Busanton to the poor refugees of Geneva and Strasbourg. Major historians have dissented from this hypothesis, however, because it is incompletely substantiated. The will of David Busanton has not survived and his link with the *Bourse française* is based largely on one source, the chronicler Michel Roset, who was writing after the time of the gift.

A more serious problem with the thesis that connects David Busanton with the *Bourse* is that there is no proof that the fund was actually in operation at this early date. There are no surviving account books from this early period. They began almost five years later, on 30 September 1550. Nevertheless, circumstantial evidence is substantial that a financial arrangement to aid the poor refugees was organized about 1545, even though it might not yet have taken on the structured form that emerged with the account books of 1550. In 1545 David Busanton, a wealthy refugee, bequeathed a large sum of money to the poor. John Calvin himself wrote in a letter to Pierre Viret that he was present when Busanton died and commented on the magnitude of the gift, one that might have been made at Calvin's own suggestion. If the legacy of David Busanton was the catalyst of a project to help the poor, the evidence points toward John Calvin as a possible instigator.

Even stronger evidence suggests that a formal structure to help the poor emerged about the year 1549. The first page of the account books of 1550 lists the names of the first deacons, but these three men were already registered in the book of inhabitants of Geneva in the spring and early summer of 1549. They were in town then, and could have begun work months before their election in the fall of 1550. When Jean Budé, one of these first three deacons, retired from the accounts for a short while in 1575, it was mentioned that he had served for twenty-six years. That would place the formal organization of the *Bourse française* in 1549. Also, the first disbursement in the accounts was to Denis Raguenier, the copyist of Calvin's sermons, who had actually begun his work in 1549 and presumably was paid before the date of the opening of the account books. In addition, the first lists of donors and recipients in the account books contain substantial numbers of names that were repeated in the months that followed, as if the opening of the books was the formal recording of a procedure that was already in progress.

In sum, June 1545 was a likely point of departure because of the death of David Busanton, although the evidence for the legacy itself is more clear than its link to the *Bourse française*. There is a stronger possibility of a formal structure by 1549, because of the presence of the deacons in the city, the beginning of the work of the copyist of Calvin's sermons, and the allusion to twenty-six years of service when Jean Budé stepped down awhile in 1575. We know that by October 1550 the *Bourse* was functioning, since the surviving account books date from 30 September 1550. It is not, then, extravagant to conclude that before the formal opening of the account books some sort of fund existed, serving the poor refugees, accepting money from the wealthy, and paying the salary of Denis Raguenier. This fund was likely organized around the city pastors and the donors, who were present at the first recorded gathering of the supporters of the *Bourse* on 30 September 1550 and were intimately involved in its early functions. Perhaps the fund started with money that was entrusted by benevolent people to the ministers or to Calvin himself to help the poor. Perhaps it then grew to such proportions that a separate administration was considered advisable. Unfortunately, little is found about the *Bourse française* in the formal writings of Calvin because it did not yet exist in 1541 when he wrote his formal ideas about deacons into the Ecclesiastical Ordinances of Geneva.

Organization

The Administration: Deacons, Collectors, Auditors, and Ministers. The organization of the *Bourse française* appears from the account books to have been a gradually evolving edifice, relatively simple at the beginning, centering around the work of the three men elected on 30 September 1550 to administer the fund. They came to be called deacons. They were formally referred to by that title for the first time in the account books at a July 1554 election in the home of Calvin. These three men apparently initially included activities in their work that were later parcelled out to others, such as collecting donations. Within a short time this task was taken over by a group of collectors who canvassed the city and who apparently also maintained contact with centers of contribution abroad. During the first few years of the account books there is no evidence that they were audited, unless they were audited by the deacons themselves. Jean Budé, deacon and first bookkeeper, occasionally wrote financial summaries into the account books. At least once he signed the books with his name. Within a generation, however, the position of auditor became formalized, and the books were audited regularly. The level of honesty practiced by all concerned seems to have been high, but some doubt is cast on this by the questions raised about Jean Bude's handling of his wards' money.

Collectors, auditors, and deacons served the *Bourse française*. After their positions had developed they were formally described in a series of regulations about the fund anunciated in 1581 and written into the beginning of the account book of 1582. These regulations were, in effect, a constitution for the *Bourse*, written over thirty years as the fund evolved. The regulations described what had already developed; they did not substantially institute new procedures. This document provided for annual elections of deacons, collectors, and auditors by a plurality vote of an annual assembly of the ministers of the city and the contributors to the fund. The regularization of elections appears to have been a rather recent development in 1582. The pattern, for at least the first ten and perhaps the first twenty years of the *Bourse*, seems rather to have been to schedule elections when deacons died or to co-opt new men as the need arose. As a matter of fact, even after the formal provision for annual elections the practice of retaining the same men on the job year after year continued, at least in the post of deacon.

Alongside these relatively long-term positions was one that was considered a rotating post, that of the minister assigned to the group of deacons from the Venerable Company of Pastors. The duties of the minister on the board of deacons were twofold: to serve as a liaison between the deacons of the *Bourse française* and the Company of Pastors and to lead in the mutual censure among the deacons before the quarterly administration of the Lord's Supper in the churches of the city. His presence was also thought to enhance the credibility of the deacons among the poor.

The assignment of a minister to the deacons was evidence of the special relationship that the *Bourse française* had to the Venerable Company of Pastors. Although not spelled out in the constitution from the 1582 account book as a subordinate relationship, it seems to have been just that, especially during the early years of activity when the ministers of the city were named in the account books as instructing how money of the fund was to be spent. If the *Bourse* had originated with money that had been entrusted to the pastors for the poor, then the dominant influence of the ministers was not unnatural. Deacons could thus have been serving as administrators of funds that were ultimately considered under the jurisdiction of the Venerable Company of Pastors. Indeed, it was to the Company of Pastors that the account books were submitted for final approval after they had been audited.

It was also to the Company of Pastors that any difficulty among the deacons was to be reported by the minister in their midst, so that the ministers could advise the deacons what to do.

Despite any ultimate sovereignty resting in the Company of Pastors, the deacons themselves made so many daily administrative decisions on their own that it would be wrong to consider them lackeys of the ministers. The deacons were in effective control of the administration of the *Bourse française* because they did most of the work. Not only did they make decisions about who should be on welfare and how much they should receive, they also maintained close contact with the poor. They visited them in their homes when they were sick, and they saw that they were given proper medical care. The deacons, in effect, made house calls, sometimes on a regular weekly basis when a person was sick.

In the sixteenth century the deacons seem to have known the grassroots of their own institution fairly well. By exposing themselves to contagion at the homes of the sick, they may even have hastened their own demise! At any rate, the turnover among deacons was occasioned frequently by death rather than by retirement.

Some very competent men were called to this office. In the sixteenth century they were businessmen and nobles, well versed in the world of affairs and competent to deal with account books, legal documents, and the sophisticated people who sometimes came their way as contributors. They were expected as well, of course, to be solid Christians, and in most cases they seemed to have maintained a satisfactory, even exemplary, family life. Their wives, though not welcomed into the office of the diaconate in Geneva, were active workers in the same cause.

Wives of deacons worked alongside many other women in the *Bourse française*, for, although the *Bourse* did not select women for its administrative posts in the sixteenth century (the possibility could hardly even have been considered), it did provide ample opportunity for women to be active in welfare work. Women appeared, individually and under their own family names, among the contributors, the recommenders, and the hosts. They gave money in their own right, recommended individuals to the deacons for help, and hosted refugees in their homes.

The deacons enjoyed a broad circle of contacts both in Geneva and abroad. They were willing to give generously of their time, and the first generation, at least, could afford the time. They were foreigners and excluded from many of the important but time-consuming positions in the city that were reserved for native Genevans. They represented diverse areas of France, as did the collectors, whose wide range of contacts facilitated their work.

It was through these far-flung contacts that the *Bourse* was able to become an international organization. It was dependent not just on local funding in

Geneva, but on sympathetic individuals wherever Reformed churches were found in regions that maintained contact with Geneva. The deacons had friends in France, especially. Any traveler was able to bring in funds from abroad, merchants on business and couriers on diverse errands. Thus an international network of mutual support was established that strengthened individual Reformed churches scattered at some distance from each other. This network reinforced these churches at times when they might otherwise have collapsed. It made survival possible for members of these churches whose lives were endangered, since they could escape to Switzerland and return home when home was safe.

Employees of the Bourse française. Serving the administrators of the fund, who were all volunteers, was a cadre of personnel who were paid for their services. They were usually paid on a fee for services or on a piecework basis. These employees included a wide variety of people, from medical personnel on the most educated end of the spectrum to wet nurses and message carriers at the other extreme. Of all these employees, the only one apparently fully supported by his salary from the *Bourse* was the copyist of Calvin's sermons, Denis Raguenier, and, after him, a man called Paris. Others were paid a salary that probably supplemented other income. Many were paid specifically for the task they performed, such as the early apothecaries and barber-surgeons. From the early 1560s, however, the doctor was given a fixed amount per month that was occasionally supplemented when he had more than his ordinary share of work to do.

There was a whole cadre of additional supportive personnel—guardians to care for the sick, foster parents for the orphaned, child care personnel for children whose mothers were ill, and wet nurses to nourish the infants of women who had died or who were unable to nurse their babies. This was likely less a professional staff than an ad hoc collection of those who were willing to help out or who needed the income. The pay was very low. For these jobs the deacons often employed their own poor.

The deacons employed people on the welfare rolls for other tasks as well: poor women worked as seamstresses, sewing clothes for the poor, perhaps from the cloth that the deacons brought. Poor people carried messages and brought in wood, and if a poor person had special skills, they were sometimes utilized. The deacons, on the whole, seemed to use consistently the services of some reliable skilled people rather than conscientiously to spread out all the possible work to diverse welfare recipients. Thus there were, in effect, *Bourse* craftsmen and women who were called on when the deacons needed something made, just as there were *Bourse* medical personnel who were called on when the deacons requested medical care for the poor.

In contrast to the general procedure of the deacons making arrangements for goods and services, aid recipients sometimes bought items themselves with funds given to them by the *Bourse* for that purpose. For instance, aid recipients sometimes bought their own shoes, had them repaired, purchased an article of clothing, or had their laundry done. This was the practice for the early years when the *Bourse* was generally more flexible.

There is no particular evidence that the deacons insisted on the rock bottom price; they probably simply sought the conventionally accepted fair price. The deacons appear to have accepted the standards of their age, paying what others paid and conforming to prevailing practices. Thus a tailor may have been paid more than a woman for sewing clothing for the *Bourse*, but that is difficult to determine from the records.

Women as a whole were employed in jobs that paid poorly, in child care, predominantly. The deacons do not appear to have consciously discriminated against women. They were merely reflecting commonly accepted values. The deacons' financial and social responsibilities made it unlikely that people who were perceived of as radicals would have been chosen for this post.

Finally, the *Bourse* hired hosts and hostesses who were reimbursed for providing housing for the refugees. The deacons used private homes and inns in which to lodge the poor and paid their rent. They also may have housed some of the poor in homes owned directly by the *Bourse*, since the fund acquired real property as the beneficiary of wills. The names of the hosts and hostesses were copied into the account books haphazardly in an attempt to identify nameless aid recipients through their host. The names of these hosts and hostesses are largely French in origin.

It appears that many of the hosts and hostesses of the poor welcomed people voluntarily with no apparent recompense. This was in line with the general philosophy of the *Bourse* to use volunteer help and gifts when possible and to make purchases and employ people only when necessary. The *Bourse française* was, after all, essentially a volunteer agency that had grown too large in its services to rely completely on unpaid help.

Donors and Donations. During the first generation of *Bourse* activity, the income of the *Bourse* came largely from contributions that were more or less voluntary. The contributors were mostly French. Many were residents of Geneva, some were visitors to the city, and others resided in France, where they had apparently heard about the fund through the network of communication among Reformed churches. There were occasional donations from members of other nationality groups and from native Genevans.

Contributions came both as outright donations from living people and as bequests from the dead. They were given either as money, real estate, or gifts in kind such as cloth, grain, or firewood. Small amounts of property also escheated to the fund from the estates of poor people who had received money from the *Bourse* in exchange for the meager proceeds from their possessions after they died. There were also large bequests. It became common practice for Genevans to include one of the refugee funds in their wills. They also typically contributed to the city hospital and the academy. This custom was encouraged by the city's notaries, who were responsible for reminding people of their charitable obligations when they drew up their wills. Some bequests also lapsed into the hands of the deacons by default when the original heirs failed to meet the demands in a will and the *Bourse* was the next eligible party. This occurred particularly when an heir left town or the Reformed religion against the will of a parent or relative who had stipulated that the heir stay in Geneva or within the Reformed Church.

In these various ways the *Bourse française* inherited substantial sums of money and property, and the real possessions of the fund grew beyond the immediate needs of the poor for a place to live and clothes to wear. The deacons then rented and sold what they could not use directly. They thus became involved in the management of property.

But some gifts came to the *Bourse* with strings attached, with specifications as to how the money was to be spent or for whom it was intended. Sometimes the limitations were so strict that the gift amounted to a trust given by one individual for another, administered through the good offices of the deacons. The deacons of the *Bourse française* thus were also viewed as esteemed members of the community who could safely be entrusted with the responsibility for other people's money.

Altogether the work of the deacons was increased by the legal negotiations over contested wills and the pursuit of errant bequests. These responsibilities were compounded by the accumulation of capital and real estate that had to be managed. The duties of the deacons combined with their responsibilities as trusted members of the community made them very busy people, but their active role in the community helped the *Bourse*. It enhanced the credibility of the welfare fund they represented and made it a reliable charitable institution in which the well-meaning donor could have confidence. Donations depended in part on the public image of the deacons.

The credibility of the deacons thus encouraged direct benevolence toward the *Bourse française* or toward similar deacons' funds in Reformed churches elsewhere. Another powerful incentive in Geneva was the expectation that one should give to the poor. While the notaries encouraged people to remember the city's charities when they drew up their wills, well before people reached that point in life the collectors for the *Bourse française* in various quarters of the city had contacted and asked them for donations. The collectors were responsible for knowing the people from whom they were expected to collect donations. They were not above putting pressure on the well-to-do. People were also encouraged to volunteer their time and hospitality. At the same time, Genevans were not supposed to give money to beggars directly. Like Reformed Protestants elsewhere, they were to divert their alms to the deacons' funds rather than deal directly with the poor.

Not only had charity practices in Geneva changed in some respects from the pre-Reformation period, but the philosophy behind charity had changed too. John Calvin and the other reformers viewed charity as a response to God's love and to the neighbor's needs. The old Catholic incentive of giving alms to the poor to merit eternal reward was undermined by the new Protestant emphasis on justification by faith. It is difficult to determine if there was any actual change in psychological motivations. In both Catholic and Protestant areas social pressure and a sense of responsibility encouraged the well-to-do to help out the less fortunate. There were practical constraints as well. In Geneva, for instance, the alternatives to almsgiving were limited by the city's ban on begging and system of policing near the church doors where beggars were likely to accumulate. Collection boxes were located in the churches for those who wanted to contribute as they entered or left church. The proceeds went to the city hospital and the deacons' funds.

In the Genevan system of charity, donors were at least one step away from the poor who received their gifts, but they did not abdicate entire control of their contributions. Not only did the donors lend a hand as hosts, but they also taught the poor new skills, took them on as apprentices, and employed them. The *Bourse française* also held periodic meetings of the contributors to elect officers. On a more routine level the deacons honored recommendations made by contributors of individual poor people who needed help. That the *Bourse* was not an anonymous institution over which the contributors had no control must have appealed to the first generation of French immigrants, especially since in mid-sixteenth-century Geneva these immigrants found few civic outlets for their capabilities because many offices were barred to them.

Recipients. Much less is known about individual aid recipients than about donors, because of the virtual anonymity of the recipients in the account books. They were largely unknown people who were relatively absent from the city records of the period. Although a name appears here and there in the consistory minutes or the criminal records, the enduring record of many of them was simply their name on a welfare roll.

Although it is difficult to pin down individual aid recipients, the characteristics of the welfare group as a whole are retrievable. The deacon-bookkeeper recorded individual characteristics of aid recipients for the first decade or so of accounting, apparently to identify the people with whom he dealt. He also commented on the circumstances that brought people to him for help, perhaps to explain his expenditures. He identified people by their profession or craft and by the extenuating situations that brought them to Geneva. He recorded if they were sick, handicapped, aged, widowed, orphaned, unemployed, inadequately clothed, or burdened with children. He told why they had requested help—if they needed a loan, a gift, a tool, care for their children, a Bible, money for a trip, money for school, or apprenticeship fees.

This information was not provided systematically for every aid recipient. The deacon was not attempting, after all, to compile statistics. Yet he left enough data to indicate that, in general, the recipient group was composed largely of women, children, and unemployed men. These were the very individuals not included in the book of inhabitants of Geneva, whose lists of foreigners living in town emphasized able-bodied males. The welfare rolls, like the book of inhabitants, also indicated many people's geographic origins.

The piecemeal entries in the account books do not tell the whole story of what the aid recipients of the *Bourse française* were like. Some additional information about them is located in the criminal records, the consistory minutes, and the notes of the deacons. The aid recipients are not found with frequency in the criminal records. They did not apparently misbehave enough to make the public records. The comments about the exceptional cases of welfare recipients who got into trouble reveal that those who were helped by the deacons were expected to behave well. They were expected to be worthy of that aid—that is, honest, upright, God-fearing people in Geneva to live according to the "Reform of the Word." They were to appreciate whatever aid was offered to them, and they were to help themselves and other needy people, such as orphans, as much as they could. Failure to meet these expectations could get them into trouble. They could be suspended from the welfare rolls or terminated. Certain conditions beyond their control, such as mental illness, could be their nemesis, since it was not always understood by the sixteenth-century mind.

Other restrictions on aid were largely geographic and religious in nature. Aid recipients were supposed to be refugees from elsewhere, usually France, as the name of the fund indicates. They were also expected to be Protestants worshiping in the Reformed tradition.

The *Bourse française* was thus conceived of as a fund for a specific category of poor people, the worthy poor who had come to Geneva for the sake of their religion. This group was thought to be in temporary straits, composed of people who were not at fault for their predicament.

Despite these intended restrictions on whom the *Bourse* would aid, in practice it was fairly inclusive in its early years. People received money from the deacons who did not fit the expected categories: a Jew, a native Genevan, and many refugees of non-French origin. The account books reveal a fair degree of spontaneity on the part of the early deacons. This was especially true when people needed an immediate helping hand, such as when overnight travelers came to the door. The deacons seem at times to have helped almost everyone who came their way, without exception.

Toward the seventeenth century this flexibility gave way to a more rigid system, however. Stricter limitations were possible as deacons' funds were founded for other nationality groups. Funds were established in Geneva for the Italians, the English, and the German-speaking people. The various welfare institutions in the city specified ethnic groups and subgroups for whom they agreed to care. The city hospital was largely for Genevans. When regional and national boundaries changed in Europe in the vicissitudes of peace and war, the welfare funds shifted their responsibilities accordingly. Questions then arose about where people had come from and whether or not to shift a welfare recipient from one fund to another if his or her region of origin had changed sovereignty. If people in need presented themselves to the wrong fund, they could be shuttled over to the correct fund. Sometimes the welfare institutions disagreed about which was responsible for someone. Perhaps welfare had come to be thought of as a right rather than a privilege, and the welfare institutions had taken precautions to protect themselves. Children of couples who married across nationality lines presented a problem, as did men who had served as soldiers for regions from which they did not originate. Who was responsible for assistance in such cases? As the welfare system in post-Reformation Geneva matured, it lost some of its flexibility, until eventually in the mid-nineteenth century some Genevans thought the deacons' funds were parochial because of their religious and ethnic limitations. These people forced the merging of the *Bourse française* with the city hospital. The last meeting of the deacons of the *Bourse* was on 14 September 1849.[17]

In mid-sixteenth-century Geneva during the first generation of the *Bourse française*, the welfare situation apparently still allowed generosity to express itself freely. Limitations were apparently applied with common sense in a spirit of charity. This is not to say that the deacons were foolishly open-handed. The deacons of the mid-sixteenth century were no more eager to give their limited funds to the undeserving than were their later counterparts. Thus, even in the early days, certain criteria were used to identify those genuinely in greatest need. A second dominant criterion was worthiness. This may have encouraged an ingratiating hypocrisy, but high standards of conduct for the aid recipients possibly eliminated some of the stigma of accepting welfare. These standards, together with the knowledge that unworthy recipients were subject to removal, may have left a veil of propriety for aid recipients of the *Bourse française*.

Other factors may have contributed to a good public image for the poor on the rolls of the *Bourse française*. Funds from the *Bourse* were often a stopgap measure for recipients who later found employment and made their own way in life. This might have encouraged the public to think of the poor as redeemable from poverty, rather than in a state of chronic need. The type of people on the welfare rolls also may have shaped the public image of an aid recipient. That some ministers received aid may have lent respectability to the predicament. Surely the presence of the highborn on the rolls, even for a short time, must have lent a certain dignity to everyone's plight, even though there is evidence that the highborn were treated with special consideration and allowed more money, as if they were in a special category. It is also not impossible that the presence of so many able-bodied refugees on welfare, who were needy only because they had been uprooted, improved the general conceptions of the causes of poverty and the plight of the poor.

For whatever reason people received money from the deacons, that it was a fund for religious refugees must have redeemed their pride. It was a special fund founded for a unique and lofty purpose. Surely members of a community as conscious of its heritage as is modern-day Geneva can appreciate finding their ancestors' names on the welfare rolls of the *Bourse française*. There is no embarrassment because of the special historical situation that created this particular welfare fund.

Functions

The description of how the *Bourse* was organized and the composite pictures of its donors and recipients goes far to indicate some of the probable functions of the fund. It is, however, possible to be more specific. The deacon-accountant's minute details of his expenditures during the early years of *Bourse* activity reveals how money was spent rather exactly. The early functions of the *Bourse française* emerge along two general lines: as expenditures for the poor and as expenditures for the Venerable Company of Pastors. The *Bourse française* was both welfare fund and church budget.

The expenditures for the poor ranged in duration from the overnight viaticum given to travelers to lifelong welfare support. Lifelong support was granted to people who were unable to fend for themselves because they were sick, disabled, or aged. Between these two extremes there was a wide range from partial to full support for long or short periods of time to widows, orphans, unemployed able-bodied men, and families who were unable to meet all their expenses. According to need, the deacons provided a weekly handout, clothes, firewood, a Bible or Psalter, a place to stay, a mattress, bedclothes, and occasionally an allotment of grain. They apparently did not provide ready-made bread until late in the seventeenth century when the deacons arranged with the city hospital to use their ovens. Besides meeting these needs of daily subsistence, the *Bourse* also met extremities by providing medical care, drugs, guardians for the sick, hospitalization, wet nurses for infants, and foster homes for older orphans. To teach people to read and provide them with a trade, the deacons paid school and apprenticeship fees.

The *Bourse* provided these services both for those they took under full charge and to others who were apparently in temporary straits. Many people received partial aid from the deacons or occasional help when an emergency arose. Some people seemingly came when they were confronted with an expenditure that was larger than they could afford such as an apprenticeship fee or expenses for the birth of a baby.

Although the deacons gave out a considerable amount of aid in emergencies, they were apparently not eager to let people become dependent on the fund for long periods of time unless it was necessary. Rehabilitation was the order of the day, and the special nature of the *Bourse's* clientele made turnover possible as able-bodied refugees found jobs and became self-supporting. To help them toward this goal, the deacons trained and retrained people, bought tools, and even occasionally paid out large sums to procure shop space for refugees to set themselves up in business, but in general the deacons were parsimonious in their efforts to get people back into the work force. They appeared to pay for what was needed but not more, and they seemed to prefer loans to outright gifts. For some of these loans there were guarantors to protect the fund in case the original borrower defaulted. Some of this money may have been repaid in multiples of the original gift as thankful refugees recovered a means of livelihood and became contributors.

There is evidence that the deacons wanted to know specifically how money was to be spent and hesitated to give out sums that were not earmarked to a particular end. This is supported by the exactness of the expenditures listed in the account books and by the deacons' apparent surveillance of those whom they granted aid. For instance, if the deacons supported children while they were growing up, they apparently wanted some say in those children's future, particularly when they came to the age of apprenticeship. They especially wanted to make sure that young people were appropriately trained for gainful employment. There is some evidence of conflict between a parent, usually a widow, and the deacons when a child reached the age of apprenticeship. The deacons clearly had an advantage in these and similar situations, because they could withhold or threaten to withhold welfare payments. They sometimes did this to enforce their will.

Some of the deacons' actions offend our twentieth-century sense of fairness, but they were surely acting in ways appropriate to the more paternalistic age in which they lived. In addition to using welfare payments to control recalcitrant aid recipients, other apparent practices were acceptable then but seem out of step with modern notions. For instance, the deacons may not have treated people equally; the amounts of money given to recipients of long-term aid do not seem to be equal, that is, people on the welfare rolls at the same time in apparently similar circumstances got different sums of money. This was particularly evident in the case of widows. There are several possible explanations for this apparent inequality, however. Some widows might have had more dependents than others, since the account books for the first decade do not list the actual number of dependents. The exact size of a family is therefore impossible to determine. The account books reveal only a difference in payment. On the other hand, there may have been inequalities in the welfare payments. Perhaps the deacons felt that some people had greater needs or were more deserving than others, such as those who had undergone religious persecution or the shamefaced poor of high birth. Whatever the reasons, the early *Bourse française* does not appear to have been completely egalitarian.

The deacons appear to have accepted the social stratification of their society, yet they offered the dispossessed certain opportunities to rise from the bottom of the social hierarchy. By paying school and apprenticeship fees, the deacons opened the doors to literacy, livelihood, and advancement to some very poor people. Teaching the poor to read so that they could read the Bible may have helped break the barrier of literacy between the bourgeoisie and those they considered beneath them.

The *Bourse française* was democratic in some respects—in the educational opportunities it offered to the poor and in the aid it offered in the early years to people who were not French refugees. What is impressive in these years is the flexibility with which aid was distributed, not the restrictions limiting those who could be helped. The early fund was remarkably comprehensive and versatile, particularly in short-term assistance, but also in long-term support.

The usefulness of the *Bourse* was apparently enhanced by its willingness to give attention to any legitimate request. From its inception, it appears to have been ready to move into the world of the larger church to take on the tasks of what the modern world would consider the budget of a church. The deacons paid the salary of the copyist of Calvin's sermons, helped with the arrangements for the production of the Psalms of Théodore de Bèze, and sent messengers and books into France.

Apparently the community behind the *Bourse* allowed it a scope broad enough to meet diverse needs as they arose. The open-mindedness and generosity of the *Bourse* in its early years was due in part to the nature of the people who were involved in its activities, particularly the deacons. These were an exemplary group, especially Jean Budé, the son of the great French humanist Guillaume Budé. It is in Jean Budé's hand that the first account books were kept, and it is among his relatives and friends that many of the first people active in the *Bourse française* were recruited. He, together with the other deacons, superintended it through the 1550s and early 1560s, when the refugee population increased dramatically and the *Bourse* became solidly engaged in its missionary activities in France.

So many members of the Budé family were involved in the *Bourse française* that to some extent it seemed like a family affair, but it included the families and friends of the other deacons and contributors as well. The *Bourse française* was a community affair, the product of the collective efforts of the French immigrants to Geneva in the mid-sixteenth century. In fact, that community extended beyond Geneva into France and elsewhere, linked by that growing international network of communication and mutual support that constituted the Reformed Church of the sixteenth century.

The importance of the *Bourse française* transcended the local scene. Within the first generation of its founding, similar deacons' funds were created by Reformed churches across the Continent and in England. The parent institution in Geneva provided a model and an inspiration, keeping morale alive and offering a place of refuge to Reformed Christians faced with persecution and war in the increasingly foreboding world. The *Bourse française* was a linchpin in the organizational structure of Reformed churches providing financial links and strengthening the survival skills of that persistent minority, the Reformed Church of early modern Europe.

EVALUATION OF THE *BOURSE FRANÇAISE*

How should one evaluate this institution? How does it stand up under considerations of fairness and equity? How did it compare to social welfare institutions in other parts of Europe? Did it succeed?

There is a human tendency, to which even historians succumb, to become infatuated with a person or institution that one studies. This temptation is particularly compelling with an institution as magnanimous as the *Bourse française*. As one notes how the hard-working deacons died in the ranks one by one, one sympathizes with them and their welfare efforts. Can one criticize the *Bourse française*?

Certainly if one applies modern standards of fairness and equity, the *Bourse française* would fall short. It awarded special treatment to the shame-faced poor, it did not understand mental illness fully, and it favored Protestants. But there were good reasons for this behavior. Treating some people in a special manner simply reflected the prevalent hierarchical view of society. The deacons at least understood depression or melancholia, even if they were intolerant of those who acted like fools. And the *Bourse* was founded to help religious refugees; how could it not favor Protestants?

The modern individualist might condemn the deacons for coercing aid recipients to follow their advice. Was it not a misuse of power to remove people from the welfare rolls because they would not conform or obey? In reality, these practices were not unique to the *Bourse française;* they were part of the era.

What if one compares the *Bourse française* to other welfare institutions of the era? What stands out? One distinguishing feature of the *Bourse française* was that it served people who were not native to Geneva—the foreign poor, unlike most social welfare systems of the era that preferred to concentrate on the local poor. In the seventeenth century it would become somewhat exclusive about which foreign poor it helped, but in the sixteenth century the deacons seem to have had an open hand, especially before other ethnic deacons' funds were founded for the Italians, English, and German-speaking refugees to Geneva. These refugee funds were an ingenious way of enabling the wealthier of each ethnic group to help their poorer compatriots. The refugee funds may have saved Geneva as a city of refuge by taking the burden off the indigenous welfare system and the general hospital. The deacons' funds dissipated at least some of the hostility that native Genevans felt toward the influx of foreigners. The settlement of these refugees, in fact, would revolutionize the economic life of Geneva by bringing in craftspersons and artisans. Geneva built its economy on the skills of the refugees in the seventeenth and eighteenth centuries.

Somewhat more difficult to evaluate is the effect of this welfare activity on the people involved. Can one hypothesize that lives were transformed? Surely, at the very least, some benefactors must have gained a more tolerant attitude toward the poor since religious persecution had driven some of the refugees, even ministers, to Geneva and welfare.

The most outstanding feature of the *Bourse française* in comparison to other welfare institutions was its international scope. It was the hub of a wide network of Reformed churches. Churches outside Geneva sent money and refugees to the *Bourse;* the *Bourse* in turn sent them books and messengers. In the sixteenth century the *Bourse* functioned like a bank, receiving funds and distributing publications. It assured Protestant Christians a place of refuge. In this role the *Bourse* became a resource to the Venerable Company of Pastors of Geneva, whose eyes were always fixed on France. The *Bourse française* became a part of the larger effort to evangelize all of France led by the French pastors of Geneva. That project was only partially realized in the sixteenth century. Then the *Bourse* pulled back into its social welfare role. For several centuries the account books kept their secret of the larger role of the *Bourse française* during the lifetime of John Calvin, just prior to the Wars of Religion in France.

Appendix A
Payments to Paris, Copyist of John Calvin's Sermons, from the "Great Book of the Assisted," 1561–1564

Paris qui escrivoit les sermons

Le 7 fébvrier 1561 30 s.	fl.	2.	6.	0
Le 21 dudit moys 30 s.	fl.	2.	6.	0
Le 7 mars 1561 30 s.	fl.	2.	6.	0
Le 21 dudit moys 30 s.	fl.	2.	6.	0
Le 4 apvril 1561 30 s.	fl.	2.	6.	0
Le 18 dudit moys 30 s.	fl.	2.	6.	0
Le 2 may 1561 30 s.	fl.	2.	6.	0
Le 16 dudit moys 24 s.	fl.	2.	0.	0
Le 30 dudit moys 30 s.	fl.	2.	6.	0
Le 13 juing 1561 30 s.	fl.	2.	6.	0
Le 27 dudit moys 30 s.	fl.	2.	6.	0
Le 1 juillet 1561 4 s.	fl.	0	4.	0
Le 11e dudit moys 30 s.	fl.	2.	6.	0
Ladite [?] 13 s. 6 d.	fl.	1.	1.	6
Le 25 juillet 1561 45 s.	fl.	3.	9.	0
Le 8 aoust 1561 45 s.	fl.	3.	9.	0
Le 22e dudit moys 45 s.	fl.	3.	9.	0
Le 5e septembre 1561 45 s.	fl.	3.	9.	0
Le 19e dudit moys 45 s.	fl.	3.	9.	0
Le 1er octobre 1561 60 s.	fl.	5.	0	0
Le 17e dudit moys 60 s.	fl.	5.	0	0
Le 31e dudit moys 60 s.	fl.	5.	0	0
Le 23e novembre 1561 60 s.	fl.	5.	0	0
Le 25 dudit moys 60 s.	fl.	5.	0	0
Le 12e decembre 1561 60 s.	fl.	5.	0	0
Le 24e dudit moys 60 s.	fl.	5.	0	0
Le 5 janvier 1562 66 s.	fl.	5.	6.	0
Le 19 dudit moys 66 s.	fl.	5.	6.	0

	fl.		
Le 6 fébvrier 1562 6 fl.	fl.	6.	0	0
Le 1 mars 1562 7 fl. 6 s.	fl.	7.	6.	0
Le 3e apvril 1562 8 fl. 9 s.	fl.	8.	9.	0
Le 17e dudit moys 8 fl. 9 s.	fl.	8.	9.	0
Le 1er may 1562 6 fl. 3 s.	fl.	6.	3.	0
Le 15e dudit moys 9 fl. 3 s.	fl.	9.	3.	0
Le 29e dudit moys 9 fl. 3 s.	fl.	9.	3.	0
Le 12e juing 1562 9 fl. 3 s.	fl.	9.	3.	0
Le 10e juillet 1562 9 fl. 3 s.	fl.	9.	3.	0
Le 21e dudit moys 9 fl. 3 s.	fl.	9.	3.	0
Le 7e aoust 1562 9 fl. 3 s.	fl.	9.	3.	0
Le 21e dudit moys 9 fl. 3 s.	fl.	9.	3.	0
Le 4 septembre 1562 9 fl. 3 s.	fl.	9.	3.	0
Le 18e dudit moys 9 fl. 3 s.	fl.	9.	3.	0
Le 2e octobre 1562 9 fl. 3 s.	fl.	9.	3.	0
Le 25e dudit moys 9 fl. 3 s.	fl.	9.	3.	0
Le 9e novembre 1562 9 fl. 3 s.	fl.	9.	3.	0
Le 23e dudit moys 9 fl. 3 s.	fl.	9.	3.	0
Le 11e décembre 1562 9 fl. 3 s.	fl.	9.	3.	0
Le 4 janvier 1563 9 fl. 3 s.	fl.	9.	3.	0
Le 22e dudit moys 9 fl. 3 s.	fl.	9.	3.	0
Le 5e febvrier 1563 9 fl. 3 s.	fl.	9.	3.	0
Le 10e dudit moys 9 fl. 3 s.	fl.	9.	3.	0
Le 1er mars 1563 9 fl. 3 s.	fl.	9.	3.	0
Le 15e dudit moys 9 fl. 3 s.	fl.	9.	3.	0
Le 2e apvril 1563 9 fl. 3 s.	fl.	9.	3.	0
Le 16e dudit moys 9 fl. 3 s.	fl.	9.	3.	0
Le 30e dudit moys 9 fl. 3 s.	fl.	9.	3.	0
Le 14e may 1563 9 fl. 3 s.	fl.	9.	3.	0
Le 25e dudit moys payé à Boniface appoticaire pour dedit Paris 9 s.	fl.	0	9.	0
Le 28e dudit moys 9 fl. 3 s.	fl.	9.	3.	0
Le 11e juing 1563 9 fl. 3 s.	fl.	9.	3.	0
Le 25e dudit moys 9 fl. 3 s.	fl.	9.	3.	0
Le 9e juillet 1563 9 fl. 3 s.	fl.	9.	3.	0
Le 23e dudit moys 9 fl. 3 s.	fl.	9.	3.	0
Le 6e aoust 1563 9 fl. 3 s.	fl.	9.	3.	0
Le 20e dudit moys 9 fl. 3 s.	fl.	9.	3.	0
Le 3e septembre 1563 9 fl. 3 s.	fl.	9.	3.	0
Le 10e dudit moys payé audit appoticaire pour ledit Paris et sa femme 35 s.	fl.	2.	11.	0
Total	441.	4.	6	

776v

Le 17e septembre 1563 9 fl. 3 s.	fl.	9.	3.	0
Le 1 octobre 1563 9 fl. 3 s.	fl.	9.	3.	0
Le 15e dudit moys 9 fl. 3 s.	fl.	9.	3.	0
Le 29e dudit moys 9 fl. 3 s.	fl.	9.	3.	0
Le 12e novembre 1563 9 fl. 3 s.	fl.	9.	3.	0
Le 26e dudit moys 9 fl. 3 s.	fl.	9.	3.	0
Le 10e decembre 1563 9 fl. 3 s.	fl.	9.	3.	0
Le 24e dudit moys 9 fl. 3 s.	fl.	9.	3.	0

Le 7 janvier 1564 9 fl. 3 s.	fl.	9.	3.	0
Le 21ᵉ dudit moys 9 fl. 3 s.	fl.	9.	3.	0
Le 4ᵉ febvrier 1564 9 fl. 3 s.	fl.	9.	3.	0
Le 18ᵉ dudit moys 9 fl. 3 s.	fl.	9.	3.	0
Le 3ᵉ mars 1564 9 fl. 3 s.	fl.	9.	3.	0
Le 11ᵉ dudit moys payé audit appoticaire pour ledit Paris 16 s.	fl.	1.	4.	0
Le 17ᵉ dudit moys 9 fl. 3 s.	fl.	9.	3.	0
Le 31ᵉ dudit moys 9 fl. 3 s.	fl.	9.	3.	0
Le 14ᵉ apvril 1564 9 fl. 3 s.	fl.	9.	3.	0
Le 28ᵉ dudit moys 9 fl. 3 s.	fl.	9.	3.	0
Le 12ᵉ may 1564 9 fl. 3 s.	fl.	9.	3.	0
Le 26ᵉ dudit moys 9 fl. 3 s.	fl.	9.	3.	0
Le 14ᵉ juing 1564 10 fl.	fl.	10.	0	0
Le 10ᵉ aoust 1564 10 fl.	fl.	10.	0	0
Le 11ᵉ octobre 1564 20 fl.	fl.	20.	0	0
Le 26ᵉ decembre 1564 40 s.	fl.	3.	4.	0

Paris who writes down the sermons

The 7 February 1561 30 s.	fl.	2.	6.	0
The 21 of the said month 30 s.	fl.	2.	6.	0
The 7 March 1561 30 s.	fl.	2.	6.	0
The 21 of the said month 30 s.	fl.	2.	6.	0
The 4 April 1561 30 s.	fl.	2.	6.	0
The 18 of the said month 30 s.	fl.	2.	6.	0
The 2 May 1561 30 s.	fl.	2.	6.	0
The 16 of the said month 24 s.	fl.	2.	0	0
The 30 of the said month 30 s.	fl.	2.	6.	0
The 13 June 1561 30 s.	fl.	2.	6.	0
The 27 of the said month 30 s.	fl.	2.	6.	0
The 1 July 1561 4 s.	fl.	0	4.	0
The 11th of the said month 30 s.	fl.	2.	6.	0
The said [?] 13. 6 d.	fl.	1.	1.	6
The 25 July 1561 45 s.	fl.	3.	9.	0
The 8 August 1561 45 s.	fl.	3.	9.	0
The 22d of the said month 45 s.	fl.	3.	9.	0
The 5th of September 1561 45 s.	fl.	3.	9.	0
The 19th of the said month 45 s.	fl.	3.	9.	0
The 1st of October 1561 60 s.	fl.	5.	0	0
The 17th of the said month 60 s.	fl.	5.	0	0
The 31st of the said month 60 s.	fl.	5.	0	0
The 23d of November 1561 60 s.	fl.	5.	0	0
The 25 of the said month 60 s.	fl.	5.	0	0
The 12th of December 1561 60 s.	fl.	5.	0	0
The 24th of the said month 60 s.	fl.	5.	0	0
The 5 January 1562 66 s.	fl.	5.	6.	0
The 19 of the said month 66 s.	fl.	5.	6.	0
The 6 February 1562 6 fl.	fl.	6.	0	0
The 1 March 1562 7 fl. 6 s.	fl.	7.	6.	0
The 3d of April 1562 8 fl. 9 s.	fl.	8.	9.	0
The 17th of the said month 8 fl. 9 s.	fl.	8.	9.	0
The 1st of May 1562 6 fl. 3 s.	fl.	6.	3.	0

The 15th of the said month 9 fl. 3 s.	fl.	9.	3.	0
The 29th of the said month 9 fl. 3 s.	fl.	9.	3.	0
The 12th of June 1562 9 fl. 3 s.	fl.	9.	3.	0
The 10th of July 1562 9 fl. 3 s.	fl.	9.	3.	0
The 21st of the said month 9 fl. 3 s.	fl.	9.	3.	0
The 7th of August 1562 9 fl. 3 s.	fl.	9.	3.	0
The 21st of the said month 9 fl. 3 s.	fl.	9.	3.	0
The 4 September 1562 9 fl. 3 s.	fl.	9.	3.	0
The 18th of the said month 9 fl. 3 s.	fl.	9.	3.	0
The 2d of October 1562 9 fl. 3 s.	fl.	9.	3.	0
The 25th of the said month 9 fl. 3 s.	fl.	9.	3.	0
The 9th of November 1562 9 fl. 3 s.	fl.	9.	3.	0
The 23d of the said month 9 fl. 3 s.	fl.	9.	3.	0
The 11th of December 1562 9 fl. 3 s.	fl.	9.	3.	0
The 4 January 1563 9 fl. 3 s.	fl.	9.	3.	0
The 22d of the said month 9 fl. 3 s.	fl.	9.	3.	0
The 5th of February 1563 9 fl. 3 s.	fl.	9.	3.	0
The 10th of the said month 9 fl. 3 s.	fl.	9.	3.	0
The 1st of March 1563 9 fl. 3 s.	fl.	9.	3.	0
The 15th of the said month 9 fl. 3 s.	fl.	9.	3.	0
The 2d of April 1563 9 fl. 3 s.	fl.	9.	3.	0
The 16th of the said month 9 fl. 3 s.	fl.	9.	3.	0
The 30th of the said month 9 fl. 3 s.	fl.	9.	3.	0
The 14th of May 1563 9 fl. 3 s.	fl.	9.	3.	0
The 25th of the said month paid to Boniface the apothecary for the said Paris 9 s.	fl.	0	9.	0
The 28th of the said month 9 fl. 3 s.	fl.	9.	3.	0
The 11th of June 1563 9 fl. 3 s.	fl.	9.	3.	0
The 25th of the said month 9 fl. 3 s.	fl.	9.	3.	0
The 9th of July 1563 9 fl. 3 s.	fl.	9.	3.	0
The 23d of the said month 9 fl. 3 s.	fl.	9.	3.	0
The 6th of August 1563 9 fl. 3 s.	fl.	9.	3.	0
The 20th of the said month 9 fl. 3 s.	fl.	9.	3.	0
The 3d of September 1563 9 fl. 3 s.	fl.	9.	3.	0
The 10th of the said month paid to the said apothecary for the said Paris and his wife 35 s.	fl.	2.	11.	0
Total		441.	4.	6

776ᵛ

The 17th of September 1563 9 fl. 3 s.	fl.	9.	3.	0
The 1 October 1563 9 fl. 3 s.	fl.	9.	3.	0
The 15th of the said month 9 fl. 3 s.	fl.	9.	3.	0
The 29th of the said month 9 f. 3 s.	fl.	9.	3.	0
The 12th of November 1563 9 fl. 3 s.	fl.	9.	3.	0
The 26th of the said month 9 fl. 3 s.	fl.	9.	3.	0
The 10th of December 1563 9 fl. 3 s.	fl.	9.	3.	0
The 24th of the said month 9 fl. 3 s.	fl.	9.	3.	0
The 7 January 1564 9 fl. 3 s.	fl.	9.	3.	0
The 21st of the said month 9 fl. 3 s.	fl.	9.	3.	0
The 4th of February 1564 9 fl. 3 s.	fl.	9.	3.	0

The 18th of the said month 9 fl. 3 s.	fl.	9.	3.	0
The 3d of March 1564 9 fl. 3 s.	fl.	9.	3.	0
The 11th of the said month paid to the said apothecary for the said Paris 16 s.	fl.	1.	4.	0
The 17th of the said month 9 fl. 3 s.	fl.	9.	3.	0
The 31st of the said month 9 fl. 3 s.	fl.	9.	3.	0
The 14th of April 1564 9 fl. 3 s.	fl.	9.	3.	0
The 28th of the said month 9 fl. 3 s.	fl.	9.	3.	0
The 12th of May 1564 9 fl. 3 s.	fl.	9.	3.	0
The 26th of the said month 9 fl. 3 s.	fl.	9.	3.	0
The 14th of June 1564 10 fl.	fl.	10.	0	0
The 10th of August 1564 10 fl.	fl.	10.	0	0
The 11th of October 1564 20 fl.	fl.	20.	0	0
The 26th of December 1564 40 s.	fl.	3.	4.	0

SOURCE: AEG, Arch. hosp., Kq 1, fols. 776ᵛ, 967.

Appendix B
Selected Expenditures from the Extraordinary Accounts of the *Bourse française:* August 1559–November 1562

Toute despence extraordinaire despuis le premier aoust 1559

A deux femmes des ministres absens,	5 f		
Pour une douzaine et demye de nouveaulx testamens de Monsieur Maccard,	4 f	6 s	
A trois pauvres chez Monsieur de Normandye,	3 f	1 s	
Rendu à Monsieur de Normandye,	12 f		
Rendu encores à Monsieur de Normandye,	7 f	4 s	
Rendu à Monsieur de Normandye,	36 f		6 d

Despence extraordinaire pour les pauvres au moys de septembre 1559

A Denys pour la relieure de 2 douzaines de catechismes en cuyr,	4 f	
A luy mesmes pour 15 nouveaulx testamens partie en cuyr partie en parchemin,	5 f	
Rendu tant à Monsieur de Normandye comme à Monsieur de Sainct Germain par les mains de Monsieur de la Touche,	33 f	2 s
A ung pauvre garçon bourguignon pour le conduyre jusques à Basle par l'ordonnance de la Compaignie,		15 s
A ung jeune homme pour aller à Lyon par l'ordonnance de la Compaignie,		20 s
Rendu à Monsieur de Normandye,	32 f	8 s

Despence extraordinaire pour les pauvres au moys d'octobre 1559

Item j'ay rendu à Monsieur de Normandye 19 écus pistoletz qu'il avoit avancez pour

189

ung ministre qui a esté envoyé en Gascoigne dont il y a la cedule de Antesignanus [Pierre Davantes] pour responce, valent lesdits 19 écus pistoletz,	95 f		
A Maistre Françoys venu de Lausanne pour rendre à Maistre Pierre Viret,	10 f		
Item pour le louaige d'une maison pour les femmes d'aucuns ministres envoyez en France laquelle apartient au Prevost de Clugny,	52 f	1 s	
Rendu à Monsieur de Normandye qu'il a avancé à plusieurs jours,	21 f	8 s	
Plus à luy mesme encores pour une aultre partye,	29 f	2 s	

Despence extraordinaire pour les pauvres au moys de novembre 1559

A la femme de Maistre Helye ministre absent chargee de cinq petiz enfans,	4 f		
Pour l'amenaige de neuf cordes de boys au logis de Monsieur de Normandye à 7 sols la corde,	5 f	3 s	
A ung pauvre homme chez Monsieur de Normandye,		9 s	
Rendu à Monsieur de Normandye,	15 f		
A Piramus qui est venu de Paris estant echapé de la main des bourreaulx et tyrans,	20 f		
A un pauvre allemand recommandé par Monsieur de Beze pour retourner en son pais,	5 f	2 s	6 d
A ung bon homme de ceste Eglise par la communication du conseil de Monsieur Calvin,	30 f		
A Julienne pour la façon des abiz qu'elle a faiz oultre 3 florins qu'elle a receuz de Monsieur de Normandye,	4 f	3 s	
Au filz de Gohier pour ung nouveau testament grec relié,		15 s	
A plusieurs pauvres par l'ordonnance de la Compaignie,		31 s	
Item et à Maistre Jacques Chapel, minister,	2 f	6 s	
Item et envoyé à Estienne Girar par son homme par lequel il m'envoya demande argent une portugaloise, 5 écus sol et 8 testons valant le tout ensemble,	104 f	2 s	6 d
Chez Monsieur de Normandye distribué à diverses personnes,	4 f		

Item donné à ung pauvre verrier chez
Monsieur de Normandye,   12 s

Rendu à Monsieur Remé [*sic;* René] qu'il a
avancé par ordonnance de la Compaignie,   11 f   6 d

A Baltazar pour la façon des abiz qu'il a faiz
oultre 2 florins qu'il a receu de Monsieur
de Normandye, je lui ay encores baillé,   4 f   6 s

A ung pauvre garçon que nous avons
envoyé exprez à Grenoble,   2 f   3 s

Rendu à Monsieur de Sainct Germain qu'il a
baillé pour envoyer à ung pauvre
prisonnier de Grenoble,   5 f   2 s   6 d

Despence extraordinaire pour les pauvres au moys de decembre 1559

Item rendu à Monsieur de Normandye,   10 f   7 s

Baillé mercredy 12e chez Monsieur de
Normandye,   3 f   4 s   6 d

A Pierre Bourgeoys presté soubz le credit
de Monsieur René,   10 f

Le dimanche 17 chez Monsieur de
Normandye à plusieurs pauvres,   3 f   9 s   6 d

A ung bon personnaige de ceste Eglise,
Chaperon,   20 f

A ung quidam recommandé par Monsieur
Viret lequel s'en alloit en Angleterre,   2 f   4 s   4 d

Item et le mercredy 20e chez Monsieur de
Normandye à plusieurs pauvres,   7 f

Samedy à la fin du preche . . . la
Compaignie donné à plusieurs pauvres,   5 f

Dimanche 24 baillé chez Monsieur de
Normandye,   18 s

Item et le mardy 26e chez Monsieur de
Normandye,   4 f   8 s

Mercredi chez Monsieur de Normandye,   6 f   4 s

Au pauvre Pyramus donné encores,   10 f

Monsieur de Normandye rendu,   13 f   2 s

A plusieurs pauvres chez Monsieur de
Normandye le dernier decembre,   7 f   8 s

Du moys de janvier 1560

A Charles Hernes par ordonnance de la
Compaignie pour avoir du cuyr pour
travailler,   5 f

A Denys libraire pour la relieure de
cinquante psalmes à 2 sols . . .   8 f   4 s

Mercredi chez Monsieur de Normandye à
plusieurs pauvres,   23 s

A ung pauvre garcon pour avoir porté des fagoz,			9 d
A Henry Gon pour quelques fagoz qu'il a envoyez chez Monsieur de Normandye,		18 s	
Dimanche chez Monsieur de Normandye pour plusieurs pauvres,	6 f	3 s	
Encores cedit mesme jour à ung pauvre chez Monsieur de Normandye,		10 s	
Item à Jehan de Tere pour lever quelque petite marchandise,	5 f		
A Denys sur la relieure de 50 psalmes,	5 f	6 s	3 d
A Maistre Symon,		12 s	
Mercredy 17e chez Monsieur de Normandye,	6 f	2 s	6 d
Dimanche 21e chez Monsieur de Normandye,	2 f	7 s	
A Denys libraire encores pour parchever la relieure de 50 psalmes,	2 f	9 s	9 d
Rendu à Monsieur de Normandye,	22 f	7 s	
A plusieurs pauvres chez Monsieur de Normandye dimanche 28e,	6 f	6 s	
Mercredy 30e chez Monsieur de Normandye,	9 f	3 s	

Despence extraordinaire faicte au moys de fevrier 1560

Dimanche 4e chez Monsieur de Normandye,	8 f	4 s	
Item et le lundy 5e par commandement de la Compaignie,		20 s	
Le mercredy 7e chez Monsieur de Normandye,	6 f	2 s	
A Denys libraire pour la relieure de 24 nouveaux testamens,	6 f		
A Hierost lequel a esté prisonnier, par l'ordonnance de la Compaignie,	5 f		
A Denys libraire pour la relieure de deux douzaines de testamens,	6 f		
Dimanche 11 febvrier chez Monsieur de Normandye,	4 f	6 s	
Mercredy 14e chez Monsieur de Normandye,	9 f		
Dimanche 18 chez Monsieur de Normandye,	8 f		
Mercredy chez Monsieur de Normandye,	2 f	8 s	
A ung pauvre soldat recommandé,		12 s	

	f	s	d
Dimanche 25ᵉ chez Monsieur de Normandye,	11 f	2 s	

Despence extraordinaire au mois de mars 1560

	f	s	d
Dimanche chez Monsieur de Normandye, y comprins ung pauvre garçon frere du beau frere du grefier,	11 f	4 s	
A Jehan de Tere pour les enfans qu'il enseigne,		18 s	
Mercredy 6ᵉ chez Monsieur de Normandye,	2 f	5 s	
A Trucheron pour quelques parties,		12 s	6 d
Mercredy 20ᵉ chez Monsieur de Normandye,	3 f	3 s	
Envoyé à ung pauvre homme prisonnier à Grenoble par Monsieur Perlier[?],	5 f		
Rendu à Monsieur de Normandye pour plusieurs parties qu'il a frayées,	19 f	11 s	
A Piramus,	2 f		
A plusieurs pauvres chez Monsieur de Normandye le dimanche dernier de ce moys,	3 f	4 s	
A Salomon Camuz[?] par ordonnance de la Compaignie pour payer sa maison,	6 f		

Despence extraordinaire pour les pauvres au moys d'apvril 1560

	f	s	d
A quelques pauvres chez Monsieur de Normandye le mercredy 3ᵉ,		21 s	
A quelques pauvres par l'ordonnance de la Compaignie,	2 f	6 s	
Le dimanche 7ᵉ chez Monsieur de Normandye,	3 f		
Du coste du Monsieur René tant pour ce voyaige comme pour ce qu'il avoyt avancé la sepmaine passee,	28 f	9 s	
A plusieurs pauvres personnes sur la sepmaine,	2 f		
A plusieurs pauvres chez Monsieur de Normandye le mercredy 17ᵉ,		9 s	3 d
A plusieurs pauvres chez Monsieur de Normandye le dimanche 21ᵉ,	3 f	11 s	11 d
Dimanche 28ᵉ chez Monsieur de Normandye,	9 f	3 s	3 d
Item encores à une aultre ascavoir Pierre Conseil,		18 s	9 d
Rendu à Monsieur de Normandye,	12 f		

Despence extraordinaire faicte pour les pauvres au moys de may 1560

A ung aultre pauvre chez Monsieur de Normandye,		9 s	
Mercredy 15e chez Monsieur de Normandye,	7 f	7 s	
Presté à Monsieur de Besze[?] pour Maistre Jehan Randon mallade,	52 f	1 s	
A Maistre Jacques Chapel par ordonnance de la Compaignie,	5 f		
Dimanche 26e chez Monsieur de Normandye,	10 f		
Mercredy 28e chez Monsieur de Normandye à plusieurs pauvres,	4 f	5 s	
A la femme de Monsieur Barthelemy qui est allé à Chartres[?] et puis à Dieppe,	2 f		

Despence extraordinaire pour les pauvres au moys de juin 1560

A Maistre Jacques Chapel le dimanche 2e,	4 f	8 s	
Dimanche 9e chez Monsieur de Normandye à plusieurs personnes,	11 f	11 s	9 d
Rendu à Monsieur de Normandye pour plusieurs parties,	15 f	7 s	6 d
Mercredy 12e chez Monsieur de Normandye,	2 f	3 s	
A plusieurs pauvres chez Monsieur de Normandye,	2 f		
Dimanche 23e chez Monsieur de Normandye,	8 f		9 d
Mercredy 26e chez Monsieur de Normandye,	13 f	5 s	3 d
Ce mesme jour chez Monsieur de Normandye,	4 f	6 s	9 d

Despence extraordinaire pour les pauvres au moys de juillet 1560

Mercredy 10e chez Monsieur de Normandye,	6 f	6 s	
Ledit mesme jour rendu à Monsieur de Normandye,	41 f	6 s	
A ung quidam par les mains de Monsieur Autin [or Antin?],		31 s	3 d
Dimanche chez Monsieur Normandye,	6 f	6 s	
Dimanche 21e chez Monsieur de Normandye à plusieurs pauvres,	10 f	7 s	6 d
A ung pauvre jeune homme pour faire son voyaige en Normandye,		18 s	
Chez Monsieur de Normandye à plusieurs pauvres par les mains de Monsieur Paré,	5 f	4 s	

	f	s	d
Rendu à Monsieur de Normandye pour argent qu'il avoyt avancé à plusieurs foys et mesmes pour Maistre Jacques Besson auquel a esté donné 3 écus pour lui,	28 f		3 d
Du dimanche precedent 28 chez Monsieur de Normandye,	11 f		
Le mercredy 31 chez Monsieur de Normandye,	6 f	9 s	

Argent debourcé extraordinairement pour les pauvres ou moys d'Aoust 1560

	f	s	d
Chez Monsieur de Normandye le dimanche 4ᵉ,	12 f		
A Denys libraire pour les nouveaulx testaments avancé,		27 s	
Mercredy chez Monsieur de Normandye,	9 f	8 s	
A Denys libraire pour le parachevement de la relieure de 2 douzaines de nouveaulx testamentz,	3 f	9 s	
A Jehan de Tere pour s'en aller au pays,	12 f	11 s	
A Monsieur Maccard pour 24 nouveaulx testamenz,	6 f		
A Monsieur René pour payer la chambre d'ung ministre,	8 f	7 s	
A Denys pour la relieure de 38 testamentz,	6 f	4 s	
Samedy 31ᵉ après le preche baillé,	3 f	8 s	

Despence extraordinaire pour les pauvres au moys de septembre 1560

	f	s	d
Dimanche premier jour dudit moys chez Monsieur de Normandye,	8 f	6 s	
Dimanche 8ᵉ chez Monsieur de Normandye,	6 f		
Mercredy 11 chez Monsieur de Normandye,	5 f	8 s	
Dimanche 15ᵉ chez Monsieur de Normandye,	5 f	11 s	
A Monsieur René pour rendre au Prevost[?] Bergevin qu'il avoit baillé en nostre nom à quelques compaignons,	7 f	6 s	
A ung jeune homme de Provence par ordonnance de la Compaignie,		15 s	
Mardy 17ᵉ par ordonnance de la Compaignie,	3 f	9 s	
Mercredy chez Monsieur de Normandye,	11 f	9 s	9 d
Dimanche 22ᵉ au matin baillé chez Monsieur de Normandye,	3 f		
A Pierre Helon de Rene en Bretaigne,	5 f		

	f	s	d
Rendu à Monsieur de Normandye pour plusieurs parties,	68 f	2 s	
Plus baillé à deux foys chez Monsieur de Normandye, livré par les mains du Sieur Boucher 10 florins, l'autre par Monsieur du [sic: de] Paré 12 florins 6 sols en mon absence pour ce,	22 f	6 s	
Item pour troys douzaines et demye de nouveaulx testamentz de feu Monsieur Maccard à 3 sols piece,	10 f	6 s	6 d
Dimanche 29e chez Monsieur de Normandye baillé par les mains de Monsieur du Paré,	10 f	3 s	6 d

Despence extraordinaire pour les pauvres au moys d'octobre 1560

	f	s	d
Chez Monsieur de Normandye le mercredy 2e,	7 f	7 s	9 d
A Monsieur de Paré pour 8 bibles en françoys,	9 f	4 s	
Item au bon homme de Bretaigne, Pierre Helon,	5 f		
Relieure, pour cinq bibles en petit volume à Monsieur de Paré,	4 f	2 s	
Pour la relieure de troys petites bibles,		30 s	
Mercredy 16e chez Monsieur de Normandye à plusieurs pauvres,	11 f	10 s	
Rendu à Monsieur de Normandye,	5 f	11 s	
A ung pauvre homme pour s'en aller à Nismes,		14 s	
A Monsieur Cordernis[?] par ordonnance de la Compaignie,	16 f		
A troys aultres chez Monsieur de Normandye mercredy, 30e,	2 f		
A Maistre Jehan du Taulne[?] par les mains des collecteurs d'Anjou,	5 f		

Despence extraordinaire pour les pauvres au moys de novembre 1560

	f	s	d
Encores au libraire qui aprens le mestier à Balthasar pour ce second moys comme il luy a esté accordé,	5 f	3 s	
A deux pauvres garçons pour s'en retourner en France,		15 s	
Donné à une pauvre Provençale recommandée par Monsieur Du Four,		8 s	
Pour la relieure de 2 douzaines psalmes,	4 f		
A Anthoine Ogier pour une bible,		9 s	2 d

A ung bon homme d'Anjou Taulne[?] par
    les mains de ceulx de la cueillette,   5 f

Dimanche 23e,   19 s

Au libraire pour la relieure de 18 psalmes,   3 f

Despence extraordinaire pour les pauvres au moys de decembre 1560

    A deux pauvres personnes mercredy 3e,   12 s

    A plusieurs personnes le mardy 17e,   2 f   6 s

    Rendu au Sieur Jehan Personne 15 florins 6
        sols qu'il avoit avancé par nostre
        ordonnance à plusieurs pauvres mallades,   15 f   6 s

    Rendu à Monsieur de Normandye,   5 f   1 s

    Donné à troys pauvres personnes,   22s   6d

    Mercredy donné à troys pauvres personnes,   12 s

    Encores pour la façon de quelques chemises,   5 s

    A ung jeune homme de Grenoble pour s'en
        aller au pays,   4 f

Despence extraordinaire pour les pauvres au moys de janvier 1561

    Pour la relieure de deux nouveaulx
        testamens et 22 Psalmes,   4 f   2 s

    A Mademoyselle du Plessix par
        l'ordonnance de la Compaignie,   5 f   6 s   3 d

    A ung pauvre ministre fugitif de la vallee
        d'Augroigne [a valley of Piedmont,
        "Angrogna" in Italy],   5 f

Despence extraordinaire faicte pour les pauvres au moys de febvrier 1561

    Mercredy chez Monsieur de Normandye,   4 f

    Mercredy 26e chez Monsieur de
        Normandye,   9 f

Despence extraordinaire pour les pauvres au moys de mars 1561

    A Loys Mile pour relier quelques livres
        qu'il avoyt mis en gaige,   12 s

    A ung pauvre garçon pour s'en retourner à
        Paris,   6 s

    Rendu à Monsieur de Paré qu'il avoyt
        avancé par ordonnance de la Compaignie,   10 f   8 s

Despence extraordinaire pour les pauvres au moys d'apvril 1561

    A Pierre Cousturier pour s'en retourner à
        Paris par ordonnance de la Compaignye,   10 f   6 s

    A une pauvre femme du ministre envoyé à
        Coutance,   2 f

    Au ministre d'Angroigne,   15 f

Despence extraordinaire faicte pour les pauvres au moys de may 1561

    A ung pauvre trouvé prez la maison de la
        ville pour le louaige d'une chambre,   8 f

A la femme de Jacques Vilet[?] pour leur ayder à louer une chambre,		15 s	
A Jehan Singlant pour s'en aller jusques à Lyon,	2 f	1 s	
Rendu à Monsieur de Normandye,	3 f		

Despence extraordinaire pour le moys de juing 1561

A Monsieur de la Court pour avoir transcrypt les Psalmes de Monsieur de Baise pour envoyer en court,	12 f	6 s	
A luy mesme pour avoir transcript le privilege desdits Psalmes,		8 s	
Pour une douzaine de bibles achaptees de Madamoyselle du Plessis,	12 f		
Rendu à Monsieur de Paré qu'il a fourny en diverses parties,	7 f	2 s	
A Maistre Pierre pour avoir mis les Psalmes en musicque,	10 f		
A Jehan Parran par ordonnance de la Compaignie,	2 f		

Despence extraordinaire faicte pour les pauvres au moys de juillet 1561

Rendu à Monsieur de Beze qu'il avoyt bailé encores à Maistre Pierre le Chantre pour les psalmes en muscique oultre les 10 florins cy dessuz,	20 f	5 s	

Despence extraordinaire pour les pauvres au moys d'aoust 1561

Dimanche 3, à plusieurs pauvres en la place Sainct Pierre,		34 s	6d
Donné à Cornille pour une foys par ordonnance de la Compaignie,	50 f		
Audit Cornille mesme encores ledyt jour feust advisé de luy donner encores ving cinq florins,	25 f		
A Maistre Jehan Le Roux pauvre eschollier par l'ordonnance de la Compaignie,		15 s	
Dimanche en la place Saint Pierre à plusieurs pauvres,	3 f	2 s	
A Monsieur de Paré rendu pour la relieure de plusieurs nouveaulx testamentz et paletes,	4 f	5 s	
A celluy qui a transcript la premiere copie des Psalmes de Monsieur de Beze avant que Monsieur La Court les escripvit pour les envoyé à la Court,	12 f	6 s	

Argent debourcé extraordinairement pour les pauvres au moys de septembre 1561

Rendu au Sieur Jehan Personne qu'il avoyt
avancé à Maistre Bevigne[?] à plusieurs
foys,   16 f

A Monsieur le greffier,   15 s

Despence extraordinaire pour les pauvres au moys d'octobre 1561

A Paris,   5 f

Au libraire pour deux bibles et cinq
volumes,   20 s

A Jacques Bruyere suyvant ce qui avoyt de
long temps esté ordonné,   5 f   3 s   9 d

Despence extraordinaire pour les pauvres au moys de novembre 1561

Toute despence extraordinaire pour les pauvres au moys de decembre 1561

Despence extraordinaire pour les pauvres au moys de janvier 1562

A Noel pauvre boulanger qui luy a esté
ordonné par la Compaignie,   50 f

Item et encores à Noel le boulanger par
l'advis a esté accordé pour s'acquieter
envers ung nommé Bastier,   25 f

Rendu à Jehan Personne pour quelques
argent qu'il a avancé pour quelques gens
de son quartier,   12 f   2 s

A Maistre Aynierant[?] pour les Psalmes
envoyez à Monsieur de Beze asçavoir
pour la relieure de 44,   48 f   9 s

Item pour le ruban oultre celluy que ledit
Aynierant a fourny,   3 f

A Symon lequel porta lesdits livres avancé
premierement,   10 f

                                                                            1
A luy encores en partant,   13 f   6 s   7 d   florin*

                                                                            ung
Pour la toille ciree pour l'emballaige   9 s   3 d   florin

A Symon encores pour le parachevement de
son voiaige au retour de Paris où il
demoura 32 ou 34 [sic; 33] jours,   19 f   6 s

Despence extraordinaire pour les pauvres au moys de febvrier 1562

Despence faicte extraordinairement pour les pauvres au moys de mars 1562

A Thomas Dourteau [sic; Courteau] pour
une douzaine de Psalmes pour envoyer à
Monsieur de Beze,   5 f

A ung pauvre garçon pour la relieure de
quelques Psalmes encores,   1 s

Despence extraordinaire pour les pauvres au moys d'apvril 1562

---

*In the original manuscript, these one florin entries are located to the right of the columns
ordinarily used by the bookkeeper.

Despence extraordinaire pour les pauvres au moys de may

Despence extraordinaire pour les pauvres au moys de juing 1562

Despence extraordinaire pour les pauvres au moys de julliet 1562

A Robinet pour la relieure de 56 Psalmes
par accord faict par Monsieur René, 2
sols, 6 deniers,   11 f   8 s

Despence extraordinaire pour les pauvres au moys d'aoust 1562

A Maistre Artus ledit jour baillé pour ses
peines d'avoir travaillé aux comptes des
Psalmes pour les pauvres six pistolletz,   30 f   7 s   6 d

Despence extraordinaire pour les pauvres au moys de septembre 1562

Aux officiers qui ont revus les libraires à
troys diverses fois pour le faict des
Psalmes,   22 s   6 d

Despence extraordinaire pour les pauvres au moys d'octobre 1562

A ung ministre de Mascons,   5 f   3 s   9 d

A quelques aultres comme il feust ordonné
par la Compaignie le mercredy 13e,   4 f   4 s

Despence extraordinaire pour le moys de novembre 1562

Rendu à Jehan Combez pour une hallebarde
et une espee qu'il a achaptee a ung pauvre
homme par le commandement de la
Compaignie,   26 s

SOURCE: AEG, Arch. hosp. Hj 2, August 1559–November 1562, passim.

Appendix C
Payments to Paris, Copyist of Calvin's Sermons, from the "Great Book of the Assisted," 1568–1575

Le 3 janvier 1568 8s	8 s	
Le 7e dudit moys 1 coupe de bled		
Le 21e dudit moys 1 coupe de bled		
Le 18e dudit moys 1 coupe de bled		
Le 3e mars 1568 1/4 de bled		
Le 17e dudit moys 1/4 de bled		
Le 31e dudit moys 1/4 de bled		
Le 14e dudit moys 1/4 de bled		
Le 28e dudit moys 1/4 de bled		
Le 8e may 1568 12 s	1 f	
Le 11e dudit moys 30 s	2 f	6 s
Le 12e dudit moys 1/4 de bled		
Le 25e dudit moys 24 s	2 f	
Ledit jour 1/4 de bled		
Le 9e juing 1568 1/4 de bled		
Le 22e dudit moys 6 s		6 s
Le 23e dudit moys 1/4 de bled		
Le 3e juillet 1568 15 s	1 f	3 s
Le 7e dudit moys 1/4 de bled		
Le 21e dudit moys 1/4 de bled		
Le 2e aoust 1568 15 s	1 f	3 s
Le 7e dudit moys 12 s	1 f	
Le 13e dudit moys 7 s		7 s

Le 18ᵉ dudit moys 1/4 de blé			
Le 31ᵉ dudit moys à l'appoticaire 20 s 6d	1 f	8 s	6 d
Le 1 septembre 1568 1/4 de bled			
Le 15 dudit moys 1/4 de bled			
Le 28ᵉ dudit moys 4 s		4 s	
Le 12ᵉ octobre 1568 10s		10 s	
Le 23ᵉ novembre 1568 5 s		5 s	
Le 15ᵉ decembre 1568 6 s		6 s	
Le 4ᵉ janvier 1569 6 s		6 s	
Le 18ᵉ dudit moys 12 s	1 f		
Le 15ᵉ febvrier 1569 5 s		5 s	
Le 15ᵉ mars 1569 8 s		8 s	
Le 12ᵉ apvril 1569 5 s		5 s	
Le 10ᵉ may 1569 5 s		5 s	
Le 7ᵉ juing 1569 5 s		5 s	
Le 19ᵉ juillet 1569 5 s		5 s	
Le 30ᵉ aoust 1569 5 s		5 s	
Le 8ᵉ novembre 1569 12 s	1 f		
Le 22ᵉ dudit moys 12 s	1 f		
Le 6ᵉ decembre 1569 12 s	1 f		
Le 20ᵉ dudit moys 12 s	1 f		
Le 3ᵉ janvier 1570 12 s	1 f		
Le 14ᵉ febvrier 1570 12 s	1 f		
Le 28ᵉ dudit moys 12 s	1 f		
Le 5 apvril 1570 8 s		8 s	

	266 f	8 s	6 d
	441 f	4 s	6 d
	708 f	1 s	
Au fueillet 776	25 f	5 s	9 d
	733 f	6 s	9 d
Au fueillet 967	708 f	1 s	
Le 9ᵉ may 1570 15 s	1 f	3 s	
Le 6ᵉ juing 1570 12 s	1 f		
Le 4ᵉ juillet 1570 30 s	2 f	6 s	
Le 15ᵉ aoust 1570 12 s	1 f		
Le 10ᵉ octobre 1570 8 s		8 s	
Le 7ᵉ novembre 1570 6 s		6 s	
Le 19ᵉ decembre 1570 12 s	1 f		
Le 16ᵉ janvier 1571 12 s	1 f		
Le 30ᵉ dudit moys 12 s	1 f		

Le 13ᵉ febvrier 1571 12 s	1 f		
Le 27ᵉ dudit moys 10 s		10 s	
Le 27ᵉ mars 1571 12 s	1 f		
Le 10ᵉ apvril 1571 12 s	1 f		
Le 24ᵉ dudit moys 12 s	1 f		
Le 8 may 1571 12 s	1 f		
Le 22ᵉ dudit moys 12 s	1 f		
Le 5 juing 1571 12 s	1 f		
Le 13ᵉ dudit moys 12 s	1 f		
Le 19ᵉ dudit moys 12 s	1 f		
Le 3ᵉ juillet 1571 12 s	1 f		
Le 31ᵉ dudit moys 12 s	1 f		
Le 11 septembre 1572 12 s	1 f		
Le 23ᵉ dudit moys 9 s		9 s	
Le 5ᵉ novembre 1572 (pour luy ung bas de chausses)			
Le 6ᵉ dudit moys 5 s		5 s	
Le 17 aout 1575 18 s 9 d	1 f	6 s	9 d
	25 f	5 s	9 d
Au fueillet 967	708 f	1 s	

The 3 January 1568, 8 s.		8 s
The 7th of the said month, one cutting of grain,		
The 21st of the said month, one cutting of grain,		
The 18th of the said month, one cutting of grain,		
The 3d of March 1568, ¼ of grain,		
The 17th of the said month, ¼ of grain,		
The 31st of the said month, ¼ of grain,		
The 14th of the said month, ¼ of grain,		
The 28th of the said month, ¼ of grain,		
The 8th of May 1568, 12 s.	1 f	
The 11th of the said month, 30 s.	2 f	6 s
The 12th of the said month, ¼ of grain,		
The 25th of the said month, 24 s.	2 f	
The said day, ¼ of grain,		
The 9th of June 1568, ¼ of grain,		
The 22d of the said month, 6 s.		6 s
The 23d of the said month, ¼ of grain,		
The 3d of July 1568, 15 s.	1 f	3 s
The 7th of the said month, ¼ of grain,		

The 21st of the said month, ¼ of grain,			
The 2d of August 1568, 15 s.	1 f	3 s	
The 7th of the said month, 12 s.	1 f		
The 13th of the said month, 7 s.		7 s	
The 18th of the said month, ¼ of grain,			
The 31st of the said month to the apothecary, 20 s 6 d.	1 f	8 s	6 d
The 1 September 1568, ¼ of grain,			
The 15 of the said month, ¼ of grain,			
The 28th of the said month, 4 s.		4 s	
The 12th of October 1568, 10 s.		10 s	
The 23d of November 1568, 5 s.		5 s	
The 15th of December 1568, 6 s.		6 s	
The 4th of January 1569, 6 s.		6 s	
The 18th of the said month, 12 s.	1 f		
The 15th of February 1569, 5 s.		5 s	
The 15th of March 1569, 8 s.		8 s	
The 12th of April 1569, 5 s.		5 s	
The 10th of May 1569, 5 s.		5 s	
The 7th of June 1569, 5 s.		5 s	
The 19th of July 1569, 5 s.		5 s	
The 30th of August 1569, 5 s.		5 s	
The 8th of November 1569, 12 s.	1 f		
The 22d of the said month, 12 s.	1 f		
The 6th of December 1569, 12 s.	1 f		
The 20th of the said month, 12 s.	1 f		
The 3d of January 1570, 12 s.	1 f		
The 14th of February 1570, 12 s.	1 f		
The 28th of the said month, 12 s.	1 f		
The 5 April 1570, 8s.		8 s	
	266 f	8 s	6 d
	441 f	4 s	6 d
	708 f	1 s	
from page 776	25 f	5 s	9 d
	733 f	6 s	9 d
At the page 967	708 f	1 s	
The 9th of May 1570, 15 s.	1 f	3 s	
The 6th of June 1570, 12 s.	1 f		
The 4th of July 1570, 30 s.	2 f	6 s	
The 15th of August 1570, 12 s.	1 f		

The 10th of October 1570, 8 s.		8 s	
The 7th of November 1570, 6 s.		6 s	
The 19th of December 1570, 12 s.	1 f		
The 16th of January 1571, 12 s.	1 f		
The 30th of the said month, 12 s.	1 f		
The 13th of February 1571, 12 s.	1 f		
The 27th of the said month, 10 s.		10 s	
The 27th of March 1571, 12 s.	1 f		
The 10th of April 1571, 12 s.	1 f		
The 24th of the said month, 12 s.	1 f		
The 8 May 1571, 12 s.	1 f		
The 22d of the month, 12 s.	1 f		
The 5 June 1571, 12 s.	1 f		
The 13th of the said month, 12 s.	1 f		
The 19th of the said month, 12 s.	1 f		
The 3d of July 1571, 12 s.	1 f		
The 31st of the said month, 12 s.	1 f		
The 11 September 1572, 12 s.	1 f		
The 23d of the said month, 9 s.		9 s	
The 5th of November 1572 (for him a pair of stockings)			
The 6th of the said month, 5 s.		5 s	
The 17 August 1575, 18 s 9 d.	1 f	6 s	9 d
	25 f	5 s	9 d
from page 967	708 f	1 s	

SOURCE: AEG, Arch. hosp., Kq 1; pages are actually folios.

Appendix D
Guidelines of the *Bourse française*
January 1581

C'est l'ordre qui a esté tenu jusques icy pour la plus grande part en l'election des diacres et en l'administration des deniers de la Bourse des pauvres estrangers confermé tant par l'advis des ministres de ceste Eglise qu'approbation desdictz diacres et bonne partie des contribuans à ladicte Bourse assemblés pour ce faict le cinquiesme de janvier 1581.

1. Que le nombre des diacres sera de cinq pour le present et leur charge annuelle et qu'au commencement de chascune annee on eslira ou confermera ceulx de l'annee precedente tous ou partie.

2. Qu'on eslira les plus propres que faire ce pourra selon la reigle de l'Apostre (Romains 12, 8, et 1 Timothee 3, 8), assavoir par la pluralité des voix tant des ministres de ceste Eglise que des contribuans à la Bourse qui se trouveront avec eulx, estans pour ce faire appelez par les collecteurs.

3. Que les diacres adviseront de commettre à l'ung d'entre eulx la recepte et distribution des deniers appatenans à ladicte Bourse tant des ordinaires qui seront recueillis par les collecteurs chascun en sa dizaine que de tous aultres quelz qu'ilz puissent estre, et ce pour le temps de demye annee sauf à continuer la mesme recepte à ung mesme par leur advis pour une aultre demye annee consecutive si besoing est et que celuy qui recevra lesdictz deniers enrigistera les sommes par luy reçuees pour en rendre bon et loyal compte.

4. Que les diacres s'assembleront une foys la sepmaine d'ordinaire tant pour distribuer les aumosnes qu'ilz adviseront estre requises pour les pauvres vefves et aultres estans en necessité selon la condition d'ung chascun, comme pour pourvoir à tous aultres affaires concernans la subvention desdictz pauvres. Et quand aulx affaires extraordinaires survenans, qu'ilz y advisent le plus diligemment et commodement que faire ce pourra selon

l'exigence du cas, faisans debvoir de visiter soigneusement les personnes desdictz pauvres mesmement quand il y en aura des malades, donnans ordre qu'iceulx malades soyent pensez par les medecin, chirurgien et appoticaire qu'ilz emploieront pour cest effect.

5. Qu'ilz advisent aussy entre eulx à la subvention des passans selon qu'ilz jugeront estre le plus propre et convenable.

6. Et affin que les pauvres respectent tant mieulx et comme ilz doibvent lesdictz diacres en leur administration, qu'il y ayt ung des ministres de ceste Eglise choisi par iceulx ministres, lequel par l'espace de six moys assiste en leur assemblee et lequel quand il y escherroit quelque dificulté la rapporte à l'assemblee desdictz ministres pour y adviser, suyvant l'advis desquelz ministres lesdictz diacres se reigleront après avoir esté ouys en la Compagnie d'iceulx ministres.

7. Que celuy qui aura receu et manié les deniers de ladicte Bourse dresse ses comptes au bout de sa demye annee et les rande aulx auditeurs d'iceulx comptes, puys estans signés par lesdictz auditeurs, les presente à la Compagnie des ministres affin qu'ilz soyent signez aussy par deulx d'iceulx, puys qu'ilz let mettent en l'armoire des papiers des pauvres afin qu'on puisse tousjours monstrer comment on c'est gouverné en ceste administration.

8. Qu'on eslise troys auditeurs des comptes ou que l'on conferme ceulx qui auront esté esleuz en la mesme façon qui a esté dit des diacres. Le semblable se face aussy des collecteurs quand il y escherra.

9. Que de Cene en Cene il y ayt censure en ladicte compagnie des diacres le ministre deputé avec eulx recueillant les voix et sujet le premier à censure afin de s'acourager et advertir fraternellement en leur debvoir.

10. Qu'au temps des elections susdictezs se fera lecture des presens articles à l'entree afin que toute l'assemblee entende mieulx comment il y fault proceder.

Source: AEG, Arch. hosp., Kg 19, fol. 1.

Appendix E
Notarial Documents Pertaining to Jean de Borne in His Appeal to the Deacons of the *Bourse française* for His Inheritance from Damoiselle Gabrielle de Borne

Quictance de 243 florins, 13 sous, 4 deniers, faicte par noble Jehan de Borne en faveur des seigneurs, diacres, et administrateurs des deniers aulmosnes aux paouvres estrangers de Geneve.

(Receipt of 243 florins, 13 sous, 4 deniers, made by Noble Jean de Borne in favor of the lords, deacons, and administrators of the alms money of the poor foreigners of Geneva.)

Au nom de Dieu sachent tous qui ces presentes letres verront liront et ourront que l'an mil cinq cens soixante six et le vingthuictieme jour d'apvril par davant moy Jehan Ragueau notaire public et bourgeoys de Geneve soubzigné et les tesmoings soubznommés s'est personnellement constitué noble Jehan de Borne, lequel, ayant requis Spectables Jehan Budé, Jehan Dallamont, Yves Bergevin et Regnauld Anjorrant diacres et ayans charges de l'administration des aulmones des paouvres estrangers de ceste cité de Geneve de luy delivrer la somme des deux tiers de cent escutz à raison de cinquante solz l'escut dont l'ung des tiers luy a esté legué et quant a l'aultre tiers à luy apartenant comme substitué à Catherine Jehanne legataire avec luy pour l'aultre tiers et despuys decedee; et le tout par le moyen du testament et legatz en iceluy coutenuz faictz par defuncte noble Gabriele soeur de pere d'iceluy Jehan. Et à ces fins exhibe et produict ausdictz diacres une attestation datee du sixieme d'apvril present moys signee par Spectable Pierre d'Airebaudoze d'Anduse de Chambrun. Item une aultre attestation du sep-

208

tieme de ce mesme present moys soubzignee par Spectables Jehan Terouch[?] ministre en l'Eglise de Sablieres et Barthelemy Maurin et Jehan Bernard juges audit lieu de Sablieres. . . .

(In the name of God knowing all to whom these present letters will come, will be read, and will be opened, that in the year 1566, and the twenty-eighth day of April before me, Jean Ragueau, public notary and bourgeois of Geneva, the undersigned, and the below named witnesses, Noble Jean de Borne personally established himself, who, having requested of Spectable Jean Budé, Jean Dallamont, Yves Bergevin, and Regnauld Anjorrant, deacons in charge of the administration of the alms of the poor foreigners of this city of Geneva, to deliver to him the sum of two-thirds of one hundred ecus at the rate of fifty sous the ecu of which one of the thirds was willed to him and as for the other third [it] belongs to him as substitute for Catherine Jeanne, legatee, with him for the other third and since then deceased, and all by means of the will and legacy contained in it made by the defunct Noble Gabriele, sister of the father of this Jean, and to this end exhibited and produced to the said deacons an attestation dated from the sixth of April, this present month, signed by Spectable Pierre d'Airebaudoze of Auduze of Chambrun. Also another attestation from the seventh of the same present month signed below by Spectables Jean Terouch[?] minister in the church of Sablieres and Barthelemy Maurin and Jean Bernard, judges in the said place, Sablieres. . . .)

Item une aultre attestation en date du dixhuictieme de ce present moys d'apvril soubzignee par Spectable Marcial Malzieu ministre de la Parolle de Dieu a Sainct de Marveroux[?] pour tesmoigner qu'il est demourant en l'eglise reformee selon la Parolle de Dieu qui est a Sablieres au pays de Vivarez et ha graces à Dieu bon tesmoignage de ladicte Eglise et aultres et qui doibt suffire pour la condition dudit legat consideré que du temps dudit Testament ledit testateur ne se pouveyt encores asseurer ny estre advertye de ce qu'il a pleu à Dieu elargir sa faveur pour establiz ladite Eglise de Sablieres et aultres Eglises reformees audict pays de Vivarez et autres lieux de France et soubz mesme reformation et reglement qui sont les Eglises ausquelles se rapporte ladicte condition joinct que ledit de Borne sert de diacre et maistre d'escolle en ladicte Eglise de Sablieres et lesquelles charges il ne peult delaisser pour accomplir plus precisement ladite còndition; ce qui ne reviendroyt aussi à plus grand profict ou edification de l'Eglise. Sur laquelle requeste lesdictz diacres ayans veu lesdictes attestations et icelles communiquees aux spectables ministres de ceste Eglise et suyvant leur advis et en consideration des raisons susdictes et du coutenu esdictes attestations enclinans à ladicte requeste ont consenty de delivrer comme de faict en ma presence ladicte somme des deux tiers de cent escutz a esté delivree audict noble Jehan de Borne par noble Charles de Joan seigneur de Jonvillier au nom desdictz spectable Budé, Dallamont, Bergevin et Anjorrant comme diacres susdictz . . .

(Again another attestation on the date of the eighteenth of this present month of April signed by Spectable Marcial Malzieu, minister of the Word of God at Saint of Marveroux[?] in order to witness that he remains in the church reformed according to the Word of God that is at Sablieres in the country of Vivarais and has, thanks to God, a good testimony from the said church and others that ought to suffice for the condition of the said legacy considering that at the time of the said will the said testator could not yet ascertain nor be informed that it pleased God to extend his favor in order to establish the said church of Sablieres and other Reformed churches in the said country of Vivarais and other places of France under the same reformation and rule as are the churches to which the said condition relates. Also, the said de Borne serves as deacon and master [teacher] of the school in the said church of Sablieres which charges he can not forsake in order to accomplish more precisely the said condition; that also would not amount to the church's greatest profit or edification. On this request the said deacons having seen the said attestations and these communicated to the spectables ministers of this church and following their advice and in consideration of the above said reasons and that the contents of the said attestations, inclining to the said request, consented to deliver as fact in my presence the said sum of two-thirds of one hundred ecus, delivered to the said Noble Jean de Borne by Noble Charles Joan, lord de Jonvillier, in the name of the said spectable Budé, Dallamont, Bergevin and Anjorrant as the above said deacons . . .)

SOURCE: AEG, Not. Jean Ragueau, vol. 8, fols. 240–42.

Appendix F
Text of a Genevan Decision for Five Boys in a Case of Sodomy, 7–16 March 1554

Veu les confessions et confrontations des cinq jeunes garçons faictes en la présence de noz magnifiques seigneurs syndiques, et de nous soubsignés touchant le crime de sodomie et après avoir le tout bien entendre consideré et examiné et conferé ensemble nostre advis est: que ledit crime est suffisamment verifié contre lesdits garçons respectivement et que iceluy crime est des plus attroces et abhominables que on trouve poinct comme appert par l'Escripture saincte et par le droict. Aussi c'est une chose trop estrange et monstrueuse en telle jeunesse. Toutefoys trouvons difference de crime et de peine entre lesdits garçons car les deux plus jeunes ont esté seulement patientz d'icelluy crime et pour leur grande jeunesse n'ont peu apprehendez tant facilement l'horreur et attrocité dudit crime que les aultres troys, neantmoingtz ne peuvent en tout estre exemptes de la peine car ilz ont desjà quelque jugement et capacité de raison. Parquoy et afin qu'a l'advenir il aye horreur et souvenance de leur mal pour en eviter la reitteration semble sauf meilleur advis qu'ilz doibvent estre baptus de verges en lieu secret et en la presence de nosdicts seigneurs et aulcungs de leurs parens afin que lesdits jeunes garçons souffrantz telle peine en la presence de leursdits parens ayent à l'advenir crainte d'eulx et se rendent plus subjectz à leurs castigations et admonitions et pour leur donner mieulx à congnoistre la grace qu'on leur a faicte et l'habomination de leur mal sera bon de leur representer la peine du feu en bruslant quelques fagotz davant eulx avec grande commination de ladite peine du feu s'ilz y retournent et du tout soyt faict registre.

Au reste quant aux aultres troys plus aagés, consideré leurdit aage que trouvons estre capable dudit crime joinct leur habitude et corpulence et congnoissance qu'ilz avoyent d'icelluy crime et de la peine dudit crime avec la longue continuation et reiteration non seulement avant avoir veu executer à mort et brusler le dernier sodomite, mais aussi apres ladite execution, comme ilz ont tous troys confessé, ce qui demonstre leur grande et . . . malice par laquelle aulcung d'eux auront desja attente à stuprez de petites filles, à ces causes ne trouvons que par le droict la jeunesse les puisse exempter de la peine dudit crime. Car quand les loix parlent d'excuser les delictz de jeunesse, elles font expresse declaration des enfans qui s'entend de ceulx qui ne sont assez capables de raison et ne sçavent bonnement qu'ilz font, et non pas de ceulx qui sont puberes ou prochains de puberté et capables de malice pour pouvoir commettre et perpetrer telz crimes, et pourtant suyvant la disposition de droict ne pourons trouver qu'ilz ne meritent la mort. Toutefois non pas taut rigoureuse que si lesdits garçons eussent esté plus aagés et suffiroit à rigueur de droict pour rendre la peine correspondante à tel crime et moins rigoureuse pour leur jeunesse qu'ilz feussent noyés.

Toutefois s'il faisoit à vos excellences leur faire grace de mort semble neantmoings qu'ilz ne peuvent estre exemptés de peine corporelle publique et exemplaire car n'est possible que ledit crime soyt caché et cellé et y auroit plus grand danger et scandals en l'impunité ou couverture de la peine qu'en la punition publique et exemplaire. Attendu aussi qu'il fault craindre l'ire de Dieu qui n'a voulu. . . . tel crime et en tant de personnes pour le laisser impuny mesme et tel lieu. Et seroit danguer que nostredit seigneur manifestast avec plus horrible punition ce que les hommes auront voulu cacher et que son ire envellopast plusieurs aultres. Parquoy nous semble que lesdits troys plus grands garçons pour le moings meritent d'estre fouettés publiquement par les carrefours la corde au col et qu'en quelques lieux publics où ilz seront fouettés soyt allumé ung feu pour leur demonstrer la peine que meritoit tel crime abhominable et qui leur sera signifiee et comminé en cas de recidivation. Et afin qu'après ladit peine du fouet ilz ne soyent en horreur au public pour certain temps seront mis et enserrés en quelque lieu où bon vous semblera et une partie audit temps nourris au pain et à l'eaux et, si bon vous semble, les bulles en garde aux parens sera avec commination d'observer ce qui leur sera enjoint.

> Jehan Calvin
> Abel Poundin
> Daniel Colladon
> François Chevallier

(Having seen the confessions and confrontations of the five young boys made in the presence of our magnificant lord syndics and of ourselves undersigned, touching the crime of sodomy and after having heard, considered, and examined everything well and conferred together, our advice [is] that the said crime is sufficiently verified against the said boys respectively and that this crime is of the most atrocious and abominable that one finds as [it] appears by the Holy Scripture and by the law. Also, it is a thing too strange and monstrous in such youth. Yet we find a difference of crime and of punishment between the said boys because the two youngest only endured this crime and because of their great youth could not have understood very easily the horror and atrocity of the said crime as the other three did. Nevertheless, they could not entirely be exempted from the punishment because they already had some judgment and capacity of reason. For this reason and to the end that in the future one has horror and remembrance of their evil in order to avoid the reiteration of it, [it] seems without better advice that they ought to be beaten with switches in a secret place and in the presence of our said lords and some of their parents to the end that the said young boys suffer such pain in the presence of their said parents to have in the future fear of them, and to be rendered more subject to their castigations and admonitions and to give them better understanding of the grace that one made them and the admonition of their evil. [It] will be good to represent to them the pain of the fire by burning several faggots before them with grand commination of the said pain of the fire if they return to it and [that] of everything a record be made.

For the rest, as for the three other older [boys], having considered their said age, we find [them] to be capable of the said crime, in addition to their habit and corpulence and understanding that they have of the said crime and of the punishment of the said crime with the long continuation and reiteration not only having seen executed to death and burned the last sodomite, but also, after the said execution, as they have all three confessed, which demonstrates their grand and . . . malice by which each of them has already tried to debauch young girls. In these cases we do not find that [their] youth can through the law exempt them from the punishment of the said crime, because, when the laws speak of excusing the misdemeanors of youth, they make express declaration of children who are to be understood to be those who are not enough capable of reason and do not know well what they are doing and not of those who are pubescent or near puberty and capable of malice in order to be able to commit and perpetrate such crimes, and yet following the disposition of the law we cannot find that they merit death, not yet so rigorously as if the said boys had been older and would suffer at the rigor of the law in order to render the punishment that corresponds to such a crime and less rigorous for their youth that they be drowned.

Yet, if it pleases your Excellencies to render them mercy from death, it seems, nevertheless, that they cannot be exempted from corporal public punishment and example, because it is possible that the said crime be hidden and concealed, and there would be greater danger and scandal in the impunity or covering of the punishment than in the public and exemplary punishment. Hear also that it is necessary to fear the anger of God who does not want . . . such crime and in so many persons to leave it unpunished even in such a place, and there would be a danger that our said Lord would manifest with more horrible punishment what men would have wanted to hide and that his anger would envelop several others. Therefore, it seems to us that the said three older boys at least merit to be whipped publicly through the intersections, the cord at the neck, and that in several public places where they are whipped that a fire be illuminated in order to demonstrate to them the punishment that such an abominable crime merits and that will signify to them and menace them in case of recidivism and to the end that after the said punishment of the whipping, they be in horror to the public. For a certain time [they] will be put and locked up in such a place where it will seem good to you and a part of the said time nourished with bread and water, and if it seems good to you, the bulls in keeping to the parents will be in commination to observe what will be enjoined to them.

> Jehan Calvin
> Abel Poundin
> Daniel Colladon
> François Chevallier)

SOURCE: AEG, Proc. Crim. 502, loose manuscript of three pages, fols. 1–2.

Appendix G
A Résumé of the Confessions and Sentencing of Charles Lourdois and His Wife, Jeanne Varrot, and an Opinion in the Case by Germain Colladon, 8–27 August 1568

Procès Criminel 1469

Charles Lourdois de Meaux . . . Jehanne, fille de feu Jehan Varrot, dudit Meaux, femme dudit Lourdois. Lesquels estans constitués prisonniers ont volontairement confessé: premierement ladite Jehanne qu'il y a environ deux ans que pour avoir mellieur moyen et commodité de nourrir leurs enfans dont ilz ont bon nombre, elle s'abandonna à larrecins et despuys y a tousjours continué en plusieurs et divers lieux usant de toutes les commodités qu'elle en pouvoyt avoir . . . et desrobe plusieurs sommes tant en or que testons et autre monoye soyt en changeant quelques especes ou au marché ou à la boucherie ou mesmes en prenant du vin à pot. Desquelz larrecins elle a despuys nourry et entretenue avec quelque peu de labeur que faisoient toutte leur famille se traittans plus largement qu'il ne leur apartenoyt tant en viandes que acoustremens et meubles dont ilz ont amassé bonne quantité. Oultre ce qu'ilz ont heu argent d'abondant jusques à en prester en un seul lieu la somme de vingt escuz.

Le tout en sceu et consentement dudit Charles son mary, auquel elle s'est souvent declaré luy disant qu'il seroyt cause qu'elle seroyt pendue, sans que touttesfois iceluy ayt jamais tasché d'y remedier estant bien content d'estre entretenu par ce moyen.

Davantage ont tous deux confessé qu'encores qu'ilz ayent esté en charge à la bourse des paouvres l'espace de 14 ans, ilz ne laisserent pour tant l'annee passee, qu'ilz estoient qui dist est bien garni de leurs larrecins, de charger ladite Bourse des medecines et fraiz à eux fournis par l'apoticayre en une leur maladie.

Sentence de Charles Lourdois et de sa femme:

Condamnés "à estre liés, menés et fouettés de verges par tous les carrefours de ceste cité et autour d'icelle jusques a effusion de sang fasson accoustumee et en oultre marqués et flettris de leurs armoiries chacun sur l'espaule droitte et de là estre bannis, comme ilz les bannissent perpetuellement de leur ville et terres d'icelle à les debvoyr vuider dans trois jours et n'y jamais revenir à peine d'estre pendus et estranglés et c'est pour servir d'exemple aux autres qui telz cas voudroient comettre. . . .

Prononcé le 27 d'avril 1568

Germain Colladon

Veu les procez criminelz faicts contre Charles Lourdoys et Jehanne Varrot sa femme . . . et confessions faictes par lesditz Lourdoys et sa femme . . . qu'ilz soyent venus fort pouvres en ceste cité dès long temps et ayant ceste[?] chargés de plusieurs enfans et qu'ilz se soyent faict baillee l'ausmoune ordinaire de la Bourse des pouvres estrangers jusques y a environ ung an, joinct qu'ilz n'ont peu grandement gaigner de leur travail, toutefoys se sont trovés bien . . . avoir presté sommes notables mesmes jusques à vingt escuz pour une foys à ung boucher et d'autre argent sur une foule et encore s'est trouvé jusques à quinze escuz d'or contant en leur maison quand ilz ont esté prins et se trouve aussi qu'ilz se sont bien traictés et ont tenu propoz de bailler bon mariage à leur fille pour laquelle ilz ont achepté drapz de hault pris.

Consideré aussi le larrecin que tous deux ensemble ont faict en abusant tant impudemment des biens et ausmounes des pouvres par si long temps dont se trouvera sur les livres des dyacres desdites ausmounes que dès l'an 1559 ilz ont receu seize solz à chascune distribution et quelques foys d'advantage, plus ladite femme et leurs enfans ont . . . estre vestus aux despens desdites ausmounes et mesmes y a seulement environ ung an qu'ilz ont faict payer sur lesdites ausmounes le medecin et appoticaire qui les avoit visités et traictés, . . . ce qui est ung larrecin qualifié et espece de sacrilege.

Parquoy et attendu que telz larrecins ont esté continues par long temps et à plusieurs foys semble que tous deux meritent d'estre pendus et estranglés à la mort.

Colladon

Procès Criminel 1469

(Charles Lourdois of Meaux . . . Jeanne, daughter of the deceased Jean Varrot of the said Meaux, wife of the said Lourdois, who being constituted prisoners have voluntarily confessed:

First, the said Jeanne about two years ago in order to have a better means and way of feeding their children, of whom they have a good number, abandoned herself to thefts and since then has always continued in several and diverse places using all the means at her disposal . . . and has stolen several sums as much in gold as testons and other money either in changing some cash or at the market or at the butcher's or even in taking some wine from a pot, with which thefts she since nourished and maintained their entire family with very little labor, treating themselves more generously than suited them as much with meat as with clothing and furnishings of which they have amassed a good quantity. Also, that they had had money of such an abundance to the point of loaning in one sole place the sum of twenty ecus.

Everything [was done] with the knowledge and consent of the said Charles, her husband, to whom she often confessed, saying to him that he would be the cause that she would be hung, without each time [his] ever having attempted to prevent her, being well content to be maintained by these means.

Moreover, both have again confessed that although they were supported by the *Bourse* of the poor for the space of fourteen years, they permitted, however, last year, which as was said was well garnished with their thefts, to charge the said *Bourse* for expenses and medicines furnished to them by the apothecary in their illness.)

Sentence of Charles Lourdois and of his wife:

Condemned (to be bound, led, and beaten with switches through the intersections of this city and around here until the effusion of blood in the accustomed fashion and further marked and branded on their arms each on the right shoulder and from there to be banished, as they banish them perpetually from their city and lands from which they must evacuate in three days and never come back there at the pain of being hung and strangled, and it is in order to serve as an example to the others who would want to commit such an act. . . .) Pronounced 27 April 1568.

Germain Colladon:

(Seen, the criminal procedures made against Charles Lourdoys and Jeanne Varrot, his wife . . . and confessions made by the said Lourdoys and his wife . . . that they came very poor into this city a long time ago and charged with several children and that they put themselves in the charge of the ordinary alms of the fund of the poor foreigners for about one year, joined to that that they have so little greatly gained from their work. Yet, they found it good . . . to loan notable sums, even up to twenty ecus once to a butcher and other money to a fool, and besides there was found up to fifteen ecus of gold in their house when they were taken, and it is also found that they are well treated and intended to give a good marriage to their daughter for which they bought high-priced cloth.

Consider also the theft that the two together made in abusing so shame-lessly the goods and alms of the poor for such a long time by being found on the books of the deacons of the said alms. Since the year 1559 they have received sixteen sous at each distribution and sometimes more. Plus, the said woman and their children have . . . been clothed at the expenditure of the said alms and only about a year ago they had the doctor and apothecary who visited them and treated them paid by the said alms. . . , which is a qualified theft and kind of sacrilege.

For that and understood that such thefts have continued for a long time and several times, it seems that the two of them merit being hung and strangled until dead.)

Colladon

Appendix H
Real Estate Transactions from the Family Papers of Jean Budé de Vérace

17 décembre 1551	Archat par Jean de Budé de biens sur le fief de Nicolas de la Biellée.
17 novembre 1556	Acquis par Jean de Budé à Nicolas et Amblard de Lonnex de la Terre . . .
26 juin 1571	Acquis de Jean de Budé de Pierre Delapierre.
27 septembre 1573	Vente a Jean de Budé par Jean Thuril de Gaillard . . . de 3 poses pour 172 florins.
18 décembre 1573	Acquis pour Jean de Budé de Claude Debarge à Thonex.
27 octobre 1573	Acquis par Jean de Budé . . . pour deux poses pré et vigne, lieudit au Chatellet, prix: 120 florins.
1 janvier 1577	Vente à Jean de Budé d'une vigne par Jean Turil de Gaillard.
12 mars 1582	Vente à Jean de Budé par Guillaume, d'une maison . . . prix 1700 florins.
14 décembre 1583	Achat par Jean de Budé à Bertrand, d'une vigne . . .
29 avril 1584	Achat à Pierre Polliens par Jean de Budé d'une vigne.
10 septembre 1584	Achat à Bertrand, fils de feu Pierre Polliens, par Jean de Budé d'une vigne.
31 janvier 1585	Achat à Pierre Du Cimitiere par Jean de Budé d'une pièce de Terre au Salève.
25 février 1587	Achat par Jean de Budé d'une vigne.
9 décembre 1607	Achat à Claude Debornand par Jean de Budé d'une vigne.

SOURCE: AEG, Arch. de famille, 3e série, Budé de Vérace.

Appendix I
The Will of Marguerite de Morel, Wife of François Budé

. . . ordonné que Noble damoyselle Catherine Budé, vefve du defunct noble Jehan Anjorrant, luy vivant president en la court du Parlement à Paris, soeur dudict defunct noble François Budé, ensemble ses enfans, famille et compagnye demoure tant que à elle plairra en la maison dudict defunct son mary comme elle y a esté receue honnorablement et fraternellement par sondict mary declarant que telle a esté la volonté de sondict defunct mary à laquelle elle s'est conformee et desire, veult et ordonne que sesdits enfans se conforment, leur enjoignant de l'honnorer et aymer comme leur tante l'accommedant de meubles comme elle a faict despuys sa venue jusques à ce jourd'hui, priant aussi ladicte damoyselle Catherine Budé et, en son absence, damoyselle Marguerite Budé, vefve de feu noble Guillaume Trye, tantes desdictes Jehanne et Judith de icelles addresser, conduire et enseigner en la craincte de Dieu, les leur recommandant comme leur niepces. Item et pour la tutele, gouvernement et administration des personnes et biens de sesdictes deux filles, ladite testatrice suyvant la volonté dudict defunct son mary a nommé et nomme Nobles Jehan Budé, seigneur de Verace et Regauld Anjorrant, seigneur de Sully et chascung d'eulx tant conjoinctement que divisement tellement que ce qui aura esté commancé par l'ung puisse estre poursuivy et mené à fin par l'aultre, les leur recommandans, les supplians aussy de conserter à sesdictes filles les biens meubles qu'ilz cognoistront se pouvoir maintenir et estre gardez pour la commodité et necessité de sesdictes filles et pour l'honneur de leur maison, sans les vendre, suyvant en ce la volonté dudict defunct son mary, laquelle il leur avoyt declaré et à elle testatrice aussy ung peu auparavant son deces et comme ilz sçavent, s'asseurant en telle chose comme aussy a faict sondict mary de leur prudhommye et loyaulté et qu'en toutes choses ilz procureront le bein profict et honnoeur

220

de sesdictes filles et de leur maison et derechef selon la volonté dudict defunct son mary prye et requiert ledit noble Anjorrant de prendre la charge de la conduicte de sesdictes filles par le conseil et advis de noble et magnifique seigneur Galeaz Carraciol, marquiz de Vico, et dudict seigneur de Verace, les supplians tous de continuer la bonne affection et amityé qui a esté entre eulx et ledict defunct, noble François Budé son mary, envers sesdictes filles, voulant aussy suyvant la volonté dudict defunct son mary que sesdictes deux filles demourent en leurdicte maison et y soient nourries et entretenues avec telle conduicte et conseil que dessus sans estre distraictes d'icelle maison sinon que la necessité du temps, profict et biens desdictz enfans requist changement selon l'advis et conseil des susdictz. Item et pour l'execution de son present testament ladicte testatrice a nommé et nomme les susdictz noble Jehan Budé, seigneur de Verace, et Regnauld Anjorrant, seigneur de Sully.

(. . . ordered that Noble Damoiselle Catherine Budé, widow of the deceased Noble Jean Anjorrant, who, when he was alive, was president in the court of the Parlement at Paris, sister of the said deceased Noble François Budé, together with her children, family and company, live as long as it pleases her in the house of the said deceased, her husband, as she had been honorably and fraternally received there by her said husband, declaring that such had been the will of her said deceased husband, to which she conforms and desires, and wants and ordains that the said children conform, enjoining them to honor her and love her as their aunt, accommodating her with furniture as she did since her coming to this day, requesting also the said *Damoiselle* Catherine Budé and in her absence *Damoiselle* Marguerite Budé, widow of the deceased Noble Guillaume Trye, aunts of the said Jeanne and Judith, to address, guide, and teach them in the fear of God, recommending them to them as their nieces.

Also, for the guardianship, government and administration of the persons and possessions of the said two girls, the said testatrix, following the will of the said deceased, her husband, named and names, Nobles Jean Budé, Lord of Verace, and Regauld Anjorrant, Lord of Sully, and each of them as much conjointly as separately, so that that which will have been begun by one of them can be followed and led to the end by the other, recommending them to them, supplicating them also to conserve to said girls the movable possessions that they are aware of in order that they maintain and are kept for the comfort and necessity of her said girls and for the honor of their house, without selling them, following in this the will of the said deceased, her husband, which he had declared to them and to herself, testatrix, also, a little before his death, and as they know, assuring her in such a matter as also did her said husband, of their valor and loyalty and that in all things they will procure the welfare, profit, and honor of her said girls and of their house and again once more according to the will of the said deceased, her husband, entreats and requests the said Noble Anjorrant to take charge of the conduct of her said girls with the counsel and advice of noble and magnificent Lord Galeaz Carraciol [Galeazzo Caracciolo], Marquis de Vico, and of the said Lord of Vérace, supplicating them all to continue the good affection and friendship that has been between them and the said deceased, Noble François Budé, her husband, toward her said girls, wanting also, following the will of her said deceased husband, that her said two girls remain in their said house and be nourished there and maintained with such guidance and counsel as above stated without being separated from this said house unless the needs of the age, profit, and welfare of the said children require change according to the advice and counsel of the above said. Also, for the execution of her present will, the said testatrix named and names the above said Noble Jean Budé, Lord of Vérace and Regnauld Anjorrant, Lord of Sully.)

SOURCE: AEG, Not. Jean Ragueau, vol. 11 (1569), pp. 1001–5.

Notes

CHAPTER 1. THE *BOURSE FRANÇAISE* AND ITS SETTING: AN INTRODUCTION

1. Significant literature on the problem of the Reformation's impact on charitable activity includes Paul Bonenfant, "Les origines et le caractère de la réforme de la bienfaisance publique aux Pays-Bas sous le règne de Charles-Quint," *Revue Belge de Philosophie et d'Histoire* 5 (1926): 887–904 and 6 (1927): 207–30; Natalie Zemon Davis, "Poor Relief, Humanism, and Heresy," in *Society and Culture in Early Modern France: Eight Essays by Natalie Zemon Davis* (Stanford, Calif.: Stanford University Press, 1975), pp. 17–64; Jean-Pierre Gutton, *La société et les pauvres: l'exemple de la généralité de Lyon, 1534–1789* (Paris: Société d'Edition "Les Belles Lettres," 1970); W. K. Jordan, *Philanthropy in England, 1480–1660: A Study of the Changing Pattern of English Social Aspirations* (London: George Allen and Unwin, 1959); Robert M. Kingdon, "The Deacons of the Reformed Church in Calvin's Geneva," *Mélanges d'histoire du seizième siècle offerts à Henri Meylan* (Geneva: Librairie Droz, 1970), pp. 81–90; Robert Kingdon, "Social Welfare in Calvin's Geneva," *American Historical Review* 76 (February 1971): 50–69; and Carter Lindberg, "'There Should Be No Beggars Among Christians': Karlstadt, Luther, and the Origins of Protestant Poor Relief," *Church History* 46 (1977): 313–34.

See especially the excellent recent book by Elsie Anne McKee, *John Calvin on the Diaconate and Liturgical Almsgiving* (Geneva: Librairie Droz, 1984). McKee's special emphasis is the diaconate, whereas this volume is concerned with the archival documentation of the actual practice and functioning of the *Bourse française*. McKee offers a precise and insightful discussion of current literature on the historiographical issues in sixteenth-century poor relief. A general sociological change was under way, shifting the burden of poor relief from the uncertain, inequitable, and quite subjective dependence upon almsgiving to a somewhat more stable and rational process of care for the poor that would eventually be based on tax income and other public revenues in addition to revenues from the secularized endowment of the church. The Reformation accelerated the process in some areas. The reformers took up the ideas. The process toward public support of the poor was moved along through their persistence and strong emphasis on regular care for the poor. McKee's emphases are on alms in sixteenth-century Protestant worship, the exegetical history of Biblical texts that refer to the diaconate (pp. 139–84), and diaconal themes in Calvin's thought. She uses printed works and manuscript materials. This study relies almost entirely on unedited archival sources and includes a considerable quantity of original transcriptions from these sources.

2. J. Nolf, *La réforme de la bienfaisance publique à Ypres au seizième siècle* (Ghent: Librairie Scientifique E. Van Goethem, 1915), p. xi.

3. See the vivid description of begging in Davis, "Poor Relief, Humanism, and Heresy," pp. 24–27.

4. On John Geiler see E. Jane Dempsey Douglass, *Justification in Late Medieval Preaching: A Study of John Geiler of Keisersberg*, Studies in Medieval and Reformation Thought, vol. 1 (Leiden: E. J. Brill, 1966).

5. Juan Luis Vives, "On Assistance to the Poor," in *A Sixteenth-Century Urban Report*, ed. Alice Tobriner, Social Service Monographs, 2d ser. (Chicago: School of Social Service Administration, University of Chicago, 1971), pp. 33–57.

6. Many scholars attribute changes in welfare in Nuremberg to the Lutheran influence there even though the city was still Roman Catholic when the changes occurred. See, for instance, the reference to the new alms ordinance in the year 1522 in Gottfried Seebass, "The Reformation in Nürnberg," in the *Social History of the Reformation*, ed. Lawrence Buck and Jonathan Zophy (Columbus: Ohio State University Press, 1972), p. 25.

7. See Brian Pullan, *Rich and Poor in Renaissance Venice: The Social Institutions of a Catholic State to 1620* (Cambridge: Harvard University Press, 1971), and Gene Brucker, "Bureaucracy and Social Welfare in the Renaissance: A Florentine Case Study," *Journal of Modern History* 55 (1983): 1–21.

8. Nolf, *La réforme de la bienfaisance publique*, p. xii.

9. These were the comments of one Bishop Godeau in his *Discours sur l'établissement de l'Hôpital général* as quoted in Wilma Pugh, "Social Welfare and the Edict of Nantes: Lyon and Nîmes," *French Historical Studies* 8 (Spring 1974): 375.

10. Martin Luther, "Ordinance of a Common Chest, Preface, 1523," trans. Albert T. W. Steinhaeuser, rev. Walther I. Brandt, in *Luther's Works*, ed. Jaroslav Pelikan and Helmut Lehmann, vol. 45, *The Christian in Society II*, ed. Walther I. Brandt (Philadelphia: Muhlenberg Press, 1962), p. 173; "Ordenung enns gemennen tastens: Radschlag wie die genstlichen gutter zu handeln sind," in *D. Martin Luthers Werke: Kritische Gesamtausgabe (Weimar Ausgabe)* (Weimar: Hermann Böhlaus Nachfolger, 1891), 12: 11–30.

11. Martin Luther, "134: To Elector Frederick, Leisnig, August 11, 1523," in *Luther's Works*, vol. 49, *Letters II*, trans. and ed. Gottfried Krodel (Philadelphia: Fortress Press, 1972), pp. 45–47; "Nr. 643, Luther an Kurfürst Friedrich, Leisnig, 11 August 1523," in *D. Martin Luthers Briefwechsel (Weimar Ausgabe)* (Weimar: Hermann Böhlaus Nachfolger, 1933), 3 : 124–26. For a discussion of Luther and poor relief see Harold Grimm, "Luther's Contributions to Sixteenth-Century Organization of Poor Relief," *Archiv für Reformationsgeschichte* 61 (1970): 222–33.

12. On Strasbourg see Otto Winckelmann, *Das Fürsorgewesen der Stadt Strassburg vor und nach der Reformation bis zum Ausgang des sechzehnten Jahrhunderts* (Leipzig: Heinsieu, 1922).

13. See, for instance, Pullan, *Rich and Poor in Renaissance Venice;* Jordan, *Philanthropy in England, 1480–1660,* and Leslie Goldsmith, "Poor Relief and Reform in Sixteenth-Century Orleans" (Ph.D. diss., University of Wisconsin, Madison, 1980).

14. Archives d'État de Genève, Archives hospitalières, Dd 1, Livre des legatz faictz tant aux paouvres de l'Hospital general de Geneve, au College, que aux paouvres estrangiers. Dès le premier janvier 1580, 1580–1637, hereafter cited as AEG, Arch. hosp., Dd 1.

15. AEG, Arch. hosp., Ka 1–Ka 6, Bourse française, Livres Memorials des Diacres (6 April 1612–30 December 1691).

16. Bibliothèque Publique et Universitaire de Genève, Manuscrits suppl. 816 (41), Mémoires, notes, et documents sur la Bourse et l'Église italiennes, no. 8, "Libro di Memorie Diverse Della Chiesa Italiana Raccolte Dà Vincenzo Burlamachi" (1550–1669), hereafter cited as BPU, Manuscrits suppl. 816, pp. 1–113.

17. AEG, Manuscrits historiques, no. 223, Henri-Leonard Bordier, "Les Registres de la Bourse Française de Genève commençant au premier octobre 1550: Extraits des dits registres depuis le premier octobre 1550 jusqu'au premier octobre 1566" (October 1876).

18. "Ordonnances ecclésiastiques," in *Registres de la Compagnie des Pasteurs de Genève au temps de Calvin*, published under the direction of the Archives of the State of Geneva, vol. 1, *1546–1553*, ed. Jean-François Bergier (Geneva: Librairie Droz, 1964), pp. 7–8. In English translation see "Draft Ecclesiastical Ordinances," in *Calvin: Theological Treatises*, ed. J. K. S. Reid (Philadelphia: Westminster Press, 1954), pp. 64–66.

CHAPTER 2. IDEOLOGY AND ORIGINS OF THE *BOURSE FRANÇAISE:* JOHN CALVIN

1. For Calvin's social and economic thought see André Biéler, *La pensée économique et sociale de Calvin* (Geneva: Librairie de l'Université, Georg, 1961). For Calvin's political

thought see Harro Höpfl, *The Christian Polity of John Calvin* (Cambridge: Cambridge University Press, 1982).

2. Calvin sets up these four offices in his *Ecclesiastical Ordinances* of 1541. "Ordonnances ecclésiastiques," pp. 1–13; "Projet d'ordonnances ecclésiastiques, septembre et octobre 1541," in *Ioannis Calvini Opera Quae Supersunt Omnia*, ed. Guilielmus Baum, Eduardus Cunitz, and Eduardus Reuss, vol. 10, in *Corpus Reformatorum*, vol. 38 (Brunswick: C. A. Schwetschke and Sons, 1871), cols. 15–30; Emile Rivoire and Victor van Berchem, eds., *Les sources du droit du Canton de Genève*, vol. 2, *1461–1550* (Arau: H. R. Säuerlander & Cie., Imprimeurs-Éditeurs, 1930), pp. 377–90; in English translation, "Draft Ecclesiastical Ordinances," pp. 56–72. John Calvin also described the four offices in book 4, chapters 3–5 of *Institution de la religion chrétienne*, ed. Société Calviniste de France (Geneva: Labor et Fides, 1958), 4:53–100; for an English translation, see John Calvin, *Calvin: Institutes of the Christian Religion*, ed. John T. McNeill, trans. Ford Battles, Library of Christian Classics (Philadelphia: Westminster Press, 1960), 2:1053–1102.

3. See the letter of the Company of Pastors of Geneva to the churches of Normandy, 30 November 1564: "Nous adjoustons encores ce mot, qu'il nous semble qu'en tel cas, et generalement, il est bon que ceux qui sont commis à administrer la Parole ne soyent embrouillés des mises ne receptes, mais qu'on les entretienne sobrement et honnestement, soit par le moyen des diacres (qui seroit bien le meilleur) soit par autres moyens, selon la circonstance des temps et des lieux." (We add yet this word, that it seems to us that in such a case, and generally, it is good that those who are committed to administer the Word are not embroiled in investments or receipts, but that one keeps them soberly and honestly, either by the means of the deacons [which really would be the better] or by other means, according to the circumstance of time and place.) "Lettre de la Compagnie des Pasteurs de Genève aux Églises de Normandie," in *Registres de la Compagnie des Pasteurs de Genève*, vol. 2, *1553–1564*, ed. Robert M. Kingdon (Geneva: Librairie Droz, 1962), p. 140.

4. On the office of doctor see Robert W. Henderson, *The Teaching Office in the Reformed Tradition: A History of the Doctoral Ministry* (Philadelphia: Westminster Press, 1962).

5. Acts 6:1–6. Traditionally this text has been considered an account of the instituting of the first deacons. For a development of this argument and the subtleties in the interpretation of the text see McKee, *John Calvin on the Diaconate*, pp. 140–58.

6. 1 Tim. 3:8–13. See McKee, *John Calvin on the Diaconate*, pp. 159–84.

7. Deacon was the former occupation of three of the eighty-eight pastors sent from Geneva to France, 1555–62, listed in Robert Kingdon, *Geneva and the Coming of the Wars of Religion in France, 1555–1563* (Geneva: Librairie E. Droz, 1956), p. 142.

8. On the origins of the city hospital see Kingdon, "Social Welfare in Calvin's Geneva," pp. 52–57.

9. Ibid., pp. 59–60.

10. The handouts occurred every Sunday from 6:00 to 7:00 A.M. according to article twenty-nine of thirty-nine articles for the hospital, entitled "From the General Alms" and dated 10 March 1552. Article thirty provided for a prayer before the distribution:

De l'aumosne generale:
Item que quand lesditz paouvres seront assemblés tous ensemble que le ministre dudit Hospital doibge [sic] faire une priere affin que les paouvres recongnoissent quy c'est qu'envoie le bien que l'on leur distribue et ceulx quy le maintiennent et cella soit faict tous les dimenches avant que dystribuer ladite aumosne.

(Also that when the poor are assembled all together that the minister of the said hospital must make a prayer in order that the poor recognize who it is that sends the goods that one distributes to them and those who maintain it and that that be done every Sunday before distributing the said charity.)

AEG, Arch. hosp. Aa 2, "Registre des deliberations des Procureurs de l'Hospital" (23 March 1552–12 November 1560), fol. 4ᵛ. The following entries were made for books for children in the accounts of the hospital:

Item du 30ᵉ de janvier 1560 à Monsieur Jean Pynault pour les enfans de ceans ascavoir pour ceux de la 4ᵉ et 5ᵉ classe deux grammayres de Monsieur Quor[?] a 8 sols 6 deniers pièce . . .
Item pour lesdits enfans six payres de pseaumes à 3 sous 3 deniers piece . . .

(Also from the thirtieth of January 1560 to Monsieur Jean Pynault for the children of his [charge], that is to say for those of the fourth and fifth class, two grammars from Monsieur Quor[?] at 8 sous, 6 deniers the piece . . . Also for the said children six pairs [twelve] of Psalms at three sous, three deniers the piece . . .)

AEG, Arch. hosp., Fe, vol. 4, fol. 62ᵛ.

11. The first account book is entitled "Registre des pauvres" (Register of the poor), and the first page of the account books is dated 30 September 1550. The opening paragraph refers to the penultimate day of September for the commitment to office of three men to keep the accounts for the poor.

30 septembre 1550, pour tenir le compte de l'argent qui a esté receu pour les pauvres depuis le temps que la Compaignie commist à ceste office le seigneur Maldonnade, Monsieur de Thillat, et moy, qui feust le penultiesme jour de septembre l'an 500 cinquante [sic 1550], la Compaignie assemblee chez les freres de Burcy [Bury?] et d'Aimery [d'Aimen?]

(30 September 1550, in order to keep the account of the money that has been received for the poor since the time that the Company committed to that office the Lord Maldonnade, Monsieur de Thillat, and myself, which was the penultimate day of September, the year 500 [sic 1550], the Company assembled at the home of the brothers de Burcy [de Bury?] and d'Aimery [d'Aimen?])

AEG, Arch. hosp., Kg 12 (30 September 1550–September 1551), fol. 1.

12. The text describing the election reads as follows:

Annee commençant au moys de julliet 1554, le jeudy, 5ᵉ dudict moys, julliet, la Compaignie estant assemblé chez Monsieur Calvin, aprez avoir invocqué le nom de dieu, feurent eleuz diacres pour l'administration du bien des pauvres: Monsieur de Sainct Jeremie [sic, Germain], Monsieur René, Monsieur de La Touche, et moy [Jean Budé], conformé comme au paravant.

(The year beginning in the month of July 1554, Thursday, the fifth of the said month, July, the Company being assembled at the home of Monsieur Calvin, after having invoked the name of God, were elected deacons for the administration of the goods of the poor, Monsieur de Saint Jeremie [sic, Germain], Monsieur René, Monsieur de La Touche, and me [Jean Budé], confirmed as before.)

AEG, Arch. hosp., Kg 15 (July 1554–July 1555). The quotation is from the first page of the manuscript, although no page or folio number is shown. Hereafter unnumbered pages or folios will be identified by their location in the manuscript or by their date if they carry one.

13. Calvin's reference to the age of sixty was biblical: "Let a widow be enrolled if she is not less than sixty years of age, having been the wife of one husband" (1 Tim. 5:9; this and all succeeding English biblical translations are from the Revised Standard Version). See a full discussion of the role of the widows in an "Exegetical History of the Diaconate IV: Phoebe and the Widows (Rom. 16:1–2 with 1 Tim. 5:3–10)," in McKee, *John Calvin on the Diaconate*, pp. 205–23.

14. The ordinances dated from 5 January 1581. They were recorded at the beginning of the account book for 1582. AEG, Arch. hosp., Kg 19 (1582), fol. 1. For a transcription of these ten ordinances see "Reglement de la Bourse française," in *Registres de la Compagnie des Pasteurs de Genève*, vol. 4, *1575–1582*, ed. Olivier Labarthe and Bernard Lescaze (Geneva: Librairie Droz, 1974), pp. 353–54. A comparison can be made between these ordinances and those of 1562 of the Reformed church of Paris, *Police et ordre gardez en la distribution des deniers ausmonez aux pauvres de l'Eglise reformee en la ville de Paris, Bulletin de la Société d'Histoire du Protestantisme Français* 1 (1853): 255–59. Hereafter the *Bulletin* will be cited as *BSHPF.*

15. The registers of the city council of Geneva of 25 June 1545 state that Calvin "reported the death of a Frenchman, Monsieur David, who died in his house and willed to the poor of Strasbourg one thousand ecus and to the poor of Geneva one thousand ecus, asking attestation of his passing and last will." The council "ordered that his request be approved."

Sur ce que ledit sieur Calvin ministre a exposé le trespas de feuz Monsieur David qu'estoy françoy qu'est trepassé en sa mayson et a legué aux pouvres de Estrabourg mille escus et aux pouvres de Geneve mille escus demandant attestation de son trespas et derniere volonté, ordonne que sa requeste luy soyt oultroyé.

AEG, Registres du Conseil, vol. 40 (8 February 1545–7 February 1546), fol. 161; the Registres du Conseil will hereafter be abbreviated as Reg. Conseil. An alternate transcription of this quotation can be found in Baum, Cunitz, and Reuss, eds., *Ioannis Calvini Opera*, vol. 21, *Corpus Reformatorum*, vol. 49 (Brunswick: C. A. Schwetschke and Sons, 1879), col. 355.

16. Emile Doumergue, *Jean Calvin, Les hommes et les choses de son temps*, vol. 5, *La pensée ecclésiastique et la pensée politique de Calvin* (Lausanne: Georges Bridel, Éditeurs, 1917), p. 256.

17. The historian Henri Grandjean questions the association of the legacy of David Busanton with the *Bourse française*. Henri Grandjean, "La Bourse Française de Genève (1550–1849)," in *Étrennes Genevoises 1927* (Geneva: Edition Atar, 1927), pp. 46–47. He also cites J. A. Gautier as concurring with him:

Cela ne signifie point que le legs de Busanton ait constitué le premier fonds de la Bourse française, ni que ce personnage en ait été le fondateur, ainsi qu'on l'a souvent prétendu d'après un passage d'un recueil de notes manuscrites du XVIIIᵉ siècle conservé aux Archives de Genève (n° 3), passage reproduit dans les *Calvini op.*, Annales, p. 355, et qui n'est qu'une amplification du text de Roset.

(That does not signify that the legacy of Busanton constituted the first funds of the *Bourse française* nor that this person was its founder, as has often been alleged after a passage from a collection of manuscript notes of the eighteenth century preserved in the Archives of Geneva [no. 3], a passage reproduced in the *Calvin op.*, Annales, p. 355, and which was only an amplification of the text of Roset.)

Jean-Antoine Gautier, *Histoire de Genève des origines à l'année 1691*, vol. 3, *1538–1556* (Geneva: Rey & Malavallon, 1898), p. 231n. The text in question is as follows:

Commencement de la Bourse françoise à l'occasion d'un legs de 1000 écus fait par David Busanton qui en légua autant, aux pauvres de Strasbourg dont plusieurs étrangers réfugiés firent un fonds et un ordre de contribution pour la continuer et établirent des diacres et des receveurs de chaque nation qui rapportoient en une bourse les contributions, ce qu'étant entendu en France plusiers gens de bien y contribuerent et envoierent leur aumone. *(Archives de Genève).*

(Beginning of the *Bourse française* on the occasion of a legacy of 1000 ecus made by David Busanton who willed as much to the poor of Strasbourg of which some foreign refugees made a foundation and an order of contribution in order to continue it and established deacons and collectors from each nation who brought the contributions back into a fund. That being heard in France, several good people contributed to it and sent their alms. [*Archives of Geneva*])

Baum, Cunitz, and Reuss, eds., *Ioannis Calvini Opera*, vol. 21, *Corpus Reformatorum*, vol. 49, col. 355. This identical text appeared in Henri Bordier's manuscript of selected transcriptions from the *Bourse française* account books. The Bordier manuscript is three years older than volume 21 of the works of Calvin. Bordier cites as his source volume 3 of a collection of manuscript volumes of the archive. He entitles his own manuscript, "Les Registres de la Bourse Française de Genève commençant au premier octobre 1550, extraits des dits registres depuis le premier octobre 1550 jusqu'au premier octobre 1566." This manuscript is listed in the Genevan archive catalog of historical manuscripts as "Extraits des comptes des caissiers de la Bourse française de Genève, octobre 1550–octobre 1566, par Henri-Léonard Bordier, archiviste-paléographe (1817–1888)." This manuscript was a part of a purchase in 1934 from Th. Dufour. AEG, Manuscrits historiques, no. 223 (October 1876), p. 108 or fol. 55v. There is a dual system of pagination by page and folio.

18.

Cela fut des premières occasions que peu de temps après les estrangiers venus pour la Parole de Dieu establirent ung ordre de contribution entre eulx pour faire l'aumosne aux pauvres & commirent des diacres & recepveurs de chascune nation ou contrée, qui raportoient le tout en une bourse & en administroient ès disetteux & mallades & faisoient aprendre des mestiers aux jeunes gens & aux autres qui n'avoient moyen de vivre. Plusieurs bons personnages de la France y ont envoyé de bonnes sommes, tellement que cest ordre a esté entretenu jusques aujourdhuy avec grand fruit & soulagement de ceux qui estoient destituez de tous autres moyens humains, ès extrémitez des persécutions.

(That was the first occasion that a little time afterwards the foreigners who had come for the Word of God established an order of contribution among themselves in order to give alms to the poor and committed deacons and collectors from each nation or country who brought everything back into a fund and administered it to the destitute and sick and made young people and others who did not have a means of livelihood learn trades. Some good people from France sent sizable sums to it so that this order has been maintained until today with great fruit and solace to those who were destitute of all other human means, in extremity from the persecutions.)

Michel Roset, *Les chroniques de Genève*, ed. Henri Fazy (Geneva: Georg, Libraires de l'Institut, 1894), p. 309.

19. Michel Roset was born in Geneva on 15 June 1534. When the legacy was made he was still a boy and was sent off to Zurich to study in October 1547. When he presented his chronicle to the city council of Geneva in 1562 he was still a young man in his twenties and could have experienced personally merely the last few years of *Bourse* activity. He described that accurately. Henri Fazy, "Michel Roset, Notice Biographique," in Roset, *Les chroniques de Genève*, pp. xvi–xviii, 8.

20. For an account of the long and close friendship between Pierre Viret and John Calvin see Robert Linder, *The Political Ideas of Pierre Viret* (Geneva: Librairie Droz, 1964), pp. 28–31, 39, 41.

21. Calvin to Viret, June 1545:

Optimo fratri meo Petro Vireto Lausannensis ecclesiae pastori fidelissimo.
Quum mihi redditae sunt tuae literae *David* noster animam agebat, quam paulo post reposuit in manum Christi), singulari adeoque mirabili fidei constantia. Testamentum eius ubi veneris leges. Cave nos longius protrahas.

Letter 656, in Baum, Cunitz, and Reuss, eds., *Ioannis Calvini Opera*, vol. 12, *Corpus Reformatorum*, vol. 40 (Brunswick: C. A. Schwetschke and Sons, 1873), col. 98.

22. Order on the general hospital and distribution of alms:

Suyvant la requeste de Monsieur Calvin ministre a esté ordonné que les procureurs de l'Hospital doybgent ballier par escript tout le revenuz dudit Hospital et ceulx esqueulx l'on destribue l'aulmone, et puys que le seigneur sindicque Curteti ensemble les commis paravant sus tel cas deputés doybgent proceder à mestre ordre sus tel cas.

(Following the request of Monsieur Calvin, minister, it has been ordered that the procurators of the hospital should lay down, in writing, all the revenue of the said hospital and those to whom one distributes alms, and then that the Lord Syndic Curteti, together with the deputies committed previously in such a case, should proceed to put order in such a case.)

9 March 1545, AEG, Reg. Conseil, vol. 40, fol. 42.

23. "Pouvres estrangiers: Ordonné que les deux guets nouvellement constitués doybgent assembler tous les pouvres estrangiers vers Rive et à ung chascun d'iceulx soyt donné l'aulmone de pain et puys leur soyt faict commandement de non plus revenyr en Geneve." (Poor foreigners: Ordered, that the two patrols newly constituted should assemble all the poor foreigners toward Rive and that each of them be given alms of bread and then a command to no longer return to Geneva.) 15 June 1545, AEG, Reg. Conseil, vol. 40, fol. 149.

24. "Bolsec déclare que Calvin était un peu voleur 'gardian de la bourse des pauvres,' faisant courir des bruits 'pour attraper deniers,' distribuant à Viret 25 écus, à Farel 20 écus, sur les 2000 légués aux pauvres par David de Haynault. 'On ne peut savoir que devindrent les 1500 autres.'" (Bolsec says that Calvin was a little bit of a thief, "keeper of the fund for the poor," making lots of noise "in order to snare money," distributing to Viret twenty-five ecus, to Farel twenty ecus, on the two thousand willed to the poor by David of Hainaut. "One can not know what became of the other fifteen hundred.") Bolsec, *Vie de Calvin*, 1582, pp. 14–15, quoted in Doumergue, *Jean Calvin*, 5:256, n. 4.

25. "A l'escripvin des sermons baillé 2 écus d'or au soleil [hereafter referred to as "écus" or "écus sol"] sur les sermons qu'il a baillez pour le moys de septembre dont la bouce estoit en arriere, 2 écus sol." (To the writer of the sermons, given, two ecus d'or au soleil for the sermons that he gave for the month of September of which the *Bourse* was in arrears, two ecus sol.) AEG, Arch. hosp., Kg 12, fol. 2. For documentation of the beginning of the copying of Calvin's sermons by Denys Raguenier see Kingdon, ed., *Registres de la Compagnie des Pasteurs de Genève*, vol. 2, *1553–1564*, p. 115.

26. AEG, Arch. hosp., Hj 2 (August 1559–July 1570), p. [2] of December 1560.

27. "Item, a esté trouve en la boite 32 sols, 6 deniers." (Also, found in the box, 32 sous, 6 deniers.) AEG, Arch. hosp., Kg 12, vol. 1ᵛ.

28.

Calvin à une dame: Iay receu les dix escuz que vous avez icy envoye pour subvenir auz pouvres fideles qui ont necessite. Ie les ay mis en bonne main pour les distribuer selon vostre intention. Dieu veille accepter ceste aumosne de voz mains comme un sacrifice de bon odeur, et face que vous ioyssiez quelque iour des biens spirituelz dont il a fait participans ceux auquelz vous secourez en leur pouvrete terrienne . . . 12 de ianvier 1549.

(Calvin to a woman: I received the ten ecus that you sent here to support the faithful poor who are in need. I have put them in good hands in order to distribute them according to your intention. Would that God accept these alms from your hands as a sweet-smelling sacrifice and make you rejoice some day from the spiritual goods of which he made participants those whom you supported in their terrestrial poverty . . . 12 January 1549.)

Letter 1119, in Baum, Cunitz, and Reuss, eds., *Ioannis Calvini Opera*, vol. 13, *Corpus Reformatorum*, vol. 41 (Brunswick: C. A. Schwetschke and Sons, 1875), cols. 149–52.

29. AEG, Arch. hosp., Kg 12, fols. 2–6.

30. The three men who were chosen were the Lord Maldonnade, Monsieur de Thillat (du or de Thillac or Tillac), and Jean Budé. They were registered in the book of inhabitants as follows:

Guy de Serignac, surnommé de Tillac, du royaulme de France au pays de Gascoigne, seneschausée d'Armagnac, le 3 de may 1549. Noble Pierre de Maldonnade, natifz de Blaton, comtée de Haynault, le 3 de may 1549. . . . Noble Jehan Budé, natifz de la ville de Parys, filz de messire Guillaume Budé, conseiller et maistre des Requestes ordinaires de la maison du Roy de France, faicte le 27 junii 1549.

(Guy de Serignac, surnamed de Tillac, of the kingdom of France in the country of Gascony, seneschalsy of Armagnac, the 3rd of May, 1549. Noble Pierre de Maldonnade, native of Blaton, county of Hainaut, the 3rd of May, 1549. . . . Noble Jehan Budé, native of the city of Paris, son of Messire Guillaume Budé, counselor and master of the ordinary petitions of the household of the king of France, made 27 June 1549.)

Paul-F. Geisendorf, ed., *Livre des habitants de Genève*, vol. 1, *1549–1560* (Geneva: Librairie Droz, 1957), pp. 2–3.

31. Calvin was listed as one of the donors in the first recorded receipts and continued to be listed regularly as a generous donor. "Item de Monsieur Calvin quatre écus sol, 4 écus sol." (Also, from Monsieur Calvin, four ecus sol, 4 ecus sol.) AEG, Arch. hosp., Kg 12, fol. 1. He also regularly recommended people to the deacons for aid. See for instance a young barber recommended by Calvin in September 1562. "A un pauvre jeune homme barbier de Sainct Amour recommandé par Monsieur Calvin, 12 sols." (To a poor young man, barber, of Saint Amour, recommended by Monsieur Calvin, 12 sous.) AEG, Arch. hosp., Hj 2, p. [1] of September 1562.

CHAPTER 3. WELFARE, REFUGEES, PUBLISHING

1. See, for instance, the following entry for passersby: "À deux pauves passans, 6 sols" (To two poor passersby, 6 sous). AEG, Arch. hosp., Hj 2, p. [1] of April 1565.

2. See, for instance, a woodworker from England whom the deacons helped get tools and another man who was aided in setting up his trade. Note that the Englishman is already in

Geneva in September 1554; is he among the first in refuge from Mary Tudor? "A ung pauvre menuysier venant d'Angleterre pour luy ayder a avoir des outilz, 17 sols" (To a poor wood-worker coming from England in order to help him have some tools, 17 sous), 10 September 1554, AEG, Arch. hosp., Kg 15 (July 1554–July 1555), p. [4] of September 1554; "A Louis . . . pour luy ayder à monter son mestier, 5 florins" (To Louis . . . in order to aid him to mount his craft, 5 florins), AEG, Arch. hosp., Hj 2, p. [2] of October 1559.

3. See, for example, the following loans to a man with another man to back him up, to two schoolboys until they reach adulthood, and to Pierre Bourgeois: "A ung bon homme auquel a esté presté 7 florins 6 sols sur la responce de Matthieu Durval le 24e decembre, 1560, 7 florins, 6 sols" (To a good man to whom had been loaned seven florins six sous on the response of Matthieu Durval, the twenty-fourth December, 1560, 7 florins, 6 sous), AEG, Arch. hosp., Hj 2, p. [4] of December 1560; "Presté à deux escholliers sur leur adult avec respondant, 41 florins, 8 sols" (Loaned to two schoolboys on their adult [until their adulthood?] with respondent, 41 florins, 8 sous), ibid., p. [2] of October 1560; "A Pierre Bourgeoys presté soubz le credit de Monsieur René, 10 florins" (To Pierre Bourgeoys, under the credit of Monsieur René, loaned, 10 florins), ibid., p. [2] of December 1559.

4. "A Anthoine Bynet pour le louaige de sa bouticque, 5 florins" (To Anthoine Bynet for the rent of his store, 5 florins), AEG, Arch. hosp., Hj 2, p. [1] of June 1560.

5. For instance, the following two young men were recommended by Calvin: "A un jeune escolier de Louan [Louhan (modern spelling), a city in the department of Seine and Marne] recommandé par Monsieur Calvin, 16 sols" (To a young schoolboy of Louhan, recommended by Monsieur Calvin, 16 sous), AEG, Arch. hosp., Hj 2, p. [2] of June 1562; "A un autre jeune homme de Louan, malade, recommandé aussi par Monsieur Calvin, 15 sols" (To another young man of Louan, sick, recommended also by Monsieur Calvin, 15 sous), ibid., p. [2] of June 1562.

6. "A ung jeune homme pour s'en retourner au pays, 2 florins, 1 sol" (To a young man in order to go back to his country, 2 florins, a sou), AEG, Arch. hosp., Hj 2, p. [1] of September 1560.

7. "A la femme de feu Nicolas Potle[?] pour retirer ses enfans au pays avec elle ou elle pretend avoir quelque moyen de les nourir sans charger les eglises . . . , 8 florins" (To the wife of deceased Nicolas Potle[?] in order to take her children back to the country with her where she claims to have some means of feeding them without charging the churches. . . , 8 florins), AEG, Arch. hosp., Hj 2, p. [2] of May 1561.

8. "Item cedit mesme jour [le premier octobre, 1559] donné à ung pauvre jeune homme qui aprend le mestier de compositeur chez Monsieur Crespin recommandé par Meistre Jehan Fabry, 8 sols" (Also this said same day [1 October 1559] given to a poor young man who is learning the trade of compositor at Monsieur Crespin's place, recommended by Master Jean Fabri, 8 sous), AEG, Arch. hosp., Kg 12, fol. 2v. Jean Crespin was an immigrant printer and editor of Geneva who was originally trained in law but who attained lasting fame as the martyrologist of the early Reformed church. The definitive work on him is Jean-François Gilmont, *Jean Crespin, un éditeur réformé du XVIe siècle* (Geneva: Librairie Droz, 1981).

9. Section 1100, "Étrangers sans profession":

D'autant que plusieurs de ceux qui se retirent icy maintenant sont paouvres et ne veulent rien faire, chargeans la Bourse, pour y remedier arresté que desormais on n'en recoyve plus qui n'ayt estat; et que ceux qui tesmoigneront pour luy promettent qu'il ne sera en charge. Et, affin qu'ilz en puissent estre sommés, quand ce viendra qu'ilz se presenteront à la Bourse, qu'on mette à leurs lettres leurs mestiers et le nom de ceux qui auront tesmoigné pour iceux.

Reg. Conseil, vol. 63, fol. 139, in Rivoire and van Berchem, *Les sources du droit du Canton de Genève*, vol. 3, *1551–1620* (Arau: H. R. Sauerländer, Imprimeurs-Editeurs, 1933), p. 269.

10. "A une pauvre femme qui avoit loué sa chambre à quelque mallade, 14 sols" (To a poor woman who had rented her room to some sick person, 14 sous), AEG, Hj 2, p. [3] of August 1560.

11. The legal weight and price of bread is contained in the legal documents of the period. The amount of money a widow received per week is contained in the deacons' accounts. By combining the two, one can estimate the amount of bread she could afford. See, for instance, Rivoire and van Berchem, *Les sources du droit du Canton de Genève*, vol. 2, *1461–1550*, pp. 468–69.

12. The discovery that the *Bourse* continued to pay child support for the children of the first bed after remarriage of a widow came about through an attempt to trace down orphans. Some of the children who appeared to be orphans on the welfare rolls were actually living with their remarried mother. Examples include Jean, son of the deceased Anthoine Bonnefoy, and the children of the deceased Didier Breton, and of the deceased Estienne Felix; their stepfathers received money for their food. AEG, Arch. hosp., Kq 1 and Kq 2, "Bourse française, Grand Livre des Assistés," vol. 2, *1580–1599*, fols. 172, 176 , 178–79.

13. A wet nurse is a woman who cares for and suckles children who are not her own. See the following two instances of nurses paid by the deacons: "A la nourrice de l'enfant que tenoit Mademoiselle Magny, 20 sols" (To the nurse of the child whom Mademoiselle Magny is keeping, 20 sous), AEG, Arch. hosp., Hj 2, p. [1] of November 1561; "A ung pauvre homme qui a sa femme mallade pour la nourrice qui allaiste son enfant, 15 sols" (To a poor man who has his wife sick, for the wet nurse who is nursing his child, 15 sous), ibid., p. [2] of March 1562.

14. See the case of Paul du Chesne: "A Paul du Chesne pour le quartier du petit garcon qu'on luy a baillé, 5 florins" (To Paul du Chesne for the quarterly pay for the small boy whom one entrusted to him, 5 florins), AEG, Arch. hosp., Hj 2, p. [6] of October 1560.

15. See the case of Anne, AEG, Arch. hosp., Kq 2, p. 5.

16. See the case of Marie, daughter of the deceased Anthoine Breton of Lorraine, whom the deacons gave over to a Genevan and his sister for a two-year apprenticeship. In the contract the deacons agreed to pay twenty florins, ten then and ten at the beginning of the second year. Marie, in turn, was to be fed and housed during the time of the apprenticeship. The contract is dated 19 September 1566. AEG, Notaire Jean Ragueau, vol. 8 (1 January—15 October 1566), pp. 473–74. In subsequent references "Notaire" will be abbreviated to "Not." All references to the notary Jean Ragueau will be given in page numbers instead of folio numbers. He occasionally marked as foliated what is actually paginated.

17. See Paul Gonnet, *L'adoption lyonnais des orphelins légitimes (1536–1793)* (Paris: Librairie Générale de Droit & de Jurisprudence, 1935), 2 : 15–46.

18. It is difficult to determine from the entries in the account books whether the deacons are paying for an orphan or for a person for whom they had taken the financial responsibility for some other reason. See the following three examples: "A Pierre Heurtaut pour ung apretif qu'il luy a esté bailé par M. Leleu[?] et ceulx du pays à nostre consentement sur l'avance de deux écus qu'on luy a promis pour quatre moys, 2 florins" (To Pierre Heurtaut for an apprentice whom he had been given by Monsieur Leleu[?] and those of the country with our consent on the advance of two ecus that one had promised to him for four months, 2 florins), AEG, Arch. hosp., Hj 2, p. [4] of April 1561; "A Pierre le menuysier pour ung garçon que l'on a mis en mestier chez luy, 26 florins, 6 deniers" (To Pierre, the carpenter, for a boy whom one put in training with him, 26 florins, 6 deniers), ibid., p. [1] of November 1559; "A Pierre Cousturier menuysier pour le parachevement du payement de son aprentif, 5 florins, 2 sols, 6 deniers" (To Pierre Cousturier, carpenter, for the completion of the payment for his apprentice, 5 florins, 2 sous, 6 deniers), ibid., p. [3] of November 1559.

19. AEG, Arch. hosp., Kq 2, p. 83.

20. The fact that Jean Crespin had assistants who were on welfare may only have meant that he was not paying them enough. However, it is certainly possible that he was helping out some of the poor by training them but that he could not support them completely on his own and needed the deacons' help. See the case of the poor young man who was learning to be a compositor with him. AEG, Arch. hosp., Kg 12, 2ᵛ.

21. See the following payments of school fees to teachers and students (boys, girls, and a married woman): "A ung maistre d'escholle pour quatre personnes qu'il a instruites l'espace de 3 moys, 3 florins" (To a schoolmaster for four persons that he instructed during three months, 3 florins), AEG, Arch. hosp., Hj 2 p. [2] of June 1560; "A ung magistro pour des enfans qu'il a instituez par l'espace de troys moys, 3 florins" (To a teacher for some children that he instructed for the space of three months, 3 florins), ibid., p. [5] of September 1560; "Item et à Jehan de Tere pour plusieurs enfans qu'il instruit, 14 sols" (Likewise to Jean de Tere for several children that he teaches, 14 sous), ibid., p. [4] of November 1559; "A Jehan de Tere pour les enfans qu'il enseigne, 18 sols" (To Jean de Tere for the children that he teaches, 18 sous), ibid., p. [1] of March 1560; "Pour l'eschollaige d'une fille, 2 sols" (For the school fees of a girl, 2 sous), ibid., p. [1] of October 1560; "A une pauvre fille pour son eschollaige, 2 sols" (To a poor girl for her

school fees, 2 sous), ibid., p. [1] of January 1561; "A une pauvre fille pour son eschollaige, 2 sols" (To a poor girl for her school fees, 2 sous), ibid., p. [1] of December 1560; "A la fille de Clement Mailet pour son eschollaige, 2 sols" (To the daughter of Clement Mailet for her school fees, 2 sous), ibid., p. [1] of 1561; "A une petite fille pour son eschollaige, 2 sols" (To a small girl for her school fees, 2 sous), ibid., p. [1] of February 1562; "A la femme de Guillaume de Soyssons pour son eschollaige, 3 florins" (To the wife of Guillaume de Soyssons for her school fees, 3 florins), ibid., p. [2] of May 1560.

22. "A ung pauvre escholier mallade, 2 florins" (To a poor schoolboy, sick, 2 florins) AEG, Arch. hosp., Hj 2, p. [4] of 1560; "A ung estudiant provençal, 15 sols" (To a Provencal student, 15 sous), ibid., p. [2] of February 1561; "A ung jeune homme eschollier, 18 sols" (To a young man, a schoolboy, 18 sous), ibid., p. [1] of March 1561; "Encores à ung pauvre estudiant, 15 sols" (Again to a poor student, 15 sous), ibid., p. [1] of March 1561.

23. "A ung jeune eschollier s'en allant en Angleterre, 10 florins" (To a young schoolboy departing for England, 10 florins), AEG, Arch. hosp., Hj 2 p. [1] of June 1560.

24. There is, for instance, the case of a cutler named Nicolas Campin who had been released from prison in Paris, had come to Geneva, and who went back home to recover his possessions. The deacons gave him a substantial sum to do so, but required a deposit of some of his personal effects. These were given back to him when he returned. "A Nicolas Campin qui est l'ung des quatres prisoniers qui feurent relachez à Paris par arrest, presté pour aller à son pays pour chasser son bien, 10 florins, 6 sols, sur quoy il m'a laissé ses hardes pour gaige, 10 florins, 6 sols" (To Nicolas Campin who is one of the four prisoners who was released in Paris by decree, loaned in order to go to his country in order to pursue his belongings, 10 florins, 6 sous, for which he left his personal effects as a pledge, 10 florins, 6 sous). In the margin is written: "Nicolas le coustelier, on luy à rendu ses gaiges" (Nicolas the cutler, was given back his pledged effects), AEG, Arch. hosp, Hj 2, p. [1] of April 1561.

25. There was, for instance, the case of a woman whose husband, Master Helye or Helie, a minister, had been hung because of his witness for the Gospel. AEG, Arch. hosp., Hj 2 p. [3] of October 1559, p. [2] of November 1559, p. [2] of December 1560, and p. [1] of January 1561.

26. "A ung pauvre libraire venu de Paris duquel la femme est prisonniere, 2 florins" (To a poor bookseller come from Paris of whom the wife is prisoner, 2 florins), AEG, Arch. hosp., Hj 2, p. [2] of November 1559.

27. "À ung pauvre homme de Paris sortant des galleres avec l'attestation des ministre et diacres du lieu, 15 sols" (To a poor man of Paris, leaving the galleys, with the attestation of the minister and deacons of the place, 15 sous), AEG, Arch. hosp., Hj 2, p. [2] of March 1562; "A ung pauvre coustelier qui a esté prisonnier à Paris pour la parole, nommé Nicolas, 2 florins, 6 sols" (To a poor cutler who was prisoner at Paris for the word, named Nicolas, 2 florins, 6 sous), ibid., p. [3] of November 1560; "A Nicolas le coustelier qui a esté prisonnier pour l'Evangile et maintenant fort mallade, 33 sols, 9 deniers" (To Nicolas, the cutler, who was prisoner for the Gospel and now is very sick, 33 sous, 9 deniers), ibid., p. [2] of December 1560; "A Nicolas le coustelier qui a esté prisonnier à Paris, 30 sols" (To Nicolas, the cutler, who was prisoner in Paris, 30 sous), ibid., p. [5] of December 1560. Nicolas was aided by the deacons for several months in the fall and winter of 1560 before he went back to recover his possessions in the spring of 1561.

28. "A ung pauvre ministre fugitif de la vallee d'Augroigne, 5 florins" (To a poor minister, fugitive from the valley of Angroigne, 5 florins), AEG, Arch. hosp., Hj 2, p. [2] of January 1561.

29. "A quatre ou cinq pauvres mesnaiges venuz de Castelane, chassez pour l'evangile, 21 florins, 6 deniers" (To four or five poor couples come from Castelone, chased for the Gospel, 21 florins, 6 deniers), AEG, Arch. hosp., Hj 2, p. [2] of July 1560.

30. The woman in question was the wife of the minister, Master Helye (Helie). Deacon entries in her name read as follows: "A la femme de Maistre Helye pauvre ministre absent, 4 florins" (To the wife of Master Helye, poor minister, absent, 4 florins), AEG, Arch. hosp., Hj 2, p. [3] of October 1559; "A la femme de Maistre Helye ministre, 2 florins" (To the wife of Master Helye, minister, 2 florins), ibid., p. [2] of November 1559; "A la femme de Maistre Helie qui a esté pendu pour le tesmoignaige de l'Evangile, 5 florins" (To the wife of Master Helie who was hung for witnessing for the Gospel, 5 florins), ibid., p. [2] of December 1560; "A la vefve de

Maistre Helye ministre de la parolle pour une chambre, 7 florins" (To the widow of Master Helye, minister of the Word, for a room, 7 florins), ibid., p. [6] of January 1561.

31. Manuscrits Historiques, no. 223, Bordier, passim.

32. Grandjean, "La Bourse française de Genève," pp. 53–54.

33. There are many examples of instances in which the deacons rented only a bed for a person: "A la vefve de Clement Mallet pour le louaige de son lit pour deux moys, 10 sols" (To the widow of Clement Mallet for the rent of her bed for two months, 10 sous), AEG, Arch. hosp., Hj 2, p. [1] of September 1560. In the case of entire houses it is not always completely clear whether the deacons were renting a house for someone or from someone. "A Jehan Le Beuf pour le louaige de sa maison, 30 sols" (To Jean Le Beuf for the rent of his house, 30 sous), ibid., p. [2] of October 1560; "A Jehanne Champaigne pauvre vefve pour le louaige de sa maison, 2 florins, 6 sols" (To Jeanne Champaigne, poor widow, for the rent of her house, 2 florins, 6 sous), ibid., p. [2] of May 1561; "A la Huguette pour le louaige de sa maison, 2 florins" (To the Huguette for the rent of her house, 2 florins), ibid., p. [2] of October 1561.

34. AEG, Arch. hosp., Kq 2, p. 230.

35. See, for instance, a loan to a man to buy a coat in March 1560: "A Nicolas des Mares presté pour avoir ung manteau, 20 sols" (To Nicolas des Mares, loaned, in order to have a coat, 20 sous), AEG, Hj 2, p. [2] of March 1560. A few months earlier, the hospital of Geneva was employing tailors to make clothing for the poor at two sous per day and food. For instance, on Sunday 17 December 1559: "Item pour 4 journees à Jean Marne comme à Monsieur Cuve[?], couturiers pour fayre des habillemens aux pouvres à 2 sols et norry, 8 sols" (Also for 4 days to Jean Marne as to Monsieur Cuve[?], tailors, in order to make clothing for the poor at 2 sous and nourishment, 8 sous), AEG, Arch. hosp., Fe 4 (21 November 1558–4 July 1560), fol. 55^v.

36. See, for instance, the poor girl who received two sous for wooden shoes. "A ungue pauvre fille pour des sabotz, 2 sols" (To a poor girl for her wooden shoes, 2 sous), AEG, Arch. hosp., Hj 2, p. [3] of December 1560. In contrast the city hospital employed a cobbler by the day. See this entry of Sunday 17 December 1559 in the account book of the hospital of Geneva, "Item au cordaunier pour cinq journees à fere des solliers aux pouvres à 2 sols le jour, 10 sols" (Also to the cobbler for five days to make some shoes for the poor at 2 sous the day, 10 sous), AEG, Arch. hosp., Fe 4, fol. 55^v.

37. "A Balthasar pour semeler ses soulliers, 8 sols" (To Balthasar in order to resole his shoes, 8 sous), AEG, Arch. hosp., Hj 2, p. [4] of October 1560.

38. "A ung pauvre garçon pour achapter ung pannier, 2 sols" (To a poor boy in order to buy a basket, 2 sous), AEG, Arch. hosp., Hj 2, p. [2] of June 1561.

39. AEG, Arch. hosp., Kq 1 & 2, 1560–99. See AEG, Arch. hosp., Hj 2 for records of payments to the doctors and barber-surgeons.

40. There was, for instance, a poor man named Jean Lerin who came to the deacons to get money for his wife in childbed. "A ung pauvre homme Jehan Lerin pour sa femme acouchee, 12 sols" (To a poor man, Jean Lerin, for his wife in childbed, 12 sous), AEG, Arch. hosp., Hj 2, p. [1] of January 1561.

41. See, for instance, the itemized drug bill of 24 September 1582 inserted between two folios of AEG, Arch. hosp., Kq 2, fols. 315^v and 316.

42. "A Jean le Flamand pour aller changer d'air par le conseil des medecins, 30 sols" (To Jean, the Flemish person, in order to go to change air by the advice of the doctors, 30 sous), AEG, Arch. hosp., Hj 2, p. [1] of August 1562.

43. "A une garde et ung jeune garçon qui ont gardé ung mallade chez le Prevost de Cluny [?], 15 sols" (To a guard and a young boy who guarded a sick person at the prevost of Cluny's[?] house, 15 sous), AEG, Arch. hosp., Hj 2, p. [2] of January 1562.

44. Examples of accommodations include private homes, the Inn of the Crescent hosted by Henry Gon, and the city hospital itself: (1) "A une Provençale pour avoir gardé une pauvre fille qui est morte chez elle, 2 florins, 6 sols" (To a Provençal for having cared for a poor girl who died at her house, 2 florins, 6 sous), AEG, Arch. hosp., Hj 2, p. [2] of May 1561; (2) "Au filz du bon homme de Paris pour deux garçons qu'il a mallades chez luy, 15 sols" (To the son of the good man of Paris for two boys that he has sick at his house, 15 sous), ibid., p. [5] of October 1560; (3) "À Jehan de Sainct Denys mallade chez Henry Gon, 12 sols" (To Jean de Saint Denis, sick, at Henry Gon's place, 12 sous), AEG, Arch. hosp., Hj 2, p. [2] of January 1561. Hospital

and drug bills are itemized under individual names in the "Great Books of the Assisted": AEG, Arch. hosp., Kq 1 and 2, passim; in the early years payments were recorded chronologically in the account books as they were paid, but by the 1560s hospital and drug bills were also itemized by name for individual dependents of the *Bourse* in the "Great Books of the Assisted."

45. "A Monsieur René pour quelques pauvres gens qui sont à l'Hospital de Messieurs, 8 florins" (To Monsieur René for a few poor people who are at the hospital of Messieurs, 8 florins), AEG, Arch. hosp., Hj 2, p. [1] of December 1561; "Rendu à Monsieur René pour quelques pauvres personnes qui sont en l'Hospital de Messieurs, 5 florins, 8 sols" (Paid back to Monsieur René for several poor people who are in the hospital of Messieurs, 5 florins, 8 sous), ibid., p. [1] of February 1562; "A Jehan Personne pour une fille qui est à l'Hospital, 4 florins" (To Jehan Personne for a girl who is at the hospital, 4 florins), ibid., p. [2] of February 1560; "Encores à Monsieur René pour deux en l'Hospital, 5 florins" (Again to Monsieur René for two in the hospital, 5 florins), ibid., p. [1] of February 1562. There is a parcel of bills from the city hospital to the *Bourse française* from the first quarter of 1596 in AEG, Arch. hosp., P 239, dossiers 2940–73 (1596–1846), dossier 2941.

46. The city hospital no longer had enough room for the poor of the *Bourse française* and offered the *Bourse* a building, rent free, on 12 February 1703. The *Bourse* furnished it and installed its own help, including a pastor. In 1707 the *Bourse* transferred this hospital to the house next door, and in 1742 the *Bourse* enlarged it with the purchase of another building. However, the *Bourse* hospital lasted less than a century. Because of financial hardship the *Bourse* closed its hospital in 1798 and placed its sick people in the country or at the city hospital. Henri Grandjean, "La Bourse Française de Genève," pp. 54–57.

47. AEG, Arch. hosp., Kg 12, fol. 2.

48. "Depuis le penultime jour de septembre 1549, je Denis Raguenier escrivain, ay recueilli les sermons de Monsieur Calvin, & iceulx fourni ez mains des Diacres ordonnez pour subvenir aux necessitez des povres François estans en l'Eglise de Genefve. . . . Sur les Actes des Apostres . . . commençant le premier desdits sermons le dimanche vingtcinquiesme jour d'Aoust 1549 au matin." Kingdon, ed., *Registres de la Compagnie des Pasteurs de Genève*, vol. 2, *1553–1564*, p. 115.

49. Bernard Gagnebin, "L'incroyable histoire des sermons de Calvin," *Bulletin de la Société d'histoire et d'archéologie de Genève* 10 (1955): 318.

50.

Denys Raguenier, filz de feu Jehan, de Bar sus Senne, escripvain, gratis, eu esgard de ce qu'il a présenté ung livre où sont huit sermons de Monsieur Calvin, réduitz en bon ordre avec l'envoy sus icelluy & dizains.

(Denys Raguenier, son of the deceased Jean, of Bar sus Seine, writer, gratuitously, in consideration that he presented a book in which [there] are eight sermons of Monsieur Calvin, reduced in good order with a presentation of this to the dizainiers.

Alfred Covelle, *Le Livre des Bourgeois de l'Ancienne République de Genève* (Geneva: J. Jullien, 1897), p. 249.

51. His last payment from the deacons reads: "A Maistre Denys pour le parachevement de ce mois, 12 florins, 6 sols" (To Master Denys for the completion of this month, 12 florins, 6 sous), AEG. Arch. hosp., Hj 2, p. [2] of December 1560. See also Gagnebin,. "L'incroyable histoire des sermons de Calvin," p. 314.

52. "Paris Prostat, escrivain—au rapport de Artus Chauvin et Jean du Pré et Monsieur Ricaud, ayant sa femme à Lyon." (Paris Prostat, writer, on the report of Artus Chauvin and Jean du Pré and Monsieur Ricaud, his wife at Lyons.) Geisendorf, ed., *Livre des habitants*, vol. 2, *1572–1574 et 1585–1587* (Geneva: Librairie Droz, 1963), p. 2; payments from the "Great Book of the Assisted" to Paris are recorded in appendix A. The following are payments to Paris and his wife from the extraordinary account books: "A le femme de Paris l'escripvain, 4 sols" (To the wife of Paris the writer, 4 sous), AEG, Arch. hosp., Hj 2 p. [1] of July 1560; "Baillé a Paris l'escripvain, 8 sols" (Given to Paris the writer, 8 sous), ibid., p. [2] of July 1561; "A Paris l'escripvain pour la copie de quatre sermons, 12 sols" (To Paris the writer for the copy of four sermons, 12 sous), ibid., p. [2] of August 1561; "A Paris pour six sermons, 18 sols" (To Paris for six sermons, 18 sous), ibid., p. [1] of September 1561; "A Paris, 5 florins" (To Paris 5 florins),

ibid., p. [1] of October 1561; "A Paris donné, 5 florins" (To Paris, given, 5 florins), ibid., p. [2] of December 1561; "A Paris l'escripvain, 5 florins, 6 sols" (To Paris, the copyist, 5 florins, 6 sous), ibid., p. [1] of January 1562; "A Paris, 6 florins" (To Paris, 6 florins), ibid., p. [2] of January 1562; "A l'escripvain des sermons, 9 sols" (To the copyist of the sermons, 9 sous), ibid., p. [1] of February 1562; "Pour deux sermons, 7 sols" (For two sermons, 7 sous), ibid., p. [1] of February 1562; "A Paris, 7 florins, 6 sols" (To Paris, 7 florins, 6 sous), ibid., p. [2] of February 1562: "A Paris pour ceste premiere distribution, 7 florins, 6 sols" (To Paris for this first distribution, 7 florins, 6 sous), ibid., p. [1] of March 1562; "A luy mesme pour l'escripture de 14 sermons, 3 florins, 16 sols" (To himself for the copying of 14 sermons, 3 florins, 16 sous), ibid., p. [1] of March 1562; "Item à Paris, 7 florins, 6 sols (Likewise to Paris, 7 florins, 6 sous), ibid., p. [2] of March 1562.

53. Purchases of paper, binding, and recopying of sermons in the account books: "A Paris escripvain pour deux rames de papier, 2 florins" (To Paris, the writer, for two reams of paper, 2 florins), AEG, Arch. hosp., Hj 2, p. [1] of September 1561; "Item et pour quatre rames de papier qui ont esté livrees à Paris depuis le 10ᵉ novembre, 4 florins" (Likewise, and for four reams of paper that have been delivered to Paris since the tenth of November, 4 florins), ibid., p. [1] of March 1562; "A Maistre Denys l'escripvain, 4 florins, 9 sols, 6 deniers. A luy mesmes pour la relieure du premier volume des sermons sus Job, 7 sols, 6 deniers" (To Master Denis, the writer, 4 florins, 9 sous, 6 deniers. To himself for the binding of the first volume of the sermons on Job, 7 sous, 6 deniers), AEG, Arch. hosp., Kg 15 (July 1554–July 1555), p. [8] of July 1554; "Pour quatre sermons mal escriptz que j'ay faict rescripe, 13 sols" (For four sermons badly written that I had rewritten, 13 sous), AEG, Arch. hosp., Hj 2, p. [2] of March 1562; "Au garçon qui a transcript les sermons, 3 sous" (To the boy who transcribed the sermons, 3 sous), ibid., p. [3] of March 1562; "Au garçon lequel escript les sermons comme a esté promis pour retirer ses chemises, 7 sols" (To the boy who wrote the sermons as had been promised for getting back his shirts, 7 sous), ibid., p. [1] of March 1562.

54. See, for instance, a 9 July 1563 permission to print the Psalms given to a printer of Metz in Lorraine in exchange for a portion of the profits to be given to the poor of Geneva and a portion to the poor of Metz, the latter percentage to be determined by the Reformed church of Metz. AEG, Not. Jean Ragueau, 5 (January 1562–20 February 1564): 1035–37.

55. The text of the consignment of the manuscript sermons of Calvin to the college of 22 November 1613:

A esté representé par Monsieur Lemaire que Monsieur le recteur du College desireroit que l'on remeist en la biblioteque les manuscripts des sermons de feu Monsieur Calvin sur divers livres de la Bible avec offre que advenant qu'il s'en retire quelque benefice, que ce sera pour les pauvres de seans. A esté advisé que selon ledit offre, il luy sera remis lesdictz manuscript avec inventaire d'iceulx au près duquel il fera sa promesse.

(It has been presented by Monsieur Lemaire that Monsieur, the rector of the College, would desire that one put in the library the manuscripts of the sermons of the deceased Monsieur Calvin on diverse books of the Bible with an offer that in the event that he takes back from it some benefit, that it will be for the poor here. It has been advised that according to the said offer, the said manuscripts will be delivered with an inventory of them, to which he will make his promise.)

AEG, Arch. hosp., Ka 1, p. 54. For additional information see Bernard Gagnebin, "L'Incroyable histoire des sermons de Calvin," pp. 311, 319–34.

CHAPTER 4. INTERNATIONAL ACTIVITIES

1. For information on the missionary pastors sent to France see especially Kingdon, *Geneva and the Coming of the Wars of Religion*.

2. AEG, Arch. hosp., Hj 2.

3. The account book immediately preceding AEG, Arch. hosp., Hj 2 was AEG, Arch. hosp., Hj 1 (August 1557–February 1559). It contained only receipts and so-called "ordinary" expenditures, the weekly welfare handouts. The account book containing the extraordinary expenditures for these years has apparently been lost. Early in the 1550s both kinds of

expenditures were contained in one account book, but then the accounts were divided. Because one of the two books is missing for 1557–59, it is impossible to determine exactly when the clandestine activities began in full force. Later account books are also missing, specifically from August 1570 through December 1578—the years that immediately followed the account book that contains the evidence of missionary activities.

4. Laurent de Normandie was born in John Calvin's hometown, Noyon, France (in Picardy, not in Normandy as his name might otherwise suggest), of a noble family, son of Jean de Normandie. He studied law at the university of Orléans as did Calvin. Were they already friends? Their stay in Orléans apparently overlapped. Laurent de Normandie returned to Noyon, where he was lieutenant of the king and mayor. In 1544 he was a witness at the marriage of Théodore de Bèze along with Jean Crespin, the future martyrologist. He himself married Anne de la Vacquerie. In 1548 he followed de Bèze and Crespin across the Jura to Geneva. His wife, their three young children and some servants followed. Shortly afterwards his father (in France), his wife, and his daughter died.

Despite these personal losses, Normandie established himself in Geneva and made friends. He asked for the right of habitation on 2 May 1549. By 10 July 1550 John Calvin and Laurent de Normandie were fast friends. Calvin cited the tragic deaths in the family of Normandie in a preface, "Jean Calvin à Monsieur Laurent de Normandie son singulier et entier ami, salut." (John Calvin to Monsieur Laurent de Normandie, his singular and absolute friend, salutations.) In 1550 Laurent de Normandie also bought a house on the cathedral square, one that formerly belonged to the canons of the cathedral, and on 14 September 1550 he married Anne Colladon in a marriage celebrated by Calvin himself at the Sunday morning service. They had three children, two sons and a daughter. (Two sons survived from his first marriage.) He solicited the right of bourgeoisie 8 September 1551. The small council lowered the price of admission from sixty to twenty ecus, but it was not until 15 April 1555 that he was received as a bourgeois: "Spectable Laurent de Normandie, filz de feu Jehan, natif de Noyon, docteur ès droictz, ayant regard aux agréables services qu'il a faict, 20 escus, 1 seillot." (Spectable Laurent de Normandie, son of the deceased Jean, native of Noyon, doctor in Law, regarding the agreeable services that he did, 20 ecus, 1 seillot [Covelle, Le Livre des Bourgeois, p. 242].)

He performed a mission for the city to Berne and Lyons. He was sworn in as an attorney on 1 October 1555, but his chief preoccupations were elsewhere, like others with a similar education in this first generation of the Reformed in Geneva such as John Calvin and Jean Crespin.

Laurent de Normandie was primarily a financier of books; he arranged for their publication and sale. He was especially known because of his support of colporteurs who carried illegal religious books to France. He would advance the colporteurs books and await payment on return. If the colporteur lost his life, Normandie would absorb the loss so that the man's family would not. (Colportage was dangerous work.) He became a member of the Council of Two Hundred on 7 February 1559. He seemed to have many friends. He took on responsibilities for them as executor of their wills and guardian of their children. He was executor of the will of Etienne Girard and of John Calvin; the latter responsibility he shared with Calvin's brother Antoine. Laurent de Normandie asked Antoine in his will to aid his wife in the guardianship of his children and in the administration of his goods.

While Laurent de Normandie was making his life in Geneva, the door to France was closed to him. On 7 September 1552 the Parlement of Paris condemned him to be burned alive. Since he was in Geneva, it was done in effigy. His goods were confiscated, though he made several trips to try to recover them. He wrote his will on 6 September 1565 in contemplation of the danger of a planned trip to France. He died of the plague on 14 August 1569. "Monsieur de Normandie de pres Saint Pierre apporté mort de peste" (Monsieur de Normandie of near Saint Pierre carried away dead of the plague), AEG, EC Mort, vol. 9 (11 February 1568–October 1569), p. 112.

See Jules Bonnet, Récits du seizième siècle, 2d ser. (Paris: Grassart, Libraire-Editeur, 1885), pp. 1–38. His chapter on Laurent de Normandie is based on the "Notice sur Laurent de Normandie" by Theophile Heyer in the Mémoires et documents publiés par la Société d'histoire et d'archéologie de Genève (Geneva: J. Jullien, Libraire-Editeur, 1867), 16:399–422. See also, "Normandie (Laurent de)," in Eugène and Emile Haag, La France protestante ou vies des protestants français qui se sont fait un nom dans l'histoire depuis les premiers temps de la Réformation jusqu'a la reconnaissance du principe de la liberté des cultes par l'Assemblée Nationale; Ouvrage précédé d'une notice historique sur le protestantisme en France suivi de pièces justificatives (Paris, Geneva: Joël Cherbuliez, Libraire-Editeur, 1858), 8:24–26.

5. Heidi-Lucie Schlaepfer, "Laurent de Normandie," in *Aspects de la propagande religieuse,* ed. Gabrielle Berthoud et al., (Geneva: Librairie E. Droz, 1957), pp. 176–230.

6. Paul Chaix, *Recherches sur l'imprimerie à Genève de 1550 à 1564: Etude bibliographique, économique et littéraire* (Geneva: Librairie E. Droz, 1954), p. 55.

7. Compare the entries in AEG, Arch. hosp., Hj 1 that recorded the disbursements to regular aid recipients to those in AEG, Arch. hosp., Hj 2 that recorded the disbursements to those at Laurent de Normandie's house.

8. "Rendu à Monsieur de Normandye." The sixteenth-century manuscripts recorded his name as ending with "ye." The modern French rendition of that is frequently "ie." Except for direct quotations in the original French this text uses "ie." This particular phrase was repeated frequently in account book AEG, Arch. hosp., Hj 2. See, for instance, August 1559. This document, like so many others, has no page numbers. "Rendu" could be translated in context as rendered, paid back, or delivered.

9. "Chez Monsieur de Normandy distribué à diverses personnes, 4 florins," AEG, Arch. hosp., Hj 2, p. [4] of November 1559; "Plus à luy mesme encores pour une aultre partye, 29 florins, 2 sols," ibid., p. [3] of October 1559.

10. "A Monsieur René [René Gassin, a deacon] pour payer la chambre d'ung ministre, 8 florins, 7 sols" (To Monsieur René, to pay for the room of a minister, 8 florins, 7 sous), AEG, Arch. hosp., Hj 2, p. [3] of August 1560.

11. "A deux femmes des ministres absens, 5 florins." AEG, Arch. hosp., Hj 2, p. [1] of August 1559; "Item pour le louaige d'une maison pour les femmes d'aucuns ministres envoyés en France laquelle apartient au Prevost de Clugny, 52 florins, 1 sol," ibid., p. [2] of October 1559.

12. "Item j'ai rendu à Monsieur de Normandye 19 écus pistoletz qu'il avoit avancez pour ung ministre qui a esté envoyé en Gascoigne dont il y a la cedule de Antesignanus pour responce, 95 florins," AEG, Arch. hosp., p. [1] of October 1559. Antesignanus was probably Pierre Davantes, classicist, who used a system of musical notation by numbers to publish in 1560 the Psalms of David as translated and arranged by Théodore de Bèze and Clement Marot. Eugène and Emile Haag, *La France protestante publiée sous les auspices de la Société de l'histoire du protestantisme français et sous la direction de Monsieur Henri Bordier,* 2d ed. (Paris: Sandoz & Fischbacher, 1886), vol. 5, cols. 163–70.

13. "A Christofre Saupon pour luy ayder à achapter une bible, 12 sols" (To Christopher Saupon in order to aid him to buy a Bible, 12 sous), AEG, Arch. hosp., Hj 2, p. [2] of May 1561; "A ung pauvre garçon pour ung livre grec, 3 sols" (To a poor boy for a Greek book, 3 sous), ibid., p. [2] of April 1560; "A ung jeune homme pour une grammaire grecque, 10 sols" (To a young man for a Greek grammar, 10 sous), ibid., p. [2] of March 1560; "A ung pauvre garçon pour ung livre en françoys, 5 sols" (To a poor boy for a book in French, 5 sous), ibid., p. [2] of June 1561.

14. "Au bon homme de Paris pour achepter des Pseaumes [sic] de la plus grosse letre, 10 sols" (To the good man of Paris in order to buy the Psalms of the largest letter, 10 sous), AEG, Arch. hosp., Hj 2, p. [2] of March 1562.

15. AEG, Arch. hosp., Hj 2, p. [2] of May 1561.

16. "Pour les Psalmes envoyez à Monsieur de Beze asçavoir pour la relieure de 44, 48 florins, 9 sols. . . . A Symon lequel porta lesdits livres, avancé premierement, 10 florins. . . . A Symon encores pour le parachevement de son voyaige au retour de Paris où il demoura 32 ou 34 [sic; 33] jours, 19 florins, 6 sols," AEG, Arch. hosp., Hj 2, p. [3] of January 1562.

17. For more information see Eugénie Droz, "Antoine Vincent: La propagande protestante par le psautier," in Berthoud et al., eds., *Aspects de la propagande religieuse,* pp. 276–93.

18. AEG, Arch. hosp., Hj 2, January, February, August 1560.

19. Chaix, *Recherches sur l'imprimerie à Genève de 1550 à 1564,* pp. 76–77.

20. "A Piramus qui est venu de Paris estant échapé de la main des bourreaulx et tyrans, 20 florins" (To Pyramus, who has come from Paris, having escaped from the hand of the executioners and tyrans, 20 florins), AEG, Arch. hosp., Hj 2, p. [2] of November 1559.

21. On the editors and printers of sixteenth-century Geneva see Eusèbe H. Gaullieur, "Etudes sur la typographie genevoise du XVe au XIXe siècles, et sur l'introduction de l'imprimerie en Suisse," in *Bulletin de l'Institut National Genevois* (Geneva: Kessmann, Editeur, Librairie de l'Institut Genevois, 1855), 2:3–292; on the Candolle family see Alphonse de Candolle, *Recherches sur les Candolle et Caldora de Provence et de Naples* (Geneva: Imprimerie

Charles Schuchardt, 1885).

22. AEG, Arch. hosp., Hj 2, August 1559–September 1560. Note that "f" indicates florin(s), "s" indicates sou(s), and "d" indicates denier(s). The original French for these quotations is in appendix B.

23. "Rendu à Jehan Combez pour une hallebarde et une espee qu'il a achaptee a ung pauvre homme par le commandement de la Compaignie, 26 sols" (Paid back to Jean Combez for a halberd and a sword that he bought from a poor man by the order of the Company, 26 sous), AEG, Arch. hosp., Hj 2, p. [1] of November 1562.

24. AEG, Arch. hosp., Kq 1. This is the first of two "Grand Livres des Assistés" covering the latter part of the sixteenth century. These books appear to have been a later effort to arrange by name of recipient the expenditures that had originally been entered into the accounts in chronological order. Their completion may have been the occasion for doing away with some of the original running accounts in the ordinary account books.

25. The transcription of the original French for table 1 is in appendix B. The text for the entries are found in sequence in AEG, Arch. hosp., Hj 2, August 1559–November 1562, passim. Note that the sums of money have been changed from roman to arabic numerals and that "f" indicates florin(s), "s" sou(s), and "d" denier(s).

26. Compare this disproportionately large room rent of eight florins to other room rents, such as the one for 15 sous that follows.

CHAPTER 5. PASTORS AND DEACONS

1. For a specific recommendation by Calvin see AEG, Arch. hosp., Hj 2, p. [1] of September 1562.

2. See, for instance, the expenditures for October 1550, AEG, Arch. hosp., Kg 12, fol. 2ᵛ.

3. "A une pauvre femme d'auprez de Poumier [an ancient abbey near Geneva, now a restaurant; the modern spelling is Pommier], femme de Jehan Le Roy, attendant la Compaignie, 3 sols." AEG, Arch. hosp., Kg 12, fol. 2ᵛ.

4.

Sur laquelle requeste lesdictz diacres ayans veu lesdictes attestations et icelles communi-quees aux spectables ministres de ceste Eglise et suyvant leur advis et en consideration des raisons instrictes et du contenu esdictes attestations enclinans à ladicte requeste ont consenty de delivrer comme de faict en ma presence ladicte somme des deux tiers de cent eseutz a esté delivree audict Noble Jehan de Borne par Noble Charles de Joan, Seigneur de Jonvillier, au nom desdictz Spectable Budé, Dallamont, Bergevin et Anjorrant comme diacres sus-dictz. . . .

(On which request the said deacons, having seen the said attestations and communicated them to the *spectable* ministers of this church and following their advice and in consideration of the above stated reasons and of the contents of the said attestations, inclining to the said request, have consented to deliver as fact in my presence the said sum of two-thirds of one hundred ecus delivered to the said Noble Jean de Borne by Noble Charles de Joan, Lord of Jonvillier, in the name of the said Spectable Budé, Dallamont, Bergevin and Anjorrant as the above stated deacons. . . .

AEG, Not. Ragueau, vol. 8 (1 January–15 October 1566), pp. 240–42.

5. "Ung des ministres de ceste Eglise." AEG, Arch. hosp., Kg 19 (1582), fol. 1. The ten ordinances were copied into the first folio of the account book for 1582, but the introductory paragraph states that they were confirmed a year earlier by a meeting of the ministers and contributors on 5 January 1581. They were read aloud a year later on 11 January 1582 at a similar assembly:

C'est l'ordre qui a esté tenu jusques icy pour la plus grande part en l'election des diacres et an l'administration des deniers de la Bourse des pauvres estrangers confermé tant par l'advis des ministres de ceste Eglise qu'approbation desdictz diacres et bonne partie des contribuans à ladicte Bourse assemblés pour ce faict le cinquiesme de janvier 1581.

(It is the order that has been held to until now for the most part in the election of the deacons and in the administration of the deniers of the *Bourse* of the poor foreigners confirmed as much by the advice of the ministers of this church as the approbation of the said deacons and a good part of the contributers to the said *Bourse* assembled for this fact the fifth of January 1581.)

Ibid., fols. 1 and 1^v.

6. "Afin de s'acourager et advertir fraternellement en leur debvoir." AEG, Arch. hosp., Kg 19, fols. 1–1^v.

7. "Affin que les pauvres respectent tant mieulx et comme ilz doibvent lesdictz diacres en leur administration." AEG, Arch. hosp., Kg 19, fol. 1.

8. AEG, Arch. hosp., Kg 19, fol. 1^v.

9. AEG, Arch. hosp., Kg 15, fol. 1.

10. The information on the number of deacons in the seventeenth century is from Grandjean, "La Bourse Française de Genève," p. 48.

11. Sometimes the deacons' soliciting of funds was more than informal. For instance, in 1567 Jean Budé was sent to the other Protestant cantons of Switzerland to ask for support for the refugees. Shortly thereafter, Berne sent 650 ecus and some grain to distribute to the poor. This was recorded in the registers of the city council on 1 January 1568. Jean-Antoine Gautier, *Histoire de Genève des origines à l'année 1691*, vol. 4, *1556–1567* (Geneva: Ch. Eggimann, Imprimeurs, 1901), p. 614.

12. Most donations from living people seem to have been entered monthly into the receipts of the deacons and thus would have passed by way of a collector or a deacon. A few were recorded in the notarial documents, such as a donation of 2 April 1557 from Dame Anne de Remy (?) made in her habitation on the rue des chanoines to the deacon René Guassin [Gassin]. "Aux dessusdictz ayans la charge susdite et en contemplation desdictz paouvres Noble René Guassin l'ung d'iceulx ayans ladicte charge present et acceptant . . . la somme de cinquante cinq angelotz . . ." (To the above mentioned having the charge of the aforesaid and in contemplation of the said poor, Noble René Guassin, one of those having the said present charge and accepting . . . the sum of fifty-five *angelotz* . . .). AEG, Not. Ragueau, vol. 2 (20 June 1556–8 April 1558), pp. 127–129.

13. "Au tondeur qui a tondu deux pieces de draps que l'on nous avoit donnees, 14 sols, 6 deniers" (To the shearer who sheared two pieces of cloth that one had given us, 14 sous, 6 deniers). AEG, Arch. hosp., Hj 2, p. [1] of January 1561.

14. "Pour le change de troys écus, 9 deniers" (For the change of three ecus, 9 deniers). AEG, Arch. hosp., Kg 12, fol. 66. A recent well-illustrated work on the money of Geneva is by Bernard Lescaze, *Genève: sa vie et ses monnaies aux siècles passés* (Geneva: Crédit Suisse, 1981).

15. "De la part de ceulx de Provence par les mains de Monsieur René, 28 florins, 11 sols, 6 deniers" (On behalf of those from Provence by the hand of Monsieur René, 28 florins, 11 sous, 6 deniers). AEG, Arch. hosp., Kg 14, January 1554. Although it may be that "those from Provence" were residing in Geneva, it seems more probable that entries like this referred to money from foreign regions, particularly when the individual who brought them in the collection frequently traveled there.

16. One such legacy from France was that of the "defunct Spectable Maistre François Felix," minister near Nîmes in sixteenth-century Languedoc, 17 October 1565. AEG, Not. Ragueau, vol. 7 (1 March 1564–31 October 1565), p. 852.

17. See, for instance, the cases of individuals who had given money to the poor. The deacons paid off the outstanding debts of the deceased before allocating the rest to the poor.

"Rendu à Monsieur de la Bessonnaye pour acquist d'argent que luy devoit feu Monsieur de Vesignon qui a institué les pauvres ses heriters, 5 florins, 8 sols, 9 deniers" (Rendered to Monsieur de la Bessonnaye for quittance of the money owed to him by the deceased Monsieur de Vesignon who instituted the poor his heirs, 5 florins, 8 sous, 9 deniers). AEG, Arch. hosp., Hj 2, p. [3] of July 1560; "Rendu à la femme de Lassere pour les parties d'ung quidam duquel les pauvres on eu quelque argent qu'il avoyt laissé 15 florins, 1 sol" (Rendered to the wife of Lassere for the shares from a certain person from whom the poor had had some money that he had left, 15 florins, 1 sou). AEG, Arch. hosp., Hj 2, p. [1] of July 1561.

18. See his comments on the attempts by executors of one Pastor Agnet to turn aside a part of the goods willed to the poor. Letter 552, "Calvinus Ministris Neocomensibus," in *Ioannis*

Calvini Opera, ed. Baum, Cunitz, and Reuss, vol. 11, *Corpus Reformatorum*, vol. 39 (Brunswick: C. A. Schwetschke and Sons, 1873), cols. 715–17.

19. See, for instance, the case of Jean Bourdel: "A Jehan Bourdel vinaigrier pour quatre livres, 7 sols, qui luy estoient deux par les heritiers de Monsieur Jehan le Piccart, 9 florins, 9 deniers" (To Jean Bourdel, vinegar-maker, for four pounds, 7 sous, that was his, due from the heirs of Master Jean le Piccart, 9 florins, 9 deniers). AEG, Arch. hosp., Hj 2, p. [1] of June 1560.

20. The Lieutenant of Justice put a large sum in the hands of the deacons until the heirs came.

Rendu à Lassere la somme de cent trente florins, 9 sols pour ung pauvre homme heritier d'ung quidam qui estoit mort chez ledit Lassere duquel l'argent avoyt esté mis entre nos mains par l'ordonnance de Monsieur le Lieutenant attendant lesdits heritiers, laquele partie j'ay icy couchee pour ce qu'elle me estoys chargé au papier de recepte asçavoir de 70 livres dont je avoys baillé audit Lassere 15 florins, 1 sol, pour des parties, pour le reste montant 133 florins, 8 sols; 133 florins, 8 sols, 6 deniers.

(Paid back to Lassere the sum of 130 florins, 9 sous for a poor man, heir of a certain person who died at the said Lassere's house, of whom the money had been put between our hands by the ordinance of Monsieur the Lieutenant awaiting the said heirs, which part I have written down here for that which was charged me in the receipt, that is to say of 70 pounds[?], of which I had given to the said Lassere 15 florins, 1 sou, for some parties, for the sum remaining mounts to 133 florins, 8 sous: 133 florins, 8 sous, 6 deniers.)

AEG, Arch. hosp., Hj 2, p. [2] of December 1561.

21. "Procuration de Noble Jehan Budee et Jehan Dallamont comme diacres et administrateurs des deniers aulmosne aux paouvres faicte à honorable Jehan Clavet (ou Clanet) et Anthoine Montlhery" (Procuration of Noble Jean Budé and Jean Dallamont as deacons and administrators of the deniers, alms for the poor, made to honorable Jean Clavet [or Clanet] and Antoine Montlhery), 17 October 1565. AEG, Not. Ragueau, 7:851–53.

22. See, for instance, AEG, Arch. hosp., Kq 2, fol. 283.

23. AEG, Arch. hosp., Kg 19, fol. 1.

24. The building was in the rue des chanoines, today the rue Calvin. It was a house bought by the deacons on 30 December 1583 from the widow of Thomas Courteau, a refugee printer, for the sum of two thousand florins. Here they held their meetings and distributed their alms. Hélène Mayor, "La Bourse française de Genève au moment de la révocation de l'Edit de Nantes" (Mémoire de licence, University of Geneva, May 1983), p. 47.

25. See, for instance: "A Jehan cousturier pour sa femme mallade et pour ung tablié de cuyr pour son aprentif, 20 sols" (To Jean, dressmaker, for his sick wife and for a leather apron for his apprentice, 20 sous). AEG, Arch. hosp., Hj 2, p. [2] of November 1559. See also: "A Supplin de Vie qui a sa femme en couche, 12 sols" (To Supplin de Vie who has his wife in labor, 12 sous). AEG, Arch. hosp., Hj 2, p. [2] of January 1560.

26. "Et quand aulx affaires extraordinaires survenans, qu'ilz y advisent le plus diligemment et commodement que faire ce pourra selon l'exigence du cas . . ."; "Qu'ilz advisent aussy entre eulx à la subvention des passans selon qu'ilz jugeront estre le plus propre et convenable." AEG, Arch hosp., Kg 19, fol. 1.

27. See the following examples of deacons advancing money to the poor: "Rendu à Monsieur de Paré pour la visite du Plaimpalaix [*sic;* Plainpalaix] du jeudy 14ᵉ qu'il avoit avancee à mon absence, 19 florins" (Paid back to Monsieur de Paré for the visit of Plaimpalaix [*sic;* Plainpalaix] of Thursday, the fourteenth, that he had advanced in my absence, 19 florins). AEG, Arch. hosp., Hj 2, p. [2] of March 1560; "Item j'ay ce jourdhui rendu à Monsieur René qu'il avoit avancé pour la visite du Plaimpalaix [*sic;* Plainpalaix] precedente asçavoir du 7ᵉ dudit present moys et aultres memes parties, 28 florins, 2 sols" (Also, I have today paid back to Monsieur René what he had advanced for the preceding visit of Plaimpalaix [*sic;* Plainpalaix] that is to say, of the seventh of the said present month and also for other parties, 28 florins, 2 sous). AEG, Arch. hosp., Hj 2, p. [2] of March 1560; "Rendu à Monsieur de Paré qu'il a avancé à plusieurs foys, 26 florins, 2 sols, 9 deniers" (Paid back to Monsieur de Paré that he advanced several times, 26 florins, 2 sous, 9 deniers). AEG, Arch. hosp., Hj 2, p. [1] of February 1561; "Rendu à Monsieur d'Allamont pour ce qu'il a baillé à plusieurs fois, 10 florins, 5 sols" (Paid back to Monsieur d'Allamont for what he gave several times, 10 florins, 5 sous). AEG, Arch. hosp., Hj 2, p. [3] of March 1562.

28. The case of Guillaume Maurice is cited in the "Registres du Conseil" of Geneva on 22 April 1580:

Guillaume Maurice de Paris a esté renvoyé du Consistoire d'autant qu'ayant receu un teston de la main des Diacres de la Bourse il l'auroit porté au jeu de la paume et l'auroit joué, . . . est un faineant et qui ne veut travailler et un moqueur n'estant comparu a esté arresté qu'il soit appellé et ouy apres disner.

(Guillaume Maurice of Paris was sent away to the consistory for as much as having received a teston from the hands of the deacons of the *Bourse*, he carried it to the tennis court [It is not certain that "jeu de la paume" meant tennis court in sixteenth-century Geneva.] and played with it. . . . [He] is a good-for-nothing who does not want to work and a mocker. Not having appeared, it was decreed that he be called and heard after dinner.)

AEG, Reg. Conseil, vol. 75, fol. 73ᵛ.

29. "Benoiste, femme de Louys Arnault, le dernier jour d'apvril 1580, payé à Maistre Boniface appoticaire pour ladite Benoiste douze solz. . . . Ladite Benoiste s'en est allee sans dire adieu et a emporté les linceux qu'on luy avoyt pretés" (Benoiste, wife of Louys Arnault, the last day of April 1580, paid to Master Boniface, apothecary, for the said Benoiste, 12 sous. . . . The said Benoiste departed without saying goodbye and carried away the linens loaned to her). AEG, Arch. hosp., Kq 2, fol. 230.

30. "Deposé que quand le sieur feu Mardonat trespassa eté dict à son advis que le dyable avoict ceste belle proye" (Deposed that when the deceased Lord Mardonat died, it was said, in her opinion, that the devil had this fine prey). 11 October 1554, AEG, Registres du Consistoire (hereafter Reg. Consist.), 9 : 153. See the first receipts of the account books for the beginning of Maldonnade's contributions to the *Bourse*, "Item receu de Monsieur Maldonnade, 6 sols. . . . Item Monsieur Maldonnade a mis en la boete ung florin, 12 sols" (Also received from Monsieur Maldonnade, 6 sous. . . . Also Monsieur Maldonnade put one florin in the box, 12 sous). AEG, Arch. hosp., Kg 12, fol. 1ᵛ.

31. See, for instance, a poor man of Paris coming to Geneva with the attestation of the minister and deacons of the place and a woman recommended by the collectors: "A ung pauvre homme de Paris sortant des galleres avec l'attestation des ministre et diacres du lieu, 15 sols" (To a poor man of Paris, leaving the galleys, with the attestation of the minister and deacons of the place, 15 sous). AEG, Arch. hosp., Hj 2, p. [2] of March 1562.

"A Nicolle Lescuyere recommandee par les collecteurs de Meaulx et encores ung aultre recommandee pauvre mesnaige, 2 florins" (To Nicolle Lescuyere, recommended by the collectors of Meaux and also another poor couple, recommended, 2 florins). AEG, Arch. hosp., Hj 2 p. [1] of January 1560.

32. For a discussion of the welfare system and how it worked in France, see Wilma J. Pugh, "Social Welfare and the Edict of Nantes: Lyon and Nîmes," *French Historical Studies* 8 (Spring 1974): 349–76.

33. For an account of the population of Geneva in the sixteenth century see Alfred Perrenoud, *La Population de Genève du seizième au début du dix-neuvième siècle: Etude démographique* (Geneva: A. Jullien, 1979).

34. "A ung pauvre Hebreu qui s'en alloit en angleterre, 4 florins, 9 sols, 6 deniers" (To a poor Hebrew who was going to England, 4 florins, 9 sous, 6 deniers). AEG, Arch. hosp., Kg 14, 18 August 1553.

35. AEG, Arch. hosp, Kg 19, fol. 1. For consistent records of visits to the sick poor see especially the book of extraordinary accounts that covers from 1559 to 1570. AEG, Arch. hosp., Hj 2. For example, "A Monsieur René pour visiter quelques mallades extraordinairement, 6 florins, 3 sols" (To Monsieur René in order to visit a few sick people, extraordinarily, 6 florins, 3 sous), p. [1] of October 1560.

36. "Ledit jour (lundy 17ᵉ) pour la visite des mallades du costé de Monsieur René, 18 florins" (The said day [Monday the seventeenth] for the visit of the sick of the side of Monsieur René, 18 florins); "De nostre coste que j'ai rendu à Monsieur Dalamont, 8 florins" (Of our side that I paid back to Monsieur Dalamont, 8 florins). AEG, Arch. hosp, Hj 2, p. [1] of November 1561.

37. The two deacons who died were the first to be appointed along with Jean Budé. The first was Guy de Serignac, known as Monsieur de Thillat (du Tillac, or du [de] Thillac). He died on

12 October 1552, AEG, Etat civil: Registres des Décès (hereafter EC Morts), 1:81. The second was Pierre Maldonnade (Mardonat), known as "le seigneur Maldonnade." He died sometime during the year of 1554. There is no death notice registered for him, but his name as a participant in the *Bourse* seems to have disappeared from the account books after March 1554, when the accountant mentioned that someone was lodged with him. There was no mention that he was dead, but he did not make a contribution that month to the *Bourse*. AEG, Arch. hosp., Kg 14, p. [1] of March 1554. He was probably dead by the time of the new election of deacons in July 1554, and he was surely dead by August 1554 when it was recorded in the account books that the deacons received money from his will through the hands of his wife. "Item receu du testament de Monsieur de Maldonnade par les mains de sa femme, 10 écus soleil vallant 47 florins, 11 sols" (Also received from the will of Monsieur de Maldonnade by the hands of his wife, 10 ecus sol worth 47 florins, 11 sous). AEG, Arch. hosp., Kg 15, p. [1] of August 1554.

38. Jean Budé died on 5 July 1587. He was about seventy-two years old. EC Morts, 18:103.

39. AEG, Arch. hosp., Kg 19, fol. 1.

40. For example, note this purchase of cloth in the ancient measure of "aunes." An aune is "3 pieds, 7 pouces, 10 lignes 5/6" or 1 meter, 182 centimeters.

"A Maistre Pierre Le Picque pour cinquante aulnes de toile qu'il a achaptés à Lyon pour les pauvres à 6 sols l'aune, 25 florins" (To Master Pierre Le Picque for 50 *aunes* of cloth that he bought in Lyons for the poor at 6 sous the *aune*, 25 florins); "A luy mesme pour trente et une aulne de toile à 5 sols ung quart moins, 12 florins, 3 sols, 3 deniers" (To himself for thirty-one *aunes* of cloth at five sous a quarter less, 12 florins, 3 sous, 3 deniers). AEG, Arch. hosp., Hj 2, p. [2] of September 1560; "Item et le 18ᵉ decembre pour 34 aulnes de toile à 5 sols l'aulne, 14 florins, 2 sols" (Likewise and the eighteenth December for 34 *aunes* of cloth at 5 sous each, 14 florins, 2 sous), AEG, Arch. hosp., Hj 2, p. [3] of December 1560.

41. AEG, Arch. hosp., Kg 19, fol. 1.

42. Antoine gave a smaller inheritance to Samuel and David because they had been disobedient, especially David.

A scavoir ledict Samuel et David pour ung chef . . . ledict Samuel prendra les deux tiers et ledict David l'aultre tiers et ainsy eulx deux ne prendront en ses biens non plus que ung de ses aultres enfans et heritiers. Ce que ledict testateur a faict et ordonné parce que lesdictz Samuel et David luy ont esté desobeissans et notamment ledict David. . . . Item et dautant que ledict testateur a contracté et faict accord pour et touchant le bein de Samuel, David, Anne et à eulx appartenans à cause de leur feu mere, il veult et entend qu'ilz l'acceptent parce qu'il n'a rien faict que pour leur profict et avec authorité de justice. Item veult et ordonne que tous lesdictz siens enfans ne puissent demander ny quereler l'ung envers l'aultre aulcune chose pour la succession dudict defunct Spectable Maistre Jehan Calvin son frere et leur oncle que la somme de deux cens escutz.

(That is to say, the said Samuel and David, for one count . . . the said Samuel will take the two thirds and the said David the other third and thus the two of them will not take nor inherit in his goods more than one of the other children and heirs, that which the said testator did and ordered because the said Samuel and David were disobedient to him and especially the said David. . . . Also and inasmuch as the said testator has settled and made an agreement for and touching the welfare of Samuel, David, Anne, and Susanne, his children, and to them appertaining because of their deceased mother, he wants and expects that they accept it because he did nothing except for their profit and with the authority of justice. Also he wants and orders that all the said, his children, cannot ask nor quarrel the one with the other about one thing from the succession of the said deceased Spectable Master John Calvin, his brother and their uncle, than the sum of two hundred ecus.)

18 March 1569, AEG, Not. Ragueau, vol. 11 (1 January–28 October 1569), pp. 240, 243.

Samuel, David, Anne, and Susanne were the children from Antoine's first wife and Jean, Dorothea, and Marie from the second wife. These latter three were still young, so he willed them each forty ecus more to help raise them. Marie got thirty ecus more because she was forgotten in the inheritance from John Calvin. Jean got two cups of silver as his uncle John Calvin had wished, one of which had come from Laurent de Normandie and the other from Guillaume Trye. Antoine's wife was put in charge of the three minor children with the help of Laurent de Normandie, who received a small silver box that Antoine had gotten from his brother John Calvin. He willed ten florins to the hospital and twenty florins to the *Bourse française.* Antoine appeared apologetic that so little remained from John Calvin's estate, but he said that by the time he had paid his brother's debts and legacies and sold the furniture very little remained. 28 March 1569, Not. Ragueau, 11:239–44.

43. See the section on Robert Estienne and his sons in Eusèbe H. Gaullieur, "Etudes sur la typographie genevoise du XVᵉ au XIXᵉ siècles, et sur l'introduction de l'imprimerie en Suisse," in *Bulletin de l'Institut National Genevois* (Geneva: Kessmann, Editeur, Librairie de l'Institut Genevois, 1855), 2:180–210.

44. For an exegetical discussion of this verse and of women deacons, see McKee, *John Calvin on the Diaconate*, pp. 205–23.

45. See, for instance, the receipts of March 1554: "D'ung quidam logé chez Monsieur Maldonnade, 5 sols" (From a certain person lodged at Monsieur Maldonnade's house, 5 sous). AEG, Arch. hosp., Kg 14, p. [1] of March 1554.

46. "Item receu du testament de Monsieur de Maldonnade par les mains de sa femme, 10 écus sol vallant 47 florins, 11 sols." From the "Recepte pour les pauvres au moys d'aoust 1554." AEG, Arch. hosp., Kg 15, p. [1] of August 1554.

47. "A la dame Anne chez Madamoyselle Tagault[?], 2 florins" (To the dame, Anne, at Madamoiselle Tagault's[?] house, 2 florins). AEG, Arch. hosp., Hj 2, p. [1] of February 1561 and p. [1] of November 1561. "A une Provençale pour avoir gardé une pauvre fille qui est morte chez elle, 2 florins, 6 sols" (To a Provençal for having cared for a poor girl who died at her house, 2 florins, 6 sous). AEG, Arch. hosp., Hj 2, p. [2] of May 1561.

48. This English translation is from *Calvin: Institutes of the Christian Religion*, ed. John T. McNeill and trans. Ford Lewis Battles (Philadelphia: Westminster Press, 1960), 2:1061. "Car les femmes ne pouvaient exercer d'autre office public, que de s'employer au service des pauvres (I Tim. 5: 9–10). . . . il y aura deux genres de diacres: les premiers serviront l'Eglise, en gouvernant et dispensant les biens des pauvres; les seconds, en servant les malades et les autres pauvres." (John Calvin, *Institution de la religion chrétienne*, book 4, p. 62).

49. For a discussion of the office of widow and Calvin's views in an historical and exegetical context, see McKee, *John Calvin on the Diaconate*, pp. 205–23; for a consideration of Calvin's views of the role of women in the church in a broader sense, see Jane Dempsey Douglass, *Women, Freedom, and Calvin* (Philadelphia: Westminster Press, 1985). For an overview of the role of women in early modern Geneva see Thérèse Pittard, *Femmes de Genève aux jours d'autrefois* (Geneva: Editions Labor et Fides, [1946]). For the place of women in the world of work of early modern Geneva, see Liliane Mottu-Weber, "Apprentissage et économie genevoise au début du XVIIIᵉ siècle," *Revue suisse d'histoire* 20 (1970); 321–53. By the same author see "Les femmes dans la vie économique de Genève, XVIᵉ–XVIIᵉ siècles," *Bulletin de la Société d'histoire et d'archéologie de Genève* 16 (1979): 389–90; "Rouets, navettes, et dévidoirs à l'Hôpital général de Genève (XVIᵉ–XVIIIᵉ siècles)," in *Sauver l'âme nourrir le corps: De l'Hôpital général à l'Hospice général de Genève, 1535–1985*, ed. Bernard Lescaze (Geneva: l'Hospice général, 1984), pp. 113–31.

50. For instance, the widows of Denys Gillet and Pierre Marcel were foster mothers. AEG, Kq 2, fols. 3, 5, 7, 21, 31.

51. See I Timothy 5:3–16:

3. Honor widows who are real widows. 4. If a widow has children or grandchildren, let them first learn their religious duty to their own family and make some return to their parents; for this is acceptable in the sight of God. 5. She who is a real widow, and is left all alone, has set her hope on God and continues in supplications and prayers night and day; 6. whereas she who is self-indulgent is dead even while she lives. 7. Command this, so that they may be without reproach. 8. If any one does not provide for his relatives, and especially for his own family, he has disowned the faith and is worse than an unbeliever.

9. Let a widow be enrolled if she is not less than sixty years of age, having been the wife of one husband; and she must be well attested for her good deeds, as one who has brought up children, shown hospitality, washed the feet of the saints, relieved the afflicted, and devoted herself to doing good in every way. 11. But refuse to enrol younger widows; for when they grow wanton against Christ they desire to marry, 12. and so they incur condemnation for having violated their first pledge. 13. Besides that, they learn to be idlers, gadding about from house to house, and not only idlers but gossips and busybodies, saying what they should not. 14. So I would have younger widows marry, bear children, rule their households, and give the enemy no occasion to revile us. 15. For some have already strayed after Satan. 16. If any

believing woman has relatives who are widows, let her assist them; let the church not be burdened, so that it may assist those who are real widows.

52. Doumergue, *Jean Calvin*, vol. 5, *La pensée ecclésiastique et la pensée politique de Calvin*, pp. 304–7.

53. For more information on the city governors, see E. William Monter's discussion of the structure of Genevan politics. He is impressed with the ease with which the French refugees were assimilated, but considers a period that encompasses more than a generation, whereas this study of the *Bourse* emphasizes 1550–1562, those few years that include missionary activity in France. *Studies in Genevan Government, 1536–1605* (Geneva: Librairie Droz, 1964), pp. 85–121.

54. For a discussion of the origins of the Candolle family, see Alphonse de Candolle, *Recherches sur les Candolle et Caldora de Provence et de Naples* (Geneva: Imprimerie Charles Schuchardt, 1885).

55. The Budé family, for instance, started to buy up land, vineyards, and pasture as soon as they arrived in Geneva and continued land transactions, at least through the death of Jean in 1587. See, for instance, an exchange of a meadow or pasture for a vineyard on 19 February 1558: Budé ceded "une piece de pré contenant deux sextines" (a piece of meadow containing two "sextines") situated near Thonex; Marmet Caveussin ceded to him "une piece de vigne et terre contigues contenant une pose ou environ au territoire de Troys Vernaz" (a piece of vineyard and the contiguous ground containing about a *pose* in the territory of Troys Vernaz). Since the meadow was worth more than the vineyard, Marmet paid Budé 7 ecus sol. AEG, Not. Ragueau, 2:185–87. (This volume binds together two protocols of the notary; this citation comes from that beginning 19 June 1557, which is the second protocol in the volume.)

56. For the precision on Pierre Maldonnade I thank Jean-François Gilmont of Belgium; and for Budé and de Thillac, Geisendorf, ed., *Livre des habitants*, 1:2.

57. AEG, Arch. hosp., Kg 19, fol. 1.

58. "Pour tenir le compte de l'argent qui a esté receu pour les pauvres depuis le temps que la Compaignie commist à ceste office le seigneur Maldonnade, Monsieur de Thillat, et moy, qui feust le penultiesme jour de septembre l'an 500 cinquante [sic], la Compaignie assemblee chez les freres de Burcy [Bury?] et d'Aimery [d'Aimen?]." AEG, Arch. hosp., Kg 12, fol. 1.

59. AEG, Not. Ragueau, vol. 3 (28 December 1559–27 August 1560), pp. 291–96.

60. EC Morts, vol. 1, p. 81.

61. AEG, Arch. hosp., Kg 15, p. [1] of the manuscript.

62. Olivier Fatio and Olivier Labarthe, eds., *Registres de la Compagnie des Pasteurs de Genève*, vol. 3, *1565–1574* (1969), pp. 87, 100.

63. Olivier Labarthe and Bernard Lescaze, eds., *Registres de la Compagnie des Pasteurs de Genève*, vol. 4, *1575–1582*, pp. 23, 37, 77.

64. "De Monsieur de Normandye pour luy et ceulx de sa charge, 20 florins, 2 sols, 1 denier" (From Monsieur de Normandie for himself and those of his charge, 20 florins, 2 sous, 1 denier). AEG, Arch. hosp., Kg 14, p. [1] of November 1553.

65. AEG, Not. Ragueau, 11:46–47.

66. Theophile Heyer, "Notice sur Laurent de Normandie," in *Mémoires et documents publiés par la Société d'histoire et d'archéologie de Genève* (Geneva: J. Jullien, Libraire-Editeur, 1867), 16:399–422.

67. The phrase used to refer to the deacons varied somewhat, but was basically, "diacres et administrateurs de la Bourse des paouvres estrangers." See, for instance, the title of a notarial act of 2 March 1564. AEG, Not. Ragueau, 7:8.

68. The full quotation reads:

Les travaux préparatoires exigés par la publication partielle de la correspondance de Calvin furent le dernier acte et, pour ainsi dire, le couronnement de la vie de Jonvillers [sic]. Ces travaux accomplis, il rentre dans l'ombre, et son nom n'est cité que de loin en loin dans les registres des conseils de la république.

(The preparatory work required by the partial publication of the correspondence of Calvin was the last act and was, so to speak, the crowning achievement of the life of Jonvillers [sic]. These works accomplished, he returned to the shadows, and his name was cited only here and there in the registers of the councils of the republic.)

Jonvilliers was John Calvin's secretary and, therefore, inherited the responsibility to see that his correspondence was published. A note to this passage reads: "*Registres*, 20 avril 1574, et 24 mars 1575 et 10 mai 1580. A cette dernière date Jonvilliers est chargé, avec Fabri et Th. de Bèze, de revoir les règlements des imprimeurs" (Registers, 20 April 1574 and 24 March 1575 and 10 May 1580. At this last date Jonvilliers is charged, with Fabri and Theodore de Bèze, to review the regulations of the printers). There is no indication of what these "registres" might be. The account books of the *Bourse française* for the 1570s are missing. Jules Bonnet, "Les amitiés de Calvin," *Récits du seizième siècle*, 2d ed. (Paris: Grassart, Libraire-Editeur, 1875), p. 137.

69. AEG, Not. Rageau, 11:215–16; AEG, Arch. hosp., Kg 19, fol. l^v.

70. John Calvin, *Leçons ou commentaires et expositions de Jean Calvin, tant sur les révélations que sur les lamentations du prophète Jérémie. Le tout fidèlement recueilli, premièrement en latin par Jean Budé et Charles de Jonvillier et depuis translaté nouvellement en françois* (Lyons: Cl. Senneton, 1565).

71. The documents used in compiling this list include the records of the Genevan notaries for the period, the registers of the city council and of the consistory, the *procès criminels*, the registers of the city pastors, the death records, and of course the account books of the *Bourse française*. AEG, Arch. hosp., Kg 12–19 and Hj 1 and 2 (30 September 1550–December 1582).

72. Pierre Maldonnade [Maldonnat] came to Geneva from the Low Countries and was registered in the book of inhabitants on 3 May 1549: "Noble Pierre de Maldonnade, natifz de Blaton, comtée de Haynault, le 3 de may 1549." (Noble Pierre de Maldonnade, native of Blaton, county of Haynaut [actually the province of Hainaut, district of Tournai], 3 May 1549). Geisendorf, ed., *Livre des habitants*, 1:2. Several Protestants from the Low Countries existed with the name of Maldonnade or a variant. They belonged, it seems, to two families. Maldonnade is mentioned in 1544 in the correspondence of Calvin. Letter 1415, "Valérand Poullain à Jean Calvin, à Genève. De Strasbourg, 28 novembre 1544," in *Correspondance des Réformateurs dans les pays de langue française, recueillie et publiée avec d'autres lettres relatives à la Réforme et des notes historiques et biographiques*, ed. A.-L. Herminjard, vol. 9, *1543–1544* (Geneva: Georg, Libraires-Editeurs, 1897), pp. 343 n.10, 382. Pierre is a close relative of Daniel de Maldonade implicated in 1550 in a trial for heresy at Namur. L.E. Halkin, "Guillaume de Gulpen et Daniel de Maldonade," in *Etudes d'histoire et d'archéologie namuroises dédiées à Ferdinand Courtoy* (Namur, 1552), 2:641–61. For the information on "Maldonnade" in the Low Countries I am grateful to Jean-François Gilmont of Brussels, Belgium.

73. Jean Budé was entered into the book of inhabitants on 27 June 1549. Geisendorf, ed., *Livre des habitants* 1:3. He was entered with his brother François into the book of the bourgeois on 2 May 1555:

2 mai 1555—Nob. Françoys et Jehan Budé, frères, filz de feu Guillaume, natifz de Paris, leur très scavant pere est bien cogneu d'ung chaqu'ung, 40 escus 2 seillots.

(Noble François and Jehan Budé, brothers, sons of the deceased Guillaume, native of Paris, their very knowledgeable father is well known, from each, 40 ecus, 2 *seillots* [waterbuckets].)

Covelle, *Livre des Bourgeois*, p. 242. Jean Budé died at about seventy-two years of age on 5 July 1587. EC Morts, 18:103. For the Budé family see Haag and Haag, *France protestante*, vol. 3 (1852), pp. 74–77; 2d ed., vol. 3 (1881), cols. 371–82.

74. "Le 12e devant l'Esvechee Guy de Serignac, seigneur du Tillac" (The 12th before the Bishop's house, Guy de Serignac, Lord du Tillac). 12 October 1552, EC Morts, 1:81.

75. Guillaume Prevost is entered in the *Livre des habitants* on 29 November 1552 and in the *Livre des Bourgeois* on 23 August 1560: "Guilleaume Prevost, de Paris." Geisendorf, ed., *Livre des habitants*, 1:25: "Nob. Guilliaume Prevost, filz de Jehan, de Paris, Jehan, David, & Jacques, ses filz, 6 escus 1 seillot" (Noble Guilliaume Prevost, son of Jean, of Paris, Jean, David, and Jacques, his sons, 6 ecus, 1 *seillot*). Covelle, *Livre des Bourgeois*, p. 267. Henri Naef referred to him as "Noble Guillaume Prevost, seigneur de Sainct Germain (le beaufrère d'Hotman et l'ami de Calvin" (Noble Guillaume Prevost, Lord of Saint Germain [the brother-in-law of Hotman and the friend of Calvin]). *La Conjuration d'Amboise et Genève*, Extrait des Mémoires et documents de la Société d'histoire et d'archéologie de Genève (Geneva: A. Jullien, Georg, Libraires-Editeurs, 1922), pp. 527–28, n. 2. Guillaume Prevost appears repeatedly in the

documents of Geneva and in the account books of the *Bourse française*. The death records reveal that a Guillaume Prevost, "passementier," lost a daughter on Saturday, 9 March 1555, on the Bourg de Four. AEG, EC Morts, 1:203. The notarial documents reveal that he bought a house on the rue Pelleterye from his mother-in-law on 18 March 1558. AEG, Not. Ragueau, 2:201–3. There was also a procuration enabling others to sell for him vineyards, lands, barns, and other goods and possessions. 24 February 1562, AEG, Not. Ragueau, 5:88–90. In the account books he appears as a donor, advancing money to the sick whom he visited: "qu'il a avancé a plusieurs mallades qu'il a visitez, 5 florins, 3 sols, 6 deniers" (that he advanced to several sick people whom he visited, 5 florins, 3 sous, 6 deniers). AEG, Arch. hosp., Kg 14, 15 September 1553.

76. René Gassin was entered into the *Livre des habitants* in December 1552. He was entered into the *Livre des Bourgeois* on 22 April 1555. "Reception de René Gassin, docteur ès droictz, originaire de la ville de Salon de Crau en Provence, faicte le dernier de decembre 1552" (The reception of René Gassin, Doctor of Laws, originating from the city of Salon de Crau in Provence, done the last of December 1552). Geisendorf, ed., *Livre des habitants*, 1:22. "Spect. Regné Gassin, filz de feu Bertrand, de Saillon de Craux en Provence, 12 escus 1 seillot" (The honorable René Gassin, son of the deceased Bertrand, of Saillon de Craux in Provence, 12 ecus, 1 *seillot*). Covelle, *Livre des bourgeois*, p. 241. See also Haag and Haag, *France protestante*, 2d ed., vol. 5 (1886), col. 23. René Dagulles or d'Aguilles, "gentilhomme provençal," appeared in the account books under both names already in August 1552: "De Monsieur René, 20 sols . . . De la parte de ceulx de Provence par les mains de Monsieur Daguilles de René, 4 écus sol, 10 sols vallant 20 florins" (From Monsieur René, 20 sous . . . From the part of those of Provence by the hands of Monsieur Daguilles of Rene, 4 ecus sol, 10 sous, worth 20 florins). AEG, Arch. hosp., Kg 13 (October 1551–September 1552), p. 101. He may have been acting as a collector for the *Bourse* at that time. He appears surely to have been doing so by February 1554: "De Monsieur René pour ceulx de sa charge, 30 florins, 11 sols" (From Monsieur René for those of his charge, 30 florins, 11 sous). AEG, Arch. hosp., Kg 14, p. [1] of February 1554. An earlier entry in the death registers dates from November 1551: "Le 29ᵉ en la taconnerie Thomas fils de Maitre René Gasin" (The 29th in the taconnerie [near the Cathedral of St. Pierre] Thomas, son of Master René Gasin). AEG, EC Morts, 1:46. The sixteenth-century records did not typically have an acute accent in *René*. Where it was not there it has been added. René was also spelled "Regnier."

77. Monsieur de La Touche was entered into the book of inhabitants on 3 May 1549 and in the book of the bourgeois on 21 October 1555: "Maturin et François Buynard, freres, natifz de l'evesché de Vannes en Bretaigne, le 3 de may, 1549" (Maturin and François Buynard, brothers, native of the Bishopric of Vannes in Brittany, the third of May, 1549). Geisendorf, ed., *Livre des habitants*, 1:2. "21 oct. Nob. Francoys Buynard, seigneur de la Touche, 15 éscus l seillot" (21 October [1555] Noble François Buynard, Seigneur de la Touche, 15 ecus, 1 *seillot*). Covelle, *Livre des Bourgeois*, p. 244. Monsieur de la Touche kept the accounts from 21 August 1556 to the last Friday in October of that year. He appears to have continued to function as a deacon at least until September 1559. "Rendu à Monsieur de la Touche, 22 sols, 6 deniers" (Paid back to Monsieur de la Touche, 22 sous, 6 deniers). AEG, Arch. hosp., Hj 2, p. [1] of September 1559.

78. Antoine Popillon, called Monsieur Paré, de Paré, or du Paret, was entered into the book of inhabitants of Geneva on 3 May 1549 and into the book of the bourgeois on 13 January 1556. "Anthoine Popillon, natifz de Molins en Borbonoys, le 3 de may 1549" (Antoine Popillon, native of Molins in Burgundy, the third of May 1549). Geisendorf, ed., *Livre des habitants*, 1:3. "13 janvier: Noble Anthoine Popillon, de Bourbonoys, 10 escus 1 seillot" (13 January: Noble Antoine Popillon, of Burgundy, 10 ecus, 1 *seillot*). Covelle, *Livre des Bourgeois*, p. 248. His wife was apparently Izabeau de Merne. 5 August 1663, AEG, Not. Ragueau, 5:1104–17. They lost at least one child before baptism on 21 July 1566. AEG, EC Morts, 6:164. Antoine Popillon was usually referred to as Monsieur Paré in the deacons' account books. The acute accent over the 'e' has been added where missing. The entries in the account books make clear that he was a deacon; notarial documents support this by referring to him as such. 5 June 1561, AEG, Not. Ragueau, vol. 4 (1560–61), pp. 253–54. 8 December 1562 and 5 September 1563, ibid., vol. 5 (1562–64), pp. 503–4, 1243–47. 23 August 1563, ibid., vol. 6 (10 May 1563–March 1564), p. 18. 2 March 1564, ibid., 7:6–8. There is no clear evidence that after 1564 he was a deacon although his infant son died in 1566 in a house he had purchased in 1561 in the rue des

chanoines so he was apparently not dead in 1564. For the exact location of the house see 3 May 1561, ibid., 4:210–12.

79. Jean Dalamont (d'Alamont or Dallamon) apparently became a deacon shortly after his young wife died of a fever and he became a bourgeois of Geneva. He had at least three marriages. A marriage contract dates from 5 October 1559. He married Noble Damoiselle Catherine des Marins, daughter of the deceased Noble Jean des Marins, of Brie in France, and of Noble Damoiselle Estienette de Villers, native of the same place. The marriage contract was signed in Geneva in the hotel of honest Henry Jacquet on the Place Molard. 5 October 1559, AEG, Not. Ragueau, 3:209–12. His wife died at twenty-eight years of age on a Wednesday, the twenty-fourth of an undetermined month in 1560. The exact date is difficult to determine from the death records that cover 1560 to May 1561. AEG, EC Morts, 3:91. Haag and Haag cite the date as 24 April 1560. *France Protestante*, 2d ed., vol. 1 (Paris: Sandoz and Fischbacher, 1877), col. 70. On 9 September 1560 Dalamont married Françoise, daughter of Jean de Saint-Simon. His third marriage was with Antoinette Bouchade on 9 December 1571. Dalamont became a bourgeois of Geneva on 30 January 1561. "Noble Jehan d'Allamont, filz de Jehan, de Sathenay au duché de Bar [Meuse], 6 escus, 1 seillot" (Noble Jean Dalamont, son of Jean, of Stenay in the duchy of Bar, 6 ecus, 1 *seillot*). Covelle, *Livre des Bourgeois*, p. 268. He was a member of the Council of Two Hundred in 1564. Dalamont appears for the first time in the account books in a role that seems to be that of a deacon on 3 November 1561: "De nostre coste que l'on rendu [*sic*] à Monsieur Dalamont, 8 florins" (From our part that one paid back to Monsieur Dalamont, 8 florins). AEG, Arch. hosp, Hj 2, p. [1] of November 1561. He appears to have continued in that capacity until his death or shortly before his death. Fatio and Labarthe, *Registres de la Compagnie des Pasteurs de Genève*, 3:87, n. 3. The notarial documents in which he appears as a deacon of the *Bourse française* include the following: 5 September 1563, AEG, Not. Ragueau, 5:1244; 23 August 1563, ibid., 6:18; 2 March 1564, ibid., 7:6–8; 17 October 1565, ibid., p. 851; 25 September 1565, AEG, Not. François Vuarrier, vol. 5 (1537–67), fol. 279; 28 February 1566, AEG, Not. Ragueau, 8:133–35; 28 April 1566, ibid., p. 240; 27 November 1566, ibid., p. 647; 20 March 1569, ibid., 11:215; 13 May 1570, ibid., vol. 13 (1 January–24 June 1570), pp. 293–94.

Other notarial documents are also of interest, such as the will of his wife Catherine des Marins and a procuration to recover an inheritance in France that he acquired through her after her death. AEG, Not. Ragueau, 7:980–81.

Jean Dalamont died 26 August 1572. EC Morts, 12:10.

80. Yves Bergevin was entered into the book of the bourgeois of Geneva on 20 January 1561 without charge, in consideration of his work on the city's fortresses. "Noble Yves Bergevin, filz de feu Noble Adam, natifz de Aulbigni au pays de Sarlogne, gratis, en considération qu'il fert beaucoup à la Seigneurie pour les forteresses & peult servir à l'avenir au besoing." (Noble Yves Bergevin, son of the deceased Noble Adam, native of "Aulbigni" in the country of "Sarlogne," free, in consideration of how much he does for the *Seigneurie* for the fortresses and that he can serve in the future if there is need). Covelle, *Livre des Bourgeois*, p. 268. He married Gabrielle Brossequin, the widow of Spectable Master Philibert Grené. Their marriage contract is dated 1 March 1564. She was the daughter of Pierre Brossequin, bourgeois of Geneva, and before that he had been a royal notary in the city of Bourges in France. She was, like her husband, native of "Aulbigni." AEG, Not. Ragueau, 7:1. The notarial entries that cite him as a deacon are 25 September 1565, AEG, Not. Vuarrier, vol. 5 (1537–67), fol. 279; 28 February 1566, AEG, Not. Ragueau, 8:133–35; 19 September 1566, ibid., pp. 473–74; 27 November 1566, ibid., p. 647; 3 November 1568, ibid., vol. 10 (1568), p. 472; 19 January 1569, ibid., 11:40–41; 20 March 1569, ibid., pp. 215–16; 19 April 1969, ibid., p. 293; 18 June 1570, ibid., vol. 14 (1570), fol. 2ᵛ.

81. Regnauld or Renaud Anjorrant, Lord of Souilly, was from a Parisian family, an old noble family of Berry in France. He was the first of the family to become Protestant. He was the sixth and youngest child of Louis Anjorrant and Madelaine, his second wife. Renaud's older brother Jean was also from the second wife or "second bed," an expression for the children of the second spouse. Jean had been a president of the Parlement of Paris and the husband of Catherine Budé. There were two sisters, Madelaine and Isabeau, between Jean and Renaud, and two older brothers, Raoul and Claude, from the "first bed." Their mother's name was Marguerite. Haag and Haag, *France Protestante*, 2d ed., 1:266–67.

Renaud was received as an inhabitant of Geneva on 10 December 1554. "Regnault Aniourat, natifz de Parys" (Regnault Aniourat, native of Paris). Geisendorf, ed., *Livre des habitants*, 1:43. He was entered in the *Livre des Bourgeois* on 31 January 1556. (The date of 30 January 1556 is given in Jacques Augustin Galiffe, *Notices généalogiques sur les familles genevoises depuis les premiers temps jusqu'à nos jours* (Geneva: Imprimerie Ch. Gruaz, 1836), 3:12. "Regnaulx Anjorrant, filz de feu Loys, natifz de Paris, 10 escus, 1 seillot" (Regnaulx Anjorrant, son of the deceased Loys, native of Paris, 10 ecus, 1 *seillot*). Covelle, *Livre des Bourgeois*, p. 250.

Renaud married Geneviève, daughter of Françoise Brachet and of Guillaume Aubelyn, Lord of la Bruyère, on 12 December 1559. He was a member of the Council of Two Hundred of Geneva in 1570. Renaud died 25 August 1572. His wife outlived him by twenty years; she died at the age of seventy on 26 August 1592. They had three children: Jean (who was a godson of John Calvin and died at a young age), Jacob, and Marie. Galiffe, *Notices généalogiques*, 3:10–13.

The notarial references to Renaud reveal that he bought a house on 17 January 1559, the year he married. It was located on the rue de la cité. AEG, Not. Ragueau, 3:20–22. The notarial records that refer to him as a deacon date from 1566, but it is possible that he became a deacon before that. He may have been a fourth deacon in 1564 and 1565 for when it is only possible to confirm the names of three deacons. The *Bourse* seems to have had four deacons most of the years since the election in Calvin's house on 5 July 1554. 28 February 1566, AEG, Not. Ragueau, 8:133–36; 28 April 1566, ibid., p. 240; 19 September 1566, ibid., pp. 473–74; 27 November 1566, ibid., p. 647; 20 March 1569, ibid., 11:215–16. He was a deacon until his death. An election to replace him and Jean Dalamont was held on 3 September 1572. Fatio and Labarthe, *Registres de la Compagnie des Pasteurs de Genève*, 3:87, n. 2. For the Anjorrant family see Haag and Haag, *France Protestante*, 2d ed., vol. 1, cols. 266–75.

82. Charles de Jonvilliers was born c. 1517 at Chartres, France. His father was Rougier (Rogerin) de Jouan, Lord of Jonvilliers, and his mother was Magdeleine (Madeleine) Imbault (Imbaut). He had three sisters: Marie, who married Jean Budé, and Jeanne and Gabrielle, who married Roman Catholic men and stayed in France. He never married. He studied at the University of Paris. The departure of the Budé family for Geneva in 1549 moved him to go too, despite his mother's reluctance. In April 1550 he was in Italy studying law in Padua with Louis Budé. He was in contact with Italians of Reformed leanings and especially with the group at Ferrara, of the household of the Duchess Renée, daughter of Louis XII of France. Bonnet, *Récits du seizième siècle*, 2d ed., pp. 102–42.

He returned to Geneva in 1551 and was received inhabitant on 28 August 1551. "Charles de Jonville, natif de Chartres du pays de France, *le 28 augusti 1551*" (Charles de Jonville, native of Chartres of the country of France, 28 August 1551). Geisendorf, ed., *Livre des habitants*, 1:15. His mother followed him to Geneva, and the two of them lived with Marie and Jean Budé. In her will of 12 February 1558 Magdelaine Imbault left one hundred pounds to Jean Budé for food, maintenance, and compensation for having lived in his house since 23 March 1551. She left the same amount to her son Charles because he had had less of her belongings than his sister Marie had had. She left possessions in France for her daughters in France. To the poor foreigners of Geneva she left fifty pounds. 12 February 1558, AEG, Not. Ragueau, 2:174–78.

Charles was entered into the *Livre des Bourgeois* on 30 January 1556, "Charle De Jonvillier, filz de feu Rougier, 10 escus, 1 seillot" (Charle De Jonvillier, son of the deceased Rougier, 10 ecus, 1 *seillot*). Covelle, *Livre des Bourgeois*, p. 250. He became a member of the Genevan Council of Two Hundred in 1563. He was a friend of John Calvin. Indeed, he was Calvin's personal secretary for over ten years. Many of Calvin's letters were thus dictated to Charles de Jonvilliers and are in his handwriting. This was despite Calvin's initial reluctance to let someone else do his writing for him for fear of being accused of negligence or pride. Bonnet, *Récits du seizième siècle*, 2d ed., pp. 118, n. 2, 119–20.

The position of Latin secretary to Calvin made Jonvilliers largely responsible for collecting and preserving Calvin's correspondence as well as for editing, with Jean Budé, Calvin's Old Testament commentaries. He also translated from Italian into French a book of a preacher of Piedmont that he dedicated to Galeazzo Caracciolo, Marquis of Vico, an Italian who settled in Geneva. The book was Agostino Mainardi, *L'Anatomie de la Messe* (Geneva, 1562).

He was extremely moved by the death in 1564 of Calvin, for whom he had an intense devotion and affection, but he was close to others as well. Jean Budé, his brother-in-law, referred to him as "my brother" in the account books: "de mon frere de Jonvil" (from my brother, de Jonvil). AEG, Arch. hosp., Kg 15, p. [1] of February 1555. Jean Budé willed Charles de Jonvilliers his nourriture, maintenance, expenditures, and habitation in both his city and country houses and asked that his children be guided in their affairs by his advice and counsel, continuing in friendship, honor, and reverence for him as for their mother.

> Je luy donne et legue sa nourriture, entretenement, et despence de bouche avec son habitation à sa commodité en mes maisons de la ville que des champs . . . que tous mes enfans se conduisent en leurs affaires par son advis et conseil et qu'ils continuent en son endroict l'amitye que je luy ay toujours portée, dont je lez charge expressement comme de l'honneur et reverence qu'ils doibvent porter à leur mere . . .

7 July 1587, AEG, Not. Jean Jovenon, vol. 6, fols. 212^v and 213.

Charles de Jonvilliers died on 20 May 1590 at the age of about seventy-four. He willed thirty florins to the Bourse française, fifteen florins to the college, and ten florins to the hospital. Bonnet, Récits du seizième siècle, 2d. ed., pp. 138–41.

His sister Marie outlived him. She died 10 December 1602. She willed one hundred florins to the Bourse française and one hundred florins to the hospital, both of which were collected. 10 December 1602, AEG, Not. Olivier Dagoneau, vol. 1 (1591–1608), fols. 457–58^v.

Despite these accomplishments, a nineteenth-century biographer, Jules Bonnet, called Charles de Jonvilliers a person of secondary rank, living through another's life. Bonnet, Récits du seizième siècle, 2d ed., pp. 102, 141. Bonnet did not take into account Jonvilliers's service as a deacon, a post in which he was first found in the notarial records in 1569 and in which he died. The notarial records that mention him as deacon include 20 March 1569, AEG, Not. Ragueau, 11:215–16; 10 March 1570, ibid., 13:183–84; 16 April 1578, Not. Jovenon, vol. 4 (1 January 1577–20 October 1580), fols. 162–63. By the 1570s the registers of the Company of Pastors recorded the deacons' names with some regularity. There was an election on 3 September 1572 that elected Jonvilliers among others. Fatio and Labarthe, Registres de la Compagnie des Pasteurs, 3:87. On 26 May 1575, the same deacons were confirmed. Labarthe and Lescaze, Registres de la Compagnie des Pasteurs, 4:23. In the election of 28 December 1576 he was confirmed rather than elected anew:

> . . . les nations assemblee sont confermé Monsieur de Verace, de Jonvilliers, Louys André et Campefleur, Monsieur de Fequieres en la charge de diacres pour l'annee suivante et ont esleu Monsieur de Candoles pour leur assister en la place d'Artus Chauvin qui a prié d'estre decharge.
>
> (. . . the nations assembled confirmed Monsieur de Vérace, de Jonvilliers, Louis André, and Campefleur, Monsieur de Fequières in the charge of the deacons for the following year and elected Monsieur de Candoles in order to assist them in place of Artus Chauvin who asked to be discharged.)

Ibid., p. 77. Charles de Jonvilliers was again mentioned as a deacon in 1583, and in the years 1586–1590. He may have been a deacon continuously since there are gaps in the record. Olivier Labarthe and Micheline Tripet, eds., Registres de la Compagnie des Pasteurs, vol. 5, 1583–1588 (Geneva: Librairie Droz, 1976), pp. 26, 100, 141, 177; Sabine Citron and Marie-Claude Junod, eds., Registres de la Compagnie des Pasteurs, vol. 6, 1589–1594 (Geneva: Librairie Droz, 1980), pp. 3, 44, 169.

83. Antoine Calvin was the brother of John Calvin, whom he followed to Geneva. They lived in the same household. He was entered into the Livre des Bourgeois on 3 August 1546, thirteen years before his famous brother and a decade before many of the French refugees. He did not have to pay anything because of his brother:

> Anthoine Calvin, filz de feuz Girard, de Noyons, gratis, en contemplacion que Monsieur Jehan Calvin, ministre de Genève, prend grand poierne à l'avancement de la parolle de Dieu & a maintenyr l'honneur de la Cité.
>
> (Antoine Calvin, son of the deceased Girard, of Noyon, free, in contemplating that Monsieur John Calvin, minister of Geneva, takes great pain for the advancement of the Word of God and the maintenance of the honor of the city.)

Covelle, *Livre des Bourgeois*, p. 226. He was an editor, an administrator of the hospital, a member of the Council of Two Hundred, and a deacon of the *Bourse française* from 3 September 1572 until his death on 2 February 1573. See Doumergue, *Jean Calvin*, vol. 3, *La ville, la maison et la rue de Calvin* (Lausanne: Georges Bridel, Editeurs, 1905), pp. 568–75.

84. Sire Louys André was entered into the *Livre des Bourgeois* on 31 December 1557: "Loys André, filz de feu Michiel, natifz de Vaux en Languedoc, 10 escus, 1 seillot" (Loys André, son of the deceased Michiel of Vaux in Languedoc, 10 ecus, 1 *seillot*). Covelle, *Livre des Bourgeois*, p. 259. Loys André was a merchant. He was elected deacon on 3 September 1572 after the death of Renaud Anjorrant and Jean Dalamont. He appears to have remained a deacon until at least 1579. His wife, Dame Nycole Le Grain, made her will on 26 September 1587 and at that time was referred to as a widow. She left fifty pounds to the *Bourse française*, and twenty-five pounds each to the college and the hospital. AEG, Not. Jovenon, vol. 6 (1586–90), fols. 272–75^v; Fatio and Labarthe, *Registres de la Compagnie des Pasteurs*, 3:87; Labarthe and Lescaze, *Registres de la Compagnie des Pasteurs*, 4:77; Haag and Haag, *France Protestante*, 2d ed., vol. 1, cols. 235–41.

85. Philippes du Pas is cited in Doumergue as "le sieur de Feuquières" who in 1564 suggested revisions in the city walls of Geneva. *France Protestante* says only that the name "Pas" was of the "seigneurie de l'Artois," one of the oldest families of the country, that of the marquis de Feuquières. Philippes was elected a deacon on 6 February 1573 and remained in that office until at least 1577, returning again on 7 January 1591. Doumergue, *Jean Calvin*, 3:123–24; Haag and Haag, *France Protestante*, 8:148; Fatio and Labarthe, eds., *Registres de la Compagnie des Pasteurs*, 3:100; Labarthe and Lescaze, eds., *Registres de la Compagnie des Pasteurs*, 4:23, 45, 77; Citron and Junod, eds., *Registres de la Compagnie des Pasteurs*, 6:63. The account of the 1573 election says it began with prayer, followed by the election, an exhortation by Théodore de Bèze to be charitable, and finally an action of grace toward the Lord.

86. There are two people by the name of Artus Chauvin in the book of inhabitants but one is nine months after the election of 6 February 1573 on 16 November 1573. The other is dated the 22 May 1554 "honn. Artus Chauvin, du pays de Bourdelles, libraire" (the honorable Artus Chauvin, of the country of Bourdelles, [Dordogne] dealer in books). On 4 September 1572 Artus Chauvin is a supporter of "Paris Prostat, escrivain." This could be the Paris who copied Calvin's sermons. Perhaps he had just come from Lyons since his wife was there at this time and there was a gap in payments to him by the *Bourse française* from 31 July 1571 to 11 September 1572. This may have been an effort to regularize his presence in Geneva. As a dealer in books Chauvin was not allowed to print them himself. He asked to set up a printing press in his own house but was told he needed to be a bourgeois to do that. He had other presses print what he published. He specialized in the official publications for the city. In 1562 he also published in Lyons. Chauvin is apparently a deacon from 6 February 1573 until 28 December 1576 when he asks to be discharged. Geisendorf, ed., *Livre des Habitants*, 1:160, 2:2; Haag and Haag, *France Protestante* (Paris: Librairie Fischbacher, 1884), 4:27; Fatio and Labarthe, *Registres de la Compagnie des Pasteurs*, 3:100; Labarthe and Lescaze, *Registres de la Compagnie des Pasteurs*, 4:60, 77, 81; Chaix, *Recherches sur l'imprimerie à Genève de 1550 à 1564* (Geneva: Librairie E. Droz, 1954), pp. 160–61.

87. Labarthe and Lescaze, *Registres de la Compagnie des Pasteurs*, 4:37, 42, 58, 60, 77, 81.

88. Bernardin de Candolle was of a noble and very old family of Provence that may have been related to a family of Naples. The authors of *France Protestante* state that it is the oldest family they know, because they can find records back to the thirteenth century. The family held responsible positions, especially in Marseilles. Bernardin is one of twelve brothers and sisters. He became a canon of Forcalquier but then adopted the reform, married a woman named Anne Rigaud, and came to Geneva where he was entered into the book of inhabitants on 26 May 1552, "Bernardin de Candolle, escuyer, de Marseille, a esté receu pour habiter." (Bernardin de Candolle, squire, of Marseilles, has been received to live here.) He became a bourgeois of Geneva 9 May 1555. He became a member of the Council of Two Hundred, 1562, and of the consistory, 1575. He was apparently a deacon of the *Bourse Française* from 28 December 1576 until his death 2 July 1585. He was already a donor in the 1550s. He was a collector for the *Bourse* in 1575 and 1582 and apparently other years. In at least 1582 he was both a collector and a deacon at the same time, and in 1583 he was a deacon and an elder on the consistory. After his wife died he married in 1571 Sara Gassin, daughter of René Gassin, a former deacon. He had no

children, but he drew his relatives to Geneva. After a trip to Germany he came back with the proposal from a community of Jews numbering in the thousands to resettle in Geneva in exchange for which they would provide defense for the city, prosperity, and money. The proposal was rejected. In his will he left three hundred florins to the *Bourse française*, one hundred to the hospital, and one hundred to the collège. He also treated his relatives generously, particularly his nephew Piramus de Candolle, who was a teenager, on the condition that he live in Geneva, marry a Protestant woman, and continue in the textile business. From Piramus the Candolles of Geneva descended. Augustin-Pyramus is perhaps the most famous, a botanist. Geisendorf, ed., *Livre des habitants*, 1:23; Covelle, *Livre des Bourgeois*, p. 243. Galiffe, *Notices Généalogiques*, 2:567–99; Labarthe and Lescaze, *Registres de la Compagnie des Pasteurs*, 4:16, 17, 77, 89, 261; Labarthe and Tripet, *Registres de la Compagnie des Pasteurs*, 5:100, 218, 225, 226, 229; Gabriella Cahier and Michel Grandjean, *Registres de la Compagnie des Pasteurs de Genève*, vol. 7 *1595–1599* (Geneva: Librairie Droz, 1984), p. 55; Haag and Haag, *France Protestante*, 3:183–98; 2d ed., 3:687–706; Doumergue, *Jean Calvin*, 3:623 n. 9; 16 April 1578, AEG., Arch. hosp., Not. Jovenon, 4:162.

CHAPTER 6. VOLUNTEERS AND PAID PERSONNEL

1. The section in the Ecclesiastical Ordinances on deacons reads as follows:

> Le quatriesme ordre du gouvernement ecclesiasticque, asscavoir des dyacres
>
> Il en y a eu tousjours deux especes en l'eglise ancienne. Les uns ont esté deputez à recevoir, dispenser et conserver les biens des povres tant aulmosnes quotidiennes que possessions, rentes et pensions. Les aultres pour songner et penser les malades et administrer la pitance des povres, laquelle coustume nous tenons encore de present. *Et affin d'eviter confusion*, car nous avons procureurs et hospitalliers, *que l'un des quatre procureurs dudict hospital soit recepveur de tout le bien d'icelluy et qu'il ait gaiges competans, affin de exercer mieulx son office.*

"Ordonnances Ecclésiastiques," in *Registres de la Compagnie des Pasteurs de Genève*, ed. Bergier, 1:7.

> (The fourth order of ecclesiastical government, that is, deacons
>
> There were always two kinds in the ancient church, the one deputed to receive, dispense and hold goods for the poor, not only daily alms, but also possessions, rents and pensions; the other to tend and care for the sick and administer allowances to the poor. [This custom we hold now, and in order to avoid confusion, because we have procurators and hospitalers, that one of the four procurators of the said hospital be receiver of all the goods and that he have an adequate salary, in order to better exercise his office.])

"Draft Ecclesiastical Ordinances," in Reid, ed., *Calvin: Theological Treatises*, p. 64. Bracketed section is my translation.

2. For more on the functions of the deacons of the city hospital of Geneva see Robert M. Kingdon, "Social Welfare in Calvin's Geneva," *American Historical Review* 76 (February 1971): 50–69. Kingdon suggests that John Calvin utilized the model of the supervisors of the city hospital to support his description of two types of deacons: trustee deacons (procurators) and deacons who cared for the poor (hospitalers). For his carefully reasoned argument see "The Deacons of the Reformed Church in Calvin's Geneva," In *Mélanges d'histoire du XVIe siècle offerts à Henri Meylan* (Geneva: Librairie Droz, 1970), pp. 81–90. The most recent book on the city hospital of Geneva is *Sauver l'âme, nourrir le corps*, a collection of essays in commemoration of its four hundred and fiftieth anniversary, gathered under the supervision of Bernard Lescaze.

3. AEG, Arch. hosp., Kg 19, fol. 1.

4. Ibid., fol. 1ᵛ. Labarthe and Lescaze, *Registres de la Compagnie des Pasteurs de Genève*, 4:16–17.

5. From the deacons' receipts of November 1553 and January and September 1554: "De Monsieur de La Touche pour ceulx de son quartier, 11 florins, 1 sol, 6 deniers"; "De Monsieur de Normandye pour luy et ceulx de sa charge, 20 florins, 2 sols, 6 deniers"; "Du bailly Potier

pour ceux d'Orleans, 10 florins, 9 sols, 3 deniers"; "De ceux de Lyon par les mains du signeur [*sic;* seigneur] Estiene Tremblé, huict escuz sol et 19 sous tournois, vallant, 40 florins, 3 sols, 9 deniers." AEG, Arch. hosp., Kg 14, pp. [1, 2] of November 1553. "De la part de ceulx de Provence par les mains de Monsieur René, 28 florins, 11 sols, 6 deniers." AEG, Arch. hosp., Kg 14, p. [1] of January 1554.

    6. The mid-sixteenth century manuscripts do not seem to support the contention of Henri Grandjean that these offices could overlap. The office of auditor and that of deacon did not appear to overlap from 1550 to 1582. See Grandjean, "La bourse française de Genève," p. 48. Information on who the auditors were, to the extent that it is available, comes from the account books of the *Bourse* and the election of deacons, auditors, and collectors of 11 January 1582. AEG, Arch. hosp., Kg 19, fol. 1ᵛ.

    7. Ibid.

    8. "Premier Registre 1550: Registre de la recepte et despence des pauvres depuis le premier octobre mille cinq cents cinquante, Bude" (First Register, 1550: Register of the receipt and expenditure of the poor since 1 October 1550, Budé). AEG, Arch. hosp., Kg 12, front cover of the book; the transcription of the account books by Henri Bordier, dated 1 October 1876, includes a copy of Jean Budé's signature that he says he copied from the anterior plate of the second account book. The transcription reads as follows:

1551

Papier journal de recepte et despence pour les pauvres depuis le moys d'octobre m. cinq cens cinquante et ung.
Livre journal de la despence des pauvres et de la recepte ordinaire depuis le moys d'octobre m. cinq cens cinquante et ung pour jusques en l'année suyvante.

BUDE

(Paper journal of receipt and expenditure for the poor since the month of October 1551.
Journal book of the expenditure for the poor and of the ordinary receipt since the month of October 1551 until into the year following.

BUDE)

In Bordier's transcription the signature of Budé is large and ornate. AEG, Manuscrits historiques, no. 223, fol. 17 or p. 31.

    9. Only one extraordinary account book survives for the 1560s. AEG, Arch. hosp., Hj 2.
    10.

Davantage fut ordonné que lesdicts diacres anciens [Jean Budé and Charles de Jonvilliers] rendroyent le conte de leur administration precedente, pour lequel ouyr furent esleus Jean Truchet, Simon Le Maire et Jean Ternault. Furent faictes par Monsieur de Besze plusieurs exhortations vives pour remontrer les faultes qui se commettent au cas de donner, afin qu'on s'eschauffast à mieux faire que devant.

(Moreover it was ordered that the said old deacons [Jean Budé and Charles de Jonvilliers] render the account of their preceding administration for which accounting were elected Jean Truchet, Simon Le Maire and Jean Ternault. Several lively exhortations were made by Monsieur de Bèze in order to show the faults that were committed in the case of giving, to the end that one rises to do better than before.)

Fatio and Labarthe, *Registres de la Compagnie des Pasteurs de Genève*, vol. 3, *1565–1574*, p. 87.

Ledict Tillier [Pierre] aussi s'offrant a esté esleu pour auditeur des contes des deniers des povres avec ceux de l'annee passee à sçavoir Jean Truchet, Jean Ternaut et Jean Boucher.

(The said Tillier [Pierre] also offering to be elected as auditor of the accounts of the pennies of the poor with those of the past year that is to say Jean Truchet, Jean Ternaut and Jean Boucher.)

Labarthe and Lescaze, *Registres de la Compagnie des Pasteurs de Genève*, vol. 4, *1575–1582*, p. 77.

11.

Somme totalle de le despence: 222 florins 3 sols 6 deniers, par ainsy doibt la recepte à la despence pour avoir plus mis que receu. Cy 127 florins 5 sols 6 deniers, qui vallent soixante et une livre troys solz 6 deniers tornois.

(Sum total of the disbursements: 222 florins, 3 sous, 6 deniers, thus the receipts owe to the disbursements for having put out more than received. Here 127 florins, 5 sous, 6 deniers, which is worth sixty-one pounds, three sous, 6 deniers *tournois.*)

29 June 1551, AEG, Arch. hosp., Kg 12, fol. 60.

Somme de toute la despence extraordinaire du present moys monte 465 − 7 − 5. La distribution monte 309 − 0 − 6 qui vallent les deux ensemble sept cens septante quatre florins sept sols unze deniers. La recepte ne monte que 609 − 10 − 8. Parquoy me deu pour avoir plus amployé que receu la somme de 164 − 9 − 3.

(Sum of all the extraordinary expense of the present month mounts 465 − 7 − 5. The distribution mounts 309 − 0 − 6 which is worth, the two together, seven hundred seventy-four florins, seven sous, eleven deniers. The receipt mounts only 609 − 10 − 8. Therefore, it will be owed to me for having employed more than received, the sum of 164 − 9 − 3.)

AEG, Arch. hosp., Hj 2, pp. [3 and 4] of September 1561.

Somme de toute la despence extraordinaire monte 179 − 6 − 0. La distribution monte 301 − 2 − 3, qui vallent les deux ensemble quatre cens huictante florins, huict sols, 3 deniers. Le recepte monte 443 − 8 − 2 . . . Pourtant sera deu pour avoir plus amployé que receu la somme de trente sept florins, je dy 37 − 0 − 0.

(Sum of all the extraordinary expenses mounts 179 − 6 − 0. The distribution mounts 301 − 2 − 3, which is worth, the two together, four hundred eighty florins, eight sous, 3 deniers. The receipt mounts 443 − 8 − 2. . . . Still the sum of thirty-seven florins will be due for having employed more than received, I say 37 − 0 − 0.)

AEG, Arch. hosp., Hj 2, p. [2] of November 1561.

12.

Les exhortations ont esté faites à ce qu'on s'esvertue d'une aultre sorte pour assister aux povres, et pour mieux faire entendre à chacun la necessité qui en est, a esté arresté de se retrouver tous ensemble vendredy prochen pour voir par les contes combien la mise surmonte la recepte et comme tout s'en va espuisé si Dieu n'y pourvoit et si chacun ne s'esforce de sa part.

(Exhortations were made to the effect that one does one's utmost of another sort in order to assist the poor, and in order to better make each one hear the need that there is, it has been decided to meet again all together next Friday in order to look at the accounts, how much the expenditures mount over the receipts and how everything is going to be exhausted if God does not provide and if each one does not strain to do his part.)

Labarthe and Lescaze, *Registres de la Compagnie des Pasteurs de Genève,* vol. 4; *1575–1582,* p. 37.

13. See the first folio of the first surviving account book: AEG, Arch. hosp., Kg 12, fol. 1–1ᵛ.

14. "De Madamoiselle de Boynville ung ducat valant 5 florins, 2 sous, 6 deniers." AEG, Arch. hosp., Kg 15; in the sixteenth century a *damoiselle* or a *madamoiselle* is not necessarily an unmarried woman. These terms designated rank in society. *Damoiselle* was used in contrast to *bourgeoisie* and to *dame.* A *damoiselle* was a woman of the lesser nobility, "de rang moyen." Edmond Huguet, *Dictionnaire de la langue française du seizième siècle* (Paris: Librairie Ancienne Honoré Champion, 1932), 2:701; Ibid. (Paris: Didier, 1961) 5:69–70.

15. The transcription of the title of AEG, Arch. hosp., Kg 14 is: "Livre de despence et recepte ordinaire pour les pauvres depuis le premier juillet 1553" (Book of the expenditures and ordinary receipts for the poor since the first of July 1553).

16.

Receu de Monsieur de Verace	165 f		
De Mademoiselle de La Roche	9 f	9 s	6 d
De quelque autre particulier par les mais de Monsieur de Villeneufve	5 f		
(Received from Monsieur de Vérace	165 f		
From Mademoiselle de La Roche	9 f	9 s	6 d
From some other particular person by the hands of Monsieur de Villeneuve)	5 f		

AEG, Arch. hosp., Hj 1.

17. AEG, Arch. hosp., Hj 2.

18. AEG, Arch. hosp., Kq 1 and 2.

19. See, for instance, Boniface, an apothecary regularly employed by the deacons in the 1560s. "A Messire Boniface apoticquaire pour les parties des pauvres depuis le moys de febvrier, 63 florins, 5 sols" (To Monsieur Boniface, apothecary, for the parties of the poor since the month of February, 63 florins, 5 sous). AEG, Arch. hosp., Hj 2, p. [2] of March 1562.

20. See, for instance, folio three of the first account book: "Item à ung apoticaire . . ." (Also to an apothecary . . .). AEG, Arch. hosp., Kg 12, fol. 3.

21. AEG, Arch. hosp., Kg 19, fol. 1.

22. "Au medecin pour le parachevement de ceste anné, 11 écus pistolez valent 55 florins" (To the doctor for the completion of this year, 11 ecus pistoles, worth 55 florins). AEG, Arch. hosp., Hj 2, p. [3] of September 1560.

23. AEG, Arch. hosp., Ka 6, "Délibérations des Diacres de la Bourse française et Livre de Mémoire" (1 March 1680–30 December 1691), p. 392.

24. Ibid., p. 424; 18 April 1614, AEG, Arch. hosp., Ke 1, "Livre des Reglements contenant un receuil des plus importantes deliberations prises par Messieurs les Diacres de la Bourse françoise sur divers cas proposés ou autrement representés dans leur assemblée concernant la direction des pauvres refugies françois . . . autres qui en dependent et conformement aux livres de Memoire de la ditte Bourse des années 1612 à 1 . . . [no closing date is written here] inclus," p. 11.

25. "A ung serrurier pour ouvrir une chambre du Plaimpalaix, 1 sol, 9 deniers" (To a locksmith in order to open a room of Plainpalais, 1 sou, 9 deniers). AEG, Arch. hosp., Hj 2, p. [3] of December 1560.

26. There is a three-year gap in payments to Paris beginning at the end of 1564, the last year of Calvin's life, then he again received assistance from the *Bourse,* this time in money, grain, clothing, and payments for apothecary bills from 3 January 1568 to 31 July 1571 and from 11 September 1572 to November 1572. Then there is another gap of three years and a final payment of 7 August 1575. It is possible that some of this time was spent in Lyons. On 4 September 1572 Paris Prostat, writer, became an inhabitant of Geneva. His wife was in Lyons. Geisendorf, *Livre des habitants,* 2:2. See appendix C for the payments to Paris from "The Great Book of the Assisted," 1568–1575.

27. See, for instance, Baltazar and Julienne. AEG, Arch. hosp., Hj 2, pp. [2 and 4] of November 1559.

28. The first of the following payments, which pays three sous per sermon, could indicate that Paris was paid per sermon, but it seems more likely that he received an ordinary salary as indicated in the second quotation in which he buys a coat to be paid back on his "ordinary." The third citation, which refers to a boy who was given 2 florins, 6 sous, might indicate that a boy was paid a fixed amount to transcribe the sermons that Paris had already copied down. In a sense the boy could be considered a piecework employee. "A Paris l'escrivain pour unze sermons qu'il a fait transcrire au pris de trois sols piece, 2 florins, 9 sols" (To Paris, the writer, for eleven sermons that he had transcribed at the price of three sous each piece, 2 florins, 9 sous). AEG, Arch. hosp., Hj 2 p. [1] of April 1562. "A Paris l'escrivain presté pour avoir un manteau qui luy fauldra rabattre sur son ordinaire, 7 florins" (To Paris the writer, loaned in order to have a coat that he should pay back on his ordinary salary, 7 florins). AEG, Arch. hosp.

Hj 2, p. [1] of April 1562. "Au garçon pour dix sermons cy encores, 2 florins, 6 sols" (To the boy for ten sermons or more, 2 florins, 6 sous). AEG, Arch hosp., Hj 2, p. [1] of April 1562.

29. See, for instance, the large purchases, apparently of cloth, from Lord Estienne Girard. "Item: et le lundy 25ᵉ au seigneur Estienne Girard sur les parties des pauvres en plusieurs espece doit la somme de septante sept livres quatorze sols, que valent, 161 florins, 10 sols, 6 deniers" (Likewise and Monday, the twenty-fifth, to the Lord Estienne Girard for the portions of the poor in several kinds, owed the sum of seventy-seven pounds, fourteen sous, worth, 161 florins, 10 sous, 6 deniers). AEG, Arch. hosp., Hj 2, p. [4] of December 1559. See also ibid., p. [2] of February 1560.

30. *Le Chien Vert.* The Inn of the Green Dog put up many of the poor, but association with the *Bourse* did not prevent it from appearing regularly in the consistory records with pregnant serving girls and cases of blasphemy and drunkenness. On 13 November 1550, there was a question of a pregnancy by Jean Lullin. Reg. Const., vol. 5, fol. 80. On 21 May 1551, the host of the Green Dog reported a case of blasphemy. Reg. Consist., vol. 6, fol. 36. In January 1553, a man's son apparently made an unwise offer of marriage to a loose woman at the *Chien Vert* that his father wanted the consistory to absolve. Reg. Consist., vol. 7, fol. 132.

Jaquet, dit Henry Gon, hôte du Croissant. The *Croissant* is an inn located, apparently, on the Place du Molard. "Anri Gon hoste du Croyssant au Mollard" (Henry Gon, host of the Crescent at the Molard). Reg. Consist., vol. 8 (1553–54), fol. 26ᵛ. Like the innkeeper at the *Chien Vert*, Henry Gon and his children were involved as witnesses before the consistory for suspicious activities on their premises. Appearing before the consistory on 25 May and 1 June 1553, Pierre, the son of Henry Gon, saw one Martin Le Grieur leaving their stable alone followed shortly thereafter by a girl. The door had been barred from the inside a short while before, apparently by these two. The consistory wanted more evidence. Reg. Consist., vol. 8, fols. 26ᵛ and 27ᵛ. Henry Gon had appeared himself the year before as a witness to report on the after dinner conversation of one Richard, who had said he had slept with a girl. Reg. Consist., vol. 7, fol. 125. "A Balthasar pour payer chez Henry Gon[?], 12 sols" (To Balthasar for paying at Henry Gon's[?] place, 12 sous). AEG, Arch. hosp., Hj 2, p. [5] of September 1560.

Other lodging places in Geneva include *La Lanterne, La Tête Noire,* and *Le Lyon Dore.* Reg. Consist., vol. 6, fol. 45; vol. 8, fol. 28; and vol. 9, fol. 196.

31. Master Giles Bobusse or Monsieur Bobusse received monthly payments from the *Bourse* for the people he put up. They included a broad spectrum of individuals from the very poor to Didier Rousseau. On 6 April 1551 Didier Rousseau was given four ecus sol to pay Monsieur Bobusse: "Item à Dydier Rousseau pour acquicter de la pension de Monsieur Bobusse jusques au 17ᵉ de ce moys, 4 écus sol, vallant 19 florins, 2 sols" (Also to Didier Rousseau to pay the boarding-house of Monsieur Bobusse until the seventeenth of this month, 4 ecus sol, worth 19 florins, 2 sous). AEG, Arch. hosp., Kg 12, fol. 40ᵛ; Bobusse continued to be involved in *Bourse* activities during 1559–61, the years when the French refugees were trying to evangelize France.

32. For details on life in Geneva during this period see René Guerdan, *Genève au temps de Calvin* (Geneva: Editions du Mont-Blanc, 1977).

33. "Au logis de Monsieur Crespin, 7 sols." AEG, Arch. hosp., Kg 12, fol. 3ᵛ. "A une pauvre religieuse, 12 sols" (To a poor nun, 12 sous). AEG, Arch. hosp., Hj 2, p. [1] of February 1561. "A une pauvre religieuse, 12 sols" (To a poor nun, 12 sous). AEG, Arch. hosp., Hj 2, p. [3] of February 1561. "A une religieuse comme il luy a esté ordonné, 12 sols" (To a nun as it has been ordered to her, 12 sous). AEG, Arch. hosp., Hj 2, p. [3] of March 1561. "A une religieuse chez la femme de Crespin, 12 sols" (To a nun at the home of the wife of Crespin, 12 sous). AEG, Arch. hosp., Hj 2, p. [1] of August 1561.

34. For the French of the guidelines of the *Bourse française* see appendix D.

CHAPTER 7. DONORS

1. Anne Marie Piuz, "Les depenses de charité d'une ville au XVIIIᵉ siècle: Le cas de Genève," in *Domanda e Consumi, Livelli e Strutture (Nei Secoli XIII–XVIII) Atti della "Sesta Settimana de Studio" (27 aprile–3 maggio 1974),* ed. Leo S. Olschki (Florence: Istituto Internazionale di Storia Economia "F. Datini", 1978), pp. 205–12, and "Charité privée et mouvement des affaires à Genève au XVIIIᵉ siècle," *Colloque FrancoSuisse d'Histoire Economique et Sociale*

(Geneva: Librairie de l'Université, 1969), pp. 71–77. These articles by a Genevan economic historian are an example of the uses to which the manuscripts of the *Bourse française* and the city hospital have been put to study philanthropy and charity in Geneva for a period somewhat later than that covered here.

2. *Fragmens biographiques et historiques, extraits des registres du Conseil d'Etat de la République de Genève, dès 1535 à 1792* (Geneva: Manget et Cherbuliez, Imprimeurs-Libraires, 1815), 5 August 1584.

3. D'Andelot's name appears in the receipts in February 1559 making a donation by means of the hands of Monsieur Dupont: "par les mains de Monsieur Dupont." AEG, Arch. hosp., Hj 1.

4. Anthoine and Guillaume Chiccand were both procurators of the city hospital, Antoine from 1546 to 1550, Guillaume from 1556 to 1561. Both men were also syndics. Kingdon, "The Deacons of the Reformed Church in Calvin's Geneva," pp. 88–89.

5. The city council tried several times to take over the direction of the *Bourse française*. On 9 February 1676 it ordered, without success, that one of its members take charge of the *Bourse française*, "afin que les deniers y soyent bien administrés" (in order that the deniers are well administered). On 13 January 1680 the city council insisted that the deacons take an oath in the council. On 28 April 1721 a member of the city council and a member of the Council of Two Hundred were to preside over the assembly of the *Bourse*. The same order was made on 24 December 1721. The Company of Pastors resisted and in an order of 26 January 1722 were left with the supervision of the deacons of the *Bourse*. Grandjean, "La Bourse française de Genève," p. 49.

6. Eugène Choisy, *L'état chrétien calviniste à Genève au temps de Théodore de Bèze* (Geneva: Ch. Eggimann, 1902), pp. 69, 70, 84–85, 88.

7. Ibid., p. 84.

8. Galeazzo Caracciolo's monthly donations were quite regular; from September 1551 to February 1559 there were only short lapses in his record. He made three trips to his native Italy during that time, departing in the springs of 1553, 1555, and 1558. At the time of the first and third of these trips large lump sums were handed over to the deacons, apparently to compensate for his regular monthly donation. The fact that he, an Italian, was giving to a French fund at all is of interest. He was a supporter and participant in both the Italian and French communities in Geneva and an interesting figure in Genevan life. AEG, Arch. hosp., Kg 12–17 and Hj 1, September 1551–February 1559 in the monthly receipts, passim.

Galeazzo Caracciolo, the Marquis of Vico, was born in July 1517, the only son of one of the most important families of the kingdom of Naples. His mother was of the Caraffa family that gave Pope Paul IV to the church. Paul IV was Galeazzo's great uncle. Galeazzo married Dona Vittoria at twenty years of age and had six children. He was charged with several missions by Emperor Charles V, who conferred on him the title of chamberlain. He came under the influence of three men who, though still within the Church of Rome, were the bringers of new ideas to Naples: the Spanish humanist, Juan Luis Vives; the superior general of the Capuchins, Bernardino Ochino; and the Augustinian, Peter Martyr Vermigli. Under the preaching of Peter Martyr he had an experience that might be called a conversion. With the threat of persecution, Ochino and Martyr left Italy along with others who went into exile. Galeazzo himself was criticized by his father and his wife for his views. On 21 March 1551 he left his family for the court of Charles V and then went secretly to Geneva. The city council announced his arrival in June 1551 as a person who had left his parents and possessions in order to be able to profess freely the Reformed religion. On 15 June he was received as an inhabitant of Geneva and warned that he was to live in subjection as the others do. Jules Bonnet, *Nouveaux récits du seizième siècle* (Paris: Grassart, Libraire-Editeur, 1870), pp. 171–89.

That note of hesitance on the part of the city did not endure as Carracciolo proved himself a good and loyal citizen. On 11 November 1555 he became a bourgeois of Geneva with no fee:

Nob. Galeas Carraciolo, filz de magnif. seigneur Collatonio Galeas, marquys de Vyco au royaume de Naples, gratis, attendu qu'il est homme honnorable & renommé, & prince & excellent en Italie, que est venu icy pour l'Evangille.

(Noble Galeas Carraciolo, son of the magnificent Lord Collatonio Galeas, Marquis of Vico, in the kingdom of Naples, free, considering that he is an honorable and renowned man, and a prince and excellent in Italy, who has come here for the Gospel.)

Covelle, *Livre des Bourgeois*, p. 245. In 1559 he became a member of the Council of Two Hundred and of the consistory.

Caracciolo's family back in Naples was eager for him to return. He encouraged his wife to join him. He was willing to move to another area where they both could practice their religion, for she was Catholic. She refused. After his third trip to Italy and her refusal, he asked for a divorce. Geneva would grant divorce for prolonged desertion or for adultery at this time, but adultery was not an issue in this case. Calvin sent the question on to other theologians. Finally the city council granted him a divorce on 14 August 1559, and allowed Caracciolo the right to remarry in three months. The decision was confirmed on 17 November 1559 after his wife was notified. He then married a widow of Rouen, Anne Framery, on 15 February 1560. He was forty-four years old at the time; he lived to be sixty-nine. He died on 7 May 1586. Bonnet, *Nouveaux récits du seizième siècle*, pp. 189–207. See also Benedetto Croce, "Il Marchese di Vico," in *Vite di Avventure, di Fede e di Passione*, 3d ed. (Bari: Gius, Laterza and Sons, 1953), pp. 187–291.

In addition to his participation in the affairs of Geneva and his friendship with the French refugee community, Caracciolo supported the Italian community in Geneva. He and other Italians who arrived in 1551 were a boost to the small Italian congregation that had been allowed to begin meeting together in October 1542 in the Chapel of the Cardinal d'Ostie (l'Auditoire de Philosophie). In 1551 they were permitted to organize on a more formal level on the condition that expenses would come out of their own money. Caracciolo gave his support to this Italian church. He ultimately willed to it two-thirds of a house in his will of 4 May 1577. He supported the *Bourse italienne* as well, willing it one-fourth of his revenues after the death of his second wife. This *Bourse* was said to have dated from 1542 with the gathering of the Italian congregation. It had its deacons and its poor, and it had church expenses to meet as well. In 1555 the congregation of Italians was allowed to move to the Church of the Madeleine. BPU, Manuscrits suppl. 816, nos. 6 and 7, "Notes sur la Bourse italienne," pp. 24–26; BPU, Manuscrits suppl. 821, "Liste de personnes qui ont fait des donations par testament à l'Eglise et à la Bourse des Italiens établis à Genève," p. 80.

9. This is not to say that many sixteenth-century people were ignorant of inflation. On this subject see the comments of Miriam Chrisman in "Urban Poor in the Sixteenth Century: The Case of Strasbourg," in *Social Groups and Religious Ideas in the Sixteenth Century*, ed. Miriam Chrisman and Otto Gründler (Kalamazoo: The Medieval Institute, Western Michigan University, 1978), p. 65.

10. Louis Binz, *Brève histoire de Genève* (Geneva: Chancellerie d'Etat, 1981), p. 32. See this excellent brief survey for further information on the history of Geneva, especially its economic and political history. The following are some examples of the price of funerals from the account book, AEG, Arch. hosp., Hj 2: "A une pauvre femme pour enterrer son enfant 3 sols" (To a poor woman in order to bury her child, 3 sous), p. [2] of November 1560; "Pour enterrer ung homme, 6 sols" (In order to bury a man, 6 sous), p. [1] of January 1561; "Pour avoir faict enterrer Guillan [sic] Roux, 6 sols" (For having had Guillan [sic] Roux buried, 6 sous), p. [3] of March 1561; "Aux porteurs pour avoir enterré une pauvre femme du Plaimpalaix [sic], 6 sols" (To the porters for having buried a poor woman of Plainpalais, 6 sous), p. [1] of May 1562.

11. Choisy, *L'état chrétien calviniste à Genève*, pp. 69–70, 73, 83–85, 88.

12. Jean-Pierre Gaberel, *Histoire de l'Eglise de Genève depuis le commencement de la Réformation jusqu'à nos jours* (Paris: Joël Cherbuliez Libraire, 1862), 3:359.

13. It is interesting to note that it was by the order of the Company (of Pastors?) that the Breton was placed for room and board with one Jacques Gerard, tinsmith. AEG, Arch. hosp., Kg 12, fols. 22ᵛ–23ᵛ.

14. AEG, Arch. hosp., Kg 13, fols. 36–37.

15.

Maistre Jacques Perrin escollier habitant de Geneve, lequel certain bien advisé de sa pure et libre volonté et tant pour luy que pour ses hoirs au ayans cause de luy a confessé et par ses presentes confesse avoir heu et receu des diacres et commis à l'administration des biens des paouvres estrangers de ceste cité de Geneve par les mains de noble Anthoine Popillon seigneur de Paray l'ung d'iceulx present, stipulant et acceptant audit nom pour luy et ses compagnons absens avec moydit notaire assavoir la somme de 10 livres tournoys et ce pour la pension et nourriture ou partye d'icelle de Anthoine Chanluin escollier, filleul de defunct Anthoine Rebut luy vivant imprimeur de Geneve. Lequel Rebut a icelle somme laissée audit Chanluin par son testament.

(Master Jacques Perrin, student, inhabitant of Geneva, who, being well advised of his pure and free will and as much for him as for his heirs or those dependent on him, confessed and by these present confesses to have had and received from the deacons committed to the administration of the goods of the poor foreigners of this city of Geneva by the hands of noble Antoine Popillon, Lord of Paray, one of those present, stipulating and accepting in the said name for him and his absent companions with myself the said notary, that is to say, the sum of ten pounds tournois and this for the room and board or part of it of Antoine Chanluin, student, godson of the defunct Antoine Rebut himself living, printer of Geneva. The said Rebut has left this sum to the said Chanluin by his will . . . 5 June 1561.)

AEG, Not. Ragueau, vol. 4 (1560–61), fols. 253–54. Jacques Perrin was received *habitant de Genève* on 8 May 1559. Geisendorf, ed., *Livre des habitants*, 1:172. He was of the diocese of Metz. He is number 39 under the year 1559 in *Le Livre du Recteur de l'Académie de Genève (1559–1878)* in Latin as "Jacobus Perrinus, Lotharingus." Ed. Suzanne Stelling-Michaud (Geneva: Librairie Droz, 1959), 1:82. He is also called in French "Jacques Perrin de Lorraine." Ibid. (Geneva: Librairie Droz, 1976), 5:126.

16.

Procuration de Noble Jehan Dallamont . . . nome . . . ses procureurs generaulx et certains messengers . . . asçavoir noble Jehan Budé et honnorable Francois Marcaiz et aultres qui seront inserez au blanc absens, . . . demander . . . et recepvoir de noble Adrian de Lymes ou soit de noble damoiselle Loyse des Marins sa femme et de noble damoiselle Jacqueline des Marins soeurs de ladyct defunct noble damoyselle . . . lequel testament fut receu par moydit notaire l'unzieme d'apvril l'an mil cinq cens soixante . . . et ce pour telles sommes de deniers ou aultrement ainsy que bon semblera à sesdictz procureurs desdictz accordz, transactions et appoinctemens et de ce que en sera receu en faire et passer quictance et aultres instrumens soubz et avec telles clauses, obligations et submissions que sesdictz procureurs et chascung d'eulx cognoistront estre à faire et expedient aux fins et pour les choses susdictes elire et convenir d'arbitres et pour iceulx nommer les honnorables ministres diacres et anciens de l'Eglise reformee de Meaulx. . . . 11 decembre 1565.

(Procuration of Noble Jean Dalamont . . . names . . . his general procurators and certain messengers . . . that is to say the Noble Jean Budé and honorable François Marcaiz and others who will be inserted in the blanks . . . asks . . . and receives of Noble Adrian de Lymes or of Noble *damoiselle* Loyse des Marins, his wife, and of Noble *damoiselle* Jacqueline des Marins, sisters of the said defunct Noble *damoiselle* . . . whose will was received by me, the said notary, the eleventh of April, 1560 . . . and this for such sums of deniers or otherwise as thus seem good to the said procurators of the said accords, transactions, and emoluments; and from that which will be received to make of it a receipt and other instruments with such clauses, obligations, and submissions as the said procurators and each of them understand to be that which is to be done and expedient to the ends, and for the above-mentioned things to choose and to convene the arbiters and for these to name the honorable ministers, deacons, and elders of the Reformed church of Meaux.)

December 11, 1565, AEG, Not. Ragueau, 7:979–81.

17. For Robert Estienne's will and codicil see AEG, Not. Ragueau, 3:185–91.

18. The will of Gabrielle de Borne was an example of a sixteenth-century will that restricted the religious affiliation and movement of prospective heirs. In Gabrielle de Borne's will three prospective heirs would lose their inheritances if they left the Reformed church of Geneva or that of a Reformed country. These were her bastard nephew or brother, Jean de Borne, and two women, Catherine Jeanne and Martha. In such a will some provision needed to be made for the legacy if the heirs did not fulfill the testator's requests. Happily for the foreign poor of Geneva the *Bourse française* was often the backup heir, as in this particular will. Restrictive as the conditions might have seemed, at least outside of the sixteenth-century context, the testator does not appear to have been unfeeling. She commented on the loss the would-be heirs had sustained on leaving the country of their birth and their possessions to come to Geneva for the Word of God. They were now poor, and she left them this inheritance as a way of providing charity and alms:

Noble damoyselle Gabrielle de Borne . . . habitant de ceste cité de Geneve . . . laisse à noble Jehan de Borne son frere bastard et à nobles Catherine Jehanne natifve d'Orange et Martha de La Vernarde pour charité et aulmosne dautant qu'elle les cognoissoyt paouvres mesmes pour avoir laissé le pays de leur nativité et leur bien s'estans retirez en ceste cité de Geneve pour la parolle de Dieu la somme de cent escutz sol de valeur de cinquante solz tournoys piece entre luy et elles, à diviser egallement . . . soubz condition toutesfoys que iceulx legataires demourent et se tiennent en l'Eglise de Geneve ou aultre de ce pays reformee selon l'Evangile . . . et au cas que tous lesdits legataires . . . habandonneroyent l'Eglise du Seigneur où sa parolle seroyt preschee se retirant au pays de la papaulté, elle les privoyt et dementoyt dudict legat et donnoyt iceluy qui estoyt ladicte somme de cent escutz aux paouvres estrangers icy en ceste Eglise de Geneve retirez pour la parolle de Dieu et voloyt ladicte somme estre baillee aux seigneurs diacres pour en faire distribution . . .

(Noble damoiselle Gabrielle de Borne . . . inhabitant of this city of Geneva . . . leaves to Noble Jean de Borne, her bastard brother, and to Nobles Catherine Jeanne, native of Orange, and Martha of La Vernarde for charity and alms for as much as she knows them to be poor even for having left the country of their birth and their possessions, having retreated into this city of Geneva for the Word of God, the sum of 100 ecus sol worth 50 sous tournois each between him and them to divide equally under the condition yet that these heirs remain and hold fast in the church of Geneva or another of this country reformed according to the Gospel . . . and in the case that all the said heirs abandon the church of the Lord where his Word is preached retreating to the country of the papacy, she deprives and denies them the said legacy and gives that which is the said sum of one hundred ecus to the poor foreigners here in this church of Geneva, having retreated for the Word of God and wants the said sum to be given to the Lord deacons to make distribution of it . . .)

AEG, Not. Ragueau, vol. 8, fols. 134–35.

19. For further documentation on the inheritance of Jean de Borne from Gabrielle de Borne see appendix E: (1) a receipt from Jean de Borne to the deacons of the *Bourse française*, (2) a notarial document confirming the presentation of attestations on behalf of Jean de Borne, and (3) a notarial document acknowledging an attestation from a pastor in France that Jean de Borne was a deacon and teacher in a church of Sablieres in France.

20. AEG, Arch. hosp., Ke 1, p. [7].

21. The teaching of the Roman Catholic church about purgation after death after the Council of Trent of the sixteenth century was that there is a "state" of purgation after death, but by late medieval times the notion of a "place" of purgation had already taken over, enflamed by works such as Dante's *Purgatorio* in the *Divine Comedy* and also by the art of the period. For a history of the notion of purgatory in the popular mentality see Jacques Le Goff, *The Birth of Purgatory*, trans. Arthur Goldhammer (Chicago: University of Chicago Press, 1984).

22. Choisy, *L'état chrétien calviniste à Genève*, pp. 256–57.

23. See, for instance, Brian Pullan, *Rich and Poor in Renaissance Venice*. See also Maureen Flynn, "Charitable Ritual in Late Medieval and Early Modern Spain," *The Sixteenth Century Journal* 16 (Fall 1985): 335–48; see mention of the confraternities of Geneva in J. B. G. Galiffe, *Genève historique et archéologique* (Geneva: H. Georg, Libraire-Editeur, 1869), p. 34.

24. See, for instance, this text in the laws of Geneva of 7 September 1574 for "Pigney": "Ascavoir qu'ilz retireront à eulx les paouvres . . . et les entretiendront de leur pouvoir; et pour ce faire, que chacun sera cottisé selon sa faculté pour subvenir aux necessitées" (That is to say that they withdraw to themselves the poor . . . and maintain them with their capacities; and, in order to do this, that each person will be assessed according to his ability to support his needs). Rivoire and van Berchem, *Les sources du droit du Canton de Genève*, 3:312.

25. For a description of medieval poor law and the church in Britain see Brian Tierney, *Medieval Poor Law: A Sketch of Canonical Theory and Its Application* (Berkeley and Los Angeles: University of California Press, 1959).

26. Of the studies that have used wills to study charitable bequests, the pioneering research of W. K. Jordan, *Philanthropy in England, 1480–1660*, is a useful study of a country in religious transition. See also W. G. Bittle and R. Todd, "Inflation and Philanthropy in England, a Reassessment of W. K. Jordan's data," *Economic History Review*, 2d ser., 29 (1976): 203–10. See also J. A. F. Thomson, "Piety and Charity in Late Medieval London," *Journal of Ecclesiastical History* 16 (1965): 178–95. For a broader bibliography of publications on the Reformation, especially books relative to cities, see Kaspar von Greyerz, "Stadt und Reformation: Stand und

Aufgaben der Forschung," and the bibliography, "Verzeichnis Zitierter Publikationen," *Archiv für Reformationsgeschichte* 76 (1985): 6–63.

27. Vives, "On Assistance to the Poor," pp. 44–48.

28. Calvin's suggestion for an industry for the poor is in AEG, Reg. Conseil, vol. 39, fols. 84ᵛ–85. For the silk industry at the hospital see Liliane Mottu-Weber, "Des vers à soie à l'Hôpital en 1610: Un bref épisode de l'histoire de la soierie à Genève," *Revue du Vieux Genève* 12 (1982): 44–49.

29. Donation of Dame Anes de Remy(?). April 2, 1557, AEG, Not. Ragueau, vol. 2, fols. 127–29.

30. See for instance the Ecclesiastical Ordinances of Geneva of 20 November 1541 and 3 June 1576:

> Au surplus, pour empescher la mendicité, laquelle est contraire à bonne police, il fauldra que la Seigneurie commette quelcungs de ses officiers, et ainsi avons ordonné, à l'issue des eglises, pour oster de la place ceulx que vouldroient resister.

> (In addition, in order to prevent begging, which is contrary to good policing, it will be necessary that the magistrates commit several of its officers, and thus have ordered, at the issue of the churches, in order to remove from the place those who would like to resist.)

Rivoire and van Berchem, *Les sources du droit du Canton de Genève*, vol. 2, *1461–1550*, p. 385.

> CLXIII. Que pour empescher la mendicité, laquelle est contraire à tout bon ordre et police, on y tienne la main par tous les meilleurs moyens qu'il appartiendra.

> (CLXIII. That in order to prevent begging, which is contrary to all good order and policing, one holds it in hand by all the best means that appertain.)

Ibid., vol. 3, *1551–1620*, p. 346.

31. One suspects, for instance, that poor people aided on the Court of St. Pierre might have come to the cathedral to ask for money since churches were a popular place to beg in this period. Did the deacons prevent them from begging by coming to their aid or were they already begging when the deacons helped out? "A troys pauvres personnes cedit jour en la court Saint-Pierre, 1 florin, 6 sols" (To three poor people this day on the Court Saint Pierre, 1 florin, 6 sous). AEG, Arch. hosp., Hj 2, p. [3] of February 1561.

32. Le Blanc was convicted and burned for sodomy. There is considerable information on his case, including his plea for clemency, in the criminal records of sixteenth-century Geneva. AEG, Procès Criminel 502 (7–16 March 1554), n.p. Hereafter "Proc. Crim."

The file for the criminal procedure of Lambert Le Blanc contains a statement on boys involved in the case, a part of which seems to be in the handwriting of John Calvin, whose signature is found first among the signatories on a loose manuscript of three pages. The story of these boys is known today, perhaps because of the exemplary fire in their punishment and John Calvin's participation in the decision. The fate of Lambert Le Blanc has had less attention. A phrase from the case appears in the dictionary of sixteenth-century French: "Commination . . . sera bon de leur representer la peine du feu en bruslant quelques fagotz devant eulx avec grande commination de la dicte peine du feu silz y retornent. Calvin, *Lettres*, 1922 (XV, 67)" (Commination . . . it will be good to represent to them the pain of the fire by burning several faggots before them with grand commination of the said pain of the fire if they return to it. Calvin, *Lettres*, 1922 [XV, 67]. Huguet, *Dictionnaire de la langue française du seizième siècle*, 2:368. The text from the original manuscript describing the fate of the five boys is in appendix F.

33. See, for instance, Jean-Pierre Gutton, *La société et les pauvres: L'exemple de la généralité de Lyon, 1534–1789* (Paris: Société d'Edition "Les Belles Lettres," 1970), pp. 215–18.

34. For an example of a city working for welfare change see the article on Lyons by Natalie Zemon Davis, "Poor Relief, Humanism, and Heresy," pp. 17–64.

35. "Bourse française, Livres memorials des diacres," AEG, Arch. hosp., Ka 6 (1 March 1680–30 December 1691), pp. 412–15.

36. "1020. Enregistrement des actes portant lods et des testaments . . . 4 août 1562":

> . . . Arresté qu'on dresse un livre en la chancellerie, attaché à un pulpitre, auquel tous notaires seront tenus de venir registrer la designation de tous instrumens portans lodz, dix

jours après la reception d'iceux. . . . Plus soyent tenus lesdicts notaires, sur lesdictes peines, venir registrer audict livre tous legatz en faveur de l'Hospital ou des paouvres, ou du College, dix jours après le deces du testateur duquel ils auront receu le testament; ou bien, s'ils n'en avoyent heu notice, avant qu'expedier les testamens.

(. . . Ordered that one set out a book in the chancellery, attached to a lectern, to which all the notaries will have to come to register the designation of all instruments bearing *lods*, ten days after the reception of them. . . . Plus, the said notaries have, on the said penalties, to come to register in the said book all the legacies in favor of the hospital or of the poor, or of the college, ten days after the death of the testator of whom they will have received the will; or indeed, if they have not had notice of it before expediting the wills.)

Rivoire and van Berchem, *Les sources du droit du Canton de Genève*, 3:132. The book of legacies from the sixteenth century dates from 1580 and continues until 1637. "Livre des legatz faictz tant aux paouvres de l'Hospital general de Geneve, au College, que aux paouvres estrangiers. Dès le premier janvier 1580" (Book of the legacies made as much to the poor of the general hospital of Geneva, to the college, as to the poor foreigners. From the first of January 1580). AEG, Arch. hosp., Dd 1.

37. AEG, Arch. hosp., Kg 12–17 and Hj 1 (30 September 1550–February 1559); AEG, Notarial records, and consistory records; the extraordinary expenditure account book that covers August 1559–July 1570 contains no receipts, AEG, Arch. hosp., Hj 2. Hence the limitation of this list of donors to 1550–1559.

38. Charles Borgeaud, *Histoire de l'Université de Genève*, vol. l, *L'Académie de Calvin, 1559–1798* (Geneva: Georg, Libraires de l'Université, 1900), pp. 25, 32, 45, 50, 66, 72–73, 638.

39. Eugénie Droz, *Chemins de l'hérésie: textes et documents* (Geneva: Slatkine, 1976), 4:124, 328.

40. Several members of the family took refuge in Geneva at diverse times. The first was Guillaume Le Cointe, seigneur de Boinville, received inhabitant in 1553, married to Catherine, daughter of the deceased Jean de Marigny of Liege, with whom he had eleven children, of whom those surviving in 1561 were three sons and one daughter. Galiffe, *Notices généalogiques*, vol. 3 (1836), p. 287.

41. Droz, *Chemins de l'hérésie*, 4:75–202.

42. Kingdon, *Geneva and the Coming of the Wars of Religion*, p. 61. Alain Dufour, Fernand Aubert, Henri Meylan, Arnaud Tripet, Alexandre de Henseler, Claire Chimelli, Mario Turchetti, and Béatrice Nicollier, eds., *Correspondance de Théodore de Bèze* (Geneva: Librairie Droz, 1978), 9:161, n. 13.

43. Heyer, *L'Eglise de Genève, 1535–1909*, p. 430.

44. Henri Naef, *La Conjuration d'Amboise et Genève* (Geneva: A. Jullien, Georg, Libraires-Editeurs, 1922), p. 130, n. 3.

CHAPTER 8. RECIPIENTS

1. Perrenoud, *La population de Genève*, p. 37.

2. A segment of the Marian exiles in Frankfort objected to the Edwardian prayer book. Calvin himself requested on 10 June 1555 that the city council of Geneva allow them to set up an English congregation in Geneva. The refugees arrived on 13 October 1555. They shared the church of *Marie la Nove* or *l'Auditoire* where the Scottish Church worships today on the Court of St. Pierre. Dan G. Danner, "The Marian Exiles and the English Protestant Tradition," in *Social Groups and Religious Ideas in the Sixteenth Century*, ed. Chrisman and Gründler, pp. 96–97.

3. For a description of many of these refugees see F. Fournier-Marcigny, *Genève au XVIᵐᵉ siècle; La vie ardente du premier Refuge français, 1532–1602* (Geneva: Les Editions du Mont-Blanc, 1942).

4. There is a useful chapter on the connection of poverty to crime in its broad social, economic, and geographical context entitled "Misère et banditism" in Fernand Braudel, *La Méditerranée et le Monde méditerranéen à l'époque de Phillippe II* (Paris: Libraire Armand Colin, 1949), pp. 643–60.

5. Alain Dufour, "Le mythe de Genève au temps de Calvin," in *Histoire politique et psychologie historique* (Geneva: Librairie Droz, 1966), pp. 88–89.

6. Although precise statistical information on poor people in early modern Europe is difficult to find, good descriptions are available on the condition of the poor in Europe as a whole. For early modern see especially Gutton, *La société et les pauvres;* for an earlier period see Michel Mollat, *Les pauvres au moyen âge: Etude sociale* (n.p.: Hachette, 1978). See Mollat also on the notion of poverty in the Middle Ages, "La notion de pauvreté au moyen âge: Position de problèmes," *Revue d'histoire de l'Eglise de France* 52 (1966): 6–24.

7. For Geneva's aid to those serving on the galleys in the seventeenth and eighteenth centuries see Michel Grandjean, "Genève au secours des galériens pour la foi (1685–1718)," in *Genève au temps de la Révocation de l'Edit de Nantes, 1680–1705*, Mémoires et documents publiés par la Société d'histoire et d'archéologie de Genève (Geneva: Librairie Droz, 1985), pp. 399–438. For galley service in France in a somewhat later period see Paul Bamford, *Fighting Ships and Prisons: the Mediterranean Galleys in the Age of Louis XIV* (Minneapolis: University of Minnesota Press, 1973); André Zysberg, "La société des galériens au milieu du XVIIIᵉ siècle," *Annales: Economies, Sociétés, Civilisations* 30 (January–February 1975): 43–65.

8. "A ung qui a esté serviteur de Monsieur de Beze, 2 sols, 6 deniers" (To one who was a servant of Monsieur de Bèze, 2 sous, 6 deniers). AEG, Arch. hosp., Hj 2, p. [4] of April 1561.

9. For more information on the refugee population, see chapter 3, which describes the aid recipients to some extent to explain what was done on their behalf; for the statistical use of the account books of the *Bourse française* in the seventeenth century see Cécile Holtz, "La Bourse française de Genève et le Refuge de 1684 à 1686," in *Genève au temps de la Révocation de l'Edit de Nantes*, pp. 448–74; her charts of the receipts and expenditures of the *Bourse française* from 1679 to 1700 were possible to assemble because of the more complete account books of this period, pp. 493–500.

10. AEG, Arch. hosp., Hj 1, August 1557; for further comment on the regional disparity of the refugees to Geneva see Robert Mandrou, "Les Français hors de France aux XVIᵉ et XVIIᵉ siècles," *Annales: Economies, Sociétés, Civilisations* 14 (1959): 662–75.

11. "A ung pauvre Flament passant, 6 sols" (To a poor Flemish person, in passage, 6 sous). AEG, Arch. hosp., Hj 2, p. [3] of January 1560.

12. "A ung pauvre espaignol arrivé de nouveau recommandé par Monsieur Puerins, 5 florins" (To a poor Spaniard, come again, recommended by Monsieur Puerins, 5 florins). AEG, Arch. hosp., Hj 2, p. [2] of November 1559.

13. AEG, Arch. hosp., Kg 14, 18 August 1553.

14. For the Italian refuge to Geneva see J. B. G. Galiffe, *Le refuge italien de Genève aux XVIᵐᵉ et XVIIᵐᵉ siècles* (Geneva, 1881).

15. For the German fund and church see H. Fehr, *La communauté réformée allemande de Genève et la paroisse protestante de langue allemande de l'Eglise Nationale: documents divers et notices historiques* (Geneva: Imprimerie Gutenberg, 1917).

16. For the English in Geneva and the names of the deacons of the English church see John Burn, *Livre des anglois à Genève* (London: n.p., 1831), pp. 12–13; for the description of a deacons' fund in England for the support of refugees from the Continent see W. J. C. Moens, "The Relief of the Poor Members of the French Churches in England as Exemplified by the Practice of the Walloon or French Church at Sandwich (1568–72)," *Proceedings of the Huguenot Society of London* (10 January and 14 March 1894), pp. 321–39.

17. Henri Heyer and Louis Johannot, *Les diaconies de la ville de Genève, leur origine et leur activité de 1850 à 1900 avec le tableau des membres: rapports présentés à la séance annuelle du Consistoire et des diaconies le 27 novembre 1900* (Geneva: Librairie Henry Kündig, 1901), p. 8.

18. Jérôme Sautier, "Politique et refuge—Genève face a la Révocation de l'Edit de Nantes," in *Genève au temps de la Révocation de l'Edit de Nantes*, p. 47.

19. The following ruling of 27 January 1682 on the hospital and the *Bourses* describes the division of responsibility among the various welfare funds of Geneva:

Réglemens par raport à l'Hospital et aux Bourses, approuvés en Conseil le 27 janvier 1682. Premierement l'Hospital devra assister tous les pauvres de la Ville, de la souveraineté et territoire d'icelle.
La Bourse Françoise devra assister tous les pauvres françois, y compris ceux des petites

souverainetés qui sont enclavées dans la France, savoir: Avignon, Oranges et Dombes, et autres si aucunes y a.

La Bourse Italienne devra assister tous les pauvres italiens, comme aussi ceux des petites souverainetés possédées par le roy de France, de l'Italie, comme Pignerol, vallées de Piémont et toutes autres places et lieux de l'Italie, nonobstant qu'elles soyent possedées par quels princes que ce soit.—Item devra assister tous les Espagnols et tout ce qui depend de l'Espagne, y compris la comté de Bourgogne.

La Bourse Allemande devra assister tous les pauvres allemans et tous ceux qui dependent de l'Empire, y compris l'Alsace, Lorraine, la Suisse du pays allemand, Hollande et tout le Pays Flamand, Angleterre, Suede et Pologne, Dannemarc, Norvege, Hongrie, Transilvanie.

(Rules in connection with the hospital and the *Bourses* approved in council 27 January 1682.

First, the hospital should help all the poor of the city, of the sovereignty, and of this territory.

The *Bourse française* should help all the poor French, including those of the small sovereignties that are enclaves in France, that is to say: Avignon, Orange, and *Dombes*, and others, if there are any.

The *Bourse italienne* should help all the poor Italians, as also those of the small sovereignties possessed by the king of France, such as *Pignerol*, the valleys of Piedmont, and all other places and localities of Italy, notwithstanding those that are possessed by whatsoever princes. Also [the *Bourse italienne*] should help all the Spaniards and all those who are dependents of Spain, including the county of Burgundy.

The *Bourse allemande* should help all the poor Germans and all those who are dependents of the Empire, including Alsace, Lorraine, the German regions of Switzerland, Holland and all the Flemish countries, England, Sweden and Poland, Denmark, Norway, Hungary, Transylvania.)

Rivoire and van Berchem, *Les sources du droit du Canton de Genève*, vol. 4, *1621–1700* (Arau: H. R. Sauerländer, Imprimeurs-Editeurs, 1935), p. 477.

20. "A ung pauvre Genevoys mallade par les mains de . . . Bastie par ordonnance, 12 sols" (To a poor sick Genevan by the hands of . . . Bastie by ordinance, 12 sous). AEG, Arch. hosp., Hj 2, p. [2] of September 1560.

21. Holtz, "La Bourse française de Genève et le Refuge de 1684 à 1686," p. 441.

22. Choisy, *L'état chrétien calviniste à Genève*, pp. 69, 72–73, 85.

23. After the French edicts of 1568 against the "pretended reformed" religion, Théodore de Bèze corresponded with Heinrich Bullinger. All the small villages in Berne's territory were full of refugee families but the four churches in Geneva still had many of them. Choisy, *L'état chrétien calviniste à Genève*, pp. 69, 72.

24. Holtz, "La Bourse française de Genève et le Refuge de 1684 à 1686," pp. 487–89.

25. "De l'angloys qui est chez Monsieur Maldonnade, 7 sols, 6 deniers" (From the Englishman who is at Monsieur Maldonnade's, 7 sous, 6 deniers). AEG, Arch. hosp., Kg 13, fol. 101. Note this collection taken up in November 1553 for a poor man from England: "De luy [Monsieur de Normandy] pour quelque queste qu'il a faict . . . pour ung pauvre homme venu d'angleterre, 2 florins" (From him [Monsieur de Normandie] for some collection that he made . . . for a poor man come from England, 2 florins); AEG, Arch. hosp., Kg 14, p. [1] of November 1553; "A ung pauvre menuysier venant d'Angleterre pour luy ayder a avoir des outilz, 17 sols" (To a poor woodworker coming from England in order to help him have some tools, 17 sous). 10 September 1554, AEG, Arch. hosp., Kg 15, p. [4] of September 1554.

26. Geisendorf, ed., *Livre des habitants.*

27.

D'autant que plusieurs de ceux qui se retirent icy maintenant sont paouvres et ne veulent rien faire, chargeans la Bourse, pour y remedier arresté que desormais on n'en recoyve plus qui n'ayt estat; et que ceux qui tesmoigneront pour luy promettent qu'il ne sera en charge. Et, affin qu'ilz en puissent estre sommés, quand ce viendra qu'ilz se presenteront à la Bourse, qu'on mette à leurs lettres leurs mestiers et le nom de ceux qui auront tesmoigné pour iceux. R. C., vol. 63, vol. 139.

Rivoire and van Berchem, *Les sources du droit du Canton de Genève*, vol. 3, *1551–1620*, p. 269.

28. AEG, Not. Aimé Santeur, vol. 5 (1568–70), fols. 32–33. This will is published in Eugène Ritter, "Didier Rousseau, le quartaieul de Jean-Jacques," *BHSPF* 42 (1893): 281–92. Didier was a bookdealer from Paris where he may have fled potential persecution because of the prohibition by the crown of selling books from Geneva, Germany, and elsewhere that had not been examined by the faculty of the theology of Paris. He became an inhabitant of Geneva on 24 June 1550 and was identified as a wine merchant. "Didier Rousseau, de Parys, vendeur de vin, *24 junii 1550* (Didier Rousseau, of Paris, wine seller, 24 June 1550). Geisendorf, ed., *Livre des habitants*, 1:16; he was entered into the book of the bourgeois of Geneva on 22 April 1555 for a relatively high price of twenty ecus. "Didier Rosseau, filz de feu Anthoyne, de Paris, librayre, 20 écus, 1 seillot" (Didier Rousseau, son of the deceased Antoine, of Paris, bookdealer, 20 ecus, one *seillot*). Covelle, *Livre des Bourgeois*, p. 241. There are *procès criminels* against Didier Rousseau, one for having irregular dealings in the wine trade for which he received three days in prison, and another for having sold wine and left his house when he and his wife were sick and there was fear of catching the plague. AEG, Proc. Crim., 1070 (1562) and 1489 (1568); for additional data on Didier Rousseau see Chaix, *Recherches sur l'imprimerie à Genève de 1550 à 1564*, p. 221; for the Rousseau Family, see Galiffe, *Notices généalogiques*, 2d ed., vol. 2 (Geneva: J. Jullien, Libraire-Editeur, 1892), pp. 412–31.

29. "A Madamoyselle du Plessix par l'ordonnance de la Compaigne, 5 florins, 6 sols, 3 deniers" (To Madamoiselle du Plessix by the ordinance of the Company, 5 florins, 6 sous, 3 deniers). AEG, Arch hosp., Hj 2, p. [2] of January 1561; "A la Dame Anne, 2 florins" (To the dame, Anne, 2 florins). AEG, Arch. hosp., Hj 2, p. [2] of January 1561; Madamoiselle de la Tour is in the account book for 1582, AEG, Arch. hosp., Kg 19, fol. 9; Mangis Merlin and Monsieur Hennequin are in the second of the "Great Books of the Assisted," AEG, Arch. hosp., Kq 2, fols. 206, 302.

30. Richard C. Trexler, "Charity and the Defense of Urban Elites in the Italian Communes," in *The Rich, the Well Born, and the Powerful: Elites and Upper Classes in History*, ed. Frederic Jaher (Urbana: University of Illinois Press, 1973), pp. 99, 104.

31. For a less positive view of the effects of the Reformation on education as a whole see the criticism of the work of W. K. Jordan in J. A. F. Thomson, "Piety and Charity in Late Medieval London," *Journal of Ecclesiastical History* 16 (1965): 195.

32. "A ung pauvre medecin mallade comme il luy a esté ordonné pour chacun moys, 4 florins" (To a poor sick doctor as it has been ordained to him for each month, 4 florins). AEG, Arch. hosp., Hj 2, p. [1] of November 1559; "A Maistre Anthoine de Montcles[?] pauvre medecin comme il luy a esté ordonné, 4 florins" (To Master Antoine de Montcles[?], poor doctor, as it was ordained for him, 4 florins). AEG, Arch. hosp., Hj 2, p. [1] of December 1559; "A Maistre Anthoine de Montcles, 4 florins, 6 deniers" (To Master Antoine de Montcles, 4 florins, 6 deniers). AEG, Arch. hosp., Hj 2, p. [2] of January 1560; "A Monsieur Anthoine de Montcles medecin, 4 florins" (To Master Antoine de Montcles, doctor, 4 florins). AEG, Arch. hosp., Hj 2, p. [1] of February 1560.

33. "A Monsieur René pour payer la chambre d'ung ministre, 8 florins, 7 sols" (To Monsieur René in order to pay for the room of a minister, 8 florins, 7 sous). AEG, Arch. hosp., Hj 2, p. [3] of August 1560.

34. For an example of a minister fleeing persecution see the case of Master Bernard: "Baillé a Maistre Bernard ministre, 7 florins, 6 deniers" (Given to Master Bernard, minister, 7 florins, 6 deniers). AEG, Arch. hosp., Hj 2, p. [2] of October 1559; "Il a esté ordonné à Maistre Bernard pauvre ministre chassé pour la parolle par chacun moys, 10 florins à luy baillé pour ce present moys le premier jour, 10 florins" (It has been ordered for Master Bernard, poor minister, chased for the Word, 10 florins for each month. To him given, for this present month, the first day, 10 florins). AEG, Arch. hosp., Hj 2, p. [1] of December 1559; "Le premier dudit moys baillé à Maistre Bernard, 10 florins" (The first of the said month, given to Master Bernard, 10 florins). AEG, Arch. hosp., Hj 2, p. [1] of January 1560.

35. The "Great Book of the Assisted" specifies the profession or craft of the individual welfare recipients at the top of the page, right after their names. AEG, Arch. hosp., Kq 1.

36. For information on the missionary pastors sent from Geneva see Kingdon, *Geneva and the Coming of the Wars of Religion*.

37. For a detailed account of the French political scene in the latter half of the sixteenth

century see N. M. Sutherland, *The Huguenot Struggle for Recognition* (New Haven: Yale University Press, 1980).

38. Choisy, *L'état chrétien calviniste à Genève*, pp. 72–73.

39. Ibid., pp. 69–70, 85, 88.

40. Ibid., p. 239.

41. Olivier Fatio, "L'Eglise de Genève et la Révocation de l'Edit de Nantes," in *Genève au temps de la Révocation de l'Edit de Nantes*, pp. 186–87; for the preaching of refugee pastors see also Edouard Montet, *Genève et les pasteurs française réfugiés en 1685* (Geneva: Imprimerie Rémy Schira, 1884), p. 10.

42. For a more detailed analysis of how Genevan pastors were paid in the sixteenth century see Jean-François Bergier, "Salaires des pasteurs de Genève au XVIᵉ siècle," in *Mélanges d'histoire du XVIᵉ siècle offerts à Henri Meylan* (Geneva: Librairie Droz, 1970), pp. 159–78.

43. The eleven pastors, in order according to the first "Great Book of the Assisted" were: (1) Jean Boulier, AEG, Arch. hosp., Kq 1, fol. 56; (2) Jean Gadovin, ibid., fol. 142ᵛ, 324ᵛ, 374ᵛ; (3) Master Jacques Bourdier, ibid., fol. 310ᵛ (note that the Jacques Bordier who was a pastor near Geneva was not born until 1591 and was active in the seventeenth century [Henri Heyer, *L'Eglise de Genève, 1535–1909*, p. 428]); (4) Bonaventure Minet, AEG, Arch. hosp., Kq 1, fol. 374ᵛ; (5) "Le ministre de Macon," ibid., fol. 524; (6) Monsieur de Larz, "ministre de La Chante" (listed in the index as "Monsieur de Lery, ministre de la Charité"), ibid., fol. 551ᵛ; (7) Leonard Moret (Morel in the index), ibid., fol. 556; (8) Master Jean Le Blanc, ibid., fol. 694ᵛ; (9) Master Jean de Laulnaz, "ministre de Saint Mezan" (listed in the index as Master "Jehan de Laulnay"), ibid., fol. 799; (10) Pierre Ralliet "ministre de Monnaz," ibid., fol. 908ᵛ; (11) Master Louys Corbel, "ministre de Moratel," ibid., fol. 948.

Jean Gadovin received aid from 13 September 1574 until 29 February 1576 when his widow, Marguerite, received aid. She remarried Pierre Forcet on 15 October 1577 bringing with her three children from the first marriage: Pierre, Jacque, and Marie. She continued to receive aid at the same rate after the remarriage until June 1578. The children received aid from July 1579 to August 1580 except for Pierre, who received no aid in 1579. He would have been about fourteen years of age at that time because he was baptized on 18 March 1565. He did, however, receive aid from 1 January to 12 September 1586. Note that the aid to the children did not cease with the remarriage of their mother. Ibid., fols. 142ᵛ, 324ᵛ, 374ᵛ; AEG, Arch. hosp., Kq 2 (1580–99), pp. 13, 15, 17.

Jacques Bourdier received aid from 11 November 1574 to the end of the first "Great Book of the Assisted" in December 1579. Later his children, Eleazard and Marie, were orphaned and continued to receive aid. AEG, Arch. hosp., Kq 1, fol. 310ᵛ and Kq 2, p. 29.

The unnamed minister of Macon received aid from 29 October 1562 to 3 March 1563 over a period of four and one-half months. AEG, Arch. hosp., Kq 1, fol. 524.

Monsieur de Larz, "minister de la Chante," was listed in the index as "Monsieur de Lery, ministre de la Charite." He received aid from 24 January 1573 to 23 March 1575. Ibid., fol. 551ᵛ. There was a Jean de Léry who was well known for his journal of the Calvinist expedition to Brazil in 1557. He became a missionary pastor to Nevers, France, by a decision of the Company of Pastors on 11 November 1564. That would have been over eight years before the record in the "Great Book of the Assisted" of aid to Monsieur de Lery. He became a bourgeois of Geneva on 5 August 1560, shortly after his return from Brazil. He was then sent to Belleville, from which he probably returned after the first war of religion in France. This was followed by the mission to Nevers. It is uncertain when he returned from Nevers, but he was minister at La Charité in 1572. A number of Protestants were killed there in the St. Bartholomew's Day massacres. He retreated to Sancerre and experienced the siege and famine that he later recorded. Haag and Haag, *France protestante*, vol. 6 (1856), pp. 556–68.

For his writings or the use of his writings by others see Jean de Léry, *Histoire d'un voyage fait en la terre du Brésil*, ed. Jean-Claude Morisot (Geneva: Librairie Droz, 1975); Jean de Léry, *Le voyage au Brésil de Jean de Léry 1556–1558* (Paris: Payot, 1927); Frank Lestringant, "Calvinistes et cannibales: Les Ecrits protestants sur le Brésil français (1555–1560): Première Partie: Jean de Léry ou l'élection," *BSHPF* 126 (1980): 9–26; Frank Lestringant, "Calvinistes et cannibales: Les Ecrits Protestants sur le Brésil français (1555–1560): Deuxième Partie: La 'réfutation' de Pierre Richer," *BSHPF* 126 (1980): 167–92; Claude Levi-Strauss, *Tristes Tropiques* (Paris: Librairie Plon, 1955); Oliver Reverdin, *Quatorze Calvinistes chez les Topinambous:*

Histoire d'une mission genevoise au Brésil (1556–1558) (Geneva: Librairie E. Droz, 1957); Janet Whatley, "Food and the Limits of Civility: The Testimony of Jean de Léry," *The Sixteenth Century Journal* 15 (1984): 387–400; and Janet Whatley, "Savage Hierarchies: French Catholic Observers of the New World," *The Sixteenth Century Journal* 17 (1986): 319–30. For Jean de Léry's *Histoire mémorable de la ville de Sancerre,* see the edition published in Géralde Nakam, ed., *Au lendemain de la Saint-Barthelémy: guerre civile et famine* (Paris: Anthropos, 1975).

Leonard Moret, listed in the index as "Morel," received aid in September 1562 and December 1563. AEG, Arch. hosp., Kq 1, fol. 556.

Jean Le Blanc received aid from 19 February 1571 to 31 December 1571 and then again on 14 May 1572. Ibid., fol. 694ᵛ.

Jean de Laulnaz (Laulnay) "de Saint Mezan" received aid from 18 October 1560 to 7 July 1563. Ibid., fol. 799.

Pierre Ralliet, "ministre de Monnaz," received grain and money in September 1568. Ibid., fol. 908ᵛ. There was a Pierre Ralliet in the book of inhabitants. He was "natifz de Rincourt, Cité de Bourge. Lundi, dernier Octobre 1558." Geisendorf, ed., *Livre des habitants,* 1:138.

Louys Corbel, "ministre de Moratel," received aid in May and July 1568. The payment of 26 May was quite large, twenty-six florins, about five or ten times what others received. AEG, Arch. hosp., Kq 1, fol. 948.

A number of pastors' widows and children also received aid. Among them were the widow of Claude François, minister at Metz, 5 April 1574; the widow of Monsieur Clement, 25 June and 13 July 1573; and Anne Valbisquot, widow of Monsieur Elie, 15 November to 26 December 1560. Ibid., fols. 367, 468, 829. There was a "Claude Francoys" in the book of inhabitants "de Mez en Lorrenne," but he was listed as "mercier et gantier ([haberdasher and glover]), primo septembris 1551." Geisendorf, ed., *Livre des habitants,* 1:17. Among the children were Samuel, son of Monsieur Jean Caltet (Valtet), who received aid in October 1575 and August 1577; Samuel, son of Monsieur Joachim Massot; and the son of Louys Vincent, who received aid from 2 March to 30 September 1573. AEG, Arch. hosp., Kq 1, fols. 265ᵛ, 375, and 526ᵛ.

44. Jean Boulier was not an insignificant figure. He was important enough to be sent forth from Geneva to France as a pastor, and he was in communication with the Genevan Company of Pastors from his post in Lyons. Kingdon, *Geneva and the Coming of the Wars of Religion,* pp. 136, 138, 140, 142, 146; Kingdon, *Registres de la Compagnie des Pasteurs de Genève,* 2:93, 96; Fatio and Labarthe, *Registres de la Compagnie des Pasteurs de Genève,* 3:5, 29.

Jean Boulier or de la Roche accepted a position at Vandoeuvres and Cologny where he served as a minister in 1560. Previously he had served as a minister at Lyons, France, in 1558. The church at Lyons subsequently asked for him back, and he served there again from 1562 to 1565. He is perhaps better known for his ministry there, but he was entered into the book of the inhabitants of Geneva on 30 October 1572, and he and his family appeared in the registers of the Company of Pastors, the consistory records, and the account books of the *Bourse française;* Geisendorf, ed., *Livres des habitants,* 2:49; Kingdon, *Registres de la Compagnie des Pasteurs de Genève,* 2:93, 96; Heyer, *L'Eglise de Genève, 1535–1909,* pp. 229, 430; Haag and Haag, *France protestante,* 2d ed., vol. 2 (Paris: Librairie Sandoz and Fischbacher, 1879), cols. 1014–15. Kingdon, *Geneva and the Coming of the Wars of Religion,* pp. 32, 81; 30 July 1579, AEG, Reg. Consist., vol. 31, fols. 367ᵛ–368; AEG, Arch. hosp., Kq 1, fol. 56, and Kq 2, fol. 200.

45. "Item Jehan Boulier dict de la Roche ministre de la parolle de Dieu est mort d'un catarre avec viniellose agé de 87 ans, le 26 de janvier [1580], en la cité" (Also, Jean Boulier, called de la Roche, minister of the Word of God, is dead of a catarrh with viniellose, at the age of 87 years, the 26th of January, in the city). AEG, EC Morts, vol. 12 (1572–80), p. 219.

46. "Je suis le Diable," Labarthe and Lescaze, *Registres de la Compagnie des Pasteurs de Genève,* 4:125.

47.

Spectable Jehan Boullier de Lholme près Aulthing ministre de la parolle de Dieu appellé en Consistoyre d'aultant qu'estant ung homme ancien mal aisé de sa personne et chargé de famillie et auquel ayant estees faictes bonnes remonstrances, assavoyr de s'occuper de quelque besogne ou bien de tacher d'instruire sa famillie ayant esté trouvé chez luy sa famillie mal instruicte, mesmes ung sien fils de l'aage de neuf à dix ans ne scait ne lire ne escripre, mesmes luy ayant esté donné terme pour adviser à tacher de fayre quelque chose. Il n'a volu y entendre, ains a retiré de la Bourse des paouvres bien cinq centz livres dès peu de temps qu'il est venu du pais, qui luy ont estees [one word omitted] et en somme apprès l'avoyr exorté à fayre quelque chose et honneste train, il a respondu par deux ou troys foys fort rudement à Monsieur de Beze luy ayant dict [three words omitted] mes escritz valent bien d'estre receus et vous mesprisés tout et en somme a parlé fort orgeullieusement à la Compagnie.

(Spectable Jean Boullier of *Lholme* near *Aulthing*, minister of the Word of God, called into the consistory for as much as [he] was an old man, ill at ease with his person, and charged with family and to whom were made good remonstrances, that is to say, to occupy himself with some need or even to try to instruct his family, it having been found at his house that his family was poorly instructed, even that one of his sons of the age of nine or ten years did not know how to read or write, even though a limit had been given to him in order to advise him to try to do something. He didn't want to hear it, as [he] had withdrawn from the *Bourse* of the poor five hundred pounds even, in the little bit of time that he had come from the country, that had been to him [one word omitted] and, in summary, after having been exhorted to do something in an honest way, he responded two or three times very rudely to Monsieur de Bèze having said to him [three words omitted] my writings are indeed worth being received and you scorn everything, and in sum [he] spoke very conceitedly to the Company.)

30 July 1579, AEG, Reg. Consist., vol. 31 (17 January 1577–18 February 1580), fols. 367^v–368.

48. The family name appeared in the great book of the assisted on 6 September 1565. Aid was given several times per month until 28 April 1566 and then again on 29 November 1573. There were also entries for the family in the extraordinary account books of the deacons during this period. However, the first entry was to the son of Jean Boulier rather than to Jean himself. Although there was no indication in the entries that followed that it was his son who was being given aid, it may well have been. For the entries from 1565 to 1573 see AEG, Arch. hosp., Kq 1, fol. 56; the entries in the extraordinary account book were to his son. "Au filz de Maistre de la Roche, ministre, 24 sols . . . Au filz de Monsieur le ministre de la Roche, 24 sols" (To the son of Master de la Roche, minister, 24 sous . . . To the son of Monsieur the minister de la Roche, 24 sous). 17 and 24 February 1566, AEG, Arch. hosp., Hj 2, pp. [2] and [4] of February 1566; see also Kq 2, fol. 200, for "Huguette Galee veufve de Monsieur Jean Boulier dit la Roche" (Huguette Galee widow of Monsieur Jean Boulier called la Roche); assistance to her and her sons continued. AEG, Arch. hosp., Kq 2, fols. 200–203; for the admission of Jean de la Roche to the hospital see Labarthe and Lescaze, *Registres de la Compagnie des Pasteurs de Genève*, 4:156.

49. See also, "A la femme de Maistre Godart ministre, 15 sols" (To the wife of Master Godart, minister, 15 sous). AEG, Arch. hosp., Hj 2, p. [2] of April 1561.

50. AEG, Reg. Consist., vol. 31, fol. 368.

51. See, for instance, the government workers of Florence in Gene Brucker, "Bureaucracy and Social Welfare in the Renaissance: A Florentine Case Study," *Journal of Modern History* 55 (March 1983): 1–21.

52. For a history of medicine in Geneva in early modern times see Léon Gautier, *La médicine à Genève jusqu'à la fin du XVIIIme siècle,* Mémoires et documents publiés par la Société d'histoire et d'archéologie de Genève, 2d ser., 10 (Geneva: J. Jullien, Georg, Libraires-Editeurs, 1906).

53. Pullan, *Rich and Poor in Renaissance Venice,* pp. 64–77.

54. This resolution is found in the deacons' "Livre de memoire des années 1658 à 1661, 1663 à 1680," AEG, Arch. hosp., Ka 5, p. 113.

55. For use of this long title to refer to the *Bourse française* in notarial documents see, for instance, the will of the deacon Jean Budé: "la bourse des pouvres estrangers francoys refugies en ceste cité pour la parole de Dieu." 7 July 1587, AEG, Not. Jovenon, vol. 6, fol. 210. There were other variants. The will of François Budé, brother of Jean, referred to "la Bourse des paouvres François estrangers retirés en ceste cité pour la reformation de l'Evangile" (the *Bourse* for poor French foreigners who have retreated into this city for the reformation of the Gospel). 8 May 1569, AEG, Not. Ragueau, 11:338.

56.

Mescredy doze de julliet 1559 . . . Il y a sept ou huit ans qu'il dit à Monsieur Daiguilles (d'Aiguilles) qu'il ne voloit point bailler son argent pour nourrir palliardz et putains . . . il estait fasché d'avoit perdu beaucoup de son bien et on ne luy donnoit rien.

(Wednesday the twelfth of July 1559 . . . Seven or eight years ago he said to Monsieur Daiguilles [d'Aiguilles] that he did not want to give his money to nourish debauchers and prostitutes . . . he was angry to have lost so much of his goods and to have been given nothing.)

AEG, Proc. Crim., première série, 838 (11–13 July 1559). Recognition for this citation and the transcription of the case of Esprit Nielle should go to Gabrielle Berthoud, professor emerita of the University of Neuchatel.

57.

Huguette Martin, femme dudit Jehan Boullier, appellee en Consistoire [one word omitted] tant que le mauvays mesnage qui est entré en leur maison peult venir de son costé, et elle a respondu qu'elle a bien prins de la peyne et en a mesmes beaucoup apprés ses enfans en nombre desquelz elle en a cinq et à present est enceinte d'une [word omitted], parlant fort arrogamment de cestre affayre disant que Dieu nous jugera [one word omitted] ayant mesmes dicts que les dix francz qu'on a donné à son mary luy ont estés donnés en escus legiers qui ne valoint pas quarante solz, ains que nos [one word omitted] joint advertis du faict et les personnes y renvoyees à lundy prochain et en oultre bonnes remonstrances luy ont estés faictes à luy et à ladite femme. Ladite femme a arrogamment respondu à Spectable Theodore de Beze luy disant qu'il luy avoyt reprochee ung teston qu'elle avoyt bien gagné, aussi a dict [one sentence omitted] et qu'on l'a appelée pour la fayre avorter de l'enfant qu'elle porte.

(Huguette Martin, wife of the said Jean Boullier, was called into the consistory [one word omitted] for as much as the marital discord that entered into their house could come from her side, and she responded that she had had enough grief and had even learned a lot about it [from] her children, in number of whom she has five, and at present [she] is pregnant with one [one word omitted], speaking very arrogantly of this affair, saying that God will judge us [one word omitted], having even said that the ten francs that one had given to her husband had been given to him in light ecus that were not worth forty sous, so that our [one word omitted] are notified of the fact and the persons sent away until next Monday and besides good remonstrances were made to him and to the said wife. The said wife arrogantly responded to Spectable Théodore de Bèze saying to him that he had reproached her for a teston that she had indeed earned. She also said [one sentence omitted] and that one called her in order to make her abort the child that she carries.)

AEG, Reg. Consist., vol. 31 (17 January 1577–18 February 1580), fol. 368.

58. The percentage of *procès criminels* retained in the Genevan archives for the sixteenth century varies. Bernard Lescaze, a Genevan scholar, estimates that there are 10.18 percent for the year 1572, much less than the 47 percent conserved for 1562 and the 53 percent for 1552 cited by E. William Monter in "Crime and Punishment in Calvin's Geneva, 1562," *Archiv für Reformationgeschichte* 64 (1973): 281–87.

59. AEG, Proc. Crim., 2d ser., no. 1618.

60. J. H. Hexter, "Utopia and Geneva," in *Action and Conviction in Early Modern Europe: Essays in Memory of E. H. Harbison*, ed. Theodore Rabb and Jerrold Seigel (Princeton: Princeton University Press, 1969), p. 78. Choisy, *L'état chrétien calviniste à Genève*, p. 71.

61. The entire incident is recorded in a *procès criminel* listed under the husband's name, Charles Lourdois: AEG, Proc. Crim., no. 1469, 8–27 August 1568. (There is an error in the classification. The *procès* is from the month of April.) The information was taken by the lieutenant of justice against Jeanne Varrot. The *procès* contains several responses from Jeanne and from Charles Lourdois, *foulon de drap*. Appendix G contains a resume of their confessions, the sentence, and an opinion by Germaine Colladon who recommended the death penalty.

For Germain Colladon, see his biography by Erich-Hans Kaden, *Le jurisconsulte Germain Colladon ami de Jean Calvin et de Théodore de Bèze*, Mémoires publiés par la Faculté de Droit de Genève 41 (Geneva: Librairie de l'Université, Georg, 1974).

62. The family had apparently received aid from the *Bourse française* over a period of thirteen years beginning in 1554 to within a year of their conviction and banishment of 1568. Ironically, in the early years Charles Lourdois was referred to as a "good man": "A ung bon homme de Meaulx nommé Charles Lourdoys, 7 sols, 6 deniers. . . . A Charles Lourdoys pauvre homme de Meaulx, 4 sols" (To a good man of Meaux named Charles Lourdois, 7 sous, 6 deniers. . . . To Charles Lourdoys poor man of Meaux, 4 sous). AEG, Arch. hosp., Kg 15, pp. [4] and [8] of

September 1554. The assistance for this family continued regularly from 12 January 1560 to 28 August 1567, with additional entries for clothing and the apothecary. AEG, Arch. hosp., Kq 1, fol. 141.

63. Although Charles Lourdois apparently began to receive payments from the *Bourse française* in 1554 he was not received as an inhabitant of Geneva until 13 June 1558, giving some idea of how delayed the entry into the book of inhabitants of Geneva might have been for some individuals. At that time he was listed as native of Meaux, by profession a fuller. Geisendorf, ed., *Livre des habitants*, 1 : 126. His name is also found in the criminal records at an earlier date, but as an accuser rather than a defendant. He accused Claude Bally of making bad merchandise, something which in those days could be punished. Cities set certain standards for goods produced within their domain. The products of Claude Bally were inspected by experts, and he was released: "Procédure contre Claude, fils de Philibert Bally, bourgeois, sergier, accusé par Charles Lourdois de fabriquer de mauvaises marchandises. . . . Sur le rapport des experts chargés de visitez ses produits il est relâché" (Procedure against Claude, son of Philibert Bally, bourgeois, serge-weaver, accused by Charles Lourdois of making bad merchandise. . . . On the report of the experts charged with visiting his products he was released). AEG, Proc. Crim. no. 1367 (27 June–15 July 1566).

64. René Gassin was the deacon who reported to the procurators of the hospital, as recorded in a memorandum of the hospital contained in a criminal process: "Memoire de l'Hospital du lundi premier de febvrier 1558, Magniffiques puissans et très redoubtez princes et Seigneurs, sachez que le present est remyse devant voz exellences, La Loubiere, laquelle de voz benignes graces avyez logé en l'hospital là-bas, Monsieur Regné Gassin, dyacre des Françoys a notiffié aux freres procureurs de l'hospital que ladite est yvronesse, larronesse, medisante, babillarde et an tout et par tout scandaleuse" (Magnificent, powerful, and very feared princes and lords, know that the present is remitted before your excellencies, La Loubière, whom of your kind grace [you] have lodged in the hospital there. Monsieur René Gassin, deacon of the French, notified the brothers, procurators of the hospital, that the said is a drunkard, thief, beggar, chatterer, and in all and by all scandalous); AEG, Proc. Crim., 2d ser., no. 1192 (1 February 1558), fol. 1. La Loubière received aid from the *Bourse française* as early as March 1552 on a regular basis: "A La Laubiere, 6 solz. . . . A La Laubiere, 5 solz. . . . A La Laubiere, 6 sols" (To La Laubiere, 6 sous. . . . To La Laubiere, 5 sous. . . . To La Laubiere, 6 sous). AEG, Arch. hosp., Kg 13, fols. 55, 57ᵛ, 58ᵛ.

65. Jean-Etienne Genequand, "La prison de Saint-Antoine, ancienne maison de discipline," *Revue du Vieux Genève* (1981), pp. 52–54. On the city hospital in the early seventeenth century see Micheline Tripet, "L'Hôpital général au temps de l'Escalade," *Escalade de Genève* 53 (1980): 173–90.

66.

Comme il s'est trouvé diverses personnes qui ont fait des plaintes à quelques uns de Messieurs les diacres de la mauvaise conduitte de Catherine Chevallier qui a esté ellevé au despens de la bourse et entretenue jusques à present et comme elle s'est trouvee convaincue de divers larrecin et d'avoir engagé plusieurs effects, a avisé de prier Monsieur le Sindique de l'Hospital de permettre qu'elle fust mise à la dissipline, ce qu'ayant accordé, elle y a esté conduitte ce jourd'huy.

(Since diverse persons are found who made complaints to some of Messieurs the deacons of the bad conduct of Catherine Chevallier who has been brought up at the expense of the *Bourse* and supported up to the present and as she is found convicted of diverse larcenies and of having pawned several objects, it was advised to ask Monsieur the Syndic of the hospital to permit that she be put in the discipline. This being accorded, she was conducted there this day.)

AEG, Arch. hosp., Ka 6, "Livre de Memoire commencé le premier mars 1680 et finy le 30ᵉ decembre 1691." 12 November 1683, p. 217.

67. See, for example, the case of a widow named Marie, widow of Nicolas Clerisseau. She was received at the hospital of Geneva sometime after 11 January 1585 by the city fathers at their expense because the deacons of the *Bourse française* did not want to support her. In turn she was chased from the hospital on 10 November 1589. "Messieurs l'ont receue à l'Hospital à leurs

despens apres leur avoyt esté remontré que les diacres ne vouloient entretenir des folles. . . .
Ayans esté chassee de l'Hospital le 10ᵉ de novembre 1589" (Messieurs received her at the
Hospital at their expense having been shown that the deacons did not want to support
fools. . . . Having been chased from the hospital the tenth of November 1589). She again
received assistance from the deacons of the *Bourse française*, 6 December 1596. AEG, Arch.
hosp., Kq 2, fol. 166–66ᵛ.

68. The record book of the session of the deacons of April 1613 contains an entry to the effect
that a Monsieur Grenet, representing the pastors, presented the case of the daughter of
Madamoiselle Favre [or Faure], who was "afligee de maladie melancolique." The deacons
determined that she was to receive 10 florins per month.

> Monsieur Grenet a representé, de la part de Messieurs les pasteurs de ceste Eglise, la necessité
> qui est en Mademoiselle Favre [ou Faure] et sa fille, ladite damoiselle afligee de maladie
> melancolique, et qu'il seroit besoing de pourveoir pour sa subvention jusques à ce que
> Messieurs Durand, ses freres, y ayent donné ordre, offrant ledit sieur Grenet au nom desdits
> sieurs pasteurs de payer et rendre ce que luy aura esté fourni. A esté advisé que l'on delivrera
> auxdits sieurs pasteurs dix florins par moys pour ladite damoiselle à la susdite condition.

> (Monsieur Grenet has presented, on the part of Messieurs, the Pastors of this church, the
> need that Mademoiselle Favre [or Faure] is in and her daughter, the said damoiselle afflicted
> with melancholy illness, and that he would have need of means for her subvention until
> Messieurs Durand, her brothers, have supplied an arrangement, the said lord Grenet offering
> in the name of the said pastors to pay and to give back that which will have been furnished.
> [It] has been advised that one will deliver to the said lord pastors ten florins per month for the
> said damoiselle on the said condition.)

AEG, Arch. hosp., Ka 1, No. 11, "Livre memorial de ce qui s'est advise en la compagnie des
diacres de la bourse de pauvres estrangiers francois . . ." (6 April 1612–30 September 1616),
p. 33.

69. The deacons' minutes from the seventeenth century record the case of a woman, Sarra
Melier, who thanked them for the aid they gave her from 13 March 1615 to 12 February 1616.
She promised to pay them back when she could. In another instance, the deacons recorded the
case of a woman, Elizabeth Haultin, who thanked them on behalf of someone else, Bartheleme
Haultin, who was apparently her relative and recently deceased.

> Sarra Melier delaissee de Jeremie Pitet a remercié de l'assistance qu'elle a receue des deniers de
> ceste bourse depuis le 13 mars 1615 jusques à present, laquelle a promis rembourser ceste
> bourse lorsqu'elle aura le moyen, comme elle promect seans l'horsque l'assistance luy fut
> accordee, le susdit jour comme appert cy davant. [12 February 1616]

> (Sarra Melier, abandoned by Jeremie Pitet, said thank you for the assistance that she received
> from the pennies of this *Bourse* since 13 March 1615 to the present, that she promised to
> reimburse to this *Bourse* when she has the means as she promised here when the assistance
> was accorded her, the said day as appears here before. [12 February 1616])

"Elisabet Haultin a remercié de l'assistance faicte cy davant à Barthelemie Haultin" (Elisabet
Haultin said thank you for the assistance made before to Barthelemie Haultin). The seventeenth-century record book in which these instances were recorded is a manuscript entitled
"Livre memorial de ce qui s'est advisé en la compagnie des diacres de la bourse des pauvres
estrangiers François ès annees 1612–1613–1614–1615 à 1616." It contains the decisions made at
the Monday meetings of the deacons. Next to the title on the first page in parchment is the
number "11." This may mean that there were ten volumes preceding it at one time. AEG, Arch.
hosp., Ka 1 (6 April 1612–30 September 1616), pp. 206, 226; the volumes in this series of
deliberations of the deacons include:

Ka 1   6 April 1612–30 September 1616
Ka 2   6 January 1617–18 December 1626
Ka 3   1 January 1627–27 December 1641
Ka 4   3 January 1642–4 October 1658
Ka 5   11 October 1658–26 February 1680
Ka 6   1 March 1680–30 December 1691

They are cited in the archive as Arch. hosp., Ka 1 (no. 11)–Ka 6, Bourse française, Livres Memorials des Diacres, 6 April 1612–30 December 1691.

70. "Benoiste femme de Louys Arnault le dernier jour d'apvril 1580 payé à Monsieur Boniface appoticaire pour ladite Benoiste douze solz"; "Ladite Benoiste s'en est allee sous dire adieu et a emporté les linceux qu'on luy avoyt prestés." (Benoiste, wife of Louys Arnault, the last day of April 1580, paid to Monsieur Boniface, apothecary, for the said Benoiste, twelve sous); (The said Benoiste left without saying goodbye and carried off the linens that we had loaned to her). AEG, Arch. hosp, Kq 2, fol. 23; for Françoise see ibid., fol. 247^v.

71. AEG, Reg. Consist., vol. 31, fol. 368.

72. For greater detail on the various provisions in Geneva to feed the poor, including food policy, see William C. Innes, *Social Concern in Calvin's Geneva* (Allison Park, Penn.: Pickwick Publications, 1983); for more on the application of the concept of social control in the early modern setting see the section on carnivals as social control in Peter Burke, *Popular Culture in Early Modern Europe* (New York: Harper and Row, 1978), pp. 199–204. For a work that links more strongly Calvin's theology and economic thought with social reform see W. Fred Graham, *The Constructive Revolutionary: John Calvin and His Socio-Economic Impact* (Richmond, Va.: John Knox Press, 1971); for a tightly reasoned evaluation of the contribution of Calvin and the Reformation to views on economics and poverty see Roger Stauffenegger, "Réforme, richesse, et pauvreté," *Revue d'histoire de l'Eglise de France* 52 (1966): 47–58; on grain reserves in Geneva and the sixteenth-century policies leading up to the foundation of a grain storage system see Hermann Blanc, *La Chambre des Blés de Genève, 1628–1798* (Geneva: Georg, 1941), pp. 13–36.

73. AEG, Arch. hosp., Kq 2, fol. 83.

74. Ibid., fol. 220.

75. Ibid., fol. 259.

76. Choisy, *L'état chrétien calviniste à Genève*, p. 88.

77. Pullan, *Rich and Poor in Renaissance Venice*, p. 627.

78.

Ceux que Dieu nous a icy envoiés qui sont réfugiés pour la parole de Dieu, ne savent où aller; ils iront à la papaulté. Il y a des impotens, vefves et petis enfans; quant M^{rs} les mettront dehors et s'ils meurent, cela sera sus leurs coffres. Remonstrans que l'église de Dieu est le refuge des paouvres, ce sont ceux desquels N^{tre} Sr Jésus Christ parle disant: Vou m'avez vu nud, etc.

Choisy, *L'état chrétien calviniste à Genève*, p. 246.

79. Ibid.; Nancy Roelker, "Les femmes de la noblesse huguenote au XVIe siècle," in *Actes du Colloque l'Amiral de Coligny et son temps (Paris, 24–28 octobre 1972)* (Paris: Société de l'histoire du protestantisme français, 1974), p. 228.

80. The edict of the city council reads as follows:

Edict sur les mariages, 18 août 1550

Icy est esté parlé et faict advys à cause que d'aulcungs estrangiers viennent souvent en ceste ville et amenent des femmes que l'on ne scait si ce sont leurs femmes ou non d'où y a dangeur de paillardise, pourquoy est arresté que tous ceulx là qu'il viendront et amenerrot des femmes qu'il doibgent faire apparoitre legitimement de leur mariage; aultrement il doignet etre presentés en la congregation et soit faict comment de feu le seigneur de . . . qu'il fust representé et amené en l'Eglise.

(Edict on Marriages, 18 August 1550

Here has been discussed and a judgment made because of some foreigners who often come into this city and bring women of whom one does not know if they are their wives or not, from which there is danger of extramarital sex. For that reason it is ordered that all those there who come and bring women must prove the legitimacy of their marriages. Otherwise they must be presented in the congregation and do as the deceased *seigneur* de . . . who was presented and brought into the church.)

AEG, Reg. Conseil, vol. 45, fol. 70.

81. AEG, Arch. hosp., Ka 1, p. 31.

82. Choisy, *L'etat chrétien calviniste à Genève*, p. 89.

83. John T. McNeill, *The History and Character of Calvinism* (New York: Oxford University Press, 1954; reprint, 1979), pp. 178–79.

84. Natalie Zemon Davis, "Scandale à l'Hôtel-Dieu de Lyon (1537–1543)," in *La France d'Ancien Régime: Etudes réunies en l'honneur de Pierre Goubert* (Toulouse: Société de Démographie Historique et Editions Privat, 1984), 1 : 175–87.

85. For more on the spirit of religious refugees see a thoughtful essay by Gottfried Locher, "The Theology of Exile: Faith and the Fate of the Refugee," in *Social Groups and Religious Ideas in the Sixteenth Century*, ed. Chrisman and Gründler, pp. 85–86, 92.

86. AEG, Arch. hosp., Hj 2, p. [3] of November 1560; AEG, Proc. Crim. 982.

87. AEG, Proc. Crim. 2d ser., 975.

88. AEG, Arch. hosp., Kg 13, fols. 64^v, 77^v. AEG, Proc. Crim., 2d ser., 1005.

89. "A la femme Pierre de Chesne d'Auvergne, 5 sols" (To the wife of Pierre de Chesne of Auvergne, 5 sous). AEG, Arch. hosp., Kg 14, p. [7] of December 1553. AEG, Proc. Crim., 2d ser., 1134. There is a "Pierre Du Chesne" who is listed as a printer from "Chatre sous Montlhéry près Paris" in Chaix, *Recherches sur l'imprimerie à Genève de 1550 à 1564*, pp. 177–78.

90. AEG, Arch. hosp., Kg 13, fols. 55, 57^v, 58^v. AEG, Proc. Crim., 2d ser., 1192, fol. 1.

91. "A Guillaume Maillard drappier, 8 sols" (To Guillaume Maillard, draper, 8 sous). AEG, Arch. hosp., Kg 13, fol. 66^v; AEG, Proc. Crim. 1296.

92. AEG, Proc. Crim. 1192.

93. AEG, Proc. Crim. 505.

94. AEG, Proc. Crim. 1070, 1489.

95. AEG, Arch. hosp., Kg 15, p. [5] of November 1554. AEG, Proc. Crim., 2d ser., 1155.

CHAPTER 9. JEAN BUDÉ AND THE *BOURSE FRANÇAISE*

1. "Noble Jehan Budé, natifz de la ville de Parys, filz de messire Guillaume Budé, conseiller et maistre des Requestes ordinaires de la maison du Roy de France, faicte *le 27 junii 1549*." Geisendorf, ed., *Livre des habitants*, 1 : 3.

2. McNeill, *History and Character of Calvinism*, p. 99. For more on Calvin and Budé see Josef Bohatec, *Budé und Calvin: Studien zur Gedankenwelt des französischen Frühhumanismus* (Graz, Austria: Hermann Böhlaus Nachf., 1950).

3. Both editions of *France Protestante* cite Matthieu Budé as living in Geneva and being employed by Henri Estienne, in contrast to Doumergue who bases the death of Matthieu in 1547 on Calvin's correspondence. For more on the Budé family see Doumergue, *Jean Calvin*, 3 : 606–10. Eugène de Budé, *Vie de Guillaume Budé, fondateur du Collège de France (1467–1540)* (Paris: Librairie Académique Didier, 1884), pp. 278–300. Haag and Haag, *France Protestante*, 3 : 74–77; 2d ed., 3 : 371–82. John Calvin, "869: Calvin à une dame," in *Ioannis Calvini Opera Quae Supersunt Omnia*, ed. Baum, Cunitz, and Reuss, vol. 12, *Corpus Reformatorum*, vol. 40, cols. 452–55.

4. For the purchase and sale of land of the Budé family during the sixteenth century see the family papers of Jean Budé de Vérace. AEG, Arch. de famille, 3e série, Budé de Vérace, 1550–1745, 23 pièces parchemin.

5. Labarthe and Lescaze, *Registres de la Compagnie des Pasteurs de Genève*, 4 : 37, 42, 77.

6. Sometimes Jean Budé was absent. For instance, in February 1561 Jean Budé paid back René Gassin for money he had advanced to the poor and to the doctor in Jean's absence. "Rendu à Monsieur René qu'il a fourny pour les pauvres 3 moys entiers mesmes ce qu'il a fourny au medecin en mon absence, 101 florins, 5 sols, 11 deniers" (Reimbursed to Monsieur René that he furnished for the poor for three entire months even that which he furnished to the doctor in my absence, 101 florins, 5 sous, 11 deniers). AEG, Arch. hosp., Hj 2, p. [4] of February 1561.

7. "Pour ma mere et pour moy, 6 florins." AEG, Arch. hosp., Kg 12, fol. 44^v; "Pour mon frere et pour moy, 6 florins." AEG, Arch. hosp., Kg 14, p. [2] of July 1553; "Item de Monsieur Varennes de son cousin" (Also from Monsieur Varennes from his cousin); "Item et de Monsieur de la Planche" (Also from Monsieur de la Planche); "De son cousin" (From his cousin). 30

September 1551, AEG, Arch. hosp., Kg 12, fol. 1; "D'ung quidam logé chez Monsieur Maldonnade, 5 sols" (From a certain person lodged at Monsieur Maldonnade's house, 5 sous); AEG, Arch. hosp., Kg 14, p. [1] of March 1554.

8. AEG, Arch. hosp., Kq 1 and 2.

9. See, for instance, this reference of 23 March 1562: "Le bâtiment du Collége, duquel ont eu soin Ami de Château et Jean Budé, étant fort avancé, arrêté de les récompense leur peine, et de donner à ce dernier 25 écus . . ." (The building of the College, of which Ami de Château and Jean Budé have had charge, being very advanced, [it is] ordered to recompense them for their effort and to give to this last twenty-five ecus . . .). *Fragmens biographiques et historiques, extraits des registres du Conseil d'Etat de la République de Genève, dès 1535 à 1792*, p. 30. For Jean Budé's service to the city as an ambassador see Gautier, *Histoire de Genève des origines à l'année 1691*, 3:518; 4:145, 248–49, 364, 455, 509–11, 514–16, 536, 600; Budé, *Vie de Guillaume Budé, fondateur du Collège de France (1467–1540)*, pp. 295–96; Doumergue, *Jean Calvin*, 3:609.

10. Calvin described Jean Budé as "lun des plus familiers amys que iaye, et homme seur auquel on se peult fier iusquau bout" (one of the most intimate friends that I have and a reliable man in whom one can rely to the end). John Calvin, "4067. Calvin à la Duchesse de Ferrare," *Exhortations écrites à l'occasion du retour de la Duchesse de Paris à Montargis*, in *Ioannis Calvini Opera*, ed. Baum, Cunitz, and Reuss, vol. 20, *Corpus Reformatorum*, vol. 48, col. 231.

11. ". . . l'amitié des hommes distingués, Nicolas des Gallars, Laurent de Normandie, Colladon, le marquis de Vico, qui composaient, avec les frères de Budé, la société habituelle du réformateur (. . . the friendship of distinguished men, Nicolas des Gallars, Laurent de Normandie, Colladon, the Marquis de Vico, who composed, with the brothers Budé, the habitual society of the reformer). Bonnet, *Récits du seizième siècle*, 2d ed., pp. 118–19.

12. "La premiere et seure adresse pour nous conduire à la cognoiscance de bien c'est de avoir volunté de Luy obeyr comme il est escript: Si aucun[?] veut obeyr à sa volunté il cognoistra et jugera de toute doctrine si elle est de Dieu ou non, 7e Jehan. Secondement est à noter que c'est une vraye seurté pour cognoistre qu'elle est une doctrine quand par icelle nous glorifions Dieu, 7e Jehan." AEG, Arch. hosp., Kg 12, last existing page. See John 7:17–18: "If any man's will is to do his will, he shall know whether the teaching is from God or whether I am speaking on my own authority. He who speaks on his own authority seeks his own glory; but he who seeks the glory of him who sent him is true, and in him there is no falsehood."

13. AEG, Proc. Crim. 769 (11–24 October 1558), 1037 (17–18 May 1562), 1741 (14 March–10 April 1584).

14. AEG, Proc. Crim., 2d ser., 1929, p. 70.

15. LaBarthe and Lescaze, *Registres de la Compagnie des Pasteurs de Genève*, 4:174.

16. Ibid.

17. Galiffe, *Notices généalogiques*, 3:86.

18. ". . . l'infirmite et imbecillite de sa main droite." 7 July 1587, AEG, Not. Jovenon, vol. 6 (1586–90), fol. 215; elsewhere in the will it refers to the gout and debility of his right hand: "de gouttes et debilite de sa main droite." Ibid., fol. 208v.

19. "Damoyselle Marye de Jonvilliers ma femme bien aymee . . ." The expression "my beloved wife" is common in Genevan wills of this period. Ibid., fol. 211.

20. Jean Budé's will reads as follows: "en consideration et recognoissance de la bonne et singuliere amitié que j'ay tousjours portee [*sic;* There is an acute accent over the first 'e' of "portée" in the manuscript] et que je porte à Noble Charles de Jonvilliers, mon cher et bien aymé beau frere, et de la droite affection qu'il a tousjours portee à ma maison et au bien et soulagement de moy et de mes enfans que je le prie de vouloir continuer . . ." Ibid., fols. 212v, 213.

21. Jean Budé's will reads, "l'honorer et respecter en toutes choses comme un bon enfant bien instruit en la crainte de Dieu doibt . . ." Ibid., fol. 213v.

22. "Premierement je donne et legue à la Bourse des pouvres estrangers francoys refugiés en ceste cite pour la parole de Dieu six cens florins et à l'Hospital general dudyt Geneve cent florins et au College de ladyte cité pareille somme de cent florins" (First I give and will to the *Bourse* of the poor French foreigners who have taken refuge in this city for the Word of God, six hundred florins, and to the general hospital of the said Geneva, one hundred florins, and to the college of the said city, a like sum of one hundred florins). Ibid., fol. 210.

23. "Jehan Du Lac mon filliol" (Jean Du Lac, my Godson). Jean Budé was probably referring to his son-in-law, Noble Jean Favre, "Sieur Du Lac en Auvergne," the husband of his recently deceased daughter, Marie. AEG, Not. Jovenon, vol. 6, fol. 212ᵛ.

24. See, for instance, this notarial entry for a vineyard. 19 February 1558, AEG, Not. Ragueau, 2:185–87.

25. See appendix H for real estate transactions from the family papers of Jean Budé de Vérace, AEG, Arch. de famille, 3ᵉ série, Budé de Vérace, 1550–1745.

26. See a procuration of François Budé to Jean Budé, his brother, for proof of inheritance of property in France for the children of Guillaume Budé who were living in Geneva. François gave to Jean the responsibility of following up on an inheritance:

Pour, au nom dudit constituant, demander, exiger, poursuyvre et recepvoir . . . les biens, droictz, noms et actions a luy competans et appartenans au Royaulme de France soyt par tiltre de succession, donation, legatz, testamens paternelz, maternelz, fraternelz et aultrement par quelque tiltre et moyen que ce soyt.

(In order, in the name of said constituant, to ask, exige, pursue and receive . . . the goods, rights, names and actions to him belonging and appertaining in the Kingdom of France be it by title of succession; donation; legacy; paternal, maternal, or fraternal will; or otherwise by whatever title and means that there are.)

"Procuration de François Budé à Jean Budé son frère" (Procuration of François Budé to Jean Budé, his brother). 21 February 1566, AEG, Not. Ragueau, 8:122–24.

27. Jean Budé's will reads, "de la rente que j'ay sur la maison de ville de Paris jusques à la somme de mil livres tournois pour une foys . . ." (of the annuity that I have on the city hall of Paris to the sum of one thousand pounds tournois for one time . . .). AEG, Not. Jovenon, vol. 6, fol. 212.

28. Thomas Brady, Jr., *Ruling Class, Regime and Reformation at Strasbourg, 1520–1555* (Leiden: E. J. Brill, 1978), p. 51.

29. See appendix H for the French transcription of table 6.

30.

En premier lieu, je rends graces à mon Dieu par nostre Seigneur Jesus Christ de ce qu'il luy a pleu me retirer des tenebres horribles et de ce gouffre infernal où j'estois plongé soubz la tirannye de l'Anthechrist romain quand, par sa pure bonté et selon qu'il avoit ordonné dez le commencement, il m'a introduict en sa vraye Eglise soubz le regne et empire de nostre Seigneur Jesus Christ par la mort et sacriffice duquel tous mes pechés me sont pardonnez. Et combien que de moy mesmes je soy une pouvre et miserable creature qui ne sens en moy que toute matiere de mort et condemnation, neanmoings je scay que le sang d'Iceluy est ma vraye purgation et son merite et obeissance m'ont acquis la vraye et unique justice par laquelle je m'attendz et tiens asseuré que Dieu me recoignoistra et recevra comme son enfant avecq tous ses saints au jour de nostre Seigneur Jesus Christ. Telle est ma foy et asseurance sellon son sainct evangille, en laquelle je suis prest de rendre mon ame à Dieu quand il luy plairra m'appeller a soy, tenant au reste en general toute la doctrine contenue au vielh et nouveau testament comme elle est sommairement comprinse en la confession de foy faicte en ceste Eglise de Geneve, receue et approuvee par toutes les Eglises de France et aultres, detestant toutes aultres doctrines contraires à icelle qui n'ont nulle certitude et ferme fondement en l'Escriture. Item: je desire et veux que incontinent après mon decez mon corps soit ensevely chrestiennement à la maniere acoustumée en ceste cité de Geneve en attendant le jour de la bienheureuse resurrection. Et quant aux biens qu'il a pleu à Dieu me donner en ce monde, je en dispose et ordonne par ce present mon dernier testament solempnel et par escript en la maniere suyvante. . . .

AEG, Not. Jovenon, vol. 6, fols. 290–290ᵛ.

31.

L'an mil cinq cens huictante sept le neufieme jour du moys de mars par devant moy notaire public juré de Geneve soubzigné et en presence des tesmoings apres nommés s'est person-nellement establi Noble Jehan Budé, seigneur de Verace, bourgeois de Geneve, lequel de son bon gre estant, par la grace de Dieu en son bon sens et entiere memoire, combien qu'il soit detenu de maladie corporelle a dit et declairé que le contenu cy dans cez feulles de papier qu'il m'a exibees ainsi closes et cachettees est son dernier testament qu'il a dicté et fait coucher ainsi par escript ne pouvant escrire ne signer à cause de l'infirmité et imbecillité de sa main droite.

(The ninth day of the month of March, the year 1587, before me the undersigned sworn public notary of Geneva, and in the presence of witnesses, afterwards named, personally appeared Noble Jean Budé, Lord of Vérace, bourgeois of Geneva, who, being of his own good will, by the grace of God, in his good sense and entire memory, however much he is held back by corporal illness, said and declared that the contents here in these sheets of paper that he exhibited to me thus closed and sealed is his last will that he dictated and had laid down thus in writing, not being able to write nor to sign his name because of the infirmity and imbecility of his right hand.)

7 July 1587, AEG, Not. Jovenon, vol. 6, fol. 215.

32. Michel Vovelle in a study of French wills described a practice among "cultivated" people of drawing up a will before witnesses but keeping the contents private, then sealing the will and putting it away so that only after death would others know how one had disposed of one's property. Jean Budé might have used some modification of this system. Michel Vovelle, *Piété baroque et déchristianisation en Provence au XVIIIe siècle: les attitudes devant la mort d'après les clauses des testaments* ([Paris]: Librairie Plon, [1973]), p. 47.

The laws of Geneva provided for a similar procedure:

VII. Et si le testateur veult que son testament soit secret, l'ayant escript ou fait escripre, le pourra clorre et seeller de ses armoyries, et, en presence de notaire et sept tesmoins, faire declaration que c'est son testament ou disposition de derniere volonté, et requerir iceux notaire et tesmoings de souscripre sadicte declaration sur le repli d'iceluy testament; et cela faict sera ledict testament ou disposition vallable quant à la forme.

(VII. And if the testator wants his will to be secret, having written it or had it written, [he] can close it and seal it with his arms, and, in the presence of a notary and seven witnesses make declaration that it is his will or disposition of his last will, and request this notary and these witnesses to endorse his said declaration on the fold of his will; and that done, the said will or disposition will be valid as to form.)

Rivoire, *Sources du droit du Canton de Genève*, 3:222.

33. "tenté du mauvais esprit. . . ." The information about Jean Budé comes from Lambert Le Blanc's rough draft of an appeal for clemency that is contained in the file for his criminal process, AEG, Proc. Crim. 502 (7–16 March 1554), a loose manuscript in the folder, one page only. The file for the criminal procedure of Lambert Le Blanc also contains an opinion on the fate of the boys involved in the affair, a part of which seems to be in the hand of Jean Calvin, whose signature is found first among the signatories. Ibid. A loose manuscript of three pages: fols 1–2.

34. AEG, Proc. Crim. 502, three pages bound into the *procès*, fols. 13–14, and a page on which the sentence is written signed by two syndics.

35. Ibid.

36. Ibid. The rough draft of an appeal for clemency by Lambert Le Blanc.

37. Jean Budé lived until 1587, when the records report that "Noble Jean Budee, seigneur de Verase, bourgeois est mort pthisique, agee d'environ 72 ans ce 5 juillet 1587 en la rue des Chanoisnes" (Noble Jean Budé, Lord of Vérace, bourgeois, is dead, tuberculous, at the age of about 72 years this 5 July 1587, in the Street of the Canons). AEG, EC Morts, 18:103.

38. Ibid., 1:48.

39. Ibid., vol. 7 (September 1566–February 1568), p. 48.

40. Ibid., 8:121.

41. Ibid., vol. 12 (1572–80), p. 49.

42. Ibid., vol. 15 (1 May 1583–21 November 1584), p. 103.

43. Ibid., vol. 17 (1586), 20 October 1586.

44. AEG, Not. Jovenon, vol. 6, fol. 211[v].

45. Louis Budé was also known as sieur or Monsieur de la Motte (Mothe). "Item et j'ay receu

de mon frere de la Mothe, 11 sols" (Also I received from my brother de la Mothe, 11 sous). AEG, Arch. hosp., Kg 12, fol. 1ᵛ.

46. Haag and Haag, *France protestante*, 2d ed., 3:373–74. Geisendorf, *Livre des habitants*, 1:43.

47. Galiffe, *Notices généalogiques*, 3:85.

48. "Ma mere a baillé 12 sous." AEG, Arch. hosp., Kg 13, p. 36.

49. "A Marie qui a servi feu ma mere laquelle esté en couche logé au Bourg du Four, 12 sols" (To Marie who served my deceased mother, who is in childbed, lodged in the Bourg-de-Four, 12 sous). Ibid., p. 11.

50. "Pour ma mere et pour moy, 6 florins." AEG, Arch. hosp., Kg 12, fol. 44ᵛ.

51. Baum, Cunitz, and Reuss, eds., *Ioannis Calvini Opera*, vol. 14, *Corpus Reformatorum*, vol. 52 (Brunswick: C. A. Schwetschke and Sons, 1875), col. 131.

52. AEG, Arch. hosp., Kg 12, p. 51ᵛ.

53. The edition of Louis Budé's translations of the Psalms came out in the year of his death from the press of Jean Crespin. There was a preface by John Calvin touching on Louis Budé's translation and the usefulness of the Psalms. Loys Budé, *Les Pseaumes de David traduicts selon la verité Hebraique, avec annotations tresutiles* (Geneva: Jean Crespin, 1551); a modern edition came out in 1984: Théodore de Bèze, *Psaumes mis en vers français (1551–1562) accompagnés de la version en prose de Loïs Budé*, ed. Pierre Pidoux (Geneva: Librairie Droz, 1984).

54. "Le 23 en la rue de la boulangerie—Scientifique Loys Budée, Docteur." AEG, EC Morts, vol. 1 (December 1549–29 December 1555), p. 36, entry no. 8; the term *"scientifique"* attached to Louis Budé's name did not necessarily mean that he was a scientist in the twentieth-century sense of the word. In the sixteenth century *"scientifique"* was used in the sense of *"savant,"* or scholar. Edmond Huguet gives the example of "Hommes docts et scientificques" in his *Dictionnaire de la langue française du seizième siècle*, 6:724.

55. AEG, EC Morts,vol. 1 (December 1549–29 December 1555), p. 81.

56. Le testament de Noble François Budé, seigneur de Villeneufve, 8 mai 1569.:

> . . . neantmoingtz veult ordonné et enjoinct qu'elle baille après le decés de luy et continue l'aulmosne ordinaire qu'il a tousjours faicte et donnee chascung moys à ladite Bourse des paouvres françois et s'il plaisoyt à Dieu donner paix au Royaulme de France tellement qu'elle peust recouvrer le revenu de son bien, en ce cas il veult et ordonne que sadicte femme donne le double chascung moys à ladicte Bourse des paouvres estrangers. Item legue et donne à Noble Regnauld Anjorrant seigneur de Sully son amy ancien et inthime son jardin ou courtil qu'il a achepté en Plain Palays.

> (. . . nevertheless, wants ordered and enjoined that she give, after his decease, and continue the ordinary alms that he has always made and given each month to the said fund for the poor French and if it pleases God to give peace to the Kingdom of France so that she can recover the revenue of her property, in this case he wants and orders that his said wife give the double each month to the said fund for the poor foreigners. Also, [he] wills and gives to Noble Regnauld Anjorrant, Lord of Sully, his old and intimate friend, his garden and garth that he bought in Plainpalais.

AEG, Not. Ragueau, 11:338. The entire will is on pp. 337–41.

57. Marguerite de Morel was the sister of François de Morel, pastor. Marguerite de Morel and François Budé had been married less than twelve years when she died. Their marriage contract is dated 5 November 1557. AEG, Not. Ragueau, vol. 2 (1556–58), pp. 110–11; she was sick in bed when she made her will, leaving twenty-five florins to the *Bourse*, fifteen to the college, and ten to the city hospital. Marguerite assigned the care of the surviving children, Jeanne and Judith, to their aunt Catherine Budé, the widow of Jean Anjorrant, who had formerly been associated with the Parlement of Paris. Another aunt, Marguerite Budé, was to take over in her absence. Marguerite Budé was the widow of Guillaume Trye, a notary. Two deacons of the *Bourse française*, Jean Budé and Regnauld Anjorrant, were named to administer the girls' persons and belongings following the desire of the girls' father. Jean Budé was the girls' uncle and Regnauld Anjorrant, the younger brother of Jean Anjorrant, had been a good friend of the girls' father. In addition to the two daughters, the couple had at least two other children, Jozel and Natanael, who died in March of 1562, one on Monday the 16th and the other on Saturday the 21st. Both were eight months old, so apparently they were twins. Both were

reported dead of a fever. AEG, EC Morts, vol. 4 (30 May 1561–1 June 1562), pp. 102–4. For the will of Marguerite de Morel see appendix I.

58. Charles de Jonvilliers, former secretary to Calvin, began his career as a deacon in 1569 as far as the records reveal. 20 March 1569, AEG, Not. Ragueau, 11:215–16; Jean Du Lac as deacon is recorded in Labarthe and Tripet, eds. *Registres de la Compagnie des Pasteurs de Genève*, 5:100, 141, 177; Citron and Junod, eds., *Registres de la Compagnie des Pasteurs de Genève*, 6:3. The first mention of him as deacon on 6 January 1586 says he is confirmed as deacon, so he was apparently in office before that date.

CHAPTER 10. SUMMARY AND CONCLUSIONS

1. Grimm, "Luther's Contributions to Sixteenth-Century Organization of Poor Relief," pp. 225–26.

2. Ibid., p. 226.

3. Ibid., p. 229.

4. Ibid., pp. 226–29; Luther, "Ordinance of a Common Chest, Preface," pp. 169–76; "Fraternal Agreement on the Common Chest of the Entire Assembly at Leisnig," trans. Walther I. Brandt, in *Luther's Works*, ed. Pelikan and Lehmann, vol. 45, *The Christian in Society II*, ed. Brandt, pp. 178–82; "Ordenung enns gemennen tastens: Radschlag wie die genstlichen gutter zu handeln sind," in *D. Martin Luthers Werke: Kritische Gesamtausgabe (Weimar Ausgabe)* (Weimar: Hermann Böhlaus Nachfolger, 1891), 12:11–30.

5. Grimm, "Luther's Contributions to Sixteenth-Century Organization of Poor Relief," p. 229.

6. Ibid., pp. 223, 229–32.

7. Innes, *Social Concern in Calvin's Geneva*, p. 56; J. Wayne Baker, *Heinrich Bullinger and the Covenant: The Other Reformed Tradition* (Athens: Ohio University Press, 1980), p. xx.

8. André Biéler, *La pensée économique et sociale de Calvin*, Publications de la Faculté des Sciences Economiques et Sociales de l'Université de Genève, vol. 13 (Geneva: Librairie de L'Université, Georg, 1961), p. 60.

9. Miriam Chrisman, *Strasbourg and the Reform: A Study in the Process of Change* (New Haven: Yale University Press, 1967), pp. 272–83.

10. Ibid., p. 280.

11. Ibid., pp. 42–44.

12. Robert W. Henderson, "Sixteenth-Century Community Benevolence: An Attempt to Resacralize the Secular," *Church History* 38 (December 1969): 426–27.

13. Consider, for instance, the collective life of rural areas near Lyons, France, between 1600 and 1650; Jean-Pierre Gutton, "Confraternities, Curés and Communities in Rural Areas of the Diocese of Lyons under the Ancien Régime," trans. John Burke, in *Religion and Society in Early Modern Europe, 1500–1800*, ed. Kaspar von Greyerz (Boston: George Allen and Unwin, 1984).

14. Karen Norberg, *Rich and Poor in Grenoble, 1600–1814* (Berkeley and Los Angeles: University of California Press, 1985), p. 6.

15. Innes, *Social Concern in Calvin's Geneva*, p. 244.

16. Ibid.; Biéler, *La pensée économique et sociale de Calvin*; Graham, *The Constructive Revolutionary*.

17. Grandjean, "La Bourse française de Geneve," p. 60.

Select Bibliography

ARCHIVAL SOURCES

Archives d'Etat de Genève

Archives de famille, 3e série. Budé de Vérace, 1550–1745. 23 pièces parchemin.

Archives hospitalières, Aa 2. Registre des deliberations des Procureurs de l'Hospital, 1560.

Archives hospitalières, Dd 1. Livre des legatz faictz tant aux paouvres de l'Hospital general de Geneve, au College, que aux paouvres estrangiers. Dès le premier janvier 1580, 1580–1637.

Archives hospitalières, Fe 4, 1558–1560.

Archives hospitalières, Hj 1 and 2; Kg 12–19. Bourse française, Account Books, 1550–1582.

Archives hospitalières, Ka 1–Ka 6. Bourse française, Livres Memorials des Diacres, 1612–1691.

Archives hospitalières, Ke 1. Livre des Reglements contenant un receuil des plus importantes deliberations prises par Messieurs les Diacres de la Bourse françoise sur divers cas proposés ou autrement representés dans leur assemblée concernant la direction des pauvres refugies françois . . . autres qui en dependent et conformement aux livres de Memoire de la ditte Bourse des années 1612 à l . . . [no closing date] inclus.

Archives hospitalières, Kq 1 and 2. Bourse française, Grand Livre des Assistés No. 1, 1560–1579. No. 2, 1580–1599.

Archives hospitalières, P 239. Dossiers 2940–73 (1596–1846), dossier 2941.

Etat Civil. Registres des Décès. Vols. 1–18, 1549–1587.

Manuscrits Historiques. No. 223, Henri-Leonard Bordier. Les Registres de la Bourse Française de Genève commencant au premier octobre 1550: Extraits des dits registres depuis le premier octobre 1550 jusqu'au premier octobre 1566, October 1876.

Notaire: Dagoneau, Olivier. Vol. 1 (1591–1608).

Notaire: Jovenon, Jean. Vol. 4, 1577–1580, and Vol. 6, 1586–1590.

Notaire: Ragueau, Jean. Vols. 2–14, 1556–1578.

Notaire: Santeur, Aimé. Vol. 5, 1568–1570.

Notaire: Vuarrier, François. Vol. 5, 1537–1567.

Procès Criminels, 1550–1599.

Registres du Conseil. Vols. 39–75, 1545–1580.

Registres du Consistoire. Vols. 3–31, 1550–1580.

Bibliothèque Publique et Universitaire de Genève

Manuscrits suppl. 816 (41). Mémoires, notes, et documents sur la Bourse et l'Eglise italiennes. Nos. 6 and 7, Notes sur la Bourse italienne. No. 8, Libro di Memorie Diverse Della Chiesa Italiana Raccolte Dà Vincenzo Burlamachi, 1550–1669.

Manuscrits suppl. 821. Liste de personnes qui ont fait des donations par testament à l'Eglise et à la Bourse des Italiens établis à Genève.

GENERAL

Assereto, Giovanni. "Pauperismo e assistenza: Messa a punto di studi recenti." *Archivio Storico Italiano* 141 (1983): 253–71.

Baker, J. Wayne. *Heinrich Bullinger and the Covenant: The Other Reformed Tradition.* Athens: Ohio University Press, 1980.

Bamford, Paul. *Fighting Ships and Prisons: The Mediterranean Galleys in the Age of Louis XIV.* Minneapolis: University of Minnesota Press, 1973.

Baum, Guilielmus, Eduardus Cunitz, and Eduardus Reuss, eds. *Ioannis Calvini Opera Quae Supersunt Omnia.* Vols. 29–87, 1863–1900, of *Corpus Reformatorum.* 101 vols. Brunswick: C. A. Schwetschke and Sons, 1834–1968.

Bergier, Jean-François. "Salaires des pasteurs de Genève au XVIᵉ siècle." In *Mélanges d'histoire du XVIᵉ siècle offerts à Henri Meylan,* pp. 159–78. Geneva: Librairie Droz, 1970.

Berthoud, Gabrielle, A. Tricard, Eugénie Droz, R. Hari, G. Brasart-de Groër, Heidi-Lucie Schlaepfer, S. Stahlmann, E. Pommier, Natalie Zemon Davis, Robert M. Kingdon, Alain Dufour, D. Thickett, and Paul-F. Geisendorf, eds. *Aspects de la propagande religieuse.* Geneva: Librairie E. Droz, 1957.

Bèze, Théodore de. *Psaumes mis en vers français (1551–1562) accompagnés de la version en prose de Loïs Budé.* Edited by Pierre Pidoux. Geneva: Librairie Droz, 1984.

Biéler, André. *La pensée économique et sociale de Calvin.* Publications de la Faculté des Sciences Economiques et Sociales de l'Université de Genève, vol. 13. Geneva: Librairie de l'Université, Georg, 1961.

Binz, Louis. *Brève histoire de Genève.* Geneva: Chancellerie d'Etat, 1981.

Bittle, W. G., and R. Todd. "Inflation and Philanthropy in England, a Reassessment of W. K. Jordan's Data." *Economic History Review,* 2d ser., 29 (1976): 203–10.

Blaisdell, Charmaine Jenkins. "Calvin's Letters to Women: The Courting of Ladies in High Places." *The Sixteenth Century Journal* 13 (1982): 67–84.

Blanc, Hermann. *La Chambre des Blés de Genève, 1628–1798.* Geneva: Georg, 1941.

Bohatec, Josef. *Budé und Calvin: Studien zur Gedankenwelt des französischen Frühhumanismus.* Graz, Austria: Hermann Böhlaus Nachf., 1950.

Bonenfant, Paul. "Les origines et le caractère de la réforme de la bienfaisance publique aux Pays-Bas sous le règne de Charles-Quint." *Revue Belge de Philosophie et d'Histoire* 5 (1926): 887–904 and 6 (1927): 207–30.

Bonnet, Jules. *Nouveaux récits du seizième siècle.* Paris: Grassart, Libraire-Editeur, 1870.

———. *Récits du seizième siècle.* 2d ed. Paris: Grassart, Libraire-Editeur, 1875.

———. *Récits du seizième siècle.* 2d ser. Paris: Grassart, Libraire-Editeur, 1885.

Borgeaud, Charles. *Histoire de l'Université de Genève.* Vol. 1, *L'Académie de Calvin, 1559–1798.* Geneva: Georg, Libraires de l'Université, 1900.

Bouwsma, William J. *John Calvin: A Sixteenth-Century Portrait.* New York: Oxford University Press, 1988.

———. "The Quest for the Historical Calvin." *Archiv für Reformationsgeschichte* 77 (1986): 47–57.

Brady, Thomas, Jr. *Ruling Class, Regime and Reformation at Strasbourg, 1520–1555.* Leiden: E. J. Brill, 1978.

Braudel, Fernand. *La Méditerranée et le Monde méditerranéen à l'époque de Philippe II.* Paris: Librairie Armand Colin, 1949.

Brucker, Gene. "Bureaucracy and Social Welfare in the Renaissance: A Florentine Case Study." *The Journal of Modern History* 55 (March 1983): 1–21.

Budé, Eugène de. *Vie de Guillaume Budé, fondateur du Collège de France (1467–1540).* Paris: Librairie Académique Didier, 1884.

Budé, Loys. *Les Pseaumes de David traduicts selon la verité Hebraique, avec annotations tresutiles.* Geneva: Jean Crespin, 1551.

Burke, Peter. *Popular Culture in Early Modern Europe.* New York: Harper and Row, 1978.

Burn, John. *Livre des anglois à Genève.* London: n.p., 1831.

Calvin, John. *Calvin: Institutes of the Christian Religion.* Edited by John T. McNeill and translated by Ford Lewis Battles. Vols. 20–21 of Library of Christian Classics. Philadelphia: Westminster Press, 1960.

———. *Institution de la religion chrétienne.* Edition nouvelle publiée par la Société Calviniste de France sous les auspices de l'International Society for Reformed Faith and Action. 5 vols. Geneva: Labor et Fides, 1955–63.

———. *Leçons ou commentaires et expositions de Jean Calvin, tant sur les révélations que sur les lamentations du prophète Jérémie. Le tout fidèlement recueilli, premièrement en latin par Jean Budé et Charles de Jonvillier et depuis translaté nouvellement en françois.* Lyons: Cl. Senneton, 1565.

Candolle, Alphonse de. *Recherches sur les Candolle et Caldora de Provence et de Naples.* Geneva: Imprimerie Charles Schuchardt, 1885.

Carmichael, Ann G. *Plague and the Poor in Renaissance Florence.* Cambridge History of Medicine. Cambridge: Cambridge University Press, 1986.

Chaix, Paul. *Recherches sur l'imprimerie à Genève de 1550 à 1564: Etude bibliographique, économique et littéraire.* Geneva: Librairie E. Droz, 1954.

Choisy, Eugène. *L'état chrétien calviniste à Genève au temps de Théodore de Bèze.* Geneva: Ch. Eggimann, 1902.

Chrisman, Miriam. *Strasbourg and the Reform: A Study in the Process of Change.* New Haven: Yale University Press, 1967.

———. "Urban Poor in the Sixteenth Century: The Case of Strasbourg." In *Social*

Groups and Religious Ideas in the Sixteenth Century, edited by Miriam Chrisman and Otto Gründler. Kalamazoo: Medieval Institute, Western Michigan University, 1978.

Clay, C. G. A. *Economic Expansion and Social Change: England 1500–1700*. 2 vols. Cambridge: Cambridge University Press, 1984.

Covelle, Alfred. *Le Livre des Bourgeois de l'Ancienne République de Genève*. Geneva: J. Jullien, 1897.

Croce, Benedetto. "Il Marchese di Vico." In *Vite de Avventure, di Fede e di Passione*, 3d ed., pp. 187–291. Bari: Gius Laterza and Sons, 1953.

Danner, Dan G. "The Marian Exiles and the English Protestant Tradition." In *Social Groups and Religious Ideas in the Sixteenth Century*, edited by Miriam Chrisman and Otto Gründler. Kalamazoo: Medieval Institute, Western Michigan University, 1978.

Davis, Natalie Zemon. "Poor Relief, Humanism, and Heresy." In *Society and Culture in Early Modern France: Eight Essays by Natalie Zemon Davis*, pp. 17–64. Stanford, Calif.: Stanford University Press, 1975.

———. "Scandale à l'Hôtel-Dieu de Lyon (1537–1543)." In *La France d'Ancien Régime: Etudes réunies en l'honneur de Pierre Goubert*, 1:175–87. Toulouse: Société de Démographie Historique et Editions Privat, 1984.

De Klerk, Peter. "Calvin Bibliography 1985." *Calvin Theological Journal* 20 (November 1985): 268–80.

———. "Calvin Bibliography 1984." *Calvin Theological Journal* 19 (November 1984): 192–212.

———. "Calvin Bibliography 1986." *Calvin Theological Journal* 21 (November 1986): 194–222.

Douglass, E. Jane Dempsey. *Justification in Late Medieval Preaching: A Study of John Geiler of Keisersberg*. Studies in Medieval and Reformation Thought, vol. 1. Leiden: E. J. Brill, 1966.

———. *Women, Freedom, and Calvin*. Philadelphia: Westminster Press, 1985.

Doumergue, Emile. *Jean Calvin, Les hommes et les choses de son temps*. 7 vols. Lausanne: Georges Bridel, Editeurs, 1899–1927. Vol. 3, *La ville, la maison et la rue de Calvin*, 1905. Vol. 5, *La pensée ecclésiastique et la pensée politique de Calvin*, 1917.

"Draft Ecclesiastical Ordinances." In *Calvin: Theological Treatises*, edited by J. K. S. Reid, pp. 64–66. Library of Christian Classics. Philadelphia: Westminster Press, 1954.

Droz, Eugénie. *Chemins de l'hérésie: textes et documents*. 4 vols. Geneva: Slatkine, 1970–76.

Dufour, Alain. "Le mythe de Genève au temps de Calvin." In *Histoire politique et psychologie historique*, pp. 62–95. Geneva: Librairie Droz, 1966.

Dufour, Alain, Fernand Aubert, Henri Meylan, Arnaud Tripet, Alexandre de Henseler, Claire Chimelli, Mario Turchetti, and Béatrice Nicollier, eds. *Correspondance de Théodore de Bèze*. 12 vols. to date. Geneva: Librairie Droz, 1960–.

Eire, Carlos M. N. "Prelude to Sedition? Calvin's Attack on Nicodemism and Religious Compromise." *Archiv für Reformationsgeschichte* 76 (1985): 120–45.

Fatio, Olivier. "L'Eglise de Genève et la Révocation de l'Edit de Nantes, 1680–1705." In *Genève au temps de la Révocation de l'Edit de Nantes, 1680–1705*. Mémoires et documents publiés par la Société d'histoire et d'archéologie de Genève, 50: 159–311. Geneva: Librairie Droz, 1985.

———. "Genève et le Refuge." *Bulletin de la Société de l'Histoire du Protestantisme Français* 133 (1987): 115–19.

Fehr, H. *La communauté réformée allemande de Genève et la paroisse protestante de langue allemande de l'Eglise Nationale: documents divers et notices historiques.* Geneva: Imprimerie Gutenberg, 1917.

Fischer, Danielle. "L'histoire de l'Eglise dans la pensée de Calvin." *Archiv für Reformationsgeschichte* 77 (1986): 79–125.

Flynn, Maureen. "Charitable Ritual in Late Medieval and Early Modern Spain." *The Sixteenth Century Journal* 16 (Fall 1985): 335–48.

Fournier-Marcigny, F. *Genève au XVIme siècle: La vie ardente du premier Refuge français, 1532–1602.* Geneva: Les Editions du Mont-Blanc, 1942.

"1415, Valérand Poullain à Jean Calvin, à Genève. De Strasbourg, 28 novembre 1544." In *Correspondance des Réformateurs dans les pays de langue française, recueillie et publiée avec d'autres lettres relatives à la Réforme et des notes historiques et biographiques,* edited by A.-L. Herminjard, vol. 9, *1543–1544,* pp. 377–82. Geneva: Georg, Libraires-Editeurs, 1897.

Fragmens biographiques et historiques, extraits des registres du Conseil d'Etat de la République de Genève, dès 1535 à 1792. Geneva: Manget et Cherbuliez, Imprimeurs-Libraires, 1815.

Gaberel, Jean-Pierre. *Histoire de l'Eglise de Genève depuis le commencement de la Réformation jusqu'à nos jours.* 3 vols. Paris: Joël Cherbuliez Libraire, 1855–62.

Gagnebin, Bernard. "L'incroyable histoire des sermons de Calvin." *Bulletin de la Société d'histoire et d'archéologie de Genève* 10 (1955): 311–34.

Galiffe, J. B. G. *Genève historique et archéologique.* Geneva: H. Georg, Libraire-Editeur, 1869.

———. *Le refuge italien de Genève aux XVIme et XVIIme siècles.* Geneva, 1881.

Galiffe, Jacques Augustin. *Notices généalogiques sur les familles genevoises depuis les premiers temps jusqu'à nos jours.* 7 vols. Geneva: J. Barbezat et al., 1829–95.

Gaullieur, Eusèbe H. "Etudes sur la typographie genevoise du XVe au XIXe siècles, et sur l'introduction de l'imprimerie en Suisse." In *Bulletin de l'Institut National Genevois,* 2:180–210. Geneva: Kessmann, Editeur, Librairie de l'Institut Genevois, 1855.

Gautier, Jean-Antoine. *Histoire de Genève des origines à l'année 1691.* Vol. 3, *De l'année 1538 à l'année 1556.* Geneva: Rey et Malavallon Imprimeurs, 1898. Vol. 4, *De l'année 1556 à l'année 1567.* Geneva: Ch. Eggimann, Imprimeurs, 1901.

Gautier, Léon. *La médecine à Genève jusqu'à la fin du XVIIIme siècle.* Mémoires et documents publiés par la Société d'histoire et d'archéologie de Genève, 2d ser. 10. Geneva: J. Jullien, Georg, Libraires-Editeurs, 1906.

Geisendorf, Paul-F. ed., *Livre des habitants de Genève.* Vol. 1, 1549–1560. Vol. 2, *1572–1574 et 1585–1587.* Geneva: Librairie E. Droz, 1957, 1963.

Genequand, Jean-Etienne. "La prison de Saint-Antoine, ancienne maison de discipline." *Revue du Vieux Genève* (1981), pp. 52–54.

Gilmont, Jean-François. *Jean Crespin, un éditeur réformé du XVIe siècle.* Geneva: Librairie Droz, 1981.

Goldsmith, Leslie. "Poor Relief and Reform in Sixteenth-Century Orleans." Ph.D. diss., University of Wisconsin, Madison, 1980.

Gonnet, Paul. *L'adoption lyonnais des orphelins légitimes (1536–1793).* 2 vols. Paris: Librairie Générale de Droit & de Jurisprudence, 1935.

Graham, W. Fred. *The Constructive Revolutionary: John Calvin and His Socio-Economic Impact.* Richmond, Va.: John Knox Press, 1971.

Grandjean, Henri. "La Bourse Française de Genève (1550–1849)." In *Etrennes Genevoises,* pp. 46–60. Geneva: Edition Atar, 1927.

Grandjean, Michel. "Genève au secours des galériens pour la foi (1685–1718)." In *Genève au temps de la Révocation de l'Edit de Nantes, 1680–1705.* Mémoires et documents publiés par la Société d'histoire et d'archéologie de Genève, 50:399–438. Geneva: Librairie Droz, 1985.

Gray, Janet Glenn. "The Origin of the Word Huguenot." *The Sixteenth Century Journal* 14 (1983): 349–59.

Greyerz, Kaspar von. "Stadt und Reformation: Stand und Aufgaben der Forschung" and "Verzeichnis Zitierter Publikationen." *Archiv für Reformationsgeschichte* 76 (1985): 6–63.

Grimm, Harold. "Luther's Contributions to Sixteenth-Century Organization of Poor Relief." *Archiv für Reformationsgeschichte* 61 (1970): 222–33.

Guerdan, René. *Genève au temps de Calvin.* Geneva: Editions du Mont-Blanc, 1977.

Gutton, Jean-Pierre. "Confraternities, Curés and Communities in Rural Areas of the Diocese of Lyons under the Ancien Régime." Translated by John Burke. In *Religion and Society in Early Modern Europe, 1500–1800,* edited by Kasper von Greyerz, pp. 202–11. Boston: George Allen & Unwin, 1984.

———. *La société et les pauvres: l'exemple de la généralité de Lyon, 1534–1789.* Paris: Société d'Edition "Les Belles Lettres," 1970.

Haag, Eugène, and Emile Haag. *La France protestante ou vies des protestants français qui se sont fait un nom dans l'histoire depuis les premiers temps de la Réformation jusqu'a la reconnaissance du principe de la liberté des cultes par l'Assemblée Nationale; Ouvrage précédé d'une notice historique sur le protestantisme en France suivi de pièces justificatives.* 10 vols. Paris and Geneva: Joël Cherbuliez, Libraire-Editeur, 1846–58.

———. *La France protestante publiée sous les auspices de la Société de l'histoire du protestantisme français et sous la direction de Monsieur Henri Bordier.* 2d ed. 6 vols. Paris: Sandoz and Fischbacher, 1877–88.

Halkin, L. E. "Guillaume de Gulpen et Daniel de Maldonade." In *Etudes d'histoire et d'archéologie namuroises dédiées à Ferdinand Courtoy,* 2:641–61. Namur, 1952.

Harper, George W. "Calvin and English Calvinism to 1649: A Review Article." *Calvin Theological Journal* 20 (November 1985): 255–62.

Heller, Henry. *The Conquest of Poverty: The Calvinist Revolt in Sixteenth Century France.* Leiden: E. J. Brill, 1986.

Henderson, Robert W. "Sixteenth-Century Community Benevolence: An Attempt to Resacralize the Secular." *Church History* 38 (December 1969): 421–28.

———. *The Teaching Office in the Reformed Tradition: A History of the Doctoral Ministry.* Philadelphia: Westminster Press, 1962.

Hexter, J. H. "Utopia and Geneva." In *Action and Conviction in Early Modern Europe: Essays in Memory of E. H. Harbison,* edited by Theodore Rabb and Jerrold Seigel, pp. 77–89. Princeton: Princeton University Press, 1969.

Heyer, Henri. *L'Eglise de Genève, 1535–1909: Esquisse historique de son organisation suivie de ses diverses constitutions, de la liste de ses pasteurs et professeurs, et d'une table biographique.* Geneva: Librairie A. Jullien, 1909. Reprint, Nieuwkoop: B. de Graaf, 1974.

Heyer, Henri, and Louis Johannot. *Les diaconies de la ville de Genève, leur origine et leur activité de 1850 à 1900 avec le tableau des membres: Rapports présentés à la séance annuelle du Consistoire et des diaconies le 27 novembre 1900.* Geneva: Librairie Henry Kündig, 1901.

Heyer, Theophile. "Notice sur Laurent de Normandie." In *Mémoires et documents publiés par la Société d'histoire et d'archéologie de Genève,* 16:399–422. Geneva: J. Jullien, Libraire-Editeur, 1867.

Holtz, Cécile. "La Bourse française de Genève et le Refuge de 1684 à 1686." In *Genève au temps de la Révocation de l'Edit de Nantes, 1680–1705.* Mémoires et documents publiés par la Société d'histoire et d'archéologie de Genève, 50:439–91. Geneva: Librairie Droz, 1985.

Höpfl, Harro. *The Christian Polity of John Calvin.* Cambridge: Cambridge University Press, 1982.

Hudson, Elizabeth K. "The Protestant Struggle for Survival in Early Bourbon France: The Case of the Huguenot Schools." *Archiv für Reformationsgeschichte* 76 (1985): 271–95.

Huguet, Edmond. *Dictionnaire de la langue française du seizième siècle.* 7 vols. Paris: Librairie Ancienne Edouard Champion; Honoré Champion; Didier, 1925–67.

Imbert, Jean. "L'hospitalisation des protestants sous l'Ancien Régime." *Bulletin de la Société de l'Histoire du Protestantisme Français* 131 (1985): 173–87.

Innes, William C. *Social Concern in Calvin's Geneva.* Allison Park, Penn.: Pickwick Publications, 1983.

Jordan, Wilbur Kitchener. *Philanthropy in England, 1480–1660: A Study of the Changing Pattern of English Social Aspirations.* London: George Allen and Unwin, 1959.

Kaden, Erich-Hans. *Le jurisconsulte Germain Colladon ami de Jean Calvin et de Théodore de Bèze.* Mémoires publiés par la Faculté de Droit de Genève, 41. Geneva: Librairie de l'Université, Georg, 1974.

Kallemeyn, Harold. *Diacres et diaconat pendant la réforme (1517 à 1560) étude historique et théologique.* Th. M. thesis. Vaux-sur-Seine: Faculté Libre de Théologie Evangélique, 1986.

Kingdon, Robert M. "Calvin's Ideas about the Diaconate: Social or Theological in Origin?" In *Piety, Politics, and Ethics: Reformation Studies in Honor of George Wolfgang Forell,* edited by Carter Lindberg, pp. 167–80. Kirksville, Mo.: The Sixteenth Century Journal Publishers, 1984.

———. *Church and Society in Reformation Europe.* London: Valiorum Reprints, 1985.

———. "The Deacons of the Reformed Church in Calvin's Geneva." In *Mélanges d'histoire du XVIe siècle offerts à Henri Meylan,* pp. 81–90. Geneva: Librairie Droz, 1970.

———. *Geneva and the Coming of the Wars of Religion in France, 1555–1563.* Geneva: Librairie E. Droz, 1956.

———. "Social Welfare in Calvin's Geneva." *American Historical Review* 76 (February 1971): 50–69.

Kintz, Jean-Pierre. *La société strasbourgeoise du milieu du XVIe siècle à la fin de la guerre de Trente Ans 1560–1650.* Paris: Ophys, 1984.

Le Goff, Jacques. *The Birth of Purgatory.* Translated by Arthur Goldhammer. Chicago: University of Chicago Press, 1984.

Leith, John Haddon, and Charles Edward Raynal III, eds. "Calvin Studies II." Papers presented at a colloquium on Calvin studies at Davidson College Presbyterian Church and Davidson College, Davidson, North Carolina. Davidson: Davidson College, 1985.

Léry, Jean de. *Histoire d'un voyage fait en la terre du Brésil.* Edited by Jean-Claude Morisot. Geneva: Librairie Droz, 1975.

———. *Le voyage au Brésil de Jean de Léry 1556–1558.* Paris: Payot, 1927.

Lescaze, Bernard. *Genève: sa vie et ses monnaies aux siècles passés.* Geneva: Crédit Suisse, 1981.

———, ed. *Sauver l'âme nourrir le corps: De l'Hôpital général à l'Hospice général de Genève, 1535–1985.* Geneva: l'Hospice général, 1984.

Lestringant, Frank. "Calvinistes et cannibales: Les Ecrits protestants sur le Brésil français (1555–1560); Première Partie: Jean de Léry ou l'élection." *Bulletin de la Société de l'Histoire du Protestantisme Français* 126 (1980): 9–26.

———. "Calvinistes et cannibales: Les Ecrits Protestants sur le Brésil français (1555–1560): Deuxième Partie: La 'réfutation' de Pierre Richer." *Bulletin de la Société de l'Histoire du Protestantisme Français* 126 (1980): 167–92.

Levi-Strauss, Claude. *Tristes Tropiques.* Paris: Librairie Plon, 1955.

Lindberg, Carter. "'There Should Be No Beggars Among Christians': Karlstadt, Luther, and the Origins of Protestant Poor Relief." *Church History* 46 (1977): 313–34.

Linder, Robert. *The Political Ideas of Pierre Viret.* Geneva: Librairie Droz, 1964.

Locher, Gottfried. "The Theology of Exile: Faith and the Fate of the Refugee." In *Social Groups and Religious Ideas in the Sixteenth Century,* edited by Miriam Chrisman and Otto Gründler, pp. 85–92. Kalamazoo: Medieval Institute, Western Michigan University, 1978.

Luther, Martin. "134: To Elector Frederick, Leisnig, August 11, 1523." In *Luther's Works,* edited by Jaroslav Pelikan and Helmut Lehmann. Vol. 49, *Letters II.* Translated and edited by Gottfried Krodel, pp. 45–47. Philadelphia: Fortress Press, 1972.

———. "Ordinance of a Common Chest, Preface, 1523." Translated by Albert T. W. Steinhaeuser and revised by Walther I. Brandt. In *Luther's Works,* edited by Jaroslav Pelikan and Helmut Lehmann. Vol. 45, *The Christian in Society II.* Edited by Walther I. Brandt, pp. 169–76. Philadelphia: Muhlenberg Press, 1962.

Lytle, Guy Fitch, and Stephan Orgel, eds. *Patronage in the Renaissance.* Princeton: Princeton University Press, 1982.

Mayor, Hélène. "La Bourse française de Genève au moment de la révocation de l'Edit de Nantes." Mémoire de licence, University of Geneva, May 1983.

Mandrou, Robert. "Les Français hors de France aux XVIe et XVIIe siècles." *Annales: Economies, Sociétés, Civilisations* 14 (1959): 662–75.

McGrath, Alister E. "John Calvin and Late Mediaeval Thought: A Study in Late Mediaeval Influences upon Calvin's Theological Development." *Archiv für Reformationsgeschichte* 77 (1986): 58–78.

McKee, Elsie Anne. *John Calvin on the Diaconate and Liturgical Almsgiving.* Geneva: Librairie Droz, 1984.

McNeill, John T. *The History and Character of Calvinism.* New York: Oxford University Press, 1954.

Mentzer, Raymond A. Jr. *"Disciplina Nervus ecclesiae:* The Calvinist Reform of Morals at Nîmes.*" The Sixteenth Century Studies Journal* 18 (Spring 1987): 89–115.

Meyer, Christian. "Le psaulter huguenot: notes à propos de quelques éditions antérieures à son achèvement (1554–1561)." *Bulletin de la Société de l'Histoire du Protestantisme Français* 130 (1984), 87–95.

Moens, W. J. C. "The Relief of the Poor Members of the French Churches in England as Exemplified by the Practice of the Walloon or French Church at Sandwich (1568–72)." *Proceedings of the Huguenot Society of London* (10 January and 14 March 1894), pp. 321–39.

Mollat, Michel. "La notion de pauvreté au moyen âge: Position de problèmes." *Revue d'histoire de l'Eglise de France* 52 (1966): 6–24.

———. *Les pauvres au moyen âge: Etude sociale.* n.p.: Hachette, 1978.

Monter, E. William. *Calvin's Geneva.* New York: John Wiley and Sons, 1967.

———. "Crime and Punishment in Calvin's Geneva, 1562." *Archiv für Reformationsgeschichte* 64 (1973): 281–87.

———. "La sodomie à l'époque moderne en Suisse romande." *Annales: Economies, Sociétés, Civilisations* 29 (1974): 1023–33.

———. *Studies in Genevan Government (1536–1605).* Geneva: Librairie Droz, 1964.

Montet, Edouard. *Genève et les pasteurs français réfugiés en 1685.* Geneva: Imprimerie Rémy Schira, 1884.

Mottu-Weber, Liliane. "Apprentissage et économie genevoise au début du XVIIIᵉ siècle." *Revue suisse d'histoire* 20 (1970): 321–53.

———. "Des vers à soie à l'Hôpital en 1610: Un bref épisode de l'histoire de la soierie à Genève." *Revue du Vieux Genève* 12 (1982): 44–49.

———. "Les femmes dans la vie économique de Genève, XVIᵉ–XVIIᵉ siècles." *Bulletin de la Société d'histoire et d'archéologie de Genève* 16 (1979): 381–401.

Naef, Henri. *La Conjuration d'Amboise et Genève.* Extrait des Mémoires et Documents de la Société d'histoire et d'archéologie de Genève, vol. 32. Geneva: A. Jullien, Georg, Libraires-Editeurs, 1922.

Nakam, Géralde, ed. *Au lendemain de la Saint-Barthélemy: guerre civile et famine.* Paris: Anthropos, 1975.

Neuser, Wilhelm H., ed. *Calvinus Ecclesiae Genevensis Custos.* New York: Peter Lang, 1984.

Nolf, J. *La réforme de la bienfaisance publique à Ypres au seizième siècle.* Ghent: Librairie Scientifique E. Van Goethem, 1915.

Norberg, Karen. *Rich and Poor in Grenoble, 1600–1814.* Berkeley and Los Angeles: University of California Press, 1985.

"Nr. 643, Luther an Kurfürst Friedrich, Leisnig, 11 August 1523." In *D. Martin Luthers Briefwechsel (Weimar Ausgabe),* 3:124–26. Weimar: Harmann Böhlaus Nachfolger, 1933.

"Ordenung enns gemennen tastens: Radschlag wie die genstlichen gutter zu handeln sind." In *D. Martin Luthers Werke: Kritische Gesamtausgabe (Weimar Ausgabe),* 12:11–30. Weimar: Hermann Böhlaus Nachfolger, 1891.

"Ordonnances ecclésiastiques." In *Registres de la Compagnie des Pasteurs de Genève au temps de Calvin.* Published under the direction of the Archives of the State of

Geneva. Vol. 1, *1546–1553*, edited by Jean-François Bergier, pp. 1–13. Geneva: Librairie E. Droz, 1964.

Parker, Thomas Henry Louis. *Calvin's Old Testament Commentaries*. Edinburgh: T. and T. Clark, 1986.

Pelikan, Jarislav, and Helmut Lehmann, eds. *Luther's Works*. 55 vols. St. Louis: Concordia Publishing House; Philadelphia: Fortress Press (Muhlenberg Press), 1955–76.

Perrenoud, Alfred. *La Population de Genève du seizième au début du dix-neuvième siècle: Etude démographique*. Geneva: A. Jullien, 1979.

Pittard, Thérèse. *Femmes de Genève aux jours d'autrefois*. Geneva: Editions Labor et Fides, [1946].

Piuz, Anne Marie. "Charité privée et mouvement des affaires à Genève au XVIIIe siècle." In *Colloque Franco-Suisse d'Histoire Economique et Sociale*, pp. 71–77. Geneva: Librairie de l'Université, 1969.

————. "Les depenses de charité d'une ville au XVIIIe siècle: Le cas de Genève." In *Domanda e Consumi, Livelli e Strutture (Nei Secoli XIII–XVIII) Atti della "Sesta Settimana di Studio" (27 aprile–3 maggio 1974)*, edited by Leo S. Olschki, pp. 205–12. Florence: Istituto Internazionale di Storia Economia "F. Datini," 1978.

Plantinga, Cornelius, Jr. "The Concern of the Church in the Socio-Political World: A Calvinist and Reformed Perspective." *Calvin Theological Journal* 18 (1983): 190–205.

Police et ordre gardez en la distribution des deniers ausmonez aux pauvres de l'Eglise reformee en la ville de Paris. Bulletin de la Société d'Histoire du Protestantisme Français 1 (1853): 255–59.

Prestwich, Menna, ed. *International Calvinism, 1541–1715*. Oxford: Clarendon Press, 1985.

Pugh, Wilma J. "Social Welfare and the Edict of Nantes: Lyon and Nîmes." *French Historical Studies* 8 (Spring 1974): 349–76.

Pullan, Brian. *Rich and Poor in Renaissance Venice: The Social Institutions of a Catholic State to 1620*. Cambridge: Harvard University Press, 1971.

Raitt, Jill. "Beza, Guide for the Faithful Life." *Scottish Journal of Theology* 39 (1986): 83–107.

Registres de la Compagnie des Pasteurs de Genève. Publiés sous la direction des Archives d'Etat de Genève. 8 vols. to date. Geneva: Librairie Droz, 1962–. Vol. 1, *1546–1553*, edited by Jean-François Bergier. Vol. 2, *1553–1564*, edited by Robert M. Kingdon. Vol. 3, *1565–1574*, edited by Olivier Fatio and Olivier Labarthe. Vol. 4, *1575–1582*, edited by Olivier Labarthe and Bernard Lescaze. Vol. 5, *1583–1588*, edited by Olivier Labarthe and Micheline Tripet. Vol. 6, *1589–1594*, edited by Sabine Citron and Marie-Claude Junod. Vol. 7, *1595–1599*, edited by Gabriella Cahier and Michel Grandjean. Vol. 8, *1600–1603*, edited by Gabriella Cahier and Matteo Campagnolo.

Reid, J. K. S., ed. *Calvin: Theological Treatises*. Philadelphia: Westminster Press, 1954.

Reverdin, Olivier. *Quatorze Calvinistes chez les Topinambous: Histoire d'une mission genevoise au Brésil (1566–1558)*. Geneva: Librairie E. Droz, 1957.

Ritter, Eugène. "Didier Rousseau, le quartaïeul de Jean-Jacques." *Bulletin historique et littéraire de la Société de l'Histoire du Protestantisme Français* 42 (1893): 281–92.

Rivoire, Emile, and Victor van Berchem, eds. *Les sources du droit du Canton de*

Genève. 4 vols. Arau: H. R. Sauerländer, Imprimeurs-Editeurs, 1927–35. Vol. 2, *De 1461 à 1550*. Vol. 3, *De 1551 à 1620*. Vol. 4, *De 1621–1700*.

Roelker, Nancy. "Les femmes de la noblesse huguenote au XVIᵉ siècle." In *Actes du Colloque l'Amiral de Coligny et son temps (Paris, 24–28 octobre 1972)*, pp. 227–50. Paris: Société de l'histoire du protestantisme français, 1974.

Roset, Michel. *Les chroniques de Genève*. Edited by Henri Fazy. Geneva: Georg, Libraires de l'Institut, 1894.

Ruben, Miri. *Charity and Community in Medieval Cambridge*. Cambridge Studies in Medieval Life and Thought. ser. 4, no. 4. Cambridge: Cambridge University Press, 1987.

Sautier, Jérôme. "Politique et refuge—Genève face a la Révocation de l'Edit de Nantes." In *Genève au temps de la Révocation de l'Edit de Nantes, 1680–1705*, 50 : 1–158. Mémoires et documents publiés par la Société d'histoire et d'archéologie de Genève. Geneva: Librairie Droz, 1985.

Seebass, Gottfried. "The Reformation in Nürnberg." In *The Social History of the Reformation*," edited by Lawrence Buck and Jonathan Zophy. Columbus: Ohio State University Press, 1972.

Selinger, Suzanne. *Calvin Against Himself: An Inquiry in Intellectual History*. Hamden, Conn.: Archon Books, 1984.

Stauffenegger, Roger. "Réforme, richesse, et pauvreté." *Revue d'histoire de l'Eglise de France* 52 (1966): 47–58.

Stelling-Michaud, Suzanne, ed. *Le Livre du Recteur de l'Académie de Genève (1559–1878)*. 6 vols. Geneva: Librairie Droz, 1959–80.

Sutherland, N. M. *The Huguenot Struggle for Recognition*. New Haven: Yale University Press, 1980.

Thomson, J. A. F. "Piety and Charity in Late Medieval London." *Journal of Ecclesiastical History* 16 (1965): 178–95.

Tierney, Brian. *Medieval Poor Law: A Sketch of Canonical Theory and Its Application*. Berkeley and Los Angeles: University of California Press, 1959.

Torrance, T. F. "The Eldership in the Reformed Church." *Scottish Journal of Theology* 37 (1984): 503–18.

Trexler, Richard C. "Charity and the Defense of Urban Elites in the Italian Communes." In *The Rich, the Well Born, and the Powerful: Elites and Upper Classes in History*, edited by Frederic Jaher, pp. 64–109. Urbana: University of Illinois Press, 1973.

Tripet, Micheline. "L'Hôpital général au temps de l'Escalade." *Escalade de Genève* 53 (1980): 173–90.

Tronrud, Thorold J. "Dispelling the Gloom: The Extent of Poverty in Tudor and Early Stuart Towns: Some Kentish Evidence." *Canadian Journal of History* 20 (1985): 1–21.

van der Walt, Barend Johannes, ed. *Proceedings of the Second South African Congress for Calvin Research, July 31–August 3, 1984*. Wetenskaplike Bydraes of the PU for CHE. Series F: Institute for Reformational Studies; F 3: Collections, 28. Potchefstroom: Potchefstroom University for Christian Higher Education, 1986.

Venema, Cornelius P. "Heinrich Bullinger's Correspondence on Calvin's Doctrine of Predestination." *The Sixteenth Century Journal* 17 (Winter 1986): 435–50.

Vives, Juan Luis. "On Assistance to the Poor." In *A Sixteenth-Century Urban Report*, edited by Alice Tobriner. Social Service Monographs, 2d ser. Chicago: School of Social Service Administration, University of Chicago, 1971.

Vovelle, Michel. *Piété baroque et déchristianisation en Provence au XVIIIᵉ siècle: les attitudes devant la mort d'après les clauses des testaments.* [Paris]: Librairie Plon, [1973].

Whatley, Janet. "Food and the Limits of Civility: The Testimony of Jean de Léry." *The Sixteenth Century Journal* 15 (1984): 387–400.

———. "Savage Hierarchies: French Catholic Observers of the New World." *The Sixteenth Century Journal* 17 (1986): 319–30.

White, Robert. "Fifteen Years of Calvin Studies in French (1965–1980)." *Journal of Religious History* 12 (1982): 140–61.

———. "Oil and Vinegar: Calvin on Church Discipline." *Scottish Journal of Theology* 38 (1985): 25–40.

Willis, David. "A Reformed Doctrine of the Eucharist and Ministry and Its Implications for Roman Catholic Dialogues." *Journal of Ecumenical Studies* 21 (1984): 295–309.

Winckelmann, Otto. *Das Fürsorgewesen der Stadt Strassburg vor und nach der Reformation bis zum Ausgang des sechzehnten Jahrhunderts.* Leipzig: Heinsieu, 1922.

Zysberg, André. "La société des galériens au milieu du XVIIIᵉ siècle." *Annales: Economies, Sociétés, Civilisations* 30 (January–February 1975): 43–65.

Index

Abandonment: of women and children, 42, 144

Abortion: and consistory of Geneva, 140, 268 n.57

Academy of Geneva: bequests to, 26, 119, 153, 155, 175; construction of, 151; founding of, 11; Jean Boulier censured at, 138; and Jean Budé, 153, 155; John Calvin's sermons and lectures deposited there, 49; and men and boys, 44; and poor students, 136; in the sixteenth century, 41. *See also* *Collège* of Geneva; Genevan academy

Accommodations: of the *Bourse française*, 103–4. *See also* Hostesses; Hosts; Housing; Inns of Geneva

Account books: auditing of, 71; extraordinary, 97; of Jean Budé for his nieces, 152; ordinary, 97; unlined, 96. *See also* Account books of the *Bourse française*; Accountants of the *Bourse française*; Accounting; *Bourse française*: account books

Account books of the *Bourse française*: 13, 26, 108, 111, 114, 118, 120; and ambiguous disbursements, 57–69, 189–200; and anonymity of aid recipients 176; and apprenticeships, 143; auditing of, 21, 71, 94; clandestine activities in 52–53; Company of Pastors of Geneva, 70–71; Consistory records overlap, 142; deacons competent to keep, 172; and Denis Raguenier, 47; detailed, 77, 111, 128, 150–51; disorder in, 94–95; donations therein, 73, 114; exactness of expenditures in, 180; elections to the diaconate not recorded therein from 1552 to 1582, 84; of 1582, containing ten

ordinances of 1581, 71, 93-94, 97; first, 76, 83–85, 149, 169–70; future uses of, 27; and Genevan daily life, 26; home visits recorded in, 77; hosts and hostesses in, 174; incomplete, 95; individual influence, 148–50; information in, 23, 40, 46; and international activities, 50, 69; Jean Budé, 71, 150, 153, 157, 171; and John Calvin, 55–56, 59, 170, 190; keeping the secret of the missionary efforts, 183; lacuna in, 45, 73, 85, 150; Laurant de Normandie, last reference to, 154; list in, 97; listed erroneously under the hospital of Geneva, 51; lists of donors in, 170; lost, 73; and management, 26; names of individuals, 26; its overlap of names with the *Livre des habitants de Genève*, 132–33; overlap of with criminal records, 141; payments, 100; piecemeal entries, 177; and Pierre Viret, 55–56, 58, 60, 190–91; and prior financial activity, 34, 36; and purchases, 78; and receipts, 96, 107, 111; its record of daily expenditures, 86; and refugees, 128, 132; and regulations, 171; repetition of names in, 170; as rich source of information, 26; roman numerals in, 95; and shamefaced poor, 134 (*see also* Shamefaced poor); statistics from, 128, 262 n.9; storage of, 94, 105, 207; surviving, 84; three-column pattern in, 9; women's work not recorded therein, 80. *See also* Account books; Accountants of the *Bourse française*; Accounting; *Bourse française*: account books

Accountants of the *Bourse française*, 45–46; Jean Budé, 95; spelling of, 120. *See also*

291

Account books; Account books of the *Bourse française;* Accounting; Accounts

Accounting: of the *Bourse française,* 26, 94–95, 176; hospital, 34; split into ordinary and extraordinary, 97; modern, 150; in roman numerals, 95. *See also* Account books; Account books of the *Bourse française;* Accountants of the *Bourse française*

Administrators: of the *Bourse française,* 32, 36, 49, 173 (*see also Bourse française:* administration; *Bourse française:* deacons); of the hospital, paid, 21 (*see also* Hospital of Geneva: deacons). *See also* Deacons; Deacons of the *Bourse française:* Diaconate; Double diaconate

Adolescents: helped by the *Bourse française,* 43

Adoption, 43

Adultery: donors accused of, 142; grounds for divorce in Geneva, 40, 256–57 n.8; and wife of Antoine Calvin, 79

Aged people: in account books, 176; lifelong support of, 174; on welfare, 38

Agnet, Pastor: John Calvin commenting on his uncollected bequest to the poor, 239–40 n.18

Alban, Jehan de Montauldan or Montaulban: as donor, 120

Alex (widow of Pierre Herman): judged unworthy of assistance, 143

Almosenherren: Strasbourg committee for poor relief, 164

Almosenpfleger: Strasbourg parish helpers for poor relief, 164

Alms: of bread, 34; direct, 108, 116–17; discouraged in Geneva, 12; donors control through the *Bourse française,* 119; Elsie McKee on, 223 n.1; forbidden to lazy beggars by Charlemagne, 23; from Francois Budè after his death, 158, 276 n.56; in Geneva, 176; money or food given directly to the poor, 117–18; as a salvific good work of merit for eternal reward, Catholic belief, 12, 117, 164, 176; as social control, 143; as synonym for donation, 118; Venice determining need for by confraternity officers' visits, 139. *See also* Benevolence; Charity; Donations; Philanthropy

Alphonse, Monsieur: as donor, 120. *See also* Aubelin (Aulmosne), Monsieur

Alsace: refugees from aided by the *Bourse allemande,* 262–63 n.19

Amboise, Conspiracy of. *See* Conspiracy of Amboise

Anabaptists, 28, 167

André, Sire Louis (Louys): as bourgeois and deacon, 90–91, 248–49 n.82, 250 n.84.

André, Michiel: of Vaux in Languedoc, father of Louis André, 250 n.84

Angelots: as money donated to the poor, 116

Angrogna: in Piedmont, Italy, 66, 197. *See also* Angroigne; Augroigne

Angroigne (valley in Italy): fugitive minister therefrom, 67, 197, 232 n.28. *See also* Angrogna; Augroigne

Anjorrant, Claude: stepbrother of Renaud and Jean Anjorrant from the first bed, 247 n.81

Anjorrant, Isabeau: sister of Jean and Renaud Anjorrant, 247 n.81

Anjorrant, Jacob: son of Renaud Anjorrant, 247–48 n.81

Anjorrant, Jean: husband of Catherine Budé and older brother of Renaud Anjorrant, 220–21, 247 n.81; 276 n.57; and *Parlement de Paris,* 220–21, 247 n.81; 276 n.57

Anjorrant, Jean (son of Renaud Anjorrant and nephew of Jean Anjorrant), godson of John Calvin: death of, 247–48 n.81

Anjorrant, Louis: father of Renaud and Jean Anjorrant, 247 n.81

Anjorrant, Madelaine: sister of Jean and Renaud Anjorrant, 247 n.81

Anjorrant, Marie: daughter of Renaud Anjorrant, 247–48 n.81

Anjorrant, Raoul: stepbrother of Jean and Renaud Anjorrant, 247 n.81

Anjorrant, Renaud (Regnauld or Regnault), Lord of Souilly: biography, 247–48 n.81; as bourgeois, 247–48 n.81; and Council of Two Hundred, 247–48 n.81; as deacon, 89–90; death of, 90, 247–48 n.81, 250 n.84; donor, 120, 126; as executor of the will of Marguerite de Morel, 221–22; as first Protestant in his family, 247 n.81; and François Budé, 221–22; 276 n.56; as guardian of Jeanne and Judith Budé, 220–22, 276 n.57; as inhabitant of Geneva, 247–48 n.81; and Jean de Borne, 208–10; as native of Paris, 247–48 n.81; in notarial document, 238 n.4; as younger brother of Jean Anjorrant, 276 n.57

Anjorrant family, 247–48 n.81

Anjou: collectors of, 66, 196

Anne (foster child), 42, 231 n.15
Anne, Dame: as aid recipient, 134, 264 n.29; at Mademoiselle Targault's[?] house, 243 n.47. See also Anne de Remy[?]
Anne de la Vacquerie: as second wife of Laurant de Normandie, 236 n.4
Anne de Remy[?], Dame: donation by, 239 n.12. See also Anne, Dame
Annuity: of Jean Budé on the city hall of Paris, 154; living from, 110
Antesignanus (Pierre Davantes), 58, 190; as guarantor of a disbursement, 53; and Psalms of Théodore de Bèze, 237 n.12
Antichrist: Roman tyranny as, 154
Apothecaries: bills of, 98; Boniface, 98, 254 n.19, 271 n.70; of the Bourse française, 46, 70, 74, 77, 98–99, 105, 173, 207; and medicine to Charles Lourdois and Jeanne Varrot, 141, 215–18; ordered to ask reasonable rates, 99; as paid medical personnel, 98; for Paris, copyist of John Calvin's sermons, 185, 187, 202, 204
Apprenticeship: and children, 146, 180; of the children of Alex, widow of Pierre Herman, 143; conflict with deacons over, 180; with donors, 176; fees for, 43, 134, 176, 179–81; with Jean Crespin, 43; of Jean and Timothee Boulier, 140; as a start in life, 167
Arbiters: appointed to settle a will in Meaux, 258 n.16
Archives of Geneva, Switzerland: Archives hospitalières, Kg 12, Bourse française (30 September 1550–September 1551), folio 2 reproduced, 96; Archives hospitalières, Kg 15, Bourse française, p. 1 reproduced, 85 (see also Account books of the Bourse française); as depository of deacons' account books, 13; family papers, 26. See also Account books of the Bourse française
Armagnac, seneschalsy: and Guy de Serignac, deacon, 229 n.30
Armarron, Monsieur, 122. See also Coumarron, Monsieur
Arnault, Louis (Louys): as husband of Benoiste, aid recipient, 142, 271 n.70; his wife, 241 n.29
Artisans: as pastors or lay preachers, 135; in Geneva, 39; interest free loans to, 161; as refugees, 133, 183. See also Craftspeople
Artus, Master: and accounts of the Psalters, 69, 200
Assembly of the Bourse française, annual, 171

Assistance: from the Bourse française as a privilege not a right, 142; and Geneva's hospital, 34
Asylums: in pre-Reformation Geneva, 165
Attestations from deacons, pastors, or collectors, for poor people: by a minister and deacons of Paris for a former galley slave, Nicolas Campin, 232 n.27; and Jean de Borne, 113, 208–10, 259 n.19; and Nicolle Lescuyere, 241 n.31; for a poor man of Paris leaving the galleys, 241 n.31
Aubelin (Alphonse, Aulmosne), Monsieur: as donor, 120, 123. See also La Bruere, Dame de
Aubelyn, Geneviève (daughter of Guillaume Aubelyn, Seigneur de la Bruyère, and wife of Renaud Anjorrant): death of, 247–48 n.81
Aubelyn, Guillaume (Seigneur de la Bruyère): as father of Geneviève Aubelyn; as husband of Françoise Brachet, 247–48 n.81
Auditoire or Auditoire de Philosophie (Marie la Nove), Court of Saint Pierre: chapel of the Cardinal d'Ostie of, 256–57 n.8; English church in, 261 n.2; illustration of, 130; and the Italian congregation, 256–57 n.8
Auditors of the Bourse française, 70–71, 94–95, 98, 105, 207; beginning and frequency of, 94; Company of Pastors of Geneva overseeing, 171; elections of, 94–95, 105–6, 171; formalizing of the position of, 171; Jean Boucher, 94, 252 n.10; Jean Ternault (Ternaut), 252 n.10; Jean Truchet, 252 n.10; not deacons concurrently, 94, 252 n.6; Pierre Tillier, 252 n.10; role of, 170–71; Simon Le Maire, 252 n.10; three 94, 105; as volunteers, 98
Auduze (Anduse) of Chambrun: as Spectable Pierre d'Airebaudoze, 209
Augier (Ogier), Antoine: as aid recipient, a banished priest, 146
Augroigne (a valley of Piedmont): a fugitive minister from, 66, 197, 232 n.28. See also Angrogna; Angroigne
Augustinians: Peter Martyr Vermigli, 256 n.8
Aulbigni in the country of Sarlogne: Yves Bergevin from, 247 n.80
Aune (ancient measurement), 242 n.40
Autin (Antin?), Monsieur (recipient of funds), 63, 194
Autin, Seigneur Rene: as donor, 120
Autour, Estienne (Monsieur or Seigneur de

Beauregard): as donor, 120–21. *See also* Beauregard, Monsieur de

Auvergne: printer therefrom, Pierre de (Du) Chesne, 147

Avignon: refugees from, 262–63 n.19

Aynierant[?], Master: and Psalms sent to Theodore de Beze, 68, 199

Babies, 180. *See also* Children; Infants

Badges: for beggars, Nuremberg, 163

Badius, Conrad: letter from mentioning the death of Dennis Raguenier, 48

Baduel, Claude: as donor, 120

Bailiff Nicolas Potier (Pothier): as donor, 125. *See also* Potier (Pothier), Bailiff Nicolas

Bale, John, 145

Bally, Claude: and bad merchandise, 269 n.63

Bally, Philibert: as father of Claude Bally, 269 n.63

Baltazar: as *Bourse française* tailor, 254 n.27; making clothes, 59, 191

Balthasar: *Bourse française* paying to resole his shoes, 233 n.37; at Henry Gon's *Croissant*, 255 n.30; learning the trade from a bookseller, 66, 196

Banishment: from Geneva for theft, 141, 216–17; of Jeanne Varrot and Charles Lourdois, 141; of the maid of Marie de Jonvilliers, 152; of Martin Luther, 162; of the priest, Antoine Augier (Ogier), 146; of vagrants, 21

Baptisms: Genevan lists of, 26

Bar, duchy of (Meuse): as home of Jean Dalamont, 247 n.79

Barber-surgeons: and *Bourse française*, 46, 49, 74, 77, 98, 173. *See also* Surgeon

Barrault, Monsieur Pierre or Maistre Pierre: as donor, 120

Barthelemy, Master: goes to Chartes[?] and Dieppe, 56, 63, 194; wife of, 56, 63, 194

Bartholemy, Maistre: as donor, 120

Basel: as destination of travelers supported by the *Bourse française*, 55, 56, 58, 189; Nuremberg's welfare ordinances printed in, 163; pastors of, 110; as source of John Calvin's experience for Geneva, 29

Bastard cursive: handwriting of the *Bourse française*, 95

Bastie: aiding a Genevan, 263 n.20

Bastier: disbursement of fifty florins to through the baker, Noel, 68, 199

Baudechon, feu Seigneur: as donor, 120

Bayf (Baif), Monsieur Rene de (Seigneur de Cre): as donor, 120, 122. *See also* Cre, Seigneur de

Beating, spousal, 141, 147

Beaucastel, feu Monsieur, 121

Beaulieu, Monsieur de: as donor, 121, 125. *See also* Prevost, François

Beauregard, Monsieur de (Estienne Autour): as donor, 121. *See also* Autour, Estienne

Bedclothes: given out, 179; stolen, 75

Beggars: badges of, 20, 163; at churches, 20, 176; and crippling of children, 20; expulsion of, 20; few among Protestants, 23; Genevans not to give money to directly, 175; La Loubiere, 147, 269 n.64; lazy, Charlemagne forbidding alms to, 23; licensing of, 20, 163; in Nuremberg, 163; rowing on galleys, 128; self-inflicted wounds of, 20; son of Barthelemy Michau (Michault or Michaux), 147; on the streets, 117; in Zurich, presence of demeaning, 164. *See also* Begging; Mendicancy; Mendicant orders

Begging: as an art, 37; attempts to control, 20, 22, 117, 167; Catholic ordinances exempting mendicant orders from laws prohibiting, 22; in Catholic regions, 167; Charlemagne's 806 ordinance against, 23; deacons preventing, 260 n.31; in Geneva, 117, 176; laws against, 40, 117, 260 n.30; opposition to, 39, 117; as pious act, 22; prohibition of considered Lutheran, 22–23; Protestant, 167; as result of enclosure, 21; in Strasbourg, outlawed, 164; suppressed, 167; tactics of, 20; and unemployment, 21; in Wittenberg, outlawed, 161–62; in Zurich, forbidden, 164. *See also* Beggars; Mendicancy; Mendicant orders

Begnin (Begnyn, Beguin), Monsieur or Sire Jehan: as donor, 121

Belgium: Hainaut, Pierre Maldonnade from, 83

Bellegarde, feu Monsieur de: as donor, 121

Belleville: Jean de Léry in, 265 n.43

Benefactors: to the *Bourse française*, 183; intentions of, 116. *See also* Benevolence; Charity; Philanthropy

Benevolence: in Geneva, 12; toward deacons' funds in other Reformed churches and the *Bourse française*, 175. *See also* Benefactors; Charity; Philanthropy

Benoist, Seigneur Estienne: as donor, 121

Benoiste (wife of Louys Arnault): as aid recipient carrying off linens, 142, 241 n.29, 271 n.70

Bequests: of Antoine Calvin, 242–43 n.42; to the *Bourse française*, 26, 113–14, 119, 175, 242–43 n.42; to the *Bourse italienne*, 119; by default of the original heirs, 175; to the Genevan academy, 119; to Genevan charitable institutions, 26; and Genevan hospital, 119; large, 174; registered by notaries, 260–61 n.36; turned aside, Calvin's opinion, 239–40 n.18. *See also* Executors; Legacies; Wills

Bergevin, Adam (father of Yves Bergevin): of "Aulbigni" in "Sarlogne," 247 n.80

Bergevin, Monsieur de or Prevost Yves: advancing money, 56; biography of, 247 n.80; as bourgeois, 247 n.80; as deacon, 89–90; as donor, 121; and Geneva's fortresses, 247 n.80; and Jean de Borne, 208–10, 238 n.4; reimbursed, 65, 195

Berlin: printing of Nuremberg welfare ordinances in, 163

Bernard, Master (pastor): as aid recipient fleeing persecution, 264 n.34

Bernard, Francois: as debt collector for the *Bourse française*, 114

Bernard, Maistre or Seigneur Jaques: as donor, 121

Bernard, Jean (judge at Sablieres): his attestation for Jean de Borne, 208–9

Berne: city council of, 110; contacted by Geneva, 144; and refugees, 263 n.23; refusing Geneva help, 110; sending the *Bourse française* money and grain, 239 n.1; Zurich as a model for, 164

Bernier (Bernire), Francois: as donor, 121

Bernot, Monsieur: as donor, 121

Bertrand (son of Pierre Polliens): his sale of a vineyard to Jean Budé, 155, 219

Besson, Anton Charle. *See* Besson, Honorat

Besson, Honorat: as donor, 121

Besson, Master Jacques: Laurent de Normandie given money for, 64, 195

Bessonnaye, Monsieur de la: debt to paid by the deacons, 239 n.17

Bevigne, Master: advanced money by the *Bourse française*, 68, 199

Bèze, Théodore de: correspondence of with Heinrich Bullinger, pastors of Basel and Zurich, 110, 263 n.23; denouncing Jean Budé, 152; his exhortation to be charitable,

250 n.85; his exhortations to better accounting practices, 94, 252 n.10; and France, 111; his servant as aid recipient, 128, 262 n.8; insulted before the consistory, 268 n.57; Jean Boulier, speaking rudely to, 138; and Jean Randon, 63, 194; and Louis Budé's French prose Psalms, 58, 158; marriage of, 236 n.4; and printers' rules, 244–45 n.68; and Pierre Bourgeois, 67, 198; and Psalms, 48–49, 54, 168, 181, 237 n.12; and Psalters, 54–55, 69, 198–99; recommending a German, 59, 190; royalties to the poor, 55; *Salle de,* 130

Bible: binding of, 65, 196; and deacons and widows, 32–33, 81; distributed by the *Bourse française,* 179; and division of church office into four, 29; and literacy, 181; for a priest, 146; the poor owning, 74; provided, 176; purchased by the *Bourse française,* 51, 54, 65, 67–68, 168, 196, 198–99; reading to the poor, 77; the Reformation encouraging reading of, 134; sent to France, 50; and view of sodomy, 156. See also New Testament; Psalms; Psalters

Bible citations: Acts 6:1–7, deacons, 18, 225 n.5; Acts 6:8–15, Stephen, 18; Acts 7:1–60, Stephen, 18; 1 Timothy 3:8–13, deacons, 12, 18, 105, 206, 225 n.6; 1 Timothy 5:3–16, 226 n.13, 243 n.51; John 7, 151, 273 n.12; Romans 12:8, 79, 105, 206

Bienassis, Mademoiselle de (Marguerite Vernon, wife of Rene Bienassis): as donor, 121. *See also* Vernon, Marguerite

Bienassis, Rene: as husband of Marguerite Vernon, 121

Bigamy, 145

Bishops: as judges and patrons of the poor, 18; of Nîmes, 23

Black Death. *See* Plague, bubonic

Blasphemy: reported to the consistory, 255 n.30

Blaton: Pierre de Maldonnade from, 229 n.30

Blind: aided, 133, 143; and workfare, 116

Bloodletting, 46, 99

Bobusse, Master or Monsieur Giles: as host, 103–4, 255 n.31

Bolsec, Jerome: accusing John Calvin of misusing *Bourse française* funds, 34, 228 n.24

Boniface, Monsieur (apothecary for the *Bourse française*), 98, 254 n.19, 271 n.70; payments to for Paris, copyist of John Calvin's sermons, 185, 187, 202, 204

Bonnefoy, Anthoine (deceased father of Jean Bonnefoy), 231 n.12

Bonnefoy, Jean (son of Anthoine Bonnefoy): as aid recipient living with his remarried mother, 231 n.12

Bonnet, Jules: on Charles de Jonvilliers, 87, 248–49 n.82; on John Calvin's habitual companions, 151

Bonneterye, Monsieur de: as donor, 121–23, 125. See also Cluny, Prevost de; La Bonneterye; La Botiere, Francois de; Prevost de Cluny

Bonueni (Bonuemi; Bonuevi), Testament de: and donation, 121

Bookkeepers of the Bourse française, 107–8, 110–11, 118; their attempt to name all contributors, 108; their comments on the circumstances that brought the poor to them, 176; Jean Budé, 149–50, 171; recording characteristics of Bourse française aid recipients, 128, 176. See also Accountants of the Bourse française, Accounting; Accounts; Administrators; Bookkeeping; Deacons

Bookkeeping: of Bourse Française, extraordinary expenditures, 51; of Bourse française, more concise over time, 120; of Bourse française, single entry, 95; Genevan customs of, 51; and ordinary expenditures, 51; and welfare accounts, 21. See also Account Books of the Bourse française; Accountants of the Bourse française; Accounting; Bookkeepers; Deacons

Book of inhabitants of Geneva. See Livre des habitants de Genève

Books: Bourse française sending to France and Reformed areas, 181, 183; provided by the Genevan hospital for school children, 225–26 n.10

Booksellers: and Bibles, 68, 199; Denis, 54, 58, 60–61, 64, 189–92; and missionary activity in France, 86; as prisoner, 44; Psalters, 66, 69, 197, 200; teaching the trade to Balthasar, 66, 196. See also Colporteurs; Printers

Bordier, Henri (paleographer), 14; extracting names for France Protestante, 26; and Jean Budé's signature, 252 n.8; transcribing account books, 26, 44

Bordier, Jacques (Genevan pastor of the seventeenth century), 265 n.43

Borne, Gabrielle de, 113, 208–10, 258–59 n.18

Borne, Jean de (deacon and schoolteacher at

Sablieres, France), 209–10; attestations of, 113, 208–10, 259 n.19; inheritance of, 71, 113, 258–59 n.18

Borrowers, defaulting, 180

Bosquet, mon frere de (Jean Budé's brother?): as donor, 121

Botanist: Augustin-Pyramus de Candolle, 250–51 n.88

Bouchade, Antoinette (third wife of Jean Dalamont), 247 n.79

Bouchard, François (Monsieur or Vicomte d'Aubeterre): as donor, 121–22. See also d'Aubeterre

Bouche, Jehan: as donor, 121. See also Boucher, Jean; Boucher, Sieur

Boucher, Sieur: at Laurent de Normandie's, 65, 196. See also Bouche, Jehan; Boucher, Jean

Boucher, Jean, 121: as auditor, 94, 252 n.10; as collector, 94. See also Bouche, Jehan; Boucher, Sieur

Boulier, Antoine (son of Pastor Jean Boulier): as aid recipient, 140

Boulier, Jean: biography of, 266 n.44; in the Bourse française account books, 266–67 n.44, 48; and consistory of Geneva, 266–67 nn. 44 and 47; death of, 138, 140, 266 n.45; as Genevan pastor on welfare, 136, 138; as husband of Huguette Martin, 140, 143; illiterate son of, 138; marital discord of, 140; as pastor at Vandoeuvres, 136; supported by the Bourse française, 138, 140, 265 n.43; his wife, pregnant, before the consistory of Geneva, 138. See also La Roche, Jean de

Boulier, Jean (son of Pastor Jean Boulier); as aid recipient, 267 n.48; his apprenticeship with a printer, 140; censured at the Genevan academy, 138

Boulier, Timothee (son of Pastor Jean Boulier); as aid recipient, apprenticed with a passemantier, 140

Bourdel, Jean: vinegar maker, repaid a debt from a will, 240 n.19

Bourdelles: as origin of Artus Chauvin, 250 n.86

Bourdier, Eleazard (son of Jacques Bourdier): orphaned and aided, 265 n.43

Bourdier, Master Jacques: pastor, aided, 265 n.43

Bourdier, Marie (daughter of Jacques Bourdier): orphaned and aided, 265 n.43

Bourg-de-four: a servant of Jean Budé's mother lodged there, 276 n.49; as site of the hospital of the *Bourse française*, 46

Bourgeois: of Geneva, 134. *See also* individuals by name

Bourgeois (Bourgeoys), Pierre: disbursement to him for having put the Psalms to music, 67, 198; loaned money, 60, 191, 230 n.3

Bourgeoisie: literate, 181; of Geneva, 79

Bourges, France: Pierre Brossequin a royal notary in, 247 n.80; Pierre Rallet from, 265–66 n.43

Bourgogne, Jacques de (Seigneur de Falais et de Breda): as donor, 123. *See also* Bredan (Bredain, Bredehan), Monsieur de; Fallaix (Falais, Falaises), Monsieur de

Bourgoing, Francois: as donor, 121–22. *See also* d'Aignon

Bourse: See *Bourse allemande; Bourse anglaise; Bourse française; Bourse italienne*

Bourse allemande, 177–78, 262 n.14: founding of, 183; Genevan law fixing its territorial welfare responsibilities, 262–63 n.19; helping the Dutch, English, Flemish, German-speaking people of the Germanies and Switzerland, Poles, Swedes, 129

Bourse anglaise: in Geneva, 129

Bourse des pauvres estrangiers français, 24. See *Bourse française*

Bourse française, 11: and acceptance of hierarchical view of society, 180–82; accommodations of, 103–4; account books of, 13, 26, 86, 149, 169–72; accountant of, 46; accounts, ordinary and extraordinary, 57–69, 189–200; accused of supporting prostitutes, 139–40; administration of, 72, 83, 170–73; and adolescents, 43; aid as partial and stopgap, 178–79; aid recipients (*see* Recipients of *Bourse française* aid); aiding a fool, 269–70 n.67; aiding immigration, 24; and apothecary, 46, 70, 74, 77, 105, 141, 173, 207; and apprenticeship fees, 134, 180; and assistance as a privilege not a right, 142; assuring refuge, 183; auditors of, 70, 170–71; as a bank, 50, 183; and bedding, 75, 179; beginning in 1549, 169–70; bequest to, from Antoine Calvin, 242–43 n.42; bequest to, from Bernardin de Candolle, 250–51 n.88; bequest to, Charles de Jonvilliers, 248–49 n.82; bequest to, Dame Nycole Le Grain, 250 n.84; bequest to, François Budé of five hundred pounds, 158; bequest to,

from Marguerite Morel, 158, 160, 276 n.57; bequests to, 26, 111, 113–14, 119, 160; bequests inherited by default, 113–14, 175, 258–259 n.18; and Bibles, 55, 57–58, 65, 67–68, 168, 179, 189, 196, 198–99; in book of bequests of Geneva, 26; and bookkeeping, single entry, 95; books sent by to France and Reformed churches, 181, 183; a bourgeois of Geneva sent by to the hospital, 134; and bread, 179; Budé family involvement with, 25, 146, 157–58, 160, 181; and building, 75; and burials, 99; and capital, deacons' management of, 175; caring for the sick, 104; and catechisms, 168; and Catherine Chevalier, 142; as channel of funds from French congregations, 53; as charitable institution, 11; and child care, 99–101, 128, 173; and childbirth, 180; and children, 43, 128; as church budget, 47, 57–69, 179, 181, 189–200; clandestine activities of, 51–69, 189–200; clientele of, 37, 75, 180; cloth, 78; clothes, 173–74, 179; collections of, 109, 114–15, 118; collectors of, 66, 70, 72, 108–9, 115, 118, 165, 175, 196; as a Company of Pastors of Geneva resource, 55–69, 168, 170–71, 183, 189–200; compared to other welfare institutions, 45, 182–83; comprehensiveness of, 181; conforming to accepted practices, 168; and the Conspiracy of Amboise, 57; constitution of, 171 (*see also* Ordinances); contributions to, 17–20, 26, 74, 107–27, 165, 171; contributors' control and influence, 108, 119–20, 176; contributors' meetings, 176; and craftsmen and women, 173; criticism of, 139–40, 182; David (de) Busanton linked with the *Bourse* by Michel Roset, 169; deacons' characteristics and duties, 175–77; division of the deacon's office in two not applicable, 92; deacons' influence on, 25; and deacons' last meeting, 178; and deacons' selection, 79, 171; deacons' wives' role in, 80; and debts, 95; as democratic, 134–35, 181; as a departure from centralization of welfare, 12; and Denis Raguènier, 170; and discrimination favoring Protestants, 25; dissolution of, 25; distributing publications, 183; and doctors, 46, 70, 77, 98, 101, 105, 141, 173, 207, 216–18; donations to from native Genevans and non-French nationality groups, 24, 174; donors to, 107–26, 148, 151, 153, 155, 158, 160; donors' confidence in, 175; donors employing and housing the poor, 176; donors' influence on, 170; dual role of as welfare and church fund, 168; and educational opportunities, 181; and the elderly, 128; and emergency aid, 180; employees of (see Employees of the Bourse française); as employer, 40, 49; equity of, 180–82; European context of, 17, 161–68; evaluation of, 182; organization of, 25, 93–95, 170; exchange by of support for property, 145; exclusiveness of, 24; expenditures of (see Expenditures of the Bourse française); expenditures not compared to those of the Genevan city government, 27; fairness of, 180–82; families involved in, 160; far-flung contacts of, 172; and fee for services, 70, 173; first recorded gathering of supporters for, 170; flexible in early years, 25, 46, 94, 174, 181; and food, 78; foreign connections of, 93–95; and foreigners (see Foreigners); and foster homes (see Foster homes); fostering democracy, 134; founding of, 11–12, 17, 182; a fund for worthy poor who came to Geneva for their religion, 177; and funds to aid recipients to buy goods directly, 173; and Geneva, 13, 25; and the Genevan hospital, 129, 178; and Genevan law, welfare responsibilities assigned by region, 262–63 n.19; and Genevan restrictions on foreigners in public office, 82–83; and Genevans' support, 24, 109, 114–15, 181; geographic origins of aid recipients of, 128; and gifts with strings attached, 175; and grain, 179; granting any legitimate request, 181; a group effort, 157–58, 160; and guarantors for loans, 180; and guardians for the sick, 70, 173, 179; helping people recover belongings and family members, 76; history of as a collection of mini biographies, 148, 158, 160; and hospitalization and drugs, 179; hosts and hostesses, 103–4, 174; housing refugees, 103–4; housing the poor in its own houses, 174; ideology of, 27, 29, 36; importance of transcending Geneva, 182; inclusiveness of, 24, 82, 177; income of, 73; individual influence upon, 25; inheriting property, 73, 175; and inns, 70, 100, 174; international activities of, 25, 50–69, 76, 83, 86, 93–94, 107–8, 111–13, 172–73, 183, 189–200; items borrowed from, 75; and Jean Boulier, 138; and Jean Budé, animator, 151–53, 155, 181, 219; and John Calvin, 27,

48, 168–70, 183; and laundry, 46, 174; leaders of from French immigrants, 82–84; legal activities of listed under deacons' names, 26; and lifelong support, 179; and literacy, 134, 179; and loans, 60, 128, 191; and local funding, 172–73; and long-term assistance, 181; and Louis Budé's legacy, 158; and Lyons, 138; and manuscripts, 13; and mattress makers, 100; and mattresses, 179; and medical care, 46, 179; and medical personnel, 98–99; and mental illness, 188; messengers of, 55–56, 58–59, 168, 173, 181, 183, 189–91; minutes of, 26; missionary activities of, 51–54, 57–58, 83, 87, 168, 181, 189–90; as model for deacons' funds elsewhere, 25, 28, 182; and money from people's native regions, 83; more known about its donors than aid recipients, 176; no female officers of, 82; no proof of its existence in 1541 or 1545, 169–70; nonwelfare activities of, 50–69, 189–200; notarial documents of, 13; and occasional help, 179–80; organization of, 94, 169–79; origins of, 29, 32–34, 36, 169–70; and orphans, 42, 81, 179; and overnight viaticum, 169; as parochial, 25; and part-time help, 70; and pastors, 70–71, 119–20, 170–72; paying people leaving town, 76; personnel of, paid, 98–104; and philanthropy, 17, 26; and piecework, 173; pledges to, regular monthly, 158, 276 n.56; and practical considerations and ideology, 28; practices of as a part of the ear, 169–82; pragmatic evolution of, 25, 70–72, 168; precedents for, 17; presence of its first three deacons in Geneva in 1549, 169–70; primary documents of, 26; and private homes, 70, 174; and Protestant philanthropy, 160; Protestants favored by, 139, 182; and Psalms of Théodore de Bèze, distribution and production, 54–55, 168, 179; public image of, 175; as publisher, 47–50; purchasing a Greek New Testament, 59, 190; purpose of, 179; real estate of, 104; 174–75; and receipts, 95, 108, 119–120, 127, 158; record keeping of, 13, 26, 132; and recruitment of workers, 94; and Reformed church, part of its order and discipline, 24–25, 28, 168, 182; as refugee agency and fund, 12, 38; refugees (see Refugees); and regulations of 1581 in 1582 account book, 33, 171; and rehabilitation, 37, 180; as reliable, 175; religious and welfare expenditures seen by as one, 168; renting rooms, 53; 67, 197; role of during John Calvin's lifetime, 183; role of prior to the Wars of Religion in France, 183; and salary advance, 254 n.28; and school fees, 128, 134; and seamstresses, 100–101, 173–74; and shamefaced poor, 133–34 (*see also* Shamefaced poor); seventeenth-century proceedings of, 25, 129; and seventeenth-century limitations on aid, 177; and shoe repair, 173–74; and short-term assistance, 181; and sixteenth-century welfare practices, 27; special collection by, 158; spending more than it received, 95; summary about, 168–82; supporters of, 107–26; surgeon of (*see* Surgeon of the *Bourse française*); survival of, reasons for 24–25, 34, 83; and suspension from welfare, 177; tailors, 100–101, 174; and thieves, 215–18; title of, 24, 113, 139, 273 n.22; and tools, 128; transporting refugees by boat, 132; and the unemployed, 179; using the poor with special skills, 173; and variable support, 179; as versatile, 181; and viaticum to travelers, 168–69; as volunteer agency, 104, 174; and volunteers, 70, 173; as welfare fund, 38, 168, 179; and wet nurses, 100, 173; and widows, 42, 81, 179; and women workers, 172; and worthiness, 138–143, 178; and youths, 128. *See also* French fund

Bourse, Italian. *See Bourse italienne*

Bourse italienne: administered by deacons, 32; bequest to, by Galeazzo Caracciolo, 256–57 n.8; bequests to, 26, 119; and deacons' names, 26, 85; founded, 177–78, 183, 256–57 n.8; and Genevan book of bequests, 26; and Genevan law fixing welfare responsibilities territorially, 262–63 n.19; and Italian refugees, 129; as parochial, 25

Boynville, Mademoiselle de: as donor, 97, 121, 253 n.14

Boynville (Boinville, Boyenville), Monsieur de: as donor, 121. *See also* Le Coint; Le Cointe (Le Comte), Guillaume

Boysbossart (Boiboyssard, Boisbossard, Boisbossart), Monsieur or Seigneur de: as donor, 121, 123. *See also* Gorin, Pierre

Brachet, Damoiselle or Mademoiselle Francoise (mother of Geneviève Aubelyn and widow of the deceased Noble Guillaume Aubelin, Seigneur de la Bruyere): as donor, 121, 123, 247–48 n.81. *See also* La Bruere, Dame de

Branding: in Geneva for theft, 216–17; prior to banishment, of Jeanne Varrot and Charles Lourdois, 141; of vagrants, 21

Brassu, Seigneur de, 126. *See also* Varro, Michel

Brazil: Calvinist expedition, 265–66 n.43

Bread: fixed price for, 42; handed out by the *Bourse française*, 45; and water diet for crime in Geneva, 212–14

Bredan (Bredain, Bredehan), Monsieur de: as donor, 121. *See also* Bourgogne, Jacques de; Fallaix (Falais, Falaises), Monsieur de

Breton: housed by order of the Company of Pastors, 257 n.13; special collection for, 111

Breton, Anthoine (of Lorraine): as deceased father of Marie, 231 n.16

Breton, Didier: as deceased father of aid recipient children, 231 n.12

Breton, Marie (daughter of Anthoine Breton): apprenticed, 231 n.16

Brichauteau, Charles de: as donor, 121, 125. *See also* Saint Laurent, Monsieur de; Saint Martin, Monsieur or Seigneur de

Brie, France: as home of Jean des Marins and Damoiselle Estienette Villers, 247 n.79

Briquemault, Seigneur de, 126. *See also* Prignault, Adrian de; Priquemaut, Seigneur de; Villemongez, Monsieur

Britain: as origin of aid recipients, 127

Brittany: François and Maturin Buynard from, 246 n.77; Pierre Helon from, 65, 195

Bronet, Monsieur de, and his brother: as donors, 121

Brossequin, Gabrielle of "Aulbigni" (wife of Yves Bergevin), 247 n.80

Brossequin, Pierre (father of Gabrielle Brossequin): as bourgeois royal notary, 247 n.80

Bruges: Juan Luis Vive's welfare reform in, 21, 116, 163

Brusquin, Monsieur de: as donor, 121

Bruyere, Jacques: ordered paid, 68, 199

Budé, Mademoiselle (Jean Budé's sister?): as donor, 121

Budé, Anne (sister in France of Jean Budé), 157–58

Budé, Antoine (brother in France of Jean Budé), 157–58

Budé, Catherine: her arrival in Geneva, 149; living with her brother, François Budé, and sister-in-law, Marguerite de Morel, 220–21;

as wife then widow of Jean Anjorrant, 220–21, 247 n.81

Budé, Dreux (brother in France of Jean Budé), 157–58

Budé, Elisabeth (daughter of Jean Budé and Marie de Jonveilliers): as wife of Jean de Saussure, seigneur de Bussens, 157

Budé, François (brother of Jean Budé), 97: his arrival in Geneva, 149; his death and bequest to the *Bourse française*, 158; as donor, 97, 121, 126; and Galeazzo Caracciolo, Jean Budé, and Renaud Anjorrant, 221–22, 274 n.26, 276 n.56: his involvement in the *Bourse française*, 157–58; Jean Budé responsible for his daughters, 152, 221–22; and *Livres des Bourgeois*, 245 n.73; marriage contract of, 276 n.57; his monthly pledge, posthumous continuation of, 158; his wife, Marguerite de Morel, her will, 158, 220–22, 276 n.56. *See also* Villeneuve, Monsieur de

Budé, Guillaume (French humanist), 109, 181; his children, adult, 149, 157–58; as father of Jean Bude, 85, 149, 272 n.1; and Francis I of France, 149; inheritance from, 274 n.26; his widow, Isabeau de Lailly, 109, 157–58

Budé, Isabeau (sister of Jean Budé): as a nun in France, 157–58

Budé, Jacob (son of Jean Budé and Marie de Jonvilliers): death of, 157

Budé, Jean, 121, 123, 126; his absence from Geneva, 272 n.6; and Academy of Geneva construction, 151, 273 n.9; as accountant, 14, 53, 73, 78, 84, 94, 95, 150, 152, 179; as accountant for the *Bourse française*, stepping down, 149, 169–70; as administrator able to involve other people, 157; accused of being a religious bigot, 152; his affection for his wife, 153; and alms, 118; as ambassador for Geneva, 273 n.9; as ambassador to Gaspard de Coligny, the Elector Palatine, the Protestant churches of Switzerland, and the Protestant princes of Germany, 151; and book of inhabitants of Geneva, 149, 229 n.30; 245 n.73; 272 n.1; as bookkeeper for the *Bourse française*, 118, 128, 148–50, 171; of *Bourse française* animator, 25, 146, 151; as *Bourse française* deacon, 14, 49–51, 84–85, 87–91, 148, 157, 169–71, 181, 226 n.11, 241 n.37; as *Bourse française* donor, 109, 118, 121, 126, 151, 153, 155; as

Bourse française scribe, 83, 85; and Charles de Jonvilliers (brother-in-law), 153, 160, 248–49 n.82; Charles de Jonvilliers and Madelaine (Magdelaine) Imbault living with him, 248 n.82; his children, 152–54; 157; his coat of arms, 155; as congenial, 53–54, 151–53; and Council of Sixty, 151; and Council of Two Hundred, 151; cousins of, 124, 150, 157; death of, 77, 155, 157, 242 n.38, 244 n.55, 245 n.73, 275 n.37; difficulty between his wife and son, 152–53; his disabled hand, 153, 274–75 n.31; entered into the *Livre des Bourgeois* of Geneva, 245 n.73; and excessive expense accounts, 152, 252 n.10; family papers of, 26; family problems of, 152–53; flexible attitudes of, 157; and François Budé, brother 221–22, 274 n.25, 267 n.55; friends of, 150, 153; generosity of, 153–56; and Guillaume Budé (father), 181; his handwriting, 14, 95, 150, 157; ill, 274–75 n.31; as intelligent, 157; and Jean de Borne, 208–10, 238 n.4; and Jean Du Lac, his son-in-law, 154; Jeanne and Judith Budé, guardian of his nieces, 171, 220–21; John Calvin's friend and editor of his Old Testament commentaries, 151, 248 n.82; and Lambert Le Blanc, kinsman and guest, 156–57; as leader in the French immigrant community, 151; long life of, 77, 157; his library divided between his son and son-in-law, 154; magnanimous spirit of, 57, 153, 156–57; and a man fined for having ground his grain badly, 152; and Marguerite de Morel, sister-in-law, as executor of her will, 221–22; his mother, 109, 121, 158; from Paris, 82–83; and procuration to obtain goods left to the poor in France, 240 n.21; as procurator for Jean Dalamont, 258 n.16; real estate of, 149, 154–55; recording names, 150; as reliable, 151; religious convictions of, 151–55; as rentier, 154; as sensitive, 157; signing the account books, 94, 171, 252 n.8; soliciting aid from Swiss cantons, 239 n.11; thanked, 149; as typical Protestant urban aristocrat, 154; his verbosity, 150, 154; well liked, 151, 153; his will, 153–56, 248–49 n.82, 274–75 n.31. *See also* Vérace, Monsieur or Seigneur de

Budé, Jean (son of Jean Budé and Marie de Jonvilliers), 157; and Council of Two Hundred, 157; and his mother, 152–153; as representative of Geneva to Henry IV, king of

France 157; and Small Council and syndic, 157

Budé, Jeanne (daughter of François Budé and Marguerite de Morel): and Catherine and Marguerite Budé, 159–60; and Galeazzo Caracciolo, 221–22; and Jean Budé, her uncle, 152, 220–22; and Renaud Anjorrant, 220–22

Budé, Jeanne (daughter of Jean Budé and Marie de Jonvilliers): her death at the age of three, 157

Budé, Jehan (sixteenth century spelling), 121. See also Budé, Jean; Vérace, Monsieur or Seigneur de

Budé, Jozel (twin brother of Natanael Budé): as infant son of François Budé and Marguerite de Morel, 276–77 n.57

Budé, Judith (daughter of François Budé and Marguerite de Morel): and Catherine and Marguerite Budé, 159–60; and Galeazzo Caracciolo, 221–22; and Jean Budé, her uncle, 152, 220–22; and Renaud Anjorrant, 220–22

Budé, Louis (son of Guillaume Budé and Isabeau de Lailly): his arrival in Geneva, 149; his bequest to the Bourse française and, involvement, 157–58; his death, 1551, 158; as donor, 121, 123–24; his infants, dead, 158; his law studies in Padua, 248 n.82; and Pslams in French prose, 158; "scientifique", 158, 276 n.54; his widow remarried, 158. See also La Motte, Monsieur de; Mot

Budé, Madelene[?] (daughter of Jean Budé and Marie de Jonvilliers): her death, 157

Budé, Marguerite (wife or widow of Guillaume Trye): her arrival in Geneva, 149; and Catherine Budé's children, 220–21; her death at eighty-eight, 157; involvement of in the Bourse française, 157

Budé, Marie (daughter of Jean Budé and Marie de Jonvilliers): her death, 157, 274 n.23

Budé, Matthieu (brother of Jean Budé): his death, 149, 272 n.3; employed by Henri Estienne[?], 272 n.3; passing through Geneva, 149

Budé, Natanael (infant son of Francois Budé and Marguerite de Morel): death as twin brother of Jozel, 276–77 n.57

Budé, Sera (daughter of Jean Budé and Marie de Jonvilliers): her death, 157

Budé brothers: as habitual companions of John Calvin, 151

Budé family: active in the Bourse française, 25, 146, 148–53, 155–58, 160, 157–60, 181; as close, extended, 160; departure of for Geneva, 248 n.82; members and inheritance of in France, 158, 274 n.26; papers of Geneva's archive, 26; real estate and legal transactions of, 149, 154–55, 244 n.55, 272 n.4. See also de Budé; individual family members by name

Bugenhagen, Johann, 163

Bullinger, Heinrich: asking Zurich to help Geneva, 110; and Théodore de Bèze, 263 n.23; and Zurich charging the battles of Kappel to the church, 164

Burcy [de Bury?], brothers de: as hosts of the first recorded selection of Bourse française deacons, 83–84, 226 n.11. See also Saint Lauren; Sainct Martin, Noble Jacques de

Burcy (Bursy), Monsieur de: as donor, 121. See also Saint Lauren; Sainct Martin, Noble Jacques de

Bürgermeister: of Wittenberg, 162

Burgundy: boy from, 56, 58, 189; Antoine Popillon from, 246 n.78; refugees from aided by the Bourse italienne, 262–63 n.19

Burial: and Bourse française, 99; confraternities at, 115; of a deacon, 75; and Geneva, 154; as philanthropic act, 20; price of, 110, 247 n.10

Busanton, David (de): his bequest to refugees of Geneva and Strasbourg, 165, 169–70, 226–27 n.15; death of, 33–34, 36, 169, 226–27 n.15; as founder of the Bourse française, 33; and John Calvin, 169; and letter from Calvin to Pierre Viret, 228 n.21; his will, 169

Businessmen: as deacons, 172; not social revolutionaries, 101

Bussens, Seigneur de (husband of Elisabeth Budé), 157. See also Saussure, Noble Jean de

Butini (secretary of justice of Geneva), 155

Buynard, Francois (deacon), 78, 88, 124. See also La Touche, Monsieur de

Buynard, Maturin (brother of François Buynard): bourgeois of Geneva, 246 n.77

Bynet, Anthoine: store rental, 230 n.4

Caltet (Valtet), Jean (father of Samuel Caltet), 265–66 n.43

Caltet (Valtet), Samuel: as a child aided, 265–66 n.43

Calvin, Anne (daughter of Antoine Calvin, niece of John Calvin): inheritance of, 242 n.42

Calvin, Antoine (brother of John), 79; bequest of, 242 n.42; biography of, 249–50 n.83; as bourgeois and merchant of Geneva, 79, 249 n.83; as *Bourse française* deacon, 84, 90, 249–50 n.83; and Council of Two Hundred, 249–50 n.83; death of, 90; 249–50 n.83; divorce of, 79; as editor, 249–50 n.83; as executor of Laurent de Normandie's will, guardian of his children, 236 n.4; as Genevan hospital administrator, 249–50 n.83; living with John Calvin, 249 n.83; wife of, 79; his will, 242–43 n.42

Calvin, David (son of Antoine Calvin, nephew of John Calvin): inheritance of, 242 n.42

Calvin, Dorothea (daughter of Antoine Calvin, niece of John Calvin): inheritance of, 242 n.42

Calvin, Girard (father of John and Antoine Calvin): of Noyons, 249 n.83

Calvin, Jehan (sixteenth-century spelling for Jean): as donor, 121. *See also* Calvin, John

Calvin, Jean (son of Antoine and nephew of John Calvin): 242 n.42

Calvin, John: and Ann Colladon, 236 n.4; and anti-Calvinist faction, 82; and Antoine Calvin, 236 n.4, 249 n.83; and *Bourse française*, 13, 27, 29, 168–70, 183, 229 n.31; as *Bourse française* donor, 109, 121; and Budé family, 149, 151, 158, 272 nn. 2 and 3; and charity, 12, 27, 169, 176; and church office, 27, 36; and the *Collège de Montaigu*, 149; correspondence of, 34, 151; correspondence of as source of dating of Matthieu Budé's death, 272 n.3; and David (de) Busanton, 33, 169, 226–27 n.15; and deacons, 27, 36, 90, 170; deacons' election at his house, 27, 32, 84–85, 88, 170, 247–48 n.81; death of, 48, 100, 248 n.82; and delegation of responsibility, 36; and Denis Raguenier, 70, 170, 173; and double diaconate roles not applicable to the *Bourse française*, 27; and education, 11; his enemies, 82, 108–9; and English church, 261 n.2; entrusted with money for the poor, 170; estate of, 242–43 n.42; friends of, 87; and Galeazzo Caracciolo's divorce, 256–57 n.8; in Geneva, 11, 24; Genevan city

council pressured by to protect the poor, 167; and Geneva's hospital, 34, 116, 228 n.22, 260 n.28; and Guillaume Budé's widow, 149; and Guillaume Trye, 242 n.42; as a humanist, 17; his *Institutes of the Christian Religion*, 81; and Jean Budé, 151; Jeremiah commentaries of, 87; and Laurent de Normandie, 236 n.4, 242 n.42; and Louis Budé, 158, 276 n.53; and Matthieu Budé, 149; as minister, 34, 127; as Monsieur Calvin in the account books, 55–56, 59, 70, 190; negligence, his fear of being accused of, 248 n.82; not concerned with an exact replication of his ideas, 27; his opposition to hoarding of essential commodities, profiteering, speculation, 167; and Paris, copyist of his sermons, 173; picture of, 31; and Pierre Viret, 33, 169, 228 nn. 20 and 21; preaching at Saint Pierre, 137, 159; pride, his fear of being accused of, 248 n.82; the Prophets, his commentaries on, 151; recommending disbursements and poor people to the *Bourse française*, 39, 55–56, 59, 70, 190, 229 n.31, 230 n.5; and secretary, 79, 87, 248 n.82; his sermons and lectures, 34, 36, 47–49, 98–99, 114, 173, 181, 234 nn. 48 and 50; his sermons, consignment to the Genevan academy, 235 n.55; his signatures, reproduction thereof, 35; his social and economic thought, 27, 73, 116, 167, 169, 239–40 n.18; on sodomy, 211–14, 260 n.32, 275 n.33; and stewardship, 167; in Strasbourg, 23, 34, 165; his student days, 149; his theology and economic thought linked to social reform, 27, 271 n.72; and an unnamed woman, letter for a gift from, 229 n.28; his use of terms "minister" and "pastor" interchangeably, 30; and widows, 81, 101, 149; and women's role in care of poor and sick, 81

Calvin, Marie (daughter of Antoine and niece of John Calvin): inheritance of, 242 n.42

Calvin, Samuel (son of Antoine and nephew of John Calvin) inheritance of, 242 n.42

Calvin, Susanne: (daughter of Antoine and nephew of John Calvin): inheritance of, 242 n.42

"Calvin a une dame": letter to an unnamed woman, 229 n.28

Calvinism: impact of on the modern world, 38; and justification of lending money at interest, 167; and struggle against poverty, 167

Camiailles (Camiealles, Carnicalles), Jehan: as donor, 121

Camiailles, pere de (Yves?): as donor, 121

Campefleur, Monsieur de: as *Bourse française* accountant, 84; as deacon, 84, 90–91; 248–49 n.82

Campin, Nicolas: a Parisian cutler and former prisoner on the galleys, aided, 44, 232 n.24

Camuz[?], Salomon: receiving money to pay for his house, 62, 193

Candolle, Augustin-Pyramus de: botanist of Geneva, 250–51 n.88

Candolle (Candoles), Bernardin de: bequest from, 250–51 n.88; biography of, 250–51 n.88; as bourgeois, 250 n.88; as *Bourse française* collector, 93, 250 n.88; as canon of Forcalquier, 250–51 n.88; and consistory, 250 n.88; and Council of Two Hundred, 250 n.88; as deacon, 91, 93, 248–49 n.82, 250–51 n.88; as donor, 121, 250 n.88; as inhabitant of Geneva, 250 n.88; and Jews in Geneva, 250–51 n.88

Candolle, Pyramus (Piramus) de: bequest to from Bernardin de Candolle, 250–51 n.88; dancing and chess playing, 141

Candolle family, 237 n.21; as immigrants from France to Geneva, 55; as leaders in their home communities, 82; origins of, 244 n.54, 250–51 n.88

Canon of Forcalquier, 250–51 n.88. *See also* Candolle, Bernardin de

Canut: as donor, 121

Capuchins: Bernardino Ochino as superior general of, 256 n.8

Caracciolo (Carracciolo), Galeazzo: bequest from to the *Bourse italienne* and the Italian church in Geneva, 256–57 n.8; biography of, 256–57 n.8; book dedicated to him, 248 n.82; as bourgeois, 256 n.8; as *Bourse française* donor, 110, 121, 124; and Council of Two Hundred, 256–57 n.8; his divorce, 256–57 n.8; and Emperor Charles (as chamberlain to), 256 n.8; and François Budé, 221–22; and Jeanne and Judith Budé, 152, 221–22; and Genevan consistory, 256–57 n.8; and Pope Paul IV, his great uncle, 256 n.8. *See also* Le Marquis; Vico

Caraffa family: wife of Galeazzo Caracciolo, 256 n.8

Carders of wool: tools for, 39

Carion, Claude: aid recipient, inhabitant of Geneva fighting with his wife, 147

Carnivals, 271 n.72

Carre, L'Escuyer (Esquire?): as donor, 121

Catechisms: binding of for the *Bourse française*, 54, 58, 189; poor people owning, 74; purchased by the *Bourse française*, 51, 54–55, 57–58, 168, 189

Catherine Jeanne: heiress of Gabrielle de Borne, 113, 208–9, 258–59 n.18

Catholic: almsgiving, 117, 164–65, 174, 176; believers referred to as hangmen and tyrants, 152; burial, attended by Protestants, 145; charity, 115; confraternities, 22; legislation against begging, 22–23; Mass, consequences of attendance for Protestants, 145; Nuremberg welfare reform, 21; persecution of Protestants, 135–36; religious orders and welfare, 22–23; sisters, compared to Protestant deaconesses, 82; welfare administration, laicized, 166; welfare compared to Protestant, 22–23, 167. *See also* Catholic Church

Catholic Church: antipathy of Protestants toward, 154; attitude toward begging, 22; and deacons, 22; image of in Genevan wills, 154; in Nuremberg, 163; poor boxes in, 167; property of taken over by Protestants, 22–23, 163–64; remnants of in Geneva, 147; its view of laws against begging as Lutheran, 22–23, 165. *See also* Catholic

Caves, Seigneur de: as donor, 121

Caveussin, Marmet: ceding a vineyard to the Budé family, 244 n.55

Celibacy: Protestant opposition to, 23

Cenesnid (Cenefnit), Mademoiselle de: as donor, 121

Censorship: of books in France, 264 n.28

Centralization of welfare: as overall tendency, 21, 165–66

Chabart (Chabert), Maistre Anthoine: as donor, 121

Chambrun, Auduze (Anduse) of: and Spectable Pierre d'Airebaudoze, 208–9

Champaigne, Jeanne (widow): her house rent, 233 n.33

Champel: place of execution by burning in Geneva, 156

Chance: in Protestant thought of the sixteenth century, 154

Chandieu, Monsieur de (Antoine de la Roche Chandieu): as donor, 121

Chanluin, Antoine (student), 112; in receipt of a bequest, 257–58 n.15

Chapel, Master Jacques: as minister, 59, 190; as recipient of Bourse française funds, 63, 194

Chapel of the Cardinal d'Ostie: l'Auditoire de philosophie of, 256–57 n.8

Chaperon: as recipient of money from the Bourse française, 60, 191

Chaplain: at the hospital of the Bourse française, 234 n.46

Charitable institutions of Geneva: listed in the book of bequests, 26. See also Academy of Geneva; Bourse allemande; Bourse française; Bourse italienne; Hospital of Geneva

Charité, ministre de la (Monsieur de Léry [Larz]): as pastor aided by the Bourse française, 265–66 n.43. See also La Chante, ministre de

Charity: Catholic institutions of, 115; Catholic theory of, 12; as church and government responsibility, 115; and collection boxes, 118; in Geneva, 11, 178; in Geneva, bibliography for the eighteenth century, 255–56 n.1; in Geneva, practices and philosophy changed with the Reformation, 175–76; and John Calvin, 27; literature on the influence of the Reformation on, 223 n.1; Protestant, 12, 116, 259–60 n.26; voluntary, 114, 119. See also Benefactors; Benevolence; Philanthropy

Charity, Ladies of: dedicated to charity, 23

Charity, Sisters of: dedicated to charity, 23

Charlemagne (Charles the Great, Emperor): forbidding almsgiving to lazy beggars, 23

Charles V, Emperor: and banishment of Martin Luther, 162; and Galeazzo Caracciolo, 256 n.8; and law prescribing death for homosexual behavior, 156; and Nuremberg welfare legislation, 163; and welfare ordinance, 163

Charpon (Senarpont?), Monsieur de: as donor, 122

Chartres, France: as birthplace of Charles de Jonvilliers, 248 n.82; and Master Barthelemy, 56, 63, 194

Château, Ami de: building the academy in Geneva, 273 n.9

Chatelet: purchase of meadow and vineyard in by Jean Budé, 155, 219

Chatillon, Seigneur: as donor, 122. See also d'Andelot, Monsieur; Coligny, François de

"Chatre sous montlhéry près Paris": printer therefrom, 272 n.89

Chauvet, Raymond: as donor, 125. See also Remont, Monsieur

Chauvin, Artus, 90–91; biography of, 250 n.86; as deacon, 90–91, 248–49 n.82; as publisher, 250 n.86; two in the book of inhabitants of Geneva, 250 n.86

Chervault (Clairvant), Monsieur de: as donor, 122.

Chesne, Paul du: paid to keep a small boy, 231 n.14

Chess playing: and the Genevan city council, 141

Chevalier (Chevallier), Catherine: brought up at the expense of the Bourse française, 269 n.66; her larceny punished, 142

Chevallier, Francois: on sodomy, 211–14

Chiccand, Antoine: procurator (deacon) of the Genevan hospital, 256 n.4

Chiccand (Checcant, Chican, Chicquan), Guillaume: deacon (procurator) of the Genevan hospital, 1556–61, 108–9, 256 n.4; as donor, 108–9, 122; as elder on the consistory, 108–9; and John Calvin, 108–9; and syndic, 109

Childbirth: Bourse française paying expenses for, 180; as cause of seeking deacons' aid, 75, 240 n.25; and women needing care, 81

Child care: by the Bourse française, 99–101, 128, 173, 176; fees, 42; for mothers, ill and incapacitated, 99, 173; poor pay for, 174; and women, 174

Children: apprenticed, 162–63, 180; in apprenticeships they had not chosen, 146; in Bourse française account books, 128, 176; as Bourse française aid recipients, 59, 144, 177, 190; a Burgundian boy, 56, 58, 189; crippled to become beggars, 20; of deacons, 79–80, 180; disinherited, 79–80; educated by the Leisnig common chest, 163; exasperating, 152; in foster homes, 81; of French refugees, 113; funds of mishandled, 147; of Geneva called Gouliards and worthless, 147; of God, 154; of Guillaume Budé and his wife Isabeau de Lailly, 157–58; as heirs, 113; Huguenot, 131; of Huguette Martin and Jean Boulier, 138, 140; of international couples, welfare status, 178; of Jean Budé and his wife, Marie de Jonvilliers, 152–54, 157; of Jeanne Varrot and Charles Lourdois, 141; need to feed as incentive to crime by their parents, 215, 217; paid for carrying wood, 60, 192; of Pastor Jean Boulier aided, 138; of pastors aided by the *Bourse française*, 265–66 n.43; of the poor, 44; and plague, 86; pupils of Jean de Tere, 62, 193; receiving aid while living with mothers and stepfathers, 231 n.12; of refugee pastors, 136; as refugees, 39–40; of Robert Estienne, 80; with sick mothers, 173; turned out of Geneva, 144; on welfare, 43, 133; with wet nurses, 101; with widowed mothers on welfare, 45, 133; women caring for, 103. *See also* Adolescents; Babies; Infants; Orphans

"Children of the first bed": as an expression, 42

Child support: by the *Bourse française*, 43; after remarriage, 42

Christ: face of in the poor, 118; faith in, 79; truly preached, 145; yoke of, 146. *See also* Jesus Christ

Christendom: and welfare, 20

Church: as advocate of the poor, 17; ancient, as precedent for dividing the diaconate in two, 92; the *Bourse française* as part thereof, 168, 181; budget, 47, 181; classical world influence upon, 18; early, as precedent for Reformed church practices, 33; endowment (*see* Endowments); in France approving Genevan confession of faith, 154; of Geneva, model for local churches, 25; of Geneva, local needs provided for by the city, 168; of Geneva, quarterly communion services, 171; housing the homeless, 18; nursing the sick, 18; policing beggars, 176; poor boxes in, 22, 109, 118–19; and priesthood of all believers, 28; property of diverted, 23; Reformed, extension into France, 209–10; rescuing infants, 18; as responsible for charity, 115; supporting the poor, 40, 144; system of for knowing its own, 75–76; true, 154. *See also* Catholic Church; Church and state relations; Church buildings; Church of the Madeleine; Church offices; Church orders; Church property; Church reformed according to the Word of God; Churches

Church and state relations: modern conceptions of applied to the past, 38

Church buildings: Leisnig, 162; maintenance of in Geneva, 163, 168; maintenance of in Wittenberg by the common chest, 162. *See*

also Church; Church property; Endowments: church

Churches: alms boxes in, 109, 118–19; collection boxes in Geneva, 176; guardians to entrap beggars, 117; heads of household in Geneva convoked in, 115; imitating the Genevan model, 25; sending money and refugees to Geneva, 183. *See also* Catholic church; Church

Church of the Madeleine: Italian congregation of, 256–57 n.8

Church offices: in the Bible, 79; as respected positions, 112–13. *See also* Offices of the Reformed Church

Church orders: Lutheran, dividing common chest into two parts, 163; in Wittenberg, 161. *See also* Ordinances

Church property: appropriation of by Protestants, 20, 22–23, 161, 163–64; auctioned in Lausanne, 164; city council appropriation of, Nuremberg, 163; under city council control, 23, 116, 164; slipping back into private hands, 164; used for civic needs in Zurich, 164. *See also* Church buildings; Endowments: church

Church reformed according to the Word of God: as title for the Reformed church, 209–10

Cities: Basel, 29; Bruges, 21; Catholic, 117; as centers of welfare reform, 21; European pre-Reformation centralization and secularization of welfare institutions in, 165; Geneva, 21, 23–30, 33–34, 36; Leisnig, 23; Nîmes, 23; Nuremberg, 21; Protestant, 117; residency requirements for public office in, 82; revival of after Viking invasions, 20; sixteenth-century, congested, 21; Strasbourg, 21, 23, 29, 33–34. *See also* individual cities by name

City council of Geneva, 34; and alms boxes, 109; attempts to take control of the *Bourse française*, 109, 120, 256 n.5; and Berne, 144; and chess and dancing, 141; and divorce, 256–57 n.8; elders, 142; and home visits to raise funds, 115; and Jean Budé's account books, 152; and Louis Budé's legacy, 158; maintenance of church buildings by, 163; members of, 109, 114–15; members of taxed for the poor, 115; ordering an abandoned woman to leave town, 144; organizing to help the poor, 114; and pastors, 109, 136, 163, 167; records of, 26,

86–87, 108; and refugees, 127, 136, 149; its unwillingness to admit those unwilling to work, 133; wanting to diminish sanctions for Protestants who attended Catholic services, 145

City councils: appealed to for support of welfare and schools by Protestant reformers, 22; of Berne, 110; and church property, 23, 116; and education, 22, 116, 120; of Leisnig, church endowment and the common chest, 23, 163; of *Moudon,* sending money to Geneva for fugitive pastors, 110; of Neuchâtel, 110; of Nuremberg, appropriation of church endowments and property, 163; of *Payerne,* 110; Protestant, using revenues of church endowment for war and defense, 164; records of, 26; and welfare, 20–22, 116, 120, 163; of Wittenberg, advice of Martin Luther and Karlstadt and "Ordinance for a Common Purse," 162; of Zurich, 110; of Zurich, *obmann* to oversee monastic property, 164. *See also* City Council of Geneva

City hall: of Geneva, 67, 197

Claude, Le Maistre: as donor, 122

Claude, Maistre *"le coustalier":* as donor, 122

Claude, Maistre *"le tincturier":* as donor, 122

Clavet (Clanet), Jean: and procuration to obtain goods left for the poor in France, 240 n.21

Clement, Monsieur (pastor): widow of, aided, 265–66 n.43

Clergy: Catholic, and welfare, 22–23, 166; paid by the common chest, 162; and welfare, 20. *See also* Church offices; Ministers; Pastors

Clerisseau, Nicolas: his widow, chased from the Genevan hospital, 142, 269–70 n.67

Cloth: contributed to the *Bourse française,* 174; purchases of by the *Bourse française,* 46, 56

Clothing: given out by the *Bourse française,* 179; as part of welfare, 20, 45–46; given to Paris, copyist of John Calvin's sermons, 203, 205

Cluny, Prevost de: *Bourse française* disbursement to a guardian of a sick person with him, 233 n.43; as donor, 121–23, 125; renting a house to the *Bourse française,* 58, 190, 237 n.11. *See also* Bonneterye, Monsieur de; La Bonneterye, Monsieur de; La Botiere, François de la; Prevost de Cluny

Cobblers: as employees of the city hosptial, 46; not employed by the *Bourse française,* 101

Coffins: of the poor, 144

Coins: of Geneva, 102

Coligny, François de, 122. *See also* Châtillon; d'Andelot

Coligny, Admiral Gaspard de: as brother of a donor, 108; and Jean Budé, 151

Colladans, Messieurs les: as donors, 122. *See also* Colladon, Germain; Colladon, Nicolas

Colladon, Anne: as second wife of Laurent de Normandie, 236 n.4

Colladon, Daniel: and sodomy, 211–14

Colladon, Germain: as donor, 122; and John Calvin, 151; recommending death for Charles Lourdois and Jeanne Varrot, 215–18, 268 n.61

Colladon, Nicolas: as donor, 122

Collection bags: in Nuremberg, 163

Collection boxes: for *Bourse française* on Thursdays, 118; in Genevan churches, 176; in Nuremberg, 163; proceeds of in Geneva to the hospital and deacons' funds, 176. *See also* Alms boxes; Poor boxes

Collection plates: in Nuremberg, 163

Collections: for the *Bourse française,* 72; on business and diplomatic voyages, 73; for Saint Bartholomew's Day massacre, 109; special, 111, 114–15; spontaneous, 111, 118–19; in Sunday services, 23; systems for, 108, 118

Collectors of the *Bourse française:* 66, 70, 72, 196; and assigned quarters of Geneva, 93, 108, 115, 118; Bernardin de Candolle, 250 n.88; calling together ministers and contributors to elect deacons, 83, 105, 206; collecting money, 92, 94; contacting people of Geneva whom they knew, 175; their contacts abroad, 170; as contributors, 109; and couriers, 95; as deacons, 86, 92–93; duties of, 92–94, 171; election of, 105–6, 171, 207; and extraordinary contributions, 97–98; fourteen in 1582, 93; half year term of, 105, 207; their knowledge of donors' finances, 118; Laurent de Normandie, 86; Monsieur de La Touche, 93, 251–52 n.5; and ordinary contributions in each quarter of Geneva, 105, 206–7; their organizational skills, 165; their pressure on the well-to-do, 175; representing diverse areas in France, 172; role of, 170–71; reconfirmed in office, 105–6, 207; as volunteers, 98. *See also* individual names

Collège de France: Guillaume Budé, 149

Collège of Geneva, bequests: of Bernardin de Candolle, 250–51 n.88; of Charles de Jonvilliers, 248–49 n.82; of Dame Nycole Le Grain, 250 n.84. *See also* Academy of Geneva

Cologny: Jean Boulier, pastor in, 266 n.44

Colonge (Collonges), Sire de: as donor, 122. *See also* Morel, Francois de

Colporteurs: association of with Laurent de Normandie, 51–54, 109, 168; distributing Bibles, catechisms, Psalters in France, 168; from Geneva to France, 50, 54, 86

Combez, Jean: reimbursed for a halberd and a sword, 69, 200, 238 n.23

Commination: as word used by John Calvin, 260 n.32

Common chest: as depository of church property, 23; and interest free loans to artisans, 161; in Leisnig, 162; locked chest for donations to the poor, 22, 161; in Nuremberg, 163; as part of welfare reform, 22; and salaries of pastors and teachers in Lutheran areas, 23, 162; and support of orphans, 161; in Wittenberg, 162;

Communion: and censure in the company of deacons, 106, 207; quarterly in Geneva, 71, 171. *See also* Lord's Supper

Company of pastors and donors to the *Bourse française,* 83–84; ruling on aid to be granted, 139

Company of Pastors of Geneva: administering the *Bourse française,* 70–71, 139; assigning a pastor to the *Bourse française* deacons, 71, 171; *Bourse française* account books submitted to after audit, 99, 105, 171, 207; *Bourse française* expenditures on behalf of, 179, 183; and church office, 12; contacts of in France, 24; and deacons, 70–71, 171–72; denouncing Jean Budé, 152; and editors of registers, 149; influence of over the *Bourse française,* 120; and Jean Boulier, 137–38; and letter to the churches of Normandy on deacons' responsibility for church finances, 225 n.3; minutes of, 93, 95; ordering aid to Mademoiselle du Plessis (Plessix), 134, 264 n.29; ordering deacons to buy a halberd and a sword, 57, 69, 200; ordering deacons to hand over account books, 94; ordering Pierre Cousturier to return to Paris, 67,

197; recommending disbursements to the *Bourse française,* 56–63, 65–69, 74, 189–200; and refugee pastors, 136; registers of, 84–85, 87, 149; reimbursing Monsieur de Paré, 67, 197; and rules of discipline, 145; and Saint Bartholemew's Day Massacre refugees, 110; sending couriers to France, 50; sending messengers, 55–56, 58, 168, 189; supplying missionary pastors to France, 135; worrying about *Bourse française* finances, 95. *See also* Venerable Company of Pastors of Geneva

Company of the Holy Sacrament: and Grenoble hospital, 166

Confession: associated with popery, 147; public, in church, for attending a Catholic Mass, sermon, or burial, 145

Confraternities: and burials, 99; Company of the Holy Sacrament of Grenoble, 166; Congregation for the Propagation of the Faith, 166; and funerals, 115; of Geneva, 115; and hospitals, 115, 139; as institutions of social welfare, 22, 115, 166; losing control of welfare, 22; and officers' visits to members' homes, 139; and patron saints, 20; and the poor, 139, 166; preferential aid to members of, 134, 166; property of appropriated, 161; quasi-religious, quasi-social, 115; in rural areas, 166; specialization of, 166; at time of death, 115; Venice, 139, 144, 166; women's, in Grenoble, 166

Congregation for the Propagation of the Faith: as confraternity dedicated to the elimination of Protestantism, 166

Conseil, Pierre: as recipient of *Bourse française* funds, 63, 193

Consistories: composed of ministers and elders, 29; outside Geneva, 25. *See also* Consistory of Geneva

Consistory of Geneva, 12; and abortion, 140; absolving promises to marry, 255 n.30; Bernardin de Candolle as member, 250 n.88; contributors to the *Bourse française* as witnesses before, 126; elders of, 12, 108–9; and French refugees, 127; Galeazzo Caracciolo as member of, 256–57 n.8; and Guillaume Maurice, 75; and Huguette Martin, 138, 140, 268 n.57; and inns of Geneva, 255 n.30; and Jean Boulier and his wife, 138, 266–67 nn. 44 and 47; and a man who ground grain badly, 152; minutes of, aid recipients and donors therein, 127, 142,

176–77; records of, 26, 86–87; and rules of discipline, 145; weekly meetings of, 142; and woman criticizing a deacon, 75; and woman who slandered Jean Budé and his wife, 151–52

Conspiracy of Amboise: and the *Bourse française*, 57

Constitution for the *Bourse française*, 171. *See also* Ordinances

Contagion: danger of to deacons, 77

Contracts, marriage: in Geneva, 26

Contributions to the *Bourse française*, 34, 74, 78, 107–26; of cloth, 174; donor control over, 176; extraordinary, 97–98, 110–11, 113–15, 119; of firewood, 174; foreign, 91, 111; of gifts in kind and money, 174; of grain, 174; large, 115; from Lyons, 93; of Mademoiselle de Boynville, 97; monthly, 167; records of, 108–9, 111; of real estate, 174; from residents of Geneva, 174; with strings attached, 112–14; voluntary, less generous than when donors thought they bettered their life in the world to come, 165; for the worthy poor, 143. *See also* Bequests; Contributors to the *Bourse française*; Donations to the *Bourse française*; Donors; Legacies

Contributors to the *Bourse française*, 74, 78, 107–27, 171; assembly and vote of, 119; and collectors, 93; in consistory records, 127, 142; their control of the *Bourse française*, 168, 176; electing deacons, 83, 105, 120, 126; and families and friends of deacons, 181; as former aid recipients, 180; French, 174; generosity and stature of, 109–10, 172; Genevan, 109–16; hosted by Pierre Maldonnade and his wife, 80; increasing pledges, 110; and inflation, 110; influence of on the *Bourse française*, 108, 119–20; lists of, 107–9, 119–26; meetings of, 176; as members of a company running the *Bourse française*, 139; one-time, 108, 115; as recommenders of the poor to the deacons, 119, 176; unnamed, 97–98; visitors to Geneva as, 174; women as, 172. *See also* Bequests; *Bourse française*; Contributions to the *Bourse française*; Donations; Donors; Legacies to the *Bourse Française*

Convents: in Strasbourg, 165; in France, 111; in Zurich, 164

Cop, Michel or Monsieur: as donor, 109, 122

Copyist of John Calvin's sermons and lec-
tures, 98–99. *See also* Prostat, Paris; Raguenier, Denis

Copyright: difficulty of enforcing, 48

Corbel, Master Louys (minister of Moratel): as pastor aided by the *Bourse française*, 265–66 n.43

Cordernis[?], Monsieur: given florins by order of the Company of Pastors of Geneva, 65, 196

Cords of wood: at Monsieur de Normandie's, 59, 190

Cornaron, Monsieur: as donor, 122

Cornavit, Monsieur (Seigneur Amend Cornevet?): as donor, 122

Cornillaudit (Cornillaudt), feu Seigneur: his wife, bequest of to the *Bourse française*, 122

Cornille: disbursement to by order of the Company, 67–68, 198

Corporal punishment: in Geneva, 212–13

Corquilleray, Phillippe, 122. *See also* Du Pont, Claude; Du Pont, Françoys; Du Pont, Monsieur

Coumarron, Monsieur: as donor, 122

Council of Sixty of Geneva: and Jean Budé, 151. *See also* individuals by name

Council of Two Hundred of Geneva: admission of foreigners to, 82; Antoine Calvin, 249–50 n.83; Bernardin de Candolle, 250 n.88; Charles de Jonvilliers, 248 n.82; Galeazzo Caracciolo, 256–57 n.8; Jean Budé, 151; Jean Budé (son of Jean Budé and Marie de Jonvilliers), 157; Jean Dalamont, 247 n.79; Laurent de Normandie, 236 n.4; Renaud Anjorrant, 247–48 n.81. *See also* individuals by name

Counterfeiting: by an aid recipient, 141, 147

Counter Reformation: and welfare reform, 166; *See also* Catholic; Catholic church

Couriers: sent by the Company of Pastors of Geneva, 50

Courteau (Aourteau, Dourteau), Thomas: as donor, 122; as refugee printer, 69, 199; his widow, 240 n.24

Court of Saint Pierre in Geneva: *l'Auditoire* on, 261 n.2

Court proceedings of Geneva: reports of, 86. *See also* Procès criminels

Coustier, Pierre: returning to Paris by order of the Company, 67, 197

Coutance: minister sent to, 67, 197

Craftspeople: of the *Bourse française*; journeymen, 42; master, 40; as refugees, 183.

See also Artisans

Cre, Seigneur de: as donor, 120, 122. *See also* Bayf, Monsieur Rene de

Creil, Monsieur de: as donor, 122

Crescent (a Genevan inn), 103–4. *See also Croissant;* Inns of Geneva

Crespin, Jean (Jehan): apprentices of, 43, 231 n.20; death of, 20; as donor, 109, 122; employer and trainer of refugees, 40, 230 n.8; housing refugees, 104, 255 n.33; as martyrologist, 20, 230 n.8; philanthropical habits of, 27; as publisher, 20; publishing Louis Budé's translations of the Psalms, 276 n.53; wife of, 104; as witness at marriage of Théodore de Bèze, 236 n.4

Crespin, Jean (son of Jean Crespin, the martyrologist): wedding of, 141

Crime: as a result of poverty, 261 n.4. *See also* Criminal procedures; *Procès criminels*

Criminal procedures: and aid recipients, 140–42; 177, and Charles Lourdois and Jeanne Varrot, his wife, 215–27; Jean Budé mentioned in, 151. *See also Procès criminels*

Croissant: inn on the Place du Molard, 255 n.30. *See also* Crescent; Gon, Henry; Jacquet

Crulannes (Crulaines), Monsieur de: as donor, 122.

Currency: and exchange rates, 97; fees to exchange, 73; gift of to the *Bourse française,* 72–73

Curteti, Lord Syndic: requested by John Calvin to put the hospital accounting in order, 228 n.22

Cuve[?], Monsieur: as tailor, employed by the Genevan hospital, 233 n.35

Daguat (d'Aguat): as donor, 122

d'Aguile (d'Aguilhon, d'Aguilles, d'Aguillon, Dagulles, d'Aguylle, Daiguilles, d'Aiguilles, Des Aiguilles), Monsieur, 267–68 n.56; as donor, 122; his sister and sister-in-law, 122. *See also* Gassin, René (Regnier); René, Monsieur

d'Aignon (d'Agnon), Monsieur or Seigneur, 121–22. *See also* Bourgoing, Francois

d'Aimee, Seigneur: as donor, 122

d'Aimery [d'Aimen?], brother: hosting a deacon selection meeting, 83, 226 n.11

d'Airebaudoze, Pierre: of Auduze (Anduse) of Chambrun, for Jeanne de Borne, 208–9

Dalamont (d'Alamont, Dallamont), Jean: biography of, 247 n.79; as bourgeois, 247 n.79; and *Bourse française,* 77; and Council of Two Hundred, 247 n.79; as deacon, 89–90; death of, 90, 247 n.79; and Jean de Borne, 208–10, 238 n.4; and procuration, 240 n.21, 247 n.79, 258 n.16; reimbursed, 240 n.27; three marriages of, 247 n.79; his wife dies, 247 n.79. *See also* d'Allemant, Seigneur

d'Allemant (d'Allemand), Seigneur: as donor, 122. *See also* Dalamont (d'Alamont, Dallamont)

Dame: as title indicative of rank in society, 253 n.14

Dame Anes de Remy[?]: donation by, 116

Damoiselle: as title indicative of rank in society, 253 n.14

Dancing: prohibition of in Geneva, 141

d'Andelot (d'Audelont, d'Audelot), Monsieur de: as donor, 108, 122, 256 n.3. *See also* Châtillon; Coligny, François de

Danieres (Danere), Monsieur de or Seigneur de: as donor, 122

Dante Alighieri: *The Divine Comedy,* 114, 259 n.21

Data: in account books, 177

d'Aubeterre, Monsieur or Vicomte: as donor, 121–22. *See also* Bouchard, François

Davantes, Pierre (Antesignanus): as guarantor of a disbursement, 58, 190; and Psalms of Théodore de Bèze, 237 n.12

David (Damo), *feu* Monsieur: as donor, 122, 124. *See also* Laufmoins, *feu* Monsieur David

David (son of Louis Flambert), 147

Deaconesses, 80–82

Deacons: aiding families of prisoners, 49; as arbitrators, 113; becoming pastors, 225 n.7; of the *Bourse italienne,* 129; character of, 18; children of, 80; complained about, 103; death of, 75, 77, 80, 84; description of in 1 Timothy 3:8–13, 18; doing their best, 146; in the ecclesiastical ordinances of Geneva of 1541, 27, 34; of the English church in Geneva, 32, 129, 262 n.16; family instability of, 79–80; French, 79; in Geneva, 113; of the Genevan hospital, 27, 34, 80, 92; as hospitalers, 34, 92; their inconsistency in record keeping, 128; influence of, 71; institution of in Acts 6:1–6, 30, 225 n.5; as intermediaires between donors and the poor, 116–18; John Calvin's ideas on, 29; as lay workers in welfare, 22; living in a paternalistic age, 180; at Meaux, France, as arbiters for a will, 258 n.16; and medical care, 46; near Nîmes, France, 113; from other congregations as recommenders to the *Bourse française,* 76; and poor, 80–81, 139; not social revolutionaries, 101; as one of four church offices, 29; procurators, 30, 34, 92; qualifications of, 78–79, 83, 172, 175; and refugee funds, 32; respect for, 71, 78; seeing the face of Christ in the poor, 118; Stephen, 18; stingy, 103; supporting orphans and widows, 42; thankfulness toward, 75; thankless role of, 75; title's use, 86; as trustees, 73; trustworthiness of, 78, 112; two types of, 81, 92 (*see also* Double diaconate); their visitation of the poor and sick, 32–33, 139; wealth of, 71, 78; wives of, 79–80; work of, 103. *See also* Deacons of the *Bourse française;* Diaconate; Double diaconate; Hospitalers; Procurators of the Genevan hospital

Deacons' funds: contacts among, 28; Geneva as model for, 25; and money for pastors, 168. *See also Bourse française; Bourse allemande; Bourse italienne*

Deacons of the *Bourse française,* 12–13, 32, 38; absent, 86; as accountants, 51, 53, 77; and acquaintances, 160; acting on orders of Company of Pastors of Geneva, 56–58, 62–63, 65, 67, 69, 113, 120, 171, 189–200; active in the community, 175; adjusting support according to need, 45; as administrators, 72, 169–73, 244 n.67; advancing money, 75, 78; aiding families of martyrs and pastors, 49; aiding a sociological spectrum, 133; annual term of, 105, 206; and apprenticeship, 43, 179, 181; auditing account books, 94, 171, 252 n.6; autonomous, 71; and bed clothes and mattresses, 104; and begging, 260 n.31; business acumen of, 100, 172; busy, 175; and censure before Communion, 171; Christian, 172; and church finances supervision rather than pastors, 225 n.3; charismatic, 103; Charles de Jonvilliers, 79, 160 (*see also* Jonvilliers, Charles de); coercing aid recipients, 43, 182; as collectors, 93; competent, 172; confirmed by contributors and pastors, 105, 206; conservative, conforming to prevailing practices, 174; contacts of, 172; and can-

trol, 25, 143, 172, 180; and coordinated effort, 74, 139; and copyist of Calvin's sermons, 41–48, 181; corresponding with pastors of Basel and Zurich, 110; credibility of, 175; death of, 84, 172; decisions of, 71, 75, 172; and dependent people 180; dividing responsibilities, 78; as donors, 78, 109 (*see also* individual deacons by name); earliest selection of, 83–84; elections of, 84–85, 90–91, 93–94, 104–6, 170–71, 206, 248–49 n.82, 250 n.85; English, 129; exasperated, 141, 143; executors of wills, 112; their expectation that welfare recipients would behave well, 177; and fair price, 174; and family and friends, 181; family life of, 172; financial responsibilities of, 72; first generation of, 132; first three, 36, 83–84, 169–70; flexibility of, 74, 177; and fools, 182; and foster homes, 81 (*see also* Foster homes); French, 27, 160; functions of, 72, 175; generosity of, 25, 76, 103, 139, 177–78; and Genevan government, 27, 109, 120, 143–44; geographical diversity of, 83; good offices of, 175; gullible, 76; hospital, 119, 179; housing refugees, 103–4; and inadequate food allowance, 143; individual initiatives of, 74; and inequality in dissemination of money, 134, 180–81; and insufficient concern for their time, 74; as intermediaries between donors and recipients, 108, 116–17, 119; Jean Budé, 152, 171 (*see also* Budé, Jean); and Jean de Borne, 209–10 (*see also* Borne, Jean de); and Jean du Lac, 160 (*see also* Du Lac, Jean); and John Calvin, election and double diaconate, 27; judgment of, 120; their lack of insight, 142; legal activities listed under their names, 26, 72; legal procurators, 113; lending linens, money, 114, 142, 180; life money, 114, 142, 180; life expectancy of, 77; and literacy, 181; and medical care, 98, 173; meetings of, 26, 74, 99, 105, 178, 206, 270–71 n.69; minutes of, 26, 40, 118, 132, 270–71 n.69; mistakes of, 75; names of, 26, 87–91; new approved by old, 105, 206; nobles as, 172; number of, 72, 93, 105, 206; and nuns, 111; origins of, 83, 172; and over expenditure, 158; parsimonious, 180; pastoral responsibilities of, 72, 77; pastors advising and assigned to them, 71, 113, 171; and pastors sent to France, 53; paying employees, 74, 181; their perspective on the

Bourse française, 108; and the poor, 72, 76, 143, 146, 172–73; and pressure to keep foreigners in line, 145; and Psalters, 55; public image of, 175; and purchasing, 72, 78; reading the Bible and praying with the poor, 77; and real estate management, 73, 175; receiving money, 72, 74; recommendations of, 76, 119, 172, 176; reconfirmed in office, 83–84, 171; recording details on aid recipients, 56, 176–77, 179; and reimbursement, 117; removing aid recipients from the welfare rolls, 143; René Gassin, 56, 59–60, 62, 65, 191, 195 (*see also* Gassin, René); renting beds, houses, rooms, 44, 73, 104, 111; and respect and decency, 105, 142, 145, 181, 207; responsibilities of different from diaconate in ecclesiastical ordinances of 1541, 27; retirement of, 84, 172; retraining people, 180; scandalized, 141; and school fees, 179, 181; selection of, 83–85; in the seventeenth century, 131; and social stratification, 181; as sole source of money, 144; soliciting funds, 72, 111; spendthrift, 103; spontaneity of, 177; substitutes for, 86; surveillance of aid recipients by, 180; thanked, 142, 270 n.69; title of, full, 86; as trustees of other people's money, 112; unfair, 180–81; using reliable skilled people, 173; visiting the poor and sick, 72, 77, 105, 172, 206–7; as volunteers, 92, 98, 112, 142; weekly assembly of, 105, 206; and weekly handout, 179; and widows, 180; wills of, 79–80, 175 (*see also* individual deacons by name); withholding welfare to enforce their will, 180; wives of, 80, 172; and women, 80–81, 143, 172, 174; work of never done, 72; and young people, 180. *See also* Deacons; Diaconate; Double diaconate; Procurators of the Genevan hospital

Death: and confraternities, 115; of David (de) Busanton in 1545, 169–70; of deacons, 75, 77, 80, 84, 172; of foster parents, 81; at home, 20; of Jean Budé, 77, 157 (*see also* Budé, Jean death of); of Jesus Christ, 154; life thereafter 114, 165; of Monsieur de Thillat, 84 (*see also* Budé, Louis); of a nursing mother, 75; of the poor who were to be turned out of Geneva, 144; as punishment for sodomy, 212–13; rate of in the sixteenth century, 40; records of in Geneva, 26, 86, 138; of widows, 81. *See also* individuals by name

Deathbed: drafting of wills, 156

Death sentence: in the Holy Roman Empire for homosexual acts, 156

Debarge, Claude: purchase from him by Jean Budé, 155, 219

Debornand, Claude: his sale of a vineyard to Jean Budé, 155, 219

Debt collector: for the *Bourse française,* 114

Debtors: rowing on galleys, 128

Debts: public, paid by auction of church property in Lausanne, 164

de Budé, Jean. *See* Budé, Jean

Delapierre, Pierre: sale by to Jean Bude, 155, 219

Demole, Eugene: *Histoire monétaire de Genève de 1535 à 1792,* 102

Deniers: of Geneva, 95, 102

Denis: as bookseller, 54, 58, 60–61, 64; as donor, 122; and New Testaments for the *Bourse française,* 64, 195

Denmark: responsibility for refugees therefrom, 262–63 n.19

Denominational theory of social welfare reform, 22–23, 165

Depression: of aid recipient, 142; understood by deacons, 182

Des Arenes: as donor, 122. *See also* Trie, Guillaume; Varennes, Monsieur de

Des Combres (de Combes), Monsieur: as donor, 122.

Des Crignelles, Mademoiselle de: as donor, 122

Des Crignelles (Coignelles, Crignelles, Criquelles), Monsieur de: as donor, 122

Des Dant (Daut): as donor, 122

Desertion: as cause for divorce in Geneva, 40, 256–57 n.8

Des Forestz (region?): donors from, 122–24. *See also* Forestz, Monsieur de

Des Gallars, Nicholas: as companion of John Calvin, 151

Des Garennes, Mademoiselle: as donor, 122

Des Mares, Nicholas: loan to for a coat, 233 n.35

Desprit (Despoit), Monsieur: as donor, 122.

Des Roche(s), Seigneur Francois, 124. *See also* La Roche, Seigneur Francois de

Des Vaulx (region?): donors from, 122

de Vérace. *See* Vérace

Devil: deacon as his prey, 75; Jean Boulier (son of Pastor Jean Boulier) as, 138

Diaconate: absence of women in, 82; as husband-wife team, 82; Catholic tradition of different from Protestant, 22; as one of four offices of the church in John Calvin's thought, 27; as a stepping-stone to the ministry, 30, 225 n.7; as a stepping-stone to the priesthood, 30; Elsie McKee on, 223 n.1. *See also* Deaconesses; Deacons; Deacons of the Bourse française; Double diaconate; Procurators of the Genevan hospital

Dieppe: Master Bartholemy travels to, 56, 63, 194; as destination of travelers supported by the *Bourse française*, 55–56

Diet: imperial in Nuremberg in 1522, 163

Dijon, France: Huguenots not allowed worship in, 131

Dimenche: as aid recipient accused of carrying false money, 147

Disabled: guardians for, 46, 99; lifelong support for, 179; on welfare, 37–38; workfare and, 116

Disbursements of the *Bourse française*, 34; ambiguous: 55–69, 189–200; and evidence of international activity, 50–69; exceeding receipts, 253 nn. 11 and 12.; exceptional, 51; international, 55–56, 58–60, 62, 65–69, 189–91, 193–94, 196–99; at Laurent de Normandie's house, 52–54; as regular handouts, 74; undesignated, 53. *See also* Expenditures of the *Bourse française*

Discipline: and hospital detention, 142; of Reformed churches, 25

Discrimination: in dissemination of aid on the basis of religious affiliation, 25

Disinheritance: of two sons of Antoine Calvin, 79. *See also* Calvin, Antoine

Distributions: in the Acts of the Apostles 6:1–7, 18; daily, 18; frequency of, 20, 32, 44, 45; inequities in, 45. *See also* Handouts

Divorce: of Galeazzo Caracciolo, 256–57 n.8; in Geneva, 40, 256–57 n.8; granted by the Genevan city council, 256–57 n.8

Doctors: of the *Bourse française*, 46, 49, 70, 77, 98–99, 101, 105, 139, 141, 166, 173, 207, 272 n.6; as teachers and one of four Reformed church offices, 27, 29, 70; on welfare, 135. *See also* Physicians

Doctrine: knowledge of, 151; of life after death, 114 (*see also* Purgatory). *See also* Theology

Documents of Geneva: used in this study, 26

Dole: weekly, 98. *See also* Distributions of welfare aid

Dombes; *Bourse française* responsible for refugees from, 262–63 n.19

Domcevol[?], Mademoiselle de: as donor, 122

Dominicans, 22

Domques: as donors, 122

Donations: as alms, 117–18; and Catholic belief that gifts would improve the afterlife, 165; of church property returned, 23; conditional upon prayers and masses, 116; crucial, 165; currencies as, 95; by free will, 167; conserved in a locked community chest and poor boxes, 22; and social pressure, 118–19; soliciting of, 73, 111, 114–15, 119; of specie, 72; in Zurich, 164. *See also* Contributions to the *Bourse française;* Donations to the *Bourse française*

Donations to the *Bourse française*, 107–20; in account books, 26, 72–73, 114; collection of, 170; dependent on public image of deacons, 175; encumbrances to, 72, 113; English, 1552, 132; of Galeazzo Caracciolo, 110; from Genevans and non-French, 174; individual, 108–10, 115–16; from Isabeau de Lailly, 158; from living people, 72–73; long commitments to, 108–11, 115; from Mademoiselle de Boynville, 97; motivations for, 108, 113–19; in notarial documents, 114, 119; occasional, 108, 111, 113; from relatives of Jean Budé, 150, 158; solicited by collectors assigned to quarters of Geneva, 118, 175; special, 112; on Thursdays, 119; from unnamed individuals, 97–98. *See also* Contributions to the *Bourse française;* Donations; Donors to the *Bourse française*

Donors to the *Bourse française*, 36, 40, 49, 107–26, 148, 151, 153, 155, 158, 160, 174–76; accused of adultery, 142; before the collection system developed, 109; company of, 84; their confidence in the *Bourse*, 175; their contacts in France, 24; their control over contributions, 176; currencies indicating their origins, 72–73; deacons' wives as, 80; an Englishman at Pierre Maldonnade's, 263 n.25; expecting the *Bourse* to help the worthy poor, 142–43; female, 109, 113, 116; few Genevans as, 107–9; on fixed incomes, 110; foreign, 24, 111; François Budé, 158; French, 24, 107–9, 111, 113, 120–26, 174; as hosts and hostesses to refugees, 103–4; as hosts of the first recorded selection of deacons, 83; and house guests,

107; housing poor refugees, 86, 103–4, 176; their influence on the *Bourse*, 170; insuring legacies would reach the *Bourse,* 73; Italian, 110; John Calvin, 36; Laurent de Normandie, 20; listed by name, 120–26; lists of in account books, 170; more known about than about aid recipients, 176; motivations of, 116–19; network of, 110–11; one time, 108, 112, 115; as part of the *Bourse,* 104; as recommenders to the deacons, 39, 76, 119; regular monthly, 167; as relatives of other donors, 120; taking on, 176; travelers as, 107–8; usual, 111, 120–26. *See also* Contributors to the *Bourse française;* Donations; individual names of donors

Double diaconate, 27, 81, 92; in ecclesiastical ordinances, 251 n.1; in Geneva, 34; and quotation from John Calvin, 81, 243 n.48

Doumergue, Emile: citing *le sieur de Feuquières,* 250 n.85; *Jean Calvin, les hommes et les choses de son temps,* vol. 3, *La ville, la maison, et la rue de Calvin,* 19, 130, 137, 159; and the origins of the *Bourse française,* 33

Dowries, 167; from Leisnig common chest, 163

Draper: Guillaume Maillard as, 147, 272 n.91

Drugs: bills for, 46; provided by the *Bourse française,* 179

Drunkard: as aid recipient, 141–42; La Loubiere (a woman) as, 147, 269 n.64

Drunkenness: reported to the consistory by the inns of Geneva, 255 n.30

Drunks: pastors of Geneva willing to turn away, 144

Du Bois, Mademoiselle: as donor, 122

Ducat: as foreign currency donation, 97

Du Chesne, Pierre: as printer, 147, 272 n.89

Duchess of Ferrara: John Calvin's letter to, 151

Du Cimitiere, Pierre: his sale of land at the Salève (near Geneva) to Jean Budé, 155, 219

Du Clare, Francois (d'Orleans): as donor, 122

Dufour, Monsieur: as pastor of the seventeenth century, 139

Du Four, Monsieur: recommending a poor Provençal, 66, 196

Du Lac, Jean (Sieur Du Lac in Auvergne): as deacon, 160, 277 n.58; as godson and son-in-law of Jean Budè, 274 n.23; ill, 160

Du Mas, Jehan: as donor, 122, 124. *See also* Lisle, Seigneur de

Du Mont, Monsieur: as donor, 122

Du Pas, Philippes (le sieur de Feuquières): biography of, 250 n.85; as deacon, 90–91, 250 n.85. *See also* Feuquières

Du Pont, Monsieur: delivering a donation, 122, 256 n.3. *See also* Corquilleray, Phillippe; Du Pont, Claude; Du Pont, Françoys

Du Pont, Claude, 122. *See also* Corquilleray, Phillippe; Du Pont, Françoys; Du Pont, Monsieur

Du Pont, Françoys, 122. *See also* Corquilleray, Phillippe; Du Pont, Claude; Du Pont, Monsieur

Durand, Zacharie: as donor, 123

Durands, Messieurs: as brothers of a melancholy girl, 142, 270 n.68

Durval, Matthieu: as guarantor for a loan, 230 n.3

Dutch: helped by the *Bourse allemande,* 129

Du Tillac, Mademoiselle: as donor, 123, 126. *See also* Thillac, Mademoiselle de or du

Du Val, Seigneur Estienne: as donor, 123

Du Vanneau, Monsieur: as donor, 123

Du Vivier, Monsieur: as donor, 123

Ecclesiastical Ordinances of Geneva of 1541, 27; on church offices, 27, 92; deacons of the Genevan hospital in, 30, 32, 34; John Calvin's ideas about deacons in, 170; and officers to prevent begging at church doors, 117, 260 n.30

Economic historians: potential use by of *Bourse française* records, 26–27

Ecus, 47. *See also* Ecus pistoles; Ecus sol

Ecus pistoles, 53. *See also* Ecus

Ecus sol, 59, 190. *See also* Ecus

Edict: of the Genevan city council on proof of marital status, 144–45, 271 n.80. *See also* Ordinances; Laws

Edict of Châteaubriand: as prohibition of Genevan publications, 51

Edict of Nantes, 25, 45, 131, 136

Editors: missionary activity of in France, 86

Education: and the church after the fall of the Rome, 18; church property used to support, 22; primary, 11; and the Reformation, 134, 264 n.31; and school fees paid by the *Bourse française,* 43; secondary, 11

Edwardian prayer book: objections to, 261 n.2

Église prétendue réformée: French edicts

against, 263 n.23. *See also* Reformed Church

Elderly: aided, 133; in hospitals, 20

Elders, 70; as arbitrators and legal pro-curators, 113; as church officers, 27; from city councils of Geneva, 142; on consisto-ries, 25, 108–9, 142; and Huguette Martin, 140, 143; at Meaux, France, as arbiters of a will, 258 n.16; responsible for church fi-nances in the absence of deacons, 5, 29–30. *See also* Church offices

Election: of deaconesses, 81; of deacons, (*see* Elections of the *Bourse française*); ordained by God, 154

Elections of the *Bourse française*: by the as-sembly of pastors and contributors, 171; of auditors, 94–95, 105–6, 252 n.6, 252 n.10; of collectors, 106, 252 n.6; of deacons, 27, 83–85, 88, 90–91, 104–5, 171, 206, 247–48 n.81, 248–49 n.82; at John Calvin's house, 27, 84–85, 88, 247–48 n.81; in periodic meetings of contributors, 176; by a plurality vote, 83, 105, 171, 206; timing of, 83–85, 171

Elector Frederick: letter to from Martin Luther, 23. *See also* Elector of Saxony

Elector of Saxony: prescribes church order for Wittenberg, 162. *See also* Elector Fred-erick

Elector Palatine: Jean Budé as ambassador to, 151

Elie, Monsieur (pastor): widow of. *See* Valbis-quot, Anne

Emergencies: *Bourse française* help in, 74, 179–80; disrupting regularity of handouts, 75

Empire, Holy Roman: refugees from aided by the *Bourse allemande*, 262–63 n.19. *See also* Charlemagne; Charles V

Employees of the *Bourse française:* full-time, 78, 100; medical, 98, 173; piecework, 97, 100–101; wet nurses, 173; variety of, 173–74. *See also* individual crafts and profes-sions

Enard (Eynard), Maistre: as donor, 123

Enclosure: in England, 21

Endowments: church, at the time of the Prot-estant Reformation, 23, 115, 161, 164; as crucial to welfare success, 23, 165; of hospi-tals, 20; and income for the poor, 115; in Leisnig, 163; in Nuremburg, 163; Protes-tant, 116; taken by city councils and used for non-church expenses, 23, 163–64

England: aid to a schoolboy going to, 232 n.23; *Bourse allemande* responsible for refugees from, 262–63 n.19; deacons' fund at Sandwich in, 262 n.16; as destination of travelers from Geneva or supported by the *Bourse française*, 43, 55–56, 60, 129, 191, 241 n.34; Reformed churches in, 182; as route of French coming to Geneva, 132; refugees from, 129; students of theology in Geneva from, 108; and support for the *Bourse française*, 160. *See also* English

English: arrival of in Geneva, 132, 229–30 n.2; in *Auditore (Marie la Nove)*, 130, 261 n.2; church in Geneva, 129, 130, 132, 262 n.16; deacons and fund in Geneva, 32, 129, 177–78, 183, 262 n.16; donor at Pierre Maldon-nade's, 263 n.25; in Geneva, 127–29, 145–46, 261 n.2, 262 n.16; and John Calvin, 261 n.2. *See also* England

Equality: of treatment by the *Bourse fran-çaise*, 180–82

Equal opportunity: promoted by welfare, 167

Eschallat, Françoys, 123. *See also* La Boullaye

Estienne, Henri (son of Robert Estienne), 80; as employer of Matthieu Budé, 272 n.3

Estienne, Robert: children of, 80; as donor, 27, 80, 109, 123; as printer-editor, 80; wife of, 80; will of, 113, 258 n.17

Eternal life: and meritorious acts, 165. *See also* Doctrine: life after death

Etiennette of Orleans: as aid recipient striking her husband, 147

Europe: change of regional boundaries in and Genevan welfare, 178; deaconesses in, 82; food riots in, 143; Geneva as city of refuge for, 24; German-speaking areas of, 82; ho-mosexuality in, 156; pensions, 138; Protes-tant refugees in, 127; Reformed churches in, 24–25, 182 (*see also* Reformed Church); sixteenth-century, 115; and social welfare context, 161–67; socialism in, 167; welfare institutions dedicated to local needs in, 24; worthy welfare recipients in, 139. *See also* individual countries of Europe

Evaluation: of the *Bourse française*, 182

Evangelization of France, 183

Exchange rates, 97

Executors: of wills, deacons, 73

Exile: of Barthelemy Michau (Micaux or

Michault), 147; in Geneva, 165; as gift of life or death, 146; in Strasbourg, 165. *See also* Banishment; Refugees

Expenditures of the *Bourse française*, 26–27, 46, 179; daily, 86; as evidence of international activity, 50–69; exactness of, 180; extraordinary, 51, 59–69, 98; first, 96; for medical personnel, 98; monthly receipts preceding, 73; ordinary, 51. *See also* Disbursements

Extramarital sex: Genevan city council concerned about, 144–45, 271 n.80; at inn of the *Croissant*, 255 n.30. *See also* Adultery

Extraordinary accounts of the *Bourse française*, 57–69, 189–200

Fabri, Jean: and printers' regulations for the *Bourse française*, 244–45 n.68; as recommender to the *Bourse française*, 70

Fair price: sought by deacons, 174

Fairness: by the *Bourse française*, 180–82

Faith: justification by, 176

Falai(?), Monsieur de, 125. *See also* Bourgogne, Jacques de; Bredan, Monsieur de; Fallaix, Monsieur de; Pallai, Monsieur de; Salai, Monsieur de

Fallaix (Falais, Falaises), Monsieur de: as donor, 121, 123. *See also* Bourgogne, Jacques de (Seigneur de Falais and de Breda; Bredan (Bredain, Bredehan) Monsieur de; Falai(?); Pallai, Monsieur de; Salai, Monsieur de

Families; aided, 179; extended, Budé, 160; quarrels of, 79–80. *See also* individual families by name

Fanon (Favon), Seigneur: as donor, 123

Farel, Guillaume: as donor, 123

Favre (Faure), Mademoiselle: daughter of, mentally ill, 142, 270 n.68

Fay, Estienne de: as donor, 123–24. *See also* La Tour, Monsieur or Seigneur de

Fazy, James: as Genevan political figure of the nineteenth century, 25

Fee for services: and *Bourse française* employees, 70, 173

Felix, Master François (minister near Nîmes, France): his bequest to the poor, 73, 239 n.16

Ferrara (in Italy): Charles de Jonvilliers and, 248 n.82; duchess of, John Calvin's correspondence with, 151

Feuquières (Fequières), Marquis de or Monsieur de: of the seigneurie de l'Artois, 90–91, 250 n.85. *See also* Du Pas, Philippes

Financial aid: by deacons, 77. *See also* Disbursements of the *Bourse française*; Expenditures of the *Bourse Française*; Handouts

Financing: of the *Bourse française*, 110–11, 114, 118–19

Fines: for grinding grain badly, 152; for not attending a solicitation of funds for the poor, 115

Firewood, 78; given to the poor, 46, 179

Flambert, Louis: deceased father of Martha and David, 147

Flanders: aid recipients from, 262 n.11; refugees from, *Bourse allemande* responsible for, 129, 262–63 n.19; tapestry maker from, 104.

Flexibility of the *Bourse francaise:* in early years, 25, 46, 94, 174, 177, 181

Florence: pensions in, 267 n.51

Florentine, Seigneur Michel: as donor, 123

Florins: of Geneva, 48, 52–53, 95, 102

Fontaine, Monsieur de: as donor, 123. *See also* Haute Fontaine, Monsieur de

Fools: aided, 269–70 n.67; not tolerated by deacons, 182; one loaned money by Charles Lourdois and Jeanne Varrot, 216–17; a widow chased from the Genevan hospital, 142, 269–70 n.67

Forcalquier, canon of, 250 n.88. *See also* Candolle, Bernardin de

Forcet, Pierre: as husband of the widow of Jean Gadovin, 265 n.43

Foreigners, 25, 182; behaving discreetly, 145; *Bourse française* intended for, 24; employed by Geneva, 82; in Geneva, 12, 82, 145; Genevan reservations about, 24, 144, 183; poor, 182; threat of their being driven from Geneva, 34. *See also* individual nationalities; Refugees

Forestz, Monsieur de: as donor, 123

Foster homes: of the *Bourse française*, 42, 70, 81, 100, 173, 179; less than desirable, 146; widows and, 42, 81, 243 n.60

Framery, Anne: as Galeazzo Caracciolo's second wife, 256–57 n.8

France: books from Geneva sent to, 50–54, 168; *Bourse française* pays two boys to return to, 66, 196; collectors' activity in 93–94 (*see also* Collectors of the *Bourse fran-*

çaise); colporteurs in, 51–54, 86, 168; and Company of Pastors of Geneva, 183; contributions from, 73, 93–94, 107–8, 111, 165; currency of, 95; deacons' friends in, 173; deacons and collectors representing diverse regions of, 172; emigrants from (see Immigrants: French); evangelization in, 11, 183; Geneva's diplomacy with, 136; kings of (see individual names); merchants from 108; messengers to, 108, 181; missionary activity in, 53–55, 86, 181: northern and western regions of, 132; pastors from Geneva in, 50, 53, 58, 190; people recovering families and belongings in, 76; procurations in, 73; Protestant church records in, 111; Protestant pastors ordered to leave, 110, 136; recommendations from to the Bourse française, 76; Reformed Christians as a religious minority in, 152; Reformed churches, 13, 24–25, 83, 107–8, 111–13, 131, 136, 154, 160, 209–10 (see also Reformed Church); Reformed community in, 181–82; refugees from (see Refugees: French); refugees returning to, 113, 131; and support for the Bourse française, 160. See also Bourse française; French; Wars of Religion in France

France Protestante by Eugene and Emile Haag: Candolle family oldest in, 150 n.88; confusion of Antoine and François Budé in, 158; names for second edition of from Bourse française account books, 26

Francis I (king of France): and Guillaume Budé, 149

Franciscans, 22.

François, Master: from Lausanne, 56, 58, 190

François, Claude (minister from Metz): widow of aided, 265–66 n.43

Françoise (widow of Jean Guemin): selling mattress and linens lent her, 142

Francoys, Claude (haberdasher and glover): as inhabitant of Geneva, 265–66 n.43

Frankfort: Marian exiles in, 261 n.2

Frappe, Jehan: as donor, 123

Frederick, Elector of Saxony. See Elector Frederick; Elector of Saxony

French: bastard cursive handwriting, 85, 185; businessmen, 160; donors, 107–9, 111, 113, 120–26, 174; in Geneva, 24–25, 47–48, 145–46; hosts and hostesses, 174; nobles, 160; poor, 111; Protestants, seventeenth century, 131 (see also Huguenots; Re-

formed Church); signatures of Calvin, 35; spoken in Swiss cantons, 113. See also France

French fund. See Bourse française

Fribourg, 164

Fugitives: minister from Angrogna in Italy, 66, 197; from persecution, 44. See also Persecution; Refugees

Fuller: Charles Lourdois, 269 n.63

Fund for the poor French foreigners: as long title for the Bourse française, 24, 113, 139, 273 n.22

Funding of the Bourse française: foreign, 24; local, 172–73. See also Collections; Collectors of the Bourse française; Fund raising; Support

Fund raising: by the Bourse française, 111; in Geneva, 114–15. See also Collections; Collectors of the Bourse française; Funding; Support

Funeral: procession, 115. See also Burial

Gadovin, Jacque (son of Jean Gadovin): as aid recipient, 265 n.43

Gadovin, Jean: as pastor aided by the Bourse française, 265 n.43

Gadovin, Marie (daughter of Jean Gadovin): as aid recipient, 265 n.43

Gadovin, Pierre (son of Jean Gadovin): as aid recipient, 265 n.43

Galeas, Seigneur Collatonio: as father of Galeazzo Caracciolo, 256 n.8

Galee, Huguette: as widow of Jean Boulier (de la Roche), aid recipient, 267 n.48

Galiffe, J. A.: and Isabeau de Lailly's death (mother of Jean Budé), 158; and genealogy of Genevan families, 152

Galleys: John Knox and, 128; service on, 44, 128, 262 n.7

Garnier, Seigneur Francoys: as donor, 123

Gascony: a minister sent to, 53, 58, 190; Guy de Serignac from, 83, 229 n.30

Gassin, Bertrand: father of René Gassin, 246 n.76

Gassin (Gasin), René (Regnier): advancing money in Jean Budé's absence, 272 n.6; authorizing a loan to Pierre Bourgeois, 230 n.3; biography of, 246 n.76; as bourgeois, 246 n.76; as businessman, 78; and collection from Provençals, 93, 239 n.15, 251–52 n.5; as deacon, 73, 88, 122; and disbursement, 77; and donation from Dame

Anne de Remy (?), 239 n.12; as donor, 109, 122, 125; and the Genevan hospital, 147, 234 n.45; 269 n.64; paying for a minister's room, 237 n.10, 264 n.33; from Provence, 73; reimbursed, 240 n.27, 241 nn. 35 and 36; sick, 89. *See also* d'Aguile, Monsieur

Gassin, Sara: as daughter of René Gassin, wife of Bernardin de Candolle, 250 n.88

Gassin, Thomas: as son of René Gassin, 246 n.76

Gautier, Jean-Antoine: and David Busanton, 227 n.17

Geiler von Kayserberg (Kaiserberg), John: as Strasbourg pre-Reformation preacher, 21; urging poor relief, 165

Generosity: of the deceased, 115, 119. *See also* Benefactors; Benevolence; Charity; Donations; Donations to the *Bourse française;* Donors to the *Bourse française;* Philanthropy

Genesis, chapter nineteen: Sodom and Gomorrah, 156

Geneva: accounting in, 97; alms boxes in, 109, 118–19, 176; asylums in, 165; begging ban, 117, 176; book of bequests in, 26, 111, 119, 175; book of inhabitants of, 131–33 (*see also Livres des habitants de Geneve);* bookkeeping in, 95, 97; books prohibited in France, 51, 264 n.28; bourgeoisie of, 79; *Bourse française* support, 109, 114–15, 172–74; Calvinism, impact on, 38, 161; centralization of welfare in, 165; charitable institutions in, 155, 175–76; charity in, 119, 167, 175–76; church buildings in, 168; city budget of, 25, 27, 95; city council of, 12, 114, 116, 120, 141, 144 (*see also* Geneva: small council); city council of and pastors, 109, 136, 163, 167; city council supervision of the *Bourse française* in, 109, 114–15, 120 (*see also* City council of Geneva); city fathers of, 82, 136; city government asking welfare recipients to leave, 144; city government expenditures of and the *Bourse française,* 27, 95; as city of refuge, 11, 24, 33, 76, 183; city walls of, 82, 104, 144, 250 n.85; civic offices of banned to immigrants, 172, 176; civil matters in, 73; coat of arms of: half an eagle and a key, 102; coins of, 95, 102; collection of debts owed to the poor in, 114; court proceedings in (see *Procès criminels);* daily life of, 26; death records of, 48, 138; deniers, 95; economy of, 183;

errands to, 94; ethnic deacons' funds in, 183; family papers of, 26; financial records of, 27; foreign pastors in, 82; foreigners (*see* Foreigners; individual nationalities); German aid to, 110; gifts to the *Bourse française* from, 73; government of, 82–83 (*see also* City council of Geneva; Geneva: city council); grain reserve of, 271 n.72; heritage of, 179; homosexuality in, 156; hospital of (*see also* Hospital of Geneva); hospitals of, pre-Reformation, 165; hostels of, pre-Reformation, 165; independence of, 136: inflation in, 110; inhabitants of, 36, 119; inns of (*see* Inns of Geneva); laborers in, 144; laws of, 114, 117, 119, 212–13; *Livre des habitants* of (*see* Book of inhabitants of Geneva; *Livre des habitants de Genève);* map of, 19, 41; merchants from, 111; as model for Reformed institutions, 25; norms of behavior in, 143; pastors in (*see* Pastors); as plague-infested, 77; political revolution and Protestant Reformation in, 165; poor foreigners to be sent away from, 228 n.23; population of, 76, 127; pride in, 24; Protestant immigrants to, 24, 27–28, 82, 154, 157–58; as prototype, 28; providing for local church needs, 168; publishing peak in, 54; punishment for theft in, 216–17; quarterly administration of the Lord's Supper in, 171; quarters of, 115; receptive to persecuted people, 24; and the Reformation, 12, 24, 80; and Reformation motto, 102; Reformed church in (*see* Reformed Church); refugees in (*see* Refugees); residency requirements for public office in, 82, 172, 176; and Rhone River, 132; as sanctuary, 145; secularization of welfare institutions in, 165; silk industry in, 116; small council of, 82 (*see also* City council of Geneva; Geneva, city council); society in, 83; as stopover for refugees, 132; sumptuary laws of, 141; travelers through, 107–8; tribunal of the police in, 73; welfare in, 34; and welfare influence on Protestantism, 168; welfare sources in, 129; widows in (*see* Widows)

Geneva Bible: and English in Geneva, 127

Genevan Academy. *See* Academy of Geneva

Genevan families: genealogy of, J. A. Galiffe, 152. *See also* individual families by name

Genevan hospital. *See* Hospital of Geneva

Genevans: aided by the *Bourse française,* 131,

177, 263 n.20; beggars, 176; and *Bourse française* support, 24, 108–9, 174; city offices reserved by to natives, 172; as conscious of heritage, 179; criticism of, 140; and foreigners, 24, 144, 183; judging deacons' funds parochial, 178; native, 108–9, 177; in the sixteenth century, 77. *See also* Geneva

Geographic origins: and changes in sovereignty in Europe and welfare, 178; in book of inhabitants, 177; of refugees, 128, 262 n.10

Gerard, Jacques: as tinsmith, housing a Breton for the Company of Pastors, 257 n.13

German fund. *See Bourse allemande*

Germans: aiding Geneva, 110; *Bourse allemande* responsible for, 129, 177, 262–63 n.19; church of, 262 n.15; in Geneva, 145–46; one helped to go home by the *Bourse française*, 59, 190; refugees, 129. *See also* German fund; Germany

Germany: Bernardin de Candelle's trip to, 250–51 n.88; books from censored in France, 264 n.28; Lutheran churches in, 13; northern church orders in, 163; Protestant princes in, 151; refugees from, 129; southern cities of as models for welfare, 21. *See also* German fund; Germans

Gillet, Denys: his widow as foster mother, 243 n.50

Girard (Gerard, Girar), Estienne (Etienne): and *Bourse française*, 59, 190, 255 n.29; as donor, 123, 125(?); and Laurent de Normandie, executor, 236 n.4

God: active in the world, 154–55; blessing personal merit, 167; to bring peace to France, 158; calling, 146, 154; doctrine of, 151; fear of, 141, 156, 212–14; gifts, stewardship of, 167; glorified, 151, 154; and love and charity, 176; and the poor, 95, 144; thankfulness toward, 154. *See also* Christ; Jesus Christ

Godart, Master (pastor): his wife as aid recipient, 267 n.49

Godeau, Bishop: in Nîmes, France, 23, 224 n.9

Gohier: son of, 59, 190

Gomorrah: destroyed by God, 156

Gon, Henri (Henry): as donor, 123; his children as consistory witnesses, 255 n.30; as

host of the Inn of the Crescent, 103–4; keeping sick boys, 233–34 n.44; and Laurent de Normandie, 61, 192. *See also* Jacquet, Henry

Good man of Paris: his Psalter with large print, 237 n.14; his son, 233 n.44

Gorin, Pierre: as donor, 121, 123. *See also* Boysbossart (Boiboyssard, Boisbassard, Boisbossart) Monsieur or Seigneur de

Gospel, 113, 154

Gouliards: as epithet directed at Geneva children, 147

Gout: and Jean Budé, 273 n.18

Government: centralizing welfare, 20; as responsible for charity, 115. *See also* City council of Geneva; Geneva: city council

Grain: badly ground, 152; and *Bourse française*, 45, 174, 179; for Paris, copyist of John Calvin's sermons, 201–4; as pay of Genevan pastors, 136; price of, 116; reserve of, 271 n.72; in Wittenberg, 162

Grammars: provided to children by the Genevan hospital, 225–26 n.10

Grandjean, Henri: and David Busanton, 227 n.17

Grands livres des assistees (Great Books of the Assisted), Kq 1, 1560–1579; Kq 2, 1580–1599, 57, 97–98, 150–51

Greek grammar: from *Bourse française*, 237 n.13

Green Dog *(Le Chien Vert):* a Genevan inn, 103, 225 n.30

Gregorian calendar reform of 1582, 13

Grene, l'Esleu, 123. *See also* Grené, Philibert

Grené, Philibert: as deceased husband of Gabrielle Brossequin, 247 n.80; as donor, 123

Grenoble: confraternities in, 166 as destination of travelers supported by the *Bourse française*, 55, 59, 191; prisoner in, 56, 60, 62, 191, 193; young man of, 66, 197

Grule (Goute), Seigneur Henry: as donor, 123

Guarantors of loans and disbursements, 53, 58, 60, 190–91; Matthieu Durval, 230 n.3

Guard, Nicolas: and false money, 147

Guardians: of children, 101; to prevent beggars at churches, 117; of the sick and disabled, 99, 104, 173

Guemin, Jean: survived by Françoise, his widow, 142

Guerin, Seigneur Francoys Loys or Loys: as

donor, 123
Guillaume: sale of a house by to Jean Budé, 155, 219

Hainaut (Hainault): in Belgium, 83; David (de) Busanton from, 33; Pierre de Maldonnade from, 229 n.30
Handicapped: people aided, 138, 176
Handouts: coinciding with deacons' meetings, 74; direct, 117; twice a week or month, 75; unanticipated, 98; weekly, 77. *See also* distributions of the *Bourse française*
Handwriting: John Calvin's, 35. *See also* French: bastard cursive
Hanging: as punishment for return after banishment, 216–17
Haultin, Barthéleme: as aid recipient, 270 n.69
Haultin, Elizabeth: thanking deacons, 270 n.69
Haute Fontaine, Monsieur de: as donor, 123. *See also* Fontaine, Monsieur de
Health care: by the *Bourse française*, 56. *See also* Apothecaries; Barber-surgeons; Doctors; Guardians: of the sick; Surgeon
Hebrew: as aid recipient, 241 n.34 *See also* Jews
Helon, Pierre: of Rennes in Brittany, 65, 195
Hell, 114
Helye (Helie), Master: as minister hung, 232–33 nn. 25 and 30; wife of, 59, 190
Hennequin, Monsieur: as aid recipient, 134, 264 n.29
Henry III (king of France); his repression of pastors, 136
Henry IV (king of France): assassinated, 131; Jean Budé (son of Jean Budé, grandson of Guillaume Budé) as ambassador from Geneva to, 157; as a Protestant, 131, 157
Herman, Pierre: as husband of Alex, 143
Hernes, Charles: given money for leather, 60, 191
Heurtaut, Pierre: as carpenter needing an apprentice, 231 n.18
Hierost: as former prisoner and aid recipient, 61, 192
Higher prices. *See* inflation
Historians: criticism of Jean Budé by, 152; economic, and *Bourse française* records, 26–27

Hoarding of essential commodities: John Calvin's opposition to, 167
Holland: *Bourse allemande* responsible for refugees from, 262–63 n.19
Holy Roman Empire: death sentence in for homosexual acts, 156; Lutherans protected in, 28; refugees from aided by the *Bourse allemande*, 262–63 n.19
Homeless: housed, 18
Homelessness: as union with Christ, 146
Homosexuality: Lambert Le Blanc and, 156–57; and seduction of a boy beggar, 117
Honesty: and *Bourse française*, 171
Hôpital Générale de Genève. *See* Hospital of Geneva
Hospital: of *Bourse française*, 46, 234 n.46; at Nîmes, 23; chaplain of, 234 n.46; of Lyons, 146; and plague, 99. *See also* Geneva: hospital; Genevan hospital; Hospital of Geneva; Hospitals
Hospital of Geneva, 12, 24, 92, 104; and account book of the *Bourse française*, 51; aiding a drunkard and thief, 141–42; Antoine Calvin, 242 n.42, 249–50 n.83; and bread for the poor, 45; bequests to, 26, 119, 153, 155, 175, 242 n.42, 250 n.84, 250–51 n.88; and *Bourse française*, 46, 99, 104, 129, 134, 147, 178–79, 234 n.45; and collection box proceeds, 118, 176; and deacons, 34, 80, 109, 119; and deacons' funds and foreign poor, 183; as the "discipline" or place of detention, 142; drawing of, 19; as employer of tailors and seamstresses, 46; exchanging support for property, 145; founded before the ecclesiastical ordinances of Geneva, 32; and grammars and Psalters for school children, 225–26 n.10; and indigenous poor, 33, 118; as an institution to help the sick and the poor, 30; Jean Boulier in, 138, 267 n.48; and Jean Budé, 153, 155; and John Calvin's ideas about the diaconate, 27; legal welfare responsibilities of, 262–63 n.19; location of in the twentieth century near Champel, 156; on a map of Geneva, 41; ovens of, 179; and prayer before Sunday distributions, 225 n.10; recent research on, 251 n.2; in seventeenth century, 269 n.65; and silk industry, 116; Sunday assemblies of the deacon-trustees of, 119; and syndic, 142; and welfare reform, 21. *See also* Geneva: hospital; Hospital of Messieurs

Hospital of Messieurs (the city councilors of Geneva), 234 n.45. *See also Hôpital Générale de Genève;* Hospital of Geneva

Hospitaler: as administrator and deacon of the general hospital of Geneva, 21, 251 nn. 1 and 2; as one of two types of deacons, 30, 34, 92; wives of indispensable, 21–22

Hospitality: and the church after the fall of Rome, 18; donated, 175. *See also* Hosts and hostesses; Inns of Geneva

Hospitals: as all-purpose institutions, 18, 20; and confraternities, 115, 139, 166; founding of, 18, 21; pre-Reformation attempt to centralize and rationalize, 165; Protestant reformers appeal to city councils for, 22. *See also* Geneva: hospital; *Hôpital Générale de Genève;* Hospital of Geneva

Hostels: in pre-Reformation Geneva, 165

Hosts and hostesses, 172; for the *Bourse française,* 103–4, 174; French, 103; Pierre Maldonnade and his wife, 80; of refugee pastors, 186; of refugees, 98, 133

Hotman: as Guillaume Prevost's brother-in-law, 245–46 n.75

Housing: for refugees, 45. *See also* Hosts and hostesses

Huguenots, 131; rowing on galleys, 128

Humanists: Guillaume Budé, 181; Juan Luis Vives, 21; and welfare reform, 22

Hunger: and food riots, 143

Hungary: *Bourse allemande* responsible for refugees from, 262 n.63 n.19

Husband: beating of, 147; of one wife, 80

Husband-wife team: diaconate as, 82

Hutterites, 167

Hypocrisy, 178

Idolatry: and Catholicism, 154; in Geneva, 145, 166

Imbault (Imbaut), Madeleine (Magdelaine), 248 n.82

Immigrants: aided by the *Bourse française,* 24; deacons' funds and, 168; flow of, 54; French, 24–25, 47, 79, 82–83, 103, 176, 181; to Geneva, 24–25, 33, 55, 76, 79, 104, 152, 157–58, 160; men as, 133; religious, 39, 103–4; wealthy, 127. *See also* individual ethnic groups by name; Refugees

Impotent: men, 133; turned out of Geneva, 144

Inequality: by the *Bourse française,* 180–81

Infants: abandoned, 18; with dead mothers, 173

Inflation: calculated from the account books, 26–27; and hardship, 21, 110; in the seventeenth century, 131; in the sixteenth century, 20

Inheritance, 72–73, 175; of Budé family, 274 n.26. *See also* Bequests; *Bourse française:* bequest; individuals by name

Inns of Geneva: Crescent *(Croissant),* 103–4, 233–34 n.44; Green Dog *(Chien Vert),* 103; housing refugees, 46, 70, 103–4; and innkeepers, 74; named, 255 n.30; used by the *Bourse française,* 74, 174. *See also* Crescent; Green Dog; *La Lanterne; La Tête Noire; Le Lyon Dore (Doré)*

Institutes of the Christian Religion by John Calvin, 81

Institutions: charitable, 116; in Geneva, 25; hospitals, 18; management of, 21; after Viking invasions, 20; and welfare, 24. *See also* institutions under individual names

Interest: on loans, low, 167; in welfare reform, 21–22; and international activities of the *Bourse française,* 50–69, 76, 93–94, 107–8, 111–13; and colporteurs, 86; and Reformed community, 160; and scope, 183; and setting and support, 25

Invalids: on welfare, 44

Inventories: of possessions, 74

Italians: aided by the *Bourse italienne,* 177–78, 262–63 n.19; congregation in Geneva meeting in the *Auditoire,* 257 n.8; currency of, 95; as deacons, 129; as donors to the *Bourse française,* 110; fund for, 119, 177–78, 183 *(see also Bourse italienne);* Galeazzo Caracciolo, 256 n.8; in Geneva, 129, 145–46, 177–78; language, translated by Charles de Jonvilliers, 248 n.82; as recipients of aid, 127; refuge to Geneva, 262 n.14; of Reformed leanings in Ferrara, 248 n.82; as refugees, 26, 129

Jacquet, Henry: as host of the Crescent, 103, 247 n.79, 255 n.30. *See also* Gon, Henry

Jail: for having criticized the *Bourse française,* 139

Jean (dressmaker): aid for his sick wife and a leather apron, 240 n.25

Jean (a Flemish person): aided to change air, 233 n.42

Jean (son of Alex, the widow of Pierre Herman): apprenticed, 143
Jehan de Lyon: as donor, 123
Jeremiah (the Prophet): commentaries of John Calvin on, 87
Jeremie, Monsieur de (Monsieur de Saint Germain): as donor, 123
Jesus Christ: in Genevan wills, 154; quoted by pastors of Geneva, 144. See also Christ; God
Jews: and Bourse française aid, 76, 129, 177, 241 n.34; and Bernardin de Candolle proposal that a group of settle in Geneva, 250–51 n.88
Joan, Charles de: and Jean de Borne, 238 n.4. See also Jonvilliers, Charles de
Job (the Prophet): and John Calvin's sermons, 235 n.53
Job retraining: by the Bourse française, 39
Jobs: taken by foreigners, 24
John, Gospel of: Jean Budé's thoughts about, 151. See also Bible citations
Jonniane[?]: as donor, 123
Jonvilliers, Charles de: and Agostino Mainard, 248 n.82; bequest of, 153, 248–49 n.82; biography of, 248–49 n.82; as bourgeois, 248 n.82; and Council of Two Hundred, 248 n.82; as deacon, 79, 84, 87, 89–91, 160, 248–49 n.82, 277 n.58; death, 87, 248–49 n.82; as donor, 123; as inhabitant of Geneva, 248 n.82; as Jean Budé's brother-in-law, 153, 160, 248–49 n.82; and Jean de Borne, 210; John Calvin's friend and editor, 87, 248 n.82; as John Calvin's secretary, 244–45 n.68; and Jules Bonnet, 87; ordered to present account books for audit, 252 n.10; his sister, 248 n.82. See also Joan, Charles de
Jonvilliers, Mademoiselle or Damoiselle Marie (Marye) de: children of, 152–54; as donor, 123; her maid banished for theft, 152; long life of, 157; as sister of Charles de Jonvilliers, 248 n.82; as wife of Jean Budé, Seigneur de Vérace, 123, 153
Jonvilliers, Rougier de: as father of Charles and Marie de Jonvilliers, 248 n.82. See also Jouan, Rougier de
Jouan, Rougier (Rogerin) de. See Jonvilliers, Rougier de
Journeymen: marrying their masters' widows, 42
Jovenon, Jean: as notary of Geneva and will of

Jean Budé, 155
Julienne: as Bourse française seamstress, 59, 190, 254 n.27
Jura Mountains: French refugees to Geneva and, 236 n.4

Knox, John, 23, 116, 128, 130, 145–46

La Barde (La Barie, La Barre), Mademoiselle de: as donor, 123
La Bessonaye, Monsieur de: a debt paid to by the Bourse française, 239 n.17
La Biellée, Nicolas de: his sale to Jean Budé, 155, 219
La Bonneterye, Monsieur de: as donor, 121, 123, 125. See also Bonneterye, Monsieur de; Cluny, Prevost de; La Botiere, François de
La Borde, Monsieur de: as donor, 123
La Botiere, François de, 121–23, 125. See also Bonneterye, Monsieur de; Cluny, Prevost de; La Bonneterye, Monsieur de
La Boullaye, Mademoiselle de: as donor, 123
La Boullaye, Monsieur de: as donor, 123. See also Eschallat, Françoys
La Bruere, Dame de (La Bruyere, Mademoiselle de): as donor, 123. See also Brachet, Damoiselle or Mademoiselle Francoise
La Bruyere, Seigneur de, 121, 123. See also Aubelin, Monsieur or Guillaume
La Chante, ministre de: as pastor aided, 265–66 n.43. See also Larz, Monsieur de; Léry, Jean de
La Côte de Saint André: husband of a woman in Geneva preaching in, 86
La Court, Monsieur de: and Bourse française transcription of the Psalms of Théodore de Bèze, 67–68, 198
Ladies of Charity: founded in France, concerned with the poor, 23
La Gard (La Garde), Monsieur de: as donor, 123
La Huguette: house rent for, 233 n.33
Laicization of welfare: as overall tendency, 21. See also Laity
Lailly, Isabeau de (widow of Guillaume Budé): arrival of, 149; discrepancy in date of her death, 158; her servant aided, 158. See also Budé, Guillaume: his widow; Budé, Jean: mother
Laity: charity of and the poor, 20; and philanthropy, 18; in welfare and education, 22.

See also Laicization of welfare

Lake Geneva: refugees transported on, 132

La Lanterne: an inn, 255 n.30

Lalir (Labier), Seigneur Thomas: as donor, 123

La Loubiere: aided by the *Bourse française* and the Genevan hospital, 147, 269 n.64; complaints about, 269 n.64; as a drunkard, thief, beggar, chatterer, 147

La Monnoye, *Maistre de:* as donor, 123. See also Le Monneraye *(Bretagne), Maistre de*

La Motte, Monsieur de, 121, 123–24. *See also* Bude, Louis; Mot, Monsieur de

La Nailliac (Malliac), Monsieur de: as donor, 123

Lanere, Seigneur: as donor, 123

Langlis (Langlys, Lanys), Monsieur: as donor, 123

Languedoc: bequest from a minister of, 239 n.16; Michiel Andre from, 250 n.84

La Planche, Monsieur de: as donor, 124, 272 n.7. *See also* Renier (Regnier), Louis

La Planche, Monsieur de, his cousin: as donor, 124, 272 n.7

La Pommeraye, Monsieur Charles de: as donor, 124

La Porte, Monsieur de (Claude or Eustache): as donor, 124

La Prade, Monsieur de: as donor, 124

Larceny: of Catherine Chevalier, 142; of Jeanne Varrot, 141. *See also* Chevalier (Chevallier), Catherine; Varrot, Jeanne

L'Archeveque: as donor, 124

La Ripantiere (La Repauldiere, Repautiere), Monsieur de: as donor, 124–25. *See also* Ribautrere, Monsieur de

La Roche, Mademoiselle de: as donor, 124, 254 n.16

La Roche, Seigneur Estienne de: as donor, 124

La Roche (des Roche[s]), Seigneur Francois de: as donor, 124

La Roche, Jean de. *See* Boulier, Jean

La Roche Chandieu, Antoine de, 121. *See also* Chandieu, Monsieur de

L'Artois, *seigneurie de:* region in France of the name of "Pas" of the Marquis of Feuquières, 250 n.85

Larz, Monsieur de (minister of *"La Chante"*): as pastor aided, 265 n.43. *See also* La Chante, *ministre de;* Léry, Jean de

Lassere (Lacere), Seigneur (de): debt paid to, 240 n.20; as donor, 124, 240 n.20.

La Tête Noire, 255 n.30. *See also* Inns of Geneva

Latin: and secretary to John Calvin, Charles de Jonvilliers, 248 n.82 *(see also* Jonvilliers, Charles de); signatures in of John Calvin, 35

La Touche, brother-in-law of Monsieur de: as donor, 124

La Touche, cousin of Monsieur de: as donor, 124

La Touche, Monsieur de: biography of, 246 n.77; as bourgeois, 246 n.77; as collector, 93, 215 n.5; as deacon, 84–85, 88; as donor, 109, 124; as noble, 78; and Monsieur de Saint Germain, 58, 189. *See also* Buynard, Francois

La Touche, Jehan de: as donor, 124

La Tour Mademoiselle de: as aid recipient, 134, 264 n.29

La Tour, Monsieur or Seigneur de: as donor, 123–24. *See also,* Fay, Estienne de

Laurdes (Laurere), Jehan: as donor, 124

Laufmois, *feu* Monsieur David: as donor, 124. *See also* David, *feu* Monsieur

Laulnaz (Laulnay), Master Jean, *Ministre de Saint Mozan,* 265–66 n.43

Laundry: and *Bourse française,* 174

Laurent de Normandie. *See* Normandie, Laurent (Lauren) de

Lausanne: auction of church property in, 164; as destination of travelers supported by the *Bourse française,* 55–56, 58, 190; refugees from, 131–32

La Valleyere, Monsieur de: as donor, 124. *See also* Valleyere (Vallayere), Monsieur de

La Vernarde, Martha: as heiress, 113, 258–59 n.18

Laws: against begging, 117, 260 n.30; for bequests to be registered, 260–61 n.36; concerning secret wills, 275 n.32; dividing welfare responsibilities, 262–63 n.19; sumptuary, 141. *See also* Church orders; Legislation; Ordinances

Lay people in the church. *See* Laity

Lay preachers: in Reformation France, 135

Le Beuf, Jean: house rent for, 233 n.33

Le Blanc, Master Jean: as pastor aided, 265–66 n.43

Le Blanc, Messire Lambert: appeal for clemency for, 275 n.33; burned for sodomy, 156, 260 n.32; as donor, 124; and Jean Budé, 156–57; soliciting boys for homosexual acts, 117, 156

Le Bouc, Barbe (of Berry): as widow of Louis Budé and Guy de Serignac, 158

Le Coint: as donor, 124. *See also* Boynville (Boinville, Boyenville), Monsieur de; Le Cointe, Guillaume

Le Cointe (Le Comte), Guillaume, 121; as inhabitant of Geneva, 261 n.40. *See also* Boynville (Boinville, Boyenville), Monsieur de; Le Coint

Le Court, Monsieur (Andre?): as donor, 124

Le Drerur (Derier), Nicolas: as donor, 124.

Le Fer, Monsieur Nicolas: as donor, 124

Legacies: to the *Bourse française*, 73, 160; collection of, 119; of David (de) Busanton, 33–34, 36, 169–70; as extraordinary contributions, 97–98. *See also* Bequests; *Bourse française*: bequest; *Bourse française*: inheriting property; individuals by name

Legislation: on welfare, Nuremberg, 163. *See also* Church orders; Laws; Ordinances

Le Grain, Dame Nycole (widowed by Louis André): will of, 250 n.84

Le Grand, Seigneur Pierre: as donor, 124

Le Grieur, Martin: and consistory of Geneva, 225 n.30

Leipzig: Nuremberg welfare ordinances printed in, 163

Leisnig: city council control of endowment for the poor in, 23, 163; common chest of, 12, 162–63; Martin Luther and, 23, 162–63; parish assembly of, 163–64

Leleu(?), Monsieur: and apprentice for Pierre Heurtant, 231 n.18

Le Lyon Dore (Doré), 255 n.30. *See also* Inns of Geneva

Lemaire, Monsieur: and John Calvin's sermons consigned to the *Collège* of Geneva, 235 n.55

Le Maire, Simon: as auditor, 252 n.10

Le Maistre. Claude: as donor, 124

Le Marquis (de Vico). *See* Caracciolo (Carracciolo), Galeazzo; Vico, Marquis de

l'Emery (Lemerey, Jean de; l'Hemery; l'Humery; Lumery), Monsieur de: as donor, 124

Le Monneraye (Bretagne), 123. *See also* La Monnoye, *Maistre de*

Lenfant, Bailly: as donor, 124

Le Piccart, Jean: debt repaid from his estate, 240 n.19

Le Picque, *Maistre* Pierre: reimbursed, 242 n.40

Lerin, Jean: aid for his wife in childbed, 233 n.40

Le Roux, Master Jean: as schoolboy, 68, 198

Le Roy, Jean: wife of, as aid recipient, 71, 238 n.3

Léry, Jean de: aided, 265 n.43, biography of, 265–66 n.43; as bourgeois, 265 n.43; as minister of La Charité, 265 n.43; as missionary pastor to Nevers, France, 265–66 n.43. *See also* Larz, Monsieur de

Lescaze, Bernard: and *procès criminels*, 268 n.58

Lescuyere, Nicolle: recommended by collectors of Meaux, 241 n.31

Le Secretaire, Monsieur, 125. *See also* Peroulies, Monsieur le Secretaire

Letters: of recommendation, 76

Le Villain, Nocholas: as donor, 124

Levitical Code: as precedent for charity, 18

Leviticus 19:9–10: on gleanings of the field and leftover grapes, 18

Lholme (near "Aulthing"): Jean Boulier from, 266–67 n.47

Liege: Jean de Marigny from, 261 n.40

Lieutenant of justice (an official of Geneva), 73; and Jean Bude's will, 155; and money to the deacons, 240 n.20; and a *procès criminel*, 268 n.61

Life expectancy: of deacons, 77

Linens: lent to the poor, 142; not returned, 271 n.70

Lisle, Seigneur de: as donor, 122, 124. *See also* Du Mas, Jehan

Literacy: as a barrier, 134, 181; and the *Bourse française*, 134, 146; encouraging social mobility, 134, 166–67; promoted by deacons, 179, 181; in Protestant areas, 166–67

Livre des Anglois: English deacons in Geneva in, 129

Livre des Bourgeois: of Geneva, 47

Livres des habitants de Genève: able-bodied males in, 177; few aid recipients in, 177; documenting refugees, 131; Guillaume Budé, father of Jean Budé, 149; new inhabitants in, 132–33; first three deacons in, 169

Loans: by *Bourse française*, 40, 128, 176; by

Charles Lourdois and Jeanne Varrot, 215–17; guarantors of, 180 (see also Guarantors); interest on, 167; interest-free, 161; in Leisnig, 163; preferred to handouts, 39, 180

Locksmith: and Bourse française, 99; wife of ordered to leave, 144

Lonnex, Amblard de: sale of land by to Jean Budé, 155, 219

Lonnex, Nicholas de: sale of land by to Jean Budé, 155, 219

Lonnir, Jehan de: as donor, 124

Lord: punishing for ignoring sodomy, 212–14. See also God; Sodom and Gomorrah

Lord's Supper. See Communion

Lorestz: as donor, 124. See also Forestz, Monsieur de

Lorraine: Pslams of Théodore de Bèze in 235 n.54; refugees from aided by the Bourse allemande, 262–63 n.19

Lot: saved from Sodom and Gomorrah, 156

Louhan: a young man from recommended by John Calvin, 230 n.5

Louis XII (king of France): his daughter, Renée of Ferrara, 248 n.82

Louis XIV (king of France): Geneva, and, 136; and revocation of the Edict of Nantes, 131

Lourdois, Charles: accusing others of wrongdoing, 141; as aid recipient, 215–18, 268–69 nn. 62 and 63; as inhabitant of Geneva, 269 n.63; as cloth fuller and husband of Jeanne Varrot, 141; his wife's thefts, 215–17, 268 n.61

Love of neighbor: and John Calvin, 169

Low Countries: aid recipients from, 129, 262 n.11; Bruges in, 116; deacon from, 83 and Juan Luis Vives's welfare proposal, 21; Reformed church in, 13; refugees from, 129; and welfare ordinances of Charles V, 163

Lullin, Jean: paternity suit against, 255 n.30

Luther, Martin: and church property rehearsal to donors' families, 23, 116; on confraternities, 166; and education, 11; excommunication of, 162; and Leisnig, 23, 162–63; and poor relief, 12; and Wartburg Castle, 162; and Wittenberg, 161–63

Lutheran: church appropriation of Catholic property, 163–64; church in Germany, 13; church in the Holy Roman Empire, 28; church in Scandinavia, 13, 28; defined, 13;

Nuremberg welfare reform, 21–23; pastors' and schoolteachers' salaries, 23; protection by the state, 28. See also Luther, Martin

Lymes, Noble Adrian de: as heir, 258 n.16

Lyons, France: adoption in, 43; Artus Chauvin publisher in, 250 n.86; and Bourse française travelers, 55–56, 58, 189; collection in, 93, 251–52 n.5, confraternities in rural, 277 n.13; donations from, 106, 111; Edict of Nantes, Huguenots not allowed to worship in, 131; hospital in, 43, 146; Huguette Martin of, "Messieurs" requesting clemency, 140; Jean Boulier pastor in, 138, 266 n.44; and Jean Singlaut, 67, 198; Paris Prostat and his wife in, 250 n.86, 254 n.26; Reformed church in, 76, 131; welfare reform in, 165, 260 n.34

Macart, Jehan: as donor, 124. See also Maccard, Monsieur

Maccard, Monsieur: deceased, 65, 196; New Testaments from to the Bourse française, 58, 64–65, 189, 195–96. See also Macart, Jehan

Macon: minister aided, 265 n.43

Madelaine: as mother of Renaud and Jean Anjorrant, 247 n.81

Madelaine, Church of the: exterior of, 19

Magisterial reformers, 167

Magny, Mademoiselle: keeping a child and a wet nurse, 231 n.13

Mailet, Clement: his daughter's school fees, 231–32 n.21

Maillaiges (Maillaignes), Monsieur de: as donor, 124

Maillane (Maillain, Maillame, Maillant), Seigneur de, 124–25. See also Percellet, Seigneur Ardoin de; Porceller, Monsieur or Seigneur de

Maillard, Guillaume: as draper, aid recipient, 147, 272 n.91; as haberdasher from Rouen and inhabitant of Geneva, husband of the wife of the deceased Louis Flambert, 147

Mainardi, Agostino: L'anatomie de la Messe, 248 n.82

Maldonnade, Madame (Pierre's wife?): as donor, 124

Maldonnade, Nicolas (the brother of Pierre Maldonnade): as donor, 124. See also Maldonnade, Monsieur (de)

Maldonnade, Pierre: bequest of, 243 n.46; criticism of, 241 n.30; as deacon, 75, 83–84,

87–88, 226n.11, 229n.30, 241–42n.37; death of, 88, 241n.30; 241–42n.37; donation from his house guest, 243n.45, 272–73n.7; as donor, 75, 109, 124, 241n.30; and English donor, 263n.25; from Low Countries, 245n.72; and devil, 75; wife of, 80, 124; will of, 80, 241–42n.37

Mallet, Clement: his widow renting a bed, 233n.33

Malzieu, Spectable Marcial: as pastor at Saint of Marveroux(?), and Jean de Borne, 209–10

Management: of welfare institutions, 21

Mangiron (Maugiron, Catholic governor of Lyons), Monsieur de: his niece as donor, 124

Marcaiz, Francois: as procurator for Jean Dallamont (Dalamont), 258n.16

Marcel, Pierre: his widow, foster mother, 243n.50

Mares, Nicolas des: loan to for a coat, 233n.35

Marguerite: as mother of Raoul and Claude Anjorrant, 247n.81

Marguerite (widow of Jean Gadovin): as aid recipient, 265n.43

Marheron (Macheroy) (cousin of Jean Budé?): as donor, 124

Marian exiles: in Geneva, 132: from Frankfort, 261n.2

Marie (servant of Jean Budé's mother): in childbed, 276n.49

Marie (widow of Nicolas Cherisseau, a fool): and Genevan hospital, 142, 269–70n.67

Marigny, Catherine de: as wife of Guillaume Le Cointe, 261n.40

Marigny, Jean de (of Liege): as father of Catherine de Marigny, 261n.40

Marillac (Marillat), Monsieur (Pierre?): as donor, 124

Marillat, Monsieur, 124. See also Marillac, Monsieur

Marin(s), Catherine des or Damoiselle: death and will of, 247n.79; as wife of Jean Dalamont, 247n.79

Marin(s), Jean des: as father of Catherine de Brie in France, 247n.79

Marins, Damoiselle Jacqueline des: as heiress, 258n.16

Marins, Damoiselle Loyse des: as heiress, 258n.16

Marital discord: and consistory, 140,

268n.57; of Huguette Martin and Jean Boulier, 138, 140

Marne, Jean: as hospital tailor, 233n.35

Marot, Clement: Psalms of, 237n.12

Marquis (de Vico), 121. See also Caracciolo, Galeazzo; Le Marquis (de Vico)

Marriage: contracts of, 26, 79; of refugees, 144–45, 271n.80

Marrot, Monsieur: as donor, 124

Marseilles: Candolle family of, 250n.88

Martha: as daughter of Louis Flambert, 147

Martin, Huguette: as aid recipient, 140; conforming to pastors and elders, 140, 143; and consistory, 140, 268n.57; marital discord of, 138, 140; as wife of Jean Boulier, 138, 140

Martyrologist: Jean Crespin as, 20, 43

Martyrs: Jean Vernon, 109; wives and families of, 44, 49

Marveroux (?), Saint of: Spectable Marcial Malzieu from, 209–10

Mascons (Macon, Masons): minister of, 69, 200

Mass, Catholic: and Protestants, 145

Massacre of Saint Bartholomew's Day, 25, 109–10; refugees from, 25, 131, 136

Massot, Monsieur Joachim: as father of Samuel, 265–66n.43

Massot, Samuel: as child aided, 265–66n.43

Master, Pierre: as singer, 67, 198

Mattress: for poor widow, 142

Mattresses: from Bourse française, 179

Mattress makers: as piecework employees, 100

Maurice, Guillaume: as Parisian, 75; and consistory, 241n.28

Maurin, Barthelemy: as judge at Sablieres, 208–9

McKee, Elsie: on diaconate and almsgiving, 223n.1

Meadows: purchased by Jean Budé, 155, 219

Meaux, France: arbiters in, 258n.16; Charles Lourdois of, 215–16, 268nn. 62 and 63; collectors of, recommendation, 241n.31; Jean Varrot from, 215–16; Reformed church of, deacons, elders, pastors, 113

Medical care: bloodletting and, 99; and Bourse francaise, 45–46, 98–99, 172–73, 179; of Charles Lourdois and Jeanne Varrot, 215–18; in Geneva, 267n.52; inadequacy of in sixteenth century, 138; and welfare, 45. See also Apothecaries; Barber-surgeons; Doctors; Surgeons

Medieval: poor law, 259 n.25; welfare changes, 22

Meigret (Megret), Laurent, (Le Magnifique Meigret): as donor, 124

Melier, Sarra: thanking deacons, 142, 270 n.69

Mendicancy: and direct handouts, 117; as part of a religious way of life, 22; Protestant Reformation's influence upon, 117. *See also* Beggars; Begging; Mendicant Orders

Mendicant orders: Dominicans, 22; exempted from legislation against begging, 22; Franciscans, 22; religious, 117

Mental illness: *Bourse francaise* aid, 142, 269–70 n.67; fool, 269–70 n.67; in hospitals, 20; melancholy girl, 142, 270 n.68; not understood by the deacons, 182; in sixteenth century, 177

Mentality: of Jean Budé, 156–57

Merchants: Estienne Trembley, 93; Louis André, 250 n.84

Merit: in giving alms, 117; and God's reward as material possessions, 167; as incentive for almsgiving, 165

Merlin, Mangis: as aid recipient, 134, 264 n.29

Merne, Izabeau de: as wife of Antoine Popillon, 246 n.78

Messengers: of *Bourse française*, 56, 58, 168, 173, 181, 183, 189; and Company of Pastors of Geneva, 168

Messieurs: Genevan city councilors turning out the poor, 144

Metz: Claude Francois, pastor of, 265–66 n.43; and Psalms of Théodore de Bèze, 235n.54

Michau (Michault; Micaux), Barthelemy (miller of Provence): as aid recipient, 147

Middle Ages: Venice in, 139. *See also* Medieval

Mile, Loys: binding books, 67, 197

Military defense: paid for with church endowments, 164

Miller: Barthelemy Michau of Provence as, 147

Minet, Bonaventure: as pastor aided, 265 n.43

Ministers: as arbitrators, 113; as church officers, 27, 29; as helpers of the poor, 33; as legal procurators, 113; of Mascons (Mason), 69, 200; Master Jacques Chapel, 59, 190; prestige of, 71; as refugees, 135–36; sent to France, 53; sent to Gascony, 58, 190; as servants, 30; as term interchangea-

ble with pastors, 30; wives of, 53, 59, 67, 190, 197. *See also* Pastors; Pastors of Geneva

Minority church: survival of, 28. *See also* Reformed Church

Minutes: of deacons' meetings, 26, 40, 270–71 n.69

Missionary: *Bourse française* as, 50, 87, 181; pastors, former deacons, 225 n.7 (*see also* Pastors: missionaries); pastors from France, 135. *See also Bourse française:* missionary activities

Molins in Burgundy: Antoine Popillon from, 246 n.78

Mollet, Claude: as collector, deacon, 93

Monasteries: and education, 18, 163; in Strasbourg, 165; and welfare, 18; in Zurich, 164

Monks: in Geneva, 145–46

Monnaz, minister of: Pierre Ralliet as, pastor aided, 265–66 n.43

Monon, Ysabeau (Madame *la conseilliere de* Scienous or Chinon, widow of Charles Quinal): as donor, 124

Montaulban (Montauldan), Jehan Alban de: as donor, 120. *See also* Alban, Jehan

Montcles, Master Antoine de (doctor): as aid recipient, 264 n.32

Montigne, Jehan de, 124. *See also* Montiguy, Monsieur de; Villiers, Monsieur or Seigneur de

Montiguy, Monsieur de: as donor, 124. *See also* Montiguy, Jehan de; Villiers, Monsieur or Seigneur de

Montlhery, Antoine: and procuration, 240 n.21

Montrohe, Mademoiselle de: as donor, 124

Moratel, minister of: as pastor aided, 265–66 n.43

More, Thomas, 21

Morel, François de, 122; as pastor brother of Marguerite de Morel, 276 n.57. *See also* Colonge, Sire de

Morel (Moret), Leonard: as pastor aided, 265–66 n.43

Morel, Marguerite de: bequest of, 158, 160, 276 n.57; biography of, 276–77 n.57; and *Bourse française*, 157–58; and Catherine Budé, 220–21; and François Budé, 276 nn. 56 and 57; will of, 220–22. *See also* Budé, François: his wife

Moreli, Jehan, 126. *See also* Villiers (Villers),

Monsieur or Seigneur de

Morin, Pierre: as donor, 124

Mot (Mon, Mont), Monsieur de: as donor, 124. *See also* Budé, Louis; La Motte (La Mothe), Monsieur de

Mothers: ill, child care for, 173

Moudon: council of sending money for pastors of *pays de Vaud*, 110

Moulins, Monsieur de: as donor, 124

Museum of History of the Reformation, 13

Nantes: Edict of, 131; and refugees, 25

Naples: Galeazzo Caracciolo from, 256 n.8

Navet, Jean: as velvet maker of Tours, aid recipient, banished, 147

Neuchâtel: city council of, 110

Nevers, France: Jean de Léry as missionary pastor in, 265 n.43

New Testament: bound for the *Bourse française*, 54, 58, 61, 64–66, 68, 189, 192, 195–98; doctrine in, 154; Greek, 59; purchased by the *Bourse française*, 58, 65–66, 189, 195–97; terms *pastor* and *deacon* in, 30. *See also* Bible citations

New World: deaconesses in, 82; Presbyterians, Puritans in, 13

Nielle, Esprit: criticizing the *Bourse française*, 139–40

Nîmes, France: bequest from a minister near, 239 n.16; Catholic bishop of, 23; hospital of, 23; poor man departing for, 65, 196; Reformed congregations of, 76; town near, 113

Nobles: as collectors, 93; as deacons, 172; not social revolutionaries, 101

Noel: as baker, 68, 199

Normandie, Laurent (Lauren) de: biography of, 236 n.4; and *Bourse française*, 51–53, 57–67, 189–98, 237 nn. 7, 8, 9, and 12; as collector, 86, 93, 251–52 n.5; and Council of Two Hundred, 236 n.4; his death from the plague, 20, 236 n.4; as donor and activist, 20, 109, 125; as entrepreneur, 86; family papers of, 26; as financier of books and colporteurs, 20, 51–52, 86, 109, 168; his house, 52–54, 58–66, 189–97; and John Calvin, 151, 236 n.4, 242 n.42; ministers sent by, 53; paying for child care, 86; as possible deacon, 86; and Théodore de Bèze, 236 n.4

Normandy: Company of Pastors of Geneva

and, 225 n.3; young man in voyage to, 56, 64, 194

Norway: *Bourse allemande* responsible for refugees from 262–63 n.19

Notaries: and absence of documents for the poor, 127; and deacons, 84, 86; Guillaume (de) Trie, 157; Jean Jovenon, 155; Jean Ragueau, and Jean de Borne's inheritance, 208–10; and legal transactions, 78; and minute or draft of documents, 51, 86, 111, 119, 156; and protocols, 156; recording donations, 112, 114, 119; reminding clients of city welfare, 119, 175

Notre-Dame-La-Neuve: illustration of as the *Auditoire,* 130

Nour'bre, Monsieur de (Normandie?): as donor, 125

Noyon, France: John and Antoine Calvin and Laurent de Normandie from, 236 n.4, 249 n.83

Nuegler (Nueglno, Nurglne), Vincent: as donor, 125

Nuns: as aid recipients, 255 n.33; in Geneva, 145–46; at the hospital of Lyons, 146; and Jean Crespin, 104, 255 n.33; rescued, 111

Nuremberg: break of with Catholicism, 163; collection bags, plates, boxes in, 163; common chest of, 163; as model for welfare reform, 21, 163

Nurses: of *Bourse française,* 80; caring for women in childbed, 81; of the sick, 18; wet, 100–101. *See also* Wet nurses

Nursing mothers; death of, 75

Obmann: as overseer of monastic property in Zurich, 164

Ochino, Bernardino: influential over Galeazzo Caracciolo, 256 n.8

Offices of the Reformed Church: and *Bourse française,* 32; John Calvin's ideas on, 36; pastors, elders, deacons, doctor (teachers), 27, 29, 70; as return to early church practice, 30. *See also* Church offices; Deacons; Doctors: as teachers; Elders; Ministers; Pastors

Old Testament: commentaries on, John Calvin's, 248 n.82; doctrine in, 154. *See also* Leviticus

Olivier, *Maistre:* as donor, 125

Orange: *Bourse française* responsibility for refugees from, 262–63 n.19; Catherine Jeanne, heiress, from, 258–59 n.18

Orders, religious: mendicants, 37
Ordinances: of *Bourse française* of 5 January 1581 in the 1582 account books, 71, 74, 77, 79, 83, 87, 98, 104–6, 171, 206–7; of Geneva in 1541, ecclesiastical, 27, 170; of Geneva, of 7 December 1568, limitation of reception of refugees to those with a profession or craft, 40; of Leisnig, for a common chest, 162; welfare, 22, 161–63. *See also* Laws
Ordinary accounts: of *Bourse française,* 57
Organist: paid by common chest, 162
Orgier, Anthoine: given money for a Bible, 66, 196
Origins. *See* Geographic origins
Orleans: aid recipient from, 147; and collection, 93, 251–52 n.5; and donations, 107; Francois Du Clare and, 122; John Calvin and Laurent de Normandie in, 236 n.4
Orphanages: in the sixteenth century, 42
Orphans: and *Bourse française,* 43, 57, 176–77; Eleazard Bourdier, 265 n.43; foster care of, 42, 81, 173, 179; in Grenoble, and women's confraternity, 166; in hospitals, 20; infants, abandoned, 18; in Leisnig, 161–62; on welfare, 37
Orthography: not fixed, 120

Padua: Charles de Jonvilliers and Louis Budé studying law in, 248 n.82
Paleographer: Henri Bordier as, 26
Paleography: and bastard cursive handwriting, 85, 95; difficulty of, 44; and John Calvin's signature, 35
Pallai, Monsieur de: as donor, 125. *See also* Falai(?), Monsieur de; Fallaix; Salai, Monsieur de
Papacy, 113, 144
Paré (Paret), Monsieur (de): biography of, 246 n.78; buying Bibles, 65, 68, 196, 198; binding New Testaments, 68, 198; as deacon, 88–90; as donor, 125; and Laurent de Normandie, 64–65, 196, 198; in Plainpalais, 240 n.27; reimbursed, 67, 197–98. *See also* Popillon, Anthoine (Antoine)
Paris (copyist of John Calvin's sermons). *See* Prostat, Paris
Paris, France: book censorship in, faculty of theology, 264 n.28; *Collège de Montaigu* in, 149; deacon from, 83; donations from, 107; and Edict of Nantes, 131; good man from bought a Psalter, 237 n.14; Guillaume

Maurice from, 75; Jean Budé from, 149, 154, 229 n.30, 272 n.1; Parlement of, 220–21, 276 n.57; persecution in, 44; Pierre Cousturier returning to, 67, 197; Psalters of Théodore de Bèze to, 54, 69, 199; Reformed Church in, 131; travelers to supported by the *Bourse française,* 55, 67–69, 197–99; University of, Charles de Jonvilliers, 248 n.82
Parishes: and endowment, 23; and the poor, 18
Parlement de Paris: burning Laurent de Normandie in effigy, 236 n.4; Jean Anjorrant and, 220–21, 276 n.57
Parran, Jean: disbursement to by order of the Company, 67, 198
Part-time help, 70
Pas: in *France Protestante,* 250 n.85
Passersby, 108, 111; *Bourse française* handout to, 229 n.1; religious affiliation of, 139; stay of, 38; subvention of, 105, 206. *See also* Travelers; Viaticum
Pastors: as aid recipients, 53, 135–36, 138, 178; and alms boxes, 109, 118; children of aided, 265–66 n.43; and church finances, 225 n.3; on consistories, 25; dignity of office of, 136; as donors, 109, 119–20; education of, 135; fleeing persecution, 44, 135, 264 n.34; as former deacons, 225 n.7; fugitive, 110; Genevan Company of, 57; inadequate number of, 135–36; and inflation, 110; Lutheran salaries for, 23; malcontent, 136–138; at Meaux, France, 258 n.16; as missionaries to France, 50, 135; as one of four Reformed church offices, 27, 29 (*see also* Offices of the Reformed church); ordered to leave France, 136; and the poor, 115; refugee, 135–36, 183; and requests for advice, 94; room rent for, 64, 195, 264 n.33; salaries of, 23, 136, 162–63, 168; as shepherds, 30; Spectable Jean Tarouch(?) of Sablieres, France, 209; Spectable Marcial Malzieu, Saint of Marveroux, 209–10; surplus of, 135–36; widows of, aided, 265–66 n.43; of Wittenberg, 162. *See also* Ministers; Pastors of Geneva
Pastors of Geneva: and the *Bourse française,* 12, 70–71, 135, 143; advising deacons, 105, 113, 120, 207; assigned to deacons, 105–6, 171–72, 207; *Bourse française* money available to, 168; and city council of Geneva, 144, 167; and consistory, 142; contacts of,

24; and effort to evangelize France, 183; electing deacons, 83; familiar with the poor, 120; families of aided, 49–50; families of in Geneva, 53; French, 24, 168; and Huguette Martin, 140, 143; inundating Geneva, 110; and Jean Budé, 152; Jean de Borne, 209–10; messages to, 94; preferring that deacons handle financial matters, 29, 225 n.3; pressuring the city council to protect the poor, 167; recommending disbursements, 39, 55–63, 65–69, 76, 119–20, 189–200; role of in the *Bourse française*, 119–20, 170–72; salaries of, 136, 168; signing account books, 105, 207; soliciting funds, 111; urging limits on interest on loans, 167; on welfare, 136, 138; willing to send away drunks and debauchers of youth, 144. *See also* Ministers; Pastors

Patronage, 100

Paul IV, Pope: of Caraffa family, Galeazzo Caracciolo's great uncle, 256 n.8

Pawning: placing items as surety, 67, 197

Pay: as low for women, 173–74

Payerne: and city council money for fugitive pastors, 110

Pays de Vaud: pastors of, 110

Pensions: in Europe, 138; in Florence, 267 n.51; lack of, 40; of Pastor Jean Boulier, 138

Percellet, Seigneur Ardoin de, 124. *See also* Maillane; Porceller

Perlier(?), Monsieur: and prisoner at Grenoble, 62, 193

Peroulies (Polier, Poliet, Poulier), Monsieur le Secretaire: as donor, 125. *See also* Le Secretaire, Monsieur

Perrin, Ami: defeat of, 82

Perrin, Master Jacques (student), 112: bequest of, 257–58 n.15

Perrinists: as enemies of John Calvin, 109

Persecution: as cause of refugee status, 24, 44; Didier Rousseau fleeing, 264 n.28; influencing decisions on welfare, 49; in Paris, 25, 55–56, 59, 190; pastors fleeing, 135–36; 264 n.34; of Reformed Christians, 25, 182; refugees fleeing, 128; religious, 152, 181, 183

Personne, Seigneur of Sieur Jehan (Jean): as donor, 125; and girl in the Genevan hospital, 234 n.45; reimbursed, 66, 68, 197, 199

Personnel of the *Bourse française:* apothecary, barber-surgeon, doctor, 98; paid, 98–104.

See also Piecework; individual names, crafts, and professions

Pesthouse: outside the city walls, 99. *See also* Plainpalais

Petit, Loys *(espicier):* as donor, 125

Philanthropy, 175; and *Bourse française*, 17; of David (de Busanton, 33; and endowment of hospitals, the poor, 20; Genevan, 26, 118–19, 255–56 n.1; of John Calvin's contemporaries, 27; and lay people, 18; motivation for, power, social pressure, prestige and recognition, 118–19; Protestant, 110–11, 116, 160, 259–60 n.26. *See also* Benevolence; Charity

Physicians: and *Bourse française*, 139; and Venetian confraternities, 139, 166

Picardy: Laurent de Normandy and John Calvin from, 236 n.4

Picot, Nicolas (apothecary): as donor, 125

Piecework: for the *Bourse française*, 97, 100–101, 104, 173, 254–55 n.28; sewing, 42

Piedmont: *Bourse italienne* responsible for refugees from, 262–63 n.19; preacher's book from, 248 n.82

Pierre, *Maistre (le tourneur):* as donor, 125

Pierre, Master: and Psalms put to music, 67, 198

"Pignerol": *Bourse italienne* to aid refugees from 262–63 n.19

Pigney: and Genevan tax law, 259 n.24

Pilgrimage: Geneva as stopover on, 38

Pilgrims: helped, 38

Pistoles: as currency, 69, 200

Pitet, Jeremie: and Sarra Melier abandoned, 270 n.69

Place du Molard, 103

Place Saint Pierre: poor people on, 67–68, 198

Plague, bubonic: in account books, 151; Didier Rousseau and his wife and, 141, 147, 264 n.28; hospital for, 99; in fourteenth–seventeenth century, 20; two children sick with, 86. *See also* Crespin, John: his death; Normandie, Laurent: his death

Plainchamps, Monsieur de: as donor, 125

Plainpalais: deacons' visits to, 240 n.27, locksmith in, 99, 254 n.25; woman of buried, 257 n.10

Pledges: to the *Bourse française*, 109–11, 114–15, 158, 276 n.56

Plessis (Plessix), Mademoiselle du: as aid recipient, 134, 264 n.29; selling Bibles to the *Bourse française*, 67, 198; receiving money by order of the Company of Pastors, 66, 197

Poland: *Bourse allemande* responsible for refugees from, 129, 262–63 n.19

Policing: and begging, 117

Polity: in Geneva as prototype for Reformed churches, 28–29

Polliens, Pierre: his vineyard sold to Jean Budé, 155, 219

Pommier: ancient abbey near Geneva, and aid, 71, 238 n.3

Poor boxes: in churches, 22, 109, 118–19, 167; in Geneva, 34; in Wittenberg, 162

Poor houses: and confraternities, 139, 166

Poor law: medieval, 259 n.25

Poor people: aided in exchange for their possessions, 174; alms to as merit, 176; bedridden, 77, 169; Bibles and Psalters for, 32; and books, 54; and *Bourse française*, 47, 57–69, 177, 189–200; carrying messages, 173; and Catholic religious orders, 22; as Christ incarnate, 118; Christian duty toward, 33; chronic, 37, 133, 178; and the church, 17; and the common chest, 161; confraternity care of, 22, 166; and David (de) Busanton, 169; deacons and, 36, 71–72, 75, 139, 142, 146, 172–73; derelict or deserving, 138–39; description of, 37; in early modern Europe, 127, 262 n.6; employed, 70, 101, 173, 176; encouraged to do undesirable work, 144; extraordinary expenditures for, 58–59; and food riots, 143; foreign, 24, 182–83; of Geneva, 11; and Genevan city council, 167; and Genevan donors, 175–76 (*see also* Philanthropy); geographic origins of, 26; and hospital, 30; housed by donors, 86, 176; and inflation, 110; intransigent, 37; and John Calvin, 27, 48, 170; and Laurent de Normandie, 52, 59–65, 190–96; in Leisnig, 161–63; and literacy, 181; local, 182; and masses, 76; medical care of, 173; monthly contributions toward, 167; morale of, 146; not generators of permanent legal documents, 127; and pastors, 120, 170; personal possessions of, 74; and Psalters profit, 48, 55; public image of, 178; punishment of, 142; salvageable from poverty, 178; shamefaced, 166, 169, 178–79, 181 (*see* Shamefaced poor); shuttled from one welfare fund to another, 129; with special skills, 173; stereotypes of, 138; taught new skills, 176; and Théodore de

Bèze, 48; tolerance of, 183; transient, 21; visited if sick, 139; vulnerable, 144–46; and welfare, 38, 183; widows as, 32; women's care of, 81; and Zurich convent property, 164. *See also* Poverty

Poor relief: Anabaptist, 167; Catholic, 166–68; in Leisnig, 162–63; Lutheran, 160–64; in Nuremberg, new system in 1522, 163; and Reformed church, 164–66; in Strasbourg, 164–65; in Wittenberg, Luther, 161–63; in Zurich, 164. See also *Bourse allemande; Bourse française; Bourse italienne;* Social welfare; Welfare

Pope: Leo X, excommunication of Luther by, 162

Popillon, Antoine: as bourgeois, 246 n.78; biography of, 246 n.78; as businessman, 78; his children's deaths, 246–47 n.78; as deacon, 88–90, 112; delivering a bequest, 257–58 n.15; as donor, 109, 125. *See also* Paré (Paret), Monsieur de

Popism: accusations of, 141

Population: of Genevan refugees in 1550s and 1560s, 181; growth of, 20–21, 37

Porceller, Monsieur or Seigneur de: as donor, 124–25. *See also* Maillane, Seigneur de; Percellet, Seigneur Ardoin de

Portuguese: as money, 59, 190

Pose: land measurement in, 155; land sale to Jean Budé in, 155, 219

Potier, (Pothier), Bailiff Nicolas: as collector, 93, 251–52 n.5; bringing money from Orleans, 93; as donor, 125

Potle(?), Nicolas: his widow and children given travel money, 230 n.7. *See also* Potier, Bailiff Nicolas

Poundin, Abel: opinion in case of sodomy, 211–14

Poverty: Calvinist struggle against, 167; causes of, 179; and crime, 261 n.4; elimination of, 17, 117; medieval Catholic and modern Protestant institutional view of, 118; and recipients of aid, 74; as a virtue, 167

Prade, Monsieur: as donor, 125

Prayer: of deacons with the poor, 77; before Genevan hospital Sunday distributions, 225 n.10

Preachers: of Geneva, 109; lay, in early Reformation France, 135

Preaching: Genevan *Bourse française* giving out money after, 60, 191

Predestination, 154

Pregnancy: of Huguette Martin, 140, 268 n.47; of serving girls at Geneva's inns, 255 n.30

Presbyterians: in the New World, 13

Presle(s), Mademoiselle de: as donor, 125

Pretended Reformed religion: French edicts against, 263 n.23

Prevost, David: as bourgeois, son of Guillaume, 245–46 n.75

Prevost, François: as donor, 121, 125. See also Beaulieu, Monsieur de

Prevost, Guillaume, 84: biography of, 245–46 n.75; as bourgeois and son of Jean Prevost, 245 n.75; his daughter's death, 245–46 n.75; as deacon, 88; as donor, 125; as John Calvin's friend, 245 n.75; as *passementier*, 245–46 n.75; on *rue Pelleteryre*, 245–46 n.75. See also Saint (Sainct) Germain (Jeremie), Monsieur or Seigneur de

Prevost, Jacques: as bourgeois and son of Guillaume Prevost, 245 n.75

Prevost, Jean (of Paris): as father of Guillaume Prevost, 245 n.75

Prevost de Cluny. See Bonneterye, Monsieur de; La Bonneterye, Monsieur de; La Botiere, François de; Cluny, Prevost de

Prices: calculated from account books, 26–27; fair, 174

Pride: and John Calvin, 248 n.82

Priesthood of all believers, 28

Priests: as aid recipients, 146; and deacons, 30; retrained, 39

Prieur (Prien), Seigneur Guillaume: as donor, 125

Prignault, Adrian de, 126. See also Briquemault, Seigneur de; Priquemaut; Villemongez, Monsieur

Prince-bishop: of Geneva, 165

Printers: in Geneva, 54, 113, 237 n.21; Jean Boulier, apprenticeship, 140; Jean Crespin, 43, 109; Pierre Du Chesne from "*Chatre sous Montlhéry près Paris*," 272 n.89; of Psalters, 55; Pyramus Candolle, 55; Robert Estienne, 109, 113; Thomas Courteau, 240 n.24; widows of, 42. See also Publishers; Publishing

Priquemaut, Seigneur de, 126. See also Briquemault, Seigneur de; Prignault, Adrian de; Villemongez, Monsieur

Prisoners: Charles Lourdois and Jeanne Varrot, 215–18; families of, 49; at Grenoble,

56, 60, 62, 191, 193; Hierost, 61, 192; man impertinent to Jean Budé, 152, Nicolas Campin, 232 n.24; for overpricing wine, 147; Protestant, in France, 44; survivors as, 128

Procès criminels: aid recipients in 127, 146–47, 176; Didier Rousseau, 264 n.28; in Geneva, 26, 86–87, 268 n.58. See also individuals by name

Procurations: of François Budé to Jean Budé, 274 n.26; to inhabitants of France, 73

Procurator general: of Geneva, and Jean Bude's account books, 152

Procurators: of the Genevan hospital, 147, 251 nn. 1 and 2, 269 n.64; legal, 113; as one of two types of deacon in Geneva, 30, 34, 92. See also Deacons; Double diaconate; Hospital of Geneva; Trustees

Profiteering: John Calvin's oppposition to, 167

Profits, 167

Pron (Prot, Prou, Prov), Monsieur de: as donor, 125

Property: *Bourse française* inheriting, 174–75; of Catholic Church taken over by Protestants, 20, 22–23, 163 (*see also* Church property); communal ownership of, Hutterites, 167; in common chests, 161; diversion of from welfare as regions became Protestant, 23, 164; in pre-Reformation period, 161, 163–64; private, 167; for social welfare and education, 22. See also Real estate

Prophets: Jean Budé's commentaries on, 151

Prostat, Paris (copyist of John Calvin's sermons), 48, 173; advance on his salary, 254 n.28; and apothecary, 185, 187, 202, 204; *Bourse française* payments to, 168, 184–88, 199, 201–5, 234–35 nn. 52 and 53; clothing for, 203, 205, 254 n.26; grain for, 254 n.26; as inhabitant of Geneva, 250 n.86, 254 n.26; after John Calvin's death, 100; salary of, 99–100, 254–55 nn. 26 and 28; wife in Lyons, 250 n.86

Prostitutes: *Bourse française* accused of supporting, 139–40; and Grenoble women's confraternity, 166

Protestant church, 76; and Catholic welfare competition, 23, 165–66; and city councils, 164; poor boxes in, 167; records of in France, 111; and shift of welfare and education from religious orders and confraternities to deacons and trustees, 22; in Switzerland, 151. *See also* Protestant ethic; Reformation, Protestant; Protestants

Protestant ethic, 27

Protestants: aided to the exclusion of Catholics, 25, 182; and alms, 175–76; as aid recipients, 177; assured refuge, 183; and begging, 22; and celbacy, 23; and charity, 116, 259–60 n.26; and church property, 22–23, 115; and deacons, 82 (*see also* Deacons); in Europe, 127; in France, 50, 136; in *France Protestante*, 26; in Geneva, 168; and justification by faith, 176; killed, 265 n.43; and lay workers' welfare roles, 22; and literacy, 166–67; and philanthropy, (*see* Philanthropy); and private property, 167; as refugees, 24, 46, 82; rowing on galleys, 128; in Scotland, 23; theology of, eliminating merit, 165; and welfare, 22–23, 163, 167. *See also* Protestant church; Protestant ethic; Reformation, Protestant; Reformed Church.

Provençals: donations from, 239 n.15; keeping a girl who died, 233 n.44, 243 n.47; and money from the *Bourse française*, 66, 196. *See also* Provence

Provence: Barthelemy Michau (Michault or Micaux) from, 147; Bernardin de Candolle and the Candolle family from, 250 n.88; collection from those of, 93, 251–52 n.5; donations from, 107; young man from helped, 65, 195. *See also* Provençals

Providence: God's, 154, 158

Psalms: from *Bourse française*, 168; in French prose by Louis Budé, 158; permission to print at Metz, 235 n.54; production of, 181; put to music by Master Pierre, 67, 198; proceeds from, 54, 168, 235 n.54; and Théodore de Bèze, 48, 54, 67–69, 198–200. *See also* Psalters

Psalters: accounts, 69, 200; binding of, 54, 60–61, 66, 68–69, 191–92, 196–97, 199–200; *Bourse française* purchases of, 51, 54, 57, 66, 68–69, 168, 196, 198–99; from Genevan hospital, 225–26 n.10; in large print, 54, 237 n.14; of poor people, 32, 74; proceeds from for the poor, 49, 54; royalties from, 114; sent to France, 50. *See also* Psalms

Publishers: Artus Chauvin, 250 n.86; Jean Crespin, 20; Laurent de Normandie, 20. *See also* Printers; Publishing

Publishing: of catechisms, 54, 58, 189; in Ge-

neva, 37, 54; of New Testaments, 54, 58, 61, 64–66, 68, 189, 192, 195–98; of Psalters, 54, 60–61, 66, 68–69, 191–92, 196–200; Pyramus Candolle and, 55; Robert Estienne and, 80

Puerins, Monsieur: recommending a Spaniard, 262 n.12

Punishment: in Geneva, 212–13, 216–17; for the poor, 142

Purchases: *Bourse française* large-scale, regular, 78; of cloth, 98; for welfare institutions, 21

Purgation: by the blood of Christ, 154

Purgatory: images of, 114; Masses and prayers for souls in, 18, 116; as temporal punishment for sin, 12, 114, 259 n.21. *See also* Dante Alighieri

Puritans: in the New World, 13

Pynault, Jean: and grammars and Psalters for Genevan hospital school children, 225–26 n.10

Pyramus or Piramus: aided, 237 n.20; Candolle, 55 (*see also* Candolle, Pyramus; Candolle family); escape of from Paris, 55–56, 59–60, 62, 190–91

Quantification: and *Bourse française* records, 23

Quard (Girard, Guard, Quail, Quaile Quanil): as donor, 125

Quinal, Charles: his widow, 124. *See also* Monon, Ysabeau (Madame *la conseilliere de* Scienous or Chinon)

Rabier (Rabir, Rubir), Estienne: as donor, 125

Rabirius (Latin-*libraire?*), 125. *See also* Rabier, Estienne

Ragueau, Jean: as notary and bourgeois of Geneva, 208–10

Raguenier, Denis: as copyist of John Calvin's sermons, 34, 36, 47, 99–100, 173, 234 nn. 48 and 50–51; as *Bourse française* employee, 34, 170, 173, 181, 229 n.25; death of, 48; start of his work in 1549, 170

Ralliet, Pierre (minister of "Monnaz"): as pastor aided, 265–66 n.43

Ramus (Ramuz): as donor, 125. *See also* Ramuses

Ramuses (Latin for Ramus), 125. *See also* Ramus (Ramuz)

Randon, Master Jean: and Théodore de Bèze, 63, 194

Rationalization: of welfare organization, 21, 165–66

Real estate, 104; and *Bourse française*, 174–75; and notarial records, 26; turned over to the deacons in exchange for support, 145

Rebut, Antoine (printer of Geneva): bequest of, 112, 257–58 n.15

Receipts: for donations, 73. *See also Bourse française:* recipients

Receivers for the *Bourse française. See* Collectors

Recipients of *Bourse française* aid, 131–36, 138–39, 144–48; accused of crimes and indiscretions, 141, 146–47; Antoine Augier (Ogier), priest, 146; Barthelemy Michau (Micaux or Michault), 147; buying items with their aid directly, 173–74; characteristics of, 143, 176; Claude Carion, 147; and counterfeiting, 141, 147; in criminal records, 140–41, 146–47, 177; deacons' coercion of, 182; Didier Rousseau, 147; difficult, 143; Dimenche and his wife, 147; doctor, 135; drunkard, 141–42; English, 132; enhanced image because of high standards, 178; expectations of, 177; families, 179; first, 170; geographic origins of, 128; Guillaume Maillard, 147; Jacques Sylvestre, 147; Jean Budé's descriptions of, 150; Jean Navet, 147; a Jew, 177; La Loubiere, 147; laundry of, 173–74; little known about, 176; moral stature of, 146; names of, 52; nameless, 54, 174; native Genevan, 131, 177; pastors, 135–36, 138; Pierre de (Du) Chesne, 147; recalcitrant, 180, 182; refugees of non-French origins, 177; removed from welfare if unworthy, 177–78; selling articles lent to them, 142; thanking deacons, 142; unemployed men, 177; unequal treatment of, 173, 180–81; wife of a locksmith, 144–45; women, 177. *See also Bourse française;* individual aid recipients by name

Recommenders to the *Bourse française:* first, 76; John Calvin, 36; reliability of, 119; women, 80, 172

Records: baptismal, 26; *Bourse Française,* 25–26; deacons' minutes, 270–71 n.69; of Jean Budé, 26; of Laurent de Normandie, 26; and philanthropic patterns, 26, 118

Reform of the Gospel or of the Word, 76; as synonym for the Reformation, 11, 24

Reformation, Protestant: and begging, 117; and charitable activity, 223 n.1; and church property, 115, 163–64; and education, 134; 264 n.31

in France, 11, 131–35; in Geneva, 24, 115, 133, 165; influence of, 27–28; institutions of influenced by individuals, 29; limited influence of, 27–28; and literacy, 134; and persecution, 182; and preaching, emphasis upon, 137; professed allegiance toward, 76; Swiss, 11; term defined, 13; and welfare reform, 22

Reformed Church: alternate title of, "church reformed according to the Word of God," 209–10; and appropriation of Catholic endowments and property, 163–64; *Bourse française* as missionary arm and financial link of, 168, 182; communication network of, 107, 111–13, 174, 182; as a community, 108, 112–13, 160; and deacons' funds, 175, 182; in Dijon, 131; in Europe, 182; in England, 182; finances of managed by deacons not pastors, 225 n.3; in France, 13, 24–25, 50, 107–8, 111–13, 131, 160; in Geneva, 13; and heirs losing inheritance, 113–14, 175; international, 24–25, 28, 76, 173, 182–83; in Low Countries, 13; in Lyons, 131; at Metz, 235 n.54; as minority institution, 25; organizational genius in, 104; origins of, 36; in Paris, 131; as polity, 28–29; putting everyone to work, 28; in regions in contact with Geneva, 172–73; in Reims, 131; spread of, 11, 24–25, 76, 81, 113; survival of, 28, 173; in Swiss cantons, 113; in Toulouse, 131; and welfare, 12; and worship, 28; in Zurich, 164

Reformers: and church lands, 23; magisterial, 167; and welfare, 22

Refuge: for artisans and professional people, 133; second, 131; in Switzerland, 25. *See also* Refugees

Refugees: able-bodied, 39, 179–80; artisans and professional people, 133; bona fide, 76; books for, 54; and *Bourse française,* 57, 128, 132, 168; businessmen, 160; contacts of with their homelands, 93; David (de) Busanton, 169–70; as drunkards, 127; ebb and flow of, 75, 151; English (*see* English); first, 131; foreign (*see* Foreigners; individual nationalities); French, 11–12, 33, 44, 51, 109, 111, 113, 127, 129, 131, 135, 144, 160, 177, 244 n.53; on galleys, 128; in Geneva, 11–12, 17, 24–25, 32–34, 36–40, 82,

127, 132, 154, 165, 183; geographic origins of, 128, 262 n.10; housed, 70, 98, 103–4, 109, 118, 172; Italian, 26, 129; and Jean Budé, 152; large number of, 104; from the Low Countries, 129; of non-French origins, 177, 181; passing through Geneva, 55; pastors, 135–36, 183; persecution of, 183; poor, 25, 144, 165; population of growing, 110, 132; in prison, 128; records of, 132–33; registration of, 133; religious, 24–25, 32, 39, 76, 103, 107, 109, 112–13, 119, 143, 146, 179, 182; required to prove legitimacy of marriages, 144; returning to France, 131; in seventeenth century, 45, 131, 181; shop space for, 180; sick, 104; in sixteenth century, 46; skills of, 115, 154; sociological spectrum of, 133; Spanish, 129; in Strasbourg, 165; thankful, 180; as thieves, 127; unemployed, 128; on welfare, 46; wealthy, 146, 154; witnesses on behalf of, 133; for the Word of God, 144. See also individuals and countries by name

Regulations. See Church orders; Laws; Ordinances

Rehabilitation: by the Bourse française, 37, 180

Reims, France: no worship for Huguenots in, 131

Religious orders: Catholic, replaced in Geneva, 12; Ladies and Sisters of Charity, 23; teachers from, 22; and welfare, 22. See also Dominicans; Franciscans

Remé, Monsieur (misspelling of René). See d'Aguile; Gassin, René (Regnier); René, Monsieur

Remont (Raymond, Remond), Monsieur: as donor, 125. See also Chauvet, Raymond

Remy(?), Dame Anne de: donation from, 239 n.12

Renaissance: welfare changes in, 22

René, Monsieur, 56, 59–60, 62, 65, 77, 191, 195; as deacon, 84–85; as donor, 125; and Provence, 93; and Psalters, 69, 200. See also d'Aguile; Gassin (Gasin), René (Regnier)

Renée, duchess of Ferrara, 248 n.82

Renier (Regnier), Louis: as donor, 124–25. See also La Planche, Monsieur de

Rennes: Pierre Helon from, 65, 195

Resettlement: of refugees, 46

Resurrection, 154

Retirement: of deacons, 84, 172

Retraining: by the Bourse française, 40

Rhine River: town of Wesel on, 81

Rhone River: Geneva at its headwaters, 132

Ribautrere (La Repauldiere, Repautiere), Monsieur de, 124–25. See also La Ripantiere, Monsieur de

Richard, Maistre, de Vauville or Vanville: as donor, 125

Rigaud, Anne: as wife of Bernardin de Candolle, 250 n.88

Rive: drawing of entrance to Geneva at, 19; and foreigners to be sent out, 228 n.23

Robinet: binding Psalters for the Bourse française, 69, 199

Rocquebrun (Rocquebrune), Monsieur de, his uncle: as donor, 125

Rogette: as wife of the preacher at la Côte de Saint André, 86

Rolls: welfare, 76

Roman Empire, 18

Romans 12 : 8: criteria for deacons in, 79, 105, 206

Roset, Michel: as chronicler who links David (de) Busanton with the Bourse française, 33, 169, 227–28 nn. 17, 18, and 19

Rotan, Monsieur: denouncing Jean Budé, 152

Rouen: Anne Framery from, 256–57 n.8; Guillaume Maillard, haberdasher and inhabitant of Geneva, from, 147

Rousseau, Antoine: as father of Didier Rousseau, 147, 264 n.28

Rousseau, Didier: as ancestor of Jean Jacques Rousseau, 103, 133–34; biography of, 264 n.28; bourgeois bookseller, 264 n.28; and Monsieur Bobusse, 255 n.31; selling wine, 141–47; and procès criminels, 264 n.28; will of, 134

Rousseau, Jean-Jacques: ancestor of aided by the Bourse française, 133; as descendant of Didier Rousseau, 103

Roux, Guillan [sic]: burial of, 257 n.10

Rue de la boulangerie: Louis Budé's death on, 276 n.54

Rue de la cité: Renaud Anjorrant on, 247–48 n.81

Rue des chanoines (rue Calvin): Antoine Popillon on, 246–47 n.78; Bourse française building on, 240 n.24; Seigneur de Bursy, Noble Jacques de Saint Martin, on, 84

Rue pelleterye: Guillaume Prevost and, 245–46 n.75

Ruffy (Rufy), Jacques or Monsieur: as donor, 125

Rye: city council gift to the *Bourse française*, 109

Sablieres, France: Jean de Borne, deacon and schoolmaster in, 259 n.19; Judges Barthelemy and Jean Bernard of, 208–9; and Spectable Jean Terouch [?], 208–9
Sacrilege: unneeded aid from the *Bourse française* as, 141
Sainct Martin, Noble Jacques de: and selection of deacons of the *Bourse française*, 83–84. *See also* Burcy [de Bury?], brothers de; Burcy (Bursy); Saint Lauren; Saint Laurent; Saint Martin, Monsieur or Seigneur de
Saint Andre, Monsieur de: as donor, 125
Saint Bartholomew's Day Massacre, 109–10, 131; deaths in, 265 n.43; refugees from, 25, 136
Saint Denis, Jean de: sick at Henry Gon's, 233 n.44
Saint (Sainct) Germain (Jeremie), Monsieur or Seigneur de, 84, 123; as brother-in-law of Hotman, 245–46 n.75; as deacon, 84–85, 88; as donor, 125; paid back money he advanced, 56, 58, 60, 189, 191. *See also* Prevost, Guillaume
Saint Germain, *la mere de:* as donor, 125
Saint Lauren, Jacques (?), 121, 125. *See also* Burcy (Bursy), Monsieur de; Saint Laurent, Monsieur de; Sainct Martin; Saint Martin, Monsieur or Seigneur de
Saint Laurent, Madame de: as donor, 125
Saint Laurent, Mademoiselle de: as donor, 125
Saint Laurent, Monsieur de: as donor, 125. *See also* Brichauteau, Charles de; Sainct Martin; Saint Lauren, Jacques(?); Saint Martin, Seigneur de
Saint Martin, Monsieur or Seigneur de, alias de Saint Lauren, 121, 125. *See also* Brichauteau, Charles de; Sainct Martin; Saint Lauren, Jacques(?); Saint Laurent, Monsieur de
Saint Mezan, ministre de: as pastor aided, 265–66 n.43. *See also* Laulnaz (Laulnay), Master Jean
Saint Michel, a young man named: as donor, 125
Saint of Marveroux(?): Spectable Marcial Malzieu in, 209–10
Saint Pierre, Cathedral of: begging at, 260 n.31; courtyard homes at, 52, 236 n.4;

illustrations of, 130, 137, 159; Place de, 67–68, 168; refugee pastors preaching at, 136. *See also* Court of Saint Pierre
Saint Ramy (Ranvit, Rany, Ravy): as donor, 125
Saints: reception among after death, 154
Saint-Simon, Françoise de: as daughter of Jean, second wife of Jean Dalamont, 247 n.79
Saint Vincent de Paul: as French welfare reformer, 23
Salai, Monsieur de: as donor, 125. *See also* Falai (?); Pallai
Salaries: of Denis Raguenier, 170; of pastors paid by Geneva, 168
Salève: Jean Budé purchasing land at, 155, 219
Salon (Saillon) de Crau (Craux), Provence: René Gassin from, 246 n.76
Salvation: and works of merit, 117
Sancerre: siege and famine at, 265 n.43
Sandwich, England: deacons' fund in, 262 n.16
Saules (Saulx, Sautes): as donor, 125. *See also* Saulx, Madame de
Saulx, Madame de: as donor, 125
Saupon, Christofre: aid to buy a Bible for, 237 n.13
Saussure, Noble Jean de: as seigneur de Bussens and husband of Elisabeth Budé, 157
Savalier (Sanaliere, Savaliere), Monsieur de: as donor, 125
Savion (Panien, Savyon), Monsieur de: as donor, 125
Saxony: electoral, common chest of, 161–63
Scandillat, Mademoiselle de: as donor, 125
Scandinavia: Lutherans protected in, 28
School fees: paid by the *Bourse française*, 128, 134, 176, 179, 181
Schoolmaster: of a church near Nîmes, France, 113
Schools: and church endowment, 23; and city councils, 22; secondary, founding of, 11; in Wittenberg, 162
Scienous, Madame *la conseilliere de*, 124. *See also* Monon, Ysabeau; Quinal, Charles, his widow
Scientifique: as sixteenth century term, 276 n.54
Scotland: church property in, 23, 116
Scots: in Geneva, 145–46
Scottish Church: at *Auditoire*, 130, 261 n.2
Scripture: and doctrines, 154; and sodomy,

211, 213. *See also* Bible; Bible citations; New Testament; Old Testament

Seamstresses: and *Bourse française,* 46; Julienne, 59, 190, 254 n.27; paid less than a tailor, 174; as piecework employees, 70, 100–101; poor women as, 173

Secretary of justice of Geneva: and Jean Budé's will, 155

Secularization: of church property, 23

Segriynard (Seguynard), Robert: as donor, 126

Seine and Marne, department of: Louhan, John Calvin recommended young men from, 230 n.5

Serge-weaver: Charles Lourdois as, 269 n.63

Serignac, Guy de: as deacon, 83, 87, 241 n.37; death of, 245 n.74; as donor, 126. *See also* Thillat, Monsieur de

Sermons: of John Calvin, 34, 170, 173

Sertiers (Sartieres, Sertieres), Nicolas: as donor, 126

Servants: accompanying refugees, 39; chambermaid of Marie de Jonvilliers, wife of Jean Budé, 152; of Isabeau de Lailly, 158; Marie, of Jean Budé's mother, 276-49; of Théodore de Bèze, 128; in welfare institutions, 21

Sex, extramarital: by an aid recipient, 141, 146; Genevan city council concerned about, 144–45, 271 n.80; in Geneva's inns, 255 n.30; reported to the consistory, 255 n.30

Shamefaced poor: aided by the *Bourse française,* 133–34, 264 n.29; special treatment of, 168–69, 178–79, 181–82; wealthy people who fell on hard times as, 37, 166. *See also* Poor: shamefaced

Shoes: bought directly by aid recipients, 173–74; new and used, 46; repair of, 46, 101, 173–74; wooden, 233 n.36

Sick people: aided, 77; bedside care of, 81; and *Bourse française,* 176; guardians of, 46, 99, 104, 173, 179; at home, 20, 72; in hospitals, 20; lifelong support of, 179; in private homes, 46, 86; visited by deacons and widows, 32–33, and volunteers, 118; women's role in care of, 81

Sieur de Vérace: as deacon, 87. *See also* Budé, Jean

Silk industry: at Genevan hospital, 116, 260 n.28

Simon: and Psalters carried to Paris, 54, 68–69, 199. *See also* Symon

Sin: as root condition pardoned, 154; temporal punishment for, 12

Singlant, Jean: to Lyons, 67, 198

Sisters of Charity: in France, welfare, 23

Small council: of Geneva, 82 (*see also* City council of Geneva); of Geneva, attempt to centralize and rationalize welfare, 165; of Geneva, Jean Budé, son of Jean Budé, 157; of Geneva, Pierre de (Du) Chesne, 147; of Zurich, *obmann,* 164. *See also* City councils

Social agencies: as alternatives to begging, 117

Social control: through welfare, 143

Social history: medieval, 20

Socialism: in Europe, 167; women and, 82

Social stratification: accepted by deacons, 181

Social unrest: in sixteenth century 20

Social welfare: Catholic and Protestant, 22–23, 118; medieval, 22; and denominational theories, 165; equalizing opportunity, 167; and existing social order, 166; factors in success of, 165; in Geneva, 12; Genevan city council pressured by the pastors to favor, 167; organized and systematic, 118; and Protestant Reformation, 12; in Strasbourg, 164–65; in Zurich, 164. *See also* Hospital; Hospital of Geneva; Hospitals; Poor relief; Welfare

Social workers: deaconesses as, 82

Sodom and Gomorrah: and sodomy, 156

Sodomite: burned in Geneva, 211–13

Sodomy: Abel Poundin on, 211–14; as a crime, 156, 211–14; Daniel Colladon on, 211–14; François Chevallier on, 211–14; John Calvin on, 211–14; Lambert Le Blanc and, 156; *procès criminel* on, 275 n.33; punishment for, 211–14

Soldier, 62, 178, 192

Soteriology. *See* Salvation

Souilly (Sully), Monsieur or Seigneur de. *See* Anjorrant, Renaud

Soyssons, Guillaume de: his wife, school fees paid, 231–32 n.21

Spaniards: as aid recipient of the *Bourse française,* 129, 262 n.12; aided by the *Bourse italienne,* 262–63 n.19; in Geneva, 145–46; Juan Luis Vives, 21

Speculation on essential commodities: John Calvin's opposition to, 167

Stample (Stampes), Seigneur Jehan: as donor, 126

Statistics: from account books, 128, 262 n.9;

deacons not providing, 177
Stealing. *See* Theft
Stephen, Saint: as deacon and Christian martyr, 18; picked by the Apostles, 30
Stenay in the duchy of Bar (Meuse): Jean Dalamont from, 247 n.79
Stewardship, 167. *See also* Contributions to the *Bourse française;* Contributors; Donations to the *Bourse française;* Donors to the *Bourse française;* Philanthropy
Strasbourg: and David (de) Busanton's legacy to refugees, 33–34, 165, 169; French congregation in, 34; 165; and John Calvin's precedents for Geneva, 23, 29; and John Geiler von Kaysersberg, 21, 165; and Nuremberg welfare ordinances, 163; welfare in, 164–65
Students; Antoine Chanluin, 112; complaining, 136; from England, 108; inundating Geneva, 110; Master Jacques Perrin, 112; money diverted from to refugee pastors, 136; in need, 43
Support, *Bourse française,* 25; long and short-term, 45–46; from native Genevans, 24; sources of, 23
Supporters: of the *Bourse française,* first recorded meeting, 170; housing refugees, 104
Surgeon of the *Bourse française,* 46, 70, 74, 77, 98–99, 101, 105, 173, 207
Surgery: inadequacy of, 138
Swedes: *Bourse allemande* responsible for, 129, 262–63 n.19
Switzerland: aiding Geneva, 110–11; *Bourse allemande* responsible for refugees from, 262–63 n.19; escape to, 173; German-speaking, Reformed churches in, 113; Reformation in contrasted to Lutheran, 13; as refuge for Reformed churches, 25, 127; Protestant churches in, 151; refugees in, 131
Sylvestre, Jacques: as donor, 126; his wife, an aid recipient, 147
Symon, 61, 192. *See also* Simon
Syndics: of Geneva, 109; and sodomy, 211–12
Synod of Tours: and parish responsibility for the poor, 18

Taconnerie: death of René Gassin's son in, 246 n.76
Tagault, Mademoiselle: housing a dame, Anne, 243 n.47
Tailors: Baltazar, 59, 191, 254 n.27; and

Bourse française, 46; paid more than a seamstress, 174; as piecework employees, 70, 100–10
Tapestry maker: of Flanders, 104
Taulne[?], Master Jean du: receiving five florins by way of the collectors of Anjou, 66, 196
Taxation: by Catholic church, 115; by city councils, 12; graduated, 115; in Leisnig, 162; special levies, 115; for welfare, 23, 115, 259 n.24
Teachers: in Catholic religious orders, 22; Jean de Borne at Sabliere, France, 209–10; John Calvin's church offices and, 27, 29; Lutheran, salaries, 23, 162; Wittenberg, 162
Tere, Jean de: *Bourse française* helping him to his homeland, 64, 195; receiving money from the *Bourse française,* 61–62, 192–93; as schoolteacher, 231–32 n.21
Ternaut (Ternault), Jean: as auditor, 252 n.10
Terouch[?], Spectable Jean: as pastor of the church of Sablieres, 208–9
Testators: willing property to the poor, 116, 119
Thankfulness: for aid, 142, 180, 270 n.69
Theft: by an aid recipient, 141–42; by Jeanne Varrot, 215, 217; by La Loubiere, 147, 269 n.64; prevented by welfare, 143; as result of unemployment, 21
Theology: and Antichrist, 154; as active in the world, 154–55; and atonement, 154; and begging, 117; the church, 154; and confession of faith of Geneva, 154; and election, 154; and good works, 117; and Gospel, 154; and idolatry, 166; and Jesus Christ, 154; and justification by faith, 117; and knowledge of God, 151; less important than endowment in welfare success, 23; and love of neighbor, 169; and predestination, 154; and priesthood of all believers, 28; Protestant, eliminating merit, 165; and providence, 154; and purgatory, 12, 114 (*see also* Purgatory); and resurrection, 154; and saints, 154, and salvation, 117, and Scripture, 154; and sin, 12, 154; and soul, 154; and stewardship, 167; and works of merit, 117, 167. *See also* Doctrine
Thillac, Mademoiselle de or du (*ma soeur de,* sister or sister-in-law of Jean Budé): as donor, 123, 126. *See also* Du Tillac, Mademoiselle

Thillat (Thillac, Tillac, Tillat), Monsieur (de or du), 126, 158; as deacon, 83–84, 87–88, 226n.11, 229n.30, 241n.37; death of, 84, 88; as donor, 126. See also Serignac, Guy de

Thologe, La Dame de (Tholouse, the city?): as donor, 126

Thomas: as donor, 126

Thonex: and purchase by Jean Budé from Claude Debarge, 155, 219; and vineyard ceded to the Budé family, 244n.55

Thuril (Turil) de Gaillard, Jean: sale by to Jean Budé of three poses (of land): 155, 219

Tillier, Pierre: as auditor, 252n.10

1 Timothy 3:8–13: on diaconate, 105, 206, 225n.6. See also Bible citations

1 Timothy 5:3–16: quoted, 243n.51. See also Bible citations

1 Timothy 5:9: on widows over sixty, 226n.13. See also Bible citations

Tirl . . . [?], Monsieur: as donor, 126

Tithe: and Catholic Church, 115; in Judaism as precedent for welfare, 18

Tools: furnished, 40, 176, 180; woodworking, to an English person, 132

Toucheron?, Jehan or Seigneur: as donor, 126

Toulouse, France: Reformed church in, 131

Tours: Jean Navet from, 147

Transient poor, 21, 75. See also Vagrancy

Transylvania: refugees from aided by the Bourse allemande, 262–63n.19

Travelers: aided by the Bourse française, 75; bringing money, 173; legitimate, 76; overnight stay of, 37, 68, 77, 177

Tremblay (Trembley, Trembly), Seigneur Estienne: as collector, 93, 251–52n.5; as donor, 126; and Lyons, 93, 111; as merchant, 93, 111

Tremblay, Maistre Jehan: as donor, 126

Trie (Try, Trye), Guillaume (de), 122, 126; as notary, husband of Marguerite Budé, 157, 220–21, 276n.57; silver gift from to John Calvin, 242n.42. See also Des Arenes; Varennes, Monsieur de

Trousset, Marguerite: as wife of Didier Rousseau, 147

"Troys Vernaz": vineyard in ceded to the Budé family, 244n.55

Trucheron: and money for several, 62, 193

Truchet, Jean: as auditor, 262n.10

Trustees: in Leisnig, 162; and welfare, 20–22

Trusts: administered by deacons, 175

Tudor, Mary: her death and Geneva, 127

Unemployed people: aided, 57, 176–77; caused by refugee influx, 24; Jean Budé, 150; refugees, 128; support variable, 179; temporarily out of work, 37; vagrants, 21

University of Geneva: founding, 11; Genevan Academy, 49; manuscript room, 13

Universities: Protestant, 11; Wittenberg, 11, 162. See also University of Geneva

Usury: aid recipient, Jacques Sylvestre, 141, 147; Genevan pastors against, 167

Utopia by Thomas More, 21

Vacquerie, Anne de la: as wife of Laurent de Normandie, 236n.4

Vagabonds: as derelict poor, 139. See also Vagrancy; Vagrants

Vagrancy: Charlemagne's 806 law against, 23; as a result of enclosure, 21. See also Vagabonds; Vagrants

Vagrants: as the derelict poor, 138–39. See also Vagabonds, Vagrancy

Valbisquot, Anne: as widow of Monsieur Elie, pastor, aided, 265–66n.43

Valleyere (Vallayere), Monsieur de: as donor, 124, 126. See also La Valleyere, Monsieur de

Valtet (Caltet), Monsieur Jean: as father of Samuel Valtet, 265–66n.43

Valtet, Samuel, 265–66n.43

Vandoeuvres: Jean Boulier (de la Roche) pastor at, 136, 266n.44

Vannes in Brittany: François and Maturin Buynard from, 246n.77

Vanville (Vauville), Maistre Richard de, 125

Varennes, femme de Monsieur de, or mere de, or soeur de: as donor, 126

Varennes, Monsieur or Seigneur de, et son cousin: as donors, 122, 126, 157, 272n.7. See also Trie, Guillaume (de)

Varquey: as donor, 126

Varro, Michel: as donor, 126. See also Brassu, Seigneur de

Varrot, Jean (of Meaux): as father of Jeanne Varrot, 215–16

Varrot, Jeanne: as aid recipient, banished, 141; confessions and sentence of, 215–17; lending money, 141; 215, 217; and procès criminels, 268n.61; stealing, 215–18

Vaux in Languedoc: Michiel André from, 250n.84

Velu, Monsieur de: as donor, 126

Venerable Company of Pastors of Geneva. See

Company of Pastors of Geneva

Venice: charity dispensed in according to acts of piety, 139, 166; confraternities in, 144, 166; religious processions in, 139; welfare in, 166

Veqnon (Vequon), *Maistre* Jehan: as donor, 126

Verace, Mademoiselle de: as donor, 126

Vérace, Monsieur or Seigneur de, 78; as deacon, 248–49 n.82; as donor, 97, 121, 126, 254 n.82; and Madame, slandered, 151; and a man impertinent to him, 152. *See also* Budé, Jean

Vermigli, Peter Martyr: and conversion of Galeazzo Caracciolo, 256 n.8

Vernon (Vernou), Monsieur: as donor, 126

Vernon, Jean: as martyr, 109

Vernon, Marguerite (wife of Rene Bienassis), 121; as sister of a martyr, 109

Vesignon, Monsieur de: bequest of, 239 n.17

Viaticum: for travelers, 38–39, 179

Vico, Marquis de. *See* Caracciolo, Galeazzo; Le Marquis

Vie, Supplin de: handout to his wife in labor, 240 n.25

Vienne: nuns imprisoned in, 111

Vigne (Vigny), Monsieur de: as donor, 126

Vilet[?], Jacques: wife of, 67, 198

Villan, Francoys: as donor, 126

Villemongez, Monsieur: as donor, 126. *See also* Briquemault, Seigneur de; Prignault, Adrian de; Priquemaut, Seigneur de

Villeneuve (Villeneufve), Monsieur or Seigneur de: as donor, 97, 121, 126, 254 n.16. *See also* Budé, François

Villers, Noble Damoiselle Estienette de: as mother of Catherine des Marins, 247 n.79

Villiers (Villers), Monsieur or Seigneur de: as donor, 124, 126. *See also* Montigne, Jehan de; Montiguy, Monsieur, de; Moreli, Jehan

Vincent, Louys (pastor): his son aided, 265–66 n.43

Vincent de Paul, Saint: as French welfare leader, 23

Vineyards: of Budé family, 274 n.24; of Jean Budé, 155, 219; purchased by refugees, 127

Vioche, Barbe: as blind woman and aid recipient, 143

Viret, Pierre: and John Calvin, 33, 169; recommending disbursements, 55–56, 58, 60, 190–91

Vives, Juan Luis (Spanish humanist): and

Galeazzo Caracciolo, 256 n.8; and social welfare for Bruges, 21, 116, 163

Visitation: of the sick and poor, 77–78, 118

Vittoria, Dona: as first wife of Galeazzo Caracciolo, 256 n.8

Vivararis: Sablieres, France, in, 209–10

Volunteers: auditors as, 98; of *Bourse française*, 70, 92–98, 103–5, 173; collectors as, 98; deacons as, 98, 142; housing refugees, 118; visiting the sick, 118

Voyagers: to Geneva, 76

Waldensians: in *Auditoire*, 130

Wars of Religion in France, 57, 131; *Bourse française* prior to, 50, 183; refugees of, 135

Wartburg Castle: and Martin Luther, 162

Wedding: of Jean Crespin, son of Jean Crespin, the martyrologist, 141

Welfare: administrators, hiring of, 21; agencies for the poor, 117; boards of trustees, 21; Catholic, 166; Catholic and Protestant, 22–23; centralization, 12, 20, 165–66; children, 43; and church endowment, 23; city council supervision of, 21; confraternities and, 166; and deacons, 143; and egalitarian society, 166; European, 24, 161–67; and foreign poor, 28; in Geneva, 24, 36, 167, 178; and monasteries, 18; ordinances printed and sold, 22; practice of the sixteenth century, 27; pre-Reformation centralization and rationalization of, 165–66; and private property, 167; Protestant and Catholic, 22–23, 166; reform, 21–22, 166; rolls, 42, 44, 129; as social control, 143, 271 n.72; stigma of alleviated by high standards, 178; in Strasbourg, 23, 164–65 (*see also* Strasbourg); viaticum as, 39; withholding payments of, 180; and women's work, 172; and worthiness, 138, 166 (*see also* Worthiness); in Zurich, 164 (*see also* Zurich). *See also* Hospital; Hospital of Geneva; Hospitals; Poor Relief; Social Welfare

Wesel (Rhine River): deaconesses of, 81

Wet nurses for infants, 179; and *Bourse française*, 42, 70, 100, 173, 231 n.13; and fate of orphans after weaning, 43; low pay of, 173

Whipping: of Jeanne Varrot and Charles Lourdois, 141

Widow: ancient church office of absent in Geneva, 81; of Guillaume Budé, 149–50, 157–58 (*see also* Lailly, Isabeau de); of Guillaume Trye, 220–21 (*see also* Budé,

Marguerite); John Calvin's letter to, 149; of Louis Budé and of Guy de Serignac, Barbe Le Bouc du Berry, 158; miserable condition of, 144; of Nicolas Saget awarded assistance because of the transfer of a boutique, 145; of Pierre Herman, Alex, 143. *See also* individual names; Widows

Widowers: aid to, 42

Widows: in the Acts of the Apostles 6:1–7, 18; and *Bourse française*, 45, 57, 105, 176, 179, 206; and care of a blind aid recipient, 143; caring for children, 81, 86, 133; conflict of with deacons, 180; with dependents, 180; in early church, 30; in I Timothy 5:3–16, 243n.51; as foster parents, 81; Françoise, 142; gracious, 81; helping the poor, 101; and Laurent de Normandie, 86; on low incomes, 42; with no family or means of support, 81; noble, 144; and orphans, 81; over sixty years of age, 32, 81; of pastors, 138, 265–66n.43; sixty years of age, 32, 81; turned out of town, 144; unequal support of, 45, 179–80; visits to the poor and sick by, 32; wealthy, 144; as welfare recipients, 37, 40, 43. *See also* individual names; Widow

Wife: of Antoine Calvin, 79; essential for hospitaler in Geneva, 21–22; good, 80; of Jacques Vilet[?], 67, 198; of Jean Boulier, 143; of Jean Budé, 153, 157–58 (*see also* Jonvilliers, Mademoiselle or Damoiselle Marie de); of Jean Le Roy, 71; of a locksmith, an aid recipient, 144; of Maldonnade, 80; of Robert Estienne, 80. *See also* Wives; Women; women or their husbands by name

Wills, 71; of ardent Protestants, 153, 156–57; bequests in to the *Bourse française*, 114, 119, 174; bequests in to the Genevan Academy, hospital, refugee funds, 174–75; of Bonueni (Bonuemi, Bonuevi), 121; contested, 175; of David (de) Busanton, lost, 169; deacons and, 79–80; death bed, 156; and donations to the *Bourse française*, 120; execution of, 73, 112–14, 119; of Geneva as source for this study, 26; of Geneva, standard thanksgiving to God in, 154; of Jean Budé, 152–57; method of drafting in Geneva, 156; Protestant, 153–56; with restrictive clauses limiting inheritance, 114, 153, 175, 250–51n.88; 258–59n.18; revealing

refugees sense of being called by God, 146; of Robert Estienne, 80; secret, 156, 275n.32; specifying religion and place of residence of heirs, 175; of wealthy religious immigrants, 127; witnessed, 156. *See also* individuals by name

Wine: merchant, Didier Rousseau, aid recipient of the *Bourse française*, 141, 147, 264n.28; as pay of Genevan pastors, 136; stolen, 141, 215, 217

Witnesses: to refugees required so as to avoid their becoming a charge to the *Bourse française*, 133

Wittenberg: church order setting up a welfare system in, 161–62; and Martin Luther's influence, 161–62; parish preacher, Johann Bugenhagen, in, 163; poor relief in, 161–63; University of, Andreas Karlstadt, 162;

Wives: of absent *Bourse française* recipients, 56, 58, 67, 189–90, 194, 197–98; beloved, in Genevan wills, 153, 273n.19; of deacons, 79–80; of pastors, 58, 67, 136, 138, 190, 197; of recipients, 63, 67, 194, 198. *See also* Wife; Women

Women: abandoned, 133, 144–45; as aid recipients, 177; audacious, 86; blind, 143; *Bourse française* welcoming their money and work, 81, 172; and care of the poor and sick, nurses, 81; and child care, 101, 174; in childbed, 81; as deacons, 81; as deaconesses, 82; and depressed daughter, 142; discriminated against, 174; as donors; 34, 172; drunkard, 141–52; filling in for their husbands, 80; as fool, 142; in Geneva in early modern times, bibliography on, 243n.49; and heavy labor, 144; as hostesses for the *Bourse française*, 80, 172; in jobs paid poorly, 174; and John Calvin, a letter to an unnamed woman, 229n.28; as large segment of the welfare rolls, 145; married, 44; noble, 144; as nurses, 80, 82; and office of widow, 81 (*see also* Widow, Widows); ordered to leave Geneva, 144; over sixty years of age, 81; poor, 141, 173; pregnant, 140; with property, 145; as recommenders of the poor, 80, 172; renting a room to a sick person, 230n.10; sick, 81; as social workers, 82; solitary, 44; unable to nurse babies, 173; vulnerable, 144–45; wages of, 103; wealthy, 144; on welfare, 44, 70, 133; who came with men required to be married, 144–45, 271n.80; as widows, 81 (*see also* Widow; Widows); without men to support them, 144–45; and work, 80; young, 44. *See also* individuals by name

Wood: carried by the poor, 173; contributed, 174; by the cord, 59, 190; in Wittenberg, 162

Wooden shoes, 233n.36

Woodworkers: supplied with tools, 39

Workfare, 144; for the able-bodied, blind, and disabled, 116; in Geneva, 34; at Genevan hospital, 116, 260n.28; proposed by Juan Luis Vives, for Bruges, 116, 163

Works of merit: for salvation, 117

Worship in Geneva as prototype for Reformed churches, 28; as criterion for assistance in

Venice, 166

Worthiness: as criterion for welfare, 138–39, 166, 178; defined by the *Bourse française,* 138–43, 177

Ynit (Yuiv, Yvit), Anthoine: as donor, 126

Youth: laws excusing misdemeanors of, 212–13

Ypres, 163

Zurich: begging forbidden in, 164; donation from to Geneva, 110; Michel Roset in, in 1547, 228n.19; pastors of, 110; social welfare system of as a model, 164

Zwingli, Ulrich: succeeded by Heinrich Bullinger, 164